TOWARD ECONOMIC UNDERSTANDING

TOWARD ECONOMIC UNDERSTANDING

PAUL HEYNE

Southern Methodist University

THOMAS JOHNSON

North Carolina State University

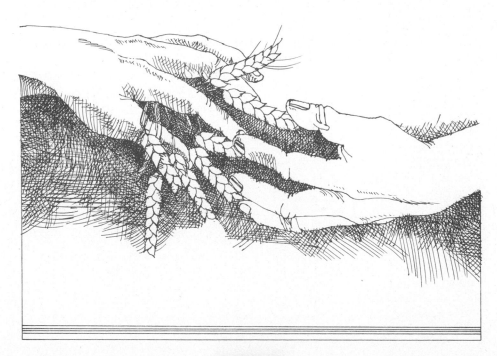

S R A

SCIENCE RESEARCH ASSOCIATES, INC.
Chicago, Palo Alto, Toronto, Henley-on-Thames, Sydney, Paris, Stuttgart

A Subsidiary of IBM

Acknowledgments

John Maynard Keynes, in *The Cambridge Economic Handbooks*. Reprinted with
the permission of the Cambridge University Press, New York.

Frank Knight, the article "Profit," in the *Encyclopedia of the Social Sciences*.
Copyright, 1930, by The Macmillan Company, New York.
Reprinted with the permission of the publisher.

I. M. D. Little, "The Economist in Whitehall," in *Lloyds Bank Review*, April 1957.
Reprinted with the permission of Lloyds Bank Ltd., London.

Alfred North Whitehead, *Adventures of Ideas*. Copyright, 1933,
by The Macmillan Company; copyright renewed, 1961, by Evelyn Whitehead.
Reprinted with the permission of the Macmillan Publishing Company
and the Cambridge University Press.

Library of Congress Cataloging in Publication Data

Heyne, Paul T
  Toward economic understanding.

1. Economics—Textbooks. I. Johnson, Thomas,
1936–   joint author. II. Title.
HB171.5.H463   330   75-31554
ISBN 0-574-19255-7

For Michelle and Sarah
and for David, Mike, and Mark

PREFACE

Why are we adding yet another book to the long procession of introductory economics texts? Readers never ask that question, of course, because they know that textbooks are written in pursuit of wealth and fame. But authors go on answering it nonetheless.

This book grew out of a much smaller one-semester introductory economics text written several years earlier by Heyne with substantial encouragement and assistance from Johnson and published by Science Research Associates in 1973 as *The Economic Way of Thinking*. (A second edition of *The Economic Way of Thinking* will appear in Fall 1976.) The success which that book enjoyed encouraged the publisher to wonder whether the same approach might not be extended to the more common two-semester course. *Toward Economic Understanding* is our attempt to produce a two-semester text employing the pedagogical principles that informed the earlier book.

Our convictions about the best way to introduce students to economics can be briefly summarized:

1. It is economic *theory* that makes economics an illuminating, useful, and fascinating subject.
2. A small amount of economic theory goes a long way and a lot of economic theory often goes nowhere.
3. Theory must be taught in the context of applications if it is to be learned and retained.

We want beginning students to <u>master a set of concepts that will help</u> <u>them think more coherently and consistently about the wide range of</u> <u>social problems that economic theory illuminates.</u> The principles of economics make sense out of buzzing confusion. They clarify, systematize, and correct the daily assertions of journalists, political figures, axe grinders, and barroom pontiffs. And the applicability of the economist's thought-tools is practically unlimited. But students won't come to appreciate any of this unless we persuade them by showing them. And that means we must teach the concepts of economic analysis as ways of answering actual questions which students are asking.

No good teacher of economics has ever found this task an easy one. It requires imagination, insight, a knowledge of current events, the ability to listen attentively, and a sense of perspective, as well as familiarity with the formal techniques of economic analysis. Those are all scarce goods. And it presupposes a conviction on the part of the teacher that economic theory really is useful for something more than answering artificial questions and passing equally artificial examinations.

Perhaps no one would disagree in principle with any of the above. If so, our practice has been far out of step with our precept. One reason is undoubtedly the obsession with formal technique that characterizes so much teaching of economic theory at all levels. The disciple will very rarely rise above the master. And if the masters in our profession are more concerned with form than with content, the effects will be felt at the principles level. We need not debate here the question of how much of what makes it into intermediate and advanced theory texts really belongs there, or how the balance should be struck in graduate theory courses between the logic-mathematics and the economics of theory. For the question of what should go into a beginning course can be answered without resolving the other questions. And that answer is: *very little.*

Most of what might go into a Compleat and Current Compendium of Economic Theory is actually refinement and elaboration of the few fundamental concepts that are useful in enabling us to understand the real world and to evaluate policy proposals. Almost all the genuinely important things that economics has to teach are elementary concepts of relationship that people could almost figure out for themselves if they thought carefully. The vast body of more advanced economics is largely composed of applications of these concepts to specific problems.

Some problems are difficult indeed and test the mathematical, statistical, and policy skills of many good minds. Our challenge, however, is getting people to *appreciate* these few, simple concepts. To do that, we must practice the virtue of restraint. We must attempt less and thereby accomplish more. An introductory course should distinguish itself as much by what it excludes as by what it incorporates. Unless it is our aim to impress students with the esoteric quality of economists' knowledge, we should teach no theory *in the introductory course* that cannot immediately be put to work in some meaningful and hopefully vivid way. Otherwise we drown the beginning student; he is made to thrash about so desperately in such deep water that he doesn't learn to swim a single stroke. Our aim should be to get him swimming and instill in him the confidence that through practice he can learn to swim better.

And so we have omitted a good deal that can be found in most of the fat textbooks through which college students are usually introduced to economics, in order to provide more applications of basic concepts and more dialogue about the social problems to which economic theory is applied. We don't present the fundamentals of accounting or the history of the labor movement, and we don't explain social security benefits, rates of population growth, or the differences between common and preferred stock. We think those are all useful things to know, but we don't want them in an introductory economics text where too many dates, definitions, and data can easily get in the way of understanding. And it's *understanding* that we're after, as the title of the book suggests.

We have, however, given more attention to political and ethical questions than most textbooks do. *Homo oeconomicus* is a fiction in which no good economist has ever believed. Economic decisions are made by real people who do not live by bread alone and whose economic activities occur in social and political contexts. Economics becomes a more difficult subject when we admit that, but it also becomes more challenging and meaningful.

Reviewers of this book who agreed wholeheartedly with our philosophy did not always agree with us about particular omissions and inclusions. Sometimes we took their advice and sometimes we did not; judgments on relevance and relative importance inevitably vary. Many of our most difficult decisions were made easier by the knowledge that this book will usually be found in the company of teachers who can amend our mistaken judgments, correct our limited vision, and assure students that nothing is certain merely because it's in print.

Our task was also made easier by the decision to produce a complementary volume entitled *A Student's Guide to Economic Understanding*. This is not simply a dull review of the text or a collection of exercises to make students read carefully. The *Student's Guide* was written to further understanding, and Heyne (author of this paragraph) believes that Johnson (author of the *Guide*) has produced something unique among study guides which teachers should also find helpful in tailoring the course more to their own preferences.

One of our most heartening experiences in the preparation of this book was discovering how many teachers of economics around the country were willing to help and how much we could learn from them. They have proved to us that a *community* of scholars still lives in this era of disciplinary professionalism, and we are deeply grateful for their unselfish assistance. They include W. H. Hutt (University of Dallas), Ronald A. Krieger (Goucher College), Donald A. Wells (University of Arizona), Robert C. Bingham (Kent State University), Thomas W. Bonsor (Eastern Washington State College), Dennis R. Starleaf (Iowa State University), John B. Egger (University of Dallas), Kenneth D. Goldin (California State University, Fullerton), Alan Randall (University of Kentucky), Edward B. Bell (The Cleveland State University), Thomas D. Duchesneau (University of Maine), Lawrence P. Nordell (University of New Hampshire), Dennis Segebarth (Triton College), Glenn Marston (Utah State University), Thomas P. Jorgens (University of Minnesota), and Martin P. Oettinger (University of California, Davis).

We also want to acknowledge once more the pioneering work of Armen A. Alchian and William R. Allen, whose *University Economics* first gave substance to the claim that economic theory could be made meaningful in an introductory course.

The special skills and the cheerful spirits of Marjorie Edens, George Oudyn, and Bruce Caldwell made our labors far lighter at every step of the way. Paul Heyne's work on the book was also facilitated by the research assistance of Margot Heyne and by a leave of absence which the Southern Methodist University School of Humanities and Sciences granted during the 1974–75 academic year.

It goes without saying but is always said anyway that we alone bear the responsibility for whatever errors and shortcomings the book contains. You should know, however, that it was Robert Bovenschulte's idea in the first place.

PAUL HEYNE
THOMAS JOHNSON

CONTENTS

The Theory of Economics does not furnish a body of settled conclusions immediately applicable to policy. It is a method rather than a doctrine, an apparatus of the mind, a technique of thinking which helps its possessor to draw correct conclusions.

JOHN MAYNARD KEYNES

THE ECONOMIC WAY OF THINKING

"Non-economists tend to be too academic. They abstract too much from the real world."

That isn't the way you usually hear it. Businessmen and college students who have sampled the writings or the courses of professional economists have all too often gone away with the suspicion that what they learned was "purely theoretical." Interesting intellectual exercise, perhaps, but not very helpful to anyone who wants to understand how an economy actually works. If you have heard comments to that effect, and are more than half-convinced of their truth, there is little chance we will persuade you otherwise in a short introductory chapter. The authors have found economics exciting and important for anyone who wants to understand the problems and possibilities of our society, but your own experience with this course will have to provide the test of that judgment.

It might be helpful, though, if you reflected for a moment on the quotation with which we began. People who sneer at "fancy theories" and prefer to rely on common sense and everyday experience are often in fact the victims of extremely vague and sweeping hypotheses. This morning's newspaper contains a letter from a young person in Pennsylvania who was once "one of a group of teenage pot smokers. Then a girl in the crowd got pregnant. Her baby was premature and deformed and needed two operations." The newspaper's adviser to the teenage lovelorn printed that letter approvingly, as evidence that the price of smoking marijuana is high.

Perhaps it is. But suppose the writer of that letter had written: "Then the Pittsburg Steelers won the Super Bowl and the Philadelphia Flyers took the Stanley Cup." Everyone would object that those events had nothing to do with the group's pot smoking. But how do we know that? If the mere fact that the young girl's misfortunes followed her pot smoking is evidence of a causal relationship, why can't we also infer a causal relationship in the case of the Steelers and the Flyers?

The point is a simple but important one. We cannot discover, prove, or even suspect any kind of causal relationship without having a theory in mind. Our observations of the world are in fact drenched with theory, which is why we usually make sense out of the buzzing confusion that our eyes and ears pick up. We actually observe only a small fraction of what we "know," a hint here and a suggestion there; the rest we fill in from the theories we hold, small ones and broad ones, vague and precise ones, well tested and poorly tested, widely held and sometimes peculiar, carefully reasoned and dimly recognized.

I. M. D. Little is a distinguished British economist who wrote the sentences with which this chapter began, in an article describing his experiences as an adviser to the British Treasury. Here is the paragraph from which they were taken:

> Economic theory teaches one how economic magnitudes are related, and how very complex and involved these relationships are. Non-economists tend to be too academic. They abstract too much from the real world. No one can think about economic issues without some theory, for the facts and relationships are too involved to organize themselves: they do not simply fall into place. But if the theorist is untutored, he is apt to construct a very partial theory which blinds him to some of the possibilities. Or he falls back on some old and over-simple theory, picked up from somewhere or other. He is also, I believe, apt to interpret the past naively. *Post hoc ergo propter hoc*[1] is seldom an adequate economic explanation. I was sometimes shocked by the naive sureness with which very questionable bits of economic analysis were advanced in Whitehall. Of course, economists may be too academic in another sense: they may not appreciate administrative difficulties, or may lack a sense of political possibility. But then, there is no danger of these things being overlooked.[2]

Thinking Like an Economist

Economics is basically a way of thinking. The theories of economists, with surprisingly few exceptions, are simply extensions of the assumption that individuals choose those options which seem to them most likely to secure their largest net advantage. *Everyone*, it is assumed, acts in accordance with that rule: miser or spendthrift, saint or sinner, consumer or seller, politician or business executive, cautious calculator or spontaneous improviser.

1. Literally, "After this, therefore because of this"; the logical fallacy of assuming that A must have caused B if A preceded B in time. The argument of the penitent Pennsylvania pot smoker is an example.

2. I. M. D. Little, "The Economist in Whitehall," *Lloyds Bank Review*, April 1957.

Economic theory, we said, is *simply* an extension of that assumption. But "simply" is a treacherous word. Did you ever have a math instructor who began: "To solve this kind of problem, we simply . . ."—when it wasn't simple to you at all? The economic way of thinking is somewhat like that. The basic assumption resembles a magician's top hat: It seems to be empty; but in practiced hands it produces a fascinating array of surprises. And once you've seen for yourself how it's done, you can go back home and astonish all your friends.

The simile of the magician's top hat is apt in another way. Economics has a reputation for being mysterious and incomprehensible. And because the subject utterly baffles so many who study it, economics has also acquired a reputation for being difficult, dull, and irrelevant. This book developed out of a growing suspicion that students have found economic theory to be mystifying and tedious largely because we economists have tried to teach them too much. We have dazzled them with complex theorems and exercises in pure logic instead of helping them to see how much their world is illuminated by economic theory.

This text is organized around a set of concepts that collectively make up the economist's basic kit of intellectual tools. The tools are all related to the fundamental assumption that we stated above and are surprisingly few in number. But they are extraordinarily versatile. They unlock such mysteries as exchange rates, monopoly, money, and speculation, all of which are generally conceded to be in the economist's province. But they also shed light on a wide range of issues that are not ordinarily thought of as economic at all: traffic congestion, environmental pollution, the workings of government, the behavior of the National Collegiate Athletic Association, and a host of others that you will encounter in these pages.

A number of jokes have been floating around for a long time about the inability of economists to agree. The one most often quoted says that if all the economists in the world were laid end to end, they would reach . . . no conclusion. The jokes have been revived in recent years as policymakers struggled with the simultaneous problems of rising unemployment and rising prices, and economists could not agree on a solution. But a more careful look at the opinions of economists reveals a range of disagreements that is actually quite small when compared with the vast area of consensus. There are two principal explanations for the erroneous belief that economists rarely agree.

One, of course, is the fact that disagreement by its very nature receives more publicity. People don't spend much time discussing points on which they agree: it's both more challenging and more fruitful to move on into disputed questions and into areas where advancing knowledge has not yet produced consensus. Because the economics profession in the United

States makes little effort to carry on controversy in secret (would we want it any other way in a democratic society?), disagreement looks much more substantial than it actually is. In addition, newspapers, magazines, and television commentators are generally more eager to publicize dissent than consensus. There's a much better market for criticism than there is for words of approval. And so an economist who wants to argue that his colleagues are off on the wrong track is more likely to obtain a forum for his views than is an economist eager to praise the accomplishments of his discipline. The situation is not unique to economics. The *New York Times* is less likely to publish an article by a physician lauding the accomplishments of medicine than an article calling attention to shoddy practices in the medical profession.

A second explanation for the tide of popular suspicion is the public's obsession in recent years with one particular economic problem: achieving aggregate stability, or checking inflation while avoiding a rise in unemployment. That is, of course, a highly visible and well publicized problem (or pair of problems). It is also an extraordinarily complex problem. How can anyone understand and prescribe for a problem created by the interaction of so many powerful and unpredictable forces? Congress, the president, the Federal Reserve Board, world food production, population growth, the weather, cartels of oil producers, international politics, labor unions, large corporations, environmental groups, the millions of producers, consumers, savers, and investors all have an impact on the price level and employment.

Some of the public's current disillusionment with economics is attributable to the thoroughly unrealistic expectation that economists ought to be able to predict and control the variables listed in the preceding paragraph. When put in that way, the expectation is absurd. By failing to recognize how much knowledge may in fact be required for the achievement of price and employment stability, we have allowed ourselves to harbor extravagant expectations. At the same time it should be admitted that those economists who eagerly claimed credit for the relatively stable price levels and low unemployment in the 1960s helped create the extravagant expectations and consequent disillusionment of the 1970s.

The economics profession is now hard at work on a variety of fronts trying to locate and describe the factors responsible for rapid price inflation and surges of unemployment. Some of the consensus that developed in the 1960s has been disrupted; certain large scale generalizations from which many hoped to construct effective stabilization policies have been called into question; more detailed knowledge is now being sought in many directions. And the resulting scene, understandably enough, seems to the lay observer more chaotic than it actually is.

Because the task of securing stable prices with high employment is so much in the forefront of public attention; because it is a task that we have by law assigned to the federal government, which draws heavily on economists for counsel; because the performance of this task entails the mastery of such a complex set of issues; and because the results will affect the decisions all of us make, well over one-third of this book will be devoted to the analysis of aggregate fluctuations.

But that should not be allowed to create the impression that economists typically disagree about the matters within their range of competence. The degree of consensus among economists is the invisible part of the iceberg and disagreement is the visible but far less weighty tip. When it comes to the understanding of economic systems and the recommendation of economic policies, the important divisions of opinion in our society are less likely to be among economists than between those who have learned to use the economic way of thinking and those who have not.

The primary goal of this book is to start you thinking the way economists think, in the belief that once you start you will never stop. For economic thinking is addictive. Once you get inside some principle of economic reasoning and make it your own, opportunities to employ it pop up everywhere. You begin to notice that sense and nonsense are all mixed up together in much of what is said or written about economic and social issues. You get in the habit of sorting the sense from the nonsense by applying the basic concepts of economic analysis. You may even, unfortunately, acquire the reputation of being a cynic, for people who habitually talk nonsense like to cry "cynic" at anyone who points out what they are doing.

But long introductions are tedious. The best way to find out about economics is to do some for yourself. Just one word of caution before you begin.

The economic way of thinking provides a *valuable but limited* perspective on human behavior and social relationships. A person who knows no economics will probably fail to understand many of the most interesting, important, and sharply contested social issues of our time. But a knowledge of economic theory is not an adequate substitute for a sense of history, a capacity for empathy, and that basic humility which is the hallmark of all good science. Alfred North Whitehead has said it most eloquently:

> The duty of tolerance is our finite homage to the abundance of inexhaustible novelty which is awaiting the future, and to the complexity of accomplished fact which exceeds our stretch of insight.[1]

1. *Adventures of Ideas,* The Free Press, 1933, 1961, p. 52.

2

SUBSTITUTES EVERYWHERE

The concept of demand

You must have read or heard statements like these many times in your life:

1. Fire safety requires that there be two exits from each apartment unit.

2. We need a new car.

3. Our state will need large amounts of additional water in the coming decade.

4. Traffic surveys have established the need for a new expressway.

5. Every citizen should be able to obtain the medical care he needs regardless of his ability to pay.

6. There is no substitute for victory.

Fire safety, water, the smooth and rapid movement of traffic, medical care, victory, and even automobiles are all "goods." We say "even" automobiles because some doubts have begun to be expressed about the goodness of automobiles in our congested cities. But you can ask the man who owns one, and a lot of young people who don't. They will assure you that a new car is very much a good. Then what's wrong with those statements?

FROM "NEEDS" TO DEMAND

The element common to all six is the notion of *necessity*. And that is what makes each statement seriously misleading.

Take the first one. Will apartment dwellers who live in units with only one exit all be injured or killed by fires? Of course not. It's just that the risk is greater with one exit than with two. But then why not three exits? Or four? Why not go the whole route and make the outside walls nothing but doors? The answer is that, while fire safety is a good, it isn't the only good apartment dwellers are interested in. Low rental costs and low heating and cooling costs are also goods, to say nothing of safety from burglars who notice that multiple exits are also multiple entrances. Moreover, there are other and perhaps better ways to increase fire safety. Extinguishers, alarm sprinklers, and large ashtrays also reduce the risk to apartment dwellers of injury or death from fire. If more than one exit is required, why not also require a fire extinguisher on every wall?

That sensible-sounding statement about apartment exits overlooks three interrelated facts: (1) Most goods are not free but can only be obtained by sacrificing something else that is also a good. (2) There are substitutes for anything. (3) Intelligent choice among substitutes requires a balancing of additional costs against additional benefits.

Costs and Substitutes

Now go back and look at the other five statements. "We need a new car." Who "needs" a new car? Obviously not everyone, but only those who value a new car more than what they must sacrifice to obtain one. That might be a vacation trip this year, new clothes, a lot of movies, and a stereo set. Is it worth it? There are plenty of substitutes for a new car, after all: an overhaul of the present one, a used car, a bicycle, a car pool, public transportation, moving closer to work, or staying home more. The intelligent consumer tries to decide upon his preferences among all these various costs and benefits. Of course, once he has made up his mind he might want to say "We *need* a new car" in the hope that the definitive tone of his statement will dissuade his wife from making her own comparison of the costs and benefits of a new one.

Consider statement 3. "Our state will need large amounts of additional water in the coming decade." Does any state really need large amounts of additional water? Dams and reservoirs, pipelines, and desalinization plants are ways of obtaining more water. But they have costs. Do the benefits justify the costs? If you think there are no substitutes for water, then you are thinking too academically. You have abstracted unrealistically from the real world. Probably you are assuming that water is only used for drinking, whereas in fact the overwhelming bulk of the water consumed in the United States goes for other uses. Since we shall use the case of water a bit later as an extended working exercise, we can pass this problem by for now. You might want to begin thinking, though, about the substitutes for water in such places of chronic scarcity as Arizona and Southern California.

You will be able to make much more sense out of the water problem and the expressway issue we take up next if you keep in mind that entities like *states* or *cities* never really want anything. Wants and goals are always attached ultimately to individuals. When someone says "The people want . . . " what does he mean? That all the people want it? A majority? Those who count? It is usually a good rule in analyzing statements like those above to ask: *Who* wants more water, or more expressways, or more fire safety?

> Things are seldom what they seem
> Skim milk masquerades as cream.

The fourth of our misleading propositions—"Traffic surveys have established the need for a new expressway"—leads into one of the vexing issues in city planning. Perhaps it would never have become such a troublesome issue had we realized that expressways have costs as well as benefits, that there are excellent substitutes for more expressways, and that intelligent city planning calls for the weighing of additional benefits against additional costs. Those who hope to derive most of the benefits from a new expressway while paying only a small percentage of the costs will not want others

to notice the full costs of the expressway or how many substitutes there really are. That is why they pretend that a traffic survey can establish "needs." But a traffic survey only shows how many cars travel given routes *at existing costs to the drivers,* including such nonmonetary costs as delay, danger, and ulcers. Suppose that the cost of downtown parking increased 500%. What do you think would happen to rush-hour traffic? Commuters would form car pools and begin using public transportation. If the cost to *drivers* of commuting were raised high enough, through parking charges, toll fees, or some other device, the need for a new expressway could turn overnight into a "need" for a rapid transit system. It's a strange kind of need that can vanish so quickly in the face of a price change.

The fifth statement sounds humanitarian and liberal. "Every citizen should be able to obtain the medical care he needs regardless of his ability to pay." But how much medical care does any person need? We might all agree that a man with an inflamed appendix and no money should have his appendectomy completely at the taxpayers' expense if he is unable to meet any of the cost himself. But what of the man with a splinter in his finger? The services of physicians are not free goods, and they would not become free goods even if every physician treated his patients without charging a fee. There just would not be enough physicians to go around if everyone consulted a doctor for every minor ill. The lower the price of visiting a physician, the smaller the sacrifice one must make to obtain his services, and the more will people substitute a trip to the doctor for such other remedies as going to bed, taking it easy, or waiting and hoping. One could rather confidently predict that lower monetary fees would result in higher fees of other sorts, like waiting in line for many hours.

What about the sixth statement: "There is no substitute for victory"? It just isn't so. That may be a good battle cry, but it's unrealistic political analysis. Victory is usually obtained by making sacrifices. If the sacrifices reach a certain intensity, people choose compromise or even defeat, although they are then inclined to *say* that they have "no choice." Once again we notice that the intelligent formulation of policy, including foreign policy, flows from a careful balancing of additional expected costs and additional expected benefits.

The word *expected* should be stressed. We live in a world of uncertainty, forced to make choices that will affect our future without knowing for sure just how they will do so. A common mistake in reasoning about economic problems is to assume that there is no uncertainty or that economic decision makers are omniscient. At last report, omniscience was still a virtue denied to mortal man. Condemned as we are to living with uncertainty, we can at least keep from making matters worse by pretending otherwise. Be alert for statements, in this book and elsewhere, that assume completely adequate information is always available. You might even notice that information, too, is a good which has costs of acquisition and for which there are substitutes available.

HARD CHOICES

A *New York Times* article on the consumer protection movement in November 1972 prompted this indignant response in a letter to the Financial Editor:

Roger Klein's smug brush-off of "consumerism" is nauseating.

For instance, he comments: "The consumer advocate begins with the premise that there are too many accidents, too much fraud and not enough information. But how does one decide on the right number of accidents, the right amount of fraud and the correct amount of information?"

The answer is a very simple one—any avoidable accident, any knowing fraud is too much. Any child burned and maimed because of flammable clothing, any infant born malformed because of thalidomide or another inadequately tested drug is too many.

But that "very simple" answer just won't do. It isn't even accepted by the writer of the letter. For *every* accident is probably avoidable. We could always further reduce the number of automobile accidents, for example, by lowering speed limits; but long before we had managed to reduce avoidable accidents to zero we would have made the automobile a slower mode of travel than walking. The fact is that each of us wants safety but that we stop wanting additional safety when the cost of obtaining it becomes too high. Of course, the social problem is complicated by the fact that we can often keep our own costs down by endangering others. Pedestrians will tend to want lower speed limits than will motorists. And since most of us are sometimes one, sometimes the other, our views on automobile speed limits aren't always consistent.

In the case of drugs, the cost of additional safety through further testing is the lives lost because a particular drug is not yet available. We cannot avoid hard choices.

The Concept of Demand

"Needs" turn out to be mere *wants* when we inspect them closely. That's an important difference, for in the case of wants we may ask: "How *urgently* are they wanted?" Economists get at this question through the concept of *demand.* Demand is a concept that *relates amounts that are purchased to the sacrifices that must be made to obtain these amounts.*

Ask yourself the following questions: How many phonograph records do you want to own? How many times do you want to go out to dinner in a year? What grade do you want from this course?

If you can answer any of those questions, it is because you have assumed some cost in each case. Suppose you said you want an A from this course and plan to get one. What difference would it make if the price of an A went up? The teacher isn't taking bribes; the price of an A *to you* (that's what counts) is the sacrifice you must make to obtain it. Would you still want an A if it required twenty hours of study a week, while a B could be had for just one hour a week? You might still want it, but you would probably not be willing to buy it at such a high price when a fairly good substitute, a B, is so much cheaper. And that is what counts. Human wants seem to be insatiable. But when a want can only be satisfied at some cost— that is to say, by giving up the satisfaction of some other wants to obtain it—we all moderate our desires and accept less than we would like to have.

The phenomenon of which we're speaking is so pervasive and so fundamental that some economists have been willing to assign it the status of a law: the law of demand. This law asserts that there is a negative relation between the amount of anything that people will purchase and the price (sacrifice) they must pay to obtain it. At higher prices, less will be purchased; at lower prices, more will be purchased.

Would you agree that this generalization can be called a *law*? Or can you think of exceptions? Genuine exceptions are rare at best. Why would anyone be indifferent to the sacrifices he must make? Or prefer more sacrifice to less? That's what a person would be doing if he took more of something as the cost of obtaining it increased.

Alleged exceptions to the law of demand are usually based on a misinterpretation of the evidence. A masochist, for example, would not provide an exception, because pain is for him a good and not a sacrifice. But what of the familiar case where the price of something rises and people increase their purchases in anticipation of further price rises? If you think about it carefully you will see that this is not an exception to the law of demand. The expectation of higher prices in the future, created by the initial price rise, has increased people's current demand for the item. It is not the higher price but the changed *expectations* that have caused people to buy more. We would observe something quite different if the initial price increase did *not* create those changed expectations. Another possibility is that changes in the price of substitutes or in available income have not been considered. When the price of beans goes up but the price of hamburger goes up even farther, people may buy more beans because they are now *relatively* cheaper.

It has sometimes been argued that certain prestige goods are exceptions to the law of demand. For example, people supposedly buy mink coats because their price is high, not low. No doubt there are people who buy some items largely to impress others with how much they can afford to pay. And people sometimes, in the absence of better information, judge quality by price, so that over a limited range, at least, their willingness to purchase may be positively rather than negatively related to price.

Even these seeming exceptions can be explained in a way consistent with the law of demand. People may be purchasing prestige rather than mere mink or judging quality by price because they have no better information. But we are not interested in rare curiosities. Whether or not you are willing to call it a law, the fact is undeniable and extremely important: increases in the price of goods will characteristically be accompanied by decreases in the total amount purchased, and decreases in price will characteristically be accompanied by increases in the amount purchased. It is a serious mistake to overlook this pervasive fact.

Money Costs and Other Costs

The price in money that must be paid for something is not a complete measure of its cost to the purchaser. Sometimes, indeed, it is a very inadequate measure, as in the case of the student who wanted an A. Economists know this at least as well as anyone else. The concept of demand definitely does not suggest that money is the only thing that matters to people. Confusion about this point has done so much to create misunderstanding that we might profitably take a moment to clarify the matter.

Consider the case of a man buying soft drinks. Assume that he can purchase them in either returnable bottles or throwaway bottles, and that a six-pack of throwaway bottles is priced at 90¢, while a six-pack of returnable bottles is priced at 80¢ plus an 18¢ deposit. Which will he buy? Which is cheaper?

It depends on the cost to him, of which the retailer's price is only one element. If he doesn't mind saving and returning bottles—that is, if the cost to him of doing so is low—he will probably find the returnable bottles cheaper and will buy them. On the other hand, if he lives in an apartment with very limited storage space, gets to the store rarely, consumes large quantities of soft drinks, and has a waste-disposal chute a few steps from his door, he may well find the throwaway bottles cheaper and will purchase them in preference to returnable bottles.

Now suppose that our hypothetical apartment dweller with a passion for pop attends an ecology conference and comes away convinced that we must recycle to survive. The cost to him of using throwaway bottles suddenly jumps, for now he suffers pangs of guilt every time he tosses a bottle in the waste-disposal chute. The added cost in moral regret may be sufficient to induce him to switch to returnable bottles.

Or it may not. Suppose that he is going on a camping trip and wants to take along a dozen bottles of pop. He must backpack them into his camp site, and backpack the empties out again if he returns the bottles. The added cost of carrying a dozen empties may be enough to overcome the added cost of an uneasy conscience so that, in this case at least, he reverts to throwaway bottles. (Hopefully he throws them in a trash can.)

But let's change the last situation. Suppose the price of throwaway bottles is not 90¢ but $1.00, $1.20, or $1.80. At some price we may confidently expect that the cost of transporting empties will become less than the combined cost of buying throwaway bottles and living with guilt. (Of course, the deposit on returnables will have to rise, too, or he will just use and discard returnable bottles.)

There are several lessons to be drawn from this tale of the pop bottles. To assert that people purchase less of anything as the cost to them increases does not imply that people pay attention only to money, or that people are selfish, or that concern for social welfare does not influence economic behavior. It does imply that people respond to changes in cost and—a crucial implication—that a sufficiently large change in price can be counted on to tip almost any balance. When someone says that Americans won't give up the convenience of throwaway bottles and cans unless the government outlaws them, he overlooks several possibilities. A widespread change in attitude toward the environment could overcome the cost of being inconvenienced. And a sufficiently large tax on throwaway containers (call it a deposit if you wish) would make convenience a luxury too expensive to enjoy very frequently.

The essential point in all this is that the money price of obtaining something is only one part, and occasionally even a very small part, of its cost. What the law of demand asserts is that people will do less of what they want to do as the cost to them of doing it increases, and do more as the cost decreases.

Self-Interest and Social Cooperation

So the law of demand suggests neither that people care only about money, which would be absurd, nor that everyone is selfish, an assertion that is close to meaningless. It is meaningless because someone can always argue that any action was done for selfish reasons: the woman who risks her life to save a neighbor's child from a burning house does so because she wants the plaudits of the community, or because she craves the inner satisfaction of being a hero, or perhaps because she decides it would be more painful to live in the knowledge she might have saved the child than to die attempting a rescue. There is no way to refute such arguments. But there is no way to prove them, either. The economic way of thinking avoids the question. It asserts through the law of demand that people will do less of anything when they must sacrifice a greater amount of *whatever* they value to continue doing it.

When the president asks people to turn their thermostats down to 68 degrees in the winter to conserve heating fuel, many of them will cooperate. Economics does not assert otherwise. On the other hand, some will ignore the request; a few will turn their thermostats *up* out of spite; many will cooperate half-heartedly and only part of the time because they suspect a lot of others are not cooperating at all; some will keep their thermostats up while reasoning to themselves that they are more cold-blooded than the average and suffer more than most people in a chilly house. One weakness of patriotic appeals is that they impose the largest burden on the most patriotic, and this hardly seems fair. The advantage of encouraging conservation by raising the price is that it gives everyone an immediate incentive to economize.

Here is an idea for you to think about. Quite a few colleges have the problem of empty classrooms at 8 A.M. and overcrowded classrooms at 10 and 11. Why not charge a little more to the student who insists upon a 10 o'clock section and turn the extra fee over to the student willing to enroll at 8? Or maybe we could offer the extra fee to the instructors to get better quality teaching at 8? What do you think would be the reaction of students to a proposal like that? How would you respond to the following reactions?

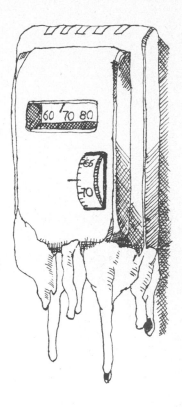

CREEDS AND DEEDS

On Washington's coldest day during the third week in January, reporters gathered in the Office of Management and Budget to be briefed on President Ford's energy conservation plan. The temperature in the room hovered near 80 degrees, according to an item in the *Wall Street Journal* of January 17, 1975.

"Some people just cannot get their eyes open early in the morning." "It wouldn't be fair; some people like to get up early, and why should they have to pay less just because they have a funny metabolism?" "Tuition is high enough already without tacking on an extra charge for 10 o'clock sections." "It wouldn't work. Money isn't everything." "That makes choosing one's classes too commercial."

Who Needs Water?

People are creatures of habit, in what they think as well as what they do. Perhaps this explains why so many have trouble recognizing the significance of substitutes and hence such difficulty in appreciating the law of demand. Water provides an excellent example.

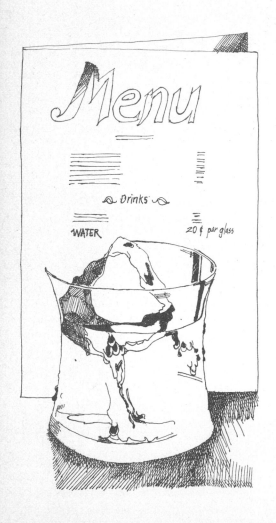

Just a few years ago there was much concern over a serious water shortage in New York City. Several years of less than normal rainfall had depleted the reservoirs from which New York obtained its water, and there was great fear that the city would run short of water during the summer unless consumption could be sharply reduced. A few hardy souls suggested that the city should install more water meters and raise the price of water. The suggestion was not taken very seriously because, as everyone supposedly knows, water is a necessity. "People won't go thirsty just because the price of water goes up a little, or even a lot," said the critics. And so New York launched a massive campaign of education plus legal threat to try to get its citizens to be more sparing in their use of water.

Lawn sprinkling and car washing were condemned. Restaurants were told not to give customers a glass of water with their meals unless they specifically asked for it. The ornamental fountains of the city were turned off—largely as a symbolic gesture, since the water in the fountains is recirculated. Citizens were asked to refrain from keeping their beer cool by letting the shower drip on it. One of the more amusing aspects of the campaign was a set of ads for a particular Scotch whiskey that urged people to drink their Scotch with water. The word *water* was crossed out in the advertisement and *soda* was written above it, with an appended admonition to save water by drinking soda.

The water shortage was not relieved by any of these measures but by a providential end to the drought. "Man proposes but God disposes." Even man might have disposed, however, had he proposed more intelligently. The basic error lay in the assumption that water is a necessity. The truth is that there are many substitutes for water, a fact which becomes glaringly obvious as soon as we break loose from the habit of assuming that people do nothing with water but drink it.

Here are just a few of the substitutes for water in New York City: dirty automobiles, brown lawns, plumbers, migration, deodorant, larger refrigerators (to hold the beer that would otherwise be cooled in the shower), plus a host of small inconveniences. The trick is to persuade people to *use* these substitutes: to call the plumber, for example, and have that leaky toilet repaired rather than allow it to continue wasting fifty gallons of water a day. To spend money on a larger refrigerator. To tolerate a dirty automobile. To put an ice cube in their glass of drinking water rather than let the tap run for several minutes to cool the water. In the case of industries using huge quantities of water, to sacrifice the advantages of a New York location in favor of locating near more plentiful water supplies. Or to install recycling equipment.

But what is the best way to induce the use of substitutes? Educational campaigns and moral exhortation can help. But how much? Most people are expert rationalizers when their own interest is involved, and it is all too easy to put off calling the plumber until the end of the month, or next month, or the month after that. Always fully intending, of course, to do one's civic duty and get that leak repaired.

What about criminal penalties for wasting water? Enforcement becomes a problem here. Are the police to stage surprise raids to catch people cooling their beer in the shower? Shall we fine a man for rinsing his tumbler too many times before taking a drink? What constitutes *criminal* waste?

A quite different approach is available. Is there any way to enlist almost everyone in a conscientious effort to seek out and use substitutes for water? A sizable increase in the price of water just might do the job. Wouldn't the careless householder call the plumber more quickly if that leaky toilet cost more per month than the plumber would charge to fix it? Wouldn't people accept dirty automobiles more readily, or at least not let the hose run the whole time they were washing the family car, if water became very expensive? There is some price for water at which it becomes cheaper to buy a new refrigerator than to use the shower as a cooler. Industries that use large quantities of water will tend to locate elsewhere if the price of water is high in their area of first choice.

And so it goes. There are substitutes for anything. A higher money price will induce some people to find and use some of those substitutes. And the higher the price, the more will substitutes be used.

A Useful Device

Many of the most useful concepts in economics can be conveniently expressed by means of graphs.

Suppose that we somehow obtained the following data on the relation between the price per gallon of water and the number of gallons that would be consumed (not swallowed!) per day in New York City at each of these different prices:

Price Charged the Consumer per Gallon	Millions of Gallons Consumed per Day
$.0035	60
.0028	80
.0021	120
.0016	160
.0012	200
.0009	240
.0003	360
.0001	450
.0000	510

We have graphed these values in figure 2A. The dots express graphically the data from the demand schedule above. If you are not accustomed to working with graphs, study figure 2A until you understand exactly how it was constructed from the demand schedule.

The graph of figure 2A also *adds* something to the information contained in the schedule. We have connected the dots by means of straight lines. The assumption underlying this procedure is that the price can be changed by very small amounts and that there will result small continuous changes in the daily consumption of water. When dealing with the total demand of a large number of consumers, it will be easy to find an individual who makes no response to a small price increase. But you can also find important changes, such as the man who gets his leaky toilet fixed.

Now use the demand curve in thinking through the following questions. (By the way, it is called a demand *curve* even though it is composed exclusively of straight lines. A straight line is simply a curve that doesn't. Like a baseball pitcher's curve that failed to "break.")

1. How much water do New Yorkers "need"? How much will they consume per day if the price of water is zero? Is there an important difference between the two questions?

2. If the price of water has been set for many years at $.0008 per gallon, how much water will the city authorities say that New Yorkers need per day? What are they assuming when they say this?

3. Suppose that New York's reservoirs are being rapidly depleted, and experts predict that the supply will become critically low before fall unless daily consumption is reduced to 180 million gallons. How could the city's water managers obtain this desired reduction in consumption?

4. Notice by how much water consumption would increase if the price were originally $.0035 and were then decreased to $.0003. Do you think that residents of the city would increase their *drinking* by this amount? How might the additional 300 million gallons per day be used?

Time Is on Our Side

If you are at all the suspicious sort of person, you will have wondered whether water consumption really would or could change in response to price changes by as much as the demand curve indicates. Changes take time. And that is an important observation. Changes in the amount purchased will be greater for any given price change the longer the time period allowed for adjustment.

Figure 2A Demand for water

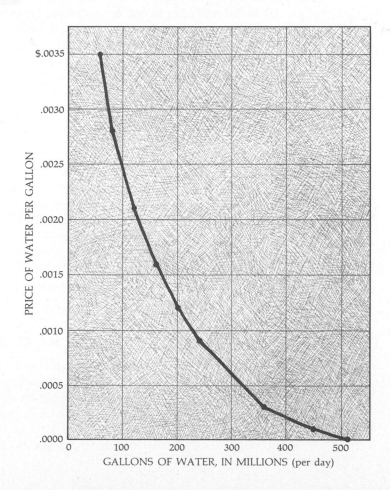

Check this out for yourself with a mental experiment. Suppose the price of water has been $.0003 a gallon for twenty years and it is raised overnight to $.0028. What substitutions for water will be made *right away*? What substitutions would you expect to observe after a month or two had passed? What substitutions would you expect to observe over the next ten years—assuming that everyone expects the price to remain at the higher level?

Try a similar mental experiment with the price of gasoline. Suppose that the federal government levied an additional tax on gasoline of 50¢ per gallon. How do you think this would affect the amount purchased in the subsequent week? In the subsequent six months? After four years had elapsed?

By taking our examples almost entirely from the area of household decisions, we may have obscured the important fact that customers include producers as well as consumers. Business firms use water and gasoline, too, and they sometimes use so much that they are exceptionally sensitive to price changes. You'll be neglecting some of the major factors that cause demand curves to slope downward to the right if you overlook the contribution producers make to the demand for many goods. In the case of water, location decisions are often made on the basis of the expected price of water, and those decisions then affect the quantities demanded in different geographic areas.

But it takes time for customers to find and begin to use substitutes. It also takes time for producers to devise, produce, and publicize substitutes. As a result, the amount by which people increase or decrease their purchases when prices change depends very much on the time period over which we are observing the adjustment. Occasionally even a rather large price increase (or decrease) will lead to no significant decrease (or increase) in consumption—*at first.* And this sometimes causes people to conclude that price has no effect on consumption. A very mistaken conclusion! Nothing in this world happens instantaneously. Man, creature of habit that he is, must be allowed a little time to prove that there are substitutes for anything.

Needs and Rights

You can't imagine how difficult it is to write a book or carry on everyday conversation without using the word *need* unless you try it. But why be so fanatical? It *is* somewhat fanatical; we admit that, and we aren't seriously asking you to purge the word from your vocabulary. Lots of people who talk about needs are kind to dogs and children, and they might conclude that anyone who denies the need for water has lost touch

THE DEMAND FOR ELECTRICITY

Electric power in the Pacific Northwest offers a good illustration of the longer run relationship between prices and quantities demanded. The heavy mountain snowfalls of the region led to the development, beginning in the 1930s, of numerous hydropower plants and a cost per kilowatt in Washington and Oregon that has run about one-half the national average. This encouraged extensive use of electricity in homes and also attracted to the region such industries as electro-process metals and chemicals that are heavy users of electricity. According to 1973 figures released by the Bonneville Power Administration, electricity use in the Pacific Northwest runs around 15,000 kilowatts annually per home compared with a national average about half that, or 7700 kilowatts per year.

with reality. Just be sure to keep in mind that the amount which is "needed" is always going to depend on the sacrifice that must be made in order to obtain it. Say *need* if you must, but mean *demand*.

And be very careful indeed about slipping from *need* into *right*. That's an additional danger that comes along with the word. Once something has been designated as a human need, we move easily to the conclusion that everyone has a right to it. But if that right is to be more than rhetorical, society must have a way to make the good available. What's the point of saying that even people who have chosen to live in a desert have a right to ample water if there's no feasible way to provide it? Or of saying that medical care without regard to one's ability to pay is a right when there aren't enough resources to provide all the care people would demand at a zero price? People already have the right to be secure in their persons and property against crimes of violence. Or they would, at any rate, if declarations were enough to make all criminals reform their ways.

CONSUMER SOVEREIGNTY?

If there are no needs, then obviously there's no greater or more urgent need for milk than there is for shag carpets or electric carving knives. There are no degrees of nonexistence. How then are we to distinguish between goods that make an important contribution to human welfare and goods that are merely frivolous? The best way to get at this question is to ask why we want to make the distinction.

The Evaluation of Wants

It would be too easy to answer that some people want to impose their tastes on others. That's too easy an answer because it implies that the distinction is only useful to cultural tyrants. But parents aren't being tyrants when they tell children that they "need" meat more than chocolate cake and should eat their meat if they aren't hungry enough for both. Surely it isn't mere arrogance to say that a family with a tight budget should cut down on cigarettes rather than on milk for the children. But what about the college professor who tells you that by spending your nights at the discotheque instead of your desk you're displaying a faulty sense of values? Now we're no longer so sure. Is the professor merely trying to impose her tastes on you? Or is she trying to summon you to obey your better self?

The concept of demand is ethically neutral. It asserts that something is desired and tells how much people are willing to sacrifice to obtain it in particular amounts. It says nothing at all about why people desire the good, where that desire came from, or whether they or society will be better off in the long run for having it. Is this a deficiency? Most economists would say that it's not. Demand is merely an analytical concept useful in describing behavior. It doesn't pretend to say anything about what people *ought* to want.

But such a defense isn't altogether accurate. The notion that people ought to have what they want to have, at least within the limits of their ability to pay, is deeply rooted in our society and just as deeply rooted in the history of economic analysis. At least since the time of Adam Smith (1723–1790), who attacked the commercial interests of his day by insisting that production and trade ought to be carried on for the sake of consumption, economists have tended to assume that the wants of consumers should direct the organization of economic activity. *Consumer sovereignty*, as it's called, has been an article of faith and a criterion by which to assess the adequacy of an economy's performance.

On first hearing it sounds eminently sensible and public spirited to insist that an economy should be organized to satisfy the wants of consumers as expressed in the various demands they bring to the marketplace. But what if many of the things that people demand are not things they really want? Of course, the shopper who impulsively buys a chrome plated sandal scraper must in some sense have wanted it at the moment of purchase. The consumer who buys a useless patent medicine because he doesn't realize that it's useless does, in a trivial sense, want what he purchases. The consumer who grabs for a high priced box of cereal because last night's TV commercial is still on his subconscious mind must want it in preference to the adjacent box with the same contents at a lower price, or he wouldn't grab it. But the examples make the critics' points. Consumers are too often foolish, shortsighted, uninformed, and easy prey for manipulative advertising. Poor candidates indeed for sovereignty. How can we defend efforts to make the economic system sensitive and subservient to consumer demands when those demands don't merit satisfaction? And they do not deserve satisfaction if they don't somehow express *genuine* human wants.

But what are "genuine" wants? John Kenneth Galbraith, a well known economist, tackled that question some years ago in a widely read book titled *The Affluent Society* (1958). He used the word *urgent* to describe wants that merited satisfaction, a good choice of words since *urgent* means "pressing for attention." And he argued that for wants to be urgent they must *originate with the individual.* Wants that are contrived by someone else cannot be regarded as urgent wants for an individual, and wants contrived in the very process of satisfying wants would seem to be doubly suspect. Wants can have "bizarre, frivolous, or even immoral origins," Galbraith argued, and still deserve satisfaction. But no case can be made for organizing society to satisfy wants if it is the process of satisfying wants that creates them in the first place.

Galbraith wasn't merely making a case against advertising, the first thing that probably comes to mind. Advertising is only the most direct way in which the system of production shapes (or tries to shape) the wants which it is supposed to fulfill. A less direct but surely more effective way is through emulation. The system of production turns out beanbag chairs; a few people see the chairs and decide that they want them; and once a few people have them, others decide that they want them, too. People usually don't know that they want something, Galbraith argued, until they see it produced, and often not until they see someone else in possession of it. That is the case, at least, in an affluent society, where "physical wants" have long since been fully satisfied.

Are There Any "Original" Wants?

The argument is appealing, but it's also dotted with pitfalls for the unwary. How many people would have wanted to read Galbraith's book if they hadn't first seen it in a bookstore or been turned on to it by an acquaintance or a reviewer? Some may even have bought it after reading an advertisement by the publisher. Shall we say that they are no better off for the book's having been produced and purchased because they wouldn't have wanted it if it hadn't been produced? Or what about the demand for musical records? No one would want them if they weren't produced. Indeed, if no one had ever produced major and minor scales, principles of harmony and counterpoint, musical instruments and people able to play them with skill, who would ever have had a craving for music? Should people's demand for books of poetry not be satisfied because their taste for poetry was created by the producers of poetry?

Galbraith is undoubtedly grasping at an important issue when he suggests that there is much about our system of production and consumption that resembles a dog track, where the greyhounds keep running but never get closer to the mechanical rabbit. But the notion of contrived versus

CIGARETTE ADVERTISING

Cigarette advertising on television was prohibited beginning on January 2, 1971. Newspaper, magazine, and billboard advertising increased after the ban on broadcast advertising, but not by enough to keep total industry expenditures on advertising from falling by 28%. That, of course, was a cost saving to the manufacturers of cigarettes. Meanwhile, cigarette consumption in the U.S. rose 3.3% in the first year after the television ban. Does this prove the ineffectiveness of advertising? If so, why are the makers of cigarettes so foolish as to continue wasting millions of dollars?

There is an alternative explanation that is consistent with what occurred. Advertising may be largely ineffective in persuading people to smoke but highly effective in persuading smokers to use one brand in preference to another. People who express concern about the social power of advertising ought to distinguish carefully between its alleged power to create new tastes and its power to alter purchasing patterns in situations where buyers have trouble distinguishing among brands.

Notice, too, that in such a situation each manufacturer has an incentive to advertise even though the industry as a whole would be better off with advertising prohibited or at least severely limited. The American Medical Association may be more astute than the Tobacco Institute which fought the television ban. The AMA condemns advertising by physicians as unethical. Perhaps the Tobacco Institute will someday discover this same profitable wisdom. New brands of cigarettes would then have as much difficulty in establishing themselves as new doctors have.

original wants doesn't capture the issue very well. There are a few wants, rooted perhaps in our animal natures, that might be called original, such as the desire for food. But even that want takes on forms that are the product of social contrivance. There's nothing natural about a demand for lobster: they're disgusting-looking creatures that almost no one would ever think of eating until he had seen one prepared. The demand for meat is unnatural in India, and the insects so much enjoyed by the Yanomamo of Venezuela are unnatural food in the United States. Archie Bunker turned down a tongue sandwich for his lunch because he wasn't going to eat anything that came out of the mouth of a cow: he asked for a hard-boiled egg instead. *All* of our wants are at least in part the product of socialization.

It may well be true that we could all be just as happy, in the United States at least, by producing and consuming less. Maybe we could even be a good deal happier. An interesting study by Richard Easterlin entitled "Does Money Buy Happiness?" supports what many have long suspected: additional goods increase one's happiness only if others in society aren't getting more, too. Put in another way, our sense of satisfaction tends to depend on what we have *relative to others* in our society.[1] If this is so, the economic system is indeed as much a squirrel cage as it is a social mechanism to serve the sovereign consumer. We could run just as far if we ran more slowly. Maybe we could even run a lot farther, by being able to enjoy a cleaner environment and a less harried existence.

Some Persistent Questions

The picture becomes still more disturbing when we notice that, in much of the world, people are actually hungry and ill from malnutrition. If the economic systems of wealthy societies are indeed chewing up resources without yielding much that is worthwhile, they are squandering resources that might have made a genuine contribution to human welfare if used in other ways for other people. Of course, we have no guarantee that those other people would use the resources wisely and humanely were we to refrain from using them: folly and shortsightedness are hardly confined to affluent consumers. All the more reason to ask, Is this consumer *sovereignty*? If it is, is it worth defending?

But what is the alternative? It's much easier to criticize social systems for their inadequacies than it is to suggest a better system that is also workable. Less consumption of trivia in the United States will not automatically produce food for Africa. We consumed far less in the 1930s than we do now, but had still less to contribute to the poor. Even if we agree

1. Easterlin's study was summarized in *The Public Interest,* Winter 1973, pp. 3–10.

that working and consuming is largely pursuit of a mechanical rabbit pro-
grammed to remain forever just out of our reach, what can we do about it?
Assuming that there are genuine human wants whose satisfaction contributes to fulfillment and self-actualization and that these have been
covered over or distorted by artificial and self-negating demands, how do
we even begin to suppress the false and nurture the true?

Some people believe that it will require a revolution. But what kind of
revolution? Political revolutions in this century have certainly demonstrated that high ideals don't by themselves create humane societies. Is it
a *social* revolution these people have in mind? But what does that mean?
Many once believed that it meant abolition of the capitalist system, and
some still do. But what do we put in its place? Socialism in the Soviet
Union has lusted after more goods at least as passionately as capitalism
and produced them less efficiently and at a high cost in political freedom.
Of course, one can always argue that the Soviet Union does not have *true*
socialism. But then what *is* "true socialism"? How does it work? How does
it transform those selfish, envious, anxious, foolish, and shortsighted
people we see today into something better?

The Importance of Limited Questions

Economists are probably just as interested in those questions as people
generally. But for the most part they don't pay a lot of attention to them
in their professional work. They take demand curves as given and assume
that the wants behind them are legitimate. The prices that people are
willing to pay for goods are assumed to represent *at least* the value of those
goods—*at least* because people often pay less than they would be willing to
pay, but presumably never pay *more* than the good is worth to them. And
that gives economists a handle with which to get an initial hold on the
problem of explaining how economic systems work.

*An economy is a social system for securing cooperation among people in obtaining
from available resources a maximum of whatever is wanted.* That definition leaves
a lot of questions wide open. Above all, it makes no attempt to specify
what should be wanted or even whose wants should be satisfied. They
could be the wants of everyone, of a privileged minority or majority, or of
an elite with the power to determine what people ought to want. Regardless of how that question is answered, every economy must secure social
cooperation.

There are more than 200 million people in the United States. There are
trillions of human resources: powerful muscles, sonorous voices, quick
wits, bursting energies in varying proportions, and all kinds of acquired
skills, interests, knowledge, and ambitions. There are trillions of non-
human resources scattered everywhere, some private property, some not;

some well known, others still undiscovered, few known to more than a handful of people. And there are an infinite number of ways in which these resources could be employed to achieve an infinitely variable constellation of purposes. How can all this be coordinated? We rarely ask that question because we've grown so accustomed to coordination. A breakdown in the system is news because we've learned to take for granted what is in reality an astonishingly complex mechanism of coordination. Think for a moment how many separate decisions had to be made and actions taken so that you could obtain a new light bulb the last time you wanted one. Miners, engineers, machinists, truck drivers, billing clerks, and more people than we can begin to list each played a small but productive part in putting a hundred watt bulb where you wanted it when you wanted it. How did they find out what they were supposed to do? How were they persuaded to do it? We could surely use more light on the significant questions that Galbraith and others are posing. But meanwhile we're going to want the kind of light that hundred watt bulbs provide. Their simple illumination will even help us in our search for a deeper illumination—a symbol, perhaps, for the importance of what seem to be trivial problems. Proposals for reconstruction of the social order must deal with the day to day problems of social coordination if they are to be of any value. And that's where the economist, with his admittedly limited questions and consequently limited answers, has something important to say.

Economizing Behavior

The concept of demand is central to the economic way of thinking because it interprets the behavior of producers as well as consumers. Producers must also choose constantly among substitutes in the process of organizing production; for producers as well as for consumers there are substitutes for everything; the demand curves for riveters, turret lathes, industrial sites, marketing agents, and all the infinite paraphernalia of production slope downward to the right just as do the demand curves for passenger automobiles, medical care, and soda pop in returnable bottles. The theory of demand is not so much the theory of consumer behavior as it is the theory of *economizing* behavior. And *everyone* economizes: the trade association lobbyist in Washington urging Congress to exclude foreign competitors as well as the supermarket shopper hesitating between pickled herring and smoked oysters. Economics explains how the economizing behavior of individuals is coordinated in a system of social cooperation.

The authors admit to a strong predisposition in favor of individual sovereignty. Notice that we did not say *consumer* sovereignty. Being a consumer is only one aspect of being human: we are also producers, dreamers,

lovers, idlers, and much else besides. We agree with those who say that individuals do not always know what they really want; but we also think that in the first instance an individual should be considered the best judge of his own welfare. We know that individuals in the process of pursuing what they want sometimes create undesirable or unforeseen consequences for themselves and others; we also think that economics helps us see why this occurs. We know that wealth and power are unequally distributed in our society (and every other known society) and that this raises questions of justice; but we also believe that economics furnishes insights into the nature, use, and control of social power and that the study of economics is therefore especially important for all those who want to improve the existing system.

Once Over Lightly

Every good has substitutes: other goods which will be used in its stead when the cost of using the original good rises, other goods for which the original good will substitute when *their* relative cost goes up.

By talking about "needs," we can sometimes win arguments we might otherwise lose. "Needs" are actually wants of many different urgencies.

People want more or less of a good as the *cost to them* decreases or increases.

The concept of *demand* is preferable to the concept of *need* because demand relates the amounts that are purchased to the sacrifices that must be made to obtain these amounts.

The "law of demand" asserts that more will be purchased at lower prices, less at higher prices—assuming that something in addition to the price has not changed to offset this consequence.

The money cost of a good is only one part of the cost that affects people's decisions.

A sufficiently large change in money cost (price) can usually overcome the effects that nonmoney costs exert on people's decisions.

A change in price will usually induce a larger change in amounts purchased when more time is allowed for consumers and producers to learn about and invent new substitutes.

The view that the economic system ought to provide what people want, or that production should be guided by demand, has long been a working assumption of economic theory. The term *consumer sovereignty,* which is generally used to describe this principle, is misleading because it suggests that the preferences of producers are unimportant; *individual sovereignty* more accurately describes the perspective from which economists have traditionally evaluated economic performance.

The economic way of thinking simply accepts individual preferences as given and provides little help to anyone who wishes to *evaluate* them. This does not mean economists approve of the way wants are formed in our society or believe individuals always want what is best for themselves or the larger society.

The concept of demand forms the basis for the theory of *economizing behavior*, behavior aimed at obtaining as much as possible from what is available.

QUESTIONS FOR DISCUSSION

1. Assume that Congress has decided to reduce consumption of nonreusable containers in order to preserve Spaceship Earth. Evaluate the following arguments that might be used in the discussion of how to go about achieving this goal.

   (*a*) "We know we cannot survive unless we stop using things and then discarding them. The only sensible approach, therefore, is a legal ban on all nonreusable containers of any kind."

   (*b*) "People will do the right thing once they understand the problem. I don't think we should start passing laws. We should assume that the American people are public-spirited and we should educate them to the facts."

   (*c*) "It has been proposed by some that we place a tax on the manufacture of containers to encourage deposit-and-return. This would not work because people just would not care about the tax. Moreover, a tax says in effect that it's all right to pollute if you're rich, but not if you're poor."

2. Most systems of hospitalization insurance substantially reduce the cost to the patient of hospitalization, sometimes to zero. How does this affect hospital use? Why? Evaluate the argument that it does not affect hospital use since "no one gets sick just because hospitals are cheap, or avoids getting sick because they're expensive."

3. In 1967 the president of the American Medical Association was quoted as saying that medical care was a privilege and not a right. Today the AMA officially proclaims that "health care is the right of everyone." What quantity and quality of health care do you suppose they're talking about?

4. Here is a classroom exercise that might be fun while also sharpening your talent for recognizing substitution possibilities. Let one person come up with two goods that seem to have no connection and challenge others to construct a plausible set of circumstances in which they would be substitutes. (Avoid the easy, though correct, answer that all goods are in the last analysis substitutes inasmuch as the acquisition of each uses up scarce time or income.)

5. If a prestigious store (Neiman-Marcus in Dallas, for example) were to put its Chanel No. 5 perfume on sale for one-fourth the current price, do you think customers would purchase more? What do you think would happen if a drugstore in a modest income neighborhood did the same thing? Suppose that each store sold Chanel No. 5 under another label, one that customers had never heard of, and offered it successively at each of the two prices. At which price do you think each store would sell more perfume?

6. If the government forbids motorists to drive more than 55 miles per hour, does everyone stay within the 55 mile limit? What are the costs of going faster? What are some of the costs of going faster that do not fall on the speeding motorist? Do these latter costs affect motorists' decisions? Why might the fact that faster driving uses up more of the nation's scarce petroleum reduce the speed of some drivers but not others?

7. Why do people live in New York City if the costs of doing so—high rents, noise, dirt, congestion, the risks of being robbed or assaulted—are so high? Is it true that most of them "have no choice"? What do you think would happen if the costs listed above were significantly reduced?

8. Do you think it's true that people sometimes want to impose their tastes on others? Disregarding the case of parents and children, do you think that's ever defensible? Are you imposing your tastes on your friends when you tell them enthusiastically about all the fun and good exercise you've had since you started playing tennis?

9. Many of the people who live in substandard housing have low incomes. Would substandard housing disappear if every family received the average income? Would everyone read more books if they were sold at a zero price?

10. One of the recurring themes of this book will be the *informational role* performed by prices. People learn about increased scarcities by paying attention to prices. How did most Americans discover in 1974 that the Arab nations were buying more sugar, the sugar beet crop in the Soviet Union had fallen short of expectations, and hurricanes had reduced the sugar cane harvest in the Gulf of Mexico region? What did people do when they found out? Why? (One of the articles reprinted in the appendix, "The Use of Knowledge in Society" by the 1974 Nobel prizewinner F. A. Hayek, is a thoughtful exploration of the price system as a social device for economizing effectively with very little information.)

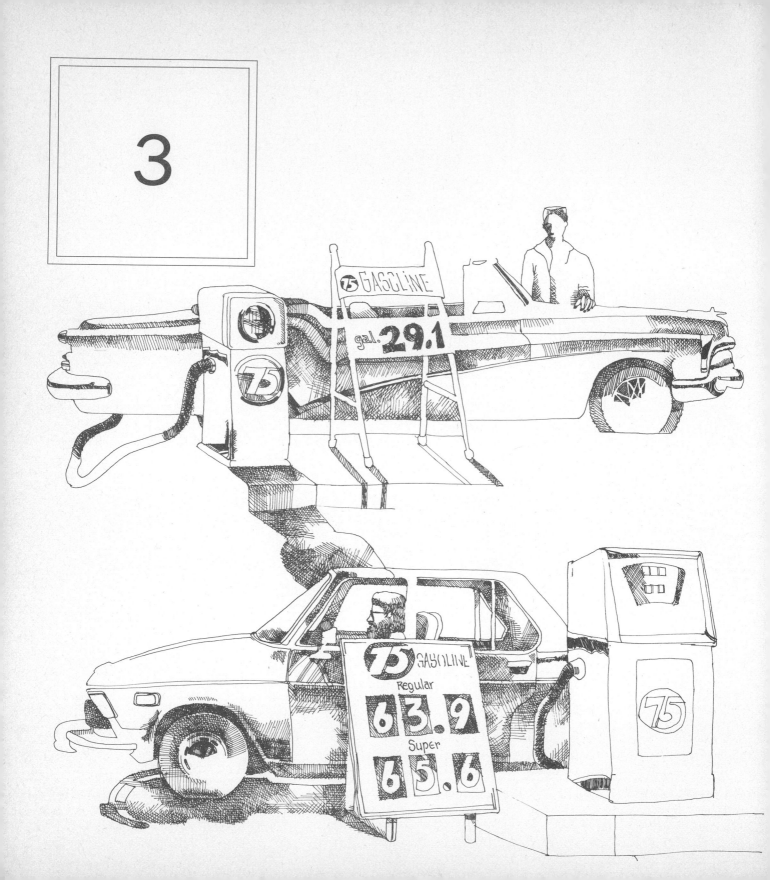

PRICES, INCOME, AND DEMAND

Americans are traveling a lot more today than they used to. That familiar statistic the Average American traveled about 75% more inter-urban miles in 1970 than he did in 1950. What has made us so mobile? Technology and restlessness? They surely played a role. But why was it that in 1970 we traveled 30% less by bus, 75% less by train, 75% more by automobile, and *nine times* as many passenger-miles per capita by airplanes?

These changes were not inevitable. In large part they were a response to higher incomes and shifts in relative prices, reflecting what the economist calls *elasticities of demand.*

PRICES AND DEMAND

It is extremely cumbersome to talk about "the amount by which people increase or decrease their purchases when the price changes." But this is an important relationship with many useful applications. So economists have invented a special phrase that summarizes the relationship. The formal title of the concept is *price elasticity of demand.*

That's an appropriate name. Elasticity means responsiveness. If the amount of any good that people purchase changes substantially in response to a small change in price, demand is said to be elastic. If even a very large price change results in little change in the amount purchased, demand is said to be inelastic.

35

Price elasticity of demand is defined precisely as *the percentage change in quantity demanded divided by the percentage change in price.* Thus, if a 10% increase in the price of eggs leads to a 5% reduction in the number of eggs sold, the elasticity of demand is 5% divided by 10%, or .5. To be completely accurate, it is *minus .5,* since price and amount purchased vary inversely. But for simplicity we shall ignore the minus sign and treat the coefficients of elasticity as if they were positive.

Whenever the coefficient of elasticity is greater than one (ignoring the sign)—that is to say, whenever the percentage change in quantity is *greater* than the percentage change in price—demand is said to be elastic. Whenever the coefficient of elasticity is less than one, which means whenever the percentage change in quantity is *less* than the percentage change in price, demand is said to be inelastic. Compulsive learners will want to know what is said when the percentage change in quantity is exactly equal to the percentage change in price, so that the coefficient of demand elasticity is exactly one. You may file away the information that demand is then *unit elastic.* (Economics is a very systematic discipline.)

You can begin to familiarize yourself with the uses of this concept by asking whether demand is elastic or inelastic in each case below. In some instances you will have to supply information from your own experience. But you have all presumably had some experience with salt and gasoline. Each case is discussed in the subsequent paragraphs.

1. "People aren't going to buy much more no matter how far we cut the price."

2. "This is a competitive business. We would lose half our customers if we raised our prices by as little as 2%."

3. The demand for salt.

4. The demand for Morton's salt.

5. The demand for Morton's salt at the Kroger Store at Fifth and Main.

6. The demand for gasoline.

7. The demand for Shell gasoline.

8. The demand for gasoline at Friendly Bob's Shell Service.

9. "The university's total receipts from tuition would actually increase if they cut the tuition rates by 20%."

10. "It's odd but true. Wheat farmers would gross more money if they all got together and burned one-quarter of this year's crop."

11. If the statement in 10 is true, does it follow that they could gross even more money by burning one-half of the crop?

Price Elasticity in Practice

1. "People aren't going to buy much more no matter how far we cut the price." If a businessman doubts that even a very large price decrease will do much to increase his sales, he believes that his demand is highly inelastic. He will not want to lower his price under such circumstances for he will lose more through the lower price than he will gain through the larger volume. But if people don't respond very much to a price cut, will they also be relatively insensitive to a price hike? If they are, a businessman out to increase his income will want to raise his price. Businessmen typically complain that prices are too low. Then why don't they raise their prices? It's a free country, isn't it? The answer, of course, is that they would usually lose too many customers if they did so. It is the elasticity of demand that determines whether or not a businessman can add to his money receipts by raising his prices.

2. "This is a competitive business. We would lose half our customers if we raised our prices by as little as 2%." The businessman making this statement is saying in effect that he faces a highly elastic demand: A 50% decline in quantity demanded would follow a mere 2% increase in price. The coefficient of elasticity is 25. The demand is very elastic indeed. Another way of putting it would be to say that his customers are extremely sensitive to any price change. And that makes it difficult for him to raise his prices, however eager he might be to do so.

3. The demand for salt. What makes demand curves elastic or inelastic? The availability of good substitutes is clearly an important factor. Another is the importance of the item in the budget of purchasers. If the expenditure on some good is large relative to the income or wealth of the purchaser, he will be more sensitive to any change in its price. Isn't that true from your own experience? Suppose you smoke and also attend movies twice a week. A book of matches costs a penny and movies $2.50. It is not likely that a 200 percent increase in match prices will have much effect on your smoking. But a 50 percent increase in the price of movies would substantially affect your movie going if you have a typical student's income.

Apply this to table salt. One pound of salt lasts a long time and costs less than 10¢. So who cares? Housewives will be relatively insensitive to any change in the price of salt. Moreover, salt has few good substitutes. You would not be inclined to put sugar on your eggs if the price of salt rose dramatically, just as you would not cut the pepper and double the salt if the price of salt fell substantially.

Adam Smith, often called the founder of modern economics, observed in *The Wealth of Nations* (1776) that "salt is a very ancient and very universal subject of taxation. . . . The quantity annually consumed by any

individual is so small, and may be purchased so gradually, that nobody, it seems to have been thought, could feel very sensibly even a pretty heavy tax upon it." Moreover, salt was one of "the necessaries of life" in Smith's terminology. We can object to the term *necessary* and express Smith's meaning more accurately: salt has few good substitutes. The result is a highly inelastic demand and an apparently irresistible temptation to governments in ancient times to levy taxes on salt.

But it's possible to exaggerate the inelasticity of even the demand for salt. Householders in wintry regions sometimes sprinkle table salt on their sidewalks or porch steps to melt the ice. If salt were ten times as expensive, many would substitute chopping and scraping for salt.

4. The demand for Morton's salt. Why would the demand for Morton's salt be less inelastic than the demand for salt? Because there are substitutes—namely, other brands of salt. The Morton Salt Company is not in the privileged position of ancient governments, which could raise the price of *all* salt. If someone in the marketing department at Morton chanced to read Adam Smith and was inspired by him to double the price, the grocery stores that are Morton's customers would tend to shift their purchases to other salt manufacturers.

5. The demand for Morton's salt at the Kroger Store at Fifth and Main. If there are more good substitutes for Morton's salt than for salt, there are even more good substitutes for the Morton's salt sold at the local Kroger store. We have moved from a very inelastic to what is probably a highly elastic demand for the same quantity. And that is why you aren't victimized when you purchase salt. You might be willing to pay $2 a pound if salt was not available at a lower price. But fortunately for you, there are many options. A seller who tried to take advantage of the fact that the total demand for salt is highly inelastic would lose his customers. The demand for *the salt he sells* will be quite elastic.

People often make the mistake of assuming that those who sell "vital necessities" could get away with charging almost any price they chose. We have learned to be suspicious of the phrase *vital necessities.* Now we see again the grounds for this suspicion. Food has as good a claim as anything to the title "vital necessity." But the relevant fact is that *no one buys food.* Housewives do not purchase a pound of "food"; they buy a pound of hamburger, or bacon, or calf's liver. And there are many sellers selling many kinds of food. All of which means that there are excellent substitutes for specific food commodities, and hence demand curves are highly elastic. So sellers are for the most part closely constrained in the prices they can charge.

6, 7, 8. The demand for gasoline, for Shell gasoline, for gasoline at Friendly Bob's Shell Service. Much of what has just been said about salt can also be applied to the demand for gasoline. Because gasoline is a more significant item than salt in the consumer's budget, we should expect the demand for gasoline to be less inelastic than the demand for salt. Once again, however, no one buys mere gasoline. There are many options, so that the proprietor of Friendly Bob's Shell Service cannot afford to raise his price even when he's complaining that he makes almost nothing on a tankful of gasoline. The demand curve with which he must live is very elastic.

Remember also what was said in the last chapter about the importance of *time:* greater substitution will occur in response to a price change the more time elapses. We can now express the same thought another way: Demand curves are more elastic over longer than over shorter periods. Gasoline provides an excellent example. If the federal government pushed up the price of gasoline across the board by imposing a large additional tax, motorists would at first grumble but pay. Then they would begin to form car pools and investigate public transportation. Still later some would move in order to be closer to work. When they replaced their present cars, many would switch from eight cylinders to four. Automobile manufacturers would meanwhile be shifting toward greater production of economy cars and less production of gas-guzzlers. Some technological changes to reduce gasoline consumption that were not economical on balance at the former price of gasoline would become economical at the higher price. These are the kinds of factors that make demand curves more elastic in the long run.

9. "The university's total receipts from tuition would actually increase if they cut the tuition rates by 20%." The university's total receipts from tuition are the product of the tuition rate and the number of students who enroll. If a 20% decrease in the tuition rate results in an increase in tuition receipts, then there must have been a *more than* 20% increase in enrollment. The percentage change in quantity demanded is greater than the percentage change in price, so demand is elastic.

This suggests a simple way of thinking about elasticity. Keep in mind that the quantity demanded will always move in the opposite direction from the price. So if a price change causes *total receipts* to move in the *opposite* direction from the price change, demand must be elastic. The change in the quantity purchased has to be larger in percentage terms than the price change, because total receipts are nothing but the product of price and quantity. And that is the definition of an elastic demand. If a price change causes *total receipts* to move in the *same* direction as the price change, demand must be inelastic. The change in amount purchased was not large enough to outweigh the change in price. And that is the meaning of an inelastic demand. You can satisfy yourself that this relationship holds by running through a numerical example.

Assume that 1000 students will enroll if the tuition is $500 per year, but only 900 will enroll if the tuition is $600 per year. Is the demand elastic or inelastic within this range of tuition charges? We notice that the university's total receipts change *in the same direction* as the price change: 1000 × 500 is less than 900 × 600. So the demand is inelastic by the rule given above. We can confirm this with a little arithmetic. The percentage change in quantity demanded is 100 enrollments divided by 950. (A percentage change is the change divided by the base: we chose the average of 1000 and 900 as the base, because we want to get the same answer whether we raise the price from $500 to $600 or lower it from $600 to $500.) The percentage change in price is $100 divided by $550—where we again use the average of the two values between which we're moving as the base. The coefficient of elasticity is $^{11}/_{19}$, or .58.

Now assume instead that enrollment falls from 1000 to 800 as a result of the tuition increase from $500 to $600. In this case total receipts and price are moving *in opposite directions:* 1000 × 500 is greater than 800 × 600. So the demand must be elastic. A few calculations will verify this conclusion. The percentage change in quantity is now 200 divided by 900; the percentage change in price is again 100 divided by 550. (The units don't matter; they cancel out.) The coefficient of elasticity is $^{11}/_{9}$, or 1.22.

Do not jump to the conclusion that the university will always be in a better financial position, given an elastic demand, if it lowers its tuition. True, lower tuition charges will mean larger receipts whenever demand is elastic; but a larger enrollment probably also means larger costs. The university must decide in such a case whether the addition to total receipts will be larger than the addition to total costs. But problems of pricing strategy must be deferred until we reach chapters 10 and 11.

10. "It's odd but true. Wheat farmers would gross more money if they all got together and burned one-quarter of this year's crop." The logic of

number 9 applies also here. Farmers can only gross more money while selling less wheat if the percentage change in price is greater than the percentage change in the amount sold. Demand would have to be inelastic. The only difference is that we have reversed the causal relationship assumed up till now. We have been tacitly assuming that sellers set the price and buyers respond. This is not always the best way to look at the price-quantity relationship. In some industries, such as agriculture for the most part, it is more useful to assume that the quantity available for sale will determine the price. We'll be talking a lot about this in chapters 10 and 11. For now it is only important to notice that the relationship between changes in total sales and changes in price depends on the elasticity of demand.

Farmers may never have heard about elastic or inelastic demands. But when they lobby for government controls on production, they are usually very much aware of the relation between price and the amount that is sold. You can, like Molière's famous M. Jourdain who spoke prose for forty years without knowing it, make good use of demand elasticities without ever having heard the term.

11. Could wheat farmers do even better by burning one-half of the crop? The elasticity of demand will almost certainly not be the same at all the different positions along a demand schedule or curve. As a general rule, demand will be more elastic at higher prices (and smaller quantities) than at lower prices (and larger quantities). Why? Basically because people tend to be more sensitive to price changes when the price in question is large (relative to their incomes) than when it is small. Consequently, if farmers somehow agreed upon a scheme for destroying wheat in order to raise its price, at some point they would run into an elastic demand. And as soon as the demand turned from inelastic to elastic, total receipts would go down as a consequence of further price increases.

This relationship may become clearer to you if you examine a straight-line demand curve. Along the upper left portion of the demand curve, any price change of a given amount will be a *smaller percentage change* than it will be along the lower right portion of the curve. At the same time, the *percentage change* in quantity demanded will be getting *larger* as we move from the lower right portion of the curve to the upper left. Since elasticity of demand is the ratio of these percentage changes, the coefficient of elasticity must be increasing continuously as we move up and back along a straight-line demand curve.

The Myth of Vertical Demand

But enough of such technicalities. In the six statements with which we began chapter 2, what was being implicitly assumed about the elasticity of

demand? Our objection to each statement, you recall, was that it ignored the fact that all goods have substitutes and that substitution does occur when prices change. In other words, demand curves are *not* completely inelastic. A completely inelastic demand curve would graph as a vertical line. You would be wise not to look for such demand curves in the real world.

You would also be wise to look out for people who argue as if completely inelastic demand curves are the rule. Here are some additional examples to give you practise in being wary.

"The Mona Lisa is a priceless painting."

Don't believe it. If the French government decided to sell the Mona Lisa at auction, it would be bought at a finite price. No doubt wealthy collectors would be eager to buy it, and might even carelessly say something like "I'd give *anything* to get it." The inaccuracy of their speech would be demonstrated as the bidding proceeded and the collectors, one by one, dropped out of the auction.

"National security requires four million men in uniform."

That sounds like a Pentagon statement. We might put the Pentagon to a hypothetical test by asking the chairman of the Joint Chiefs of Staff whether he would still insist on four million servicemen if the cost of maintaining a military establishment of this size rose to $100 billion annually. If he refused to budge and kept insisting that the Pentagon demand is completely inelastic at four million men, we could shrug our shoulders and recall what the law of demand does and does not assert. It asserts that people find substitutes for anything when the cost *to them* increases. It does not assert that people become willing to reduce their purchases when *someone else* must pay a higher price. If the salaries of generals were made to vary inversely with the total number of men in the army, the military demand for personnel would prove to be far more elastic than the Pentagon is now willing to admit.

"Cleaning up air pollution will be costly. But we cannot weigh money against clean air."

The assumption once again is that the demand for some good, in this case clean air, is completely inelastic. But anyone who thinks about it for a moment will see that it obviously is not. There are degrees of clean air. How clean do we want the air to be? "As clean as possible" is no answer because we can always make the air cleaner. We could get rid of all factories, all cars, and all home heating systems. If we wanted still more cleanliness in our air, we could start getting rid of people who perspire excessively. But long before this point we would all have noticed that the demand for clean air is not perfectly inelastic. Clean air is a good. But there are costs involved in obtaining it. Intelligent pollution-control programs seek to balance the benefits of additional clean air against the additional costs that must be incurred to get it.

The law of demand can be expressed in the language of elasticity: There is no such thing as a completely inelastic demand over the entire range of possible prices. Most purchasers will respond at least a little to changes in the cost to them, and *all* purchasers would respond to a sufficiently large change. If this seems too obvious to bother mentioning, consult your daily newspaper for evidence that it is by no means obvious to everyone. Well-intentioned people and some not so well intentioned talk constantly of basic needs, minimum requirements, and absolute necessities.

Demand curves are rarely as inelastic as orators suppose. That does not imply, of course, that they are always elastic. That is a more difficult question to be answered by looking at each case. But as we shall subsequently discover, it is a very important question for anyone who wants to decide how well our economic system functions.

Estimating Elasticity

When the oil exporting countries of the Middle East imposed their embargo on sales to the United States in 1973, the price elasticity of demand for gasoline became an issue in the newspapers. Some gloomily predicted a short run elasticity as low as .2, which means that a 20% reduction in sales would require a 100% increase in the price of gasoline. Optimistic estimates predicted an elasticity of .4, in which case a 50% increase in price would still be necessary to reduce consumption by 20%. Other estimates tended to range between .2 and .4. Let's take a look at the difference that elasticity makes.

The average retail price of gasoline in 1972 was very close to 36¢. Under the most optimistic estimate cited above, the price would have to rise to 54¢ to cut purchases back to available supply if the supply were reduced by 20%: a 20% reduction in quantity demanded divided by a 50% increase in the price yields an elasticity coefficient of .4. With a demand elasticity of only .3, the price would have to rise to 60¢. And it would have to go all the way to 72¢ under the conditions of the most unfavorable estimate, an elasticity of .2.

None of these estimates was put forward in 1973 with a great deal of confidence; we simply had no experience in the United States with changes of this magnitude in the price of gasoline. And extrapolation is risky in cases of this sort. The fact that a 10% price increase has in the past led to a 3% reduction in consumption does not mean that a 100% increase will yield a 30% reduction. We can be certain, in fact, that if the relative price of a good rises far enough, the demand for it will eventually become

AN IMPORTANT NOTE ON *RELATIVE* PRICES

From the beginning of the book, whenever we've talked about a change in the price of some good we've meant a change in its *relative price: its price in relation to other goods.* For the last decade or so the United States has experienced a general rise in prices. The average of *all* prices has been going up as a result of forces we'll begin to examine in chapter 16. Now if all prices rise by the same percentage, then relative prices do not change at all. Since we're trying to understand the way in which relative prices guide consumer and producer decisions, we have to distinguish the change in a good's price that was caused by general inflation from the change caused by an alteration in the scarcity of that particular good.

Take the case of gasoline prices. An increase from 36¢ per gallon for regular at the beginning of 1972 to 58¢ at the end of 1974 was a 61% increase (using the original price as the base). But the average of *all* prices paid by consumers rose 26% over this period. The increase in the relative price of gasoline was therefore only about 35%. That is equivalent in its effects to an increase of only $12\frac{1}{2}$¢, from 36¢ to about 48¢.

Or take the price changes from 1955 to 1974. The average price of gasoline in 1955 was 29¢. From 29¢ to 58¢ is a 100% increase. When we deduct the rate of increase in the general price level between 1955 and 1974, however, the change in the relative price of gasoline was only about 6%. In short, gasoline was not actually much more expensive in 1975 at 58¢ than it had been in 1955 at 29¢ a gallon. And it's the relative price that matters.

Unless the text specifically states otherwise, all references to price changes will mean changes in relative price. In other words, the price of everything else will be assumed not to change when we ask about the consequences of a change in the price of lobster, copper, or the services of elevator operators.

elastic. That is because at higher prices any good makes a larger dent in people's budgets and they consequently become more sensitive to changes in its price. Someone with a weekly take home pay of $150 may ignore the fact that he is now spending $9 a week rather than $6 on gasoline because its price has gone up; he is less likely to ignore an increase from $20 to $30 in his expenditures for gasoline. His budget is more likely to compel a cut in gasoline consumption in the second case. And every gallon not consumed will now free a larger portion of his income for other purposes.

A TECHNICAL NOTE ON
THE CALCULATION OF PERCENTAGE CHANGES

Is a price increase from 36¢ to 72¢ a 100% increase? That depends on how you interpret percentage changes, a matter on which there is unfortunately no uniform practice. Note that a decrease from 72¢ to 36¢ is only a 50% change—when we use the original value as the base in calculating the percentage change. For some purposes that is a misleading way of handling percentage changes because it arbitrarily makes every increase seem larger than an identical decrease. The bias arises from the fact that when the original value is chosen as the base, a smaller base is always used for increases than for decreases. We have already suggested a way to avoid this bias: by selecting as the base neither the original nor the subsequent value but the average of the two. Then the percentage change will be the same going up as coming down. By *this* method of calculation a 100% increase from a price of 36¢ is an increase to $1.08 and a 100% decrease from $1.08 returns the price to 36¢. The change in price of 72¢ is exactly 100% of the average of $1.08 and 36¢. The point is worth your attention because percentage changes are a common way of making comparisons; but the comparisons can be quite misleading when the percentage changes are large and the precise method by which they were calculated is not stated. For small percentage changes the bias introduced through choice of a base is less significant.

INCOME AND DEMAND

One of the reasons for the low elasticity of demand for gasoline is that its price *relative to income* in the United States had been falling for many years. The average price of gasoline was about 29¢ a gallon in 1955 when per capita disposable income was $1666. This means that it took $145, or 8.7% of per capita disposable income, to buy 500 gallons of gasoline in 1955. For 500 gallons of gasoline to use up 8.7% of income in 1973, its price would have had to be 73¢ a gallon. So it's not surprising that the driving habits of Americans did not change drastically in 1974 even when the price of gasoline rose to about 60¢ a gallon.

The elasticity of demand for a good will depend, then, upon its price *relative to income* as well as upon the range of available substitutes. The low elasticity of demand for gasoline results from the fact that its price has been declining substantially relative to income for many years and that the substitutes for gasoline don't appeal strongly to a lot of people. Let's apply this reasoning to a hypothetical case. Suppose we want to make ourselves less vulnerable to political blackmail by oil exporting nations. A more elastic demand reduces vulnerability. We could increase the elasticity of demand by raising the price of gasoline substantially (through an additional federal tax) or by improving the quality of such substitutes as public transportation systems, which use far less fuel per passenger ride. The higher cost of driving would presumably increase the demand for public transportation, and the tax could be used to finance improvements that would in turn make public transportation a more attractive substitute.

The other principal factor upon which demand elasticity depends is time, as we've mentioned previously. Time permits consumers to search out acceptable substitutes and gives producers a chance to contrive new ones. Elasticity is a measure of responsiveness or flexibility, and everything is more flexible over a longer than a shorter time. Some of the 1973 estimates on the elasticity of demand for gasoline *given one year* for adjustments to occur were in the vicinity of .8. A 20% reduction in the quantity demanded would require only a 25% increase in the price if elasticity were .8.

Demand versus Quantity Demanded

In using the concepts of demand and elasticity it's important to keep an eye on other factors that may be changing along with the price. Elasticity measures the responsiveness of the quantity demanded to changes in the price on the assumption that nothing has occurred to change the demand curve itself. The demand curve for any good depends upon people's tastes and preferences, their incomes, and the properties of substitutes. *With the demand curve given and constant,* the specific quantity that will be demanded depends upon the price.

You can avoid a very common confusion by carefully observing the distinction between *demand* and the *quantity demanded.* Demand is a relation between quantity demanded and price. The demand for gasoline is expressed by a series of prices and a series of corresponding quantities that would be demanded (or amounts that would be purchased) at those prices during some period of time, expressed either in a schedule or a curve. A movement from one row (or line) of the schedule to another, or from one point on the curve to another, should always be called a change in the *quantity demanded,* not a change in the *demand.* The latter would be a change in the schedule itself, a shift in the curve caused by a change in tastes and preferences, or income, or the perceived properties of substitutes. The relative prices of substitutes are among their most important properties.

If this seems a terribly abstract or pedantic distinction, try your hand at locating the error in the following argument. It arises from a failure to observe the distinction.

> If the government puts a large new tax on gasoline so that its price goes up, the demand will fall. But when the demand for anything falls, its price tends to fall. So we can't be sure that the tax will actually raise the price of gasoline.

Can you spot the error? It's in the main clause of the first sentence. The demand will *not* fall. Only the *quantity demanded* will fall. So the next two sentences are mistaken conclusions. When the quantity demanded falls in response to the price increase, that's the end of the matter. Of course, the higher price may over time call forth new substitutes, and the appearance of new substitutes is capable of causing the demand curve to shift—a true change in demand.

If a combination of rising incomes, environmental concern, and new interest in outdoor exercise induces more people to want bicycles, the demand for bicycles will increase. And both the price and quantity demanded may well increase as a consequence. This actually occurred in 1971. You have grasped the distinction between demand and quantity demanded if you see clearly why this in no way contradicts the law of demand. An increase in demand, or a shift upward and to the right in the demand curve, will pull up both price and quantity demanded. But it was still true with the high demand of 1971, as it had been with the low demand of 1969, that a smaller quantity of bicycles was demanded at higher than at lower prices. And this is what the law of demand asserts.

Income Elasticity of Demand

Price elasticity of demand is the oldest child in a rather large family of elasticity concepts. The size of the family should not surprise you. Economics is useful because change occurs; it attempts to predict or understand the consequences of changes. Elasticity concepts provide a way of focusing on particular change relationships and of discussing them in quantitative terms. So new children are born regularly into the elasticity family as economists pursue their varied investigations. We won't try to introduce you to the whole family (an impossible task anyway given the birth rate), but one more member is worth meeting at this time.

Income elasticity of demand is a close companion to price elasticity of demand. Its definition is analogous: *the percentage change in quantity demanded*

divided by the percentage change in income. If a 20% increase in your income leads to a 15% increase in your expenditures on housing, the income elasticity of your demand for housing is ¾ or .75. Notice that the coefficient of elasticity in this case could be greater than unity, between zero and unity, or less than zero (negative). If a 20% increase in your income leads to an 80% reduction in your oleomargarine consumption (because you're now buying butter), the elasticity coefficient will be minus 4. We cannot ignore the algebraic sign in the case of income elasticity of demand; for while more income *permits* more consumption, it need not *result* in more consumption of any particular commodity. Suppose that we put income on the vertical axis as we did with price. Curves expressing the relationship between *price* and quantity demanded slope downward to the right, expressing the inverse relationship between these two variables and yielding negative coefficients of elasticity. But a curve that shows the relationship between *income* and the quantity demanded of some good can slope upward to the right or be vertical or slope upward to the left. A single such curve, expressing, say, the responsiveness of Homer Iliad's weekly hamburger purchases to changes in his income, might well resemble a backward "C". The income elasticity of Homer's demand for hamburger could thus be shown as positive, zero, or negative, depending on the income range under consideration. Let's reflect on Homer's habits to convince ourselves that this is quite plausible.

When Homer's income was very low, he yearned for meat but could rarely afford it. When he got a 5% raise, he doubled his consumption of hamburger, displaying an income elasticity of demand of 20 (100% divided by 5%). Homer's coefficient declined as his income rose further, both because any absolute change in income is a smaller percentage change when income is higher and because at higher income levels Homer could afford more expensive cuts of meat. As Homer's income rose still further he eventually reached a point where more income didn't lead to any more hamburger consumption at all. As his wealth increased, Homer began substituting steaks and roasts for hamburger, something he would have liked to do even when he was poor but couldn't do because he wasn't wealthy enough.

When the quantity of a good demanded decreases as income increases, the good is called an *inferior good.* This is a technical term and not a judgment about intrinsic value. Almost any good could be an inferior good for someone at some income level. For a rich man who buys a Cadillac annually but then becomes *filthy* rich and shifts to a Rolls Royce annually, a Cadillac is an inferior good. You could easily find similar if less spectacular cases from your own experience.

The concept of income elasticity of demand is particularly useful when we are examining changes in the composition of demand over longer

CHANGING CONSUMPTION IN THE UNITED STATES

Indices of per capita consumption,
in physical units (pounds, miles, etc.)
(1950 = 100)

	1950	1960	1970
Meat	100	113	129
Wheat flour	100	87	81
Butter	100	70	50
Oleomargarine	100	154	180
Beer	100	96	114
Distilled spirits	100	126	176
Bachelors degrees[1]	100	81	160
Dental service[2]	100	135	183
Intercity passenger travel	100	130	173
by automobile	100	136	174
by airplane	100	287	885
by bus	100	61	71
by train	100	58	26

Source of data from which calculations were made: *Statistical Abstract of the United States.*

1. World War II and veterans' educational benefits produced an unusually large number of degrees in 1950.
2. Dollar expenditures adjusted for price changes.

periods of time. The income elasticity of demand for automobiles has proved to be positive and quite large, with consequences of far-reaching importance for every country that has found itself thrust by rising affluence into the Automobile Age. The income elasticity of demand for food is typically positive but less than one, so that the agricultural sector will tend to decline in relative size as a society becomes wealthier. And this, too, tends to have significant social and political implications. Long range social planning and long range business planning must both pay attention to income elasticities of demand. If the demand for vacations is highly elastic with respect to income, that is important information for the Department of the Interior, which manages our national parks, and for all the private industries that cater to vacationers.

A Note on Luxuries and Necessities

We're all familiar with the distinction between luxuries and necessities. At least we are until we approach more closely and begin to look at the distinction carefully. Then it has a disturbing tendency to fade like a highway mirage.

Through two chapters now we have been insisting that the concept of "needs" is misleading. A need, we have argued, implies a perfectly inelastic demand curve, something not likely to be found in the real world where people shift about among substitutes as relative prices change. But if *perfectly* inelastic demand curves do not exist, there certainly are some *very* inelastic demand curves. Salt is an example we've already used. An antibiotic such as penicillin is another. Or insulin for a diabetic. Whatever economists might say, most people would call those necessities. Lots of people speak of necessities and contrast them with luxuries and seem to understand one another well enough. Shall we yield to common sense (or at least common speech) and allow the word *necessity*? We could keep it on a short leash, perhaps, by defining necessities as products for which the demand is *very* inelastic.

The trouble with this conciliatory suggestion is that it doesn't work. Whatever people mean in common speech when they distinguish between luxuries and necessities, it surely isn't captured by the distinction between goods in highly elastic versus highly inelastic demand.

Governments tax cigarettes heavily because they are *not* considered to be necessities *and* because the demand for them is inelastic. If the demand were highly elastic, smokers would sharply curtail their purchases in response to the tax-induced price increase and governments would not collect much revenue from the tax. Nicotine addicts may indeed think of cigarettes as necessities; however, the surgeon general and most legislators don't use the word that way.

If we want to use language to communicate effectively we had better not call heroin a necessity because some people's demand for it is extremely inelastic.

If we're determined to relate the notion of necessities and luxuries in some fashion to the concept of elasticity, we would do better by tying it to income elasticity of demand. One could make a case for defining a luxury as a good for which the income elasticity of demand is positive and greater than one. Goods are luxuries for people, then, when the quantity of the good they demand increases more than in proportion to increases in their income. That will fit many of the goods that common sense dubs luxuries. But not all by any means! That definition would make dental care, clothing, and shoes a luxury for many people. Some dental care might sensibly be called a luxury. We would all concede that some clothing and shoes are luxuries. But are we really willing to decide whether orthodontic work is a luxury or a necessity by checking on the income elasticity of demand for it?

GRANTS FOR SPECIFIC PURPOSES

A foundation grants $200,000 to a university for the purchase of laboratory equipment and stipulates that none of the money may be used to increase salaries.

A private charity gives food to poor families rather than money because the organizers of the charity fear some of the money might be used for frivolous purposes.

The federal government provides money to state and local governments to hire new public employees as a way of reducing unemployment and stipulates that the grants must be used to create jobs.

In none of these cases can the donors be certain that their gifts or grants will be used in the way they intend.

If the university had planned, prior to receipt of the grant, to spend $150,000 on laboratory equipment, it would have to spend $350,000 after the grant to fulfill the foundation's intentions. If, instead, it spends only $200,000 on laboratory equipment, then the foundation grant has had the effect of freeing $150,000 for such other purposes as salary increases. The net result of the grant will be $50,000 more for laboratory equipment and the rest for whatever purposes the university administrators choose.

Gifts of food enable poor families to allocate a portion of their food budget to other purposes, so the charitable organization cannot be sure of increasing families' food consumption by the amount of the food donated.

State and local governments may use federal grants intended for the expansion of public service employment to pay employees with federal rather than state and local funds. Jobs that would have been added in the absence of the grant will now be added without raising taxes and some "new" jobs will be created that merely replace already existing jobs.

An increase in income raises the demand for *all* goods that are not inferior goods in the technical sense. And this can occur even if, as in the case of the food distribution, the increased income does not take the form of money. One conclusion to be drawn: It isn't as easy as many suppose for donors to control the behavior of those they are helping. (Is that good or bad?)

It's certainly legitimate to make up a personal or household budget by dividing goods into those we would not want to do without even if their prices went much higher or our incomes fell drastically, and goods we would quickly stop buying if either of those things happened. We might also, as a matter of public policy, want to establish categories of goods, such as elementary education, that we think ought to be available to people regardless of their willingness or ability to pay for them. But it would be confusing to call such goods necessities, to suppose that they are goods in highly price-inelastic demand, or to ignore all goods for which the income elasticity of demand is greater than one. Medical care provides an instructive example. Few household budgeters would call the doctor a luxury. And current social policy in America suggests that we do want to make some medical care available to people as a matter of right and without regard to their ability to pay. The difficult question is determining how much and what kind. Hair transplants, ear piercings, and face lifts are medical services. We don't clarify the issue by dumping all medical care into the category "necessity," for the same reason that we wouldn't be making sense if we called caviar a necessity because it's food and no one can survive without food.

Perhaps we should recognize that the word *luxury,* like the word *necessity,* often conceals the speaker's real meaning, maybe even from the speaker himself. If that's so we have a good reason for trying to do without both words and for substituting some other phrase that more effectively communicates our meaning. Wouldn't public discussion of national health care policy or state spending for education or welfare programs or military budgets and much else besides gain in clarity and effectiveness if we could no longer hide behind the ambiguities of "necessity" and "luxury" and had to say exactly what we mean?

Once Over Lightly

Price elasticity of demand is a measure of the percentage change in the quantity of a good demanded relative to the percentage change in its price.

Demand is (price) elastic when the percentage increase in quantity demanded is greater than the percentage decrease in price. Demand is inelastic when the percentage change in quantity demanded is smaller than the percentage change in price.

Price elasticity of demand depends upon the importance of the price relative to one's income, but even more upon the quality and price of available substitutes.

More separate sources of supply for a good imply better substitutes for any particular unit of the good and hence a more elastic demand.

Total receipts or expenditures move in the opposite direction from price when demand is elastic and in the same direction as price when demand is inelastic.

The concept of "needs" implies a perfectly inelastic demand curve—an extremely rare phenomenon.

Changes in income cause demand curves to shift. The income elasticity of demand for a good is the percentage change in the quantity demanded divided by the percentage change in income. It can vary over a wide range of negative or positive values.

The demand for a good refers to the *schedule of relationships* between price and quantity demanded and must be distinguished from the quantity or amount that is demanded. The quantity of a good demanded changes with its price. But a true change in demand will alter *both* price *and* quantity demanded.

It is the *relative* price of a good, its price in relationship to the prices of other goods, which determines the quantity demanded at various prices and income levels.

The technical term *inferior good* refers to any good for which the quantity demanded varies inversely with income. This term does not evaluate the quality of a product.

QUESTIONS FOR DISCUSSION

1. John loves butter and thinks that oleo tastes like soap. George can't tell the difference. Whose demand for butter is likely to be more elastic?

2. Would the elasticity of a crowd's demand for cold lemonade be affected by the proximity of a drinking fountain?

3. How do you think the development of other copying machines affected the elasticity of demand for Xerox machines?

4. Is the demand for prescription drugs elastic or inelastic? Why? Do you agree with the statement sometimes made that the prices charged for prescription drugs can be freely set by the manufacturers, since people must buy whatever the doctor prescribes?

5. How does ignorance affect elasticities of demand?

6. How might the development of science and technology affect demand elasticities?

7. Does a society's transportation system in any way affect elasticities of demand? How?

8. What is the elasticity of demand for water in New York City, according to figure 2A? (Be careful—the elasticity varies.)

9. The demand for aspirin at currently prevailing prices seems to be highly inelastic. What do you think would happen to the elasticity of demand if the price of aspirin relative to everything else were five times as high? Fifty times as high? Why?

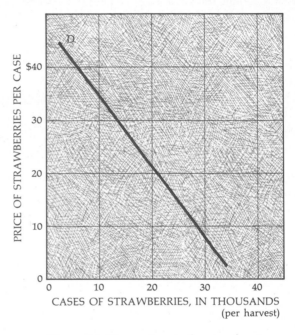

Figure 3A Demand curve for strawberries

10. Figure 3A shows a hypothetical demand curve for strawberries.

    (*a*) What price per case would maximize the gross receipts of strawberry growers? (Peek at part *d* of this question rather than waste too much time trying all sorts of different prices. The price that maximizes gross receipts will be found at the midpoint of a straight-line demand curve when the curve is extended to the axes. If you see why, good. If not, it's a bit of knowledge with only academic usefulness anyway.)

    (*b*) If the total quantity of strawberries harvested determines the price in conjunction with the demand, what size crop will result in this price?

    (*c*) What would the gross receipts of strawberry growers be if the crop turned out to be 30,000 cases?

    (*d*) Can you prove that the demand for strawberries is elastic above a price of $24 per case and inelastic below that price?

(*e*) If strawberry growers can make more money by selling fewer than 30,000 cases, why would they ever market that much? Why wouldn't they destroy some of the crop rather than "spoil the market"?

11. Higher prices for beef, automobiles, or television sets will lead to a reduction in the *amount of each demanded*. Think of some specific changes (such as in tastes, prices of substitutes, quality of complements) that would cause the *demand* for each to increase so that more might actually be demanded at higher prices. Why is this completely consistent with the law of demand?

12. A change in expectations can cause a change in demand. Explain how this could lead to a situation where a price decline was followed by a *decrease* in the amount purchased.

13. To what factors would you attribute the changing consumption patterns shown in the table on page 49? Which do you think are primarily attributable to changes in per capita income? How would you explain the changing patterns of butter and oleomargarine consumption?

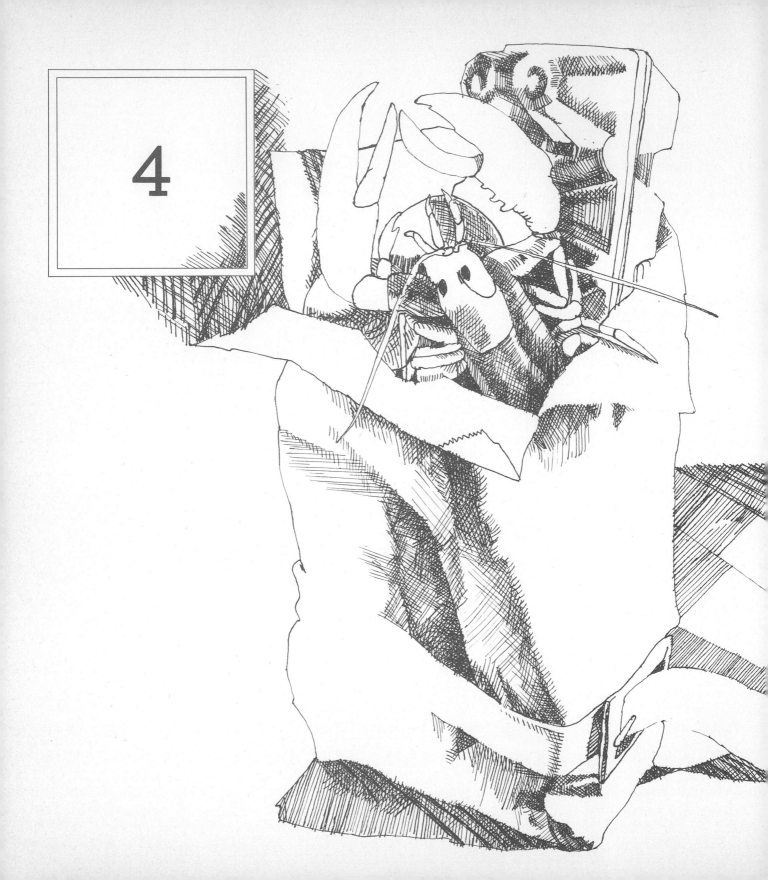

SCARCITY AND THE PRICE SYSTEM

A chapter should not begin with definitions, for definitions are boring and put students off. So don't read these definitions. Skip immediately to the next paragraph. But remember, if you get confused for a moment, that the three key terms of this chapter have been defined in the initial paragraph. A good is *scarce* whenever there is not enough available for everyone to have all he wants without having to sacrifice something else he wants in order to obtain it. A *shortage* exists when the quantity demanded at the prevailing price is greater than the quantity available. A *surplus* exists when the quantity demanded at the prevailing price is less than the quantity available.

But don't stop to memorize this. Go right on to learn about lobster, copper, sugar, house rents near army bases, and the problem of becoming president.

THE CONSEQUENCES OF SCARCITY

No one blames the thermometer for low temperatures or seriously proposes to warm up the house on a cold day by holding a candle under the furnace thermostat. People do, however, often blame high prices for the fact of scarcity and act as if scarcity could be eliminated by pushing down prices through legislation or by moralizing.

To the lover of lobster, its high price does indeed look like the cause of its scarcity. Lobster rarely appears in our house because its price is high. But what would happen if the lobster lovers' lobby pushed a bill through Congress which placed a ceiling price on lobster well below the currently prevailing price? Would lobster be any less scarce? Lobster fans would now *want* to buy more lobster. But would they succeed? The low ceiling price might in fact cause lobster to disappear from most of the stores in the country.

Contrary to the doctrine now being propounded by some who are impressed with the enormous wealth of the United States, even we, the wealthiest people in the world, have not ended scarcity. Nor is it likely that we ever shall. We may learn to be more content with fewer material goods, or we may manage to produce and distribute material goods in such abundance that no one any longer gives much thought to acquiring more. But even then we would not have abolished scarcity. For the present and the foreseeable future, we shall have to live with the fact that the means of satisfying our wants fall far short of the wants themselves.

So we must *economize.* We must allocate our resources intelligently to obtain from what we have as much as possible of what we want. We must learn to *manage* scarcity since we cannot hope to abolish it. The management of scarcity does include scaling down or otherwise altering wants as well as expanding production. It's often possible to loosen the pinch of scarcity merely by reevaluating one's objectives and discovering that a particular goal really isn't worth the cost of attaining it, or that the want behind the desire for some good can actually be satisfied in another and less difficult way. But the management of scarcity, especially in an economy as large and diversified as ours and with as many different resources and infinitely varied preferences, will remain an enormously complex social task. In this chapter we want to gain an understanding of those complexities by exploring some of the implications of scarcity. We shall notice that scarcity is quite different from shortage, and that something can be scarce even when a surplus of it exists.

The Meaning of Scarcity

The climate of Gazebo, a fictitious South Sea Island, is perfect for growing both oranges and pineapples. But since there are far more pineapple plants than orange trees on the island, 50,000 pineapples are harvested each month and only 5000 oranges. Which is more scarce?

We cannot tell from the information given. Scarcity is a *relationship*. If the people of Gazebo love pineapples and hate oranges, pineapples could be more scarce despite their greater abundance. Scarcity is a relationship between availability and desirability, or between supply and demand.

If pineapples in Gazebo were considered unfit for human consumption, and there was no way to sell them to others, they would not be scarce at all. No one speaks of the scarcity of garbage—except hog farmers, perhaps, for whom garbage is not garbage.

If everyone can have all that he wants of some good without being required to sacrifice anything else that is also wanted, that good is not *scarce.* It is a *free good.* There are obviously not many free goods available in our society, despite the song that says the best things in life are free. Perhaps the best things in life cannot be purchased with money; but that does not make them free goods.

If anything is scarce, it must be rationed. That means that a criterion of some kind must be established for discriminating among claimants to determine who will get how much. The criterion could be age, eloquence, swiftness, public esteem, willingness to pay money, or almost anything else. We characteristically ration scarce goods in our society on the basis of willingness to pay money. But sometimes we use other criteria in order to discriminate.

Harvard College each year has many more applicants than it has places in the freshman class, so Harvard must ration the scarce places. It discriminates on the basis of high school grades, test scores, recommendations, and other criteria.

Only one person at a time can be president of the United States. Since many more people than that want the position, we have evolved an elaborate system of discrimination in the form of conventions and elections. Although there is considerable doubt about just what the criteria for discrimination are, the system does discriminate. We end up every fourth year with only one satisfied candidate.

Joe College is the most popular man on campus and has coeds clamoring for his favor. He must therefore ration his attentions. Whether he employs the criterion of beauty, intelligence, geniality, or something else, he must and will discriminate in some fashion.

But the other side of discrimination is competition. Once Harvard announces its criteria for discrimination, freshman applicants will compete to meet them. The criteria for selecting a president are studied carefully by the hopefuls who begin competing to satisfy those criteria long before the election year. If the coeds eager to go with Joe College believe that beauty is his main criterion, they will compete with one another to seem more beautiful.

Competition is obviously not peculiar to capitalist societies or to societies that use money. The point is of fundamental importance: *competition results from scarcity* and can only be eliminated with the elimination of scarcity. Whenever there is scarcity, there must be rationing. Rationing is allocation in accord with some criteria for discrimination. Competition is merely what occurs when people strive to meet the criteria that are being employed.

Of course, the criteria employed do make a difference. If a society rations on the basis of willingness to pay money, members of that society will strive to make money. If it uses physical strength as a primary criterion, members of the society will do body-building exercises. And if the better colleges and universities use high school grades as an important criterion for selection, high school students will compete for grades. They might be competing for grades to acquire other goods as well (status among classmates, compliments from teachers, use of the family car); but it is odd for colleges to complain of grade grubbers when their own rationing criteria promote grade grubbing.

Scarcity and Prices

Monetary prices are the most common rationing device in our society. The high price of lobster both reflects the fact that lobster is scarce *and* rations out to eager gourmets the limited quantity available. What happens when the price of lobster is not allowed to rise to the level that reflects its actual scarcity? Suppose that our lobster lovers' lobby managed to get a law through Congress setting $1 a pound as the maximum price that could be charged for lobster.

The quantity demanded would immediately increase. Lobster lovers would race to the grocery stores in anticipation of inexpensive epicurean delights. But many would find only frustration. Someone else would have gotten there first. The lower price does nothing to increase the number of lobsters available and, in the long run, it will reduce the amount of lobster that reaches the grocery stores and fish markets as lobstermen find it more profitable to do something other than trap lobsters. The lobster lovers' lobby did nothing to make lobster less scarce. They only suppressed the rationing device. They put ice cubes on the thermometer, so to speak; they did not turn on the air conditioning. They mistook a symptom (the high price) for the cause of their discontent (the scarcity of lobster).

But since lobster is still scarce, it must still be rationed. When price was prevented from serving as the discriminatory criterion, swiftness took its place. Those who were first to the stores took home the lobster, and the rest had none. Later on we might expect friendship with the butcher or fishmonger to become an important discriminatory criterion. And if this happens we would expect the social popularity of these tradesmen to increase as lobster lovers start competing to satisfy the new rationing system. Fishmongers will be seen at all the more glittering social events, and party givers will call months in advance to be sure of their butcher's presence. Proximity to Maine will be another rationing device. Why pay the cost of shipping lobster any farther if New Englanders are willing to buy all that is available? When the lobsters no longer come to the people, the people will have to go to the lobsters.

Copper in Klutz

Scarcity is an inescapable fact of life, but shortages are avoidable. *A shortage is defined by economists as a situation in which the quantity demanded is greater than the quantity supplied.* Since the quantity demanded depends on the price (later we shall see that the quantity supplied also depends on price), it is possible to eliminate any shortage merely by allowing the price to rise.

We can see what this means and gain further practice in working with graphs by using figure 4A. The following discussion will be understood easily by anyone who follows it with a finger on figure 4A. The line labeled OD is the original demand for copper in the hypothetical country of Klutz. It shows the number of pounds of copper that will be purchased each month in Klutz at prices between roughly $1.35 and $.25 per pound. The line labeled LD is the demand for copper in Klutz at some later date. It is the demand after a major change (an expansion, let us say, in the country's electrical supply network) causes copper users to be willing to pay more to obtain any given quantity of copper. Another way of de-

CAN PRICE CONTROLS *RAISE* PRICES?

What happens when the government "freezes" prices? One consequence is that certain items disappear from the market. Any item whose price is frozen below the market clearing level will be in short supply and hence not always available to purchasers looking for it. Beyond that, however, price controls tend to cause the gradual disappearance of just barely profitable goods. Often these are "bottom of the line" commodities: cheaper grades of paper, lumber, or fabric and many other low-quality items that are demanded for uses where higher quality serves little purpose. If a firm isn't able to produce as much as it can sell, it will concentrate its resources on producing the items that generate the largest profit. This often compels other producers to adopt inefficient production techniques that raise costs and prices. An example is the steel products company forced to use beautifully grained hardwood lumber in its shipping pallets because the grade it formerly used is no longer available.

A question: Has a price freeze really frozen prices when buyers can't obtain the items they want and have to accept (and pay for) goods with more quality than they can use?

scribing the difference between OD and LD is to say that, with LD, copper users want to buy more copper than before at each and every price.

We might begin by asking how much copper was needed in Klutz at OD. The question is meaningless, of course. Klutz has a highly developed economy and every industrialized economy uses large amounts of copper. But it is still misleading to say that Klutz needs any particular amount of copper per month. As the graph indicates, more or less will be demanded as the price is lower or higher.

Suppose now that exactly 10,000 pounds of copper become available to Klutz users each month. Will this be enough? Will there be a shortage of copper? Not if the price is 85¢ per pound. At this price copper users will want to buy 10,000 pounds per month, exactly the amount available.

What would happen if the monthly supply fell for some reason to 8000 pounds? If the price did not rise, some prospective purchasers of copper would be unable to obtain as much as they want. In order to get more, some would offer to pay a slight premium, and the price would rise. It would tend to continue rising as long as anyone who was willing to pay a

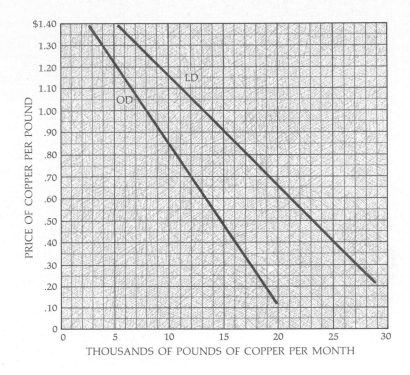

Figure 4A Copper in Klutz

higher price (if necessary) could not obtain all the copper he wanted at the existing price. But as the price rises, some prospective purchasers alter their plans. They decide they now want less copper than they originally planned to purchase. The price is bid up by the competition of those who want more than is available to them. And as it rises, the amount demanded declines. At a price of $1.05 per pound, the quantity demanded equals the quantity supplied. $1.05 per pound is the *equilibrium price* for the new situation of reduced supply. It is the price that "clears the market." This means that all purchases that people want to make *at the prevailing price* can be made, while purchases that people are willing to make only at some lower price cannot be made.

Do prices really change in the way described above, or is this just part of the mythology of economists? The picture we have given is a simplified one. It describes quite accurately the way some prices change, but not others. We shall examine later what happens in the very common situation where sellers have some power to set prices. But we can pass by for now the question of whether this process is "typical" in order to focus on our principal concern at the moment: the relation between scarcity and shortage or surplus.

THE CONCEPT OF "EQUILIBRIUM"

A price at which the quantity of a good demanded equals the quantity offered for sale is called an *equilibrium price*. The price is said to be "at equilibrium" or "in equilibrium" because the various factors pushing it in each direction just balance each other at that price. When the quantity demanded equals the quantity supplied, those who would like to see the price at a higher or lower level don't have the ability to make it go higher or lower; and those who have the ability lack the desire.

In Figure 4A, when suppliers have 10,000 pounds they want to sell and demand is OD, the equilibrium price is 85¢. Sellers would like to get more; but any seller who holds out for more than 85¢ won't find a buyer. Demanders would prefer a lower price; but no copper will be available to those bidding less than 85¢.

Economists make frequent use of the equilibrium concept. But equilibrium is a theoretical construct to assist us in thinking clearly; it is not something we can observe. Economists would say that a price of 60¢ with the supply fixed at 10,000 pounds and the demand at OD is a *disequilibrium* price because some suppliers *and* some demanders would prefer a higher price. If purchasers are willing to pay more, the price will presumably rise from the 60¢ level.

But if the government threatens to fine or imprison any purchaser who pays more than the legal ceiling price, can we be sure that purchasers will in fact be willing to pay more than 60¢ a pound? With legal penalties taken into account, perhaps the 60¢ price is an equilibrium price by the definition above.

The point is that equilibrium or disequilibrium depends upon which factors we choose to include in our analysis. Almost any price might qualify as an equilibrium price under the appropriate assumptions. We shall see in chapters 20 and 23 that the equilibrium concept can confuse discussion at times by concealing critical assumptions.

What would have occurred if the government of Klutz had decided that copper was an essential commodity and therefore its price could not be allowed to rise? When the supply fell from 10,000 pounds per month to 8000 pounds, a shortage would have appeared: the quantity demanded at the legally fixed ceiling price would exceed by 2000 pounds per month the quantity supplied. The shortage is a clear consequence of the ceiling price and can be eliminated by removing the ceiling.

Suppose that with the supply at the lower level of 8000 pounds and the price effectively fixed at 85¢ per pound, the demand shifts from OD to LD. How large will the shortage now be? Purchasers will want to buy 16,000 pounds. The shortage will therefore be 8000 pounds per month.

Would you like to see a shortage turn into a surplus before your very eyes? Let the demand continue at LD and the monthly supply at 8000 pounds. And let the government of Klutz now decide that since copper is an essential commodity its price must be supported at $1.30 a pound. If you wonder how a government can argue first for a low maximum price and then for a high minimum price both on the grounds that copper is an essential commodity, remind yourself once again that those who talk about "essential" commodities are often not much interested in logical conclusions.

If the government supports the price of copper at $1.30 a pound by offering to buy for stockpiling all of the supply which cannot be sold at that price, then 1000 pounds will have to be added each month to the government's stockpile. *Voilà!* A surplus. It's easy once you learn the trick, as many governments other than that of Klutz have often demonstrated. *A surplus,* in case you are still looking for the formal definition, *is a situation in which the quantity supplied exceeds the quantity demanded.*

Notice that copper is still scarce despite the surplus. Surpluses do not necessarily mean that scarcity has been overcome. They may only mean that prices are not being allowed to decline. It's tempting to assert that just as any shortage can be eliminated by a large enough increase in price, so any surplus can be eliminated by a large enough decrease in price. But that could be misleading unless you realize that the price decrease might have to be so large as to make the equilibrium price negative. Suppliers might have to pay demanders to take the commodity away. If that sounds silly, how do you think we eliminate surpluses of trash?

Supply Curves: A Brief Introduction

We've been assuming in the copper case that the problem is to allocate a *monthly output* of copper among competing demanders. That assumption simplifies the exposition. But you know very well that the output of goods like lobster or copper is not fixed and unalterable. We mentioned a few paragraphs back, in parentheses, that the quantity supplied also depends upon the price. In other words, there are supply curves as well as demand curves. Chapter 5 will launch us into reflection on the nature of costs and the relationship between costs and supply curves. But a little anticipation at this point will be helpful.

Figure 4B adds a supply curve (S) to figure 4A. It's a relatively inelastic supply curve: throughout the range of quantities and prices shown, a

FOILING THE BUDGET MAKERS

If you're a producer making use of a scarce resource that may soon be put under government non-price rationing, be careful about economizing in your use of that resource. The most common way to determine each user's quota is to base it on the amount used in some previous period. That means the producer who anticipates the imposition of a rationing system should reverse the old rule of survival, "Waste not, want not." Those who waste the least *before* controls will experience the most acute wants *after* controls.

The Soviet Union has accumulated a good deal of experience relevant to this problem under its system of input allocations called "planning by material balances." The directors of Soviet enterprises, in addition to paying rubles for the inputs they received, were not allowed to purchase most inputs without an authorization from the government. The allocation of these authorizations thus became the focus of concern for enterprise directors, who padded orders, hoarded inventories, and made sure never to end the planning period with a visible surplus of any scarce input.

The same process operates within most large organizations. As department heads and division chiefs look ahead to next year's budget allocations, they try to make sure they fully use up everything they were allocated for the current year lest some superior conclude that they didn't "need" as much as they were assigned. This problem tends to arise whenever the users of scarce resources are not required to pay the full cost of what they use. A price system, on the other hand, under which resource users must bid what they want away from others, avoids this in two ways. It sets prices at levels that reflect goods' scarcities and, by compelling users to pay those prices, induces them to take full account of the cost of their decisions.

change in price will be accompanied by a smaller percentage change in the quantity supplied.

Price ceilings and price supports will lead to even larger shortages and surpluses when the quantities supplied as well as those demanded are reponsive to price changes. Look at figure 4B. With demand at LD, the market clearing price will be 95¢ a pound. An effective price ceiling of 80¢ would create a monthly shortage of 4000 pounds, by inducing demanders to want an extra 3000 pounds each month while prompting suppliers to reduce their offerings by 1000 pounds per month.

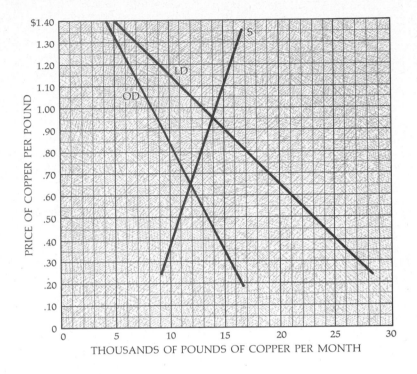

Figure 4B Supply and demand for copper

Price Rationing and Non-Price Rationing

Shortages and surpluses that persist for any extended period of time will almost always be found to be a consequence of failure to allow prices to perform their rationing function. Since rationing is a necessary consequence of scarcity, some other method of rationing will come into play when a price is set at a level that does not reflect actual scarcity. A few years ago the United States government tried to hold down the price of copper in the face of rising demand and a diminished supply. New discriminatory criteria came into operation, such as willingness to stand in line, ability to influence sellers, and dishonesty (thefts of copper increased significantly). Are these rationing devices any better than price?

It is hard to see in what way they might be better. One important consequence of rationing by means of price is that it allocates the scarce commodity to those who are willing to pay more. If you assume that some prospective buyers are willing to pay more than others because they plan to use the copper in products for which consumers are willing to pay more, rationing by means of price has a tendency to allocate scarce commodities toward those uses for which consumer demand is greatest. And that makes sense.

Remember the law of demand and the phenomenon of substitutability on which it ultimately rests. At a low, fixed price, copper users have little incentive to economize in its use by finding copper substitutes. When the price of copper is allowed to rise, a long chain of substitutions is set in motion. Home builders may cut down on the number of bathrooms, for example, in order to hold down the cost of the houses they are constructing. New home buyers may look at the cost of an additional bathroom and decide, all things considered, that three aren't really much better than two. Scarcity calls for economizing. Higher prices for copper encourage everyone who uses it to do exactly that.

Allocating Housing Space

You will get a better sense of what happens when prices are not allowed to ration effectively if we run through an example more within your own experience. Suppose that the army suddenly reactivates a large military base far from any large population center. Small towns in the vicinity of the base will experience a large increase in the demand for housing from military personnel and their dependents who prefer to live off the base. Housing will become more scarce, and rental prices will begin to rise.

If rental prices are allowed to rise, people will want to purchase less housing space. Renters will lease smaller apartments or double up with friends. Some personnel will change their minds and elect to live on the base. Some dependents will decide to locate farther from the area of the base. Some military families will settle for being together just on weekends. Moreover, owners of living space will economize, too. People who own large houses will open up their basements and spare bedrooms to renters. This means, in effect, that they will be demanding less housing space for their own use. All of these economizing activities will alleviate the shortage and, if rental prices rise high enough, eliminate it completely. The scarcity will still exist; there is no way to eliminate it, and few ways even to reduce it substantially in the short run. But the challenge is to live with scarcity by economizing effectively. Higher prices stimulate a more effective coping with the problem of scarcity by inducing people to substitute other goods for housing space in an area of acute scarcity.

It has been argued in cases just like this that rent controls should be imposed to keep greedy landlords from exploiting the situation. But if legal rent ceilings are imposed, the price of housing will be prevented from performing its rationing function. A shortage will appear. The quantity demanded (at prevailing and legally fixed rentals) will exceed the quantity available. Some way will have to be found to ration out the short supply. We can easily predict some of the rationing devices that will appear.

Families with children will be discriminated against. Why rent to people

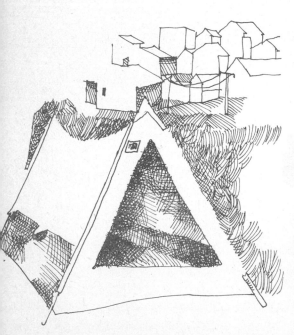

with children who are more likely to damage the property when at the same price you can find plenty of renters without children?

People who are noisy or have other habits offensive to landlords will be discriminated against. Why tolerate unpleasant tenants when there are plenty of pleasant ones around?

Members of minority races will be discriminated against for the same reason, if landlords tend to harbor racial prejudices.

Discrimination will occur also on the basis of agility, personal influence, friendship with someone who has an apartment he plans to vacate, and all sorts of bribes, legal or illegal.

There will be a decline in the quality of accommodations from the tenants' standpoint. Landlords will provide minimum heat. They will refuse to paint. They will insist on large deposits and extract large breakage fees from tenants.

Moreover, with rent controls, we would have less reason to expect that housing would go to those most desirous of obtaining it. At $75 a month the single soldier who wouldn't much mind living on the base might wind up nonetheless with an apartment in town, thus depriving the newly married army couple of an apartment for which they would be willing to pay $125. If rents are allowed to rise, those who care less buy less, leaving more for those who care more. That at least makes more sense than rationing without regard to intensity of desire.

HOW MUCH MEDICAL CARE IS "NECESSARY"?

William Sherman, a reporter for *The New York Daily News*, conducted an experiment a few years ago that vividly demonstrates some of the dangers in calling medical care a necessity. He borrowed a Medicaid card and presented himself at a private clinic in New York City, claiming to have a cold. After visiting the clinic twice on successive days (and rejecting an invitation to return for a third visit), he had been examined by three physicians, had been subjected to a cardiogram, X rays, three blood tests, and two urinalyses, and had collected six drug prescriptions.

We should not conclude that the clinic behaved irresponsibly. A responsible physician wants to take as few chances as possible with a patient's health, and will therefore tend to run a lot of tests and prescribe generously *if someone else is paying all the bills*. A physician who knows that the patient must pay for tests or prescriptions will order them only if there is a higher probability of their serving some useful purpose.

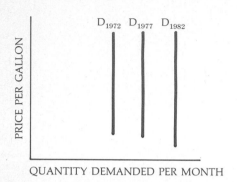

Figure 4C Projected growth in demand

MANAGING SCARCITY: A CASE STUDY

When the "energy crisis" became front page news in 1973, "finding the villain" became a favorite indoor sport. But there is one villain at whom we too rarely point an accusing finger: the public and its careless way of thinking about scarcity. Too many people have been talking and acting as if prices contributed nothing to the appearance of the crisis and can make no contribution toward its solution.

An alarming number of commentators on the energy problem continue to speak of national "needs" and to predict future increases in energy consumption from past increases in a purely mechanical way. But how much energy is demanded depends upon its price, and the rate at which consumption will increase (or decrease!) in the coming years depends upon what happens to prices over those years. Let's take gasoline as our example again. Figure 4C pictures the way many people seem to view the situation.

Given all the evidence of a high income elasticity of demand for gasoline, that may be a reasonable sort of projection. But it's a projection that fails to take into account the consequences of the very problem it gloomily forecasts.

Increasing demand creates a problem only if supply cannot keep pace. But that means increasing scarcity and increasing scarcity leads to higher prices and hence a slowdown in the rate at which the quantity demanded increases. A lot of commentators have chosen to ignore the distinction between demand and quantity demanded. And that's evidence that they are ignoring the role that higher prices can play in rationing a scarce supply and keeping a problem from becoming a crisis. But *how much higher* will prices have to go?

We learned very quickly after the announcement of the oil embargo that the number of miles Americans will choose to drive their automobiles depends, among other things, on how much they must pay for gasoline. Our recent experience doesn't provide good data on the demand curve for gasoline because the monetary price wasn't the only component of cost that rose for the consumer. Waiting in line is also a cost, and that went up—sharply in some parts of the country. Being stranded on a trip is a cost, too, and many people who might have been willing to pay a high price for their gasoline were not willing to run the risk of an infinitely high price (none available at all) on a Sunday excursion far from home. Patriotism or public spirit played some role, too, in reducing consumption. So did the reduced highway speed limits. So while we have evidence that the higher price did reduce consumption, we don't know just how much it contributed.

We have even better evidence that the higher price will reduce *future*

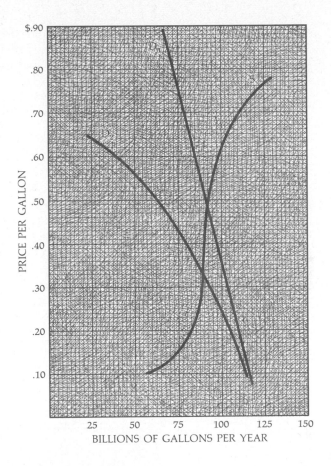

consumption. Automobile dealers suddenly found customers clamoring
for cars that got good gasoline mileage; and Detroit learned that the
American motorist, supposedly infatuated hopelessly with power and
size, was a fickle lover after all. With astonishing rapidity, considering the
apparent depth of the previous commitment, Americans abandoned acceleration to court the new status symbol of economy.

Of course, the fact that higher prices *can* eliminate shortages doesn't
prove we should let them do so. It surely doesn't prove that price increases
should be allowed to bear the whole burden of adjustment. Let's put the
tools of demand and supply to work in a systematic way to see if we can
sort out the effects of alternative policy approaches. We'll make some
assumptions about the shape of the demand and supply curves that will
serve to demonstrate the nature and direction of the effects we might
anticipate.

Let D_1 in figure 4D represent the initial demand for gasoline. If 100 billion gallons are supplied each year, a price of 36¢ will clear the market. If the supply is suddenly cut to 90 billion gallons, the price will rise to 52¢.[1] Is that an intolerable increase? Should the price be held down with legal ceilings?

Protecting the Poor

Yes it should, some argue, because poorer people cannot afford to pay that much more for gasoline. Someone who consumes 20 gallons per week will have to pay an extra $3.20 each week for gasoline. And that certainly can put a crimp in the budget of someone whose weekly take home pay is less than $100. But will the poorer people actually pay an extra $3.20? Or will they reduce their consumption of gasoline? By cutting consumption to about 14 gallons per week, they could avoid increasing their expenditures for gasoline. Isn't it reasonable to infer that poorer people, precisely because they have less income, will be among the more effective economizers on automobile use when the price of gasoline rises? Cutting back on automobile use is a sacrifice, of course; and it's a sacrifice poor people may be compelled to make while the more affluent blithely pay an extra $3.20 that they scarcely miss and go on consuming their 20 gallons per week. And many think that's unfair.

What will be the costs of a legal ceiling price at 36¢? And how will these costs be distributed? In the absence of a formal rationing system, as we have recently seen, rationing will occur partly through queuing. Motorists will spend more time (and burn more gasoline!) searching for supplies and waiting in line. The ten-gallon limit was not an effective rationing system at all, of course. It simply forced motorists to search farther and wait in line longer and encouraged the practice of "topping out"—adding a few gallons to keep the tank full—a practice that wasted the time of station attendants and added to the length of queues. Searching and waiting are just as real costs as the money paid. And as costs to purchasers, they did have the effect of reducing the quantity demanded.

Dead Weight Costs

But searching and waiting are dead weight costs: no one benefited from them.[2] A monetary cost, on the other hand, is a benefit to the seller. By

1. The price elasticity of demand between those points is .29 if we use the midpoints as bases in calculating the percentage changes in both price and quantity demanded. Since the percentage changes are fairly large, especially in the case of price, it might be better to use the midpoints rather than calculate the changes as percentages of the original values.

2. Except sadists! Or people who aren't sadists but do dislike automobiles and who derived a sort of gleeful pleasure from seeing the long lines. It is perhaps worth noting that economic analysis has traditionally rejected the possibility that people might derive satisfaction from the discomfiture of others.

this criterion, rationing through higher search and queue costs is clearly inferior to price rationing.

Is it nonetheless more equitable? Before deciding we would want to consider the distribution of those queuing costs. People who worked from 8 to 5 encountered long lines on their way to work and closed pumps at all the other times they were free. But those who worked bankers' hours or had adult family members who didn't work at all could slip into the stations at slack times and avoid the cost of waiting. Was that equitable?

It may be more important, though, even from the standpoint of equity, not to concentrate exclusively on what will happen next week or even next month. A higher price for gasoline encourages people to shift to smaller cars, to make up car pools, to use public transportation, perhaps even to relocate closer to work if they anticipate a permanently higher price.[1] The curve labeled D_2 shows what might happen to the demand as a result of these kinds of adjustments. The price could conceivably fall below the original price despite the reduction in supply. We aren't predicting this result, since the curve will tend to move upward and to the right due to rising incomes even while it's tipping backward due to the kinds of adjustments we've described. But it's possible, especially with a commodity like gasoline whose rate of consumption depends so very much on decisions made earlier: private decisions to own a gas-guzzler, live in the suburbs while working in the city, or not bother with hunting for a car pool, and collective decisions on what kind of public transportation system to have. If a higher price for gasoline increases the demand for public transportation and the public transportation system is dramatically improved in response to that demand, people might be weaned from their automobiles and not go back to them even though the price of gasoline fell below its former level. In the example depicted by the curves of Figure 4D, the price would at first rise to 52¢ as a result of the reduced supply, then fall gradually to 32¢ as the demand declines over time toward D_2.

Some of the concern expressed for the poor by those who wanted price ceilings rather than price rationing has to be seriously questioned. It's not only that the poor tend to buy relatively little gasoline. Cheap gasoline and the automobile oriented society that it fosters have imposed a burden on the poor by contracting or eliminating public transportation systems. Viewed in this context, the proposal for a large hike in the federal gasoline tax could be supported by people who want to reduce the cost of transportation for low income people. Such a tax, by announcing a higher

1. It's hard to imagine many people selling their houses in order to move closer to the office or factory. But remember that location relative to work is a factor when people are choosing a place to live, that Americans move frequently, and that over a period of years significantly higher transportation costs will, therefore, result in a lower average distance between residence and workplace.

price for gasoline as a matter of policy, independent of the vagaries of international diplomacy and new oil discoveries, would encourage a more rapid reorientation of society from its dependence on the automobile. Individuals and communities tend to delay major adjustments as long as they have grounds for hope that the situation will "correct itself." Price controls have the unfortunate effect of encouraging this kind of reaction.

Price and Supply

We've omitted the impact of suppliers' responsiveness to higher prices because we haven't yet discussed the costs which are the basis of supply curves. But we don't want to suggest even for one chapter that the amount of gasoline available for consumption is not affected by the price. Common sense suggests what subsequent chapters will demonstrate: supply curves slope upward to the right. How steeply does the supply curve slope in the case of gasoline? What's the price elasticity of supply? Estimates differ enormously, both for the short run and the long run. There are people who believe that the high prices for oil obtained by the Organization of Petroleum Exporting Countries will lead to a flood of new production that must eventually undercut the OPEC price. Even if these predictions are much too optimistic, we can be certain that supply is not *completely* price-inelastic. And that's an additional reason for allowing a rising price to ration in a time of increased scarcity. The added production that the higher price calls forth moderates the scarcity and prevents the price from rising further.

We assumed in figure 4D that 100 billion gallons were originally being supplied per year when the price was 36¢, and that this was cut to 90 billion, forcing the price up to 52¢. But will the quantity supplied remain at 90 billion gallons in the face of a price this much higher? It isn't likely. OPEC does not, after all, control all the world's oil reserves, and may even have trouble controlling the production of its members as higher prices give them a powerful incentive to increase their sales. Even a modest increase in output will go a long way toward holding down the price when demand is as inelastic as shown by D_1 in figure 4D; and a supply curve as inelastic over the relevant range as S could nonetheless keep the price from remaining long above 48¢. At higher prices the supply curve has been drawn to show greater price elasticity, on the assumption that there's a greater probability of a breakdown in OPEC's ability to control production at very high prices.

Taxes as Rationing Devices

Some people objected to handling the gasoline scarcity by means of higher prices and argued that higher prices would mean windfall gains for oil companies. This line of argument led to the recommendation that the price of gasoline be raised to a market clearing level by means of a higher tax. The higher tax would restrict consumption without enriching the supposedly undeserving suppliers of gasoline. Passing over the question of *which* suppliers are "undeserving" and why (as well as some additional complications created by the fact that the tax would transfer purchasing power from consumers to the government), we note that the proposal does allow the price to do its rationing job. Of course, the government will have to search for the precise size tax that will lead to a market clearing price: it doesn't have the advantage of seeing the demand curves in figure 4D, an advantage reserved to the writers of textbooks and others who solve only hypothetical problems. It can, however, ignore the curve S; since the government rather than suppliers will collect the higher price, no additional supply will be forthcoming. With the rate of supply constant at 90 billion gallons, no price controls, and an additional tax of 16¢ per gallon, the price will rise to 52¢ with demand at D_1 and eliminate the shortage; but suppliers will still get only 36¢, eliminating any windfall gains.

An interesting proposal aimed at preventing windfall gains while also protecting low income consumers called for the issue of ration coupons that could be freely bought and sold. Customers would then pay 36¢ plus one coupon for a gallon of gasoline. The supply of coupons would be restricted to match the available supply of gasoline. Since suppliers would not be receiving a higher price under this system, the amount of gasoline available would not increase: only 90 billion gallons would be available for allocation. With demand at D_1, therefore, the price of a ration coupon good for one gallon of gas might go to about 16¢, bid up to that level by consumers who wanted to buy more than their allotted share of gasoline. Consumers willing to use less than their allotment would sell coupons at the market determined price to those who wanted to use more. And surely business firms, given the enormous variation in their demands, would be active traders in the coupon market. Don't assume that the poor would sell to the rich. It isn't that simple. Some low income people would be unwilling to restrict their consumption and would end up buying coupons from higher income people who *were* willing to do so. We can't predict with any confidence how such a scheme would redistribute income. We can and should note, however, that the gainers would *not* be gasoline suppliers. Those who paid 52¢ for gasoline (36¢ to the station, 16¢ for the coupon) would be transferring income to other gasoline consumers; and so the flow of gasoline to the pumps would not increase.

Would this be an equitable system? Before answering be sure you know exactly how the allotments are going to be distributed. One book of ration coupons per person is overly generous to families with a lot of small children. One per licensed driver discriminates in favor of families with several license-packing teenagers. One per car isn't fair to the large family with a single car but may provide the family with two or three cars more gasoline than they ordinarily use. Moreover, by allotting ration coupons to cars the government will increase the demand for clunkers; cars will be kept indefinitely in order to obtain the associated gasoline ration. The real dilemmas begin, however, when we ask about the allocation of coupons to industrial, commercial, and agricultural users. Their situations vary so widely that it would be an impossible task to determine the proper quantities each should receive. Remember, finally, that a system widely regarded as unfair will be that much harder to administer.

REFLECTIONS ON PRICE SYSTEMS

If a good is scarce, it will be rationed. Some kind of discriminatory criteria will be used to allocate the good among competing claimants. The social choice, therefore, is never between rationing and nonrationing but among alternative rationing systems. It's a bit misleading to talk about "the social choice," however, because societies rarely discuss the options and make a conscious choice. Most people just take for granted that what *has been* is what *ought to be.* But in periods of rapid inflation, when a lot of prices rise significantly above the levels to which people are accustomed, or when particular goods suddenly become much more scarce and their prices jump sharply, people start to entertain doubts about rationing by means of price. They begin to call for price controls; and that is in effect a call for an alternative rationing system.

It's even more than that, in reality; for relative prices determine the organization of production as well as the distribution of the product. There is in fact no larger, more important, or more difficult issue in economics than the evaluation of the price system. On this, at least, the defenders of capitalism and of socialism (at least among economists) have historically agreed. Defenders of capitalism have usually extolled the efficiency of an economic system in which prices are set by supply and demand and have called attention to the degree of individual freedom that this permits. Proponents of socialism, on the other hand, have often objected to the injustice of such a system and have argued that it enslaves people to an economic order which no one controls.

When scarce goods are rationed by means of money prices, rich people can buy milk for their pets while poor people cannot get milk for their children. This is the traditional and still the most common argument against price rationing. Those who have money can satisfy their most trivial wants while those who lack money may have to go hungry and ill-clothed. It is a compelling argument. (Remember, however, that poor resource allocation occurs within families as well as among families. Malnutrition is sometimes found in children of wealthy families.) But what are the social alternatives?

Creating an Alternative System

It's difficult if not impossible to keep the word *need* from sneaking into any description of an alternative. But even if we relax our prohibition against that word in order to concede that little children need milk, we will not solve the problem. *How much* milk does a child need? What *age* child are we talking about? And how much milk should *adults* receive? We could, if we chose to, establish nutritional schedules for every age and allocate milk in accordance with those schedules. But our problems would only have begun.

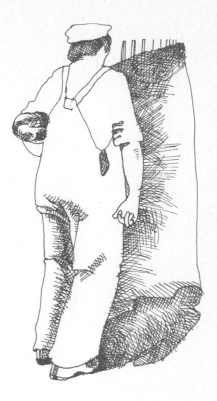

Bread, clothing, and fuel for domestic heating are just a few of the goods that would crowd in for consideration after milk had been rationed. Would we want to grant equal rations of these goods to people without regard to their size, occupation, or the winter temperatures where they reside? That may be equality but it hardly seems like equity. And what about such divergent personal characteristics as basal metabolism? Some people eat like horses and find cold weather invigorating; others eat like birds, set the thermostat at 80 degrees Fahrenheit, and still shiver without a woolen sweater. How could the rationing authorities take such differences into account? They probably could not do so, and would be compelled to perpetrate some glaring injustices by treating all people alike.

Some of these inequities could be eliminated, after the initial equal distribution of "necessities," by allowing the young man with the high basal metabolism to trade a little clothing and fuel oil to the old man with poor circulation in exchange for some bread. It's hard to imagine that such exchanges would *not* take place, even if they were prohibited; and since they can obviously increase the welfare of both parties to the exchange, why shouldn't they be allowed?

But another question arises now. How will the hungry horses *locate* the shivering birds and vice versa? A lot of time could be consumed under such a system in searching for people with whom to barter and in negotiating the terms of exchange. Who will be willing to give how many loaves of bread for a wool sweater (which has to *fit!*) or a gallon of fuel oil (useless, of course, in natural gas furnaces)? While the potential advantages of exchange would be considerable under such a system, the cost of arranging satisfactory transactions, in time and effort, would be a significant barrier to extensive trade. Many beneficial barter transactions would not be made simply because people had not found one another.

Evolution toward a Price System

This difficulty could be partially overcome through the development of trading centers. Unless they were rigorously prohibited, such centers would undoubtedly evolve rather quickly. The hungry horses could then exchange clothing for bread at the trading centers, while the shivering birds went there to exchange bread for clothing. The trading centers could pay for the scarce resources used in operating them by giving, let us say, 25 loaves for a sweater and asking 26 loaves when they in turn resold the sweater. The hungry horses would be delighted with 25 loaves, since their own limited contacts probably wouldn't turn up anyone willing to give more than 20; and the shivering birds would gladly sacrifice 26 loaves since on their own they probably couldn't find anyone demanding fewer than 30.

If most goods in this society continued to be rationed by means of money prices, money would be in demand and the trading centers would probably just buy and sell for money rather than engage in barter. People would bring their extra rations into the trading center whenever the prices being quoted there made the money (and what it would buy) more attractive to them than the goods, and would purchase extra rations from the trading center when they found the goods more attractive than the money.

Perhaps you've noticed by now that we have been describing the evolution of a price rationing system. Step by step, in a perfectly logical way, people would transform a rationing system based on "need" into one that used money prices, simply by searching for ways to improve their welfare. If *all* goods were allocated according to "need" and *nothing* sold (originally) for money, an extensive network of trading centers would develop because the opportunities to gain from exchange would be so vast and so numerous while the cost to individuals of making the exchanges on their own would be quite high. If the government failed to provide money, even that difficulty could be at least partially overcome: a commodity like cigarettes might be called into service.[1]

Unless the government checked this evolution by prohibiting exchange or by forbidding the formation of trading centers (the latter step would inhibit exchange by making it a far more costly activity), a system of rationing by means of money prices would evolve out of a system of rationing according to "need." Of course, everyone would in effect have a minimum guaranteed income, which could be stated either in terms of the goods in his basic ration *or* the money those goods could be exchanged for at the trading centers. The same effect on income distribution could be achieved in a far less cumbersome fashion, however, simply by providing

---

1. The reader who finds this a little farfetched is urged to read R. A. Radford on "The Economic Organization of a P.O.W. Camp," reprinted in the appendix.

every citizen with a minimum money income and allowing prices to continue their rationing function.

We observed earlier that the demand for price controls was in reality a demand for an alternative method not only of rationing scarce goods but also of organizing production. Most people who want the government to control the price of beef or gasoline or to protect consumers in general against "price gouging" have in mind no such sweeping reforms, however. Basically they want the price system to continue functioning: they just want a few of its rough edges blunted by political intervention.

Economics and Politics

Price rationing is for the most part an impersonal process. When the price of gasoline rises as a result of a larger demand or a smaller supply, those who are willing to pay the higher price get as much gasoline as they want and those who are unwilling do without. Race, sex, religion, political beliefs, length of hair, character, and temperament are irrelevant.

A price ceiling set below the market clearing level alters the situation. Since station operators now have more customers than they are able to satisfy, they can, if they wish, discriminate in favor of regular customers. Or they can discriminate against afternoon and weekend customers by opening their pumps only on weekday mornings. This also has the effect of discriminating against people who work from eight to five: they must purchase gasoline on the way to work, and that forces them to leave home earlier and burn up both gasoline and patience in long queues. Rationing systems of this kind are highly arbitrary and offend most people's sense of justice. Rationing by queuing is also inefficient, as we have pointed out, since the real costs that are borne by those who must wait in line are dead weight costs; they do not become income for someone else as does a higher money price.

And so private rationing systems devised by sellers usually lead to a demand for rationing through the political process. What are the principal advantages and disadvantages of political rationing?

Its main advantage lies in the fact that people tend to regard political rationing as basically equitable, at least in its early stages. When the government takes over and allocates scarce supplies, everyone gets his "fair share"; at least everyone is *more likely* to get his fair share than under other systems. Or so many people apparently believe. The belief is important whether it is true or not. But political rationing systems seem to have rather short useful lives. It is extraordinarily difficult to devise a system for allocating gasoline and diesel fuel that will guarantee adequate supplies to "essential" users, distribute what remains in an equitable fashion, and protect the interests of firms in the supply system. Truck drivers will

not agree, for example, that agriculture is a more "essential" industry than transportation. And if they aren't given what they want and sincerely believe they deserve, truck drivers will feel justified in demonstrating how essential their services are by going on strike. They also know that a 55 mile per hour speed limit on large trucks that have been designed for higher cruising speeds forces them to burn more fuel, not less, and they resent being compelled to pay these higher costs just so motorists won't have to bear the indignity of being passed by a truck. Of course, the 55 mile limit will not stick if too many motorists conclude that it is unfair, which they are more likely to do if they are frequently passed on the highway by large trucks. So how do the government rule makers arrive at efficient and equitable decisions that are also *perceived* as efficient and equitable?

They will inevitably rely on past allocations as a basic guide. For example, they may allocate to each geographic area for the current year some percentage of the quantity it consumed last year. That seems fair at first glance, a reasonable way of spreading the shortage. But it is not fair at all when the shortage has itself altered the geographic pattern of consumption. As a direct consequence of a gasoline shortage, for example, fewer motorists take long trips. With fewer people on the highways, the demand may actually decline in rural areas along major highways while rising in urban areas, leading to patterns of surplus *and* shortage. That is neither efficient nor equitable.

According to a February 1974 wire service story, the mayor of a West Virginia coal town decreed that any gasoline truck passing through the city would be stopped and unloaded. In itself the incident means little; as a symptom of the basic disadvantage of political rationing it may be significant. When government allocates scarce resources, an impersonal rationing system is replaced by one managed by human beings in a very visible way. What people might previously have accepted as unfortunate but inevitable, like "acts of God," now come to be seen as under human control and therefore avoidable. Criticism focuses on the government allocators; the inequities of their decisions, real or imagined, are widely advertised; the system is increasingly regarded as "fixed" and therefore unjust; and laws perceived as unjust do not command allegiance. The West Virginia mayor no doubt felt himself fully justified in confiscating some other area's gasoline for the sake of his community. But rationing on the basis of a lot of individual and highly biased perceptions of efficiency and equity is clearly not a viable system in the long run.

Perhaps the most significant feature of the government price and wage controls introduced in August 1971 and retained in a wavering fashion into 1974 was precisely that they wavered. They were imposed with fanfare. That apparently quieted the rumblings of those who believed the government had an obligation to control "price gouging" and check inflation.[1] They were then quietly relaxed. That enabled prices to continue performing their allocative function. This is hardly an ideal procedure. But the intelligence and understanding, or ignorance and misunderstanding, of citizens finally determine the shape of public policy in a democratic society.

Once Over Lightly

Scarcity is a relationship between availability and desirability. A good is scarce when there is not enough available for everyone to have all that he wants at no cost.

Scarce goods must be rationed in some way.

Every rationing system must employ criteria of some kind to discriminate among those who want scarce goods.

Competition is the attempt to satisfy whatever discriminatory criteria are being used to ration the scarce goods.

Rationing by the criterion of monetary price encourages people to acquire money. The social consequences of this will largely depend on the discriminatory criteria that must be satisfied in a society in order to obtain monetary income.

A shortage of a good exists when the quantity demanded is greater than the quantity supplied (at a given price). A shortage can always be eliminated by a sufficiently large price increase.

A surplus of a good exists when the quantity supplied is greater than the quantity demanded. If a surplus still existed when the price of a good was zero, that good would not be scarce.

Rationing a good by means of monetary price discriminates in favor of those who receive high monetary incomes, whether through diligence, luck, genius, or knavery. But it also discriminates in favor of those who want the good more strongly and are therefore willing to give up a larger portion of their monetary income to obtain it.

An equilibrium price is a price that adjusts the *intentions* of buyers and sellers until the quantity people want to purchase is equal to the quantity people want to sell. Economists make extensive use of the equilibrium concept as a way of predicting the consequences of particular sets of circumstances. An equilibrium is never observed; it is deduced from the assumptions the analyst is using and may therefore change if the assumptions are expanded or otherwise altered.

1. Nothing in this discussion should be allowed to give the impression that government is powerless to control inflation. We are postponing examination of the causes of inflation until chapter 17. There you will begin to see that the federal government has substantial power to affect the overall price level.

When prices are held below their market clearing level, purchasers must often pay the cost of waiting in line in addition to the money price. Queuing is a dead weight cost because the loss to the purchaser is not a gain for the seller.

The diversity of human wants is by itself enough to create the potentiality of gains from exchange. An economic system in which goods are bought and sold for money facilitates extensive exchange.

Many people discern important inequities in a social system that rations by means of money prices. The advantages and disadvantages of such a system must be compared with the advantages and disadvantages of alternative and *feasible* systems.

QUESTIONS FOR DISCUSSION

1. Many ceiling prices were fixed by law in World War II. How were scarce goods rationed?

2. Why was the sale or barter of ration stamps in World War II prohibited? Who would gain and who would lose if citizens were allowed to exchange ration allotments?

3. State colleges and universities usually set a very low tuition. How do they ration scarce facilities? Who do you think gains from this system? Why might professors and administrators of state schools prefer *not* to have scarce facilities rationed by means of higher price (tuition)?

4. There are no toll charges for driving on many urban expressways during the rush hour. How is the scarce space rationed?

5. Parking space is often sold on college campuses at a zero price. How is the scarce space rationed? If all students who bring cars onto the campus are charged $10 a year by the college as an automobile registration fee, is the fee a rationing device?

6. If the supply of turkeys in a particular November turned out to be unusually small, do you think a turkey shortage would result? Why or why not?

7. (*a*) There is currently much concern about a growing surplus of college teachers. How could the surplus be reduced or eliminated? Do you think this is likely to occur? Why or why not?

   (*b*) Notice that a surplus of college teachers can also be viewed as a shortage of college teaching positions. How will the scarce supply of positions be rationed if the price (salary of teachers) is not allowed to perform this function?

8. How do you account for the fact that people were deeply concerned about world food shortages in 1974 when only five years earlier the governments

of Australia, Canada, and the United States had been worrying about surpluses?

9. If you travel through the Western states in the summer, you are much more likely to encounter a shortage of camping spaces than of motel rooms. Why?

10. When motels raise their rates "during the season" and reduce them "off season," are they exploiting customers or promoting a better allocation of resources?

11. The government did not impose controls on sugar prices in 1974, and the price per pound rose about 600%. Did the high price cause any more sugar to be available in 1974 than would have been available at a lower, controlled price? Do you think there would have been any refined sugar available on grocers' shelves if the government had frozen the price near its original level? Where would it have gone?

12. Would scheduled airline flights be bunched as much as they are at the popular hours if airports based landing fees on the time of day as well as weight? What are the costs created by the present system with its alternating shortages and surpluses of landing and takeoff times?

13. Here are data on total energy consumption in the United States in selected years. Project energy consumption for 1975 and 1980 by making a rough extrapolation. Compare your projection for 1975 with the data for actual energy consumption. (Try looking in the most recent *Statistical Abstract of the United States*, which has a comprehensive index.)

1955	39,956 trillion British thermal units
1960	44,816
1965	53,969
1970	67,143
1975	_____
1980	_____

14. In 1972, to celebrate an anniversary, a Chicago bank offered to sell $100 bills for $80 cash to each of the first 35 customers who appeared at opening time (9 A.M.) on its birthday. How would you suppose the bills were rationed? What kind of people do you think managed to buy the cut-rate $100 bills?

15. In chapter 2 we asked you to think about a registration scheme under which students would pay more tuition for 10 o'clock classes and receive discounts for taking 8 o'clock classes. Why do colleges *not* charge higher prices for the hours in greater demand? A student willing to pay a friend $5 to stand in line for him and grab a 10 o'clock section might protest vigorously if he were charged an extra $3 to take a 10 o'clock class—even though the $3 fee gets rid of the line which he would pay $5 to avoid. If you think this is plausible after reflecting on it, how would you explain it?

16. If a ceiling price of $1 per pound were set on lobster sold at retail, where could you go to eat a lobster?

17. If the distribution of income were equalized, would everyone purchase the same quality automobile? Against whom do automobile prices discriminate?

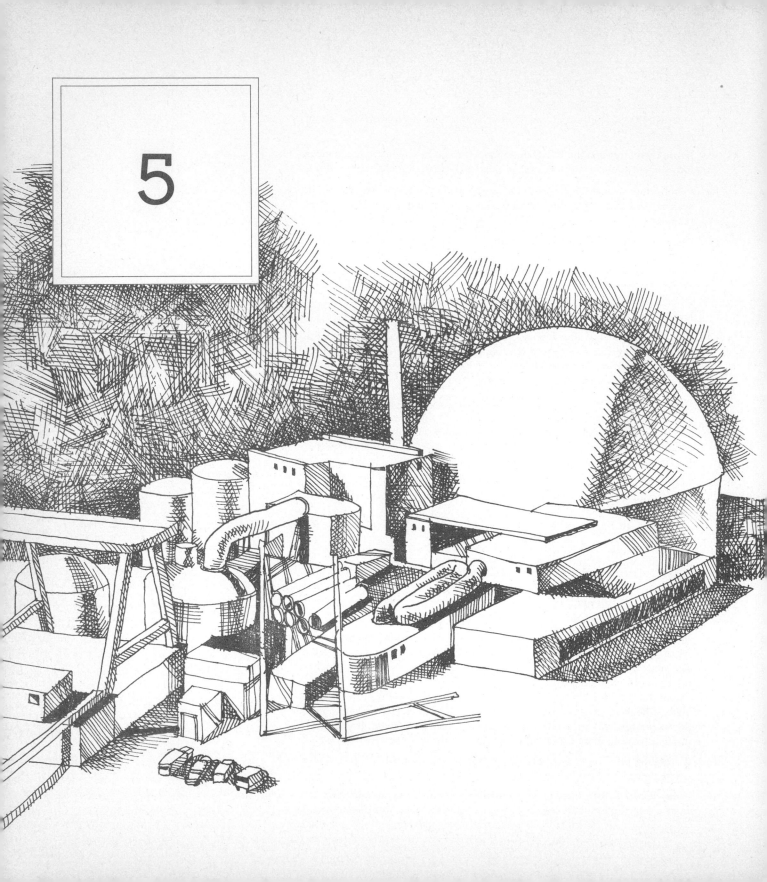

OPPORTUNITY COST

AND THE SUPPLY OF GOODS

Most of our attention has been focused until now on demand. We've been looking at the way in which prices ration available supplies by persuading people to substitute alternative goods. But what determines the available supplies, or the amount of each good offered for sale?

The answer is *cost*. But this reply raises as many questions as it answers once you begin to think about it. What do we mean by *cost*? We shall try to convince you in this chapter that it makes sense to think of *cost as the value of sacrificed opportunities*. Economists call this concept *opportunity cost*, and it ties together, as we shall see, the law of demand and the principles governing supply.

OPPORTUNITY COST: CONCEPT AND APPLICATIONS

The following exchange occurs in a college dormitory on a Monday night in the fall:

"Hey, Jack, do you want to go see the new Bergman movie? It closes after tonight."

"Golly, I'd love to but I can't. We've got a Russian test tomorrow and I'll flunk if I don't cram some vocabulary."

"Forget it. You can borrow my vocabulary cards in your free period tomorrow. An hour with the cards right before class is a B for sure."

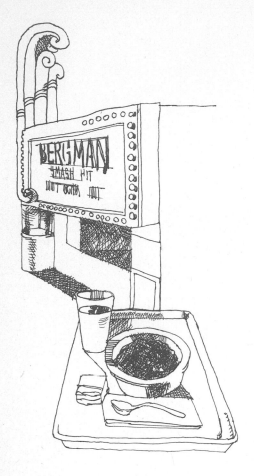

"Well—trouble is the Redskins and Miami are on TV tonight and I'd rather watch the game if I don't have to study."

"We'll go at six and be back for the kickoff."

"All right. Just let me see how much money I've got. . . . Five, six, seven, eight dollars—to last until I get paid on Thursday. And I'm out of meal tickets!"

"Eat peanut butter sandwiches! I thought you wanted to see the movie."

"I do. O.K. I'll let my stomach shrink a little until Thursday. Should we leave at quarter to six?"

The real cost of any action (going to a movie, buying a pair of jeans, manufacturing a lawnmower, moving to Halifax, raising beef cattle, building a hardware store, taking out an insurance policy) is the value of the alternative opportunity that must be sacrificed in order to take the action. The cost for Jack of going to the movie was at first calculated as a passing grade (given up!) in Russian. When his friend showed him how to reduce that cost, Jack looked at the next most valuable opportunity he would have to sacrifice if he went to the movie: watching the Monday night football game, a game he particularly wanted to see. His friend eliminated that cost for him and Jack turned to the money cost. But money wasn't the real cost. The real costs that dollars and cents represent are the opportunities given up when the money is spent in one way rather than another. The two dollars Jack will spend for the movie represent some meals he would have liked to eat but is willing to sacrifice in order to see the film.

The theory of supply in economics is not essentially different from the theory of demand. Both assume that decision makers face alternatives and choose among them, and that their choices reflect a comparison of the benefits anticipated from the alternatives. The logic of the economizing process is the same for producers as it is for consumers.

Producers' Costs as Opportunity Costs

When we think about producers' costs, asking ourselves for example why it costs more to manufacture a ten-speed bicycle than a redwood picnic table, we tend to think first of *what goes into* the production of each. We think of the raw materials, of the labor time required, perhaps also of the machinery or tools that must be used. We express the value of the inputs in monetary terms and assume that the cost of the bicycle or the table is the sum of these values. That isn't wrong. But it leaves unanswered the question of why the inputs had those particular monetary values. The concept of opportunity cost asserts that those values reflect the value of the inputs in their next best uses, or the value of the opportunities foregone by using the inputs in the production of bicycles and picnic tables.

The manufacturer's cost of producing a bicycle will be determined by what he must pay to obtain the appropriate resources. He must bid these resources away from alternative uses. Insofar as these resources have other opportunities for employment, he must pay the value of the best such opportunity. The value of these foregone opportunities thus becomes the cost of manufacturing a bicycle. This makes excellent sense. For the meaningful cost of obtaining one more bicycle is the value of what must be given up or sacrificed or foregone in order to obtain that bicycle.

Consider the case of the picnic table. Part of its cost of production is the price of the redwood. Assume that the demand for new housing has increased recently, and that building contractors have consequently been purchasing a lot more redwood lumber. If this causes the price of lumber to rise, the cost of manufacturing a picnic table will go up. Nothing has happened to affect the physical inputs that go into the table, but its cost of production has risen nonetheless. For houses containing redwood lumber are now more valuable than formerly, and the table manufacturer must pay the opportunity cost of the lumber he wants to put into his picnic tables.

The concept of opportunity cost explains also how labor enters into production costs. A worker must receive from his employer a wage that persuades him to turn down all other opportunities. A skilled worker will be paid more than an unskilled worker because and only insofar as those skills make him more valuable somewhere else. A worker who can install wheel spokes while standing on his head and whistling "Dixie" is marvelously skilled. But our bicycle manufacturer will not have to pay him additional compensation for that skill *unless* his unusual talent makes him more valuable somewhere else. That could happen. A circus might bid for his talents. If the circus offers him more than he can obtain as a bicycle producer, his opportunity cost to the manufacturer rises. In that case the manufacturer will probably wish him goodbye and good luck and replace him with another worker whose opportunity cost is lower.

If the National Basketball Association and the American Basketball Association merge into one league, what happens to the opportunity cost of physically coordinated seven-footers? With two leagues, each player has two teams bidding for his services. What either team must pay to get him is determined by what the other team is willing to pay and is based on its estimate of his value to the franchise. If the leagues merge, however, the right to hire a particular player is assigned to a single team, and the opportunity cost of a well coordinated seven-footer will fall to the presumably much lower level of his value in other lines of work. It's not surprising that owners of professional basketball teams prefer one league to two.

Let's take a less unusual case. If a large firm employing many people moves into a small town, the cost of hiring grocery clerks, bank tellers, secretaries, and gasoline station attendants in the town will tend to go up.

Why? Because grocery stores, banks, offices, and gasoline stations must all pay the opportunity cost of the resources they employ, and more valuable opportunities will have been created for these people by the entrance of the new firm. Suppose the new firm is interested in hiring women exclusively; only the opportunity cost of hiring women will increase at first. But that will pull women out of some jobs and thereby create additional opportunities for men, so that the opportunity cost of male workers will also tend to rise.

The resource that most clearly illustrates the opportunity cost concept is probably land. Suppose you want to purchase an acre of land to build a house. What will you have to pay for the land? It will depend on the value of that land in alternative uses. Do other people view the acre as a choice residential site? Does it have commercial or industrial potentialities? Would it be used for pasture if you did not purchase it? The cost you pay for the land will be determined by the alternative opportunities that people perceive for its use.

Case Studies in Opportunity Cost

Let's examine some other cases of varying costs to see how the concept of opportunity cost explains familiar but often misunderstood phenomena.

Why has the cost of a haircut gone up over the past 40 years so much more than the cost of goods generally? It's because potential barbers have alternative opportunities. If people want their hair cut by professionals, they must be willing to pay enough to bid barbers away from these alternative employments. As wage rates increase elsewhere in the economy, the opportunity cost of being a barber and hence the opportunity cost of hiring one rises also.

Why is it often so much harder to find a teenage babysitter in a wealthy residential area than in a low-income area? The frustrated couple unable to find a babysitter may complain that all the girls in the neighborhood are lazy. But that is a needlessly harsh explanation. Teenage babysitters can be found by any couple willing to pay the opportunity cost. That means bidding the babysitters away from their otherwise most valued opportunity. If the demand for babysitters in the area is large because wealthy people go out more often, and if the local girls receive such generous allowances that they value a date or leisure more than the ordinary income from babysitting, why be surprised to find that the opportunity cost of a babysitter is high?

Why did the cost of a college education rise so steeply during the decade of the 1960s? A very large part of the explanation lies in sharply increased instructional costs, made up partly of higher faculty salaries and partly of reduced teaching loads. But how did these developments come about?

Ask your friendly neighborhood professor and he will probably tell you about the long years that must be spent getting a Ph.D. and the impossibility of doing research while teaching twelve hours. Any good member of the professorial guild will assent to the virtues of those arguments, but no good economics professor will be much impressed with their cogency as an explanation of why professors earned more at the end than at the beginning of the decade, and taught less. The rapidly rising demand for professors provides the explanation. State legislatures poured money into building new colleges and expanding old ones; the federal government responded to the Sputnik scare by appropriating vast sums for higher education and for research, which gave teachers new opportunities; the World War II baby boom became a college-student boom in the 1960s; and a larger percentage of the population became persuaded that a college degree was the passport to the good life. The government and private industry meanwhile increased their demand for the services of highly trained personnel, improving a wide range of opportunities for people with extensive education. The net result was a vastly increased demand for the services of college professors. College professors, too, are scarce resources with opportunity costs. A larger number of them was obtained by bidding them away from alternative employments with the offer of higher salaries and reduced teaching loads. (Every college professor knows that it is easier to raise his income by finding a better opportunity elsewhere than by reciting his virtues to his current dean. Deans are more attentive to the recitals of professors with alternative opportunities.)

Why does the high school dropout rate decrease during a recession? The opportunity cost of remaining in high school varies with the job market for teenagers. A decline in job opportunities in a recession reduces the opportunity cost of remaining in school for some young people, and so they drop out less often. It's less costly to stay in school during a recession.

Why are poor people more likely to travel between cities by bus and wealthy people more likely to travel by air? A simple answer would be that the bus is cheaper. But it isn't. It's a very expensive mode of transportation for people for whom the opportunity cost of time is high; and the opportunity cost of time is typically much lower for poor people than for those with a high income from working.

Do you have the idea? Figure out for yourself the cost of going to college. If you include in your calculations the value to yourself of whatever you would be doing were you not in college, you have grasped the principle of opportunity cost.

To be quite certain about it, consider the case of a man who runs a small grocery store all by himself. He says that he does pretty well because he has no labor costs. Is he right? The cost of his own labor is not a monetary outlay, but it certainly is a cost. And that cost can be measured by the value of the opportunities he foregoes by working for himself.

A Note on Alternative Systems

The concept of opportunity cost is as applicable to a socialist society where resources are allocated by government planning as it is to a market economy in which relative prices guide decentralized decisions. For economic planners in the Soviet Union, the cost of building a railway from point A to point B is the value of whatever would have been done with the resources had they not been allocated to the railroad. Opportunity costs will be calculated by different means and different decision makers in a socialist society. But the concept of opportunity cost is an important aid to clear thinking for any person and for any society interested in getting the most out of available resources.

However, government officials often have the power to obtain scarce resources without bidding for them. And thereby they can sometimes conceal the real costs of a policy. There is no good reason to go abroad for an example: we have an excellent illustration in our own historical experience with the military draft.

The Cost of a Volunteer Military Force

Selective service, as it is euphemistically called, has been around in this country for a long time. While almost everyone regards it as an evil, most Americans still seem to think of it as the only way to obtain military personnel in wartime. "The country needs 3 million men in uniform, and a draft is the only way to get them."

We objected in chapters 2 and 3 to all such notions as "The country *needs* 3 million men in uniform." But we'll let it pass this time in order to ask, "Why is a draft the only way to get them?" Isn't there some wage rate for military service that would induce 3 million men to volunteer? Even in time of war? We don't draft policemen, firemen, steeplejacks, or others who do dangerous or disagreeable work. Why must we draft military personnel?

There may be good arguments for the draft, but the familiar argument that a volunteer army would cost too much is not one of them. The Department of Defense and others who worry about the relative costs of a conscripted and a volunteer military are conveniently overlooking the concept of opportunity cost. The true employment cost of creating a military force of 3 million men is *not* the wages paid to them, especially not when most of them have been conscripted against their will. It is rather the sum of the values of the opportunities foregone when these 3 million men entered the military.

What does it cost when a young man becomes a soldier? The best way

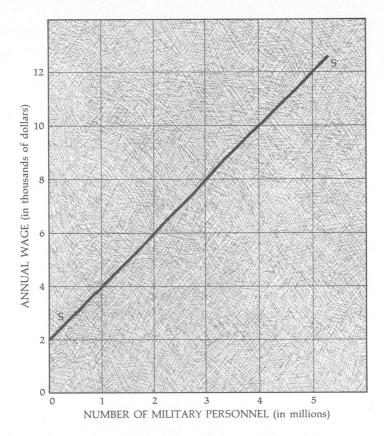

to find out would be to offer him a bribe, and to keep raising the bribe until he accepted it. If Marshall would enlist for $5000 per year, Basil for $8000, and Philip for no less than $60,000, those represent the opportunity costs of Marshall, Basil, and Philip. The social cost of drafting all three would then be $73,000, even though the government can conceal this fact by offering far less in wages and then compelling each to serve.

The opportunity cost, or the genuine cost, is a function of alternative employment opportunities foregone and all sorts of other values: preferences with respect to life style, attitude toward war, degrees of cowardice or bravery, and so on. When the government bids for military personnel, raising its offer until it can attract just the desired number of enlistments, the government in an important sense actually minimizes the cost of its program. For it pulls in those with the lowest opportunity costs of service —everyone like Marshall but no one like Philip. Under a draft this could occur only through the most unlikely of coincidences. Figure 5A provides a simple way to grasp the argument we're attempting to make.

Figure 5A Supply of military personnel

Opportunity Costs and Budget Costs

There *is* a supply curve of military volunteers, and whatever its precise nature, it will certainly slope upward to the right. Some people (those who assign low value to their available alternatives) will volunteer at a very low wage. But 3 million volunteers can be secured, on our assumptions, only if the wage offer is at least $8000 per year. That would mean a wage bill of $24 billion annually. Because taxpayers wouldn't like to have their taxes raised, congressmen wouldn't like to make such a huge appropriation. And the people in the Department of Defense care very much about the likes and dislikes of congressmen. They can cut that upsetting bill in half by offering only $4000 and compelling enlistments. The published cost will now be only $12 billion. Hurrah for cost savings!

But what of the genuine costs? The cost of the *volunteer* army under our assumptions would be $15 billion. That is the value of the area under the supply curve up to 3 million men, or the sum of the values of the opportunities foregone by those who enlisted. The other $9 billion paid out by the government is not a true cost to society as a whole. It is rather a transfer of wealth from taxpayers to members of the military who would have enlisted at a lower wage but who nonetheless receive the higher wage that is required to induce the enlistment of the 3 millionth volunteer. You should note in passing that this required wage will be lower in periods of high unemployment in the economy, when the value of alternative opportunities for volunteers decreases.

What will be the actual cost of a *conscripted* army? We can't say, except that it will certainly be larger. Only if the draft happened to hit exactly those and only those men who would have enlisted under a volunteer system would the cost be as low as $15 billion. But that is most unlikely. The more draftees who are grabbed from the upper end of the supply curve in place of men from the lower end, the higher will be the true cost of a conscripted army. For example, a man who would have volunteered at a wage of $4500 is offered $4000. He rejects the offer, and he is not subsequently drafted. Instead, a man who would only have volunteered at $12,000 is drafted. There was a "budget saving" of $500 annually and an actual loss of $7500.

The military draft fails to minimize the cost of obtaining military personnel. That may in your judgment be one of the least of its faults; or it may be outweighed in your mind by presumed advantages. But at least it's a flaw that economists can point out.

Do Costs Determine Prices?

When sellers announce a price increase to the public, they like to point out that the increase was compelled by rising costs. *The Wall Street Journal* publishes frequent announcements of this kind, and it's rare indeed when the announcement fails to include an expression of regret that higher costs made this unfortunate step necessary. In chapter 10 we'll explore more fully the principles that guide sellers when they're choosing what prices to set. In this section of chapter 5 we want to use the concept of opportunity cost to examine critically the basic notion that prices are determined by costs. We want to show you that it makes as much sense to assert that costs are determined by prices. More accurately, we shall argue here that costs are always determined in part by demand. They are not something independent of demand as so many people carelessly assume.

Demand and Cost

We can begin with an example discussed earlier in this chapter. Does it make sense to claim that the price of haircuts has gone up because barbers' wages have risen? If people weren't willing to pay a high price for a haircut, how could barbers' wages rise? The price people are willing to pay to have their hair cut professionally is one important factor that causes costs—that is, wages—to be what they are.

Plastic surgeons receive high incomes because they command a high price for their services. Is this why it costs so much to have a face lift? Not exactly. The causal relationship also runs in the opposite direction. It's the fact that people are willing to pay a high price for cosmetic surgery that makes the cost of hiring a plastic surgeon so high. Few people have the requisite skills, of course, and their acquisition is difficult and time-consuming. That's why the demand for cosmetic surgery raises the income of the surgeons rather than merely increasing the number of people willing and able to provide the service. But the cost of a plastic surgeon is obviously not something independent of the demand for plastic surgery.

When the owners of professional football teams announce in the summer that ticket prices will be raised in the fall, they like to blame this tearfully on rising costs, especially the high wages that must be paid to the players. But why do the players receive such high wages? It can't be that their work is so dangerous and grueling because it was just as dangerous and grueling in the days when players received only a few hundred dollars for the season. It's the demand, the willingness of many people to pay high prices to watch, that has pulled up the costs by making football players such valuable productive resources to the owners of professional teams. Soccer players in the United States receive far less, not because they work less hard, but because soccer isn't that popular in this country.

The Case of Land Prices

One of the most interesting cases of the relationship we're stressing is found in agriculture. The value of the real estate owned by farmers in this

country rose more than 800% between 1940 and 1974, according to data published by the Department of Agriculture. Anyone who decides to go into farming today will find that he has to pay a high price to obtain productive land. It would clearly be misleading to assert that the high cost of land is a cause of high food prices. It was the demand for land, determined in large part by the demand for agricultural products, that pulled up the cost of farming land. When farmers argue for higher government support prices for their crops because land costs so much, they are ignoring the fact that higher support prices will tend to pull up the cost of the land on which those crops can be grown.

The most dramatic case of misleading reasoning is the argument of a farmer whose land lies near a large city. As the suburbs expand, residential developers offer to buy the land for prices three or four times higher than what it's worth in agricultural production. If a farmer were to refuse to sell because he wants to stay in farming, he could hardly complain about the rising cost of his land. But farmers who *rent* land near large cities often do just that. The landowner will understandably want to sell the land to the developers unless the tenant farmer is willing to pay three or four times more rent. We can certainly sympathize with the tenant farmer dispossessed by the growth of the suburbs. But it's important that we see *why* he's being asked to pay a rent so much higher than before: it is the demand for land that is raising its cost.

Consumer Prices as Opportunity Costs

In all these examples we've tried to show that the costs of productive resources like labor and land are prices determined by demand. This is what's meant by calling them opportunity costs. We can just as easily argue that the prices of consumer goods are in reality costs, opportunity costs that measure the value of the goods in alternative uses. Take the case of lobster tails again.

Lobsters are, unfortunately, scarce. More lobsters will be brought to market as higher prices offer larger incentives to lobster fishermen; but the demand in recent years has increased considerably faster than the supply and the price has consequently risen sharply. Figure 5B illustrates what has occurred.

The higher price can be viewed as the opportunity cost of the resources engaged in bringing lobsters to market. But when the lobsters have all been brought to market on a given day, so that the supply is, for that day at least, completely inelastic, then the price can be viewed as the opportunity cost of the last potential purchaser who was persuaded by the high price to do without lobster. Think of it as follows: Lobster tails have many alternative uses, at least as many as there are potential lobster eaters. Lobsters by and large have only one function, it is true, from the aggregate point of view. (We're notorious for ignoring the values and preferences of the lobster.) But the consumption of a lobster by one gourmet prevents its consumption by another. Lobster lovers in effect bid against one another for the limited supply. As the price rises, more and more potential consumers are reluctantly persuaded to do without. The price that clears the market, that makes the quantity demanded equal to the quantity supplied, will be the price that just barely persuades the most reluctant of the disappointed lobster lovers to go home from the seafood market with ocean perch or flounder fillets. It is *his* opportunity cost that is expressed by the market clearing price.

The point of all this is that people don't pay what lobster is worth to them but rather what lobster is worth in its most valued alternative use: as food for the consumer who was just barely deterred by the price from making a purchase. It's the opportunity cost of this disappointed lobster lover that the price reflects, as well as the opportunity costs of the resources used to bring additional lobsters to market.

How many people realized in late 1974 when they were paying 75¢ a pound for sugar that the price was equal to the cost? Not the growers' cost, of course, but the opportunity cost of those sugar and candy bar lovers who were finally persuaded by the rising price to sacrifice the sweets they craved.

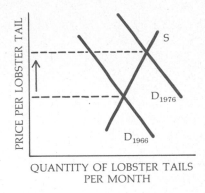

QUANTITY OF LOBSTER TAILS PER MONTH

Figure 5B Supply and demand for lobster tails

A DIALOGUE ON COST AND VALUE

Demand and supply are the two concepts that economists use continually to interpret and make sense out of the seemingly chaotic patterns of a complex and ever-changing economic system. Demand reflects human wants for goods, supply reflects the availability of goods; and every economy is a social system for matching up what's wanted with what's available.

Demand is an expression of people's preferences, the subjective valuations that they assign to things, processes, or experiences. That seems clear enough. But of what is supply an expression? Supply expresses the obstacles or difficulties that must be overcome in order to make goods available, usually characterized as costs of production. But on what do costs of production depend? What do they express? The standard answer in economics at least until the end of the nineteenth century, and probably still the standard answer most people would give today, is that costs of production reflect the human effort, the toil and trouble, that enter into the production of goods. If you agree with that, then you do not accept the concept of opportunity cost; and you're probably going to wind up in confusion or contradiction sometime when you're trying to make sense out of what you observe in the economy around you.

Human Effort and "Real" Cost

The idea that the real cost of any good is the human effort or labor or toil-and-trouble required to produce it occurs readily to anyone who begins to think systematically about economic problems. It seemed obvious, for example, to John Locke, the philosopher whose writings did so much to influence social thought in the eighteenth century and who has properly been called the philosopher of the American Revolution. Locke saw that the production of goods required natural resources and human effort, usually summarized in the concepts of *land* and *labor*. Land or natural resources was by definition something given: it was simply there to begin with. And since it was free, it could not be considered a cost of production. Of course, a natural resource that had been improved through human effort (the draining or irrigation of land, the cultivation of orchards, the digging of mine shafts) was no longer a purely natural resource. It had become land *plus* labor, with the labor embodied in the improvements.

The point is that nothing is ultimately required for the production of goods but land and labor, that land is free, and that all costs must therefore reduce to labor costs. It is the fact that something can only be obtained by the expenditure of human effort that makes it "costly," that is, not free. Or so at least almost everyone believed prior to the development of the opportunity cost concept in the late nineteenth century.

The Labor Theory of Value

The name usually given to this point of view is the *labor theory of value.* Today we associate the theory primarily with Karl Marx and his followers. But Marx was actually standing in the mainstream of economic thinking when he articulated his labor theory of value; and though that stream was soon after diverted to leave Marxists increasingly alone among economists in defending the labor theory of value, they have always had plenty of company. Anyone who judges the appropriateness or fairness of a particular price by reference to the human effort associated with it is implicitly adopting a labor theory of value: "He never works more than ten hours a week and still makes $300. It's *ridiculous!*" "The price of sugar is *absurd* when you consider how much cane one person can cut in an hour." "She *deserves* a bigger salary. She went to school for seven long years after high school."

The notion that prices depend upon costs that in turn express the amount of human effort entering into the production of a good still commends itself to people for a number of reasons. One is that it accords roughly with our sense of justice. We can't assess the fairness of any price, whether it's the price of a commodity or of human services, without a standard. And the natural standard for human beings to apply is human effort. If gizmo producers are receiving more for their product than are widget producers, it must take more people or more arduous, dangerous, or exacting labor to produce a gizmo—or else the gizmo price is a rip-off or the widget producers are being exploited. And that's why physicians point to their long years of schooling or crane operators to the heavy responsibilities resting on their shoulders whenever they're asked to justify the prices they receive for their services. It's also why so many people are indignant about the low wages paid to lettuce and grape pickers.

Perhaps the best example of the way in which human effort provides a standard for evaluation is the procedure so often employed to compare welfare between countries. We say that it takes two hours for an average American to earn the price of a pair of shoes and four hours for an average Albanian. The comparison is meaningful insofar as a unit of human effort is a meaningful standard for us.

The other principal reason for the continuing popularity of a labor-expended theory of comparative costs is the difficulty of finding a satisfactory alternative. At the beginning of his three-volume study, *Capital*, Marx lays down the postulate that if 8 bushels of wheat sell for the same price as 112 pounds of iron, there must exist in each equal quantities of something common to both. After correctly observing that "this common 'something' cannot be either a geometrical, a chemical, or any other natural property," he concludes that it can only be labor. The relative prices of commodities are the result, therefore, of the quantities of labor "embodied" in them in the process of production.

Breakdown of the Labor Theory

The trouble with this conclusion is that it doesn't square with what we all know or can readily observe. Commodities just do not exchange at ratios proportionate to the man-hours required for their production. Some commodities produced by highly skilled labor will sell at prices many times greater than other commodities produced by means of an equal number of unskilled man-hours. Marx thought he could save his theory from this fundamental objection. He argued that, in applying the theory, one must adjust the number of man-hours entering into a product to take account of skill differentials. But that makes sense only until we ask how this adjustment is to be carried out. Shall we correct the number of man-hours for skill differences by using an index of relative wage rates, so that one hour from a worker paid at $5 counts two and one-half times as heavily as an hour from a worker earning only \$2? This was the method of adjustment recommended by Marx. But it is a method that destroys the theory. For it leaves us with the question of why one worker receives two and one-half times the hourly wage of another.

Do not suppose that this can be explained in turn on the basis of length of training or irksomeness of the work. It cannot. A brilliant lawyer who breezed through law school and now loves his work probably commands a higher, not a lower, wage than the classmate who ground his way through and now plods reluctantly to the office every day. Some people acquire skills easily, almost naturally, and others only by means of long and arduous training. If they have the same skills they will tend to be paid identical wages without regard to how long or hard they studied. And no one is willing to pay a ditchdigger a higher wage until his blisters turn to calluses.

Moreover, even a high degree of skill, whether acquired easily or by arduous effort, is no guarantee that a worker will be paid a high wage. Relative wage rates for skilled and unskilled workers often change with no observable change in their skills. There just is no way to get around the fact that the valuation of goods, as reflected in the demand for them, affects costs of production. But the admission of demand into the explanation of costs undermines the basic assumption of the labor theory of value.

The theory contains an even more serious difficulty. Natural resources are, by definition, "free" in the sense that humanity gives up nothing to obtain them. But in another and very important sense they are not free at

THE LABOR THEORY OF VALUE IN TAX COURT

A case was recently brought before the United States Tax Court by an owner and trainer of trotting horses who apparently subscribed to both the opportunity cost *and* the labor theory of value. In 1965 he had bought a mare who died in 1970; and he wanted to claim a casualty loss on his income tax. He added \$7 to her value for every hour he had spent in training her, arguing that because he could earn this rate in his regular job as a heavy-equipment operator, his time was worth that amount.

He was using the opportunity cost concept to assess the value of his own time. In assuming that each hour spent with the mare added \$7 to her value, he was shifting to a labor theory of value. But a trotting horse trained by an orthopedic surgeon in her spare time is not more valuable than one trained on weekends by a filing clerk *unless* the surgeon is in fact a better trainer.

all. If they are limited in supply, then they cannot be used in one way when they are used in another. Ownership is irrelevant to the argument: whether ownership of a resource is private or communal, its *use* has a genuine cost, namely, the value of whatever cannot be produced because the resource has been employed for some other purpose. To ignore this cost is to assume that natural resources are not scarce; and that is a highly misleading assumption. But a labor theory of value offers no procedure for including these losses in the calculation of costs.

The opportunity cost theory, on the other hand, explains on the basis of a single principle how both natural resources *and* human resources affect costs. It is the value of these resources in their next best use that determines their contribution to cost in any particular use. And when producers or consumers can only obtain the resources they want by bidding them away from their next best uses, then the costs producers and consumers must pay will be equal to opportunity costs.

The Subjectivity of Costs

A theory that explains all costs as the value of foregone opportunities reduces all costs ultimately to *valuations*. It makes supply as well as demand depend upon *preferences*. The common denominator in Marx's theory of costs and prices was human labor; the common denominator in the opportunity cost theory is human satisfactions or—to use the accepted term—subjective utility. And that seems to leave the theory of prices and costs without an objective foundation, especially since the valuations upon which everything is supposed to depend are not observable. This is disconcerting. To see why it's disconcerting we can listen in on an imaginary conversation between a curious citizen and an economist.

Citizen: Why do I have to pay so much more now for medical care than I paid ten years ago?
Economist: Because costs have gone up.
C: But why have medical costs risen faster than other costs?
E: Because the cost of medical care *resources* has risen rapidly.
C: But why? It doesn't take any longer to train a doctor now than it took ten years ago.
E: True but irrelevant. The opportunity cost of doctors has risen.
C: Meaning?
E: That you must bid doctors away from more valuable opportunities than they had ten years ago.
C: What valuable opportunities?
E: The opportunities to provide medical care to other people who are willing to pay more today than they were willing to pay ten years ago.

C: But why are people willing to pay more today for medical care?

E: Because, all things considered, people now place a higher valuation on medical care relative to other goods and services than they used to.

C: How do you know that?

E: By the fact that they're willing to pay a higher price for medical care.

The economist's argument could be expanded; but no expansion along the lines of opportunity cost theory could completely avoid an appearance of circularity. The prices people pay are supposed to depend upon valuations, but valuations are only observed in the form of the prices people pay. Is this an adequate theory? Or is it a tautology that explains nothing, finally asserting merely that prices are what they are because they are the prices we observe?

Suppose for a moment that someone mounted a clever (but false) advertising campaign and convinced millions of people that the way to lasting health and happiness was through daily rubdowns by licensed masseurs. The price of rubdowns would rise, reflecting the higher opportunity cost of purchasing masseurs' services. More people would, of course, acquire training in the art or science of massage. But would anyone be better off (except the masseurs)? Wouldn't we want to say that the higher prices and larger number of masseurs reflected not the greater utility of a massage but the gullibility of consumers? And if someone replied in defense that people *are* better off whenever they *think* they're better off, the cat would be out of the bag. That's precisely the objection of those who find opportunity cost theorizing inadequate. It assumes that all valuations are valuable, regardless of their origin, nature, or consequences.

We can put the objection another way. Opportunity cost theory is rooted in individual valuations which it simply takes as given and not subject to further analysis. The labor theory of value, for all its clumsiness as an explanation of relative prices, is at least rooted in something less ephemeral, something more real and surely more observable: the external relationships between and among people and their work.

Subjective Values and Radical Critiques

The individual whose valuations provide the basic material for economic analysis conducted in terms of opportunity cost has been ridiculed as a caricature of humanity and as someone with only one characteristic: he maximizes his utility, which means that he chooses in accord with his preferences, whatever they are and however they come about, and on the basis of whatever information or misinformation he possesses. A radical American economist named Thorstein Veblen (1857–1929) described this analytical fiction in an often quoted passage distinguished both by the insight of its author and the flamboyance of his prose:

> In all the received formulations of economic theory . . . the human material with which the inquiry is concerned is conceived in hedonistic terms; that is to say, in terms of a passive and substantially inert and immutably given human nature. The psychological and anthropological preconceptions of the economists have been those which were accepted by the psychological and social sciences some generations ago. The hedonistic conception of man is that of a lightning calculator of pleasures and pains, who oscillates like a homogeneous globule of desire of happiness under the impulse of stimuli that shift him about the area, but leave him intact. He has neither antecedent nor consequent. He is an isolated, definitive human datum, in stable equilibrium except for the buffets of the impinging forces that displace him in one direction or another. Self-poised in elemental space, he spins symmetrically about his own spiritual axis until the parallelogram of forces bears down upon him, whereupon he follows the line of the resultant. When the force of the impact is spent, he comes to rest, a self-contained globule of desire as before. Spiritually, the hedonistic man is not a prime mover. He is not the seat of a process of living, except in the sense that he is subject to a series of permutations enforced upon him by circumstances external and alien to him.[1]

Marx and Veblen believed that an adequate economic theory had to do more than explain how prices were determined and the way in which relative prices affected decisions. Today their followers believe that an adequate economic theory will be based on and will contribute to the understanding of history, law, sociology, politics, psychology, and ethics as well as the whole process of social change and development. They find economic theorizing based on the concept of opportunity cost incapable of answering the questions they want raised.

On Dictionaries and Poetry

We shall for the most part reject their counsel in this book. The strength and power of the economic way of thinking stems in large part from economists' refusal to be diverted into any such ambitious program. It is true that the economic theory that has been developed on the basis of the opportunity cost concept does not offer a comprehensive view of the human situation. Its ability to explain processes of historical change is particularly limited. It does, however, describe, explain, and illuminate important aspects of social behavior. Even many Marxists now concede that it offers a better explanation of relative prices than does the Marxian theory, and that central planners in socialist countries are using clumsy

1. Thorstein Veblen, "Why Is Economics Not an Evolutionary Science?" *Quarterly Journal of Economics,* July 1898. Reprinted in Veblen's collected essays, *The Place of Science in Modern Civilization.*

and ineffective tools if they try to set prices on the basis of cost calculations reflecting anything other than opportunity cost. If prices do not reflect opportunity costs, they are misleading indicators and blind guides for economic decision makers.

We do not discard our dictionaries because they contain no poetry. Nor do we try to improve them by arranging the words in metrical rather than alphabetical order. We often use them, in fact, to gain a more appreciative understanding of poetry. But we do not claim, if we are sensible, that even the most exhaustive dictionary is a *substitute* for books of poetry. The economic way of thinking is highly useful. We take for granted that a person must know a good deal more than economic theory to discourse intelligently about human societies.

Once Over Lightly

The real cost of any good is the value of what must be sacrificed in order to obtain it. Economists call this its opportunity cost.

Insofar as resources can only be obtained through competitive bidding, costs of production will reflect the value in alternative uses of the resources employed in producing the goods. This implies that producers will want to suppress competitive bidding for the resources they use if they can find an effective way to do so.

The value of a human being may be infinite; but the wages of human beings in any task will be much closer to the value of their services in alternative employments than to infinity.

Budget costs are not always real costs because they sometimes overlook or conceal opportunity costs. People in business for themselves often overlook the opportunity costs of the resources they themselves own. And governments may be able to employ coercion in place of bidding to obtain resources at less than opportunity cost.

The law of demand and opportunity cost are opposite sides of the same coin. The monetary price of a good expresses the value of other goods the purchaser could have obtained with that sum if he had not purchased this particular good. The price that must be bid to obtain it also expresses the value of that good to the last unsuccessful bidder who gave up his opportunity to have the good when the price rose too high. Because prices express forsaken opportunities, less will be purchased at higher prices and more at lower prices.

Demand determines costs. Costs determine prices. Prices for alternative goods determine the demand for particular goods. Everything depends upon everything else in the opportunity cost way of thinking.

The labor theory of value asserts that the *real* cost of any good is the human labor that went into its production. This way of analyzing relative costs and prices is inconsistent with the opportunity cost concept and fails to explain the relative costs and prices we actually observe.

Opportunity costs are ultimately expressions of subjective valuations, which we observe only in the form of the prices people are willing to pay. Some critics object to the circularity in explaining prices by reference to valuations that are in turn only observed in the form of prices. Advocates of the labor theory of value contend that their theory, grounded in external relationships among people, provides a better foundation for explaining and evaluating *changing* economic relationships.

QUESTIONS FOR DISCUSSION

1. What effect would the expectation of a continuing high price for soybeans have on the price of field corn? How does the concept of opportunity cost aid us in seeing the relationship?

2. What is the cost per ticket to a professional baseball club that offers 50 "free" tickets to an orphanage? Does it matter *for what game* the tickets are offered?

3. Why did the cost of hiring domestic servants increase dramatically during World War II? What would you have replied to people who said that servants "just weren't available"?

4. Some people contend that the ending of the military draft reduced college enrollments. Use the concept of opportunity cost to defend this argument. How did organized draft resistance and mounting public hostility to the Vietnam war affect Congressional perceptions of the relative cost of a conscripted and a volunteer army?

5. Jim Teen, a high school junior, can caddy at the local country club for as many hours as he chooses each weekend. His father insists, however, that Jim mow the lawn each week. It takes Jim one hour to mow the lawn, it takes his younger brother Bill two hours. Can you explain why it might be more efficient for Jim to pay Bill to take over his lawn chore even though Bill is a far less skilled yardman? What sense does it make, if any, to say that it costs more when Jim mows the lawn than when Bill mows it? (This will be discussed at greater length in chapter 7.)

6. If the federal government and private foundations allocate large sums for research, will this tend to benefit or harm a small college whose faculty either does no research or cannot land any research grants? Why?

7. By taking an airplane one can go from D to H in one hour. The same trip takes five hours by bus. If the air fare is $30 and the bus fare is $10, which would be the cheaper mode of transportation for someone who could earn $2 an hour during this time? For someone who could earn $10 an hour? $5 an hour?

8. When that Chicago bank (mentioned in question 14, chapter 4) offered to sell $100 bills for $80 cash to each of the first thirty-five people who entered the bank at 9 A.M. on its birthday, four young men started the queue seventeen hours prior to opening time. What was their cost of waiting? How do you know?

9. Why might a multinational corporation with identical plants in two different countries pay different wage rates to workers in the two countries even though their skill levels were the same? Does this strike you as unjust? Why might the *higher paid* workers object?

10. Think about the cost of television commercials. What enters into the cost of a 30-second commercial plugging Friendly Fred's Ford Dealership? How do you explain the fact that the same commercial will cost $90 on Wednesday morning but $1600 on Saturday night right before "All in the Family"? Local television stations are often asked to donate time for public service spots. Does this cost the station anything? Do you think stations are more willing to donate time on Sunday morning than on weekday mornings because the owners are religious?

11. Pablo Toros became a matador after graduating from medical school because he found he could make more money fighting bulls than practicing pediatrics. Does this prove that bullfights are of more value than the health of children? Does it prove that the society in which Toros lives values bullfights more than the health of children? Does it prove that Toros values money more than the health of children?

12. Can you recall ever having used the concept of a just or fair wage? How do you assess the justice of a particular wage? Are such assessments ever important? Is it desirable that there be some consensus within a society on the criteria of a just wage?

6

SUNK COSTS, MARGINAL COSTS,
AND ECONOMIC DECISIONS

"Tuition covers only 43% of the cost of educating your son or daughter. We're counting on your annual gift to sustain operations that are fundamental to the kind of education for which our university is noted." Those sentences are from a letter sent to parents by a prestigious university whose annual tuition is over $3500. Do you think that a student paying $3500 per year in tuition is paying only 43% of the cost of her education? Would the university really save $4640 annually if she dropped out?

How do you explain the fact that people choose to drive their own cars to a business convention rather than go with someone else even though they complain that the reimbursement of 10¢ per mile doesn't cover their costs?

Can a business firm make money by selling "below cost"?

To answer these questions you must learn to distinguish between the costs that are relevant to decision making and the monetary outlays that are irrelevant and not really costs at all.

THE IRRELEVANCE OF SUNK COSTS

If the quantity of a good that is supplied depends on opportunity costs, as we stated at the beginning of chapter 5, then costs that are not opportunities foregone will not determine the quantity supplied and hence will have no way of affecting price. This is summed up in the economist's dictum: *Sunk costs are irrelevant.* It is a simple but important principle in economic analysis as well as a valuable guide to decision making for both businessmen and consumers. But what exactly is a sunk cost?

When you go into a restaurant and order the sixteen-ounce steak for $6, you incur a cost: the value of whatever you would have done with the $6 had you not ordered that steak. Now suppose that after eating awhile you realize you overestimated your appetite. You eat half the steak and find that you just don't want any more. You wish that you had ordered the eight-ounce steak listed on the menu at $4. What is the cost of leaving the restaurant with half the steak still on your plate?

It is *not,* as many would erroneously suppose, the difference between the price of the sixteen-ounce and the eight-ounce entree, or $2. You do not give up $2 in the value of foregone opportunities by leaving half the steak on your plate. You incurred the full cost of the larger steak when you ordered it; you committed yourself at that time to pay the price of the large steak and in that moment you incurred all your costs. The opportunity to spend your money on something else disappeared at that moment.

Then what is the opportunity cost of leaving half your dinner behind? That depends. What opportunity do you thereby forego? If you have a dog, it might be the price of half a pound of dog food, which is the value of the opportunity foregone when you chose not to ask for a doggie bag.

Bygones are bygones, sunk costs are sunk.

> The Moving Finger writes; and, having writ,
> Moves on; nor all your Piety nor Wit
>   Shall lure it back to cancel half a Line,
> Nor all your Tears wash out a Word of it.

Of course, we must be certain that a cost is really sunk, or fully sunk, before we decide to regard it as irrelevant to decision making. If you were to purchase a new motorcycle and immediately afterward regret your decision, what would be the cost to you of nonetheless continuing to own the motorcycle? Clearly, you would not be forced to say "I did it and now I'm stuck." You could resell the motorcycle. By not doing so you would incur a cost (a benefit foregone) equal to its resale value. The genuine sunk cost would therefore be only the difference between what you paid for it and what you can get by selling it. That is the irrelevant part of your cost. *In the economist's way of thinking it is no cost at all, for it represents no opportunity for choice.* It may be cause for bitter regret and the occasion of some education in the dangers of impulse buying, but it is no longer a cost in any sense relevant to the economics of present decisions.

Yet we all know that people do not consistently reason things out in this way. Many a person who made such a purchase and then regretted it would be tempted to retain possession of the motorcycle rather than sell it for substantially less than the original price. He might justify this action by saying "I can't afford to take the loss." But he already took the loss! He made a mistake, and his full loss occurred when he made it. If he nonetheless chooses to keep the motorcycle, he is probably practicing self-deception. He persuades himself that a motorcycle gathering cobwebs in the garage has the same value as the money he paid to put it there, and more value than the opportunities foregone by keeping it there. But the only relevant cost now is the opportunity foregone *by not selling.*

The Case of the Las Vegas Caper

Let's take another example more closely related to the business world. You own a television retail outlet and one of your suppliers is sponsoring a gigantic Dealers Contest. For every television set you buy (no returns allowed), you receive one day in Las Vegas with all expenses paid. You gleefully order 28 sets and your wife starts planning for your two-week holiday together.

Upon your return from Las Vegas you begin wondering how you will sell all those television sets. One month later you're still wondering. It seems that none of your customers is interested in that brand or model. You are about ready to give up and store the whole lot in the back workroom.

Then you get an offer from an orphanage in some distant city to take all those sets off your hands for $1000. You know that a businessman can't make money by selling below cost, so you sit down to figure out the cost of the sets. You paid $35 apiece to the supplier. Moreover, you have had them in your store for a month tying up valuable floor space. You borrowed the money to buy them from the bank at 12% annual interest. You also had various handling costs that you estimate at $100. And you spent $40 on advertising in a vain effort to move the sets. By estimating $70 as the opportunity cost of display space tied up for a month, you arrive at a figure of $1200. You write back to the orphanage that you would be willing to sell the lot at cost for $1200, foregoing any profit on the transaction in the interest of charity. The orphanage replies that $1000 is their top price since they can get the sets they want somewhere else for that price. But you are a good businessman, you know that losses don't make profits, and you refuse.

You were actually a rather poor businessman. Every one of the "costs" you enumerated in arriving at your total of $1200 was a sunk cost and hence no cost at all. *The proper stance for making cost calculations is not looking back to the past, but forward to the future.* Your costs, if you sell, will be opportunities thereby foregone, or what you can get for the sets if you do not sell to the orphanage. You know the market fairly well and you estimate you could get $280 by selling them for junk. The relevant cost of the sets is therefore $280. Your gain from selling to the orphanage is $720. Any loss that you're worrying about should be assigned to experience and the glorious memories of Las Vegas. It is irrelevant for decision-making purposes.

Building Bridges

This way of looking at matters is important enough for us to spend time on one further example. Fred Ballistics is an enterprising engineer who decides to build a bridge across the river. He owns both the access land and the bridge-building rights over the river, so he is free to build his own bridge and charge whatever tolls he pleases. After the bridge has been constructed, at a cost of $10,000, Fred starts to think about the tolls he should charge. How should he calculate the proper toll, assuming that he is interested in the bridge exclusively as a profit-making enterprise? How does the cost of constructing the bridge enter into his pricing calculations?

The answer is *not at all.* Sunk costs are sunk and therefore irrelevant. The questions Fred should now ask are future-oriented questions: What will people be willing to pay to use the bridge? What will it cost him to collect the tolls? What will he have to pay for bridge maintenance? What will he get if he sells the bridge for scrap metal? If it turns out that the demand for crossing the bridge is so small that no schedule of rates will yield revenue greater than the costs of toll collection plus maintenance, or that the annual net revenue is less than Fred could get by selling the bridge for scrap and putting the proceeds in the local savings and loan bank, Fred should scrap the bridge (assuming, remember, that he is interested exclusively in monetary income).

If it should turn out that bridge crossings are in great demand, so that Fred's enterprising venture promises to be a huge success, he should still ignore sunk costs in calculating his schedule of tolls. Sunk costs are of concern to historians, but not to economic decision makers.

THE SIGNIFICANCE OF MARGINAL COSTS

One of the economist's favorite words is *marginal.* It means in economics exactly what it means in everyday speech: situated on the border or edge. The concept is of fundamental importance in economic thinking, because economic decisions, like all effective decisions, always involve *marginal*

comparisons. That is to say, they always have to do with movements at the border, with positive or negative *additions.* A synonym for marginal, in fact, is *additional.* What will be the *additional,* or *marginal,* cost that results from this decision? And how does it compare with the marginal cost of alternative decisions?

If you think about it for a moment, you will discover that opportunity costs are always marginal costs. The term *marginal cost* does no more than bring into strong relief an aspect of opportunity cost thinking. That aspect is so important, however, that we shall want to make frequent use of the term. Later on we shall talk about marginal other things.

Marginal Does Not Mean Average

A student will have no difficulty with the marginal concept if only he does not get it mixed up with the notion of an *average.* You may have no intention of confusing marginal with average; if so, what follows may only plant in your head the seeds of a bad idea. Let's hope it doesn't. A simple production schedule of a hypothetical zerc manufacturer will illustrate the distinction:

Number of Zercs Produced	Total Cost of Producing Zercs
42	$4200
43	4257
44	4312
45	4365

A little long division reveals that the average cost (total cost per unit) if 42 zercs are produced is $100; it is $99 for 43 zercs, $98 for 44, and $97 for 45. A little subtraction reveals, however, that the cost of producing the 43rd zerc is not $99 but $57. The incremental expenditure, or the extra cost, incurred by producing the 43rd zerc, is its marginal cost. The marginal costs of the 44th and 45th zercs are $55 and $53 respectively. It is clear that marginal cost can be more or less than average cost and can even differ substantially from average cost. It should also be clear that for a zerc manufacturer trying to make production decisions, it is the marginal costs that should guide him. Shall we produce more? Or less? Marginal cost is the consequence of action; it should therefore be the guide to action.

Is a businessman then not interested in average costs? Unless a businessman can cover all his costs from revenue, he will sustain a loss. He won't willingly commit himself to any course of action unless he anticipates being able to cover his total costs. He might therefore set up the problem in terms of anticipated production cost per unit against anticipated selling price per unit. But notice that the *anticipated* costs of any decision are really *marginal* costs. Marginal cost need not refer to the additional cost of a single unit of output. It could also refer to the additional cost of a batch of output, or the addition to cost expected from a decision regarding an entire process. Decisions are often made in this "lumpy" way. Fred Ballistics, for example, would decide whether to keep the bridge in operation for another week or month, not for one more minute.

Similarly, no one plans to build a soda-bottling factory expecting to bottle only one case of soda. There are important economies of size in most business operations, so that unless a businessman sees his way clear to producing a large number of units, he will not produce any. He won't enter the business. He won't build the bottling factory at all. The entire decision—build or don't build, build this size plant or that, build in this way or some other way—is a marginal decision at the time it is made. Remember that additions can be very large as well as very small.

Whether or not the businessman casts his thinking in terms of averages, it is marginal costs that guide his decisions. Averages can be looked at after the fact to see how well or poorly things went, and maybe even to learn something about the future if the future can be expected to resemble the past. But this is history again—admittedly an instructive study—while economic decisions are always made in the present with an eye to the future.

A Case Study

"It costs about 12¢ a mile to own and operate an automobile." This statement makes little sense no matter how often it is repeated. By examining a case with which everyone is familiar, we can tie together much of what has been said in these last two chapters and see more of the implications.

Suppose that you have been asked by your college to drive your car to an intercollegiate student-government conference. You plan to attend the conference whether you drive your own car or not. The college offers you 8¢ a mile. Will it pay you to drive, or should you say no and hitch a ride with someone else? If you go about deciding by trying to calculate whether the cost to you of owning and operating a car is less than 8¢ a mile, you are being foolish. It makes no more sense to speak of the cost per mile of owning a car than to speak of the cost per mile of owning a house.

(For just the same reason it makes no sense to compute the cost per ton of owning a steel mill, or the cost per student of having a college library, or the cost per prescription of having a cash register in the pharmacy. All such attempts suggest that someone is treating costs that cannot be affected by particular decisions as if they were relevant to the making of those decisions.)

DOES BIGGER MEAN CHEAPER?

Economic folklore commonly asserts that bigger means cheaper. The larger any firm, supposedly, the lower will be its costs. Let's examine that proposition.

First of all, it clearly isn't *total* costs that defenders of this view have in mind. It's hard to think of any case where total costs would vary inversely with size. The costs in question are costs per unit.

But the concept of cost per unit is ambiguous. Does it mean the additional cost incurred by producing another unit? Or does it mean total expenses divided by the number of units produced? It's possible for the former to be constant or even increasing while the latter declines. Fred Ballistics the bridge owner would probably find that the marginal cost of traffic is constant and close to zero; but if he means by "unit cost" the wages of the toll collector plus the sums he pays regularly to the bank from which he borrowed to build the bridge divided by the number of users, that will surely decline with the volume of his business or "output."

Contrast this with the situation of a telephone company serving a large metropolitan area. As population grows and the number of customers increases, the phone company must increase the total of interconnections that it provides *more than in proportion* to the number of phones. For while two people can be connected with one link, three people require three links, four people require six links for each to be connected with every other, and so on exponentially. The technology isn't as simple as that numerical example suggests, but the example serves to show why telephone companies often encounter *rising* unit costs as their "output" increases. Because existing central switching and other connecting facilities will often have unused capacity, per unit costs (defined in *either* of the two ways above) may decline over a certain range. But when market growth requires additional facilities, unit costs can jump very sharply. The simple graph below illustrates the pattern we're describing. Would you want to describe that as increasing or decreasing costs?

One more example to illustrate the complexity of the issue and the danger of careless generalizations. An electric utility is required to provide service to all customers when they want it. So the utility must generate enough electricity for peak hours, such as 4:30 P.M. in August when factories, offices, and shops are operating, electric ranges are cooking supper, subway trains are in motion, elevators are running, and air conditioners are on all over the city. During slack hours the utility will generate the electricity it sells with its lowest cost facilities; but as demand rises toward the peak, less and less efficient facilities are brought "on stream" and costs consequently rise. Additional sales at peak hours therefore raise marginal costs. Additional sales at slack hours, on the other hand, will reduce per unit costs defined as total expenses divided by kilowatt hours sold.

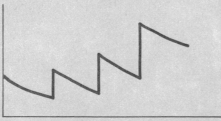

Total expenses divided by number of customers

Number of customers

Costs of purchase, license, insurance, and depreciation not due to operation are all unrelated to your decision whether or not to drive. That is why
they are irrelevant. The relevant cost is the marginal cost: How much extra
will you be out of pocket if you drive? Be sure to include not only the cost
of gas but also the costs of oil, tire wear, and mileage-induced repairs. Insofar as cost can be expected to vary proportionately with mileage driven, it
can properly be expressed as so many cents per mile. If it is less than 8¢,
as it probably would be, you make money by driving your car. As long as
the marginal cost remains less than the price paid by the college, you gain
from every additional mile "produced" and "sold."

Are the costs of purchase, license, insurance, and time-related depreciation *completely* irrelevant? Shouldn't you be allowed to cover these costs,
too? After all, you have to pay them even if they are not related to the trip
you've been asked to undertake.

You are certainly free to ask the college for as high a mileage rate as you
choose. And if you have no scruples, you are even free to trot out all your
sunk costs and wave them righteously. There is ample precedent for such
action. But the one person you don't want to confuse is yourself. Only
marginal costs are relevant to your decision, whatever the price to which
the college finally agrees.

Perhaps you've begun to suspect that it's our example that is irrelevant.
We're interested, after all, in ordinary business decisions, and whatever
may be true of the student driver as entrepreneur, businesses surely have
to cover *all* their costs, not just marginal costs. It would seem so. But it isn't
so. There is no more necessity to cover sunk costs in the business world
than there is in our case study.

The plain fact is that each year many businesses fail to cover sunk costs.
But most of them do not stop operating. We can illustrate the dilemma by
supposing that you bought your car with the intention of driving it for the
college. When you made up your mind to become a sort of taxi operator,
you hoped to make enough money to pay your way through college. So
you purchased a car, the license, and insurance. You probably would not
have done so if you expected the college to pay only 8¢ a mile. Maybe you
had reason to believe they would pay you 15¢. Your calculations in these
circumstances might have run as follows:

Purchase price:	$3000.00
License:	20.00
Insurance:	150.00
Gas and oil:	.04 per mile
Wear and tear:	.02 per mile
Chauffeur service:	2.00 per hour

Your problem now is the familiar one of adding apples and oranges. Or even worse, adding apples and velocity. How can you add $3000 to 4¢ per mile and $2 per hour? Obviously you can't.

You could, however, turn all these figures into costs per year. The license and insurance are annual costs. The purchase price could be converted into an annual figure by estimating annual depreciation and adding the annual interest charge on your initial outlay of $3000. But you can't state the other costs on an annual basis without knowing how far and how long you'll be driving. You must anticipate. Remember what we said earlier: the significant costs and benefits in economics are *expected* costs and benefits. That means they are uncertain. But uncertainty is a fact of life, and if you want to be a student entrepreneur, you will have to live with it. So you estimate that you will obtain so many miles and so many hours of business per year. You can plug in your estimate and obtain numbers for gas and oil, wear and tear, and chauffeur services per year.

Now you can do your addition and come up with a figure for the annual cost of doing business. You can then take your estimate of miles used in calculating gas and oil plus wear-and-tear charges, multiply by the rate you expect to be paid, and thereby calculate prospective revenue per year. If the anticipated annual revenue exceeds the anticipated annual cost, you take the plunge and buy a car. If it doesn't, you don't.

So sunk costs are relevant? Of course not. Until you take the plunge they aren't sunk. They are marginal. They are additions to cost which you are thinking about incurring. That's the essence of being marginal. And as long as they're marginal, they are relevant. But only that long! When you have yet to commit yourself in any way to a business operation, *all* your costs are marginal. Once you have committed yourself, the situation has

obviously changed. If you want to maximize your profits (or minimize your losses, which comes to the same thing), you must produce and sell all those units of output whose anticipated marginal cost is less than the anticipated price to be set by the college.

The parable of the student entrepreneur is applicable to any kind of decision-making situation, in business or elsewhere.

Another Note on Alternative Systems

All of this is just as applicable in a communist or socialist society as in a capitalist society. Resources will be differently allocated, and income and power differently distributed, depending on who owns the means of production. But the principles we have described are the general principles of economizing, applicable wherever resources are scarce. The central planners in a socialist state also operate within the constraints imposed by scarcity: the resources available to them have alternative uses; substitution possibilities are pervasive; one good can usually be achieved only by giving up some other good. The planners should therefore calculate the opportunity cost of contemplated actions, treating sunk costs as irrelevant and paying attention only to marginal costs.

Suppose that the minister of coal production in a socialist state is trying to decide how much coal should be mined this month. He can increase coal production by using more workers or employing them for longer hours, or by using more machinery or better machinery. The relevant cost to the society of doing so is the value of whatever is given up through his decision, or the marginal (opportunity) cost. If he obtains new machinery in order to increase coal output, society loses what could otherwise have been produced with the aid of that machinery, or what could have been produced with the resources employed in the construction of the new machinery. The real cost of increased coal production is therefore decreased production of locomotives, or cement, or farm tractors.

If the minister can expand coal production by using machinery already in place that would otherwise stand idle, the opportunity cost is much lower and may even be zero. The sunk cost of the equipment is irrelevant. Notice, though, that the marginal cost will be greater than zero if the machinery has any alternative use, including use as scrap metal.

We see the fundamental importance of evaluations in determining oportunity costs when we contemplate the costs, in such a situation, of expanding output by working the existing labor force longer hours. In a society where workers must be induced through monetary bribes (wages) to work in particular ways, the wage measures the opportunity cost. The wage must be sufficient to attract them from their (subjectively) next best alternative. But if workers can be compelled to do what the state dictates, the wage need not bear any relation to the opportunity cost as determined by the workers. (We saw in chapter 5 how that occurs under a military draft.) In moving from an eight- to a ten-hour day, the miners might be sacrificing two hours of leisure. Whether this is worthwhile would depend upon the *planners'* valuation of the extra coal produced in relation to the *planners'* valuation of the leisure foregone.

In any event, it would be clearly wrong to suppose that the cost of producing the extra coal can be determined from the *average* cost of coal production. This is worth mentioning because some socialists have argued in the past that marginal cost considerations were only relevant in an economy guided by the pursuit of private profit. It is true that in a capitalist society businessmen will not choose to produce anything whose marginal cost of production exceeds its value to the consumer as measured by its price. But it is just as true that in a socialist society the central planners and enterprise directors should produce nothing whose marginal cost exceeds its value.

The major difference lies in the different social-political rules and procedures by means of which opportunity costs and prices are calculated: for workers, consumers, government officials, or any other resource managers. One of the distinct advantages of a capitalist system characterized by substantial private ownership and control of resources is its pricing mechanism. In a capitalist system, competitive offers to buy and sell resources interact to establish scarcity prices and opportunity costs expressed in monetary units. An enormous quantity of information summarizing a vast range of alternatives is distilled into the prices that in turn guide the choices of decision makers.

In no capitalist system past or present have prices ever summarized perfectly the available range of opportunities. And under certain circumstances, as we shall see later, they may do so in a fashion so inadequate as to be politically unacceptable. The relevance of all this for making a choice between alternative economic systems is a very complex issue that cannot be resolved exclusively by economic arguments.

In any economic system, however, the following general principles will be applicable:

Real costs are opportunity costs, the value of opportunities foregone.

Sunk costs are irrelevant, because they are costs that the decision cannot affect.

Opportunity costs are always additional or marginal costs, the costs entailed by the decision under consideration.

Some method of assigning indices of value to alternative opportunities must be used in any economic system, or decision makers will be operating blindly.

Supply and demand, or the market process of competing bids and offers, creates indices of value for decision makers by placing price tags on available resources.

If supply and demand are not allowed to set prices in a centrally planned society, the planners will still want to know what prices supply and demand *would* have set so they can use scarce resources most effectively.

DIMINISHING RETURNS AND MARGINAL COSTS

How much would it cost to eliminate air pollution due to automobiles: carbon monoxide, hydrocarbons, and nitrogen oxides? To eliminate *all* such emissions we would have to eliminate automobiles. Since we aren't at all likely to accept a cost that high, the real question comes down to the cost of *reducing* emissions. That's a more complex question than it seems at first glance.

Reliable data on this issue are hard to come by, partly because many of the data will only emerge as we actually succeed in doing things we aren't yet sure how to do, partly because there are special interest groups on all sides of this question who, if they aren't consciously trying to deceive us, are probably allowing their hopes for the future to influence their reading of the future. But reliable data will not by themselves answer the question of what we ought to do or what laws we ought to pass. The data will have to be put together in a meaningful way. A little economic theory can do a lot to help with that part of the task.

The concept of *marginal* cost is especially useful here. The following table is a simplification of data published in 1973 by the Mobil Oil Company and derived from estimates by that company's engineers.[1]

% Reduction of Auto Emissions below Pre-control Levels	Extra Cost of Cars with Emission Controls
65%	$ 85
85%	235
95%	550

Diminishing Marginal Returns

Notice how cost rises at an increasing rate as we attempt to secure successive reductions in the level of emissions. 65% of the pollution can be eliminated at a cost of $85 per car. But to obtain an additional reduction of

1. Since it is in Mobil's interest to increase the demand for gasoline and since the company's argument supported policies that would reduce the demand, we may assume that vested interests have not led to any data distortion.

20%, a cost of $150 *more* per car must be incurred. To squeeze out yet an additional 10% means incurring $315 of cost *over and above* the cost incurred at the 85% level. You're looking at a case of *diminishing* returns.

We're all familiar with the phenomenon of diminishing returns because so much of what we do displays it. The first wring of your wet washcloth gets out most of the water. Another wring just as hard squeezes out far less. Still another wring will yield no more than a few drops of water. Successive applications of effort yield *diminishing marginal returns.*

We snuck in the word marginal because it makes the statement formally correct and because the marginal measure is the important measure for decision makers. *Total* returns in this case actually rise with each successive application of effort: the more wrings, the more water is squeezed out. But the extra return, or the return due to each successive application of effort, which is what we mean by the marginal return, goes down dramatically. Sensible decision makers, whether they're washcloth wringers, plate scrapers, or pollution controllers, will focus their attention on marginal returns.

Marginal Costs under Diminishing Returns

Marginal cost is simply the other side of marginal return. We can use our emission data to illustrate. We say that the marginal return from additional emission controls is diminishing because successive applications of effort, here measured in dollar costs, yield diminishing results in the form of reduced auto emissions. The first $85 of "effort" cuts pollution by 65%. But each successive $85 of effort is less and less effective in securing the returns we're after.

The concept of diminishing marginal returns expresses the return per (constant) unit of effort, or input, or cost. The concept of increasing marginal costs expresses this same reality as increasing costs per (constant) unit of return. Figure 6A shows that graphically. (For an explanation of the dots and a discussion of accurate plotting, read the footnote below.)[1]

1. We cannot calculate accurately the cost of a one percent reduction in emissions by just dividing 65% into $85, because marginal cost is increasing at an increasing rate. It turns out, in this particular example, that marginal costs (in $ per % reduction) follow very closely the relationship

$$MC = \left(\frac{76.76}{100 - p}\right)^{1.6}$$

where MC is marginal cost and p is the total percentage reduction of emissions. Note that if we had just calculated the average cost for each 1% reduction in the three ranges 0% to 65%, 65% to 85%, and 85% to 95%, our best guess would have been that these were approximately the marginal costs in the middle of the ranges. Between zero and 65% the average per unit cost is ($85) divided by (65%) or $1.31 for each 1% reduction; between 65% and 85% it's ($235 − $85) divided by (85% − 65%) or $7.50; and between 85% and 95% it's $31.50. If we

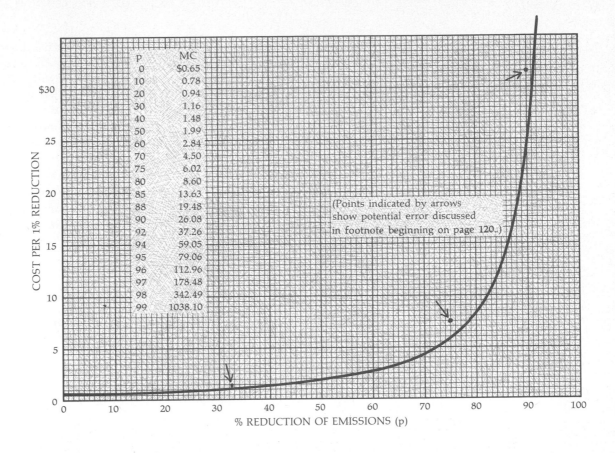

p	MC
0	$0.65
10	0.78
20	0.94
30	1.16
40	1.48
50	1.99
60	2.84
70	4.50
75	6.02
80	8.60
85	13.63
88	19.48
90	26.08
92	37.26
94	59.05
95	79.06
96	112.96
97	178.48
98	342.49
99	1038.10

(Points indicated by arrows show potential error discussed in footnote beginning on page 120.)

COST PER 1% REDUCTION (y-axis: $30, 25, 20, 15, 10, 5, 0)

% REDUCTION OF EMISSIONS (p) (x-axis: 0, 10, 20, 30, 40, 50, 60, 70, 80, 90, 100)

Figure 6A Rising marginal costs and diminishing marginal returns

Where is the best place to be on that curve? In large cities where air pollution due to automobiles is responsible for stinging eyes, lung disease, and other threats to health, beauty, and the joy of life, the lower left portion of the curve seems to portray an excellent bargain. A substantial improvement in the quality of life for city dwellers can be purchased at a modest cost. (We're neglecting for now the additional costs of car operation and maintenance that would be associated with this type of emission control program; these costs would be substantial, but their inclusion would not affect the logic of the present argument.)

hadn't taken time to estimate the equation from which figure 6A is graphed, we would have guessed that these were approximately the marginal costs at 32.5%, 75%, and 90%. These points are shown by the dots in figure 6A. Notice how these averages overestimate the true marginal costs at the mid-points of the ranges. The error isn't too bad for 0–65%, because marginal costs increase at close to a constant rate in that range; but the error becomes progressively worse. If the dots don't seem to your eye excessively far from the curve, that's because you aren't comparing cost at the dot with cost *at the corresponding percentage*. Read *down* from the dot to find the size of the inaccuracy.

The upper right portion of the curve, on the other hand, seems to portray a very poor bargain indeed. Extremely costly procedures yield modest, almost unnoticeable improvements in the quality of the air. The benefit-to-cost ratio is high in the lower left section of the curve, very low in the upper right portion. Beyond about a 70% reduction, we don't get much of a return for our efforts. Common sense suggests that the sensible stopping place will consequently be somewhere to the left of the steeply rising part of the curve.

But now from the back of the room comes a protesting voice:

"Health, beauty, and the joy of life are enormous benefits, well worth paying for. The sensible place to stop on that curve depends on how high a value one places on clean air. The trouble with economists is that they don't assign high enough values to such benefits as beauty when they do their benefit-cost analyses."

Marginal Cost for Esthetic Purposes

The point is well taken. We probably do undervalue beauty in our calculations (most of us, not just economists), because the market doesn't do an effective job of expressing the demand for beauty or other goods that everyone enjoys but no one pays for directly. We'll return to this particular problem in chapter 14. For now, however, we can respond that no matter how high a value we place on clean air, the upper right portion of that curve is probably *not* a place where we'll want to be.

Why not? Because those *marginal costs are the value of foregone opportunities.* The 315 extra dollars added on to the purchase price of a car to cover the cost of more effective exhaust controls is $315 per new car that might have been used to purchase something else, such as environmental improvements by other means. If we now add the expected annual additions to maintenance and operation costs attributable to the emission controls, and multiply by the number of cars affected each year, we arrive at a sum of money that might alternatively be used to construct excellent systems of mass public transit. If the mass transit system that is sacrificed in favor of stringent emission control devices would have reduced air pollution more than the control devices, stringent exhaust control is a bad bargain no matter how high a value we place on clean air.

The value we place upon clean air certainly does help determine how much clean air we ought to "produce" by means of public policy. But when there are alternative ways to produce a good, as there are in this case and in almost any other case one can imagine, the cost of these alternatives must be compared before we can sensibly decide how far we ought to push any one of them. The principle is obvious once it has been stated: Achieve your goals at the lowest possible cost. And that in turn entails comparing the marginal costs of alternatives. If much discussion of public

policy seems to reject this obvious and elementary rule, part of the explanation is probably to be found in our habitual neglect of the first principle of sound economic thinking: There are substitutes for anything.

How far we want to push any activity will depend upon the cost; but the cost will depend at the same time upon how far we choose to push. The case of controlling automobile emissions illustrates this dramatically. It is simply meaningless to state the cost of reducing pollution through improved exhaust systems as any single number. Marginal cost (the only kind of cost relevant to decision making) is a rising function and, after a while, a very steeply rising function of the "quantity of clean air" we choose to "produce" in this way. This kind of relationship between cost and quantity of production is not at all unusual; it is, on the contrary, as common as the phenomenon of diminishing marginal returns upon which it rests.

Marginal versus Average: An Application from Coal Mining

How much does it cost to mine a ton of coal in the United States? If you know anything at all about coal mining, you know that there are rich mines with easily accessible veins from which coal can be removed at very low cost, and there are other coal deposits, including some of which we don't yet know, that could not be mined except at extremely high cost. What is the cost? Shall we say that it's the average cost of the approximately 600 million tons of coal currently being mined annually in the United States? We could surely say that; but it wouldn't be a useful statement, and it would in fact be highly misleading.

We can gain a more adequate picture of costs by considering an imaginary mining company, Amalgamated Coal.

Amalgamated's most efficient mine is Puddle Jumper No. 1, from which 8000 tons of coal a day can be extracted at a cost of $6 per ton. PJ2, with less accessible deposits, can produce 4000 tons a day at a per ton cost of $8. PJ3 can produce 9000 tons a day at $12 per ton. And PJ4, Amalgamated's poorest mine, can produce 1000 tons a day at $20 per ton.

"Wait a minute," says the voice from the rear. "Those costs at each of Amalgamated's mines sound like average costs to me. Surely it won't cost exactly the same amount to take coal from a mine regardless of how far we go in mining it or how fast we try to take it out. You said just a few paragraphs back that cost will usually depend on how far an activity is pushed, and a coal mine doesn't look like an exception. Won't the costs at each of the mines tend to go up as the mine is more fully exploited?"

That's correct! We want to show in this example that the cost of obtaining coal does depend on the rate at which we mine it. And we ought to begin by pointing out that this rule applies to each individual mine as well as to all the mines taken together. But we also want to keep the arithmetic simple. In order to discuss the way in which costs increase as more mines are put into production, we're going to ignore the increases in cost as production goes up in each separate mine. We're assuming, in effect, that each mine produces at constant cost up to its capacity, and *cannot* produce more than that at any cost—a quite unrealistic assumption. In the back of your mind you should remember, however, that the objection from the rear was right on target this time.

So we put these slightly misleading data together to form table 6A. Notice how the table has been constructed from the data given above. No coal at all can be mined for $4. PJ1 can produce 8000 tons at $6. PJ2 produces at $8, so its 4000 tons are added to the 8000 of PJ1. At a cost of $12 three mines can be operated, yielding a total output of 21,000 tons, and PJ4 comes into production at $20.

Table 6A   COST AND OUTPUT FOR AMALGAMATED COAL

Marginal Cost/Ton	Tons/Day	Total Cost	Average Cost/Ton
$ 4	0	$ 0	—
6	8,000	48,000	$6.00
8	12,000	80,000	6.67
10	12,000	80,000	6.67
12	21,000	188,000	8.95
14	21,000	188,000	8.95
16	21,000	188,000	8.95
18	21,000	188,000	8.95
20	22,000	208,000	9.45
22	22,000	208,000	9.45

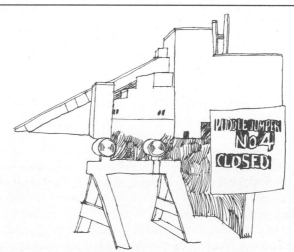

If Amalgamated operates all four of its mines, it will be producing 22,000 tons per day at a total cost of $208,000: (8000 × $6) + (4000 × $8) + (9000 × $12) + (1000 × $20). That's an average cost of $9.45 per ton. But it's a meaningless average. For if Amalgamated could only sell its coal for $9.45 a ton, it wouldn't produce 22,000 tons. PJ3 and PJ4 would not be operated, and Amalgamated would produce only 12,000 tons per day (at an equally meaningless average cost now of $6.67 per ton). Amalgamated pays attention to marginal costs, to the extra cost of mining additional coal. The cost schedule used to make production decisions is the marginal cost schedule shown above.

Table 6B introduces the marginal cost schedules of six more coal companies and sums their combined production in the final column.

Table 6B   TONS PER DAY (IN THOUSANDS)

Marginal Cost/Ton	Producing Firms							Total Output
	A	B	C	D	E	F	G	
$ 4	0	0	0	0	0	0	0	0
6	8	2	0	0	0	0	0	10
8	12	8	0	0	0	0	0	20
10	12	9	5	4	0	0	0	30
12	21	9	6	4	0	0	0	40
14	21	10	7	4	8	0	0	50
16	21	11	14	4	10	0	0	60
18	21	11	14	5	10	9	0	70
20	22	13	15	5	12	13	0	80
22	22	13	16	5	12	15	7	90

Figure 6B shows these data graphically. No coal at all can be produced from these mines at a cost below $6 per ton; but 10,000 tons can be produced daily at that cost. At $8 per ton an additional 10,000 tons, or 20,000 altogether, can be produced. And so on up to 90,000 tons at $22 per ton. (If we took account of the objection that marginal cost will tend to increase with output at *each* mine, the horizontal lines on the graph would be rising lines.)

A Picture of the Coal Industry

Figure 6C presents an imaginary marginal cost curve for the entire United States coal industry. It magnifies the picture of table 6B by thirty times and smooths out the steps in the curve. With many coal companies and many different mines, we aren't likely to observe the discontinuities that yield a step curve as in figure 6B; with a large number of mines in

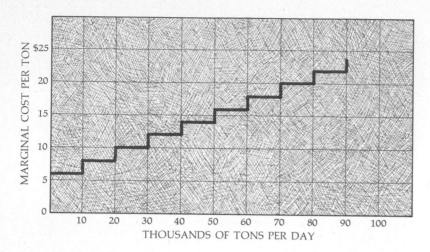

Figure 6B Cost and supply of coal

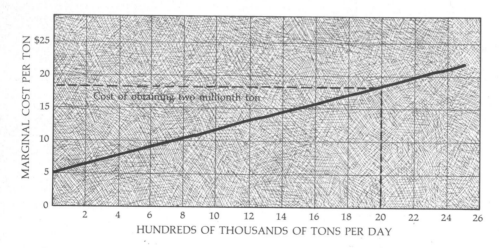

Cost of obtaining two millionth ton

Figure 6C Price, cost, and supply of coal

production, marginal cost will typically rise by small, imperceptible gradations. The fact that marginal cost rises at *each* mine will also contribute to smoothing out the steps in the curve.

You should be able to see now why average mining costs are so meaningless. Coal mine operators do not make any decisions by consulting average costs. And those who make public policy should overlook them just as consistently. If electrical utilities and other coal consumers want to burn 2 million tons per day, they will have to pay a cost high enough to secure a daily output of 2 million tons. It is the 2 millionth ton, the marginal ton, whose cost of production must be met. Otherwise it will not be produced.

PRICES, PRODUCTION, AND PROFITS

In the three months from November 1, 1973 to February 1, 1974, soft coal prices in the U.S. rose more than 100%: from about $9.80 to about $21.50. There are numerous mines in this country from which coal cannot be extracted at costs below $10 per ton but which can be operated profitably when coal is selling above $20 per ton. Many of them were being re-opened early in 1974. While the average level of coal production in the U.S. during 1973 was only 3.6% above its level in 1967, in the first six months of 1974 coal was produced at a rate 8.9% above the 1973 average.

All this resulted in large profits, of course, for the owners of the more efficient or lower cost mines. But the large profits did not *cause* the higher prices. Higher prices in this case were clearly the cause of higher profits. The higher prices were in turn caused by a larger demand operating against rising marginal costs in the industry. The sequence is: (1) increased demand; (2) higher prices; (3) increased production *and* higher profits.

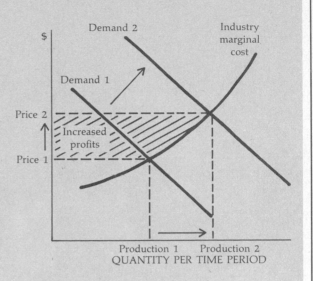

Some experts are predicting that the United States will want, by 1985, more than 4 million tons of coal per day. That will require a more extensive operation than now of less efficient mines. And that in turn will mean higher marginal costs.

Review the argument a few pages back, Another Note on Alternative Systems, if you're tempted to argue that marginal costs are crucial only under a capitalist system where producers require as incentive the prospect of personal or corporate gain. The problem is not incentive but cost. Marginal costs are opportunity costs, real costs, and they will be paid if production occurs. The method of payment can vary, of course. A socialist government might choose for reasons of its own to keep coal prices below marginal cost. But the central planners would nonetheless want to pay attention to marginal costs in deciding how much coal production to order, because it is marginal or opportunity cost that expresses the value of what is sacrificed by expanding production or what can be gained by reducing production.

Costs and Output in Agriculture

We can assemble many of these principles into a useful illustration by looking at the case of Lawrence Riley, a Kansas farmer who intends to plant his 640 acres in wheat this year. We'll assume that he has weighed the opportunity cost of planting wheat rather than sorghum or some other crop (in whole or in part), so the only question he faces is that of the intensity of cultivation. How much wheat should Riley try to grow on his land?

The actual harvest is going to depend in part on factors like the weather, over which Riley has no control. But he *can* control such factors as the quality of seed, closeness of planting, and amount of fertilizer used. By varying these expenditures, he can cause the probable yield to vary enormously. Table 6C shows Riley's calculation of the relation between total *operating* expenditures and the yield per acre. Operating expenditures do not include costs that are sunk or otherwise unrelated to production decisions, such as interest payments, taxes, or depreciation on equipment that is not attributable to use of the equipment. Operating expenditures do include, however, an implicit wage for the work Riley performs in growing wheat.

How intensively should Riley cultivate? At what yield per acre should he aim? The answer will depend upon the costs of production shown in the table *plus* the expected price of wheat. The decisive cost is the marginal cost, the additional cost that Riley incurs in trying to increase his per acre yield. Column 5, which shows marginal cost, was calculated by dividing the *changes* from row to row in column 3 (or 4) into the *changes* of column 1 (or 2). Marginal cost increases at an increasing rate in column 5 because more intensive cultivation yields progressively diminishing returns; there are technological limitations on any farmer's ability to increase the yield from an acre of land. The marginal costs are *in between* the rows because they express the cost of moving from one position to another.

Table 6C	OUTPUT AND COST ON RILEY'S WHEAT FARM			
(Col. 1) Operating Expenditures per Acre	(Col. 2: 640 acres × col. 1) Total Operating Expenditures	(Col. 3) Expected Yield in Bushels of Wheat per Acre	(Col. 4: 640 acres × col. 3) Expected Total Yield	(Col. 5: additional cost divided by additional yield) Marginal Cost per Bushel
$27.00	$17,280	18 bushels	11,520 bushels	
33.00	21,120	22	14,080	$1.50
39.20	25,088	26	16,640	1.55
45.80	29,312	30	19,200	1.65
53.20	34,048	34	21,760	1.85
62.00	39,680	38	24,320	2.20
73.00	46,720	42	26,880	2.75
87.20	55,808	46	29,440	3.55
105.80	67,712	50	32,000	4.65

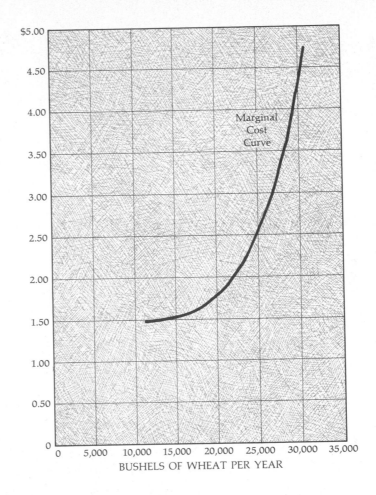

The situation Riley faces can also be shown by means of a graph. In figure 6D, *the marginal cost curve is his supply curve.* Let's see why.

If Riley expects the price of wheat to be $2 per bushel, he will want to grow any bushel that can be produced for less than $2 and no bushels that cost him more than $2 to produce. Read across from a price of $2 to the marginal cost curve; each extra bushel up to about 22,000 bushels costs less than $2 to produce. Beyond that output, extra bushels add more to Riley's costs than to his receipts. So he will produce about 22,000 bushels if the expected price is $2. He'll aim, in other words, at a yield of approximately 34 bushels per acre. If he expects the price to be $2.75 per bushel, it will be worth his while to increase production to about 26,000 bushels or approximately 40 bushels per acre.

Figure 6D Lawrence Riley's supply curve

Will Riley's marketing receipts exceed his total expenses at either or both of these prices? We don't know from the data given, because only his operating expenses are presented. But costs that are unaffected by decisions should not be allowed to influence decisions. Riley's supply curve depends exclusively upon his *marginal* costs.

Notice that if the expected price of wheat is $2 and Riley aims at a yield of 34 bushels per acre and a total harvest of 21,760 bushels, his *average* operating expenses will be about $1.565 per bushel ($34,048 ÷ 21,760). If his annual nonoperating expenses come to $10,000 per year, then his total expenses per bushel will be slightly more than $2.02. But *neither* average is relevant to his production decisions!

The Larger Picture

The price at which Riley will in fact be able to sell his wheat is going to be determined through the interaction of the market demand with the sum of the supply curves of *all* wheat farmers. Let's adopt the simplifying assumption that there are 10,000 wheat farmers altogether, each with costs exactly like Riley's. Then the *market* supply curve will be the marginal cost curve in figure 6D with the quantities on the horizontal axis multiplied by 10,000. In figure 6E we show the market supply curve along with the market demand. The equilibrium price is $2.75.

We cannot predict that the *actual* price would be $2.75 under these circumstances, because farmers' production decisions are based on *expected* prices. If farmers expected a price of $3 and weather or other unanticipated circumstances did not create a divergence between planned and actual output, they would produce about 265 million bushels. And the actual price would then turn out to be only $2.60, the highest price at which that quantity of wheat can be sold. Keep in mind that economic decisions are always based on *expected* values that may turn out to be mistaken.

We can also use this example to illustrate the point made a few paragraphs back in discussing alternative ways of organizing an economic system. Follow the argument on the graph of figure 6E. Suppose all farms are state-owned and that state planners both set wheat prices and instruct farm managers on how much wheat to grow. Suppose further that the planners order 300 million bushels to be produced and set the price of wheat at the market-clearing level of $2.15. (Check the graph to assure yourself that the market clears at $2.15.) They might congratulate themselves on the superiority of the economic system they're directing. Under private production for profit, 300 million bushels could not be obtained unless farmers were offered a price of $4.50. (Check the graph again to confirm this.) Under central planning, however, 300 million bushels are

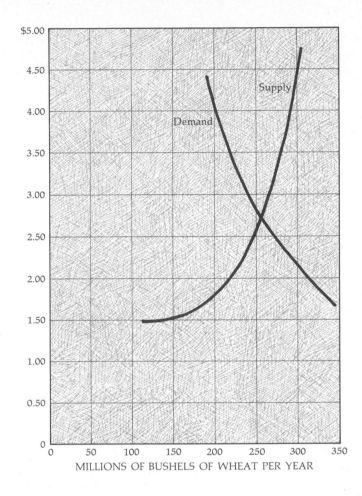

Figure 6E Supply and demand for wheat

obtained with a price of only $2.15. Moreover, that price generates $645 million in total receipts from wheat sales, which is sufficient to cover total operating costs. Isn't society better off when the marginal costs to which private producers pay attention are ignored?

In reality society is *not* better off. More wheat is presumably better than less wheat. But more wheat entails less of other goods. The objection is that the 300 millionth bushel costs society $4.50 worth of alternative goods regardless of whether individual farmers or central planners are keeping the books. It is the area under the marginal cost curve, not average cost, which represents what a society loses in other goods by expanding the production of any one good. Average costs are not opportunity costs and are therefore no more appropriate guides to central planners than they are to decision makers under a system of production for private profit. If the planners nonetheless want 300 million bushels produced and consumed, they should at least be aware of the cost to society of their decision. And that is shown by the *marginal* cost curve.

THE IDENTIFICATION OF COSTS FOR MAKING DECISIONS

It isn't the *logic* of the marginal or opportunity cost way of thinking that makes the life of decision makers difficult. The tough problem is the recognition of alternatives and the classification of costs. What are the actual marginal costs of a contemplated decision? Which of the apparent costs are in fact sunk costs and hence properly no costs at all? The logic is important, of course; that's why we've stressed it so far. In order to focus on the logic we solved all our data problems by a miraculous derivation of the "correct" numbers. But economic analysis entails more than the manipulation of numbers in accordance with formal rules. It requires first of all identification of the appropriate numbers. Here the correct answers are less certain and the solutions less neat and convincing. A knowledge of concrete circumstances is required along with enough imagination to conceive sometimes distant consequences and a wide variety of possible interrelationships. This kind of good judgment is scarce and difficult to acquire; you have a chance to practice it by turning your critical eye upon the football budget of Gungho University.

The Economics of College Football

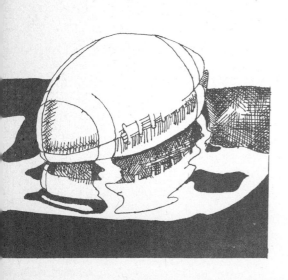

Diminishing revenues and rising costs in the 1970s persuaded many college and university administrators to take a critical look at their athletic programs. Privately owned schools in particular began to wonder out loud whether they could afford intercollegiate sports—especially football, where costs run exceptionally high. Few clear conclusions seemed to emerge from these studies. But that shouldn't surprise us. While expenditures are easy enough to compute, expenditures aren't the same thing as costs. By reasoning through a situation with which most of you probably have at least a passing familiarity, you should be able to learn more about the meaning of cost and the nature of the dilemmas that confront decision makers when they try to calculate costs and choose efficiently.

Are all these expenditures real costs? Are there significant real costs not included in these expenditure categories? Let's think about some of the classifications.

Table 6D   GUNGHO UNIVERSITY FOOTBALL BUDGET
Annual Expenditures by Category

1. Salaries and wages
2. Employee benefits
3. Supplies
4. Equipment operation and maintenance
5. Utilities
6. Advertising and publicity
7. Game expenses
8. Travel expenses
9. Insurance
10. Medical and hospital
11. Recruiting
12. Financial aid to athletes
13. Debt service

Salaries and Wages

The salaries of coaches seem clearly to be football costs. But are the salaries of trainers included in the first item? If so, do they all belong there? Knowledgeable people in college athletics say that football absorbs almost all the time of the trainers in the athletic department. But if GU were to abandon football while keeping all its other sports and still wanted one trainer for those sports, one trainer's salary could legitimately be deducted from the football budget and placed under All Other Sports. On the other hand, if the football program requires three trainers all by itself; if those same trainers can easily handle other sports in the football off season; and if the three trainers must be carried on salary throughout the year—then it's also misleading to assign the cost of one to All Other Sports. We have run at the outset into a common dilemma faced by decision makers in assigning costs, a problem for which there is often no "correct" solution: what economists call the problem of joint costs and joint supply.

The problem may arise in a slightly different form in our football budget with the salary of the athletic director. Since an athletic director presumably directs *all* sports, one could argue that the cost of his salary should be allocated among all the sports, perhaps by the amount of time he spends on each. That won't be wholly satisfactory, however, since much of the athletic director's work can't meaningfully be related to any particular sport. In addition, some universities make the head football coach the athletic director in order to be able to pay him a higher salary. Suppose the high salary they must offer to keep the head coach embarrasses the administration; the administration may be able to disguise the disconcerting gap between the coach's salary and a full professor's salary in sociology by calling him Football Coach *and* Athletic Director. If he in fact does no general administrative work and an assistant athletic director handles the actual duties, the full salary of the athletic director should be assigned to football.

Let's try item 2. Employee benefits raise the same problems as salaries and wages and maybe a few additional ones. For example, if all employees of the football program receive free tickets to home football games for each member of their families, is this a cost? That will depend on several things. If the games are always sellouts, so that each ticket given away deprives the university of ticket revenue, those tickets have a clear cost. If the games are never sellouts but all the family members would be willing to pay for tickets if they didn't receive them as gifts, the tickets also have a cost. But should we put this under revenue lost instead of cost incurred? The question reminds us that costs are always opportunities foregone: a loss of revenue is a cost. Whether we put it on the expenditure side with a plus sign or on the revenue side with a negative sign is less important than that we recognize it as a true cost and associate it with the decision that creates it. Costs are always associated with particular decisions in the opportunity cost way of thinking.

Let's jump to item 5. The costs of heat, light, water, or phone service will be partially joint costs. The only utility costs that can be assigned unequivocally to the football program are those costs that would not be incurred in the absence of a football program. Which they are won't always be clear.

The Costs of Financial Aid

The plot thickens quickly with items 12 and 13, so let's go there directly. Financial aid to athletes can be divided into tuition, room, board, and the ultimate catch-all, miscellaneous. If tuition at GU is $2000 per year, and every football player receives free tuition, should the cost be figured at $2000 times the number of football players? Not unless GU actually does incur $100,000 in additional costs by providing 50 football players with a year of schooling. That isn't at all likely. The marginal cost of an extra student is not zero; while one more student could no doubt be educated at no *discernible* cost, that only warns us to calculate the marginal cost as the cost of educating an additional *group* of students, divided by the number in the group. It's more than zero but it's almost surely less than $2000 a year. To determine the real cost of this part of the football program GU will have to obtain data on the cost of providing its educational services to undergraduates, data broken down to show the quite different costs of different curricula since these do vary considerably and are not patronized equally by football players. Engineering education, for example, is both relatively costly and relatively unused by athletes.

What about the other financial aid costs? Consider the dormitory space assigned to football players. Some universities overbuilt dormitories in the 1960s and now have rooms to spare. It costs much less to provide a room to a football player when the room would otherwise be vacant than when its use by the athlete displaces an alternative user. GU officials in charge of repaying the loans with which surplus dorms were built will understandably want to charge the football program the full amount of the usual room rental. "We have to cover construction costs," they'll argue, "and the football program must pay its share." But sunk costs do *not* have to be covered, as we know; and it isn't the football program but GU itself that is committed to paying for the dormitories. The top administrators of GU should at least be clear on the real costs of what's going on.

The last item in the budget covers principal and interest payments on such facilities as the GU football stadium. Should it also include a portion of the payments for the coliseum, which is used occasionally for football players' practice and which contains all the coaches' offices? We won't even try to answer that question because there's a far more important one that arises prior to it: Are principal and interest payments genuine costs?

The cost of the football stadium was incurred when it was originally built. It's like the cost of a new home. The monthly payments of the owner and mortgagee are not costs of the house, as proved by the fact that the house would not cease to exist if these payments weren't made. Monthly payments are costs of *possession;* a default will not remove the house but will abolish the owner's right to use it. Since the owner is interested in possession and use, he makes the monthly payments on time. But they should be viewed as costs of possession and use and not as costs of construction.

The Dilemma of the Stadium

Go back to the football stadium. The costs of its construction were all incurred when steel and cement and construction workers were bid from other uses and employed in the stadium. There's no way to take that all back. The stadium is a sunk cost.

But now the analogy with the house and the mortgage doesn't work exactly. If GU defaults on its payments, the stadium will probably not be repossessed because it's unlikely that any alternative user exists in the area who would be willing to pay the mortgage holder for the right of possession and use. The mortgage holder might have no better option than to let GU go on playing games in the stadium even though it has defaulted on its payments. So those debt service charges, which are not costs of the stadium itself, might not be costs of continued possession either.

Of what are they the costs? That's hard to say. They may be in part costs of maintaining GU's credit rating, or of avoiding suits and liens, or of retaining the good will of people who don't believe universities ought to default on mortgages, or of retaining the administrators' sense of integrity.

We are in no way suggesting that GU should default on its payments and say to the bondholders, "What are you going to do about it?" We are trying to make the point that these payments are *not* marginal opportunity costs of the football program unless abandonment of football would cause them to disappear. Stadium *upkeep* is another matter, of course; and opportunities to use the stadium for intramural sports, a health spa, or a miniature golf course, insofar as they are excluded by its use for football games, are also real costs of the football program. But the key consideration here is that mortgage payments should not enter into the administration's calculations when it's trying to decide *whether the football program should be kept or abandoned.* Those payments will be due on the same date and in the same amount whether GU plays football or not. They are consequently irrelevant to the decision.

This analysis brings us to an important conclusion. Even if revenues from football fail to cover all debt service, GU could be gaining net revenue from its football program. The football budget will show red ink, it's true; but administrators who let red ink determine their decisions *when the red ink arises from sunk costs* are making bad decisions.

Further Complications

A college president's lot in the era of big time football is not an easy one. It becomes far more difficult than even this analysis suggests when the president and his administrative colleagues must also assess the effect of the football program on gifts and student enrollments. Such revenue sources may partially disappear if football is dropped, in which case those revenue losses (expected and uncertain, unfortunately) must be seen as a cost of *abandoning* football. That cost may justify a lot of additional red ink in the football budget. But football red ink often infuriates professors and serious students, and their anger also imposes costs on the beleaguered administration of GU.

The purpose of this exercise was to give you practice in analyzing costs and distinguishing genuine or marginal costs, which ought to affect decisions, from pseudo-costs, which should not. This is the kind of analysis-of-the-past mixed with prediction-of-the-future through which all business decision makers must go in trying to decide which activities to undertake and which practices to halt. If the exercise has also helped you understand why university athletic budgets are so often treated as classified documents, that's a bonus.

THE COSTS OF MAIL SERVICE

Are we subsidizing "junk mail"? The rising price of postage stamps and the rising flood of advertisements in their mailboxes have convinced some people that they're being made to pay part of the costs of third class mail service, and they don't like it. But what *is* the cost of delivering an unwanted ad when the carrier had to stop anyway to deliver a first class letter? Congress is sympathetic; its guidelines to the United States Postal Service state that each class of mail should "bear the direct and indirect postal costs attributable to that class" plus a reasonable share of the common costs. But how can those costs be determined? The argument seems to go on endlessly with each side offering radically different data to support its case.

George M. Wattles tried to get at the relevant costs through a careful study of postal operations coupled with a survey of about 200 experienced postal supervisors. What he attempted to measure was "avoidable cost" for each class of service, defined as the reduction in total cost that would occur if that class of service were discontinued. If the goal is to make sure that one class of users isn't paying higher rates just to cover the costs of another class, avoidable cost would seem to be the most appropriate concept. The marginal cost of delivering an advertisement is a meaningless notion. But the marginal cost of providing the whole advertisement-delivering service is a useful piece of information.

Wattles found, by the way, that the avoidable costs of second, third, and fourth class mail *exceed* their respective revenues by about 60%, 36%, and 40%. So you're subsidizing advertisers all right, but you're paying an even larger subsidy for newspapers and magazines (second class).

The study titled "The Rates and Costs of the United States Postal Service" appeared in the *Journal of Law and Economics*, April 1973. Wattles' procedure sounds like a good one for getting at another long-standing controversy where meaningless data have been used to "prove" both sides of the case: Are our highway taxes subsidizing long-haul trucking companies?

Once Over Lightly

Costs that are not affected by a decision are irrelevant to that decision. Costs that have already been incurred cannot be affected by present decisions: they are sunk costs and hence irrelevant to decision making.

The cost of a decision is the value of the opportunities foregone if that decision is made.

Opportunity costs are marginal costs, not average costs; they are the additional costs the decision entails.

Cost calculations, like all economizing decisions, must be made by looking to the future, not to the past.

If costs per unit are to be used in economic calculations, the units must be related to decisions. The cost per mile of owning a car or the cost per bushel of owning a farm are both meaningless because "owning" is not a decision that produces either miles or bushels (though it may be a precondition for such decisions).

Because economic decisions are based on future or expected costs and benefits, they always entail some degree of uncertainty.

When expanded production of any good requires the increasing use of resources less well suited to the task, marginal costs will increase as the rate of production increases. This can also be stated as the law of diminishing returns: The attempt to secure additional output by using additional inputs in a situation where *all* inputs cannot be increased proportionately leads to diminishing marginal returns.

Where the price of a good is set by market demand and market supply, the marginal cost curve of a producer is that producer's supply curve of the good. The market supply is the sum of all the producers' marginal cost curves.

Producers do pay attention to marginal costs when production decisions are guided by the desire for profit. But marginal costs are equally relevant to efficient decisions when production is not undertaken for profit.

Profit maximization by business firms and efficient resource use in a society both require the ability to identify the true marginal costs of alternative decisions.

QUESTIONS FOR DISCUSSION

1. A recent news report from London stated that British doctors, while dissatisfied with some aspects of their country's National Health Service, generally appreciated the fact that they could treat patients under this system "without regard to cost." Comment.

2. Physicians in the United States must typically go through four or more years of training after college before they can practice. Does this cost affect the prices doctors receive for their services? Explain.

3. A study of the New York City housing situation revealed that many landlords are abandoning apartment buildings they own because, under rent controls, they cannot get enough revenue to cover their costs. What costs are relevant to such a decision?

4. An official of the National Association of Letter Carriers recently complained that postal service was deteriorating because "management has as its objective delivering mail at less expense." He argued that the postal system should not be expected to break even because "it's a service for the people, not a profit-making organization." Comment.

5. An airline is thinking about adding a daily flight from Denver to Billings. It has estimates of the number of passengers who would use the flight. What costs should and should not be considered in deciding whether the anticipated revenue is sufficient to make the flight profitable?

6. If you were the television dealer introduced in this chapter and you were trying to decide whether to display the sets in your showroom, how would you go about estimating the cost of the display space? Why would you *not* be interested in the cost per square foot of construction as you tried to decide? Under what circumstances *would* data on construction costs become relevant to your decision making?

7. The economist's rule "Sunk costs are irrelevant" is like a string around your finger. It reminds you to consider only marginal costs, but it cannot identify the marginal costs. That requires informed judgment. You could sharpen your judgment by trying to enumerate and assess the marginal costs of retaining or not retaining your college apartment over the summer vacation. Try to calculate the minimum rental from subleasing that would persuade you to retain it for fall reoccupancy.

8. Your boss tells you in an angry voice, "I don't care what you learned in economics. If you don't include all our sunk costs in your report and recommendation, I'll fire you." Are the sunk costs now irrelevant to your decision making? yes but I'll put them in anyway

9. Should the casualties already incurred in a war be taken into account by a government in deciding whether it is in the national interest to continue the war? This is obviously not a trivial question. And it is a much more difficult question than you might at first suppose, especially for a government dependent on popular support.

10. The Board Chairman of the Tennessee Valley Authority complained in November 1974 that "prices charged for coal in today's market bear no reasonable relationship to the cost of producing it." What do you think he

meant by cost of production? He also complained that TVA got no response when it asked for competitive bids from coal producers: "They don't need to compete because they can sell all the coal they want at their prices." If that's true, is it possible for the price of coal to be higher than its opportunity cost? What opportunities were determining the price TVA had to pay for coal? He also commented: "This country cannot afford to let something as vital to our well-being as coal be used to maximize profits." Do you think the prices charged for coal were harmful to the national well-being? What price structure for coal is most in the national interest?

11. In its 1973 annual report Phelps Dodge Corporation said it would exhaust the copper in Lavender Pit (Arizona) by mid-1974 and close the mine at that time. But the June 1974 price of copper was 25% higher than the January price, and the mine kept on operating. Did the higher price put additional copper in the pit? What would a geologist mean by the statement, "I can't tell you how much ore is in that mountain until I know the price of copper"?

12. The American Petroleum Institute estimated that proved U.S. oil reserves at the beginning of 1975 were 34.25 billion barrels. Petroleum geologists have estimated that 300 billion barrels of oil lie beneath the ground in fairly well known locations within the United States. How would you reconcile these two vastly different estimates? The API defines "proved reserves" as the amount of oil likely to be recoverable from known reservoirs *under current economic conditions.* Can you suggest an easy way to increase the nation's proved reserves?

13. If it's true that tuition charges cover about one-half the cost of a student's education at a nonpublic university, why are so many financially pinched schools currently recruiting additional students? How would you reconcile that claim (tuition covers only one-half of cost) with the university treasurer's statement that "this year's budget deficit was due to an unanticipated decline in enrollments"?

14. Mr. Hemline insists that the hall light be kept on all night to ward off burglars. Mrs. Hemline thinks that's absurd but wants the hall light on in case the children get up in the middle of the night. How should they allocate the cost of burning the hall light between burglary prevention and child protection? Why might anyone ever want to make such an allocation?

15. A Department of Agriculture official said early in 1975 that farmers were no longer pouring on all the fertilizer the ground will take because of the sharp rise in fertilizer prices. Why might higher prices cause a particular farmer to use *less* fertilizer rather than cut out its use altogether? How will higher fertilizer prices affect U.S. agricultural output? Do you think price controls on fertilizer would help maintain U.S. farm output and thus hold down food prices? (Hint: The U.S. government had put a ceiling price of $75 a ton on domestic sales of a certain phosphate fertilizer at a time when foreign buyers were offering to pay $110 a ton.)

16. The schedule below shows the relation between the amount of fertilizer applied to a hypothetical field and its resulting crop yield. How does this illustrate diminishing marginal returns?

Units of Fertilizer	Yield in Bushels
0	1000
1	1160
2	1240
3	1280
4	1300

The text states that marginal cost is the other side of marginal return. Can you translate the diminishing marginal returns in the schedule above into a schedule of rising marginal costs of production? (How much fertilizer does it cost to produce another bushel?) If the crop is expected to sell for $1.00 per bushel, how low would the price of fertilizer have to be to persuade the farmer to use 4 units? *20 dollars or less*

Marginal decision making goes to = or almost.

7

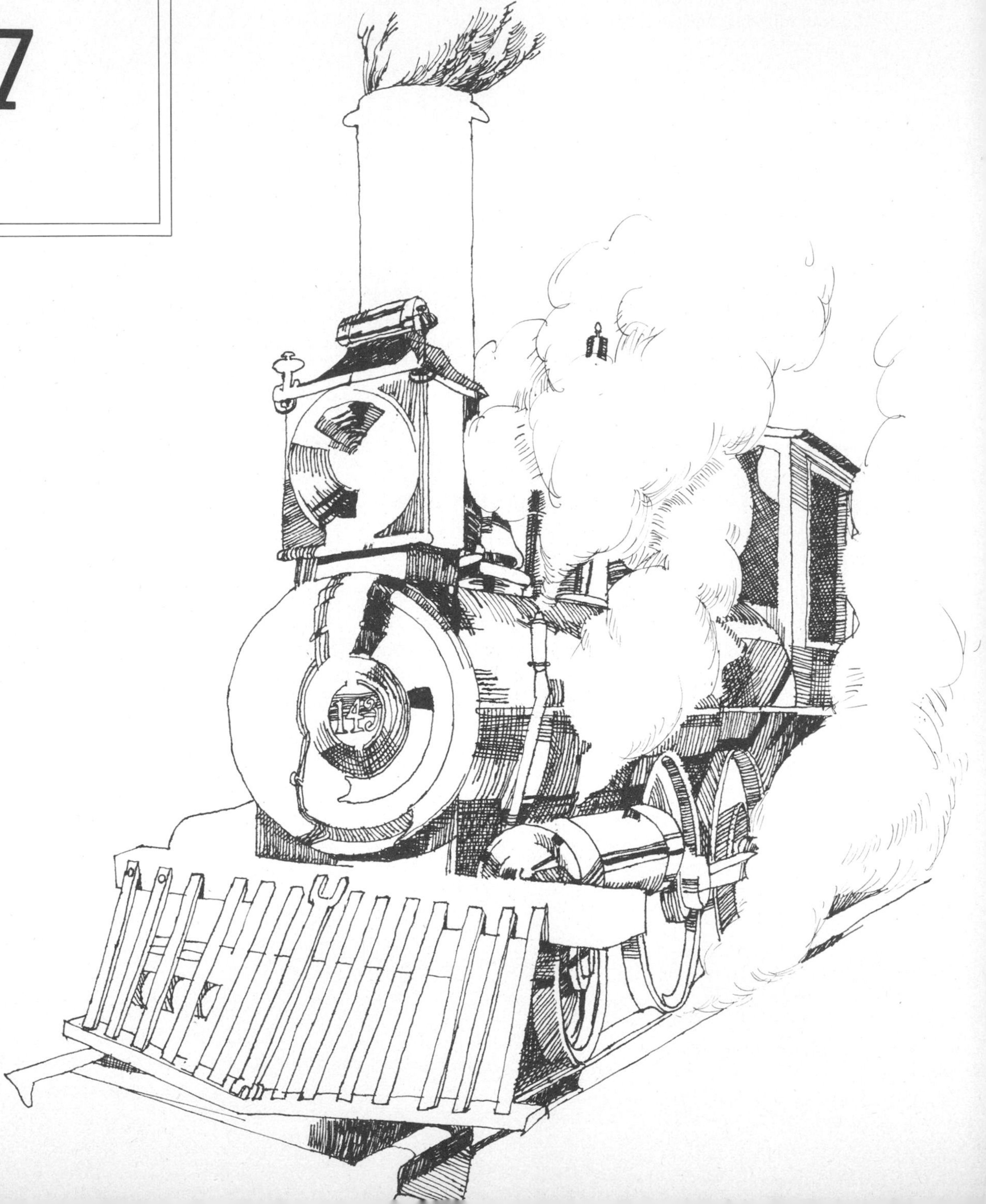

EFFICIENCY,
COMPARATIVE ADVANTAGE,
AND WELFARE

Efficiency is something almost everyone favors. But what is it? In earlier chapters we talked a great deal about efficiency even when we didn't use the word. It is time now to haul the concept into the open for scrutiny. Efficiency is another of the pervasive concepts in the economist's way of thinking.

EFFICIENCY AND THE MATERIALIST FALLACY

Is a diesel locomotive more efficient than a steam locomotive? Most people would say yes. But what reasons would they give for their answer?

If efficiency is to have any precise meaning, it must be understood as a ratio of one thing to another. Engineers use a definition of efficiency that seems to satisfy this test. They define efficiency as the ratio of the work done by a machine to the energy supplied to it, and that ratio is usually expressed as a percentage. From the engineering standpoint, the diesel locomotive is therefore more efficient than the steam locomotive because, per unit of potential energy contained in its fuel, the diesel does more work.

This definition is somewhat unsatisfactory, however, when we think about it more critically. Efficiency cannot be simply the measure of energy output to energy input because, by the laws of thermodynamics, that ratio is always unity for any process. It is rather a measure of *work done* in relation to energy input. But what constitutes "work done"? Doesn't that depend on what is *wanted*? What qualifies as "work"? Engineers actually call a steam engine less efficient than a diesel because with a steam engine a higher percentage of the energy input is *wasted*. Strictly speaking, however, even wasted energy does work. It just doesn't do any *useful* work. That means it doesn't do work that anybody *wants* done. All of which implies that efficiency is not a purely objective or technological matter, but depends inevitably upon valuations.

It is sometimes said that our society places too high a value on efficiency. That's almost like saying that we place too high a value on what we value, which doesn't make much sense. We may be excessively infatuated with technology, but that is quite another matter. A mindless obsession with technology is very different indeed from a concern for efficiency.

The Meaning of Efficiency

Efficiency is inescapably an evaluative term. It always has to do with the ratio of the *value* of output to the *value* of input. Efficiency will always have an objective component, of course; our likes and dislikes don't determine the potential heat in a pound of fuel. But physical facts *by themselves* can never determine efficiency. It follows that the efficiency of any process can change with changes in valuations, and because everything depends upon everything else, any change at all in any subjective preference is in principle capable of altering the efficiency of any process.

Let's go back to the question of the relative efficiency of diesel and steam locomotives. Each can be put into operation only with the use of a large number of inputs: not only coal or oil and locomotive operators, but also all the inputs used in manufacturing the locomotives, the inputs that went into the fabrication of these inputs, the inputs that went into the fabrication of the products that were inputs in the process of producing the products that were inputs in the manufacture of the locomotives, and so on without any discernible limit. Anything that changes the value of anything that contributes to a locomotive's operation can in principle alter its efficiency.

We don't need any far-fetched illustrations to make the essential point. An increase in the price of oil relative to coal, if it is large enough, can by itself transform their relative efficiencies so that a coal-fired steam locomotive becomes more efficient than a diesel. It follows that these relative efficiencies depend on the demand for and supply of oil and coal, and hence on such factors as the motoring habits of the general public, the political situation in oil-producing countries, United States policy on import quotas, and the value placed on the environmental effects of strip-mining coal. Perhaps it never occurred to you that the relative efficiency of the old steam locomotive was affected by the efforts of the United Mine Workers!

To test your grasp of the principle at work here, examine each of the statements below. Ask yourself what kind of change would be capable of creating or reversing the situation. The possibilities are limited only by your imagination.

1. Math can be taught more efficiently with programed text-books than with teachers.
2. It is more efficient to cultivate corn with a tractor than by hand.
3. It is inefficient to use trained lawyers as court stenographers.
4. It is more efficient to cut down trees with a chain saw than with an ax.

If you thought through these statements, you should have noticed the possibility that changes in printing costs or teachers' salaries, tractor prices or farm labor wages, alternative opportunities available to people trained in law and in shorthand, and even, in the fourth case, changes in attitudes toward noise in the forests are capable of altering relative efficiencies. If you failed to notice these things and more, try again at the conclusion of this chapter.

Some Myths Concerning Wealth

Trading has long had an unsavory reputation in the Western world. This may reflect the enormous influence of Aristotle and his medieval followers, who thought there was something unnatural about exchange for monetary gain; but it is more likely the result of a deep-seated human conviction that nothing can *really* be gained through mere exchange. Agriculture and manufacturing are believed to be genuinely productive: they seem to create something genuinely new, something additional. But trade only exchanges one thing for another. It follows that the merchant, who profits from trading, must be imposing some kind of tax on the community. The wages or other profit of the farmer and artisan can be obtained from the alleged real product of their efforts, so that they are entitled in some sense to their income; they reap what they have sown. But the merchant seems to reap without sowing; his activity does not appear to create anything and yet he is rewarded for his efforts. Trading, some have thought, is social waste, the epitome of inefficiency.

This line of argument strikes a deeply responsive chord in many people who still retain the old hostility toward the merchant in the form of a distrust of the "middleman." Everybody wants to bypass the middleman, who is pictured as a kind of legal bandit on the highways of trade, authorized to exact his percentage from everyone foolish or unlucky enough to come his way.

However ancient or deep-seated this conviction of the unproductiveness of trade, it is completely erroneous. There is no defensible sense of the word *productive* that can be applied to agriculture or manufacturing but not to trading. Exchange is productive! It is productive because it promotes greater efficiency in resource use.

Many have taken a fatal wrong turn at the very beginning in considering this question by assuming that exchange, unless it is fraudulent or coerced, is always the exchange of *equal values.* It just isn't so. The exact reverse is true: Exchange is never an exchange of equal values. *If it were, it would not occur.* In an informed and uncoerced exchange (and that is the kind we want to consider), both parties gain by giving up something of lesser for something of greater value. If Jack swaps his basketball for Jim's baseball glove, Jack values the glove more than the ball and Jim values the ball more than the glove. Viewed from either side, the exchange was unequal. And that is precisely the source of its productivity. Jack now has greater wealth than he had before, and so does Jim. The exchange was productive because it increased the wealth of both parties involved.

"Not really," comes a voice from the rear. "There was no real increase in wealth. Jack and Jim feel better off, it's true; they may be happier and all that. But the exchange didn't really produce anything. There is still just one baseball glove and one basketball."

We must be respectful but wary toward that small voice. What does wealth consist of? What constitutes production? Many people have drifted into the habit of supposing that an economic system produces "material wealth," like cars, houses, basketballs, breakfast cereals, and ball-point pens. But none of these things is wealth unless it is available to someone who values it. Additional water is additional wealth to a farmer who wants to irrigate; it is not wealth to a farmer caught in a Mississippi River flood. A food freezer may be wealth to an American housewife but not to an Eskimo. The crate in which the freezer was delivered is trash to the housewife but a treasure to her small son who sees it as a playhouse.

Economic growth consists not in increasing the production of *things,* but in the production of *wealth.* Material things can contribute to wealth, obviously, and are in some sense essential to the production of wealth. (Even such "nonmaterial" goods as love and peace of mind do, after all, have some material embodiment.) But there is no necessary relation between the growth of wealth and an increase in the volume or weight or quantity of material objects. The indefensible identification of wealth with only material objects must be rejected at root. It makes no sense. And it blocks understanding of many aspects of economic life.

So the small voice from the rear was confused. Both Jack and Jim do have greater wealth after their exchange, and in a sense no different from the sense in which each would have greater wealth if a ball and a glove rained down on them like manna. For people who hate sports, of course, such a rainfall would not be wealth but an unnatural disaster.

Recall what we concluded earlier about efficiency: it is measured by the ratio of one *value* to another, not by physical ratios of any sort. You can think of Jack and Jim's exchange as an act of production. Jack used the basketball as an input to obtain the output of a baseball glove. For Jim the glove was the input and the ball the output. The result of the productive process (the exchange) was an output value greater than input value for both parties. Nothing further is required to make an activity productive. The exchange expanded real output.

EFFICIENCY AND THE GAINS FROM TRADE

The preliminary work has been done. We're ready now to introduce you to the principle of *comparative advantage,* a concept that sums up almost everything we've been talking about thus far. We'll allow Smith and

Brown to make the introduction. They are suburban neighbors, each with a large lawn and a sizable flower garden. Every Saturday afternoon during the summer, Smith and Brown reluctantly go out to mow their lawns and weed their gardens.

But Smith always finishes earlier despite the fact that the lawns and gardens are identical in size. He is a strong and agile man who can mow his lawn in 40 minutes and weed his garden in 80 minutes. Brown takes two hours to mow his lawn and another two hours to weed his garden, so he is still toiling while Smith is sipping lemonade. You should have these data clearly before you as you proceed, so we'll summarize them in a little table:

Smith

Lawn: 40 minutes
Garden: 80 minutes

Brown

Lawn: 120 minutes
Garden: 120 minutes

We're ready for the question: Is it possible for either or both to get to the lemonade sooner on Saturday by engaging in a little trade?[1] We're all familiar with the advantages of specialization. If the mason builds the carpenter's chimney and the carpenter builds the mason's garage, they each gain by taking advantage of their own and the other party's special skills. That's familiar enough.

But it doesn't seem to fit the case of Smith and Brown. For Brown appears to have no special skills, to be less efficient than Smith in both mowing and weeding. So it would appear, but appearances are misleading.

Suppose that Smith gave up all weeding and instead confined his yard-work to mowing first his own lawn, then Brown's. He could then finish his yard work in just 80 minutes, a gain of 40 minutes for Smith. If Brown meanwhile weeded both gardens, he would still be working 240 minutes, for no gain or loss. Smith has gained from trade with Brown and without inflicting any loss on Brown.

The Principle of Comparative Advantage

What happened? Nothing very unusual. Smith just happens to be a more efficient mower than Brown and Brown a more efficient weeder than Smith. Like the mason and the carpenter. So each specialized in that

1. We shall assume that neither Smith nor Brown has a preference for one kind of chore over the other and that the use of different tools is not a factor in the problem. Dropping these assumptions would add complexity without affecting the underlying principles.

activity in which he was more efficient and they exchanged services. Each pursued his comparative advantage, which means that he specialized in the activity in which he was more efficient. It is a *comparative* advantage, because each is more efficient in one activity than the other activity only *in comparison* with his neighbor. But that is what matters.

Whoa! The small voice from the rear is stirring again. "But Brown is *not* a more efficient weeder than Smith. The clumsy slob is less efficient than Smith in *both* activities." That small but helpful voice has erred again. It just is not true that Brown is less efficient than Smith in both activities. He really is more efficient than Smith in weeding.

Proof is provided by the arithmetic calculation which shows that Smith added to his wealth (his lemonade sipping time) by specializing in mowing and then trading with Brown. And he did not do it at Brown's expense, for Brown's wealth was not reduced. No such gain would be possible if Brown were not more efficient than Smith in weeding—which implies, of course, that Smith is *less* efficient than Brown in weeding.

Nonsense? No—just a momentary paradox. The paradox disappears when we remember to wear the spectacles of opportunity cost. What is the cost to Smith of weeding a garden? It is two lawns left unmowed. And the cost to Smith of mowing a lawn is one-half a garden unweeded. The cost of anything is the opportunity thereby foregone; the cost of weeding is therefore to be expressed in this case in terms of mowing, and the cost of mowing in terms of weeding.

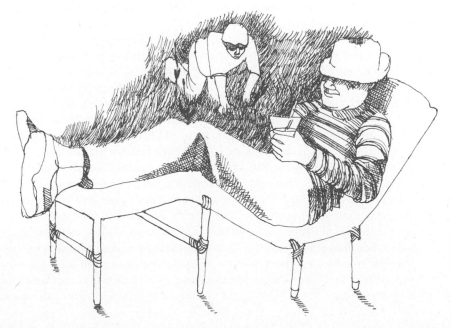

What about Brown? The cost to him of mowing a lawn is one garden left unweeded and the cost of weeding a garden is consequently one lawn left unmowed. We can now determine who is the more efficient or lower-cost producer of weeded gardens by comparing relative costs.

The cost of a garden weeded by Smith is two lawns unmowed. For Brown it is one lawn unmowed. One is less than two. Brown is therefore the lower-cost or more efficient producer of weeded gardens.

We aren't just playing with words, as demonstrated by the crucial fact that either or both can increase their wealth if Brown specializes in weeding and the two engage in trade. Common sense resists this conclusion only because Brown takes *more time* to weed a garden than does Smith. Suppose, someone objects, that we express the costs in man-hours. Then Brown's cost will be one and one-half times as high as Smith's, and common sense will be salvaged. But only at the expense of everything we have argued for! Such an approach assumes that the real measure and determinant of value is the labor embodied in a commodity. But the assumption fails completely to explain relative prices. The cost of any commodity, in the economist's way of thinking, is not what is embodied in it, but what is given up in order to obtain it. It is the value of what is sacrificed, or of the opportunities foregone.

But could we not take leisure, the third good in our problem, as the measure of cost? Let's examine this possibility. Smith gives up 80 minutes of leisure to weed a garden, Brown gives up 120. By this measure Smith is the more efficient producer of weeded gardens and common sense is again salvaged.

You may take this route if nothing else will satisfy you. But if you take it too far you will end up in confusion. Since leisure or lemonade-sipping time is a valued opportunity, the cost of mowing a lawn or weeding a garden can legitimately be expressed in terms of the leisure time given up. But the fact that Smith sacrifices less leisure than Brown to do a job does not prove that Smith is more efficient in some absolute sense. For Smith's leisure may be more valuable than Brown's! It makes sense to measure costs ultimately in terms of leisure only if we believe that leisure is "the ultimate good" *and* if we can assume that an hour of leisure is of equal value to everyone. This sort of absolutism does have a psychological appeal. There is a streak of egalitarianism in almost everyone which wants to assert that one person's leisure counts for exactly as much as any other's. And that conviction is remarkably resistant to all sorts of evidence suggesting that it just isn't so. Question 9 at the end of this chapter has been included for everyone who has trouble freeing himself from the presupposition that labor time or its opposite, leisure, is the proper ultimate measure of cost. And it's important to shake loose from the presupposition because opportunity cost thinking recognizes *no* absolute measures of value: the value of *every* good must finally be expressed in terms of other goods.

The Terms of Trade

We stated a few paragraphs back that Smith or Brown or both can gain from specialization and exchange. In the one case we worked through, Smith appropriated the entire gain. That was a result of the specific terms of trade: the relative prices at which mowing and weeding were exchanged. The terms of trade were one garden for one lawn. At that price, Smith appropriated the entire gain from trade.

Satisfy yourself that you understand what we're doing by calculating the terms of trade that would assign the entire gain to Brown. If Brown weeded his own garden plus only half of Smith's, Brown would be working 180 minutes altogether. Smith would be left with two lawns to mow (80 minutes) plus half of his garden to weed (40 minutes), so he would be no better or worse off. The terms of trade that assign the whole gain to Brown are thus

$$1 \text{ L} = \tfrac{1}{2} \text{ G, or } 1 \text{ G} = 2 \text{ L}$$

The argument is consistent with what you know about relative prices. The people who gain from an increase in the price of a good relative to other goods are those who specialize in its production. Brown likes to see the price of a weeded garden rise from one mowed lawn to two for the same reason that any producer likes to see the price of his specialty increase.

Of course, at some intermediate price ratio they could share the gain from trade. If

$$1 \text{ L} = \tfrac{3}{4} \text{ G, or } 1 \text{ G} = 1\tfrac{1}{3} \text{ L}$$

Smith could gain 20 minutes and Brown 40 minutes from specialization and trade. (Don't conclude that Brown gains more! That requires the doubtful assumption that leisure is equally valuable to both. Turn to question 9 for the antidote.)

OPPORTUNITY COSTS
AND COMPARATIVE ADVANTAGE

Let's work through another example of a somewhat different kind. Imagine a society with only two goods and three producers. The goods are xylophones and yams, which in this hypothetical society satisfy respectively all wants of the spirit and of the flesh. We shall abbreviate them as X and Y. The three producers are Ann, Ben, and Cal. Each is capable of producing in one week the following quantities of X and/or Y.

> Ann: 40 X or 20 Y or any linear combination in-between (20 X and 10 Y, 38 X and 1 Y, 1 X and 19.5 Y, *etc.*)
>
> Ben: 15 X or 15 Y or any linear combination in-between
>
> Cal: 5 X or 10 Y or any linear combination in-between

Who is the most efficient of the three producers? That question has no answer. Ann is the most efficient producer of X. But Cal, for all his ineffectiveness, is the most efficient producer of Y. It's true that he can only produce half as much Y per week as Ann and $\frac{2}{3}$ the amount that Ben can produce. But he's still the most efficient producer of Y because he produces at a lower cost than either of the other two.

What are their respective production costs? When Ann produces 1 Y, she gives up the production of 2 X. The opportunity cost of a Y is therefore 2 X when it's produced by Ann. Ben's cost per unit of Y is 1 X. And Cal's is only $\frac{1}{2}$ X. Obviously Cal is the lowest cost producer of Y. Or we could say that the input required to secure an output of 1 Y is respectively 2 X, 1 X and $\frac{1}{2}$ X when it's produced by Ann, Ben, and Cal respectively. Since the ratio of output value to input value is greatest for Cal, he's the most efficient Y producer. If common sense resists that conclusion, it's because common sense isn't accustomed to thinking in terms of cost as the value of foregone opportunities. But this only shows that common sense sometimes must be tutored.

Suppose you were appointed Emergency Minister of Wartime Production in this society and given authority to assign all producers to their tasks in accordance with your estimate of national "needs." There's no way you could get more than 60 X or more than 45 Y from this "economy." If you decided to order only X or only Y production, you wouldn't have to do any thinking. But if you decided to order some mixture of the two goods, such as 20 Y plus all the X you could obtain from the resources left over, how would you go about it?

You would want to assign Cal to Y production first, and when he gave you only 10 Y, order Ben to devote $\frac{2}{3}$ of his resources to Y production. You would then have your 20 Y (10 from Cal, 10 from Ben), plus 45 X (5 from Ben and 40 from Ann).

If the minister in such a situation never had the advantage of a course in economics and naively assigned Ann to produce the 20 Y, he would end up with 20 Y but only 20 X rather than 45 X. And that would be because he had assigned the least efficient producer to the task of turning out Y.

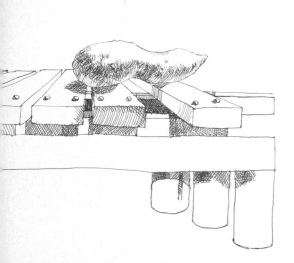

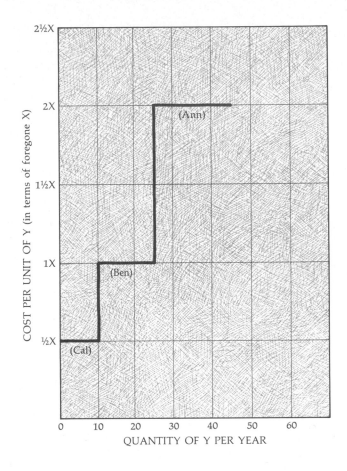

Deriving a Supply Curve

We could give the minister an assist by showing him the supply curve
for Y production, derived from the schedule of each producer's opportunity costs. Cal can produce up to 10 Y at a per unit cost of ½ X. Ben
can produce an additional 15 Y at a per unit cost of 1 X. And Ann can, if
requested, produce 20 additional Y at a per unit cost of 2 X. Figure 7A
shows the supply curve: the quantities that could be produced and the
associated costs. The supply curve makes it rather obvious that Ann is a
very inefficient or high cost producer of Y.

Organizing the Producers

The minister could also control production by setting prices appropriately (assuming that he has the power to enforce the prices he sets). Suppose he set the price of Y at 1.2 X and allowed all the producers to choose

their own output mix. The consumption preferences of the producers would be irrelevant. Cal, for example, might have no taste at all for Y and want only X. He would nonetheless choose to produce Y exclusively and exchange it for X at the established price. In this way he could obtain 12 X, while he could get no more than 5 X by producing it himself. For Cal cannot obtain an X at a cost less than 2 Y if he produces the X himself; but by specializing in Y production and exchanging for X he obtains each X at a cost of only $\frac{5}{6}$ Y.

Ann would similarly find it to her advantage to produce X exclusively. She can produce them at a cost of $\frac{1}{2}$ Y per X, but can only purchase them at the higher cost of $\frac{5}{6}$ Y per X. If she wants to consume Y, she should still produce X and purchase Y at the price of 1.2 X per Y, rather than producing Y at the higher cost of 2 X per unit of Y.

At this legally fixed price Ben would want to produce 15 Y. If he wanted X for consumption, he could obtain X through exchange at the price of $\frac{5}{6}$ Y; but he produces them at the higher cost of 1 Y per unit of X. This will result in 25 Y being produced rather than the 20 which the minister had decided on. He might therefore want to set the price at only 1 X per Y and *instruct* Ben to produce 10 Y and 5 X. Ben would be indifferent about his output mix at this price ratio since he could obtain Y or X through exchange at the same cost as that at which he could produce each good.

Market demand can "order" the various producers as effectively as can instructions from the minister. And that's where producers in a market economy typically do get their instructions. If the price of a Y is anywhere between 1 X and 2 X in our simplified example, Ann will want to specialize completely in X production, Cal and Ben completely in Y production. For by doing so all three producers are exploiting their comparative advantages. They compare the cost of obtaining goods through direct production and through exchange—which may be called indirect production—and opt for the lower cost method.

The Terms of Trade Once More

One additional point can be made before we summarize the principles we've been trying to illustrate. While any price for a Y between 1 X and 2 X will result in the same total production of 25 Y and 40 X, the producers care very much where the price lies within that range. A higher price for Y benefits those who specialize in Y production (Cal and Ben) and a lower price for Y, which equals a higher price for X, benefits those who specialize in X production (Ann). Let's compare the distribution of income at prices of $1\frac{1}{4}$ X and $1\frac{3}{4}$ X for one Y.

At a price of $1\frac{1}{4}$ X per unit of Y, Cal can obtain 10 Y or 12.5 X, Ben can obtain 15 Y or 18.75 X, and Ann can obtain 32 Y or 40 X. At a price of

$1\frac{3}{4}$ X, however, the possibilities for Cal expand to 10 Y or 17.5 X and the possibilities for Ben expand to 15 Y or 26.25 X; but Ann's possibilities are reduced to $22\frac{6}{7}$ Y or 40 X.

A Summary of Principles

The principles illustrated here have far-reaching implications. Let's list some of them:

Wealth can be increased by means of trade.

People specialize because they can increase their wealth by doing so. They specialize in activities in which they have a comparative advantage.

Relative prices help people to determine where their comparative advantages lie.

Relative prices determine the distribution of income or the gains from specialization and trade.

Anything that prevents voluntary exchange promotes inefficiency by preventing the specialization that increases total wealth.

Comparative Advantage, the Economist's Umbrella

The term with which economists summarize everything we have been discussing in this chapter is *comparative advantage.* It might even be thought of as a term to summarize the entire collection of concepts presented thus far. To pursue comparative advantage means simply to sacrifice that which is less valuable for the sake of something more valuable.

Why do demand curves slope downward to the right? Because people pursue their comparative advantage. A rise in the price of any good means that its users will now be able to obtain the satisfaction it provides at a *relatively lower cost* by using some substitute.

How is the opportunity cost of any resource established? Through the pursuit of comparative advantage. People bid for a resource after estimating the potentiality of that resource *relative to other resources* for providing whatever it is they're after.

Why are only marginal costs and not sunk costs relevant to decision making? Because marginal costs reflect the *comparative advantages of alternative decisions,* while sunk costs can never do more than reflect the comparative advantages of past decisions. But no one makes decisions with the hope of affecting what happened yesterday.

It is comparative advantage—the advantage resources have over other resources in particular uses relative to other uses—that determines the

THE USE OF AGRICULTURAL LAND

In 1972 wheat sold at an average price of $1.76 per bushel, field corn at an average price of $1.57 per bushel. Why did any farmers choose, then, to grow corn rather than wheat?

In 1972 the average yield per acre in the United States was 32.7 bushels for wheat and 97.1 bushels for corn. Wheat therefore offered an average revenue of $57.55 per acre while corn offered $152.45. The question changes now: Why did any farmers choose to grow wheat rather than corn?

If we look only at those states in which at least one million acres were harvested, corn yields varied in 1972 from Georgia's 52 bushels per acre to Iowa's 116. Wheat yields varied between 22 bushels per acre in Texas and 47.4 bushels in Washington. Moreover, the prices of these crops varied from state to state, largely because of differences in quality. When we use average state prices, Georgia corn farmers earned $82.68 per acre and Iowa corn farmers $191.40 per acre. Texas wheat farmers earned $34.32 per acre on average and Washington wheat farmers earned $96.70 per acre.

That's a very different picture from the one in the preceding paragraph. On a nation wide basis, wheat yielded a revenue per acre that was only 38% of the corn yield. But Washington wheat yielded 17% *more* revenue per acre than Georgia corn.

All of this ignores differences in cultivation costs, of course. They must be taken into account in a complete explanation of farmers' planting decisions. But the first point we're making here is that farmers do not plant average quality land and receive average yields.

State averages are still highly misleading because the productivity of land in alternative uses varies enormously within each state and even on a single farm. Cultivation costs also vary considerably with crop, terrain, climate, and other factors. Efficient decisions, decisions that maximize the ratio of output value to input value, therefore require a detailed knowledge of particular circumstances. This is a kind of knowledge that cannot be adequately conveyed through statistical aggregates and hence cannot be made readily available to central planners. (See F. A. Hayek's discussion of the knowledge problem in Appendix 1.)

Texas farmers, for example, harvest between 15 and 20 million acres each year, producing a wide variety of grains, fibers, feeds, vegetables, and fruits. The table below, based on U.S. Department of Agriculture data, gives some idea of the range and variation in agricultural production within just one state.

Who decides which land will be devoted to the growing of what crops, and on what criteria are these decisions based?

| | Acres Harvested (1000) | | |
Crop	1970	1971	1972
Upland cotton	4870	4700	5150
Corn for grain	557	552	460
Winter wheat	2267	1496	2000
Oats	764	222	360
Barley	170	66	60
Rye	39	27	35
Rice	467	468	468
Sorghum grain	5886	5827	5420
Hay	2350	2220	1970
Peanuts	306	297	304
Soybeans	158	103	210
Commercial vegetables for fresh market	226	197	198

The efficient use of land requires attention to variations in soil, temperature, and rainfall; the productivity and cost of resources complementary to the land such as fertilizer, machinery, seed, and particular types of labor; and the expected prices of the alternative crops that can be grown. Do you think these decisions could be made efficiently by central planners? Could the planners obtain in a usable form the information they would require? Why do you suppose it is that the agricultural sector of their economy has been a persistent and grave disappointment to Soviet central planners?

The justly celebrated productivity of American agriculture depends in large part upon the retention of decision making power by the people on the spot, the individual farmers who are the only people in a position to estimate the opportunity costs associated with the varied uses of all the resources under their command. The social coordination of these decisions then takes place primarily through changes in relative prices. A continuous feedback between decentralized decisions and the prices that reflect the social outcome of these decisions guides the allocation of resources.

To round out the picture we should add that *some* information important to agricultural production *can* be efficiently gathered by government. Information on new production techniques, new seed varieties, and the planting decisions of all farmers together is both highly useful and too costly for any individual farmer to acquire on his own. Government agencies have contributed significantly to the development of farm productivity in the United States by accumulating such information and disseminating it to producers.

THE "OBVIOUS" SOLUTION
ISN'T ALWAYS THE BEST SOLUTION

How can resources be allocated efficiently by a central planning authority when each resource has potential uses of which the planners aren't even aware? We think the following advertisement by the Celanese Corporation neatly points up the dilemma. It appeared under the heading, "Maybe some farmers are better off without propane."

If the energy crisis highlights one fact, it's the need for examining all the alternatives to a problem before coming up with a solution everyone has to live with.

Consider, for example, the allocation of propane.

This critically short hydrocarbon is used by farmers to dry high-moisture grain, before storage, to prevent mold.

When it became known that propane was in short supply, the authors of early allocation proposals came to some quick conclusions:

1. That food is basic.
2. That food storage requires propane.
3. That farmers must be given top priority for propane to dry their grain.

While such thinking is logical, we think it ignores what could be an even better solution. At least as far as grain-fed livestock are concerned.

And that is to use propane to protect grain without drying.

You see, Celanese makes a liquid grain preservative which we market under the brand name Chemstor.

It can be sprayed on corn and other cereal grains to protect them from mold, without drying.

In fact, Chemstor-treated grains can be stored in the open when silos aren't available.

Moreover, Chemstor, which occurs naturally in most living things, is itself a nutrient. It's totally metabolized. And accelerates the weight gain of cattle and improves their feed efficiency.

Livestock seem to love it.

Now, as it happens, Chemstor is made in part from propane.

But about the same amount of propane needed to dry a ton of grain will treat three tons of Chemstor-sprayed grain.

We cite this not in the hope that you will rush out and buy a tank car of Chemstor. But rather because it illus-

trates the trade-offs that should be considered when
allocating petroleum as a fuel and as a material.

The U.S. petrochemical industry makes a lot of such
useful products. Most of which offer more enduring values
than simply burning the equivalent amount of petroleum
as a fuel.

To make the best use of our natural resources, the
nation needs policies that consider all of these factors.

Then we'll all be better off.

When the price system is allowed to reflect competitive bids,
the less valuable uses of a scarce resource will fall into line
behind the more valuable uses. In the absence of a price system
to summarize information and give signals to producers, allocative mistakes become far more likely.

most efficient way to employ a society's resources. And the pursuit of
comparative advantage will lead decision makers actually to employ
resources in the most efficient way *if* the relative costs decision makers
must pay reflect opportunity costs.

The economic way of thinking may at root be nothing more than the
ability to think consistently in terms of comparative advantage.

EFFICIENCY AND ECONOMIC GROWTH

We began this chapter by pointing out that almost everyone favors
efficiency. *Almost* everyone? If efficiency is the relationship between the
value of output and the value of input, how can anyone be against it?
Efficiency is simply economy, choice of the best available means. Surely
no one is in favor of inefficiency, of waste, of achieving goals by using
something less than the best available means.

Efficiency has become controversial in recent years largely because the
term is widely used to mean something more narrow than what we've
been discussing. We often read, for example, that our obsession with
efficiency has led us to neglect the effect of our actions upon the environment. Another suggestion offered with increasing frequency is that we
should begin sacrificing some efficiency in our factories and offices in order
to make work more meaningful for people. In both these cases, however,
it is not efficiency as we have defined it which is under attack so much as
the failure to include in our calculations all the relevant inputs and outputs.
If environmental damage results from a production process, the value of
inputs is understated when those costs are not included. The problem is

ADAM SMITH ON SPECIALIZATION

Adam Smith believed that "division of labor" was the most important source of increases in a nation's wealth. Chapter I of book I in *The Wealth of Nations* is titled "Of the Division of Labor" and opens with these words: "The greatest improvement in the productive powers of labor and the greater part of the skill, dexterity, and judgment with which it is anywhere directed or applied seem to have been the effects of the division of labor."

But is specialization an unmixed blessing? Toward the end of *The Wealth of Nations* Smith revealed his misgivings.

In the progress of the division of labor, the employment of the far greater part of the people comes to be confined to a very few simple operations. But the understandings of the greater part of men are necessarily formed by their ordinary employment. The man whose whole life is spent in performing a few simple operations has no occasion to exert his understanding, or to exercise his invention in finding out expedients for removing difficulties which never occur. He naturally loses, therefore, the habit of such exertion, and generally becomes as stupid and ignorant as it is possible for a human creature to become. The torpor of his mind renders him not only incapable of relishing or bearing a part in any rational conversation, but of conceiving any generous, noble, or tender sentiment, and consequently of forming any just judgment concerning many even of the ordinary duties of private life. Of the great and extensive interests of his country he is altogether incapable of judging. (Quoted with some omissions from book V, chapter I, part III).

The realization that raising productivity and making work a humanly fulfilling activity might be conflicting goals is as old as the science of economics.

then not efficiency but faulty social calculation. The same objection applies to the second case: if we fail to include the boredom and frustration of work in determining the value of inputs or, alternatively, fail to count the satisfactions of meaningful work in the value of output, we are leaving out data that are relevant to genuine efficiency.

A mere quibble about words will contribute nothing to the understanding and resolution of social issues. But sensible policy formulation depends in part on our ability to think and communicate clearly, and a consistent use of words is obviously an important aid to clear thinking and discussion. Since efficiency has a defensible meaning only in relation to values, we ought to let it take account of *all* values and not steer ourselves into a trap by confining it to the production of material objects or goods privately produced and sold. If a society turns out tons of gadgets smoothly, but simultaneously produces so much pollution, meaningless work, and nervous exhaustion that the level of human welfare declines as a result, that society is not efficient in any defensible sense of the word.

Efficiency and Scarcity

Efficiency is more important in a society the more acutely it feels the pinch of scarcity. Some are now arguing that efficiency or economy is therefore not very important in our "affluent society." But that's an extremely dubious inference. While the average level of affluence in the United States is high by any standard, many people are far below the average. It is, moreover, difficult to condone inefficiency anywhere in a world characterized by extensive poverty. On top of all this, the plain truth must be faced that most Americans do not believe themselves to be affluent and clearly want more income to purchase even more goods and services than they're now consuming.

This means that the opponents of efficiency are in reality increasing the scarcity of resources and thus making efficiency more important—at least in the short run. They are adding to the aggregate of wants currently pressing upon our limited resources. To the demand for more cars, boats, air conditioners, camping equipment, divided highways, and motley products of steel, aluminum, chrome, and plastic they are adding a demand for more trains, unspoiled beaches, open areas, clear water, clean air, less compulsion to work, and also more mineral resources left in the earth for the use of future generations. Their educational efforts may eventually lead to a reduced demand for goods of the first type; but until that happens, they are aggravating the problem of scarcity.

The Critique of Growth

The critique of efficiency as an idol is one aspect of the growing campaign against economic growth. Perhaps one must have lived through the 1950s and 1960s to appreciate fully the radical nature of the shift in thinking that has transformed economic growth within just a few years from

the answer to all social problems into the root cause of all our ills. Where we once took for granted that economic growth could bring well-being to the poor at no cost to the rich, we're no longer so sure. Above all, we have come to see the earth as a finite planet with limited resources. The new advocates of zero economic growth point out that we cannot continue indefinitely to raise our rate of natural resource use. Moreover, they argue, we are already perilously close to disaster in our present course of using up the earth's goods and choking the earth with bads; we must therefore take immediate steps to bring economic growth to a halt.

Critics of the zero economic growth partisans accuse them, on the other hand, of exaggerating the problem and substituting sweeping prophecies of doom for careful analysis. We cannot hope to settle in these pages an issue so complex and about which there is so much disagreement on the fundamental facts. We can, however, try to sort out the major arguments and evaluate at least some of the competing claims.

Relative or Absolute Scarcity?

A good place to begin is with the concept of scarcity. The answer to scarcity in the economic way of thinking is substitution. Scarcity is always particular and relative. As certain goods become more scarce, their price rises, and this induces substitution toward goods that are less scarce. But some now argue that this is a mistaken view of the situation and that scarcity is now or will soon become absolute. All resources are allegedly becoming scarce, so that the opportunities for effective substitution are rapidly disappearing. Which concept of scarcity, relative or absolute, is more relevant to our present situation?

The proponents of absolute scarcity often call upon the authority of physics and the second law of thermodynamics to prove that even the most astute practice of economy must lead eventually to the total exhaustion of usable energy. Economic growth must finally cease; the only choice we have is whether to hasten or delay the end. But even short of that distant culmination, the finite character of the earth and the improbability of our ever managing to import materials or energy from outside the earth at a faster rate than they are now entering (solar energy is, of course, our dominant import) makes scarcity finally an absolute and not merely a relative phenomenon.

But are these useful assertions? One could grant that the proponents of absolute scarcity have correctly perceived the ultimate limits to growth and still deny that the ultimate limits are the ones to which we should be giving our principal attention. The shortages of fuel, meat, lumber, sugar, and other materials that have plagued us in recent years have been imposed by limitations in our ability to cope with rapid change. The energy shortage provides an illustrative example.

Institutional versus Physical Constraints

The "energy crisis" of 1973 was precipitated by the political actions of the Organization of Petroleum Exporting Countries. Whether OPEC members reduced their petroleum production to influence Middle East diplomacy or to take advantage of an inelastic demand for oil, the result was a sudden and acute increase in the scarcity of energy resources, since energy users throughout the world had become highly dependent on oil and on OPEC as a major supplier. The point here is that the scarcity was not so much physical as institutional and political in orgin. It was a short-run crisis and could be alleviated by persuading members of OPEC to expand output, something they were clearly capable of doing if they thought it was in their interest to do so.

But wasn't this short run crisis a foretaste of a not-too-distant permanent crisis? Recoverable petroleum reserves are not infinite, and the world is burning petroleum products at a rapid and increasing rate. We cannot be certain how long supplies will last because we cannot forecast the rate at which known recoverable reserves will increase; but we can be fairly certain that at the 8% rate of growth in demand which we saw in the past decade the ratio of recoverable reserves to annual consumption will be alarmingly low before the end of the century.

This portends a crisis, however, only if we maintain our present degree of dependence on petroleum as an energy source. The proponents of relative scarcity insist that this is not likely. Rising petroleum prices will induce shifts toward other, more abundant energy sources. Known reserves of coal, for example, would last more than 2700 years at our current rate of use. Of course, we aren't using much coal presently, and the day of ultimate exhaustion will come much nearer if the world shifts substantially from oil to coal. Nonetheless, at our present rate of energy consumption, known reserves of fossil fuels (oil plus coal) should last for about 500 years. That pushes the final day of reckoning well into the future. It also abstracts, of course, from future increases in energy use and ignores the environmental problems that will accompany increased mining and burning of coal.

What about nuclear energy? New uncertainties now enter the picture, because the size of our nuclear fuel reserves depends crucially on technological factors. If the technology of the breeder reactor can be perfected, we could consume energy at our present rate for an estimated one million years. But we would also expand enormously the supply of resources for building nuclear weapons. Would it be possible to keep them out of dangerous hands? The breeder reactor creates more fuel than it consumes, and this fuel would be transported to electrical generating stations. The risk of a disastrous transportation accident or an even more disastrous hijacking may be greater than we should accept. But this problem again is clearly institutional and political rather than purely physical.

All these problems may be resolved through improvement of the technology for harnessing solar energy or through successful research on the technology of fusion. Fusion alone is capable of providing enough energy to last for an estimated fifty *billion* years at present consumption rates. And there are physicists who say that we will achieve the requisite knowledge to harness this practically inexhaustible energy source within one or two generations. They also point out that progress in this direction depends upon the allocation of research funds; if they're correct, we have additional reason to concentrate upon the institutional and political factors that limit growth.

The Costs of Substitution

Defenders of the absolute scarcity concept object to the above line of reasoning on the ground that it ignores or incorrectly takes into account the costs of substitution. For example, each alternative we have described presupposes a much greater use of electricity to heat us, transport us, and power our production processes. But generating plants, transmission lines, and electrical machinery all use scarce minerals such as iron and copper. May we not be relieving the pinch in one direction only by aggravating it in another? Analysis based on relative scarcity concentrates on one problem at a time and tends implicitly to assume away simultaneous problems in other areas. It talks about the scarcity of fuel while abstracting from the scarcity of metals, clean air, open spaces, or even the human skills that will be required to bring about extensive substitutions. In short, the relative scarcity approach denies overall scarcity by assuming an abundance of slack or excess capacity that can be brought into use whenever scarcity pinches in a particular place. This is too narrow a view, according to the proponents of absolute scarcity. They maintain that we are rapidly exhausting our substitution possibilities and that even with all available alternatives employed in their most economical way we will soon run out of room for further growth. That's why they call for zero economic growth and for educational, cultural, and political changes to create a "steady-state" economy. Such an economy would be characterized by a constant population and a constant stock of physical wealth, with the latter maintained by drawing as little as possible on limited stocks of physical resources.

It's hard to bring evidence to bear on this argument because of the uncertainty and ambiguity surrounding the notion of "all available alternatives." But the concept of relative scarcity with its emphasis on substitution continues to make sense even when we grant the strongest case that the proponents of absolute scarcity can make. It's important that we see why.

A Crucial Role for Prices

Zero economic growth advocates are also calling for substitution, and substitution on an extensive scale. They want people to pursue satisfaction less through the acquisition and use of goods that exhaust physical resources and more through activities that use such resources sparingly. As soon as you begin to think about it you realize that the possibilities for moving in this direction are infinitely varied. The obvious incentive for people to begin such moves is an increase in the cost of resource-exhausting activities relative to activities that are less resource-exhausting. If current or impending scarcities of physical resources are able to express themselves in higher relative prices or costs, each individual's efforts to economize will move society in the direction of zero economic growth.

Our point here is not that an invisible hand will automatically bring us where we ought to go. Prices cannot be expected, under our current institutional arrangements, to express adequately the social scarcity of all resources. We'll see why in chapter 14. But the point here is that whatever changes we make in our political system or our values and however enthusiastically we all join the crusade for zero economic growth, we will achieve our objectives through a process in which everyone chooses the most satisfactory among available alternatives.

Human Power and Humane Growth

It is important that we continue the debate between the proponents of relative and absolute scarcity. The future of the earth is now more under human control, for good or ill, than it has ever been. Power of such awful magnitude calls for vision, a broader and more far-sighted perspective than the economic way of thinking by itself provides. But as we think, investigate, and discuss, we will be choosing continuously among available alternatives on the basis of relative scarcities. And that will have at least three desirable consequences: (1) It will give us more time; (2) It will keep down the cost of whatever we do; and (3) It will enable us to learn more about the options we have.

The economist Alexander Eckstein proposed in 1958 that economic growth be defined as *an extension of the range of alternatives open to society.* This is a definition of growth around which we should all be able to unite. It lends no support at all to what has been aptly called "growthmania," the uncritical and really absurd assumption that a larger output of physical goods leads inevitably to a better life for all. But it preserves the word *growth,* a word with too many positive connotations to be lightly discarded, while reminding us that the greater realization of human potential is the ultimate measure of humane growth.

Once Over Lightly

Efficiency depends upon valuations. While physical or technological facts are certainly relevant to the determination of efficiency, they can never by themselves determine the relative efficiency of alternative processes. Efficiency depends upon the ratio of output *value* to input *value*.

Exchange creates wealth, because voluntary exchange always involves the sacrifice of what is less valued (input) for what is more valued (output). Exchange is as much a wealth-creating transformation as is manufacturing or agriculture.

People specialize in order to exchange and thereby increase their wealth. They specialize in activities in which they believe themselves to have a comparative advantage.

Comparative advantage is determined by opportunity costs. No person, no group, no nation can be more efficient than another in *every* activity, for even the most highly productive agents must have some activities in which they are *less* highly productive. If you're four times as intelligent as someone else, three times as strong, and twice as beautiful, then the other person has a comparative advantage in beauty—and you, handsome as you are, have a comparative *dis*advantage in beauty.

Relative prices help people decide where their comparative advantages lie insofar as relative prices reflect opportunity costs.

Relative prices also determine the distribution of income or the gains from specialization and trade.

Anything that prevents voluntary exchange promotes inefficiency by interfering with wealth-increasing specialization.

Most arguments for zero economic growth are really arguments against expanded production of certain kinds of goods or against neglect of some of the costs associated with this production.

Resource conservation and protection of the environment require more, not less, attention to efficiency.

QUESTIONS FOR DISCUSSION

1. Is it more efficient to build dams with lots of direct labor and little machinery or with lots of machinery and little labor? Why might the answer vary from one country to another?

2. Which is more efficient: Japanese agriculture with its carefully terraced hillsides, or American agriculture with its far more "wasteful" use of land? How have relative prices in the two countries brought about these different methods of farming? How have opportunity costs entered into the formation of these relative prices?

3. Attorney Fudd is the most highly sought-after lawyer in the state. He is also a phenomenal typist who can do 120 words per minute. Should Fudd do his own typing if the fastest secretary he can obtain does only 60 words per minute? Prove that Fudd is *not* twice as efficient as his secretary at typing, that he is in fact *less* efficient at typing, and that he should therefore retain a secretary.

4. The dean knows that Professor Svelte is the most capable administrator in his department, far more capable than Professor Klunk. Can you think of any reasons (related to efficiency rather than nepotism) for nonetheless appointing Klunk over Svelte as department chairman?

5. Have you ever noticed how few gasoline stations are found in the center of large cities? With such heavy traffic one ought to be able to do an excellent business. Why then are there so few?

6. The key to question 5 is the high price of land in the center of large cities. Would it make sense for the city government, which has the right of eminent domain, to take over some of this land in order to provide "vitally needed service stations"?

7. It has often been claimed that under a capitalist system business firms will sometimes continue to use obsolete equipment rather than the new, "most efficient" equipment because they have a lot of money tied up in the old equipment. Does this make sense? What is the relevance to such decisions of "money tied up"? Would an efficient enterprise manager want to behave differently under a socialist system?

8. You own and occupy a large brick house in an old residential neighborhood. The area is being rezoned to allow multiple-family occupancy and apartment buildings. How would you go about deciding whether to (*a*) continue to occupy the house as a single-family dwelling, (*b*) divide the house into several apartments, or (*c*) tear down the house and erect a new apartment complex? If you were to choose *b*, could you be accused of retarding the economy by failing to adopt the most up-to-date equipment because of your vested interest in obsolete equipment? Does this differ from problem 7?

9. Here is a problem for those still infatuated with a labor-or-leisure theory of value. Suppose we want to verify the hypothesis that, since "a man's a man for a' that," one hour of Brown's leisure is equal in value to one hour of Smith's leisure. We gather the following evidence:

    (*a*) We ask them. Brown says his leisure is worth more because he is fat and lazy. Smith agrees that Brown's leisure is worth more.

    (*b*) While Smith and Brown are sipping lemonade together, Jones across the street offers them $10 apiece to work for an hour cleaning his garage. Smith accepts with alacrity, but Brown says he won't do it for less than $20.

    (*c*) Smith often walks home from work because he has, as he says, "nothing better to do." Brown would take a cab if his car were in the shop because he is always eager to get home.

(*d*) Smith daydreams while sipping lemonade. For Brown, this is a time for imaginative creativity; he thinks up all kinds of useful ideas for the employee suggestion box at the office.

If all this evidence is not sufficient to refute the hypothesis that Smith's leisure and Brown's leisure are of equal value, what possible evidence *could* refute it? If there is no way at all of refuting or confirming a hypothesis, does the hypothesis assert anything? If it asserts nothing, why retain it? You might still want to retain a hypothesis that can be neither proved nor disproved on the basis of existing data if it is useful in some way; we do speak of "useful hypotheses." But of what use is the hypothesis that every person's leisure is equal in value to everyone else's leisure? It is seriously misleading for many purposes, and it contains implications that are contrary to a great deal of evidence.

10. How does someone living one mile from work decide whether it's more efficient to walk or drive? List some of the factors that could shift this person's estimate of the relative efficiency of walking and driving. How effective do you think the following would be in causing a person who has been driving to shift to walking?

    (*a*) Closing of the company parking lot, prohibition of on-street parking, and a large increase in the fees charged by commercial parking lots.

    (*b*) Strong recommendation from personal physician that the person walk to and from work each day.

    (*c*) Evidence that if no one drove to work the United States could become self-sufficient in energy resources by 1980.

11. "We've figured that we can get the same response from a mass mailing as from a newspaper ad. We use mass mailing because it's cheaper. Of course, that doesn't mean it's more efficient." Evaluate that argument. From whose point of view is efficiency being assessed? Under what circumstances will the cheaper way to achieve a given result *not* really be the more efficient way? If the Postal Service charges less for third class mail than the service costs, how is it promoting inefficient resource use?

12. There are six little children at a party, each with different tastes. There are six cupcakes on the tray, each with a different colored icing. "It doesn't matter which one you take," the host says to the first child, "because there's one for everybody." Right or wrong? Suppose there are only five cupcakes with different colored icing and the host says: "It doesn't matter which one you take, since there aren't enough to go around anyway." Right or wrong? How does this relate to the assertion in the text that efficiency is important whether scarcity is relative or absolute?

13. The United States used wood as a fuel in metallurgy long after the British had changed to coal. Was this evidence of technological backwardness in the United States? If the United States was technologically backward, how

would you explain the fact that all sorts of machines for woodworking were perfected in the United States in the first half of the nineteenth century? Fireplaces are often said to be inefficient ways to heat a room. Why then were they so widely used in the United States in the nineteenth century in preference to stoves? (Hint: Larger logs can be used in fireplaces.) Why did stoves become more popular as wood prices increased?

14. When important supplies of natural rubber to the United States were cut off by World War II, scientists learned to make synthetic rubber products that eventually proved better than natural rubber products. Did the war increase the intelligence of chemists? Do you think that government price supports for cotton had anything to do with the discovery of synthetic textiles?

ECONOMIZING ON INFORMATION

Middlemen, speculators, and consumer protection

"How to save about $900 and lose $3000 . . . right on your own home"
That was the headline under which the National Association of Real Estate Boards ran an advertisement urging people to use the services of a realtor in selling their homes. The ad continued:

> Don't laugh. It could happen. For instance, suppose you decide to sell your house. Yourself. You decide it's worth $15,000, and you sell it for $15,000. Great. But how did you arrive at that price? By guesswork. It takes a lot more than that to determine a property's value. It takes a Realtor who knows houses and what they're worth. Suppose he said your house was worth $3000 more. A fair price to buyer and seller. It could happen. Of course, you'd save the Realtor's fee. But at quite a cost.
>
> So when you decide to sell a house, use your Realtor. He's not just anyone in real estate. He's the professional who is pledged to a strict code of ethics. That's good. Especially if you want to make the best sale you can. Or for that matter, the best buy.

That ad is eloquent testimony to something mentioned in chapter 7: the public's deep-rooted suspicion of middlemen. The fact that the realtors thought the ad was worth running is strong evidence that such a suspicion exists, and the argument employed in the ad is further evidence. For the ad seems designed to obscure the realtors' function while defending it, almost as if the truth is more than the public would tolerate.

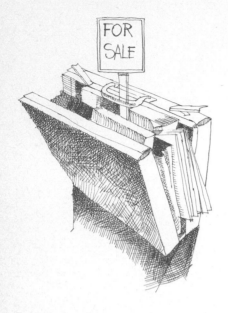

Suppose, we might ask, that the realtor said your house was worth $3000 *less:* "A fair price to buyer and seller." Isn't it just as likely that the homeowner selling his own house will guess too high as too low? Or even more likely in view of the hopeful optimism typical of so many homeowners? Then the use of a realtor will cost him twice over. And just what constitutes a "fair price"? Moreover, if realtors obtain higher prices for sellers, how can they simultaneously obtain better buys for purchasers, as the last paragraph asserts? Something is wrong with the argument.

INFORMATION AS A SCARCE GOOD

Don't criticize the Realtors Association too harshly. The plight of middlemen forced to explain their function is not an easy one. The most important fact to be noticed at the outset is that *information is a scarce good.* If you want to sell your house for as much as you can get, the appropriate buyer is the one person in the world willing to pay the highest price. That seems obvious. What isn't obvious is how you find him. You are presumably not omniscient, so you will never even discover the existence of many potential purchasers. It is almost a certainty, therefore, that when you finally do sell, you will not have found that one buyer willing to pay the very top price. Does this imply that you should keep searching indefinitely?

Information is a scarce good with its own costs of production. It simply does not pay to go on acquiring information forever before acting. A rational seller will continue acquiring information, therefore, only so long as the anticipated marginal gain from doing so is greater than the anticipated marginal cost of acquiring information. A rational buyer will behave in the same way. The reason that both can gain from using the services of a realtor is that the realtor enables each to obtain additional information at low cost. When you think about it, this seems in fact to be the primary function of middlemen: they promote efficiency and hence increase wealth by acting as low-cost producers of valuable information. Realtors provide sellers and buyers with better opportunities than they would otherwise have, by putting them in possession of additional information. That is a valuable service. (It's true that only the seller actually "hires" the realtor. But the fact that buyers go to them and make use of their multiple-listing services shows that realtors provide a service to buyers, too.)

Suppose you own ten shares of General Electric stock and want to sell it. You could go around to your friends and try to peddle it or you could put an ad in the newspaper. But it is very likely that you would obtain a higher price by using the services of a middleman, in this case a stockbroker. No doubt if you advertised long enough you could find a buyer willing to pay the price the stockbroker obtained for you. But it is most improbable that the cost of your search would be less than the broker's fee.

"Getting it wholesale" is a popular pastime for many people who think that they're economizing. Perhaps they are. If they enjoy searching for bargains (and many people do), then they may well gain from their activities. But for most people, retailers are an important low-cost source of valuable information. The retailer's inventory reveals something of the range of opportunities available, information that is often difficult to obtain in any other fashion.

BOOKS

Here's a familiar student complaint:

"I paid $12 for the book new. I didn't put a mark in it, but at the end of the semester the Bookstore offered me just $6 because they said it was a 'used book.' Then they turned around and sold the same book to some other sucker for $10.50 because they said, it was 'good as new.' Yeah! 'Good as new' when they're selling it, but just a 'used book' when they're buying it."

If the Bookstore really is taking advantage of both the selling and the buying student, why don't sellers and buyers get together directly, cut out the middleman, and pocket his profit? In the case above, a price of $8.25 would split the middleman's cut evenly between the selling and the buying student. There's no legal restriction, after all, that says books can only be purchased from the Bookstore or that compels students to sell their used texts exclusively to the Bookstore. So why *don't* the students circumvent the middleman?

The answer is that there are costs involved in sellers' and buyers' finding one another and negotiating mutually satisfactory sales agreements. Students who think these costs will be less than the Bookstore's charge often do try to cut out the middleman. Sometimes it pays off. But sometimes it doesn't.

The Bookstore offers a service at a price: a ready market for sellers and a source of supply for buyers. It even has contacts through used-book wholesalers with students on other campuses, so that a text which won't be used again on the campus where it was originally purchased can nonetheless be sold. We often have trouble recognizing the value of this service because we overlook the real costs involved in matching up supply and demand. Anyone who thinks the Bookstore is overcharging for this service is free to perform it for himself at a lower cost—if he can.

The same is true for job-placement agencies. Many people resent the fee charged by private agencies for finding them a job. But unless they felt that the information obtained through the agency was worth more than the fee, they would presumably not have used the agency's service. Employers are also willing to pay for such services, and for exactly the same reason.

A large part of the middleman's bad press stems from our habit of comparing actual situations with better but nonexistent ones. The exchanges we make are rarely as advantageous as the exchanges we could make if we were omniscient. So we conclude that the middleman takes advantage of our ignorance. But why look at it in that way? Using the same argument, one could say that the doctor takes advantage of your illnesses, and that he should receive no return for his services because he would be unable to obtain a return if you were always healthy. That is both true and irrelevant. We are neither always healthy nor omniscient. Physicians and middlemen are consequently producers of real wealth. Other prestigious persons performing similar services are lawyers, teachers, preachers, and corporation executives.

Markets Create Information

We can return now to an important point first introduced at the end of section B in chapter 6. There we asserted that supply and demand, or the market process of competing bids and offers, creates indices of value for decision makers by placing price tags on available resources. The capacity of the market to generate high-quality information at low cost is one of its most important but least appreciated virtues. Middlemen are important participants in this process.

"But what is 'the market'?" you may ask. That's a good question and not an easy one to answer in a few words. The market is clearly not a place, though it may sometimes be closely identified with a particular place. Nor is it anything one can observe in the usual sense of observation. It is finally just a set of interrelationships, or what we called a "process of competing bids and offers." Some markets, like stock markets and commodity-markets, are "well organized," which means that the bids and offers of prospective buyers and sellers are rather comprehensively assembled so that a single price tends to be established for all transactions over a wide geographic area. The market for used furniture, on the other hand, is relatively unorganized. Transactions take place at prices that vary greatly, because buyers and sellers are not in extensive contact. The market for retail groceries falls somewhere between these extremes. Hamburger prices will consequently vary more over a given area at one time than live-stock prices, but less than used furniture prices.

It is sometimes said that stock markets and commodity markets are more nearly "perfect" than retail grocery markets and used furniture markets. This is a misleading way to describe the difference, however, because it implies that the latter markets *ought to be changed* (perfection is better than imperfection). Remember, however, that such a recommendation makes sense only if the costs of improving the markets are less than the gains from more efficient exchange made possible by the improvement.

In every case, however, the relationships between buyers and sellers, whether constant and extensive or sporadic and scattered, generate prices. Each such price is a piece of potentially valuable information to other people concerning available opportunities. The more such prices there are and the more widely they are known, the wider the range of opportunities available to others.

Opportunity costs consequently decline because markets exist, which is really a way of saying that the range of opportunities available to decision makers expands. And that is a way of saying that wealth increases or that economic growth occurs. And is that not what we finally mean by an increase in wealth? A wider range of available opportunities? The freedom and the power to do more of what one wants to do?

Those who make markets—middlemen, brokers, arbitrageurs—facilitate exchange by specializing in the production of information. They do so presumably because they believe themselves to have a comparative advantage in information production. Anyone who thinks that he "knows better" is free to take advantage of his knowledge—unless, as so often occurs, legal restrictions are imposed on trading. A society that prohibits exchange or suppresses markets, whether from hostility to the trader or for some other reason, denies useful information to its members.

UNCERTAINTY AND SPECULATION

All of this is rather abstract. To make it more concrete we can examine a type of trading that probably suffers most from public misunderstanding: speculation.

The dictionary defines speculation as "trading in the hope of profit from changes in the market price." That's good enough for our purposes. The most celebrated (or, more accurately, the most execrated) speculator is probably the Wall Street "bear." He "sells short," that is, sells shares of stock he does not currently own for future delivery. He believes that the stock will go down in price, so that when the time comes for him to deliver, he can purchase the shares at a low price and sell them at the previously agreed-upon higher price.

A more important speculator is probably the commodity speculator, who may trade in such items as wheat, soybeans, hogs, lumber, sugar, cocoa, or copper. He buys and sells futures. These are agreements to deliver, at some specified date in the future, amounts of a commodity at a price determined now.

These are the spectacular speculators whose feats make the financial pages. A less publicized speculator is you yourself. You are buying education now, partly in the hope that it will increase the value of the labor services you'll be selling in the future. But the future price of your services could turn out to be too low to justify your present investment.

Another familiar speculator is the housewife who reads that the price of sugar is expected to rise and responds by loading her pantry with a two-year supply. If the price of sugar rises far enough, she gains. If it does not, she loses. She has tied up her wealth in sugar, thereby cluttering her shelves and depriving herself of the opportunity to purchase more valuable assets—an interest-bearing savings account, for example.

The motorist who fills his tank when he sees a sign advertising gasoline at two cents a gallon less than he's accustomed to pay is speculating; the price may be four cents lower two blocks ahead. And the motorist who drives on an almost empty tank in hope of lower prices up ahead is a notorious speculator.

But many people overlook the pervasiveness of speculation in order to heap blame on the "profiteers" who allegedly "take advantage" of special situations and innocent people in pursuit of their own unprincipled profit. Is the speculator really the enemy of the people he is so often alleged to be?

Consequences of Speculation

"Speculators exploit natural disasters," it is often said, "by driving up prices before the disaster occurs. And sometimes the expected disaster never even materializes." That is true. But it is only one small and misleading part of the truth. Suppose evidence begins to accumulate in early summer that the fungus called corn leaf blight is spreading to major corn-producing areas of the Midwest. A significant percentage of the year's corn crop could be wiped out as a result. People who think this is likely to occur will consequently expect a higher price for corn next year. This expectation will induce some people to hold some corn out of current consumption in order to carry it over into the next crop period when, they believe, the price will be higher. That is speculation.

Notice how many different parties engage in such speculation: farmers who substitute other livestock feed for corn in order to maintain their corn stocks at a higher level, either to avoid having to buy corn next year at a higher price or in order to sell then at the higher price; industrial users who increase their inventories now while the price is relatively low; plus people who might not know a bushel of corn from a peck of soybeans but who hope to make a profit from buying cheap now and selling dear later. There are well-organized commodity markets to facilitate this kind of transaction. The effect of all these activities is to reduce the currently marketed supply of corn; the price consequently rises. And just as the critic protested, it rises before the disaster occurs.

But that is only a part of the picture. These speculative activities cause corn to be transported *over time* from a period of relative abundance to one of greater scarcity. The price next year, when the blight is expected to have its effects, will therefore be lower than it otherwise would be. Speculators thus even out the flow of commodities into consumption and diminish price fluctuations over time. Since price fluctuations create risks for those who grow or use corn, speculators are actually reducing risk to others. More accurately, they are purchasing risk (in hope of a profit) from others less willing to take risk (and willing to pay something in the form of reduced expected returns to avoid it).

Prophets and Losses

All this assumes, however, that the speculators are correct in their anticipations. What if the expected poor harvest fails to materialize? What if an unusually large crop appears instead? Then the speculators are transporting corn from a period of lesser to a period of greater abundance and thereby magnifying price fluctuations. This is clearly a misallocation of resources, involving as it does the giving up now of some high-priced corn for the sake of obtaining later an equal amount of low-priced corn. That is not socially profitable.

But neither is it profitable for the speculators. They will sustain losses where they had hoped for gains. We should not expect them, consequently, to behave in this fashion *except as a result of ignorance.* Are speculators likely to be ignorant?

No one is omniscient. And speculators make mistakes. (Why would they otherwise be called speculators?) But living as we do in an uncertain world, we have no option but to act in the presence of uncertainty. No one escapes uncertainty and the consequences of ignorance by refusing to act or to think about the future. And if anyone thinks he knows more than the speculators, he can counter them at a profit to himself by betting against them. It is interesting and somewhat revealing to note that those who criticize speculators for misreading the future rarely give effective expression to their own supposedly greater insight by entering the market against them. Hindsight, of course, is always in copious supply—and the price is appropriately low.

As we have repeatedly tried to show, information is a scarce good. Better information means greater efficiency because it provides a wider range of opportunities and hence expanded scope for the exploitation of comparative advantage. Speculators provide information. Their offers to buy and sell express their judgments concerning the future in relation to the present. The prices generated by their activities are, like all prices, indices of value: information for decision makers on present and future opportunity costs. This information is at least as important to conservatives as it is to gamblers. It is true that the information they provide is "bad" information when the speculators are wrong. But harping on this is again a case of comparing one situation with a better but unattainable situation. Anyone who thinks he can read the future better than the speculators is free to express his convictions with money, profit from his insight, and benefit society in the process.

Meanwhile those whose ordinary business activities involve them in the use of commodities that are speculatively traded do make effective use of the information generated by the speculators. Farmers employ the prices predicted in the commodity exchanges to make planting decisions, for example. And those who use goods not ordinarily thought of as speculative commodities also take advantage of the information generated by speculators. For we all use prices as information; and prices reflect competing bids and offers inevitably based to a large extent on a (speculative!) reading of the future.

The Hedger

Let's look at all this from the standpoint of a hedger.

If you bet $10 on the Jets to beat the Rams, and then, worried about the possible loss of $10, bet $5 on the Rams to beat the Jets, we say that you're "hedging your bet." For a perfect hedge, you would bet $10 on the Rams. Of course, there would then be no point to the wager; you could neither win nor lose. And if you had wanted to avoid all risk, you could have done so more easily by not betting at all.

But economic actors don't have that option, since all economic activity entails some risk. The farmer who plants corn in May in anticipation of a high price in September when the corn is harvested incurs numerous risks: drought, excessive rainfall, hail damage, blight, plus the risk of a September price so low that even a bumper crop won't cover his costs. The commodity market offers the farmer a way to hedge against that last risk: to avoid the possibility of a loss due to a price decline by giving up the possibility of the gain that would accrue from a price increase. He does this by selling corn "futures."

The Market for "Futures"

Futures is a short term for *futures contract.* A futures contract calls for future delivery, at a price agreed upon *now*, of some specific quantity and quality of a commodity. The futures market exists side by side with the cash or "spot" market, which is the market for actual carloads of corn or other commodities delivered from country storage points. The people who buy and sell in the cash market are the people who actually use the commodity: in the case of corn, the farmers who grow it, the farmers who feed it to their livestock, firms specializing in storage, manufacturers of breakfast cereals and other food products using corn, and also exporters who make it available to users in other countries. The futures market may be entered by all these parties plus some people who are just willing to gamble on future price changes. The gamblers, who include very few actual users of corn, purchase the risk of unpredictable price changes. And that makes hedging easier for those who want to avoid risk: our corn farmer, for example, who is a producer, not a speculator by trade, and would like to reduce his risks.

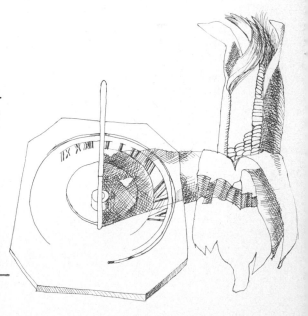

The farmer protects himself against a fall in the price of corn by using the futures market. In effect he contracts *now* to sell a crop that won't even exist for another four months. Thereby he receives assurance that the market's May estimate of September's price will be the price he actually gets when September rolls around.

Why is anybody willing to give him this kind of guarantee? It's obviously because someone believes that September's cash price will be higher than the May estimate, so that when September comes he'll be able to resell the farmer's corn at a price higher than he's committed to pay. Is the speculator taking advantage of the farmer, then? No, because the farmer is not required to sell his crop in advance. He can wait until September if he prefers and see what the price turns out to be. He then assumes the risk, however, that the price will be less than he counted on when he planted.

Still, if the speculator is willing to guarantee the September price in advance, he must know something the farmer does not know. Isn't that taking advantage in a sense? Like someone who takes bets from his friends on a football game when he's the only one who knows that the quarterback has acute appendicitis? The answer is that he *thinks* he knows more than the farmer and *hopes* he knows more but doesn't really *know* that his estimate of the September price is better than the market's May estimate. The speculator will lose if the September cash price turns out to be lower than the futures contract calls for.

There have to be speculators who think they know more than hedgers to make the futures market work effectively. And if they don't turn out to be right at least 50% of the time, they probably won't think that for long. They certainly won't be able to go on for long putting their money behind their opinions. So if you think that hedging is a good thing and, like taking out fire insurance, sensible business policy, you can't consistently be opposed to the speculators who make hedging possible.

But couldn't hedgers simply use other hedgers to buy or sell the futures contracts they want to trade? Farmers who want to protect themselves against a price decline could sell contracts to corn chip manufacturers who want to protect themselves against a rise in price. The trouble with this is that hedgers only enter the market in anticipation of actual production or use of commodities, and it just isn't likely that corn chip manufacturers will be found ready and willing to buy exactly the quantity of futures that farmers want to sell at the precise time they wish to do so. The speculative traders, who do not try to avoid risk as the hedgers do but who on the contrary actively seek to assume it, give depth to the market and thus make hedging a relatively simple, low cost transaction. So once again, if you think hedging is socially useful, you must grant some social utility to even the most swashbuckling speculator.

And hedging *is* socially useful. For example, farmers frequently require bank credit to get through the long spring-to-fall production process. They can often obtain this credit on the security of crops in the ground. But banks typically and understandably will loan more on a hedged crop than on one that is not hedged. For the same reason, a savings and loan association is willing to loan more on an insured than an uninsured house. Insurance, like hedging, reduces the cost of extending credit, because it enables the loan to be based on the rather easily ascertained value of the security rather than on the far more difficult to determine creditworthiness of the borrower. If you think that's a small difference, compare the interest rate you pay for a house or new car loan with what you would have to pay for an unsecured personal loan.

Along the same line, hedging, by reducing the risks of producers—farmers, carriers, storage specialists, processors—enables them to operate with fewer resources. A large grain elevator firm may be holding 50 million bushels of wheat at one time. As little as a 2¢ per bushel decline in the price will inflict on the firm a $1 million loss! If the firm were not able to hedge, it would have to build huge financial reserves to help it ride out price fluctuations. With hedging readily available, it can hold large grain inventories on small financial reserves and easily borrow on the security of the hedged grain.

Picking on Speculators

If hedging and speculation accomplish the socially useful functions we've described in this chapter—smoothing out fluctuations in both price and supply as well as reducing business costs by providing better information to producers of various kinds—why is the whole area under such a cloud in the public mind? And why are politicians so often eager to investigate, restrain, or punish "speculators"?[1] Some of this attitude may spring from a deep-seated hostility to "gambling." But it's hard to condemn gambling on moral grounds when, as in the case of commodity speculation, the gambler assumes *unavoidable risk* and thereby reduces the risk of those who want to avoid it. An important difference between commodity speculation and football betting is that commodity speculation does not involve the deliberate *creation* of risk.

Another cause of public hostility is probably our common preference for having our cake and eating it, too. We want to be protected against loss, but we envy and resent those who provide that protection when it turns out to be a profit rather than a loss that we avoided. Farmers, for example, complain bitterly when speculators reap the profit from an unexpected rise in commodity prices, and can usually persuade their congressmen to sympathize with them and condemn the "greedy" speculators who received "unearned" profits. Greedy they may be. But the profit is unearned only if we believe that people who purchase the risk that others don't want to bear are not performing a socially useful function.

Faulty Forecasts

It's easier to come to that conclusion if one believes that good information about the future is either unimportant or not hard to obtain. No

---

1. Richard Nixon's now famous television address of August 15, 1971, in which he announced several sharp changes of direction in government policy, included six disparaging references to speculation or speculators. It's risky to blame business, labor, consumers, other nations, or the government's own policies for creating economic problems. But it's always safe to blame speculators.

one with experience in business decision making will agree that it's un-important. The recent history of the paper industry in the United States provides one dramatic example out of many that could be mentioned. In the 1960s, papermakers had so much producing capacity that they com-peted prices down severely in efforts to market their output. The excess capacity had been installed on the basis of expected demand increases; but few producers took account of the fact that most other producers were also expanding capacity. The resulting bargain basement prices for newsprint and other paper in the late 1960s brought growth to an abrupt halt. Producers abandoned expansion plans that weren't already too far along to stop. But demand continued to grow and within a few years the situation had turned about once again. In 1973 and 1974 some newspapers cut their size and others went out of business because they couldn't obtain enough paper at a low enough price. So in 1975 papermakers were exult-ing in their newfound prosperity. And trying to take advantage of the situation by increasing production. And probably initiating capacity expansion. Were they also setting up a return to the low prices of the 1960s? They would very much like to know. So would firms that are heavy users of paper.

Committees as Seers?

It was generally agreed in 1974 that inaccurate forecasting had aggra-vated the inflation of 1973 and 1974 by allowing shortages of important resources to develop. That's why Congress enacted legislation in Septem-ber of 1974 establishing a National Commission on Supplies and Short-ages. This commission of thirteen members was asked "to provide specific recommendations . . . as to a permanent facility at the highest level of our national life fully equipped with all relevant information to perceive a potential economic crisis area and to offer alternative policy actions needed to offset or mitigate that crisis." The quotation is from the letter sent to the president by both the majority and minority leaders of the Senate upon passage of the bill. The disturbing feature of the letter and the legislation it accompanied was the assumption that the future can be forecasted if a national commission undertakes the job. But how will a bakers' dozen of presidential and congressional appointees do a more accurate job of forecasting *all* supplies and shortages than a much larger number of far more experienced people does right now in forecasting supplies and shortages in *specific industries?*

The commission or any agency it establishes will inevitably base its forecasts on information obtained from the very industries whose fore-casting failures led to creation of the commission. Where is there a better source, after all? Who is more likely to have gathered up every available bit of relevant information than those people for whom accurate forecasts can make the difference between financial success and financial ruin?

Perhaps Congress and the president were just eager to seem on top of events when they created a National Commission on "Economic Foresight," as Senators Mike Mansfield and Hugh Scott characterized it. But it's more likely that they were giving expression to the widely held view that information about the future really isn't hard to obtain. That's a strange prejudice and one remarkably resistant to the evidence.

CONSUMER PROTECTION

Every consumer purchase is risky. The consumer pays a sum of money in anticipation of a future stream of services, and those services will often not be as satisfactory as he expected when he made the purchase. The loaf of bread may prove moldy when he opens it or just less tasty than he had hoped; the new roof may leak in a driving rain; the articles in the magazine to which he took out a twelve-month subscription may turn out to be dull and uninformative; the movie rated G may give his children nightmares for a week. Since we're all consumers and nearly everyone agrees that the consumer deserves to get what he pays for, campaigns to provide more and better consumer protection are always popular. But the "purchase" of better consumer protection is also risky; the stream of actual benefits in this case, too, may fall short of what was expected when the costs were incurred.

The Caveat Emptor Principle

Caveat emptor means "Let the buyer beware." It's a legal principle which holds that the seller is not responsible for the quality of his product unless that quality is guaranteed in a warranty. The doctrine is seldom mentioned today except to condemn it. But we ought to think awhile before we decide to discard it completely. One significant virtue of the *caveat emptor* doctrine was the incentive it gave to buyers. Since the buyer had to bear the costs of his own mistakes, he had a strong incentive to acquire information about products before purchasing them. *Caveat emptor* induced each buyer to become an information collector. Now information gathering has a cost, as we know; the question for public policy is whether this cost ought to be imposed on each individual consumer or borne by someone else.

The government can and does assume some of the costs of information gathering by setting and enforcing standards. You don't carry your own scale to the grocery store because you assume the butcher's scale is accurate and his weights are honestly recorded. And you probably make that assumption because you know the butcher is liable to a fine for dishonest weighing. A little information gathering by government inspectors in this and similar cases substitutes for much more costly information gathering by individual consumers.

We often accept the word of the seller about some quality that we aren't easily able to check for ourselves by reasoning somewhat as follows: "If he were lying, somebody would probably catch him; he knows this and he also knows that the penalty for getting caught would be high—either legal action or disastrous publicity; so he's probably telling the truth." And that's another way in which we economize on the costs of information gathering. It's far from perfect; with everybody assuming that someone else is checking, no one may in fact be checking. This leaves room for dishonesty; on the other hand, it often functions as a low-cost system of quality control.

But it's a system that functions best when the qualities in question are clear in principle: like weights and volumes or chemical composition. The system begins to break down when the qualities are difficult to measure precisely (more cleaning action) or highly subjective (full-bodied flavor) or when they can only be tested over a long period of time (as with many consumer durables) or when the product is so complex (an automobile is the best example) that some defects are almost inevitable.

Ways of Gathering Information

What do we do in such cases? With relatively low cost items we tend to rely on our own cumulative experience, the testimony of friends, or sometimes the reputation of the manufacturer or retailer. The last points to an important function of brand names. By enabling consumers to blame or credit the maker, brand names give producers an incentive to provide purchasers with quality features they want even when they don't know enough to look for them. Brand names and their advertising have even been recommended recently in the Soviet Union as a way of compelling manufacturers to pay more attention to quality control.

In the case of consumer durables or automobiles, where the cost of a purchasing mistake is so great that we want good information in advance but where most of us are also unable to gather adequate information on our own, we tend to demand guarantees from the seller. We only purchase on condition that the seller replace or repair the product if it fails to perform adequately. We all know some of the inadequacies of this system: guarantees whose guarantors are unreliable or uncooperative, products that break down right after the warranty period has ended, the nuisance of frequent trips to the service center. On the other hand, the producers' desire to sell gives them an incentive to provide longer and more effective guarantees and to establish a reputation for quick, cheerful, and certain service—as well as an incentive to produce goods that won't have to be brought in for service under the warranty.

WATCHING OUT FOR LEMONS

On page 173 we attributed the often considerable difference among new book prices, used-book repurchase prices, and used-book sales prices to the costs sellers and buyers must incur to find one another. The fact that information is not a free good contributes in an additional way to the familiar gap between the prices of new and "good as new" consumer durables like automobiles.

Any automobile may turn out to be a lemon. That's only discovered through use, however. If we make the reasonable assumption that lemons will be traded in sooner than nonlemons, it follows that there will be proportionately more lemons among used than among nonused cars. Since the probability of getting a lemon when buying a "good as new" used car is therefore greater than when buying a new one, used cars can only be sold at a reduced price.

The buyer in effect demands a discount from the seller as compensation for the unrevealed information the seller may have about the car's defects. That also explains why a reputable dealer will usually be able to sell a used car for a higher price than the owner can get. The dealer makes up in part for the fact that the car is more likely to have concealed defects by offering a service warranty.

Reputation and Reliability

The reputation of the seller plays a key role in everything we have mentioned. And that comes down to the seller's desire to sell again. Producers and sellers usually have better information about product quality than do customers because they're specialists. The manufacturer of a product is obviously a specialist with ready command of detailed information about his product. As for retailers, they ordinarily buy in quantities sufficiently large to justify an investigation of product quality, so that a poor quality product will tend to disappear from the shelves. These specialists are often eager to assist the customer in his fumbling quest for information about quality, not because they love consumers but because they want future sales. And future sales will depend upon their reputation for reliability.

This analysis yields a simple prediction: Complaints by purchasers that they have been defrauded will be more frequent as sellers are less concerned about future sales. We'll leave it to you to locate examples to confirm or refute this prediction. We'll suggest only one: the sale of used residences. The first year after purchase is all too often spent by the buyer in patching, replacing, and regretting his naiveté. You can explain this on the grounds that home sellers are intrinsically less honest than businessmen; or you can explain it by granting that sellers have little incentive to share information with buyers when they have no concern for any *subsequent* sale.

Do We Want More Laws?

None of the institutions we've mentioned provide complete protection to the buyer. Even those that usually work well occasionally break down. Should we pass additional laws and create new agencies to give consumers better protection? In thinking about this question we must remember that "perfect information" is no more available to consumer protection agencies than it is to the consumers they're charged with protecting. What we really want is *more* information, but not so much information that the cost of making it available exceeds the benefits of having it.

It simply isn't possible to spell out in complete detail the characteristics of any good offered for sale. Goods have too many aspects and too many potential users. The seller may be thoroughly convinced that his fertilizer will satisfy the most exacting user, but only because he never dreamed that the purchaser wanted it for an indoor planter and would find the smell intolerable. The baker who congratulates himself for adding chemical preservatives to his product isn't thinking at all about the rare person who is allergic to those preservatives. Shall we hold the bookseller liable for failing to inform a purchaser that the language of the book he is buying will offend him or that the color of its binding will clash with the decor in his den?

The Ambiguity of Quality

Moreover, "quality" is not an either/or characteristic of goods. Even the marvelous one-horse chaise of Oliver Wendell Holmes's deacon broke down after a century. It *could* have been made to last longer. Was it therefore a poor quality chaise?

Or take something as simple as a golf ball. What is "quality" in a golf ball? The straight driver wants distance, but that's a mixed blessing for the erratic slicer to whom twenty additional yards means a longer hike into the rough on the right. The hacker wants a tough cover that will resist the hatchetlike blows of his two-iron; but the good golfer always hits the ball with the face of the club and is looking for other features. What's the value of durability to a golfer who has never in his wandering and aquatic career worn out a ball before he lost it?

What do ash trays add to the quality of a nonsmoker's automobile? Shall we say that soles on children's shoes that last two years are of higher quality than soles that last only one year if children's feet grow half an inch in half a year? Are telephone receivers that leak magnetic waves lower quality than those that don't? If you're hard of hearing and your hearing aid has a device that picks up conversation from magnetic leakages, these leakages, classified as "garbage" by the phone company, are for you the essence of a high quality receiver.

Quality and Standardization

It's much easier to certify that a product is what it ought to be if everyone agrees on what it ought to be. That's probably why the demand for more precise product descriptions and guarantees is associated with a demand for more standardization. But standardization has costs, too. A standard size loaf of bread, to take one actually disputed case, will either be so large it goes stale before the person who lives alone can finish it or so small that large families wind up paying more in packaging costs.

There's even something to be said in defense of product failures! Consider the case of light bulbs. A particular production process yields bulbs with a certain average life, a few with a much longer life, and a few dismal failures that burn out quickly. The bulbs with a shorter life will be marketed because no one knows which they are. (They can't *all* be tested because testing burns them out. The manufacturer must take a sample and employ the procedures of statistical inference to determine the quality of his products.) Now a more careful and expensive production process could surely reduce the variation in expected life and hence the number of failures. But would the result justify the additional cost? We could well end up getting less light bulb life for our money on an average than we do now. An occasional dismal failure is therefore part of the price we pay for low cost production processes.

The Regulation of Advertising

This may be as good a place as any to raise the difficult question of advertising and its regulation. In chapter 2 we encountered the argument that advertising reduces social welfare by *creating* wants that must then be satisfied. That claim is almost surely exaggerated unless one includes in "advertising" all of the social practices by which we induce one another to want things that we hadn't previously thought of. The question here, however, is one about the *quality of information* that commercial advertising provides.

The very idea that advertising provides information apparently offends some people. But information is what you're looking for when you consult

the Yellow Pages to find a plumber, look up the movie ads to see what's playing, run through the want-ads in searching for an apartment, or watch for a refiner's trademark when you're driving at night on a nearly empty tank. Of course, the informational content of advertisements will vary widely. A long and closely printed description of a new piece of machinery placed by its manufacturer as an advertisement in a trade journal is one thing; a thirty-second TV commercial for laundry soap is almost another genus. But where is the line between informing and persuading, or between rational persuasion and psychological manipulation?

What about *truth* in advertising? Is there a clear line between truthful assertions and hopeful claims? The economist George Stigler once observed somewhat cynically that "the typical university catalogue would never stop Diogenes in his search for an honest man." And one can at least wonder whether the college professor who is so critical of misleading and exaggerated claims by business advertisers applies the same rigorous standards to the personal resumes that he prepares annually for the information (?) of his dean. Two wrongs do not make a right. But criticism should also begin at home. And it's usually easier to appreciate the ambiguities of an ethical dilemma when we ourselves are involved than when we're judging the behavior of people of whom we don't quite approve.

Who Guards the Guardians?

If the government is to exercise supervision over advertising, it must be in possession of workable criteria for distinguishing warranted from unwarranted claims. The history of the Federal Trade Commission shows how difficult it is to find criteria that can be widely and effectively applied at an acceptable administrative cost. Can the regulators avoid "straining at gnats and swallowing camels"?

And will the regulators also control political advertising? How would you compare the truth-to-malarkey quotient of television commercials for business products with the truth-to-marlarkey quotient of commercials for politicians seeking elective office? Do you suppose that a government agency *could* regulate political advertising?

Would you like to ponder a really tough question? Try this one. Are laws regulating advertising consistent with the First Amendment to the Constitution? Congress shall make *no law* abridging freedom of speech or the press, says the Bill of Rights, and the Fourteenth Amendment extends that prohibition to the states. How then can advertisers be required by a government agency to withdraw claims that they cannot authenticate to the satisfaction of the agency? Some have argued that the First Amendment was only intended to protect political speech. Perhaps that is so. It is doubly ironic, then, that corporations have been criticized for running advertisements designed specifically to influence legislation, and that the

WHO SHOULD BE RESPONSIBLE FOR GATHERING INFORMATION?

Information gathering is an activity with opportunity costs. But since those costs vary for different people depending on their skills and interests as well as their situation, it makes sense to encourage those with a comparative advantage in information gathering to specialize in that activity. The argument in the text suggests that by completely abandoning *caveat emptor* we would leave no incentive for consumers to gather information even in situations where they have an enormous comparative advantage over sellers.

Consider the case of clothing. The seller will usually have a comparative advantage in acquiring information on such characteristics as durability, response of the material to alternative cleaning processes, and resistance to wrinkling. The buyer has a clear comparative advantage, however, in acquiring information on the suitability of the clothing for the buyer's intended uses and its compatibility with other wardrobe items. If the seller must guarantee the clothing against consumer dissatisfaction regardless of the source, the buyer will have less incentive to acquire information prior to purchase and the seller will be pressed to gather information in whose production he has a comparative *dis*advantage.

The argument in the text is for *shared responsibility*, not because this is a more equitable arrangement but because it's likely to be a more efficient arrangement, one that reduces total social costs. There is a close analogy with the legal principle of contributory negligence. A consumer who tries to pull matted grass from under his rotary lawnmower without shutting off the engine should not be allowed to recover damages from the manufacturer of the mower for the loss of his fingers. If even the most foolish behavior by users does not exempt the manufacturer from the payment of damages, eventually manufacturers will produce only foolproof lawnmowers—which are going to be far more expensive than present rotary mowers.

government has been asked to prohibit precisely that kind of advertising.[1]

But we only wanted to raise the questions. To answer them in a satisfactory way would obviously carry us much farther afield than we can

1. For a provocative examination of the First Amendment issues raised by government regulation, see the essay by R. H. Coase, "The Market for Goods and the Market for Ideas," *American Economic Review*, May 1974, pp. 384–91.

go in an introductory economics text. It may be helpful in weighing the problems of advertising and its regulation to remember, however, that *the scarcity of information* is the heart of the problem. It is the scarcity of information that makes advertising useful, that permits advertising to be misleading or deceptive, and that makes its regulation difficult. Any solution that would allow advertisers to disseminate only true and relevant information presupposes that someone knows exactly what is true in every case and relevant to every situation. That comes awfully close to assuming that, for at least someone, perhaps the Federal Trade Commission, information is not a scarce good.

Caveat Emptor and Caveat Venditor

In view of the fact that information is a good, but a *scarce* good, we would probably be wise not to surrender altogether the doctrine of *caveat emptor.* The consumer who knows that he must bear at least a portion of the cost associated with poor choices will have an incentive to use the information available to him and to acquire further information when it can be obtained at low cost. People who are not held responsible are, after all, tempted to behave accordingly—irresponsibly. And if we want to make the *seller* beware—*caveat venditor*—we should remember that wary consumers can be extremely effective in persuading sellers to accept responsibility. Even government regulation to protect the consumer can hardly be effective without the active and astute assistance of at least some consumers. Laws rarely enforce themselves; that's why we have police. Given the multiple dimensions of products, the variety of tastes people have, the ambiguities in the concept of quality, the sheer number of market transactions that occur each day, and the fact that even the best will in the world can be ineffective in the absence of adequate information—given all this, we probably have no alternative but to rely heavily on consumers themselves for consumer protection.

Once Over Lightly

An opportunity of which you're unaware is not a real opportunity. Information is therefore a valuable resource whose possession enables people to increase their wealth.

Information is a scarce good whose production usually entails costs. The efficient decision maker accumulates additional information only as long as the anticipated marginal benefit is greater than the marginal cost.

A great deal of economic activity is best understood as a response to the fact that information is a scarce good. The much abused "middleman" is in large part a specialist in information production. Just as the real estate broker enables prospective buyers and sellers to locate one another, so the typical retailer provides customers with knowledge of the goods sellers are offering and brings sellers into contact with those who want the sellers' offerings.

The common habit of viewing the middleman as an unproductive bandit on the highway of trade stems from the erroneous assumption that information is a free good.

Everyone who makes a decision in the absence of complete information about the future consequences of all available opportunities is a speculator. So everyone is a speculator.

People who think they know more than others about the relationship between present and future scarcities will want to buy in one time period for sale in the other. If they are correct, they gain from their superior insight and also transport goods through time from periods of lesser to periods of greater scarcity. If they're wrong in their predictions, they perversely move goods from periods of greater to periods of lesser scarcity and suffer the penalty of a personal loss on their transactions.

Because prices are summary indicators of scarcity, they are valuable information. Those whose buying and selling activities create prices are generating information that is useful to others.

Hedging is an attempt to reduce risk by selling a portion of the possible gain and possible loss from a course of action to someone else. Those who purchase risk enable others to reduce their risk.

The way in which a society assigns risk or allows people to buy and sell risk helps determine the manner in which resources will be allocated.

People who are protected against the consequences of mistakes will have less incentive to avoid mistakes. People who are required to bear the consequences of mistakes made by others will search for ways to prevent others from making mistakes.

QUESTIONS FOR DISCUSSION

1. If you found that you could reduce your bills for new clothing 10% by buying exclusively from catalogs, would you do it? Are there some articles of clothing you would be more willing to buy from a catalog than others? Why? What kinds of information does a clothing retailer supply?

2. Evaluate the following paragraph from a newspaper article:

    One sure way to save money on groceries is to eliminate the middleman by buying directly from farmers and other suppliers. That is what a group of socially motivated and normally hungry people have decided to do by forming a grocery cooperative.

3. Would you expect prices for goods of similar quality offered in garage sales to vary more than prices for goods offered in regular retail outlets? Why?

4. A man approaches you in a busy airport terminal, shows you a handsome wristwatch which he says is worth $135, and offers to let you have it for $25. Would you buy it? Would you be more willing to buy it if you had better information? What do you "know" when you buy a watch from an established local jeweler that you do not know in this situation?

5. Are you speculating when you buy fire insurance on your home? Could you save money by getting together with your friends to form an insurance cooperative, thereby eliminating the necessity of paying something to a middleman (the insurance company)? What kinds of useful information do insurance companies provide?

6. You find out in late December that you can probably make $1000 on a business deal if you can gain the good will of a client by getting him two tickets to the Super Bowl game. You manage to buy two well-located seats from a scalper for $250. Were you cheated by the scalper? Would you be glad that scalpers exist? Why do so many people dislike scalpers intensely?

7. In February 1972 the price of beef in grocery stores rose rapidly, contributing to an overall increase in the cost of groceries and pushing up the index of consumer prices at a time when the government had announced its determination to stop inflation. The president of the United States publicly blamed the middleman. Why?

8. Are you speculating when you buy a house? Are you hedging when you buy a house? Explain how the purchase of a house entails assuming additional risk of one kind and reducing risk of another kind.

9. Suppose that March corn futures were selling at $2.65 in July of the preceding year when the July cash price was $2.80. The cash price for March corn eventually turned out to be $2.50. Explain what probably happened to cause this sequence of prices and what its consequences were.

10. When a magazine sells you a three-year subscription, who is "selling short" and who is "buying long"? What risks does this entail and who bears them?

11. Does advertising provide information? Try to find examples of highly informative and extremely noninformative advertising. What effects does noninformative advertising have? Suppose that a product manufacturer's advertising does nothing but repeat the brand name in musical jingles to make consumers aware of the product's existence. Will the benefits to the manufacturer of this kind of advertising campaign depend in any way on the quality of the product?

12. How would you prefer to handle the issue of government regulation of advertising? Try to be clear about the criteria you would want used and the practical procedures for applying these criteria.

13. Prices for eyeglasses are significantly lower in states that permit them to be advertised than in states which prohibit such advertising. Why? Who do you think supports laws against advertising the prices of prescription drugs?

14. The Federal Trade Commission has held that words like *mink, diamond,* or *leopard* cannot be used in the advertising of synthetics, even when the advertising clearly states that the product is an imitation. What consequences would you predict?

15. Should *all* fraud be prohibited? Would you say that fraud has been prohibited when laws have been enacted against it but the laws are not enforced in a majority of cases? Is the prevention of fraud subject to diminishing marginal returns? Is there an "optimal amount" of fraud?

16. Do you think the rule *caveat venditor* should be substituted for *caveat emptor* in the case of garage sales? What consequences would you predict if this were done? If you would be opposed to such a substitution in the case of garage sales but would generally favor it for sales of new products, explain why you make the distinction.

17. Do you agree or disagree with the claim in the text that buyers of used residences are among the most frequently and severely defrauded purchasers of goods? Do the prices of used relative to new houses reflect this situation in any way? Do you have any ideas for reducing the amount of deception involved in the sale of used residences?

9

FRESH LEMONADE 5¢

FRESH
LEMONADE
5¢ A GLASS

THE SIZE OF FIRMS AND
THE QUESTION OF MONOPOLY

The term *administered prices* was first introduced to public discussion in the late 1930s in order to make a distinction between prices that were set by supply and demand and prices supposedly established by "administrative action." Since that time the term has been widely used, especially by critics of "big business." Some of these critics have accused professional economists of ignoring the dominant role of "administered prices" in the American economy, and of pretending that prices are all set by supply and demand. According to most of these critics, the American economy is today largely controlled by monopolists and oligopolists, who pay no attention to supply and demand, but instead use their market power to manipulate prices according to their own selfish and narrow interests.

It is impossible to evaluate any of these claims without first obtaining a clearer notion of what is meant by such terms as *administered prices* and *monopolist*. We have consciously steered around these issues as much as we could in the preceding chapters. The tactic that usually enabled us to do so was the implicit assumption that there were so many buyers and sellers in any market at which we were looking that none of them had any power to affect the price by his own individual action. It is now time to look more closely at issues that have been bypassed.

MONOPOLY: MARKET POWER OR LEGAL PRIVILEGE?

We begin with the word *monopoly,* the product of two Greek words meaning "sole seller." Are there any monopolists in that strict sense of the word? Try to think of something that is sold exclusively by one seller.

Telephone service is a favorite example. But is it an accurate example? There are many sellers of telephone service in the United States, as a matter of sometimes forgotten fact. Bell may have invented it, but neither the regional companies with his name nor their parent, American Telephone and Telegraph, are the only ones who sell it. Still, that may be beside the point. For any given buyer there is typically only one seller, since telephone companies enjoy exclusive selling privileges in particular areas. On the other hand, a buyer doesn't have to live in a given area; he can move to another franchise area if he prefers the product there. Back comes a justifiably impatient snort: "That's irrelevant." But it's not completely irrelevant. Moving your residence may be a prohibitively expensive way to shift your telephone patronage, and it's hard to imagine anyone actually moving just because he resents the local phone company. But that *is* a way of obtaining a substitute product. And by its absurdity, our example calls attention to the crux of the problem: the availability of substitutes.

Suppose we redefine the commodity sold by telephone companies and call it "communication services." There would be nothing intrinsically misleading about that. After all, that is why anyone wants a telephone: to obtain communication services. But if this is the product being sold, the telephone company is clearly *not* a monopolist, but rather a seller in competition with Western Union, the post office, various messenger and delivery services, loud shouting, fast running, and a national network for conversation among computers. The point of all this is simply that, if we define the commodity broadly enough, not a single commodity in the country is sold by a monopolist.

Now let's look at the other side of the coin. Suppose we define the commodity very narrowly. If telegrams are not the same thing as telephone calls, neither is a gallon of milk at the little store next door the same thing as a gallon of milk three blocks away at the supermarket. If you have no car, are rocking a screaming baby who won't stop until he gets his bottle, and have no one to leave the baby with, the milk three blocks away is a vividly different commodity from the milk at the store next door. Ask any parent of a small baby. Thus we are forced to conclude that, when the commodity is defined narrowly enough, every seller is a monopolist, since no two sellers will ever be offering completely identical products.

We are trying to convince you that the word *monopoly* is extraordinarily ambiguous. For everyone or no one is a sole seller depending on how we define the commodity being sold. Furthermore, there is no satisfactory way to decide in all cases just how broadly or narrowly the concept of a commodity ought to be defined. The Supreme Court of the United States has sometimes listened to persuasive arguments on both sides of a contested definition and then divided in its decision. Take cellophane, for example. Is it a separate commodity or should it be put in the category "flexible wrapping materials"? The answer given in cases such as this may determine whether a manufacturer is convicted under the antitrust laws.

Alternatives, Elasticity, and Market Power

So let's try another approach. What would be so bad about a sole seller if we found one? The telephone company hints at the answer when it advertises: "We may be the only phone company in town, but we try not to act like it." If we find a case where there really is a sole seller, the customer will have no alternatives. No one wants to be without alternatives. The poorer our alternatives, the weaker our position and the more easily we can be taken advantage of.

But we learned in chapter 2 that there are always some alternatives. There is a substitute for anything, even the services of the local telephone company. After all, no one "needs" a telephone. On the other hand, a phone is a valued convenience for many families and business firms. The concept from economics that suggests itself is elasticity of demand.

No seller is a monopolist in the strictest sense of the word because there is no such thing as a *perfectly* inelastic demand. No seller has any buyer totally over the barrel. On the other hand, very few sellers of anything face perfectly elastic demand curves. Anything less than complete elasticity means that the seller will retain some business when he raises his price, which in turn implies that the seller has at least a morsel of market power. Where is the line between a morsel and monopoly?

There is no clear line of demarcation unless we decide to draw one arbitrarily. Elasticities of demand reflect the availability of substitutes; other things remaining equal, the more good substitutes there are for anything, the more elastic will be the demand for it. Market power is thus seen to be a matter of degree, and to be inversely related to elasticity of demand. Defined in this way, the term *market power* has a meaning that we can talk about and use. But we have not yet found a useful definition for the word *monopoly*.

Privileges and Restrictions

Let's try another approach. In the early nineteenth century there was often no distinction made in the United States between a monopoly and a corporation. The reason was that corporations had always been created by special governmental acts. They received, whether from Crown and Parliament prior to the Revolution or from state and national legislatures afterward, special "patents," as they were called: official documents granting rights and privileges not available to others. Corporate charters were therefore called "grants of monopoly," since they gave to one party a power that was withheld from others. The East India Company was such a "monopoly," and the special privilege of selling tea in the Colonies, given to it in 1773, helped bring on the American Revolution.

Here is another and quite different meaning of monopoly, one related to acts of the state. If the state allows some to engage in an activity but prosecutes others for doing so, or if it taxes or restricts some sellers but not others, or if it grants protection or assistance to some while compelling others to make their own way unaided, the state is creating exclusive privileges. This meaning for the word *monopoly* has contemporary relevance as well as historical significance.

Many business organizations operate with monopoly grants of this kind. In fact, it is becoming increasingly difficult to find one that does not. In the name of all sorts of commendable-sounding goals—public safety, fair competition, stability, national security, efficiency—governments at all levels have imposed restrictions upon entry into various industries or

---

WHAT PERCENTAGE OF THE MARKET CONSTITUTES "MONOPOLY"?

In a very important legal decision handed down in 1945, the eminent jurist Learned Hand explored the question of whether the Aluminum Company of America was a monopoly. Long after the company's patents had expired, it was continuing to sell over 90% of the virgin aluminum marketed in the United States. Justice Hand held that 90% *was* enough to constitute monopoly, and added: "It is doubtful whether sixty or sixty-four per cent would be enough; and certainly thirty-three per cent is not."

Precise numerical criteria of this sort have a certain appeal. But any such criteria may be both too strong and too weak in their condemnation of market power. Three firms each controlling one-third of the total supply of virgin aluminum would almost certainly have substantial market power, whether or not we choose to apply the term *monopoly* to them singly or jointly. But one firm controlling 100% of the supply of uniformly shaped potato chips would not seem to have excessive market power merely by virtue of that fact.

trades. The beneficiaries of these restrictions always include the parties who can escape them. These parties will rarely agree that they enjoy a grant of monopoly power. But the effect of the restrictions nonetheless is to prevent some from competing who would otherwise do so.

We are not saying that restrictions on entry into a market are always to be condemned, or that the businesses which benefit necessarily behave badly afterward, or that society can never be better off as a consequence of restrictions on competition. We are only concerned that the restrictions be noted so that their consequences can be evaluated. They will often turn out to be different from what most people assume. We could, if we wished, use the word *monopolist* to describe any individual or organization operating with the advantage of special privileges granted by the government. The trouble is that most people no longer use the word in this way. By such a definition, the Postal Service is a monopolist, as are most public utilities, many liquor stores, morticians, and crop dusters; the American Medical Association, state bar associations, and labor unions; farmers with acreage allotments, licensed barbers, and trucking firms. The list is long indeed.

And so we are going to take the heroic step of dropping the word *monopoly* from our working vocabulary. Its meanings are too many and too vague. " 'When I use a word,' Humpty Dumpty said in a rather scornful tone, 'it means just what I choose it to mean—neither more nor less.' " *Monopoly* is a favorite word of contemporary Humpty Dumpties. And that's why we are not going to employ it. We shall try to use alternate terms that are more likely to communicate the precise situation we have in mind.

Price Takers and Price Searchers

Let's go back now to the phrase with which this chapter began: administered prices. Is there a distinction between administered prices and prices that are set by supply and demand?

It's a free country, as they say, and businesses are usually free to set their own prices. The United States Steel Corporation has substantial discretion when it prints up its price lists, and a wheat farmer from Kansas can feel quite safe from the threat of prosecution if he decides to offer his crop at $4.50 per bushel. But there is obviously an important difference that helps to explain why United States Steel keeps one eye on the government when deciding on its prices and wheat farmers do not. The difference, we shall nonetheless insist, is a difference of degree, not kind.

Take the case of the wheat farmer first. Suppose he consults the financial pages of his newspaper or tunes in for the noonday market reports and finds that number 2 ordinary hard Kansas City wheat opened at $3.25 per bushel. That news may disappoint or delight him, but there is almost

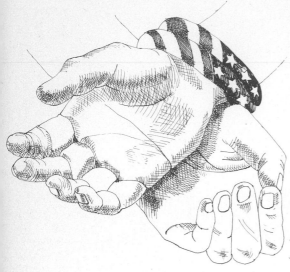

nothing he can do to change it. If he decides that the price is an excellent one, and sells his entire crop for immediate delivery, the market will feel scarcely a ripple. Even if he is one of the biggest wheat farmers in the state, he is still such a small part of the total number of those offering to buy or sell wheat that he cannot affect the price. The difference between what the closing price will be if he sells all of his crop, and what it will be if he sells only half of it, will not be as much as $\frac{1}{4}$¢.

Economists therefore call the wheat farmer a *price taker*. He cannot affect the price by his own actions. The price at the local grain elevator is determined by the actions of many buyers and sellers all over the country. If the farmer exercises his legal right to put a price tag on his wheat 2¢ higher than the market decrees, he will sell no wheat. And since he can sell all the wheat he has at the going price, he has no incentive to offer to sell any wheat at less than the going price. Price takers face perfectly elastic demand curves, or what for all practical purposes amount to perfectly elastic demand curves. The demand curves are horizontal at the going price.

Most businessmen are not in this position. They can raise their prices if they choose, without losing all their sales. And they cannot, as can the farmer, always sell everything they're capable of producing without lowering their prices. At higher prices they will sell less, at lower prices they will be able to sell more. They must choose a price or set of prices. Economists therefore call them *price searchers*. Torn between the desire for higher prices and the desire for larger sales, they must search out the price or set of prices most advantageous to them.

Price searchers include United States Steel, the trustees of a private university weighing a tuition increase, the proprietor of a local grocery store, and the little boy selling lemonade on a hot afternoon. There is a long tradition in economics of referring to all price searchers as monopolists. But this is a technical use of the word *monopolist* that is confusing to everyone except professional economists. Since the little boy selling lemonade does not face a perfectly elastic demand curve, he is not a price taker but a price searcher. It seems silly to anyone not dipped in the history of economics to call him a monopolist. So we shall not do it. The term *price searcher* captures the situation in which we're interested. Price searchers all have some market power. But it is a matter of degree, inversely related to the elasticity of the demand the seller faces.

Administered Prices Once Again

It would seem then that price searchers set their own prices, while price takers accept what the market sets. Is this the distinction between administered prices and those prices which are set by supply and demand? Not if one thinks about it carefully. *Every* seller in the last analysis sets his own price, though some sellers can do so with little or no real searching because they in effect accept the prevailing price (price takers). At the same time, price searchers are by no means free from the constraints imposed by supply and demand. United States Steel is a favorite target of those who decry administered prices, but whatever the faults or failings of the corporation, its decisions are surely conditioned by supply and demand. Supply depends on cost, and cost is taken into account by every price searcher. The supply capabilities and intentions of other steel producers will also be considered. Demand curves are never completely inelastic, so demand must be taken into account if the price searcher hopes to find what he is looking for, which is presumably the most profitable price to set. The current and prospective demands for such other products as aluminum, plywood, plastic, and cement are also relevant information to the searcher for a proper steel price, since any or all of these products may turn out to be substitutes for steel.

So we end up with no usable meaning for the term *administered prices,* either. *All* prices are administered and *all* prices are set by supply and demand. The term *administered prices* will consequently not be used in subsequent chapters. An examination of its history would reveal that it has more often been used as a polite "bad word" than as a concept to aid analysis or critical discussion. Economic problems are sufficiently complex without complicating them further by using terms that generate much heat and no light.

One other term appeared in the introductory paragraph: *oligopolist.* The dictionary suggests that an oligopolist is "one of a few sellers." The Big Three in automobiles and the major cigarette manufacturers are commonly cited as examples of oligopoly situations. But what about the daily newspapers in a large city? Or do they compete with other newspapers that can be trucked or flown in, with news magazines, billboards, television, the yellow pages? What is the commodity that allegedly has only a few sellers? Should it be broadly or narrowly defined? What about gasoline stations? Hardware stores? Automobile dealers? Shops that restring tennis rackets? How few is few? We don't have to multiply examples to discover that all the problems associated with defining a monopolist as a sole seller return to haunt us when we define an oligopolist as one of a few sellers.

There *is* a special market situation to which many economists have chosen to apply the term *oligopoly.* We'll examine and analyze that situation in chapter 11. But we shall not use the word *oligopoly,* on the grounds that, like administered prices and monopoly, it creates confusion rather than clarity and understanding.

Alternative Terms

The word *monopoly* means literally a sole seller. But we have seen that everyone is a monopolist or no one is a monopolist depending on how narrowly or how broadly we choose to define the good being sold. So we have decided to get along without the word.

The problems and issues with which we shall be concerned can be more effectively analyzed if we use the distinction between price takers and price searchers. A price searcher is *any seller facing a tilted or less than perfectly elastic demand curve.* There are as many degrees of being a price searcher as there are degrees of demand elasticity, ranging all the way to the limiting case of the price taker, who faces a perfectly elastic or horizontal demand curve.

We shall also want to talk about *sellers who enjoy special grants of privilege from the government.* We shall call them that rather than monopolists. And we shall discover that many sellers are very diligent indeed in securing such privileges, privileges that have the effect of limiting competition by hindering access of others to the market on equal terms.

THE MEASUREMENT AND SIGNIFICANCE OF SIZE

Many people who use the word "monopoly" are really employing it as a synonym for "very large business firm." But "big business"—sometimes spelled Big Business to convey a stronger implication of personified power —is as vague and ambiguous a term as monopoly, and little is gained by defining one in terms of the other. When does a corporation qualify as big? When is it *too* big? What are the best criteria for measuring size? And to what criteria should we look if we want to evaluate bigness in relation to social welfare?

The most widely used data on large business corporations are published annually by *Fortune* magazine, relying primarily on the companies' own financial statements (and hence excluding privately held companies, like Hallmark Cards, that don't publish financial statements). The data for 1973 appeared in the four monthly issues from May through August 1974, in sections on the 500 largest and the second 500 largest industrial corporations in the United States; the 50 largest nonindustrial corporations in six separate categories (commercial banking, life insurance, diversified finance, retailing, transportation, and utilities); and finally the 300 largest industrial corporations and the 50 largest commercial banks outside this country. Let's wander through these data to see what "big" might mean when applied to business corporations.[1]

Quickly now: which was the largest business corporation in the United States in 1973? You're wrong by *some* criterion no matter how you answered. Ranked by value of assets, American Telephone and Telegraph was first by a large margin, with assets of $67 billion. Its nearest rival was BankAmerica Corporation with assets of $49 billion. General Motors, the corporation many people assume to be the largest in the country, was in ninth place, after AT&T, four banks, two life insurance companies, and one other industrial corporation. GM had assets in 1973 of about $20.3 billion.

A Variety of Indicators

But assets aren't the only valid indicator of size. In fact, combining banks and life insurance companies with utilities and manufacturing firms makes the banks and life insurance companies seem more powerful and significant than they really are. A corporation like BankAmerica can hardly be considered insignificant or powerless when it holds $50 billion worth of assets. And Prudential, the largest life insurance company, with almost $35 billion in assets, is also a decidedly large corporation. But General Motors is probably far larger than either in the most meaningful sense. That is suggested, for example, by the fact that GM employed 810,920 people in 1973, more than any other company, while BankAmerica employed only 56,250 and Prudential only 58,554. General Motors had 14½ times as many employees as BankAmerica although BankAmerica had 2½ times as many assets. American Telephone and Telegraph, owner of all the Bell Systems, the nation's long-distance telephone lines, and Western Electric, a large manufacturing subsidiary, employed in 1973 almost as many people as GM: 798,934. The only industrial corporation in the United States with more assets than General Motors is Exxon, the old Standard Oil of New Jersey; but with about 25% more assets ($25 billion), Exxon had less than 17% as many employees as GM (137,000).

Are there better indicators of size than either total assets or total employees? What about total sales? By this criterion, too, General Motors comes home in first place. Its 1973 sales were $35.8 billion. Exxon was a poor second with sales of $25.7 billion, and Ford was third among industrial corporations with $23 billion. If utilities are included, AT&T's $23.5

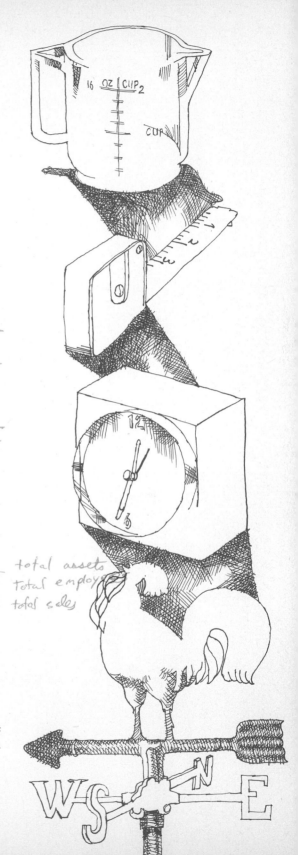

1. You might enjoy hunting through the data firsthand. *Fortune* does an excellent job of presenting the figures in a clear and interesting way. They can be found for any year in successive issues in the late spring and summer of the following year.

billion in operating revenues just noses Ford out. Banks and life insurance companies don't show up in rankings by sales because no one finds it very meaningful to measure the "sales" of financial corporations. What is it that a bank sells? Checking services, storage facilities, credit? The total fees that are paid to commercial banks for these services don't sum to an impressive amount in comparison with the total sales of firms owning far fewer assets.

The case of financial companies affords a particularly clear warning against assessing a firm's significance by its size and its size by an arbitrary criterion. The size of financial corporations is usually calculated by value of assets because that's the simplest way to do it. And within a particular industry this procedure does offer a rough measure of relative size and significance. Between industries, however, any criterion will be far less meaningful, as already shown in the case of General Motors and Bank-America. And even within a single industry like commercial banking, we might not want to assign the same power or significance to J. P. Morgan and Company and Manufacturers Hanover Corporation despite the fact that they own approximately the same amount of assets. For they have specialized in different aspects of commercial banking, as suggested by the Morgan Bank's considerably smaller number of employees (only 63% as many as Manufacturers Hanover). And any discussion of the size of financial corporations that ignores the fact that their assets are in large part the securities issued by other corporations is bound to go astray. It is at the very least illegitimate to *add* the assets of the largest financial and nonfinancial corporations, for that will involve substantial double counting.

Measuring and Evaluating Earnings

But let's go back to total sales. This is a common ranking criterion and also, for many financial commentators, a principal indicator of corporate health—at least among industrial corporations. But why should total sales be a significant measure at all? It isn't total revenue at which a firm aims but total revenue *minus total cost:* net revenue, or what *Fortune* calls net income and what most people just call profits (rather loosely—as we shall see in chapter 12). When we rank industrial corporations by their net income in 1973, Exxon beats out General Motors for first place, $2443 million to $2398 million. IBM was third with net income of $1575 million, although it was only eighth among industrial corporations in sales.

But to whom is net income significant? Ask yourself whether Avon Products' net income of $136 million in 1973 was really less than Chrysler's net income of $255 million. $136 million is less than $255 million in absolute terms, of course. But Chrysler earned its 88% larger income using assets worth more than $8\frac{1}{2}$ times as much as the assets owned by Avon.

Would we want to say that a firm earning $1000 annually on an investment of $1000 is making the same net income as a firm earning $1000 on an investment of $100,000? Not if we were thinking about investing in one of the firms. Profits or net income must be expressed as a percentage of something if they are to be used in meaningful comparisons. But as a percentage of what?

The owners of a corporation are interested in the return on their investment. As the representatives of the owners, corporation executives will also tend to look at the percentage return on investment as a good indicator of the profitability of their enterprise. But it's not at all easy to decide on the best way to measure the amount that has been invested in a firm. The value of assets would be one measure, on the assumption that the value of present assets represents the value of past investments. That won't always be the case, for assets can rise spectacularly or decline spectacularly in value as a result of factors having nothing to do with investment. Another measure is "stockholders' equity," defined by *Fortune* in its annual survey as the sum of capital stock, surplus, and retained earnings at the end of the company's fiscal year. The concept of stockholders' equity tries to get at the value of the corporation from the owners' point of view. But this base is also subject to variation with the changing fortunes of the company.

"Profit on Sales": A Misleading Indicator

The most commonly used base against which to measure profits or net income is, unfortunately, sales. That's unfortunate because total revenue from sales provides a largely meaningless base. Spokesmen for business probably use it so often because the data to calculate it are the data most easily available and because it is politically useful for making profits look small. Thus while General Motors earned 19.1% in 1973 as a percentage of stockholders' equity, it earned only 6.7% on its sales. Exxon, with 17.8% on stockholders' equity, earned 9.5% on sales. Quite apart from any intent to make profits look smaller, however, the habit of quoting the "margin on sales" (profit as a percentage of sales revenue) as an indicator of a firm's prosperity has two flaws. In the first place, it gives the impression that business decision makers *ought* to be looking at the margin on sales and trying to maximize it. But that's clearly absurd. If a firm can earn a larger net income from selling more, it surely won't refuse to do so on the grounds that this would lower its percentage return on sales. An extra dollar of net income from an extra dollar of sales is exactly as valuable as an extra dollar of net income from a dollar reduction in costs.

In the second place, any firm's net income as a percentage of sales will always be smaller, other things being equal, the farther the firm is from the beginning of the production process. If the wheat farmer, the miller, the baker, and the grocer all earn an identical net income from their contribution to the production of bread, they will all have different percentage returns on sales. Suppose they were all to net 5¢ from their contribution; the grocer's "margin on sales" would then be the smallest and the farmer's the largest, because the grocer's sales revenue includes that of the baker, the miller, and the farmer, while the farmer's includes only his own. But that's totally irrelevant to the question of which operation is most profitable.

We can check this out by looking at some of *Fortune's* data. The average level of net income for the ten largest retailing companies, when expressed as a percentage of stockholder's equity, was 11.1% in 1973. That's better than the earnings of the ten largest utilities (9.6% of stockholders' equity on average) and comparable with the earnings of the ten largest commercial banks (12.5% of equity).[1] But when the retailers' earnings are stated as a percentage of sales, they fall to only 2.3%. "Us? Big profits? Why, we only made 2.3¢ on the sales dollar. That's a very low rate of return." Not true. It's neither high nor low. It's meaningless. For the rate of return on sales is bound to be low for retailing companies simply because they stand at the end of the production chain. But a corporation near the beginning, like Newmont Mining, earned 24.2% on sales in 1973. That, too, is meaningless. The important fact is that Newmont Mining earned a very respectable 18.3% on equity.

Big Relative to What?

But after we have found meaningful criteria for measuring the size of a corporation, we must still take account of the fact that the bigness of Big Business is a relative matter. The mayor of San Francisco made the wire services when he testified before a House-Senate subcommittee in December 1974 and argued that the three largest supermarket chains should be broken up into smaller competitive units. They were so big, in his view, that they had the power to keep up the prices charged to consumers.

Safeway, A&P, and Kroger are all large corporations, if we judge by assets, sales, or number of employees. But only Safeway was big in 1973 if we look at net income. Kroger earned only 7.6% on stockholders' equity and A&P earned a dismal 2%. But is any one of them big in the sense that Mayor Alioto obviously had in mind? Big enough to control prices? If we're concerned about consumer prices, the relevant measure of size would be something like the percentage share of total grocery sales that the firm enjoys *in particular geographic areas.* And no grocery chain, not even

---

1. The retailers' average return rises above 12%, too, if the beleaguered Great Atlantic and Pacific Tea Company is removed from the list. A&P earned only 2% on equity.

the three largest chains combined, can meaningfully be said to dominate *any* metropolitan area. The important fact is that most grocery buyers have many good options, that they can shift their patronage among a number of competing stores, and that this ability restricts the power of all the stores to raise their prices. A very small, independent grocer who runs the only store in a town that is many miles from any neighboring town may well be able to charge higher prices than any Safeway store. The overall size of the Safeway chain is simply irrelevant.

Does "big business" control the economy? Would it do so if it were not subject to legal restraints? Is the power of big business increasing? What trends can we detect? What dangers can we discern? Is there anything that can and should be done to reduce or counter the power of big business? These questions are being widely asked today. They are not easy to answer, and you will find no definite answers in this book. In subsequent chapters we'll provide some ways of looking at the questions, some evidence that we hope you'll find helpful, and an historical look at government policies relating to big business and competition. But the entire discussion will be less confusing if we insist at the outset upon the distinction between *overall concentration* and *market concentration.*

Overall Concentration

When someone points out that in 1970 the 50 largest manufacturing corporations produced 24% of the total value added to the national product by manufacturing, he is talking about overall concentration. When he notes with alarm that in 1947 the 50 largest manufacturing corporations had produced only 17% of the value added, he is saying that overall concentration is a significant social indicator. There are other ways to measure overall concentration: in terms of total assets or total employees as well as value added, or by looking at the share of the largest 100, or 200, or 500. But all measures of overall concentration have this in common: They refer to the percentage of some national total that is controlled by the largest corporations in the country.

These figures are interesting, often dramatic, and possibly important. But it is not at all clear just what their importance is. Over 32% of the land area of the United States is under the control of the four largest states. So what? If you found that 75% of the wealth of the United States was owned by members of the ten largest religious or fraternal organizations in the country, would you feel threatened by this "concentration of power"? It is important that we ask: What special interests do these largest 50 (or 500) corporations have in common? What resources do they have for achieving their goals at the expense of the public interest? Are they able to collude effectively? Who exactly is placed at a disadvantage because the top 50

[handwritten margin note:] overall concentration — % some national total that is controlled by largest corporations in the country

Percentage Share of Largest Firms in Manufacturing						
Value Added by Manufacture:	1947	1954	1958	1963	1967	1970
Largest 50 firms	17%	23%	23%	25%	25%	24%
Largest 100 firms	23	30	30	33	33	33
Largest 150 firms	27	34	35	37	38	38
Largest 200 firms	30	37	38	42	42	43

Source: Statistical Abstract of the United States

manufacturing companies produce 24% rather than 17% of the value added? We are not trying to minimize the very real social challenges that concentrated power presents. We are rather suggesting that not all aggregates have equal significance.

Data on overall concentration in the American economy have been widely used over the last forty years by those who wished to argue that competition was no longer capable of ordering the economy. But overall concentration ratios do not seem to have any significant relation to competition. The concentration capable of affecting competition is market concentration.

Market Concentration

How many different sellers of a product are there in a given market? What percentage of total sales is controlled by the largest, or four largest, or eight largest firms in the market? What about the market power of buyers in a situation where there are only a few potential buyers for a product? Market power depends on alternatives: the poorer the alternatives available to buyers, the greater will be the market power of sellers. And the poorer the alternatives available to sellers, the greater will be the market power of buyers. Measures of market concentration might give us useful information for answering some of our questions about the social consequences of big business.

But *meaningful* measures of market concentration aren't easy to come by. What does it mean that the four largest automobile manufacturers control almost 100% of domestic passenger-automobile production, especially when foreign automobiles are also available in the market? What is the significance of very high concentration in tin can production when there

are so many good substitutes for cans? There are many newspapers in the United States; but most people must choose between two at best, unless they're willing to forego local news and accept the day before yesterday's sports results. Numerical measures of market concentration would be more meaningful if we knew what market was relevant to our purposes.

The Census Bureau has been providing data since the 1930s on what they call "concentration ratios." These ratios express the sales of the four largest firms in each industry as a percentage of the total sales of all firms in that industry. For the past twenty-five years, the Census of Manufactures has collected quite refined data on concentration ratios in manufacturing. What do all these data show? No clear trends toward either greater or less concentration—contrary, by the way, to the widely held popular

PERCENTAGE OF SHIPMENTS ACCOUNTED FOR BY LARGE MANUFACTURING FIRMS IN 1967				
Industry	Number of Firms in Industry	Value of Shipments (millions of dollars)	Percent of Total Shipped by	
			4 largest	8 largest
Blast furnaces and steel mills	200	$19,621	51%	69%
Motor vehicles	107	27,296	92	98
Pharmaceutical preparations	791	4,696	24	40
Petroleum refining	276	20,294	33	57
Bread, cake, and related products	3,445	5,102	26	38
Papermills	203	4,844	26	43
Meat packing plants	2,529	15,576	26	39
Toilet preparations	628	2,516	38	52
Tires and inner tubes	119	3,734	70	88
Bottled and canned soft drinks	3,057	3,173	13	20
Cigarettes	8	3,045	81	100
Farm machinery	1,526	4,300	44	56
Soap and detergents	599	2,593	70	78
Women's and misses' dresses	4,577	2,411	7	9
Shoes (non-rubber)	676	2,771	27	34
Canned fruits and vegetables	930	3,468	22	34
Wood household furniture	2,934	2,439	12	18
Radio and TV receiving sets	303	3,846	49	69
Cotton weaving mills	218	3,328	30	48

Source: Statistical Abstract of the United States

belief that concentration ratios have steadily and dramatically increased since the beginning of the century. But because of all the ambiguities illustrated in the preceding paragraph, we don't know how to interpret this relative stability over time of the concentration ratio, or whether it even shows stability in what we're actually trying to measure—namely, market power.

We long for hard numbers to counter all the vague assertions that float through public discussion of these issues. But the hardest of numbers will still require interpretation. In terms of value of assets, Exxon is the largest manufacturing corporation in the United States, about 25% larger than General Motors. But which is larger in a meaningful sense? Shall we abstract from foreign operations, or not? Shall we pay attention to relative shares of the national market—in which case GM is far larger than Exxon? How much importance should we assign to the fact that GM faces a smaller number of domestic competitors than Exxon, but that Exxon has a larger share of the world market than it does of the national market? What about political power? Is it true that the bigger they are, the more influence corporations have in Washington and in state capitals? Or is there stronger evidence for the opposite view, that larger corporations live in glass houses and are stoned for acts that smaller firms engage in with impunity?

More Questions

If it bothers you that we aren't able to provide definitive answers to these questions, get your mind off them by thinking about the following questions:

Do conglomerates (corporations formed by merging firms engaged in widely different activities) increase or decrease competition? Do conglomerates possibly pose a greater threat through their political power than their economic power?

Are larger firms more efficient than small firms? Do large firms have advantages over small firms deriving not from efficiency but from bargaining power? Do firms grow larger because they earn large net revenues, or do they earn large net revenues because they have grown large by other means?

Do the managers of large publicly held corporations represent self-perpetuating cliques? Can the shareholders of such a corporation exercise effective control over management? How and by whom are the managers of such corporations controlled?

Succeeding chapters will shed light on these questions even if they don't answer them to everyone's satisfaction. But there is one more question about the size of business firms that we want to examine before concluding this chapter. It's not the kind of question practical people are asking every day. It's a question that does have significance for policy-making, however, and for the evaluation of alternative economic systems.

ORGANIZATION AND COORDINATION: HIERARCHY AND MARKET

The basic question is this: If very large business firms are efficient economic organizations, would it be efficient to transform the entire economy into a single firm? The concept of the whole economy organized along the lines of a single firm, with all production decisions centrally planned and coordinated, has long been the vision of leading socialist thinkers. Their opponents have argued, on the other hand, that the decentralized coordination provided by many firms operating within a competitive market is more efficient and more compatible with personal freedom. But if this argument is valid, wouldn't very large firms also tend to create inefficiencies and reduce freedom? If the centralization of power characteristic of large firms is efficient, why should the further centralization called for by socialists be inefficient? And if the centralization of economic power for which socialists are calling is in fact incompatible with efficiency and freedom, why isn't the centralization of economic power achieved by large corporations also incompatible with efficiency and freedom?

Two Systems of Social Coordination

In order to get at this issue you must first recognize that there are two systems of coordination operating in the United States economy (and in every other economy, too). One is *the hierarchical system,* in which authority rests in the hands of a single superior and instructions are passed down from above. This is a characteristic feature of business firms, hospitals, churches, schools, and so-called voluntary organizations. It is what we usually mean when we use the word "organization": someone is in charge. Some *one* is ultimately in charge. There are almost always procedures for getting rid of that "one" and substituting another; so hierarchical organization doesn't imply dictatorship. But when one superior is replaced, another *one* will be installed.

This is the way a hierarchical system achieves its coordination. The activities of subordinates are under the control of a superior who must see to it that their activities mesh properly and promote the goals of the organization. These superiors may in turn be the subordinates of another superior with similar coordinative responsibilities. In a very small organization, there will be only one superior: a single-level hierarchy. But the power of any individual to coordinate effectively the activities of others is

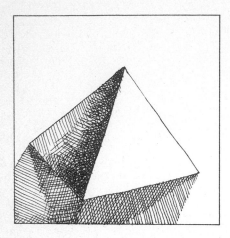

limited, so that as an organization grows it must establish a multiple-level hierarchy. With ten employees, each one answers directly to the boss. With one hundred employees, the boss can't keep track of what's going on; trying to control too much, she loses control of everything. So she creates ten foremen who will each coordinate the activities of ten production workers. She then coordinates the foremen. With two hundred employees and twenty foremen, she may find it necessary to create two divisions, appoint divisional managers to supervise ten foremen each, and confine herself to coordinating the work of the divisional managers.

Now it's a well known fact that the person way at the top doesn't really know what's going on down at the bottom, and that even when she knows she often cannot get her decisions translated into action at the operating level. This expresses a law of hierarchical organization that we can state in several ways:

Three Statements of a Single Principle

Organizational pyramids cannot be enlarged indefinitely without diminishing coordinative control.

Problems of coordination created by the fact that every individual has a limited capacity to supervise others set limits to the size to which an organization can grow without becoming inefficient.

The inevitable leakages that occur as information is transmitted up or down through a hierarchy limits the number of supervisory levels that an organization can establish and hence the size to which the organization can grow without losing efficiency.

This law of hierarchical organization doesn't say *how* large is too large. It will surely vary with the complexity and diversity of the tasks the organization has set for itself. One supervisor may be able to coordinate effectively the activities of one hundred ditchdiggers but only a dozen construction craftsmen. There probably have to be more levels of hierarchy per employee in the publication than in the circulation department of a newspaper. But the notion of the entire U.S. economy organized as a single firm staggers the imagination once its implications are grasped. Hierarchical organization simply cannot coordinate a set of activities that vast and complex. It must receive help from the other system of coordination, which we have been calling *the market system.*

Choosing between Systems

The difference between hierarchical and market coordination may be seen most clearly if we look at some alternative organizational possibilities for a single "firm." We'll take Broadbreadth University as our illustrative firm. We've chosen a university as our example because you're all somewhat familiar with its operations and to stress the fact that *all* organizations and not just business firms face the same kind of questions. Broadbreadth, as its name implies, does about everything a multiversity has ever attempted: it runs child care centers for its employees, operates a semi-professional sports program, maintains a heating and air-conditioning system,[1] manages hotels and restaurants for resident students, and dabbles in such diversified businesses as landscaping, psychological counseling, building repair, bookselling, and automobile parking. It also offers courses to students. We recited that list not to ridicule BU but to remind you how many very different tasks must be continually coordinated for BU to function effectively. Students and faculty who complain about the fact that BU has so many administrators and nonetheless runs so inefficiently should ponder the law of hierarchical organization. The variety and complexity of the tasks BU undertakes may require even more levels of administration than BU currently displays.

Alternatively, BU could spin off some of those tasks. It could get rid of *every single one of those mentioned*. "But a university has to have a bookstore, dormitories, cafeterias," says the small voice from the rear, "and it has to keep up its physical plant." That may be true. But no university has to manage those services itself. It could, if it chose, purchase them from outside contractors. And that is the essence of the market system as distinct from the hierarchical system.

BU could purchase the maintenance of its physical plant from a firm that specializes in such work, just as the owners of commercial buildings often do. It could sell its dormitories and grant a franchise to specialized firms to operate residential facilities on campus. It could lease its parking lots to the highest commercial bidder. It is no more required to have a building maintenance staff because it wants its buildings maintained than it's required to have a construction department because it occasionally wants new buildings erected. It is no more required to sell the books its students use than it is to publish them, no more required to sell the students food than to sell them clothing, no more required to own and operate parking lots than to own and operate an automobile repair shop.

We aren't saying that it is not in BU's interest to see that these services are provided. But they can usually be provided without BU's undertaking their production. Often they could be more efficiently provided by specialists with whom BU contracts; in some cases BU could just let off-campus enterprises provide the services to the individuals who want them.

---

1. Robert Hutchins once defined a university as "a series of separate schools and departments held together by a central heating system."

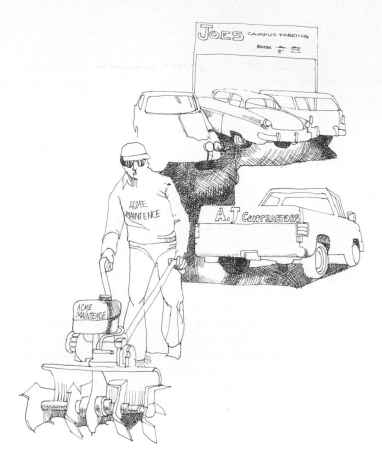

Hierarchy and Market: Advantages and Disadvantages

Hierarchical coordination and market coordination each have advantages. Members of the economics department use the services of a typist so regularly that they will usually find it more efficient to hire a permanent typist than to contract for the service each time they want some typing done. But their demand for champagne with which to entertain visiting dignitaries is so sporadic that they do not find it efficient to maintain a departmental winery. The athletic department probably owns its own baseball field but rents a golf course for varsity matches, both for reasons of efficiency. The physical education department will own the volleyballs it uses in Volleyball 110 but rent the horses for Equestrian Skills 204.

And now comes the question you've all been waiting for. Should BU dismiss its entire faculty and purchase from independent contractors the educational services it wants to provide? Let's weigh some of the advantages and disadvantages. BU could avoid carrying on its payroll a lot of

market

under-employed teachers. It could more easily adjust its payments to the quality of the instructional services provided. It could avoid many of the unpleasant and time-consuming tasks associated with administrative review of overall faculty performance. It could more easily and quickly get rid of any instructor who raised embarrassing questions or taught things that made the university's constituents unhappy. But we seem to have drifted already into disadvantages—which usually turn out to be advantages when seen from somebody's point of view.

The university would have to incur substantial costs in regularly contracting for the precise services it wants. It could be less certain of having in the area an adequate pool of competent personnel. It would have to arrange very specialized contracts in order to obtain the related services it wants from instructors: course planning, curriculum design, academic counseling, research and publications, book ordering for the library, even assistance in the evaluation of instructors.

When you think about it carefully, you realize that universities actually coordinate the activities of faculty members through a mixture of hierarchical and market organization. Most faculty are on the permanent payroll and hence members of a hierarchical system subject to supervisory control. But the tasks they are expected to perform are so varied, so difficult to specify in detail, and so dependent upon the exercise of imagination that faculty members are in large part treated as independent contractors. Just as the university could (and some do) contract with a building maintenance company to keep its physical facilities in "good order," so it contracts with faculty members to be "teachers and scholars." In each case, the detailed supervision characteristic of hierarchical coordination is rejected in favor of a contract that calls for "adequate performance," with the overall adequacy of performance subject to some minimum standards and to comprehensive review at contract time.

Back to the Original Question

Has all of this helped you better to understand the question with which we began? If the market system is as efficient as most economists say it is, why isn't all economic activity coordinated by the market through continuous contracting and exchange? Why are there firms or hierarchically coordinated organizations in the economy (what the economist D. H. Robertson aptly described as "islands of conscious power in this ocean of unconscious cooperation like lumps of butter coagulating in a pail of buttermilk")? If voluntary exchange plus the price system coordinates adequately, why do we have the "central planning" that every firm practices? And if central planning can coordinate adequately, why bother with a market system? The answer is that each system has advantages.

[handwritten margin note: expands net adv of net adv of alternative]

To turn the whole economy into a single firm by extending central planning or hierarchical coordination over the entire economy would strain the power of hierarchical coordination far beyond its breaking point. To try to get along with no firms, no hierarchical organizations, and nothing but continuous contracting and voluntary exchange would be to create vast new uncertainties and larger costs for decision makers. In short, the hierarchical system and the market system are both subject to diminishing returns or eventually increasing marginal costs. An efficient organization expands each system only as far as its net advantages are greater than the net advantages of the alternative system.

Efficient production of commodities and services is not the only criterion by which to judge a social system, of course. But we don't have to go any farther than that to see why every economic system displays a mixture of "socialism" (hierarchical coordination) and "capitalism" (market coordination).[1] The only real question for any society is the appropriate combination.

Once Over Lightly

The word *monopoly* means literally a sole seller. But whether any seller is the sole seller depends upon how narrowly or broadly we define the product. Under a sufficiently broad definition, there are innumerable sellers of every product. Under a sufficiently narrow definition, however, every seller's product differs from every other's and all sellers are monopolists. The word monopoly is therefore inherently ambiguous and will not be used in subsequent chapters.

The anti-social connotations of the word monopoly stem from the fact that the customers of a sole seller would have no alternatives and would therefore be at the mercy of the seller. Since there are in fact alternatives to every course of action and substitutes for every good, no seller ever has unlimited power over buyers. Market power is always a matter of degree.

The concept of price elasticity of demand provides a useful way of thinking and talking about the degree of market power. Demand elasticities, which can vary between zero and infinity, reflect the availability of substitutes. The more good alternatives buyers have, the more elastic are the demand curves sellers face and the more limited is the power of sellers to establish terms of sale strongly advantageous to themselves.

In the early years of the United States, a *monopoly* usually meant an organization to which the government had granted some exclusive privilege. The monopolist was thus the sole *legal* seller. While this meaning of

---

1. The quotation marks are important. For many people these would not be acceptable definitions of either socialism or capitalism.

the term is no longer common, it does have contemporary relevance since federal, state, and local governments are extensively involved in the granting of special privileges that reduce competition.

A useful distinction to make in trying to understand how prices are established is the distinction between *price takers* and *price searchers.* The price taker must accept the price decreed by the market. His buyers have such excellent substitutes for his product that any attempt to raise the price or otherwise shift the terms of sale in his own favor will leave the seller with no customers at all. The price searcher, on the other hand, can sell different quantities at different prices and must therefore search for the most advantageous price.

Competition tends to push production in price takers' markets to the point where price and marginal cost are equal. This equality indicates that resources are being allocated in such a way as to obtain the largest possible *value* of output.

The concept of *administered prices* is misleading inasmuch as almost all prices are "administered" by sellers—within the constraints imposed by their situation. The important question is whether competition imposes adequate constraints in particular circumstances.

The word *oligopoly* is at least as ambiguous as *monopoly;* whether there are just a few or very many sellers depends upon how we choose to define the product. And so the word oligopoly will also be discarded in favor of terms that are more precisely descriptive.

The absolute size of business firms is not a reliable indicator of their market power.

The profitability of a business firm over a lengthy period of time may be a meaningful indicator of market power. The most relevant measure of profitability is the ratio of a firm's net income to total investment in the firm.

Overall or aggregate concentration ratios for the economy do not measure the degree of competition in the economy. Concentration ratios must measure the degree to which a firm or group of firms dominates particular markets if they are to be used as an indicator of competition or market power.

Economies and organizations within any economy typically employ two systems of coordination. In the hierarchical system, coordination is achieved through instructions transmitted from a central authority. In the market system, there is no central authority and coordination is achieved through exchange. Hierarchical coordination becomes more difficult as the size of an organization increases, and it tends to break down into actual market coordination if pushed too far. Market coordination entails additional uncertainties and costs for decision makers and will usually yield to hierarchical coordination when the organization is small.

QUESTIONS FOR DISCUSSION

1. List some commodities or services that are sold by only one seller. Then list some of the close substitutes for these goods. How much market power is possessed by the sole sellers whom you listed?

2. List some industries, trades, or professions in which government (federal, state, or local) has imposed legal restrictions on entry. Who benefits from these restrictions? Who is harmed by them?

3. There are approximately 11,000 newspapers currently published in the United States, most of them weeklies. Only about 1800 newspapers publish daily. Of the dailies, there are only thirteen published in South Dakota. Only one of these is a morning newspaper. Is a citizen of South Dakota who wants a morning newspaper carrying state and local news therefore at the mercy of a monopolist?

4. Is the college you're attending a price searcher? How much freedom does it have in setting the tuition rate you will pay? Will your answer differ according to whether you are a freshman about to enroll or a senior about to begin your final year? Does your college enjoy any special grants of legal privilege?

5. Electric utilities are usually given exclusive franchises by the government to sell electricity in a particular area. Are they in competition with sellers of anything else? Do they compete for sales in any way with electric utility companies franchised to operate in other areas?

6. Can you think of any cases where price takers have persuaded the government to restrict entry by others into the markets where they sell?

7. Those who use the term "administered prices" do not include in this classification the prices charged by grocery stores. Nonetheless a grocer stamping prices on his products seems clearly to be "administering" his prices. Can you suggest criteria that would enable us to distinguish "administered" from "nonadministered" prices?

8. Why might it be important to have information on the size or relative size of business firms? What criterion of size is most meaningful for the purpose or purposes you've mentioned?

9. The number of steel mills in the United States is about the same as the number of paper mills. Does this imply that paper users and steel users have about the same number of alternative supply sources to choose from?

10. It has been argued that the development of the railroad in the middle of the nineteenth century substantially reduced the market power of many American manufacturing firms. Explain.

11. Manufacturers of prescription drugs have long been sensitive to the accusation that their industry isn't adequately competitive, and that its members earn huge profits by being able to charge excessive prices. As one way to counter the charge of excessive profits, the industry's trade association sometimes argues that profits should be stated as a percentage of sales rather than

investment. That argument runs counter to the one in the text. But comparing percentage returns on investment between industries will often yield absurd results, the drug industry maintains. It cites the example of a law firm that may earn $600,000 a year on a total investment of a few thousand dollars for office equipment and asks rhetorically: Should the law firm be charged with earning a 100,000% annual return on investment? What's wrong with this argument?

12. One often reads that there are "only three firms in the industry" (or five firms, or eight firms), and that this is too few for competition to be effective. How would you define an industry? Do firms in *different* industries (however defined) compete with one another? Are all the firms *within* a single industry (however defined) in competition with one another?

13. Do steel girders for bridge construction produced in Utah compete at all with girders produced in Maryland? (The phrase *at all* will usually make a statement true.) Can you think of ways in which wood products compete with steel girders?

14. Very large firms are sometimes said to have an advantage over smaller competitors because they can make for themselves more of the inputs they use. Smaller firms must purchase their inputs and consequently have higher costs of production. What's wrong with this argument?

15. How would you account for the fact that so many clothing stores are both in the business of selling clothing and the business of extending credit to consumers while so few pizza parlors have gotten into the consumer credit business?

10

PRICE SEARCHING

How does a price searcher find what he's looking for and what happens when he finds it? We're going to argue in this chapter that price searchers estimate marginal costs and marginal revenues and then try to set prices that will enable them to sell all those units of their product and only those units for which marginal revenue is greater than marginal cost. Does that sound complicated? It's just the logic of the process by which net revenue is maximized. But is it the procedure business firms actually employ? It sounds much too theoretical, like something an economist might dream up but which few real world sellers would even recognize.

$MR > MC$

MYTH AND LOGIC IN PRICE SETTING

It certainly is not the way most people assume that prices get set. The everyday explanation is a simple cost-plus-markup theory: Business firms calculate their unit costs and add on a percentage markup. A large number of price searchers will themselves describe their price setting practices in terms of the cost-plus-markup theory. Their testimony deserves to be taken seriously; but it isn't conclusive evidence. A lot of people cannot correctly describe a process in which they themselves regularly and successfully engage. Most people who ride bicycles, for example, don't know how they keep the bicycle balanced; and if asked to think about it they'll conclude that they keep the bicycle from tipping by leaning or shifting their weight slightly each time the bicycle inclines in one direction.[1] If that were the way they actually balanced, they wouldn't make it to the end of the block. In reality they balance by steering, not leaning; they turn the front wheel imperceptibly and allow centrifugal force to counter any tendency to tip. The fact that they don't know what they're doing doesn't keep them from doing it. Although they can only balance successfully by winding along a series of curves whose precise curvature will be inversely proportional to the square of the speed at which they're proceeding, many mathematical illiterates are skillful cyclists.

There are excellent reasons for doubting the cost-plus-markup theory. One is that it tells us nothing about the size of the markup. Why choose a 25% rather than a 50% markup? Why do different firms mark up their prices by different percentages? Why will the same firm vary its percentage markup at different times, on different products, and even when selling to different people? Why do sellers sometimes set their prices *below* their average unit cost?

Moreover, if firms can always mark up their prices proportionately when their costs rise, why don't they raise their prices *before* their costs rise? Are they satisfied with less net revenue when they could be earning more? That doesn't square with the perennial complaints of many price setters that they aren't making adequate profits. We all know, too, that firms are sometimes forced out of business by rising costs. That couldn't happen if every firm were able to mark up its prices to cover any increase in costs.

The popular cost-plus-markup theory is most inadequate. It just doesn't explain the phenomena with which we're all familiar. We'll return to the question of why so many people, including price searchers themselves, nonetheless hold to the theory. But we can't do that until we've gone through the economist's explanation of the price searching process.

Meet Mr. Artesian

Simple cases are best for illuminating basic principles. The complexities of actual experience can be introduced later. We shall be working for several chapters with the case of Mr. Artesian, who discovers in his front yard a flowing spring of mineral water. Many of his fellow townsmen believe that regular draughts of mineral water promote good health; they are willing to pay for the opportunity to drink from Artesian's spring.

---

1. Ask some of your friends what they do while riding a bicycle to keep it balanced. Chances are good that they will *all* give an incorrect answer unless they have been *told* how they do it.

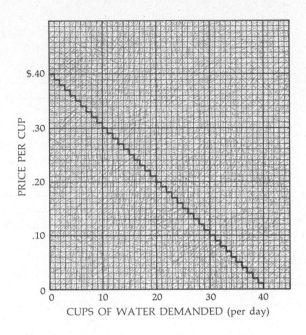

Figure 10A Demand curve for mineral water

We assume to begin with that Artesian knows precisely the community's demand for his water (an assumption we shall want to relax later). Here it is:

Price per Cup	Cups Demanded per Day
$.40	1
.39	2
.38	3
.37	4
. . .	. . .
.03	38
.02	39
.01	40
.00	40

The demand curve is graphed in figure 10A. The curve is stepped rather than smooth to enable us to read off clearly certain values we'll be interested in.

Artesian wants to sell the water and make as much money as possible. The spring produces more than 40 cups of water per day, but no more than that amount can be sold at any positive price. The remainder will be allowed to drain back into the ground. But before going into business Artesian must make an investment. He must acquire equipment to capture and dispense the water. While he *could* hire someone to do this, he estimates that the cost of hiring an attendant would be greater than the cost of renting an automated dispenser. (Don't forget that there would still be a cost for labor if Artesian tended the spring himself: the value of whatever Artesian was unable to do because he was tending the spring.)

So Artesian rents a coin-operated water dispenser for $200 per year plus 4¢ per cup dispensed. The company leasing the machine to him agrees to attach the machine, keep it serviced, provide the paper cups, and also provide an automatic change maker for customers. Artesian doesn't have to do anything except write a check at the first of each year and hold out his hand each day for the receipts, minus 4¢ per cup of water sold.

What price should Artesian set? Let's follow him as he searches for the price that maximizes his return. He sees at a glance that some prices are too high. At 35¢ per cup, for example, he would sell 6 cups, collect $2.10, surrender 24¢ to the dispenser company, and be left with $1.86 per day. He can do better by cutting his price and increasing his volume.

But he must not cut the price too far. At 10¢, for example, he would gross $3.10 and net $1.86 again. He can do better at some price in between.

If you were to examine the demand curve for a while, you would discover that Artesian's net receipts reach a maximum of $3.42 at a price of either 23¢ or 22¢, and decline gradually as he moves the price either up or down from those values. This is because the marginal revenue equals the marginal cost as sales move from 18 (at 23¢) to 19 (at 22¢).

What in the world does that mean? And what is *marginal revenue* anyway? If you are already familiar with the concept of marginal cost, you should have no trouble with marginal revenue. *Marginal revenue is the additional revenue* obtained from taking some action under consideration, in this case selling additional cups of water. But if additional cups can be sold only by lowering the price on *all* sales, marginal revenue will be less than price. To see exactly why, and in what way marginal revenue is related to demand, we're going to abandon Artesian momentarily in favor of a digression on marginal revenue.

The Meaning of Marginal Revenue

Suppose you are a price taker. The demand curve you face is then, by definition, perfectly elastic at the prevailing price. You can sell all you want to at the going price. The additional revenue you obtain, therefore, from selling one more unit, is always equal to the price per unit. *Marginal revenue equals price for all price takers.*

But suppose you are a price searcher. Your demand curve is now, by definition, less than perfectly elastic. You can sell additional units only by lowering the price. Each time you lower the price enough to sell one more unit, you gain an amount equal to the new price per unit *but you lose an amount equal to the price reduction multiplied by the number of units you could have sold at the higher price.* Gain something, lose something. Your marginal revenue is the first amount minus the second.

The following schedule will illustrate:

Price per Unit	Quantity Demanded	Total Revenue	Marginal Revenue
$6	0	0	
			5
5	1	5	
			3
4	2	8	
			1
3	3	9	
			−1
2	4	8	
			−3
1	5	5	

The logic is as simple as the arithmetic. The easiest way to grasp it is to do the calculations. When the price searcher reduces his price from $5 to $4, he sells one additional unit and so gains $4. But he loses $1 on the unit which he could have sold at $5 had he been willing to forego selling the second unit. $4 minus $1 is $3, the marginal revenue associated with the second unit. We place it *in between* the first and the second unit in the schedule to indicate that $3 is the additional revenue gained *by moving from* sales of 1 unit (at $5) to 2 units (at $4).

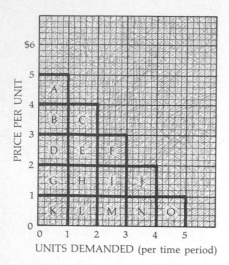

Figure 10B Step curve showing marginal revenue

Similarly, cutting the price from $3 to $2 brings him an additional $2 from the extra unit sold at this price, but loses him $1 on each of the 3 units he could have sold at the higher price. $2 minus $3 is a marginal revenue of minus $1.

If you're still awake (it's the tedium that gets you, not the difficulty), you can observe this phenomenon on a graph. Figure 10B shows the same schedule drawn as a step curve built of lettered blocks. Cut the price from $5 to $4, and you gain the blocks C, E, H, and L, but lose block A. The marginal revenue is therefore 3 blocks or $3.

Cut the price from $3 to $2, and you gain blocks J and N, but sacrifice D, E, and F. The marginal revenue is minus one block.

Marginal revenue is *less* than price for this price searcher because, to put it in common language, he "spoils his market" by expanding his sales. He can expand his sales only by reducing his price. And we're assuming here that the reduced price must be offered to *all* customers, not just to the customers he attracted through the lower price. (He cannot engage in price discrimination.)

There are questions at the end of the chapter for additional practice on marginal revenue. Be sure you understand what the concept means or you will be confused by arguments in this and succeeding chapters. Once again: marginal revenue will be *equal* to the price for all price takers. It will be *less* than the price for price searchers who cannot confine a price reduction to the customers gained by that reduction, but must also offer the reduced price to previous customers. (It would be *more* than the price only for sellers facing upward sloping demand curves. Upward sloping demand curves are barred from this book, but figuring out why marginal revenue would be higher than price in such a weird circumstance might be a useful logical exercise.)

Back to Artesian

Let's return to Artesian's search for the most profitable price. We asserted that a price of either 23¢ or 22¢ maximizes Artesian's net receipts. This can be proved by anyone willing to calculate the consequences of all possible prices. Net receipts grow gradually as the price is lowered from 40¢, reach a maximum at 23¢ or 22¢, then decline gradually through successively lower prices.

We also asserted, and thereby launched ourselves on a long digression, that marginal revenue equals marginal cost as sales move from 18 units per day to 19 units, and gave this equality as a reason for maintaining that net receipts were maximized between the prices of 23¢ and 22¢. Figure 10C shows the same information as figure 10A, and adds the marginal revenue curve derived from the demand curve on the assumption that the same price will be charged for each sale.

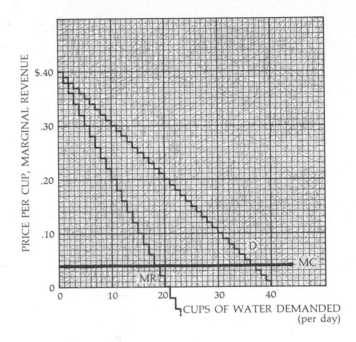

Figure 10C Marginal revenue

The marginal revenue is 40¢ from the 1st unit, 38¢ from the 2d unit, 4¢ for the 19th unit, zero for the 21st unit, becoming negative and progressively more negative after the 21st unit. You should be able to see now why net receipts are maximized at a price of either 23¢ or 22¢.

Marginal revenue is the addition to Artesian's receipts as his sales expand. Marginal cost is the addition to his costs as his sales expand. He maximizes his net receipts by selling *every* unit whose marginal revenue exceeds its marginal cost, and selling *no* unit whose marginal revenue is less than its marginal cost. Artesian stops selling, therefore, when marginal revenue equals marginal cost.

Don't allow yourself to be hypnotized by the *equality* between marginal revenue and marginal cost. Obsession with this equality has lost many a beginning economics student a good night's sleep. The equality is significant *only* inasmuch as it demonstrates the absence of an inequality! Think in terms of *inequalities* and you'll rest easily tonight.

Any unit that adds more to revenue (marginal revenue) than it adds to cost (marginal cost) is a profitable unit to sell, no matter whether it adds a lot or a little.

Suppose that Artesian is selling 17 units. Should he cut his price in order to sell 18? Is the 18th unit a profitable one to sell? The marginal cost is 4¢; the marginal revenue is 6¢. Sell it, and add 2¢ to the daily profit.

Suppose he is selling 20. Is this a profitable policy? He may well be making a profit, but the question is whether he is maximizing his profit. The marginal cost of the 20th unit is 4¢. The marginal revenue is 2¢. Do *not* sell it, and add 2¢ to the daily profit by avoiding a reduction of 2¢ from the daily profit. The principle we're using is common sense itself. Any action that yields more revenue than cost is a profitable action, and should be taken; any action that yields more cost than revenue is an unprofitable action, and should not be taken.

Doing Well and Doing Better

How does Artesian fare? Is he better off as a result of his newly discovered spring? He nets $3.42 per day as a consequence of his price searching, or $1248.30 per year. After writing the check for $200 to cover his remaining annual costs he is left with an increase of $1048.30 in his annual income. Artesian is happy.

But could he possibly fare still better? Artesian consults the demand curve (which he came to know miraculously, you recall) and notices that some cups could be sold at prices higher than 23¢. There is even one devotee of mineral water in the community who would pay 40¢ to obtain his daily draught. Moreover, water is going to waste in a frustrating fashion. There are people willing to pay more than the marginal cost of 4¢ who are excluded from purchasing by Artesian's price of 23¢. Wouldn't it be lovely, Artesian muses, if he could sell each cup for the maximum amount the customers are willing to pay. But how?

Artesian decides to place a sign by the fountain: "Please pay whatever the water is worth to you." He sets the machine to dispense a cup of water at 5¢ or more, in order to exclude those who would only be willing to pay the marginal cost or less. If the customers followed instructions, Artesian would sell 36 cups per day at prices ranging from 40¢ to 5¢, with these results:

Daily gross receipts	$ 8.10
Daily net receipts	6.66
Annual net receipts	2430.90
Annual net income	2230.90

There are stories about price searchers who try such tactics. A justice of the peace might ask each groom after the wedding to pay "whatever it's worth to you," hoping that the presence of the bride and the general awe of the occasion will prompt the groom into exuberant generosity. Charitable organizations sometimes conduct sales on this principle, hoping that philanthropic impulses will overcome each purchaser's understandable reluctance to reveal the full value of an item to him. And there exist complicated auction techniques that would accomplish a similar result. But Artesian's customers are not starry-eyed, they do not regard Artesian as a charitable enterprise, and Artesian himself is unwilling to incur the costs of running a complicated auction. So his sign is a dismal failure. His first day's receipts came to only $1.80. Each customer paid the minimum price of 5¢, and he sold 36 cups of water. Artesian's attempt to do better is summarized below. The shaded areas show his net income under each scheme.

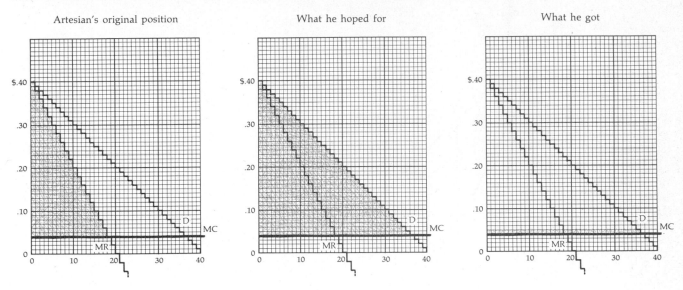

Artesian's original position   What he hoped for   What he got

CASE STUDIES IN PRICE SEARCHING

We'll come back to Artesian in chapter 11. The time has arrived to consider some applications of what we've learned.

The College as Price Searcher

College administrators often talk about the high costs of providing an education and the need for charitable contributions to make up that 50% or so of the cost not covered by tuition. Have you ever wondered why it is, then, that privately owned colleges grant tuition scholarships to needy students? If colleges are so poor that they must ask for charity, why do they simultaneously *dispense* charity? The answer is that they probably don't. Tuition scholarships for needy students may be a partially successful attempt to do what Artesian failed to do.

Figure 10D shows the demand for admission to Ivy College as estimated by the college administration. We shall assume that the marginal cost of enrolling another student is zero. That isn't accurate, but it's realistic enough for our purposes and it doesn't affect the logic of the argument in any event. Ivy College wants to find the tuition rate that will maximize its receipts.

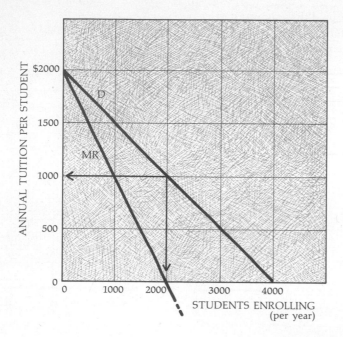

Figure 10D Demand curve of Ivy College students

If Ivy restricts itself to a uniform price for all, it will set the tuition at $1000 per year, enroll 2000 students (the enrollment at which marginal revenue equals marginal cost), and gross $2,000,000. But some students whom it would be profitable to enroll are excluded by this tuition rate; and some students who would have been willing to pay more are admitted for only $1000. Ivy's administrators wish they could charge each student what he's willing to pay. If they could find out the maximum each student or his parents would pay rather than be denied admission to Ivy, they could set the annual tuition at $2000 and then give scholarships (price rebates) to each student. The scholarship would equal the difference between $2000 and the maximum each student is willing to pay.

The problem is how to get information on willingness to pay. A student or his parents will not reveal the full value of Ivy to them if they know that candor will cause them to pay a higher price. But if willingness to pay is correlated with wealth, a solution lies at hand. Ivy announces that scholarships are available to needy students. Need must be established by filling out a statement on family wealth and income. Families will complete the forms in order to qualify for scholarship aid and will thereby provide the college with information it can use to discriminate. If the correlation were perfect between income and willingness to pay, and if families filled out the forms honestly, Ivy could discriminate with precision and increase its gross receipts to $4,000,000 (the area *under* the entire demand curve).

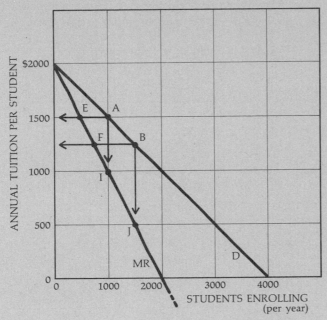

A QUICK WAY TO FIND THE
MARGINAL REVENUE CURVE

There happens to be a very simple way to construct the marginal revenue curve corresponding to any straight-line demand curve. By choosing straight-line demand curves for our illustrations we are *not* suggesting that most price-quantity relationships in the real world can be expressed by straight lines. But the use of straight lines will permit you to derive marginal revenue curves without a lot of useless effort and thus to get past the tedium and into the analysis. The marginal revenue curve always bisects a horizontal line drawn from the demand curve to the price axis. Thus for the demand curve drawn above, IJ is the marginal revenue corresponding to the segment AB of the demand curve. It was constructed by drawing horizontal lines to the price axis from points A and B, bisecting these to obtain points E and F, then drawing a straight line through points E and F and extending it through the area directly under the segment AB of the demand curve. The proof that this yields the marginal revenue curve corresponding to a particular demand curve can be constructed with the aid of very elementary geometry. But the proof won't help you understand the process of price searching. If you know a little geometry, amuse yourself by constructing the proof. If geometry has terrorized you since high school, forget the proof and just use the gimmick to draw the marginal revenue curves you want.

Marginal revenue would be equal to price despite the fact that Ivy is a price searcher. The two types of pricing are summarized below with the shaded areas again showing net income under each system.

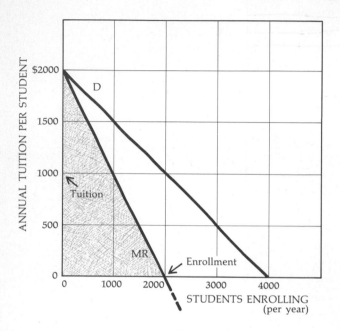 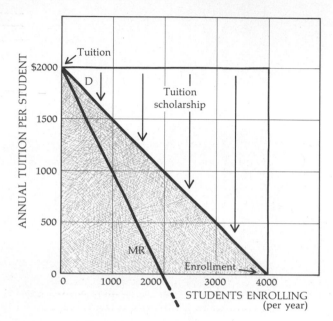

Be careful about condemning Ivy College! Notice some of the consequences of this discriminatory pricing policy. First of all, Ivy earns more income. If you approve of Ivy, why begrudge it a larger income from tuition? Is it better for philanthropists and taxpayers to cover Ivy's annual deficit than for students (or their parents) to do so through being charged the maximum they're willing to pay? Notice, too, that under a perfectly discriminating system of tuition charges, 2000 students who would otherwise be turned away are enabled to enroll at Ivy. They aren't complaining.

Setting Movie Prices

If we assume, as seems reasonable, that price searchers would like to charge each customer the most he will pay, we should expect to observe many instances of price discrimination in our society.

The local movie theater charges $4 for adults, $1.50 for students, and 50¢ for children under 12. Is this because the theater owner likes kids or because it costs him less to show a movie to kids? It is more probable that he is acting like a discriminating price searcher.

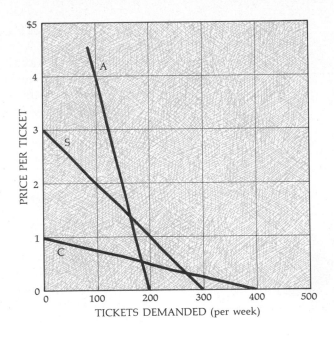

Figure 10E Demand curve for theater tickets

Let the demand curves shown in figure 10E represent the demands of adults, students, and children for tickets to the local movie theater. Children won't come at all if the price is above $1, but will come in droves as the price goes down below $1. Students start attending at prices below $3. Adults attend movies less, but will pay higher prices to do so.

Let the marginal cost of another patron be zero for the theater owner. (Why is this fairly realistic in light of what you know about sunk costs and marginal costs?) If the owner sets one price for everyone, his profit-maximizing price is $2. (The proof is a bit complicated. You could figure it out on the basis of what you know; but the marginal benefit from your efforts is likely to be less than the marginal cost of finding the solution.) He will sell 100 tickets to students and 150 to adults for a total weekly revenue of $500.

By discriminating among these three classes of customers, however, he can do better. He should charge $4 for adults, $1.50 for students, and 50¢ for children and raise his weekly receipts to $725. With this policy he sets marginal revenue equal to marginal cost *for each separate class of potential customers.* In effect, he is cutting the price to gain *additional* customers *without* offering equal price reductions to *all* customers. He is bringing his marginal-revenue curve closer to his demand curve. As a result, fewer adults will go to the movies. But maybe they'll be happier with the teenagers and the little kids out of the house more often. A total evaluation of

the discriminatory pricing policy poses a much more complex problem, of course.

Perhaps you've noticed in passing an important prerequisite for successful discrimination of the kind we've been describing. It must not be easy for low-price customers to resell to high-price customers, or for high-price customers to disguise themselves as low-price ones. And that explains why discrimination is usually observed only in situations where the seller has some effective way of identifying purchasers, and where he can make sure that the consumer of his product is the original purchaser.

Another Type of Price Discrimination

Before leaving the topic of the price searcher as a discriminating seller, we want to consider one more possibility. Additional sales are obtained through reduced prices not only by attracting new customers through reduced prices but also by inducing present customers to purchase more.

Horty Kulcher just built a new house and he wants to landscape his lot. He loves roses. But his demand curve is downward sloping. Let us assume he has this schedule:

Price per Bush	Quantity Demanded
$8	1
5	2
3	3
2	4
1	5

Assume that the owner of the garden shop pays $1.25 to obtain rose bushes from his nursery. He would like to sell 4 to Horty. On the other hand, he can only sell 4 if he offers Horty a price of $2, and it's obvious that $2 is not a profit-maximizing price for his transactions with Horty. Marginal revenue falls from $8 to $2 to *minus* $1 as the owner adjusts his price to sell alternatively 1, 2, and 3 bushes. On any sale beyond 2, marginal cost exceeds marginal revenue. Will the owner therefore settle on a price to Horty of $5?

Not if he knows Horty's demand and he's searching for the profit-maximizing set of prices! A better option is the following price schedule:

$ 8 for 1
13 for 2
16 for 3
18 for 4

In constructing this schedule we assumed that since Horty would pay $8 for the first bush and $5 for the second, he would pay $13 for two. That isn't the same as $6.50 per bush, because the price is conditional on Horty's buying two.

It would now be consistent with Horty's demand schedule for him to purchase 4 rose bushes even though the price is in a sense $4.50 a bush. Horty is caught by the fact that he can only obtain a price that low *if* he buys at least 4 rose bushes. The garden-shop owner is thereby attempting to extract the full value to Horty of each successive rose bush. In other words, he is trying to keep his marginal revenue from falling below the price.

Pity Horty if you wish. On the other hand, you might remember that Horty is paying for nothing he does not want, and that his front yard will be more beautiful as a result of the garden shop owner's "exploitation."

So how does a price searcher find what he's looking for? By (1) estimating his marginal cost and marginal revenue, (2) determining the level of output that will enable him to sell all those units of output and only those units for which marginal revenue is greater than marginal cost, and then (3) setting his price or prices so that he can just manage to sell the output produced. That sounds complicated; and it is. The logic is simple enough. But the estimates of marginal cost and especially the estimates of demand and marginal revenue are hard to make accurately. That's why price searchers are called *searchers.* And why they could sometimes be called *price gropers.*

The complexity and uncertainty of the price searcher's task helps explain the popularity of the cost-plus-markup theory. By running through a series of graphical examples, we can show the logical inadequacy of that theory and why so many people, including price searchers themselves, nonetheless hold to it.

Price groper

Markup Pricing Reconsidered

Figure 10F shows two different demand curves. The curves are drawn in such a way that the marginal revenue curves corresponding to each of the demand curves cut down across the marginal cost curve at an output of 200. (The relevant portion of each marginal revenue curve has been drawn in.) But the price will be set at $35 if the demand is D_1 and at $20 if it's D_2. Those are very different percentage markups. Price searchers select a percentage markup on the basis of the demand they face, not on the basis of the number of children they must support or their subjective estimate of what would be fair and reasonable. The more elastic the demand, the less they will be able to mark up the price over marginal cost.[1] Remember, though, that marginal cost must include such opportunity costs as the value of the price searcher's time, and not just the wholesale price of the goods.

1. The coefficients of elasticity at an output of 200 for D_1 and D_2 are 1.75 and 4 respectively.

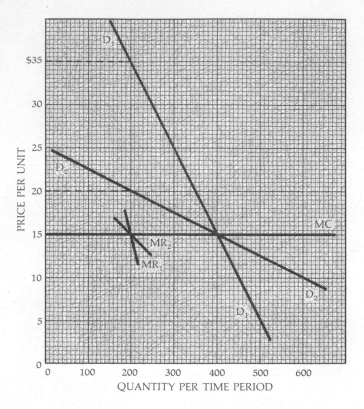

Figure 10F Demand
elasticity and markup

This is consistent with observed differences in percentage markup policies among different industries. Markups are traditionally low in grocery
retailing, for example. That's because supermarkets generally confront
quite elastic demand curves for most of the products they sell. The demand
curves are elastic because there are usually good substitutes for the products of any particular supermarket and because food is a large enough
component of most people's budgets to make them highly sensitive to
price differences. The markups are larger at convenience stores than at
supermarkets because the patrons of convenience stores typically don't
have good substitutes readily available and also are spending relatively
little at these stores. Finding the cheapest supermarket could save a shopper a considerable sum over a year or two; and that gives shoppers an
inducement to search and compare. Finding the cheapest price for a
single loaf of bread when supper is waiting on the table may well involve
more cost in time and effort than it's worth.

This way of interpreting the behavior of price searchers can even be
used to explain markup policies in the college book store, including the
different percentage markups usually employed for textbooks, typing

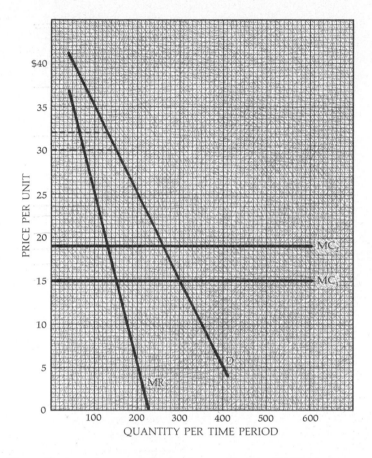

Figure 10G Rising costs and rising prices

paper, greeting cards, and class rings. The seller's estimate of demand elasticity is a key factor in price setting.

So the analysis of this chapter is superior to a simple cost-plus-markup theory of pricing in that it explains why markups vary so widely. But isn't it still true that a business firm, once it has determined the appropriate percentage markup, just adds that amount to the cost rather than searching (or groping) in the way we've described? Let's see.

What to Do When Costs Change

Figure 10G shows the demand curve for the product of a particular firm, the original marginal cost (MC_1), and a subsequent higher marginal cost (MC_2). The marginal revenue curve, drawn by using the gimmick described on page 231 (check its construction for yourself), intersects MC_1 at an output of 150: so the firm wants to produce and sell all units up to

the 150th but none beyond that. It therefore sets its price at $30. (Be sure
you use the graph to trace out each step in the argument). That's a 100%
markup over the $15 marginal cost.

Now let marginal cost rise to $19, as shown by MC_2. The firm will now
find its most profitable output to be 130, and will want to raise its price to
$32. It cannot persist in the 100% markup policy or even pass along all of
the $4 increase in cost. At least it cannot do either if it wants to earn as
much net revenue as possible. The increase in cost will lower the firm's
net revenue from $2250 to $1690. If it tries to pass along the entire $4 cost
increase by raising the price to $34, net revenue will fall further to $1650.
And if it persists in a 100% markup policy and raises the price to $38, net
revenue will be only $1330.

With marginal cost at $19:

Price	Quantity Demanded	Total Revenue	Total Cost	Net Revenue
$32	130	$4160	$2470	$1690
34	110	3740	2090	1650
38	70	2660	1330	1330

Figure 10H shows the same cost increase as in 10G and a simultaneous
increase in demand from D_1 to D_2. Given this *combination* of a demand
increase and a cost increase, the firm would be able to pass along the full
cost increase. The best price to set would become $34. That's the price at
which the firm can sell all those units and only those units for which marginal revenue is greater than marginal cost. Sometimes demand increases
and cost increases will occur together, because the same set of forces is
responsible for both. For example, in a period of general inflation, when
all costs and prices are tending to rise, a price searcher may just assume,
as a first approximation, that the demand for his product is going up at
the same rate as his costs are increasing. And so he will automatically
pass along cost increases in the form of higher prices. But for an astute
price searcher that's nothing more than a rule of thumb with which to
begin the process of searching for the most profitable price.

The cost-plus-markup theory is in general a rule of thumb for price
searchers. And this probably explains its popularity as an explanation of
the forces determining prices. Searching has to begin somewhere. Why
not begin with the assumption that the future will be like the past and that
procedures which have yielded good results in the past will continue to do
so? And so price searchers *will* try to increase their prices roughly in proportion to any cost increases they experience—but only until they discover
that they're making a mistake. The marginal cost–marginal revenue analysis of this chapter explains how price searchers recognize mistakes and
what the criteria are by which they move from rules of thumb and first
approximations toward the most profitable pricing policy.

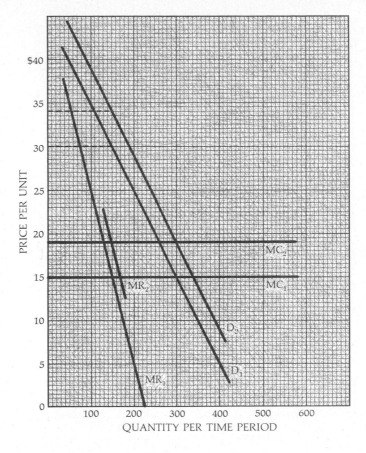

Figure 10H Rising costs, rising demand, and rising prices

Pricing for the Distant Future

The price searcher's task becomes even more uncertain and difficult when he tries to take account of what will happen over longer periods of time. Consider the case of a firm marketing a new product for which the demand is shown by D_1 in figure 10I. Production costs are shown by MC. The best price to set is $70 with output at 60—where marginal revenue equals marginal cost.

But this is a new product. Perhaps, if it were well promoted, the demand could be increased substantially—to D_2, let us say. And one of the better ways to promote a new product is to offer it at an attractive price, possibly even at a price below marginal cost for awhile. Suppose that the firm introduced its product at a price of $40 in order to sell 120. This would obviously not be the price that maximized returns in the short run; marginal revenue actually becomes negative as the firm lowers its price by enough to sell more than 100 units. But $40 might still be a good price to set if that

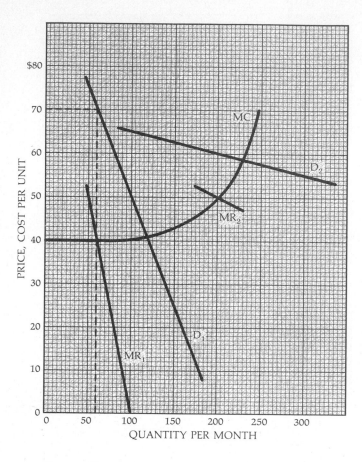

Figure 10I Price searching for a new product

price helped win general acceptance for the product, so that the demand curve after a year or so had shifted to D_2. Then the firm could raise its price and start cashing in on its promotional pricing policy. The best price to set then would be $60, with output at 200 units.

But let's push the analysis farther. MC has been drawn in such a way as to indicate that the firm is not well equipped to produce much more than 100 units per month. As it tries to increase the rate of monthly output beyond that point, it encounters rapidly rising production costs. This is inconsistent with the common belief that business firms can always lower their costs by producing in larger volume.

But that belief is mistaken. If the firm has a fixed amount of plant and machinery with which to manufacture the product, it will inevitably encounter rising marginal costs whenever the rate of production approaches "full capacity." It may have to pay overtime wages and shift differentials. It may have to skimp on maintenance procedures. It may have to pay premium prices to suppliers and sub-contractors to avoid production bottlenecks. It may have to pull resources away from other tasks for which they are better suited in order to concentrate effort on expanding output of this one product.

As the curve is drawn, the firm has no *precise* "full capacity." Marginal cost starts to rise at around 90 units per month, but more than that amount *can* be produced. At 200 units per month marginal cost is 25% higher than at 90 units and rising steeply; but additional output can still be obtained if the firm is willing to incur the costs. That's why published figures will sometimes state that a firm or an industry is operating at more than 100% of capacity. Strictly speaking, that's impossible. But if capacity is defined as that rate of output at which marginal costs begin to increase or at which they are no more than a certain percentage above their lowest level, then production at more than 100% of capacity is clearly possible. Keep in mind this ambiguity in the concept of "capacity" whenever you read figures purporting to give the rate at which an industry or even the entire manufacturing sector of the economy is operating. Such figures are always averages of estimates based on vague criteria.

capacity

Planning for Production

Producers *choose* the structure of their marginal costs—subject to error, of course—when they decide to construct a plant of a given size or to purchase equipment of a particular type and amount. How do they make that decision? In part by estimating the future demand for their product. If Henry Ford had expected to sell only a dozen cars a year, he would never have built an automobile assembly line. Not only would the initial cost have been too high for subsequent sales to cover; even the marginal cost once the assembly line was in operation would have been absurdly high for an annual production rate of twelve cars.

MC_2 in figure 10J represents marginal cost under a different set of decisions respecting plant and equipment. Does MC_2 represent lower costs than MC_1? That will depend among other things on the demand. If demand is D_1, the firm can produce any level of *desired* output at lower marginal costs with the plant and equipment yielding the marginal costs of MC_1. If MC_1 also entails a lower initial cost, as it undoubtedly will if it represents a smaller plant and less equipment, MC_1 is the structure of costs that ought to be chosen. But if demand is expected to be D_2, MC_2 may be the cost structure to choose. We cannot be certain from the data given on the graph that MC_2 is superior to MC_1 because these data don't reveal the costs of constructing the alternative plants, costs that are marginal and not sunk costs at the time the decision is being weighed. What the example illustrates is the kind of long term considerations regarding demand, costs, and their interrelations that must be taken into account by successful price searchers.

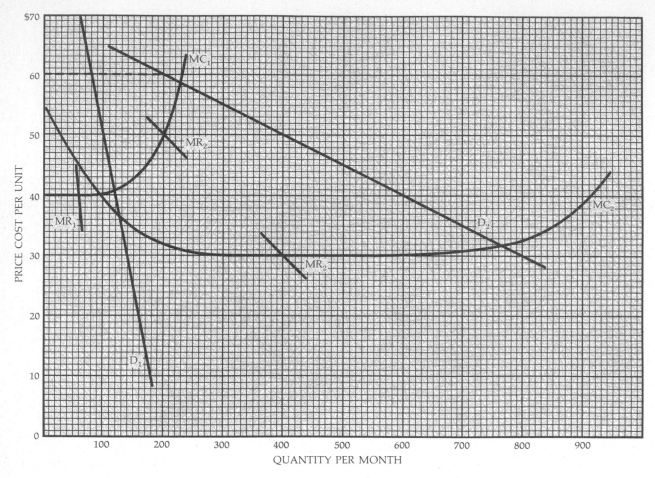

Figure 10J Choosing prices and choosing costs

SELLING BELOW COST?

Do you agree with the following paragraph?

"In order to preserve our competitive economic system, we need laws that prohibit unfair practices such as sales below cost. Large firms can often afford to sell products below cost until their rivals are driven out of business. If they are not restrained by law, we could easily wind up with an economy dominated by just a few huge corporations."

Most Americans apparently accept this argument. For our laws, at the federal, state, and local level, abound with provisions designed to prevent or inhibit price cutting. Many states have resale price-maintenance laws that not only permit but assist manufacturers and retailers jointly to establish minimum prices and to prosecute retailers who sell below these prices.[1] Many states have statutes prohibiting sales below cost that usually go by some such name as Unfair Practices Act. And regulatory commissions, ostensibly created to hold down the prices that may be charged by public utilities, often wind up enforcing minimum rather than maximum rates. This is true, for example, of the grandfather of all such commissions in the United States, the Interstate Commerce Commission (created by Congress in 1887).

It's fairly obvious why some business firms would approve that kind of legislation: they want protection against competition. But why do consumers and the general public go along? The public seems to have accepted the argument that price cutting can create "monopolies" by driving competitors out of business. And monopolies, of course, are Bad Things.

The paragraph with which this section began states the essential argument. How valid is it? Is it possible to construct a defensible case for laws that prohibit "sales below cost"? A lot of questions should immediately arise in your mind.

Determining the Relevant Cost

What is the cost below which prices should not be set? Does any one actually sell below cost? Why would anyone interested in increasing his wealth ever want to sell below cost?

Case: Lemuel Mudge, proprietor of the Thrifty Super Market, orders 1000 pounds of ripe bananas. He gets them for 5¢ a pound because the produce distributor is eager to move them before they become too ripe. Mudge advertises a weekend special on bananas: 10¢ a pound. But Monday morning finds him still with 500 pounds of bananas, now beginning to turn brown. How low can Mudge cut his price without selling below cost? The answer is *not* 5¢ a pound. That is sunk cost and hence no cost at all. If Mudge will have to pay someone to haul the unsold bananas away on Tuesday morning, his cost on Monday could be less than zero. In that case it might be to his advantage to give bananas away free. If a zero price is to his advantage, how can it be "below cost"? (By the way, did Mudge *buy* the bananas below cost?)

Or suppose Mudge bought a truckload of coffee: 1000 one-pound cans for $300. It was an unknown brand on which a local distributor offered him an attractive price. But it turns out that his customers aren't interested. He cuts the price down to 3 pounds for $1, but still can't move it success-

1. As this chapter was being written, Congress seemed on its way toward repeal of the 1937 law legalizing resale price-maintenance agreements (or "Fair Trade" practices, as their supporters have cleverly named them).

fully. Four weeks after his purchase he still has 987 cans of coffee cluttering up his shelves and storage room. If he now cuts the price below 30¢, is he selling below cost? He is not. He has no intention of replacing the cans he sells, so that each sale is that many additional cents in the till and one less can in the way. The relevant cost of a pound of coffee could well be zero. The relevant cost is, of course, the marginal cost.

Let's try a different kind of example and then return to Lemuel Mudge. It might make sense to estimate the cost of producing a steer, but does it make any sense to estimate separately the cost of producing hindquarters and forequarters? Should the price of steaks, which come from the hindquarter of a beef carcass, cover the cost of producing the hindquarter, leaving it to pot-roast prices to cover the cost of the forequarters from which they derive? The question is nonsensical. Unless it is possible to produce hindquarters separately from forequarters, one cannot speak of the cost of producing one and the cost of producing the other. Hindquarters and forequarters, or steaks and pot roasts, are joint products with joint costs. There is no way to determine the specific costs of joint products or to allocate joint costs "correctly."[1]

Back to Lemuel Mudge. Can we legitimately segregate the costs of each item sold in his grocery store? Think of his frozen-food items, for example. How much of the cost of owning and operating the freezer case should be allocated to vegetables, how much to Chinese dinners, and how much to orange juice? It's true that he could not carry frozen cauliflower without a freezer case. But if he finds it profitable to own and operate a freezer case just for the sake of the frozen juices he can sell, and if he then has some extra room in which he decides to display boxes of frozen cauliflower, it might make sense for him to assign *none* of the freezer cost to the cauliflower.

A successful businessman does not concern himself with the questions of cost allocation that have no relevance to decision making. He knows that production—and a merchant is a producer just as certainly as is a manufacturer—is usually a process with joint products and joint costs. The businessman is interested in the additional costs associated with a decision and the additional revenue to be expected from it, not in such meaningless problems as the allocation of joint costs to particular items for sale. If there is room for a magazine rack near the check-out counter, the question is: How much will its installation *add* to total costs and how much will it *add* to total revenue? If the latter is larger, the rack makes sense; and the

1. If there are techniques for growing steers with relatively larger hindquarters than forequarters, or vice versa, then it may be possible partially to distinguish the costs under appropriate circumstances. Hindquarters can be enlarged at the cost of smaller forequarters, and livestock breeders and feeders do calculate such costs. More advanced economic analysis provides techniques for making these calculations.

magazines sold need not have a price that covers utilities, rent, depreciation on cash registers, *or even the wholesale prices of the magazines.*

Mark well the italicized phrase. It may be profitable to sell a magazine for 5¢ even if it costs 10¢ to obtain it from the distributor. Why? Because the magazine display may bring in new customers who add to net revenue through their purchases of other items. Lemuel Mudge is not interested in his net revenue on any one item he sells but in the difference between total revenue and total costs. Retailers have often carried cigarettes *not* for the sake of the profit they make on the sale of cigarettes but for the sake of the profitable sales of other items that are made possible by carrying cigarettes. Similarly, hardware stores that sell odd-lot bolts, screws, and nuts lose money on each sale but expect to make up the loss through the goodwill they thereby create.

There would be little point in stressing all this were it not for the popular mythology of "selling below cost." Our argument suggests that many allegations of sales below cost are based on an arbitrary assignment of sunk costs or joint costs. Business organizations often complain about below-cost sales, of course; but that is because they dislike competition and want government to protect them from its rigors by prohibiting price cutting.

Predatory Pricing

But aren't there dangers to competition in allowing firms to cut prices as low as they wish? It is odd, but not really surprising, how often people identify the protection of competitors with the protection of competition. In reality they are more like opposites. Competitors are usually protected by laws inhibiting competition, laws that benefit privileged producers by restricting consumers and nonprivileged producers. The hobgoblin hauled out to justify this is "predatory price cutting" backed up by a "long purse."

Predatory price cutting is reducing prices below cost in order to drive a rival out of business or prevent new rivals from emerging *with the intention of raising prices afterward to recoup all losses.* It is supposedly a favorite tactic of larger firms who can stand prolonged losses, or temporary losses on some lines, because of their larger financial resources—the so-called "long purse." Economic theory does not deny the possibility of predatory price cutting. But it does raise a long list of skeptical questions, headed by all the questions we have been discussing regarding the proper definition of an item's cost.

How long will it take for such a policy to accomplish its end? The longer it takes, the larger will be the short run losses accepted by the predator firm and, consequently, the larger must be the long term benefits if the policy is to justify itself.

What will happen to the physical assets and human resources of the

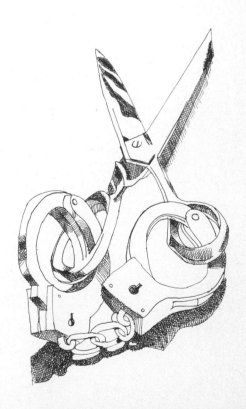

firms forced out of business? That's an important question, because if those assets remain in existence, what is to prevent someone from bringing them back into production when the predator firm raises its prices to reap the rewards of its villainy? And if this occurs, how can the firm hope to benefit from its predatory policy? On the other hand, the human resources may scatter into alternative employments and be costly to reassemble.

Is it likely that the predator firm will be able to destroy enough of its rivals to secure the degree of market power that it must have if the long run profits are to justify the short run losses? Charges of predatory pricing have most frequently been leveled against large discount houses, drug chains, and grocery supermarkets. But these sellers are not pitted exclusively against small independent competitors: they must tangle with other large discount houses, other drug chains, and other supermarkets. Perhaps A&P could cut its prices far enough and long enough to drive Lemuel Mudge out of business; but that wouldn't work on Safeway. And it's Safeway rather than Lemuel Mudge that keeps A&P executives awake at night.

We are not denying the possibility of predatory pricing in business. Well documented examples are hard to find, but it is surely possible. Minimum price laws, however, offer the *certainty* of higher prices in order to eliminate the *possibility* of higher prices: a case of accepting a known and certain evil as a way of avoiding an uncertain evil of unknown dimensions. That may or may not be a good social bargain. But since it is so often advocated by business firms that clearly stand to gain from it, we should at least approach their arguments skeptically.

A Way to Run a Railroad

Figure 10K ties the question of alleged below-cost sales to our earlier discussion of price discrimination. It pictures a railroad serving two distinct and distinguishable classes of shippers: those who ship bulky commodities and those who ship small commodities. Their demand curves are shown by D_B and D_S. The former class can easily shift to barges if the rail rates are too high; hence their demand curve shows considerable elasticity. Barges are not as suitable an option for the shippers of small commodities; their demand curve is consequently less elastic.

The bent demand curve, labeled $D_T D_T$, shows the total demand for this railroad's services. It was constructed by summing the quantities demanded by each class of shippers at the various prices. The marginal revenue curve corresponding to $D_T D_T$ cuts marginal cost at an output of 400,000 boxcar miles per month. If the railroad sets a single price for all shippers, it can do no better than to set the price at $23\frac{1}{3}$ per boxcar mile. Its total revenue will be $9,333,333 per month. Since the sum of its mar-

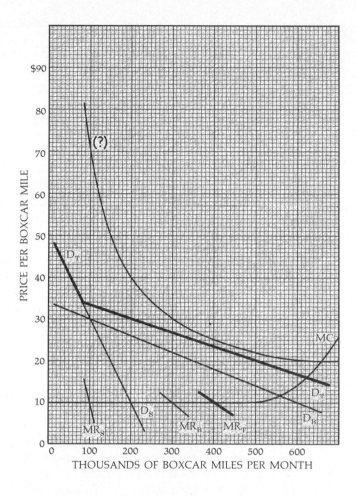

ginal costs will be $4,000,000 at this output, the railroad will be earning $5,333,333 per month.

But it can do better than that by segregating the shippers and charging each class a different rate—just as our movie theater operator did a few pages back. If it pays attention to the marginal revenue from each class of shippers, the railroad will want to sell only 100,000 boxcar miles to the shippers of small commodities and to charge them correspondingly $30 per mile. And it will want to reduce the rate charged the bulk shippers to $22 in order to sell them 300 boxcar miles. (At the single rate of $23⅓, they would have purchased 133⅓ and 266⅔ miles respectively.) The railroad's costs will be the same on our assumptions; but its total revenue will rise to $9,600,000.

Figure 10K Price discrimination by railroads

Nonmarginal "Costs"

Now marginal costs are very rarely the whole of a firm's monetary expenses. In the case of railroads, marginal costs are often a small percentage of the total monetary outlay. The railroad is expected to meet the principal and interest payments on the bonds it sold to buy its locomotives and to pay its property taxes, for example. These expenses are independent of the number of boxcar miles the railroad sells. Since they are not costs associated with decisions to sell more or less, they ought properly to be ignored in arriving at those decisions through the price searching process. There are other major expenses that are, at least in part, unrelated to the level of output: managers' salaries and roadbed maintenance are examples. But when the accountants calculate the railroad's monthly financial performance, they will add all expenditures of this kind to the expenditures incurred by actual operations and call the sum *total cost.* Past and potential railroad investors will look at this total in relation to revenue to see how the railroad is doing. The railroad's managers will also look at these totals to see how well they've been performing and whether they can expect brickbats or bouquets at the next stockholders' meeting. While sunk costs are irrelevant to decision making, they can be an embarrassing reminder of mistaken decisions made in the past.

They can even be an object of interest to the owners of barge lines. Suppose that the total of the railroad's monthly expenses *beyond its marginal costs* is a fixed $6,000,000 per month. That means the railroad will fail to reach the break-even point each month, falling short by $400,000 if it adopts the two-price policy and by more than that if it sets a single price. That's not uncommon for railroads these days. If we add this $6,000,000 to the railroad's marginal costs in order to calculate its *average total cost* at various rates of output, we will get the curve in figure 10K labeled (?). It has that quizzical label because it's a curve that shouldn't have been drawn; it makes no sense, as we argued in chapter 6, to speak of the cost per boxcar mile of something that has no relationship to boxcar miles. It's just sand in the eyes.

But sand in the eyes can be very useful to some people, which is why they kick it up. The barge lines that would like to have some of the business now going to the railroad may complain to the Interstate Commerce Commission that the $22 rate is below cost and therefore unfair competition. It's *not* below cost: it's $12 above the relevant cost, the marginal cost. But it *is* $3 below the irrelevant $25 figure that emerges when someone divides the railroad's total expenses by the number of boxcar miles it produces. And that's a good number to brandish when the barge lobby puts pressure on the Interstate Commerce Commission to raise the railroad's minimum rate schedule.

This kind of tactic is used regularly by industry lobbies wherever government agencies have some power to set minimum prices or—as in the case of imported goods—to exclude those that are being offered below some minimum price. The term of opprobrium is "dumping," which is officially defined as selling below cost. Dumping is so obviously "unfair to competitors" that the competitors are often successful in getting the government to raise the dumper's prices or exclude its products from the market. The questions too rarely asked are: Below *what* cost is the firm selling? What is the relevance of that cost figure to efficient resource allocation? How can a firm find it in its own interest to sell at prices that are actually below cost? And always with respect to the lobbyists' arguments: *Cui bono?* That's lawyer's Latin. It means, "To whose benefit?" It's not a cynical question. It's just a question that can help keep us from being taken in by special-interest arguments dressed up in public-interest garb.

Operating in the Red

Will the railroad go out of business? Even if it's allowed to set the prices that maximize its net revenue, the railroad will be spending $400,000 each month beyond its receipts. That obviously cannot continue indefinitely. But many firms, regulated and unregulated, do find themselves in positions like the one described. What could we expect to happen in such a situation?

First of all, we would expect the railroad to continue operations. For if it loses $400,000 per month by operating, it would lose $6,000,000 per month by not operating. The banks that hold mortgages on the locomotives will not be eager to see the railroad shut down when it starts to fall behind on its payments. Instead they are likely to grant an extension—in effect, lending the railroad the monthly sum by which it is delinquent in its mortgage payments. But they will simultaneously be after the railroad's managers to scrutinize their expenditures and see if some can be reduced without hurting revenue. Perhaps the railroad could lay off some personnel, though the unions are apt to resist that step. Or it could cut management salaries; management's understandable reluctance to economize here might be overcome by a threat to throw the railroad into receivership and change its top executives. Or it might postpone or skimp on maintenance, though this entails obvious risks. If no way can be found to bring expenditures down to revenue, the railroad will go more deeply into debt each year. Its creditors must then decide whether the ongoing loss from continued operation is greater than the loss they would suffer from forcing the railroad to suspend operations. Opinions and interests will differ. Local communities will not want to lose the tax revenue; but the banks may want to repossess the locomotives and sell them to another railroad.

As existing equipment wears out, the railroad will not be able to replace it from earnings and will have trouble borrowing the required funds. Eventually, therefore, the railroad may be forced to suspend operations. Or it may appeal to government for a subsidy—an appeal in which it can expect to be supported by its creditors, its employees, the communities to which it pays taxes, and the shippers who use its services. Or it may cast about for a railroad with which to merge in the hope that the merged line will be able to effect significant economies or attract additional business from shippers. The possibilities are numerous. The most important point to be noted is that *a business can be operated profitably at a loss* for an indefinite period, as long as its revenues exceed its *marginal* costs. "Profitably at a loss" is a strange conjunction of terms. What it means is that it will be to the advantage of the railroad's owners to continue operations, even though those operations steadily push the railroad more deeply into debt, as long as a shutdown would entail even greater losses. It is only through the comparison of *additions* to revenue with *additions* to cost, or marginal revenue and marginal cost, that the appropriate decision can be made.

Once Over Lightly

Price searchers are looking for pricing structures that will enable them to sell all units for which marginal revenue exceeds marginal cost.

The popularity of the cost-plus-markup theory of pricing rests upon its usefulness as a search technique and the fact that people often cannot correctly explain processes in which they regularly and successfully engage.

A crucial factor for the price searcher is the ability or inability to discriminate: to charge high prices for units that are in high demand and low prices for units that would not otherwise be purchased, without allowing the sales at lower prices to "spoil the market" for higher price sales.

A rule for successful price searching often quoted by economists is: Set marginal revenue equal to marginal cost. This means: Continue selling as long as the additional revenue from a sale exceeds the additional cost. Skillful price searchers are people who know this rule (even when they don't fully realize they're using it) and who also have a knack for distinguishing the relevant marginal possibilities. The possibilities are endless, which helps to make price theory a fascinating exploration for people with a penchant for puzzle-solving.

Firms often charge that their competitors, whether domestic or foreign, are "selling below cost" and call for the government to prevent such "predatory" practices. Most such charges only make sense if they include in per unit cost expenses that are irrelevant to the particular decisions under attack. They make a different kind of sense when we remember that sellers characteristically prefer less competition.

While the ability to sell to different parties at different prices increases the net income of a firm, it also enables some people who would otherwise be excluded to obtain goods for which they are willing to pay the marginal cost of production.

One of the price searcher's major tasks is to choose the appropriate set of marginal costs by deciding how much capacity to construct. *All* costs are marginal opportunity costs until irreversible decisions have been made.

A firm can operate at a profit while running in the red as long as its revenues exceed marginal costs. A decision to operate is a profitable decision as long as it yields smaller losses than a decision not to operate.

QUESTIONS FOR DISCUSSION

1. If you're still uncertain about the meaning of marginal revenue, here is some additional practice.

Price per Unit	Quantity Demanded
$12	1
11	2
10	3
9	4

(a) Assume that all sales take place at a single price. What is the *addition to total revenue* from selling the second unit, the third, the fourth? Why is marginal revenue less than price?

(b) What set of prices could make marginal revenue *equal* to price as shown by this schedule? (Check the case of Horty and the rose bushes.)

2. "A price searcher should set marginal revenue as far above marginal cost as possible." Explain why this statement is wrong. What is being erroneously assumed by someone who thinks that net receipts will be zero at an output where marginal revenue equals marginal cost?

3. Locate the most profitable uniform price for sellers to set in each of the situations graphed below and the quantity they will want to produce and sell. Then shade the area that represents the net income from that pricing policy. What will happen to net income in each case if the price is raised? If it's lowered? (Caution: What happens if a seller whose marginal revenue curve is the same as his demand curve raises his price?)

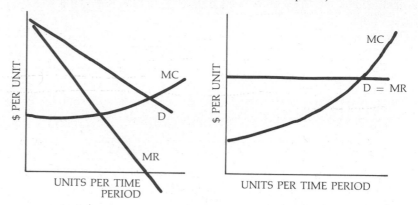

4. You want to sell at auction an antique dining room suite. There are three people who want it, and they're respectively willing to pay $8000, $6000, and $4000. Your reservation price (the price above which the bidding must go before you'll sell) is $5000. No one in the room has any information about the value of the suite to anyone else. At about what price will the suite be sold?

    Suppose you run a Dutch auction. The auctioneer announces a price well above what anyone would be willing to pay and then gradually lowers the price until a bid is received. At about what price will the suite be sold?

5. A privately owned university in the Southwest wants to increase the percentage of Mexican-Americans in its student body. Very few of them are willing to pay the university's high tuition rates, however, and the university is reluctant to spend money for scholarships. Outline a system for granting scholarships to Mexican-Americans that would not reduce the university's net income. (You will have to figure out a way of estimating the relevant marginal costs.)

6. List some cases of discriminatory pricing similar to the cases of the college and the movie theater. How do the sellers identify particular customers with the appropriate class of demanders? How do they prevent reselling?

7. You and your fiancee are shopping for wedding rings. After showing you a sample of his wares, the jeweler asks, "About what price did you have in mind?"

    (*a*) Why does he ask this question?

    (*b*) If you tell him you didn't plan to spend more than $50 on each ring, are you helping him find the rings to sell you or the price to charge for the rings you prefer?

(*c*) What might be a good technique for finding out the lowest price at which the jeweler is willing to sell the rings you like?

8. How should Artesian take account of the price he originally paid for the land on which the spring was discovered in deciding what price to charge for his water?

9. Grocery stores often run newspaper advertisements containing coupons that entitle customers to price discounts. What is the rationale for such a policy? (Hint: Price searchers would like to use lower prices to attract additional customers *without* being compelled to offer the lower price to customers already secured.)

10. Can hog growers raise the prices at which they sell when their feed costs go up? (Hog growers are typically price takers.) If feed costs are expected to remain at this higher level, what will happen after a time to the number of hogs reaching the market? How will this affect the price of hogs?

11. One store sells Wilson Championship extra-duty felt optic yellow tennis balls at $3.49 for a can of three. Another store in the same shopping center sells Wilson Championship extra-duty felt optic yellow tennis balls at $2.89 for a can of three. How is this possible? Why would anyone buy balls from the first store? Why do you think we repeated the long description in the second sentence instead of just saying "identical tennis balls"?

12. If a surgeon charges $1500 to remove the gall bladder of a wealthy patient and $500 to remove another patient's gall bladder, is she exploiting the first patient or giving a discount to the second? How does she prevent the second patient from buying several operations at the lower price and reselling them for a profit to wealthy patients?

13. Many firms use a technique called "target pricing" to decide what prices to set for new products they're introducing. The target price is a price that enables the firm to earn some targeted percentage return on its development and production costs. What must the seller know in addition to costs in order to know the return that a particular price will yield? If earnings from the sale of the product turn out to fall short of the target, should the firm raise the price? If earnings exceed the firm's expectations, should it lower the price?

14. If it's true that big supermarkets almost always have lower unit costs than small grocery stores, why does anyone ever build a small grocery store?

15. Information is a scarce good and its acquisition has a cost. How does this fact explain the frequent willingness of small firms to charge whatever prices are set by much larger firms?

16. Which of the following products are being sold below cost? With what other products are they competing? Is the competition "unfair"?

(*a*) Coffee offered without charge by a bank to its customers.

(*b*) As many cups of coffee after dinner as the diner in an expensive restaurant requests, at no extra charge.

(*c*) Commercial television programs.

(*d*) Soft drinks on an airline flight.

(*e*) A roll of film given to each adult customer during the pizza shop's first week of operation.

17. There are three elements that must all be present for a firm to be engaged in predatory pricing: pricing (1) below cost (2) in order to eliminate rivals (3) with the intention of raising prices afterward to recoup. What factors would make the last step of the process difficult to complete? Under what kinds of circumstances would it be relatively easy? Can you cite any actual examples?

18. Why did the airlines offer special reduced-rate youth fares until the Civil Aeronautics Board ordered them to stop the practice? What was the CAB's objective?

19. How should the British and French manufacturers of the Concorde supersonic commercial airliner take account of the plane's development costs in determining the prices to charge airline companies? Should they suspend production if they can't obtain a price that will cover development costs?

20. The graphs below present the marginal cost curve of a Japanese manufacturer and an American manufacturer of the same product. The demand curve facing the American manufacturer is also shown. What price would the American firm want to set? How many units would it want to sell?

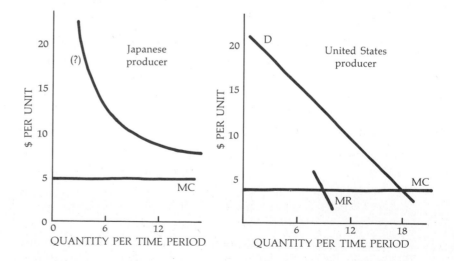

Now suppose the Japanese firm tries to sell in the U.S. market by under-cutting the American firm's price. It exports 6 units per time period at a price of $12. If the curve labeled (?) is the equivalent for the Japanese firm of the curve labeled (?) in figure 10K, is the Japanese firm selling below cost?

What kind of effect would you expect the Japanese exports to have on the American firm's demand curve?

11

MINERAL
WATER

ARTESIANS

COMPETITION AND
GOVERNMENT POLICY

Will economic competition disappear unless the government has an active program to preserve it? Or does competition preserve itself, even in the face of diligent efforts by the government to restrict it?

Is the government promoting competition when it prevents larger, more efficient, or more unscrupulous firms from driving other firms out of business? Or does the protection of competitors entail the suppression of competition?

When the government prohibits mergers, is it preventing competitors from eliminating rivals or is it barring the development of more competitive and efficient organizational forms?

What do we mean by competition and how are we to decide whether the economy or some sector of it is adequately competitive? Is competition in an industry to be measured by the number of competitors, by the practices in which they engage, or by the behavior of prices, costs, and profits and the industry's record with respect to innovation?

Those questions will not be conclusively answered in this chapter. But we hope that when you've finished thinking through the sources and consequences of competition as well as the origins and effects of government policies you will have a better sense of what the issues are.

COMPETITION: SOURCES AND CONSEQUENCES

When we last saw Artesian the price searcher, he was ruefully contemplating the consequences of an attempt to extract from his customers the full value to them of a cup of mineral water. As we rejoin him now, he has returned to the price of 23¢. He is selling 18 cups of water a day and enjoying a daily income of $3.42 from his mineral spring.

Competition Appears

Artesian's demand curve reflects the tastes and preferences of people in the community, their income, and the availability of substitutes for Artesian's mineral water. Let's see what might happen if better substitutes became available.

A good substitute for Artesian's mineral water is the mineral water of other suppliers. Perhaps there are no other springs in the community; but mineral water can be bottled and shipped in from neighboring towns. Moreover, Artesian's annual income from his spring, if it becomes known, will act as information and incentive to others. The owner of a local grocery store might decide to stock bottled mineral water in the hope of appropriating for himself some of the gains now going to Artesian. Let's assume this occurs.

The grocer can purchase bottled mineral water for $1.40 a gallon. That comes to about 10¢ per cup of the size which Artesian is selling for 23¢. The grocer thinks he can undersell Artesian and capture the bulk of his trade. What would be the best price to set?

If we knew the demand curve faced by the grocer, we could use the information we have on marginal cost to determine the profit-maximizing price for which he is searching. We assumed that Artesian knew his demand miraculously, and we could, if we wished, make the same heroic assumption for the grocer. But the assumption would now be considerably more heroic; a larger miracle would be required. For now we would have to know (a) the relative valuations placed on bottled versus fresh water; (b) the proximity of customers to Artesian and the competing grocery and the costs of patronizing one rather than the other; (c) the customer's evaluations of the advantages and disadvantages of buying two weeks' supply at one time; (d) the extent to which information is available to customers regarding these alternative supplies; and other similar factors. Moreover a fundamental uncertainty of a more radical sort is introduced by the probability that the demand facing each supplier is partially dependent on the pricing policy of the other.

Notice what this implies. The price set by Artesian will affect the grocer's demand and hence the most profitable price for the grocer to set. But the price set by the grocer will in turn affect Artesian's demand and thus alter the data with which Artesian determined his original price. What it comes to is that the best price for either one to set depends in part on the price which he himself decides to set. The neat little world of chapter 10, with its clearly defined curves, becomes blurry. Unfortunately from an analytic standpoint, but perhaps fortunately from an esthetic one, the real world is not as neatly outlined as the pictures in a coloring book.

Perhaps you recall from chapter 9 the word *oligopoly*, meaning "few sellers." We decided there that the concept of a few sellers shared all the ambiguities of the concept of a sole seller, ambiguities inherent in the problem of deciding just how broadly or narrowly to define the commodity being sold. Some economists have retained the slippery word *oligopoly* and have assigned it a very special meaning: a situation in which the demand curve of one seller depends on the reactions of identifiable other sellers, sometimes called rivals. Whether or not we choose to call this oligopoly— the usage is certainly misleading—situations of that sort, where the demand curves of different sellers are significantly interdependent, are obviously both common and important. As a result, price searchers must often plan their course of action in the manner of chess or poker players.

Effects of Competition

What can we expect to occur in such a situation? Precise predictions are impossible to make, but a number of possibilities suggest themselves:

1. Each seller will try to make his product more attractive in the hope of capturing and retaining customers. Artesian may install a bench under the shade tree by his dispenser. The grocer may offer to carry the gallon bottle to the customer's car. There are many other ways to differentiate the product, too many even to begin listing them. These actions raise the cost of doing business; but they also increase the value to the customer of what he obtains for his money.

2. Each seller will try to disseminate information throughout the community concerning the special virtues of his product. This is usually called advertising, and it has a poor reputation among many observers of the capitalist economic system. Remember, however, that information is a good, a scarce good whose possession enables people to increase their wealth by discovering more profitable exchange opportunities. Artesian and the grocer will want to spend more on advertising as long as the anticipated marginal revenue from advertising exceeds the anticipated marginal cost.

3. Artesian and the grocer may meet for lunch and agree to work together. "Why compete," Artesian asks rhetorically, "when all

we're doing is wiping out one another's profits? I'll keep my price at 23¢ per cupful, you set a corresponding price of $3.22 per gallon, and we'll just share the market." The grocer agrees and they shake hands. They don't put their agreement in a written contract, because such agreements between competing sellers to maintain prices and share markets are usually unenforceable in court and are, moreover, illegal under the laws of many states and under federal law where it is applicable. In addition, as we shall see, it might be very difficult to write a contract that would cover all the possibilities, and even more difficult to police it. So Artesian and the grocer content themselves with a "gentleman's agreement."

What might happen now? Suppose that geography, consumer tastes, and other factors are such that exactly half of Artesian's customers switch over to the grocer. Artesian will find his annual profits more than cut in half. He will sell 9 cups daily and net $1.71, or $624.15 annually. After payment of $200 to the dispenser company he is left with only $424.15 (as against $1048.30 previously). Artesian mourns the day the grocer decided to enter the mineral-water business.

Competition Reappears

But agreements of this sort are notoriously unstable. The incentives to change are so persistent that soon one or the other party will seek to circumvent the terms of the agreement. Let's see why.

Fundamentally, the explanation has to do with the inequality of marginal revenue and marginal cost. Artesian would incur only 4¢ in additional costs if he could attract just one of the grocer's customers. And he would add 23¢ to his daily revenue. That is 19¢ worth of inducement to violate the agreement (in a gentlemanly way, of course). Artesian would be willing to pay *up to* 19¢ to attract another customer, if he thought he could do so without inviting retaliation from the grocer or being forced to reduce prices to his existing customers.

He might advertise more, add vitamin C to his water, provide selective delivery service, give trading stamps, or maybe even offer secret price rebates. Meanwhile the grocer's marginal revenue is also well above his marginal cost, and the grocer is contemplating similar actions to "build volume" on mineral water. Maybe the grocer offers a special low price on paper cups to customers who buy a gallon of mineral water, thereby escaping the charge that he has violated the agreement not to reduce the price of mineral water.

Even if the gentlemen were to resist all these temptations, their agreement might still be undermined. For what is to keep some other grocer or the local druggist from doing exactly what the first grocer did? If Artesian and the grocer *do not* take these new competitors into their cartel,[1] the price of 23¢ will be undercut. If they *do* take them in, profits on the mineral-water business will be further shrunk. And the new and larger agreement would be still harder to enforce effectively, since it now involves more parties and presumably more ways to honor the letter while violating the spirit of the agreement.

The recurring lesson under this third possibility is that a downward sloping demand curve is insufficient to guarantee continuing profits. Competition (and *every* seller faces competition; remember that there is no such thing as a perfectly inelastic demand curve) tends to bring down the price, raise the quality of the product sold, and whittle away the price searcher's net income. That is why price searchers and even price takers yearn so ardently for legal restrictions on competition. Let's turn to this possibility.

Enlisting the Government

Artesian had a good thing going until the grocer found out what a good thing it was. "If people would only be loyal to their local mineral water," Artesian muses one evening, "I'd still be earning over $1000 a year from my spring." The wish becomes father to a thought and the thought inspires a course of action.

Artesian drafts a memorandum to the Town Council setting forth the following points:

1. Water is a basic necessity of life. Adequate local supplies of high-quality water must therefore be assured.

2. Mineral water is even more basic than regular water, containing as it does vital supplements to good health.

3. Unrestricted competition, especially from outside the town, can lead to irresponsible price cutting and the destruction of local mineral-water suppliers, thus depriving the town of an important industry, citizens of regular income, and consumers of assured domestic supplies of mineral water.

4. Unrestricted competition will lead to cost-cutting procedures that may threaten the purity of the mineral-water supply and hence the health and safety of the whole community. No price is too high if it guarantees pure water!

5. The Town Council should therefore pass an ordinance stipulating that every seller of mineral water within the town limits be

---

1. A cartel is an agreement among a group of sellers to regulate prices or output. There are also buyers' cartels. Chapter 13 argues that the National Collegiate Athletic Association, for example, can be viewed as a buyers' cartel.

licensed; that a license be granted only after careful scrutiny by a board of knowledgeable people in the mineral-water industry of the applicant's qualifications and ability to satisfy minimum health and safety standards; and that the board be empowered to revoke the license of any seller who engages in unethical conduct inconsistent with the public interest.

Since legislative bodies at the federal, state, and local level have often adopted just such licensing laws on the basis of very similar arguments, we shall assume that the town fathers grant Artesian's request. Market entry is now restricted and Artesian is in a more fortunate position. If he is doubly fortunate, Artesian will even be appointed chairman of the Licensing Board. Why not? He is, after all, the most experienced person in the community on the subject of mineral water.

THE PERILS OF THE PRICE SEARCHER

In the neighboring states of Maine and New Hampshire, liquor stores are owned and operated exclusively by the state. For many years, however, Maine prices were 20% to 30% higher than in New Hampshire. And as a result, Maine sold annually about 40% as much liquor as New Hampshire despite having a 25% larger population. Maine people weren't more moderate in their drinking habits; they were simply stocking up periodically during trips to New Hampshire.

So in July 1971 Maine opened a special cut-rate liquor store at its southern border just off Interstate 95. The aim, of course, was to recapture some of the business going to New Hampshire without lowering prices to those citizens who couldn't conveniently shop out of the state.

According to a *Wall Street Journal* report, the results were not what Maine anticipated. Maine residents further north understandably resented the fact that their state was discriminating against them and began calling for state-wide price reductions. Those who did drive south to obtain cut-rate liquor also resented the Maine policy and generally continued a few miles on across the border to Portsmouth, New Hampshire, to make their liquor purchases. But bar and restaurant operators, who by law can only sell liquor bought in Maine, quickly transferred their business to the new store with its sharply lower prices. The price searcher's life is apparently a perilous one even when the price searcher is the state itself.

The board will now set high standards of purity and excellence. It will probably not be so crude as to deny licenses outright. It will rather decree that bottled mineral water must be sold only in containers that have been sterilized by being boiled for 24 hours at 120 degrees centigrade (fresh water sold in cups is exempt); that stores selling mineral water must do so in separate areas so that the water does not stand closer than 25 feet to any other food or beverage by which it might be contaminated (businesses selling only mineral water are exempt); and perhaps that a tax of $2 a gallon be levied on all water sold to defray the costs of the inspection and licensing services (mineral water sold from private residences is exempt).

Entry into a market can be prevented without going so far as to prohibit it flatly. Anything that increases the costs of a supplier will restrict his supply, and the imposition of sufficiently large costs will restrict it completely. Licensing can be used to do exactly this, and often is. The prevention of competition is never given, of course, as the reason for licensing. It is always "the public interest" for which sellers profess a fervent concern when they seek to have the government impose controls on potential competitors.[1]

Restricting Competitors

Here are some actual newspaper items with names changed to protect the guilty. Who stands to gain and who to lose in each case?

"Government officials are demanding that hospitals provide registered nurses 24 hours a day or lose their Medicare certifications."

"All plumbers must spend a minimum of 140 hours a year for five years learning higher mathematics, physics, hydraulics, and isometric drawing."

"Woolen makers are arguing that, since woolen worsted fabric is essential to national defense, the government should impose quotas on imports from abroad."

"The prominent owner of a local television sales and service center said today that he welcomed the state's investigation of the television repair business and he demanded regulation of the industry. 'We must eliminate janitors, firemen, milkmen, and similar amateurs who defraud the public by providing poor quality repair service at cut-rate prices,' he argued."

"Automobile dealers are vigorously protesting Sears' application to enter the car-financing business, and are demanding that the state corporations commissioner reject the application."

"The Senate Public Health Committee yesterday rejected a bill to allow use of multiple offices and trade names in the diagnosis of eye problems and fitting of glasses. Single-office optometrists contend that, if an optom-

---

1. The appendix reprints a "parable" by Henry Manne that vividly illustrates the processes and problems to which this chapter is primarily directed.

OCCUPATIONAL LICENSING

The *Wall Street Journal* of January 8, 1975, carried an interesting feature on occupational licensing with the heading "Closed Societies?" The article reports a statement by Lewis Engman, chairman of the Federal Trade Commission, that occupational licensing has not prevented fraud, incompetence, or price gouging. Engman cited an FTC study which showed that Louisiana, which licenses television repairmen, has about the same incidence of fraud as the District of Columbia, which does not. Moreover, prices on television repairs are about 20% higher in Louisiana than in the District of Columbia.

In an effort to make licensing boards more responsive to the public interest, some states have considered legislation to require that the boards include members from outside the profession being regulated. Predictably enough, there has been strong opposition to these legislative proposals from trade and professional associations. Their argument, of course, is that people who aren't practitioners of the licensed occupation lack the technical competence to make proper decisions.

---

etrist is in his own office, his boss is his patient. If the optometrist works under a trade name, his boss is his company."

"The owner of the Piney Woods Nursing Home and secretary of the State Association of Licensed Nursing Homes accused the State Health Department last night of approving new nursing-home construction without proper investigation of the need for additional facilities or the qualifications of the applicants. 'Unqualified people, including speculators from other parts of the country, are hoping to reap big profits,' he said. 'A great surplus of beds will bring about cutthroat competition, which means nursing homes will have to curtail many needed services, resulting in lower standards detrimental to patients and the community.'"

And finally the plumbers once again, who aren't any worse than many others but seem to draw better press coverage:

"Changes proposed in the plumbing section of the city building code would require that a plumber serve as an apprentice for five years, instead of the present three, before becoming a journeyman. In addition, apprentices would have to register annually with the city and could not become apprentices after reaching the age of 25. For a plumber to become a master plumber, that is, one contracting plumbing work, he would have to take

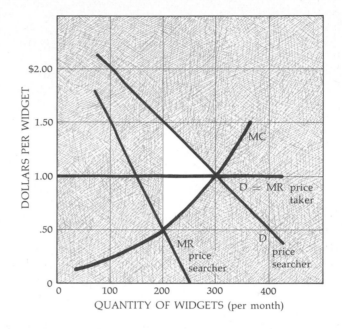

an examination. The code now requires only that a plumber seeking master-plumber status furnish bond."

Figure 11A Alternative outputs of widgets

Toward Evaluation

What general conclusions can we draw from all of this? The first observation to be made is that price searchers' markets tend to result in reduced output. To avoid spoiling his market, the price searcher foregoes some sales that could be made at prices above marginal cost. He looks at marginal revenue, not at price; and so he sells less and at a higher price than he would if he were a price taker.

Figure 11A illustrates this difference. Suppose that we have two widget-producing firms in widely separated geographic areas, each with identical marginal costs. The difference between the price-taking and the price-searching widget producers is summarized in their demand curves, also shown in figure 11A. The price taker is in a large market with many producers; the price searcher sells in a geographically isolated area.

The price taker wants to produce all units whose marginal cost is less than marginal revenue (which equals the price for him) and so produces 300 widgets per month.

The price searcher, following the same rule, wants to produce only 200 widgets per month. Any units produced beyond this add more to his costs than to his revenue. To sell 200 widgets he sets his price at $1.50. The important fact to be noticed is the *output-reducing* effect of price searchers' markets. (The law of demand predicts that restricted output will also result in higher prices.)

This reduced output represents waste in a specific sense. The marginal cost curve shows the opportunity cost of producing each unit of output. Since opportunity cost measures the value of what is given up, we can say that the area under the marginal cost curve between 200 and 300 widgets shows the gain to society from *not* producing the last 100 of 300 widgets, or what it would have cost society to produce them. The demand curve, on the other hand, measures what people are willing to pay for widgets, or the gain to society from obtaining them. Since the area under the demand curve is greater than the area under the marginal cost curve between 200 and 300, society lost more than it saved by not obtaining 100 additional widgets. The white area represents this loss of wealth. It is the difference between the value of additional widgets and the value of the alternative goods that can be produced by sacrificing these additional widgets.

The argument is admittedly somewhat formal and abstract. But it is an important argument to understand if you want to evaluate the effects of market power. In short: price searchers refrain from providing goods that could be provided at a cost below what people are willing to pay. This constitutes an inefficient use of resources.

Some further observations and words of caution can now be added.

First of all, price discrimination is capable of reducing this inefficiency. If the price-searching widget producer can find a way to do what Artesian attempted unsuccessfully with his you-set-the-price policy, and what Ivy College did more successfully through tuition scholarships, he improves the allocation of resources. Of course, he also increases his own net income, a fact that will prompt him toward more astute price searching.

Secondly, the burden of such inefficiency diminishes as price searchers' demand curves become more elastic. Since elasticity depends crucially on the availability of substitutes, legal restrictions on entry will tend to aggravate inefficiency. Restrictions on potential competitors reduce the range and diminish the availability of substitute goods, and allow the price searcher more room to increase his own wealth by allocating resources inefficiently.

Finally, for policy purposes, an efficient situation must be compared with more efficient situations that are actually attainable. We objected earlier to the frequent error of contrasting a less than ideal situation with an ideal but unattainable situation. There are costs involved in *changing* market structures, such as the cost of an investigation, prosecution, court order, and compliance under antitrust statutes. Only if these marginal costs are less than the marginal benefits can one maintain that efficiency would be increased by legal action aimed at reducing the market power of price searchers.

GOVERNMENT POLICIES TOWARD COMPETITION

The policies toward competition of federal, state, and local governments in this nation have not always been grounded in coherent economic analysis. It is relatively easy, of course, for academicians and textbook writers to point out the failings of policy makers. "Had I been present at the creation," King Alfonso X of Spain remarked in the thirteenth century, "I would have given some useful hints for the better ordering of the universe." But economists were not always present in any influential way as "antitrust" policies evolved in this country, and sometimes they gave conflicting hints when they were offered a voice in policy formation. The anomalies of antitrust policy are the anomalies we should expect when policies that significantly affect substantial economic interests evolve over many years and in many separate jurisdictions in response to political pressures and in the presence of substantial uncertainties.

The very word *antitrust*, the most common generic term for summarizing the laws and policies that affect business competition, is a strange misnomer to begin with. The "trust" was a specific legal arrangement tried out by corporations around the 1880s as a way of reducing competitive pressure. But it had already been successfully attacked in state courts and was disappearing when Congress enacted the first and most important "antitrust" law in 1890. The Sherman Act became known as the Sherman Antitrust Law because Senator Sherman was also the sponsor of other well-known bills and because the word "trust" was at that time synonymous in the public mind with schemes by powerful business interests to eliminate competition. The sweeping language of the Sherman Act in its first two sections provides good grounds for regarding it as the constitution of federal policy to preserve and promote business competition.

The Sherman Act

"Every contract, combination in the form of a trust or otherwise, or conspiracy, in restraint of trade or commerce among the several States . . . is hereby declared to be illegal. . . .

"Every person who shall monopolize, or attempt to monopolize, or combine or conspire with any person or persons, to monopolize any part of the trade or commerce among the several States . . . shall be guilty of a misdemeanor. . . ."

But it's a strange constitution that can be enacted with almost no discussion and by a nearly unanimous Congress—which happened in the case of the Sherman Act.[1] A careful examination of the law's origins leaves the

1. The Act passed both houses of Congress in 1890 with only one dissenting vote. For a comprehensive legislative history of the law, see Hans B. Thorelli, *Federal Antitrust Policy: Origination of an American Tradition* (Johns Hopkins Press, 1955).

"ILLEGAL CONSPIRACY"

distinct impression that few members of Congress thought the bill was significant, except as a ringing denunciation of sin and an assurance to the voters of each legislator's virtue. And early enforcement certainly bore the marks of indifference. When the Attorney General finally dusted the law off, he did so to use it against labor unions, to the considerable surprise and dismay of labor leaders. And the law was at first held by the courts not to apply at all to manufacturing firms because they were not strictly engaged in interstate *commerce,* the only kind of private economic activity that Congress could constitutionally regulate.[1] The law did, however, offer the prospect of triple damages to parties that could show they had been harmed by violations. So there were teeth in the law even if its jaw was not always in working order.

Clarifying the Rules

But sweeping language has its own way of becoming vague language as attempts are made to apply it. Surely Congress could not have intended the act to be applied literally. *Every* combination that restrains trade? *Every* attempt to monopolize? That could condemn competition itself. For example, if a firm cuts its prices to attract a larger share of the market, isn't it trying to monopolize? Isn't it the goal of every competitive firm to get as much business for itself as possible? And isn't that legitimate? Moreover, couldn't almost every business transaction be construed as a contract restraining trade? For every contract will be found to exclude some others. The law cried out for interpretation, and it was soon established that only "unreasonable" acts were to be condemned, with the federal courts as the ultimate arbiters of reasonableness.

In 1914 Congress added two more laws to the body of federal "antitrust" law: the Clayton Act and the Federal Trade Commission Act. Two decades of experience with the Sherman Act had convinced most members of Congress that it was necessary to spell out the rules in more detail. They also believed that even the most detailed rules Congress could write would still require expert application, and the Federal Trade Commission was created as the expert agency to interpret and apply the rules. Further rules for the governance of competition were spelled out in the Robinson-Patman Act of 1936. We'll come back to the issues raised by these rules.

The Issue of Mergers

The most important feature of the Clayton Act, at least in retrospect, was its attempt to bar a detour by which firms were circumventing the Sherman Act. If conspiring with a competitor to fix prices was illegal,

---

1. Since that time the federal courts have steadily expanded the meaning of interstate commerce until almost any economic activity at all may be federally regulated on the grounds of its tendency to affect interstate commerce. Everything in fact does.

merging with a competitor was not. A firm obviously cannot conspire with itself. And so the Clayton Act prohibited corporate mergers that might tend substantially to lessen competition. That left a large loophole, as it turned out, which wasn't closed until 1950, when Congress prohibited mergers through the acquisition of physical assets as well as through stock acquisitions. But the tough question still remained: When will a merger tend to lessen competition? When might it increase competition? And what about the relationship between size and efficiency? Do firms merge to achieve economies in production, marketing, and finance? Or do they merge in order to reduce the options of those to whom they sell or from whom they buy? Or is merger more often aimed at some quite different goal, like insurance against market uncertainties, the prestige that goes with size, or the prospect of a speculative increase in stock prices?

Economists divide mergers into three main types: horizontal, vertical, and conglomerate. If the Ford Motor Company were to merge with Chrysler, that would be a horizontal merger. If Ford merged with National Steel or bought up some of its own dealerships, those would be vertical mergers: mergers with suppliers or buyers. And if Ford merged with Xerox or Borden, that would be a conglomerate merger: the merger of firms in unrelated industries.

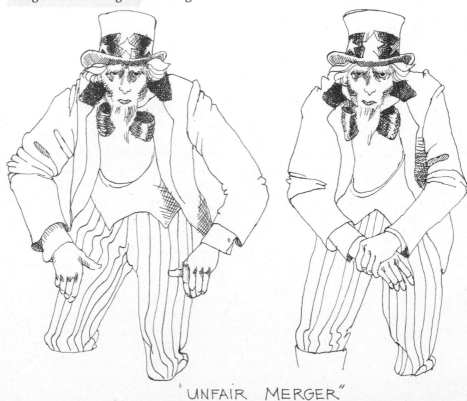

"UNFAIR MERGER"

Horizontal mergers appear to have the greatest potential for lessening competition because they combine firms that are competing for shares of the same market. By reducing the options of buyers, they decrease the elasticity of the demand faced by the merged firms and hence increase their market power.

Vertical mergers tend to have a different type of effect. The acquisition of a steel producer by an automobile producer gives one steel firm an advantage over others in selling to the automobile manufacturer. The dealerships owned by an automobile manufacturer may likewise have an advantage in purchasing from the manufacturer. Thus vertical mergers are usually criticized by firms who claim that the mergers place them at an unfair competitive disadvantage. While vertical integration does reduce the amount of competitive buying and selling of intermediate products that occurs, it is difficult to construct a convincing argument to show that it raises the final prices of goods. How could Ford increase its net income by paying more for steel from its own subsidiary than it would have to pay other suppliers? Of course, if Ford acquired ownership of its own retail outlets, it might be able to reduce competition among automobile dealers. But the problem then would be the *horizontal* merger of dealerships achieved through the vertical merger.

Evaluating Conglomerates

Conglomerate mergers are the most fashionable kind today and also the ones most difficult to assess. Why should the merger of an automobile manufacturer and a producer of copying equipment reduce competition? One answer is that it creates more opportunities for "special deals": Ford makes business cars available to Xerox at low prices that reduce Xerox's costs below those of other copying machine manufacturers, while Xerox gives Ford an advantage over Chrysler by supplying copying machines at low prices. It's again hard to see, however, in what way Ford-Xerox could gain from this kind of mutual subsidy.

Another complaint is that conglomerate mergers increase the probability of predatory pricing, which we discussed in chapter 10. The conglomerate will have that "long purse" which makes it possible for a firm to sell at below-cost prices until it has driven its competitors out of business. But predatory pricing, we have already argued, is not likely to be a source of as many advantages as some commonly assume, and it is far more often complained about than actually observed.

Conglomerates may acquire important financing advantages. They may be able to provide the capital funds for one division out of the earnings from another without going through the capital market. And insofar as larger firms are better risks, conglomerates may be able to borrow on better terms. But is this a source of increased efficiency or of socially undesirable advantages?

The political dangers associated with conglomerate mergers are also sometimes mentioned as a reason for opposing them. The centralization of financial power displayed by a large conglomerate may increase both the temptation and the ability to exert improper influence on the political process. Revelations after the 1972 presidential campaign about the illegal contributions of large corporations have increased many people's distaste for bigness in and of itself. "Power tends to corrupt," as Lord Acton observed, and money is power. The merger of a local firm into a nationwide conglomerate may also upset the relationship between that firm and local government.

Another political argument against sheer size and hence against conglomerate mergers arises from the unwillingness of the federal government to let very large corporations fail. Incompetent or irresponsible management may mean bankruptcy for smaller firms but a government subsidy for very large firms, on the grounds that the economy would be too severely hurt if the large corporation were allowed to fail. The number of jobs that would be lost is often pointed to as grounds for a subsidy. Penn Central, Lockheed, and the Franklin Bank in New York are recent warnings along this line about the dangers of bigness.

There are arguments that can be presented on the other side, however. One obstacle to increased competition in many industries is the enormous start-up costs associated with entry. Suppose that there are only two firms producing aluminum cans and that the demand for these cans is large enough and inelastic enough to allow huge profits. The two firms each recognize, without having to discuss it together, that they can both make larger profits if each will restrain itself, settle for half of the market, and

not risk spoiling the market by trying to capture a larger share. They will find it easier to maintain such a policy if they do not have to fear the entrance of additional firms. If the initial capital requirements for constructing production facilities of an efficient size are very large, the threat of potential competition is less. But that threat can be increased and turned into a reality if other large firms begin to eye the profits in the aluminum can industry. Firms in wholly unrelated industries may be able more easily to marshall the resources required for entry. A large brewer, for example, might threaten to produce its own cans, or acquire a bottle manufacturer and diversify into can production. The concentration of resources that makes conglomerates dangerous in some people's eyes may also make them continuing threats to established positions of market power.

The issues are complex, as we have often had to say. They are made more complex, however, by our ambivalence toward competition itself and in particular our tendency to equate the protection of competitors with the promotion of competition. This is nowhere better illustrated than in the history of the Federal Trade Commission and Robinson-Patman Acts.

Fair Competition

We observed earlier that Congress was determined in 1914 to spell out the rules more clearly. It did not wish to condemn size in and of itself, since size was often associated with greater efficiency. And hence it did not wish to condemn growth in and of itself, even if that growth increase a firm's market share and hence its "monopoly" power. What Congress wanted was *fair competition.* Why not go at that goal directly by proscribing in explicit terms the business practices that were *unfair?* And establishing an expert commission to act as referee? That in rough outline is the history and philosophy of the Federal Trade Commission and the laws that it administers.

"Fair competition" sounds altogether admirable. But to whom is it supposed to be fair? To consumers or to competitors? When business executives talk about unfair competitive practices, they almost invariably mean practices that put them at a disadvantage. The possibility that these same practices bring benefits to consumers tends to be overlooked. Price cutting is the prime example. A business executive who registered a protest whenever a competitor reduced prices would look ridiculous—*unless* he could construct an argument to show that the price reduction was fraudulent or based on an unfair advantage. And there are plenty of arguments to be used.

Resale price maintenance is the technical term for laws that permit manufacturers to establish minimum prices below which retailers may not sell. Many states have such laws, which not only condone collusive price-fixing but allow legal penalties against retailers who refuse to cooperate.

" FAIR COMPETITION "

This is a clear violation of the Sherman Act; but Congress has exempted resale price maintenance from coverage by the Sherman Act.[1] The term commonly used by retailers who enjoy the protection against price cutting that these arrangements give them is, not surprisingly, Fair Trade laws.

The Robinson-Patman Act is in large part grounded in the assumption that competition will disappear, leaving us the helpless victims of monopoly, if legal restrictions are not imposed upon competition. A detailed discussion of this law and of the Federal Trade Commission Act which it supplements could easily fill a separate book. Federal laws governing "trade practices" do not all have the intent of reducing competition to protect competitors; but an alarming percentage does. Or at least that is often the effect of the laws, whatever their conscious intent. Others are so difficult to interpret that they are open invitations to arbitrary decisions by federal agencies. The laws governing advertising largely fall in this category, as we saw in chapter 8. It is important to note that the most effective pressures on the Federal Trade Commission and other government agencies do not come from consumers, but from producer interests. And those are far more likely to be pressures to protect competitors against competition than to protect consumers by promoting competition. This is the principal source of the ambivalence that characterizes so much of the government's policy respecting competition.

The Effects of Antitrust Policy

Is the whole body of "antitrust" law perhaps more of a hindrance than a help to competition? There are some who come to that conclusion. There are others, heavily concentrated, it often seems, in the economics profession, who would retain the Sherman Act and the anti-merger provisions of the Clayton Act and junk the rest. Some of these defenders claim that the Sherman Act and the Clayton Act have made important contributions to the maintenance of a competitive economy. Others claim that they could make a much larger contribution if they were seriously enforced. But still other students of the American economy view them as at best a meaningless charade, at worst a set of weapons with which ignorant political appointees can do a lot of damage while assaulting windmills.

The authors of this textbook are firmly convinced that they don't know who's right. Antitrust policy is certainly full of contradictions, of cases where the right hand is doing what the left hand is undoing. State laws rarely promote competition and often fall into the hands of the competitor-protectors rather than competition-protectors. Federal enforcement of the

1. As these lines are being written, Congress is considering repeal of that exemption, first enacted in 1937. Manufacturers and retailers have increasingly found that the cost of enforcing resale price maintenance against ingenious competitors is greater than the potential gain. Former supporters of these laws are no longer willing to lobby for them.

> ## THE LOWLY PEANUT
>
> There aren't very many peanut growers in the United States, but they have a lot of political influence. And so the United States passed a law in the 1940s limiting the nation's peanut farmland to 1.6 million acres. Land cannot be planted in peanuts unless it has an acreage allotment. The allotments were granted on an historical basis: land producing peanuts when the law was passed acquired the exclusive privilege to go on producing peanuts. That was an excellent arrangement for those who owned peanut land when the law was passed. It restricted output to keep the price of peanuts high and prevented other farmers from cutting themselves in on a share of the profits by switching their land to peanut production—and bringing down the price of peanuts in the process. That would be a clear violation of the Sherman Act if it were done by anyone but the federal government.
>
> But a good thing is hard to preserve. Peanut farmers trying to increase their profits have found ways to double the output per acre over the last decade. And peanut consumption hasn't kept pace. But peanut farmers still have political clout. So the federal government, through the Commodity Credit Corporation, buys the surplus (that is, the quantity that won't be purchased at the official support price) and sells it overseas at a loss to the general taxpayer.
>
> Senator Herman Talmadge is from Georgia, a state whose largest cash crop is peanuts. He is also chairman of the Senate Agriculture Committee. And he argues that a cut in the support program would be a disaster for people who earn their living producing peanuts. Can you think of any industry that would not be grateful for a similar arrangement or to which the senator's argument could not apply?

Sherman Act and the antimerger provisions of the Clayton Act often seems to strain at gnats while swallowing camels. On the other hand, the existence of the Sherman Act, with its ringing denunciation of price-fixing conspiracies, may have retarded the development in this country of the cartel arrangements that have so often appeared in Western Europe and Japan. The economist George Stigler once suggested that "the ghost of Senator Sherman is an ex officio member of the board of directors of every large company." That statement will never meet the minimum criteria for empirical scientific truths; but good history is still a long way from being a pure science.

Once Over Lightly

A gap between the price of a good and the marginal cost of making it available is a source of potential advantage to someone. Competition occurs in the economy as people locate such differentials and try to exploit them by filling that gap with additional goods.

Competition can take more forms than we can list and usually more forms than a price searcher can anticipate and head off.

Because competition tends to transfer the gains from providing a good to purchasers and other suppliers, firms frequently try to obtain government assistance in excluding competitors, often displaying remarkable ingenuity and stunning sophistry.

The notion that government is the Defender of Competition against Rapacious Monopolists is probably more a hope than a reality. Federal, state, and local governments have created and preserved numerous positions of special privilege whose effect is to restrict competition and reduce the options available to consumers.

An adequate and balanced evaluation of that substantial body of statutes, commission decrees, and judicial holdings which makes up federal antitrust policy has not yet been published.

While price searchers' markets entail a misallocation of resources when compared with price takers' markets, the significance of that misallocation and the cost of correcting it are difficult to determine.

Since a firm that competes successfully must to some extent displace its rivals, competition may lead to the elimination of competition. On the other hand, it is impossible to preserve all competitors without restricting competition to some degree. This is the basic dilemma of government policies toward competition.

QUESTIONS FOR DISCUSSION

1. How would you account for the fact that while some observers claim competition is declining in the American economy, every business firm insists that it faces strenuous competition?

2. Consult the technical definition of *oligopoly* presented in the text. Are the manufacturers of cigarettes oligopolists by that definition? Are the owners of the gasoline stations in a small town oligopolists? Name some other sellers who are and are not oligopolists by that definition.

3. The attempt by sellers to make their product more attractive to consumers is sometimes called *product differentiation*.

(*a*) Is product differentiation a wasteful process, imposing costs on sellers that are greater than the benefits conferred on buyers? Think of cases where it probably is wasteful in this sense and other cases where it is not.

(*b*) Evaluate the following argument:

"New practices initiated by sellers to differentiate their products are liable to be wasteful from a social point of view because they are liable to entail high marginal costs and low marginal benefits. But this only means producers have already made use of the low cost–high benefit techniques of product differentiation; it does not show that the whole process of product differentiation is wasteful."

4. Why must an effective price fixing agreement between sellers include such restrictions on sales as output limitations or geographic divisions of sales territory?

5. Some states have established legal minimum prices for liquor sold at retail. Do you think this eliminates competition among retail liquor stores? Why do you think retailers in such states often lend glassware without charge to customers planning parties?

6. The realtors in an area will generally all charge the same percentage of the sales price for selling a house, a percentage established by some realtors association and adhered to by all real estate agents as a matter of "ethical practice."

   (*a*) Why would it be unethical if a realtor offered to accept 5% rather than 6% for selling your house? *Toward whom* would it be unethical?

   (*b*) How do realtors compete with one another?

   (*c*) Is an industry likely to become overcrowded if it's successful in fixing a high minimum price for its product? Is the realtor profession overcrowded in your judgment? What evidence might be used to answer this question? (From 1960 to 1973 the number of employees in the real estate industry increased 44%.)

7. A recent survey of businessmen asked them to describe the unethical practices in their own industry that they would most like to see eliminated. Of those responding, 62% mentioned "unfair pricing," "dishonest advertising," "unfair competitive practices," or "cheating customers." How would you interpret these responses? How would you define the practices they condemn?

8. Examine the paragraph in the text recounting the complaint of the nursing-home operator. How many wrong or misleading assertions can you locate in that paragraph?

9. The legislature of a large state recently considered a bill that would require all grocery stores and drug stores selling package liquor to provide separate entrances to their liquor departments. It was maintained by supporters of the bill that this was necessary to prevent minors from entering the liquor department. Who do you think lobbied for this bill? Why?

10. A study several years ago pointed out that 73% of the professions licensed by a populous Midwestern state required entrants to have "good character." Why? How can good character be determined? Who is best able to determine whether a mortician's character is sufficiently blameless to entitle him to a license?

11. Is the patent granted to an inventor a grant of special privilege? Would you favor abolition of the patent privilege? Why or why not?

12. How might laws prohibiting collusion on pricing encourage mergers? (Hint: Can a firm collude with itself?)

13. What is the difference between reducing prices to attract more customers and reducing prices in order to monopolize?

14. It is often argued that large corporations have undue political influence. It is also argued by some that large corporations are convenient political scapegoats. Which argument is closer to the truth?

15. How important is free entry in promoting efficiency, low prices, and innovation in an industry? What are some of the barriers to free entry in addition to legal restrictions?

16. Evaluate this assertion by the economist M. A. Adelman: "A useful if not very precise index of the strength of competition . . . is the resentment of unsuccessful competitors." How would you evaluate the argument by other firms in their industries that General Motors and International Business Machines ought to be broken up into several separate companies?

PROFIT

"Perhaps no term or concept in economic discussion is used with a more bewildering variety of well-established meanings than *profit.*" That sentence was written forty years ago by Frank Knight, a distinguished student of the subject, to introduce an encyclopedia article on profit. The situation has not changed greatly since then. A few years ago *The Wall Street Journal* ran a feature article entitled "Some Plain Truth about Profit." The author listed no fewer than seven distinct definitions of the word *profit* that have been employed by "economic experts," decided none of them was very helpful, and then offered his own. A month later the *Journal* published seven letters of response from its readers; their verdicts on the new definition and accompanying exposition ran from excellent through misleading to ridiculous.

So what shall we do? We shall take the coward's course and assert that *there is no correct definition of profit.* The meaning of any word depends, after all, on the way in which people use it; and it is an incontrovertible fact that people (including economists) use the word *profit* in many different senses. Rather than argue about the best definition, we'll try to help you understand the insights that lie behind some of the competing definitions. One of our principal objectives in this chapter will be to help you think more clearly and systematically about a very important phenomenon in economic life, one that has complicated our analysis before and will complicate it again: the phenomenon of uncertainty.

PROFIT: TOTAL REVENUE MINUS TOTAL COST

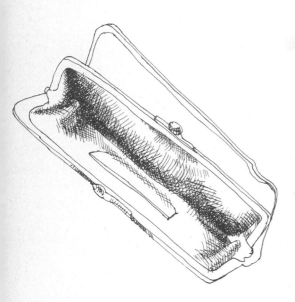

The most common definition of profit is simply *total revenue minus total cost.* That's almost everyone's intuitive definition of the term and that's how we have used it until now. When a business firm has paid all of its costs, what it has left over is profit. But before we can agree on the size of the profits, defined in this way, we must agree on what is to be counted in costs.

What Should Be Included in Costs?

Monetary outlays are not the same as costs from the opportunity cost perspective. This is clear in the case of an owner-operated business: part of the cost of doing business is the owner's own labor, even though the owner may not figure his own salary as part of his regular costs and writes no weekly payroll check to himself. If the owner pays rent for the building he uses, he will count the rental payments as part of his costs; but he may not do so if he himself owns the building. He ought to do so, however, because he is losing the amount that could be obtained from renting the building to someone else, and from the standpoint of society, too, there is a genuine cost in having the building not available for alternative uses.

The business proprietor may also be using equipment that he bought and now owns. If he bought the equipment with a bank loan, he will include his bank payments in his costs. But suppose he bought the equipment out of savings that he had previously accumulated? Then he is giving up the income that he could have obtained from letting someone else use his savings, and that is certainly part of the opportunity cost of doing business. But he may or may not decide to include this foregone income in his costs. The point is that he *should.* The income foregone represents a genuine cost both to the business proprietor and to society.

Let's next consider the accounting procedures of corporations. Corporate profits have a *legal* definition because corporations must pay taxes on their profits. But the legal definition is unsatisfactory from the opportunity cost point of view. It begins with the common sense definition of profit as revenue minus costs. But it excludes from cost the dividend payments made to stockholders of the corporation while including the interest payments made to bondholders. Are these payments that different? Both are payments for borrowed funds or for the resources that the corporation was able to purchase with those funds. The principal difference is that payments to bondholders are a contractual obligation of a fixed amount, while the dividends paid to stockholders are a kind of residual that may vary from year to year or quarter to quarter. Still, the funds loaned by the stockholders are funds not earning income somewhere else, and the resources purchased by the corporation with these funds are pulled away from alternative opportunities. Surely some portion of the dividends paid by corporations represent genuine opportunity costs, no matter how they are regarded for purposes of taxation.

Profit versus Interest

A persistent difficulty in the measurement of profits is the difficulty of deciding just how much interest a business firm is paying. The legal definition of interest isn't adequate, for payments to banks and bondholders often will not differ functionally from the payments made to shareholders in dividends or even as increases in the market price of their shares attributable to reinvestment of earnings. What we are after in trying to measure the true interest costs of a business firm is the amount the firm must pay in order to obtain the capital it uses.

Capital means goods used to produce future goods: like cash registers in retail stores, typewriters in an office, drill presses in a sheetmetal fabricating shop, or reading skills that are used to produce knowledge. In later chapters we'll take a closer look at the concept of capital and some of the ambiguities associated with its definition. But the simple definition given above is enough to get us into the puzzling phenomenon of interest.

Why Is Interest Paid?

Usury and interest were originally synonyms. Today the word *usurious* carries connotations of overreaching and grasping greed—evidence in our language of popular hostility toward the taking of interest. The hostility seems to be largely rooted in misunderstanding. Interest is not the price of using money, although that is sometimes a convenient way of expressing it. *Interest is the difference in value between present and future goods.* Once you understand why present goods are more valuable than goods in the future, you realize that interest is not something peculiar to capitalist economies, or a consequence of the avarice and monopoly power of bankers and other money lenders, or something that could be eliminated just by making more money available. Interest rates are generally talked about as if they were the cost of borrowing money, because money is the usual means by which people acquire possession of present goods. But interest would exist in an economy that used no money at all, since it is fundamentally the difference in value between present and future goods.

Why are present goods more highly valued than goods in the future? This is a question that has intrigued a number of the most distinguished minds in the history of economics, and the higher subtleties of the problem still arouse controversy in some quarters. Two facts stand out, however, whose significance can be readily grasped.

Time Preference

In the first place, individuals have on the average *a positive rate of time preference.* That is to say, people tend to place a higher subjective value on consumption in the near future than on consumption in the more distant future. Some have interpreted this as evidence of shortsightedness, or of inability to imagine the distant future with as much vividness and force as one contemplates the immediate future, or of an innate human tendency to view the future through rose-tinted glasses. Each of these interpretations casts suspicion on the ultimate "rationality" of time preference. On the other hand, given the facts of human mortality and all the contingencies of life, it is not necessarily irrational or shortsighted to prefer a bird in the hand to two in the bush. Moreover, if people have reason to believe that their income will increase over time, they could very logically conclude that giving up something now entails a larger subjective sacrifice than giving up quite a bit more of the same thing at a future date when one's income is expected to be larger. Whatever the explanation or explanations, however, there can be no doubt that people do display positive rates of time preference. To obtain 100 strawberries today, a person may be willing to give in exchange 115 strawberries one year from now. Conversely, such an individual could be persuaded to give up 100 strawberries now only by the promise of 115 strawberries or more one year hence. He displays a 15% rate of time preference. While these subjective rates of time preference vary widely from individual to individual and from one culture to another, on average they are positive in every known society. This by itself would be sufficient to create a premium on present goods over future goods and thus a positive rate of interest.

It may be instructive to consider a case of apparent *negative* time preference. This should help you grasp the principle at work. Consider a person who receives, as a gift, 100 *quarts* of strawberries. He loves strawberries, and he vastly prefers one quart now to one quart a month from now. But he does not want to eat more than one or two quarts a day, for fairly obvious reasons, so that many of these 100 quarts are without any value to him. They will spoil before he wants to eat them.

Such a person would be willing to give up strawberries now to obtain *fewer* strawberries in the future! He might go down the block offering each of 45 neighbors two quarts of strawberries apiece in return for one quart at a later date when he will be able to eat them. By this act, which seems to reveal a negative time preference, he clearly increases the value to himself of the gift he received.

Surpluses of this kind are not uncommon. How much pressure do they exert to reduce the average premium on present over future goods, or the rate of interest? Probably very little in an economy with a well-organized system for extensive exchange. If the recipient of the 100 quarts of strawberries can easily sell them (for money), and then use the money (which will not spoil after a few days) to buy strawberries as he wants them, his present surplus will not cause him to reveal a negative rate of time preference. Opportunities to exchange at low cost, which are enlarged by such institutions as money and commodity speculators, keep the rate of interest from falling.

The Productivity of Capital

The second main factor making for positive interest rates in a society—though perhaps it is only another aspect of the factor already discussed—is *the potential productivity of goods*. Suppose that Robinson Crusoe, a familiar figure in economists' arguments, can only keep himself alive from day to day by digging for clams. Five clams a day will barely enable him to keep body and soul together. And five clams a day is the most he can obtain by digging with his hands during every working hour. If he had a shovel, however, he could increase his daily output to ten clams. But a week's work is required to manufacture a suitable shovel. Since Robinson would starve if he took a week off from digging in order to make the shovel, he cannot attain this higher income level.

It is clear in such a case that Robinson would be eager to obtain 35 extra clams, and willing to give in return more than 35 clams in the future, for the opportunity to increase his productivity by first making a shovel. The shovel is capital for Robinson. And it is the shovel's value as capital—that is, its present productivity in the creation of future goods—that causes Robinson to want it and makes him willing to pay a premium to obtain it.

The Risk Factor in Interest Rates

The rates charged by banks to corporate borrowers, by department stores to customers with revolving charge accounts, or by individuals lending to savings and loan institutions all reflect the society's rates of time preference and the potential productivities of goods. But they also include risk premiums of various sizes plus differences in the cost of negotiating loans. It will cost you more per dollar to borrow from a commercial bank than it will cost a large and successful corporation.[1] This does not really mean that you are paying a higher rate of interest, however. You are paying for the costs incurred by the bank in investigating your credit standing and doing the bookkeeping entailed by your loan, as well as a kind of insurance premium that the bank collects from each borrower in anticipation of losses through costs of collection and defaults. If the bank could not charge this premium, it would not find it advantageous to make loans to customers in higher risk categories. So when legislators impose ceilings on the "annual interest" that may legally be charged by lenders, they do not reduce interest rates so much as they exclude certain categories of borrowers from contracting for loans. Since the borrowers would not contract for the loans unless they deemed them advantageous, it is difficult to discover in what way maximum-interest-rate laws benefit borrowers.

This is an important point, and not only because it corrects certain popular but mistaken notions about interest-rate legislation. The return that *any* lender will demand as a condition of lending depends on the risk he assigns to that particular loan. Commercial lenders aren't unique in that respect. Imagine two corporations, one of them General Motors and the other a shaky corporation teetering on the edge of bankruptcy. Each wants to borrow money. To do so, each issues $1000 bonds maturing in one year. At what price will the bonds be purchased?

Suppose the General Motors issue is all sold at $952. $952 now is worth $1000 at maturity (in one year) at a 5% rate of interest. The $952 price would mean, in effect, that people are willing to lend to General Motors for a 5% annual return.

But the bonds of the shaky corporation would sell for far less even if they were purchased by the same people who purchased the General Motors bonds. The probability of default is so much higher in the second case that lenders could only be persuaded to take the risk if they were offered the possibility of a very high return. If the second issue sold for $714, lenders would be demanding a 40% annual return.

---

1. When the prime rate rose to 12% in 1974, it exceeded the maximum legal rate that may be charged in some states for consumer loans. Some banks nonetheless made small consumer loans to their depositors, below the rate they could get on less risky loans to corporations, in order to retain the goodwill and continued patronage of established customers.

If all works out well, they will receive $238 more than they would have earned on a General Motors bond. But that outcome is highly uncertain: there is also the possibility they will lose most or all of the principal. The higher "interest rate" on the latter bonds should therefore be interpreted as a risk premium rather than as pure interest. Perhaps when legislators contemplate interest-rate ceilings, they should ask themselves whether they have ever purchased bonds at a heavy discount.

Consequences of Uncertainty

When we begin to think about the different rates of return that lenders will demand on risky and relatively riskless loans, we quickly get into the interesting problems raised by uncertainty. Suppose that Joe Jones puts $100 into a savings account on January 1. The bank promises 5% interest and Joe is confident that the bank will neither fail nor renege on its commitment. On December 31 he withdraws $105. He earned $5 in interest, a payment for the use of his savings.

STATE "USURY" LAWS

An article in the *Texas Law Review* (November 1971) used an interesting argument in calling for a reduction in Texas's statutory limits on interest rates for small loans. The article claimed that high rates encouraged lenders to extend credit to higher risk customers, that their defaults raised the lenders' cost of doing business, and that more responsible borrowers of larger sums then had to pay higher interest rates to cover these losses. The article also argued that high interest rate ceilings, by making credit available to "irresponsible" people, tempted them to overcommit themselves and "suffer the pains of debt difficulty."

But can lenders succeed in charging more to low risk customers to cover the costs of their loans to high risk borrowers? Won't the low risk customers simply turn to other lenders? And if lenders do in fact sustain losses on high risk loans, why do they make them?

The article (written by students, it should be mentioned) is also interesting in the transparency of its paternalism: Apparently state legislators should decide which persons in society are too immature to obtain credit. At least the authors do recognize—as is not always true with advocates of legal interest rate ceilings—that limitations on interest rates prevent higher risk borrowers from obtaining loans.

Now suppose that he lends the same $100 to a business firm that promises to pay him $5 per year for each year he leaves his funds with the firm and gives him a bond as evidence of its obligation. The firm uses his savings, we may assume, to purchase capital. This doesn't seem to differ in any significant way from the preceding case. Joe has once again received 5% per year for the use of his savings. And everyone will in fact call the $5 interest because it is a contractual obligation of a fixed amount.

Let's vary the situation once again. This time Joe lends the firm $100 and receives in return a share of common stock. Now Joe is not entitled to receive any fixed amount. Ownership of the stock entitles him merely to a share of the firm's earnings. The firm may do poorly and pay him only $2 in dividends over the year, or it may do very well and pay him $15 in dividends. That won't be called interest by most people because it was not a fixed, contractual obligation. But a good case can be made, from a functional standpoint, for applying the interest label to $5 of the dividends. For if 5% is the going rate at which the firm can borrow, and 5% is the rate of return that lenders like Joe can fairly confidently expect from lending their funds at little risk, then 5% is the opportunity cost of lending funds to firms for capital acquisitions. It is what the lender sacrifices by letting any borrower have his savings. It is what he will therefore demand as a condition of making the loan.

Unless he wants to make more than 5% and is willing to accept greater risk in the effort to do so! But if the firm subsequently pays only $2, Joe *sustains a loss.* He loses the extra $3 he could have obtained pretty much as a matter of course by purchasing a bond or putting his money in the bank. If the firm pays $15, Joe *makes a profit.* The profit is $10, not $15: the amount over and above what is available with a very high degree of certainty. To grasp the point we're making here, you must ask yourself why people lend money at 5% when there are opportunities to lend at 15%. The answer is that they can't be certain of the 15%. It might well be less, perhaps a good deal less. The higher rate of return is reserved for people who are willing to take more risk. But that implies, of course, that the higher return *was not generally anticipated.* The generally anticipated return, the rate of return that is rather confidently expected, may be thought of as the interest portion of the return. The remainder is profit.

PROFIT: THE CONSEQUENCE OF UNCERTAINTY

This is a different definition of profit from the one with which we began. *Profit* is now being defined as *the difference between the outcome that was generally anticipated when a decision was made and what finally happened.* It is not the same as interest, which is the social rate of preference for present over future goods and hence the opportunity cost of obtaining present goods. By this definition, profit as distinct from interest is not a cost at all. It is something that appears because the future is uncertain. If there were no uncertainties in life, there would never be a divergence between anticipation and realization, and there would be, by this definition, no profits at all—and no losses, since a loss is simply a profit with a minus sign, like the $3 Joe lost when the firm paid him only $2 in dividends.

Does all this sound strange to your ears? Unrelated to anything you've previously thought or read about profits? Unrelated even to economics? Stay with us. A series of examples interspersed with commentary will be used to clarify this definition and show its significance. In the process of thinking through the examples, you will discover that, however one ultimately chooses to employ the word *profit,* it is useful to have *some* concept for distinguishing between changes in wealth attributable to uncertainty and returns that are rather confidently anticipated.

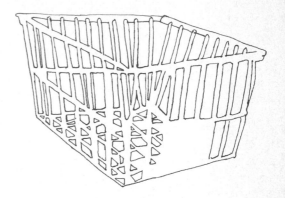

Why Do Profits Appear?

Jerry Flyer is a shrewd investor who regularly earns 10% a year on the money he invests in careful stock purchases. He purchases $1000 worth of stock on January 1. On December 31 the value of that stock plus dividends accumulated during the year is $1100. Jerry makes a zero profit. The $100 he earned should be called interest because it is the opportunity cost to Jerry of letting someone else have $1000 worth of his power to purchase present goods.

Now Jerry takes a flyer. He puts $1000 into Trustworthy Uranium, Incorporated, and one year later the stock has a market value of $1250. Jerry made a profit of $150. He might have lost, of course, and he feels very fortunate. If the stock had gone to only $1040, Jerry would have lost $60.

Notice that he expects to be able to earn 10% pretty much as a matter of course. Therefore, he would not knowingly invest for a mere 5% return, and if he were to receive only 5% he would properly call it a loss. It would be 5% per year that he did not receive because he chose to gamble on a highly uncertain stock, one that might have gone much higher (and he hoped it would) but actually ended up at only $1040.

Suppose Jerry Flyer buys a Florida lot for $2000 when he receives an advertisement that says that Florida real estate increases in value by 30% per year. At the end of the year, the market value of his lot is still $2000. Jerry lost $200, the amount by which his wealth could have been expected to increase had he followed his usual stock-purchase program. We should now begin to have doubts about Jerry's shrewdness as an investor.

If Florida real estate really can be expected to increase in value by 30%

per year, many people will be eager to buy Florida lots, as long as the alternative rate of return is, let's say, 10% per year. Their eagerness to purchase will bid up the price of the lots until the lots are no longer better buys than other available assets. If there happen to be many investors like Jerry, who uncritically accept the claims of the advertisement, their eagerness to benefit from the promised appreciation in real estate prices could even bid the present price of lots so high that price decreases rather than increases will occur subsequently. The key point is this: *The price of any marketable asset reflects the present value of generally expected future earnings.* No one can make a profit by putting his money into an asset or an operation that is *generally expected* to return more than the going rate of interest. For that would be a "good deal." And the demand for a "good deal" bids up the cost of getting in on it until it's no longer a better deal than other assets or opportunities.

Every investor knows this. The time to buy Xerox or Polaroid was before the word got around. Those who bought stock in these companies after it became widely known that they were going to earn large net revenues from the new products they had developed received no profit. The best they could hope for was an interest return on their investment. The market price of Xerox and Polaroid stock was bid up by people eager to share in those companies' future earnings, until the earnings relative to what had to be paid to share in them were no more attractive than earnings generally available in the market.

How to Get Rich

"The way to accumulate a fortune is to invest in profitable companies." This is a very misleading statement. General Motors is rightly regarded as a highly profitable corporation, because it has consistently earned large returns for many years on its original investment in plant, machinery, and other assets. But the market value of General Motors stock long ago increased to take full account of its expected high future earnings. Consequently General Motors stock is not necessarily a better buy than the stock of many companies with dismal earning records.

The way to accumulate a fortune is to invest in companies that are *going* to make large earnings that *no one else currently knows about.* And there's the rub. You must know more than others, or be able to read the uncertain future more accurately, if you hope to make large profits. Or else you rely solely on luck. But you have an equal probability of being unlucky and sustaining a large loss. The significant thing about pure luck is that it's pure.

Let's take an altogether different kind of example to drive home the essential point: that one important source of wealth or income is the successful anticipation of events that are not generally expected. Giuseppe

THE INTERESTS OF CORPORATION OWNERS AND MANAGERS

The interests of the hired managers of a large corporation are not identical with the interests of the owners. The owners primarily want maximum profits; but the managers may prefer to operate the firm to obtain for themselves high salaries, personal prestige and power, or a quiet and secure life. When ownership is scattered among many small investors, the owners may not be able to bring their voting power effectively to bear on management, so that management is left substantially free to pursue its own rather than the owners' interests. One student of the large corporation, the late A. A. Berle, Jr., coined the phrase "automatic self-perpetuating oligarchies" to characterize the managers of such corporations. But Berle may have been guilty of serious exaggeration.

The market price of a corporation's stock reflects current and potential investors' estimates of the future profits of the corporation. Investors will be less eager to own the stock of a corporation if they believe it is not being managed in the owners' best interests, and the stock will consequently have a lower market price. The gap between the actual price of the stock and what the price would be if the corporation were thought to be well managed then becomes an incentive for other corporations or wealthy investors to attempt a take-over. Their aim is to dump the offending managers, operate the company more profitably, and gain from the consequent appreciation in the stock's price.

Managers by and large know that a high market price for the stock of their corporations is the best protection for their own positions. And this constrains them to pay attention to corporate profitability and the owners' interests.

Vibrato attends a conservatory of music for three years, studying for a career in opera. At about the time of Vibrato's graduation, the public abandons all interest in opera. So Vibrato sustains a loss. We mustn't exaggerate the loss, for Vibrato may receive a generous return on his educational investment in the form of many years of listening to himself sing Verdi and Wagner. Education can prepare a person to enjoy life as well as provide him with a marketable skill. But to the extent that Vibrato paid tuition and sacrificed earnings for three years in order to earn an income in opera, the unexpected change in public tastes inflicted a loss upon him.

The very important point to be noted here is that profits and losses can and will appear almost anywhere, for anyone at all, and not just for those who invest in common stocks or real estate. Aerospace engineers suffer losses when the federal government cuts back on the space program and cancels the SST (supersonic transport). College professors receive profits when the federal government decides to spend huge sums on higher education. Authors make a profit when they hit on a product that captivates

SHOULD EMPLOYEES SHARE IN PROFITS?

"The employees of a business enterprise have no legitimate claim to share with the owners in the profits because they do not bear any of the risk." Statements like that are often made when unions point to large profits as a justification for wage increases. But is it correct to say that employees bear none of the risks of a business enterprise?

If a firm fails, its employees lose the benefits of accumulated seniority and of skills they have acquired specific to that job. There are other costs—job search, moving one's residence—that fall upon employees when the firm for which they are working lays them off.

Many players in the World Football League continued to perform in 1974 long after the team owners had stopped paying their salaries. They were investing the value of their services in the hope of a large future return if the league managed to establish itself financially. In the case of some teams, at least, the principal investors by the end of the 1974 season may not have been the owners so much as the players who had risked at least the amount of their alternative earnings in an effort to make the WFL succeed.

Employees do take risk into account in deciding whether to go to work for a firm. And if a firm's prospects are thought to be highly uncertain, employees will insist upon a higher wage as a condition of accepting employment. If the firm succeeds, they will then be receiving a wage for their labor services plus a profit for correctly anticipating the future. If the firm fails, they may receive less than the value of their labor services, or a wage minus a loss for anticipating the future incorrectly.

Few employees would be willing to work without pay for as long as some WFL players did in 1974. But that is because the WFL players continued to hope for a return considerably above what they might have earned by quitting the team and taking their next best job opportunity.

the public. Highly trained astrologers took a loss when people abandoned the belief that the stars shape individual destiny—just as some of their intellectual descendants have recently made profits from an unexpected return to older persuasions.

What Function Does Profit Perform?

The core of the argument is that profit is something quite different functionally from other kinds of income. The payment that induces someone to supply labor services is a wage. The payment that induces someone to supply the services of his money, or better, the services of what this money can obtain, is interest. These are necessary payments, in a sense. A manufacturer cannot obtain the services of people or physical property unless he is able to bid them away from alternative employments by paying their opportunity cost. But there is a kind of income that seems *both unnecessary and inevitable:* the income that accrues to people because decisions are always made in the present but only justified in the future, and the future is uncertain. "Unnecessary and inevitable" is a strange combination. But think about it.

When businessmen and others talk about the "necessity for profits," as they often do, they are almost certainly not using the word *profit* in the way that we are now defining it. A business firm will not be able to operate unless it can obtain funds with which to hire services. In that sense, such funds are necessary. It can obtain funds only by generating revenue from sales or by borrowing. It will be unable to borrow unless potential lenders believe that future sales will generate sufficient revenue to allow payment of interest on the loans. It will be easy for the firm to obtain funds if people are anticipating very large future net revenues from its operation, but difficult for it to do so if people generally are pessimistic about the firm's prospects. This is all that businessmen mean, or ought to mean, when they speak of the necessity for profits: the need for enough revenue and prospective revenue to enable the firm to pay the opportunity cost of the services required for continued operation. This much is "needed" in the sense that the business firm will not be able to operate indefinitely without it.

We must keep in mind at the same time that the *potential* of profit is an important stimulus to action. If profits could somehow always be confiscated, we would certainly observe less innovation in society and fewer resources devoted to exploration and experiment. But there is a very big difference between a *potential* profit and a profit in the pocket. The potential of a profit prompts people to search for more efficient ways of combining resources, new products for which there might be a social demand, and organizational innovations that promise to increase efficiency. If they succeed, they benefit society and receive a profit. But they may fail, and in that case they will sustain a loss.

So no business *must* make a profit. At the same time, profits and losses are inevitable. As long as there is uncertainty about the future, there will be divergencies between anticipated outcomes and what actually does occur. This is just as true of a socialist economy as of a capitalist one.

"ROYALTIES" FOR ARTISTS

A number of leading American artists have recently begun to argue that they are entitled to share in the profits when their paintings are resold at higher prices. Some are pressing Congress for legislation that would *require* the payment of "royalties" to the artist whenever the owner of a painting gained from an appreciation in its value. Others have vowed not to sell future work without a clause in the sales contract guaranteeing the painter a percentage of any profits made when the work subsequently changes hands. But would such arrangements prove financially beneficial to artists?

Contracts of this sort, whether voluntary or enforced by law, would tend to reduce original selling prices. An uncertain profit that must be shared will, after all, have a lower present value than one that does not have to be shared. Moreover, artists do gain under current arrangements from increases in the market price of previous work. If collectors bid the price of a Robert Rauschenberg painting, sold originally by the artist for $960, up to $85,000 (as happened recently), Rauschenberg gets no share of the $84,040 profit but does benefit from the effect of this sale on the price of his current work. Artists generally concede this but argue nonetheless that collectors receive an undeservedly large share of the gains. On the other hand, the prospect of occasional very large gains, by attracting more art investors into the market, increases the demand and hence the selling prices for paintings by known and unknown artists.

Artists should consider an additional factor before pushing too hard for this reform. Royalties would be collected not when paintings appreciate in value but when they are *sold* at higher prices. The royalty system might therefore discourage sales, perhaps until the artist is dead or the royalty arrangement has expired. And every artist knows how news of a high auction price for a previous work can stimulate the demand for current work.

Because the central planners in a socialist state are not omniscient, they will sometimes anticipate the future incorrectly. Their mistakes will create profits for some and losses for others. The citizens in a socialist state will also receive profits and incur losses as their actions lead to outcomes different from those that were generally anticipated. (Think of the profits that accrued to those who consistently supported Stalin in the 1930s and the losses sustained by those who misread the future.) What socialism *can* do is distribute the profits and losses differently from the way they would be distributed under capitalism.

An important task for the student of alternative economic systems is the assessment of the various consequences of different ways of distributing profits and losses. Profits and losses can be attached closely to the individuals who make decisions, or to specific other parties not involved in the decisions, or divided among many different people. Moreover, individuals can be allowed to buy and sell risk freely or they can be prevented from doing so. The efficiency of an economic system, the fairness of its operation, and the degree of freedom it allows the citizens will all be importantly affected by the way a society chooses to distribute profits and losses. But no social system can eliminate profits and losses until it learns how to eliminate uncertainty.

Combining the Two Definitions

We have now examined two different definitions of profit:

Definition 1: Total revenue minus total cost.

Definition 2: The difference between the outcome that was generally anticipated when a decision was made and what finally happened.

And here is the question: Will a firm's total revenue ever exceed its total cost in a world with no uncertainty? In other words, can there be a difference between total revenue and total cost that is *not* due to the difference between generally anticipated and actual outcomes? If the answer is *no*, the definitions are synonymous; the second definition merely explains the source of the difference between total revenue and total cost. But is *no* a defensible answer?

It's more defensible than you might at first suppose. Total cost is opportunity cost, and so it includes not only a firm's payments to others for commodities and services used, but also the implicit value of any goods—labor, land, capital—that the firm owns. Interest payments are part of the firm's costs, including that portion of its dividends which is about equal to the interest return its shareholders could have received by lending their money elsewhere. When we include *all* these opportunity costs in our calculation of total costs, there seems to be no reason why any firm would have to earn revenues in excess of costs. Firms could make zero profits and continue in business. They could even be considered successful firms and be able to borrow new funds for expansion—as long as their revenues were adequate to cover *all* their costs.

In fact, if there were some way for a firm to get into a line of business that guaranteed more in revenue than it entailed in cost, wouldn't so many people move into that line of business that the difference between revenue and cost would be competed down to zero? Remember that cost means *all* costs, including an actual or implicit payment for getting the business organized and keeping it in operation. The *certainty* of a return greater than this would surely attract new business firms. Their entry would increase output, reduce the price of the product consistently with the law of demand, and thus reduce the gap between total revenue and total cost. The gap might simultaneously be reduced from the other direction as the new entrants increased the demand and raised the cost for the inputs used in turning out the product. Only when the gap between total revenue and total cost had disappeared, or when profits had been reduced to zero, would there no longer be any incentive for new firms to enter.

In the actual and uncertain world, of course, it doesn't work that way. People see profits being made in particular lines of business but they aren't sure how to go about cutting themselves in on those profits. In a world of scarce information, the existence of such profits might not even be widely known. And so profits do exist and continue to exist without being competed down to zero. But this happens *because of uncertainty*. In the absence of uncertainty everything relevant to profit making would be generally known, all opportunities for profit making fully exploited, and profits everywhere consequently equal to zero.

PROFIT: THE CONSEQUENCE OF RESTRICTED COMPETITION

But we have left out a very important possibility! What if some profit makers, even in a world without uncertainty, were able to prevent others from entering their line of business and competing away their profits? Then total revenue could exceed total cost and continue to exceed it indefinitely.

We must therefore add a second explanation or cause of profit, something in addition to uncertainty and quite separate from it: *Profit can also arise from restrictions on the ability to compete.*

Such restrictions arise primarily from two sources and can therefore usefully be divided into two kinds: (1) Restrictions imposed by the natural scarcity of particular resources; (2) Restrictions imposed by social or political actions. We can see both kinds at work in the case of Mr. Artesian.

The Source of Artesian's Profits

Recall that Artesian was earning about $1000 per year over and above his total costs when he first got his mineral water spring into operation. This was clearly a profit by our general definition: total revenue minus total cost. But what was its cause or source?

Uncertainty

In the first instance the source of Artesian's profit was uncertainty. If it had been generally known at the time Artesian purchased the property that there was a valuable mineral spring on the premises, a spring that could net its owner more than $1000 per year, then Artesian would have had to pay more than he actually did for the land. An asset that can be confidently expected to yield its owner $1000 per year has the same value as $20,000 in a savings account earning 5% interest. So if the property had a value, let us say, of $10,000 apart from the spring, its value might be as much as $30,000 with the spring taken into account. Artesian obtained the land for $10,000 rather than $30,000 only because no one knew about the existence of the spring. The difference between the outcome that was generally anticipated when Artesian bought the lot and what finally happened, our first explanation of profit, was $1000 of extra income per year to the owner of the lot. If Artesian had incurred some costs in finding out about the spring, that would have to be subtracted from his profit.

Suppose Artesian decided to sell his land and move to Alaska. He would find people willing to bid the price up well above his own purchase price of $10,000 because they would want to obtain ownership of that $1000 per year stream of income. Of course, they aren't likely to bid the price as high as $30,000 because $1000 of net income from a mineral water spring will be regarded as a less certain prospect than $1000 in bank interest on a $20,000 savings account. Only if that $1000 could be expected with the same certainty as the bank interest would the sale price approach $30,000. Suppose Artesian is able to sell his land for $22,500. If the spring then earns its new owner $1000 in every subsequent year, the new owner also makes a profit. But *his* profit is only $475. Do you see why?

We're assuming $10,000 of the purchase price to be the value of the land for living on, raising radishes, or whatever. This was the value generally anticipated when Artesian made his purchase, and we're just assuming it remains unchanged. (It wouldn't have to. The value of the land for residential purposes could go down because the owner's privacy is destroyed by all the customers of the spring.) So we just ignore $10,000 of the purchase price and all the benefits of ownership not related to the mineral water spring. We're left with $12,500 paid to obtain the income from the spring. But now $625 of that income has to be considered a cost of doing business. $625 is the annual interest on $12,500, the amount the new owner is giving up by putting his $12,500 into ownership of the land. So if the spring continues to yield him $1000 a year, his profit—total revenue minus total cost—is only $475. On the other hand, if competition appears, as it did in chapter 11, so that his net revenue falls to $400, the new owner sustains annual losses. For $400 is only 3.2% of $12,500, and that's 1.8% less than the interest cost of owning the spring.

Restrictions on the Ability of Others to Compete

But will competition necessarily appear? We can see both kinds of restriction at work in the mineral water case. There may be in the area only one spring whose water has all the invigorating qualities so valued by Artesian's customers. Other sources may be so far away that the water can only be transported into Artesian's market area at a prohibitive cost. In such a situation Artesian could continue indefinitely to earn his $1048.30 annual profit, even though there is no longer any uncertainty about revenues and costs, because he is the owner of a naturally rare resource. Others would like to cut themselves in on Artesian's profit; but they cannot do so without access to mineral water, and Artesian has control of the only available supply.

There are many types of unique productive resources. One important type that we might tend to overlook is human skills. Very often firms will continue to earn profits year after year, despite the best efforts of their competitors, because the firms are managed with exceptional skill. Other kinds of rare resources that may restrict the ability of others to compete away a firm's profits include location, reputation, and experience.

But the restrictions imposed on competition by the natural scarcity of resources are seldom enough to satisfy firms that find themselves making profits. For one thing, there are just too many alternative ways of doing things. Even if there is no other mineral water within an economical distance, competitors could sell tomato juice fortified with vitamins and minerals and claim that it's more healthful than Artesian's water and tastes much better besides. Moreover, unless the profit-earning firm *owns* the scarce resources that give it a permanent advantage, potential competitors can try to hire those resources away. They can bid for the choice location when the current tenant's lease expires; and even if they don't manage to bid it away, they may force the firm to pay a higher rent to maintain control of the advantageous location. That would erode the firm's profit by raising its costs. If the natural scarcity that is responsible for the persistent profits happens to be managerial skills, potential competitors can try to hire away those managers. Again, even if they don't succeed, they may raise the firm's costs by forcing it to pay higher salaries to key employees. So it isn't hard to understand why profit making firms turn regularly to the government for help in imposing restrictions on competition.

Patents granted to inventors are one important type of political restriction. The purpose of a patent is precisely this: to help the patent owner earn profits over an extended period of time by prohibiting others from making use of the process that is the source of those profits. This can be justified on the grounds that new and more efficient processes would not be developed as often if the developers could not count on earning profits from their innovative efforts. The patent privilege is thus a temporary grant of privilege from the government designed to raise the wealth of successful innovators with the long run aim of raising the wealth of society.

Other forms of government restrictions on competition are usually harder to defend. We discussed this question in chapter 11 and won't rehearse what we said there. All that we're looking for in this chapter is an understanding of the sources and functions of profit. And we're ready now to put it all together.

Putting It All Together

Profit is total revenue minus total cost. That's an acceptable definition from the economist's point of view if cost is calculated as opportunity cost. Some of what is commonly called "business profits" ought to be regarded, from a functional point of view, as implicit payments to factors of production. A substantial portion of corporate profits and most of the net income of unincorporated enterprises, including professional income, is actually a payment for the use of capital, land, or labor and ought therefore to be designated as interest, rent, or wages.

What, then, is the source of pure profits? There are two sources, we have argued. One is uncertainty. Because the future cannot be accurately predicted, actual outcomes will often differ from what is generally anticipated at the time decisions are made and hostages are given to fortune. But uncertainty creates losses as well as profits, and this is a very important point to remember in assessing the size and social importance of profits.

The other source of profits is restrictions on competition. These may be due to natural scarcities or to social and political restrictions of many kinds.

That's the big picture view. If the road toward it was unusually long and tortuous, it's largely because the concept of profit is used in so many different ways and often without much thought. But the perspective one acquires by thinking carefully about the functions of profit makes the trip worth the effort. At least we hope it does.

DISCOUNTING, PRESENT VALUES, AND ECONOMIC DECISIONS

Several times in the preceding pages we used discounting procedures and the concept of present value to make our argument. The context should have made the meaning clear at the time. Let's go back now for another look at an important economic and financial concept.

Artesian was receiving a profit of $1048.30 per year from the mineral water spring discovered on his property. When he decided to move to Alaska, we assumed that he found a buyer willing to pay $12,500 for the spring (plus an additional $10,000 for the other uses of the land, which we'll ignore.) How did we arrive at a figure of $12,500? We first assumed that the buyer (let's call him Mr. Mill) was purchasing the ownership of an annual income stream of about $1000. Then we asked what such an income stream would be worth to him. We noted that he could obtain $1000 per year with negligible risk by putting $20,000 into a bank savings account that was paying 5% per year. So he clearly wouldn't be willing to pay more than $20,000 for the income from the spring. In fact, he wouldn't want to go that high because he views the income from the spring as much less certain than the income from a savings account. If Mill is to put his money into the mineral water operation, he will have to be attracted by the possibility of a return greater than the 5% he can obtain from the bank on a practically riskless investment. Mill won't have to be *guaranteed* more than 5%; guarantees are obviously out of the question on risky ventures. But the *possibility* of a better rate of return must be there. How much better will depend on Mill's perception of the risk. We assumed in setting the sale price at $12,500 that Mill was satisfied, on the basis of his assessment of the risk, with the prospect of an 8% return. For $1000 per year is an 8% return on an investment of $12,500.

Suppose Mill had seen the mineral water operation as a highly risky venture which he wouldn't be willing to enter unless he had some chance of a 25% return. Then he would only have offered $4000 for the property: $1000 (the annual income) divided by 25% (the rate of return he wants). If he wanted a 15% return, he would have offered $6667 for the property: $1000 divided by 15%.

What we're doing here is the most elementary kind of *discounting*. Discounting is *the process of obtaining present values from expected future values*. It's an important concept in the financial world as well as in the intellectual tool box of economists, and it's worth mastering. (It's also fun to play with.)

It becomes obvious as soon as you think about it that prospective purchasers of any asset will have their eye on expected future earnings, the future income or increases in wealth that can be anticipated from ownership of the asset. Their demand for the asset will reflect their estimate of

all such future earnings. That's why, for example, the stock of a corporation that isn't currently earning any revenue above its costs may still sell for a high price. Purchasers are anticipating future earnings for the corporation, and they're trying to buy themselves a share in those earnings.

What Tomorrow Is Worth Today

But income in the future is not worth as much as income now. That's what the interest rate asserts. If the pure interest rate, which means the nominal rate minus any premium for risk, is 3%, then any person with $100 now can have $103 one year from now. All he must do is surrender for a year $100 of his power to purchase goods. Whether he thinks that's a fine bargain will depend upon his personal rate of time preference.[1] Those who discount the future at less than 3% per year will want to surrender present for future purchasing power at that rate of interest. Those who discount the future at more than 3% will want to acquire present command over goods at that rate in exchange for the surrender of future command over goods.

But if the prevailing rate of interest is 3%, then future income should always be discounted at a rate no less than that. Even if you have a zero rate of time preference, so that you value future goods equally with present goods, present goods will have a higher value for you because they grow over time into more goods. At 3%, $100 now becomes $103 after one year.

It follows, then, that $103 to be received one year from now is only worth $100 in present value. The calculation in this case is so simple that it seems silly to write it out; but discounting calculations are not always so obvious, and the simple case provides the basis for understanding more complex cases.

$100 times 1.03, which is one plus the rate of discount, equals $103, the

1. Any discussion of interest rates and the relative values of present and future goods will be misleading unless all parties to the discussion are making similar assumptions about the future behavior of the general price level. In a period of long continued inflation, discussion gets confused by the implicit adoption of different expectations about future prices. If you chuckled derisively at the suggestion in the text above that 3% per year was a fine bargain, that may be because you have never experienced a stable price level and you're assuming that inflation is going to continue at 5% per year or so. But a 5% annual increase in the price level is the same thing as a 5% annual decrease in the value of money. That means that $103 one year from now in return for $100 now would be a *real* interest rate of minus 2%. And that would *not* be a fine bargain. We are always assuming no change in the value of money, or general price stability, in this chapter, and it's important for you to know that and keep it in mind. This is another instance of the problems created for economic analysis by the experience of inflation. We discussed the problem earlier in chapter 3, page 44, under "An Important Note on *Relative* Prices." You may want to review those paragraphs.

value one year from now of $100 in present value. The value of a present $100 after two years will be $100 times 1.03 multiplied again by 1.03, or $100 times 1.03^2. This is simply the familiar rule for calculating compound interest.

It follows, then, that $100 eight years from now will be $100 times 1.03^8 or $126.68. Conversely, $126.68 to be received at the end of eight years has a present value of $100: $126.68 divided by 1.03^8 equals $100.

With those basic rules in mind, let's go back to the case of Artesian and Mill. What would Mill have been willing to pay for Artesian's spring if the annual $1048.30 income was expected to continue for only ten years? (After ten years the spring is to become the property of the town.) Let's assume again that the prevailing interest rate is 5% and that Mill wants an extra 3% on this asset because of the risk he assigns to the purchase. So he's going to discount this future income at 8% in order to obtain its present value.

Now $1048.30 per year forever (financial people like to say "in perpetuity") has a present value of $13,103.75 when discounted at 8%. We merely divide the annual income by the rate of discount. But $1048.30 per year for only ten years is both less than $13,103.75 and more difficult to compute. To calculate the present value of a ten-year annuity of $1048.30 at an 8% rate of discount (an annuity is simply a sum received annually), we must determine the present value of $1048.30 one year from now, two years from now, on up to ten years from now, and then add these values. That's going to be a chore, even with a calculator. But there are tables available that one can use to simplify the calculations, and we've provided a few for you to practice with.

Look at the column under 8% in table 12A. It shows the present value at an 8% rate of discount of a $100 annuity running for various numbers of years. The first number in the column is 100 ÷ 1.08; the second number is 100 ÷ 1.08 *plus* 100 ÷ 1.08^2; the third is the previous total plus 100 ÷ 1.08^3. Jumping down to the row for a ten-year annuity, we read off the value of $671. It tells us that $100 per year for ten years has a present value of $671 when discounted at 8%. The same annuity has a greater present value at lower rates of discount, a smaller present value at higher rates. (Check that statement by looking at the other columns.)

It's a simple matter now to obtain the present value of a $1048.30 annuity. We multiply $671 by 10.483 to obtain $7034. So Mill should be willing to pay about $7034 for Artesian's spring if the town is going to take it over after ten years.

The Apartment Business

Try your hand at another problem. You have a chance to purchase an apartment building that was recently constructed. You estimate that the building has twenty years of useful life ahead of it, after which you expect

Table 12A   ANNUITY TABLE

Number of Years Annuity Is Received	Present Value of $100 Annuity, Received at the End of Each Year, for Designated Number of Years at Various Interest Rates					
	3%	5%	6%	8%	12%	20%
1	97.09	95.24	94.34	92.59	89.286	83.333
2	191.35	185.94	183.34	178.33	169.005	152.778
3	282.86	272.32	267.30	257.71	240.183	210.648
4	371.71	354.60	346.51	331.21	303.735	258.873
5	457.97	432.95	421.24	399.27	360.478	299.061
6	541.72	507.57	491.73	462.29	411.141	332.551
7	623.03	578.64	558.24	520.64	456.376	360.459
8	701.97	646.32	620.98	574.66	496.764	383.716
9	778.61	710.78	680.17	624.69	532.825	403.097
10	853.02	772.17	736.01	671.01	565.022	419.247
11	925.26	830.64	788.69	713.90	593.770	432.706
12	995.40	886.33	838.38	753.61	619.437	443.922
13	1063.50	939.36	885.27	790.38	642.355	453.268
14	1129.61	989.86	929.50	824.42	662.817	461.057
15	1193.79	1037.97	971.22	855.95	681.086	467.547
16	1256.11	1083.78	1010.59	885.14	697.399	472.956
17	1316.61	1127.41	1047.73	912.16	711.963	477.463
18	1375.35	1168.96	1082.76	937.19	724.967	481.219
19	1432.38	1208.53	1115.81	960.36	736.578	484.350
20	1487.75	1246.22	1146.99	981.81	746.944	486.958
21	1541.50	1282.12	1176.41	1001.68	756.200	489.132
22	1593.69	1316.30	1204.16	1020.07	764.465	490.943
23	1644.36	1348.86	1230.34	1037.11	771.843	492.453
24	1693.55	1379.86	1255.04	1052.88	778.432	493.710
25	1741.31	1409.39	1278.34	1067.48	784.314	494.759
26	1787.68	1437.52	1300.32	1081.00	789.566	495.632
27	1832.70	1464.30	1321.05	1093.52	794.255	496.360
28	1876.41	1489.81	1340.62	1105.11	798.442	496.967
29	1918.85	1514.11	1359.07	1115.84	802.181	497.472
30	1960.04	1537.25	1376.48	1125.78	805.518	497.894
31	2000.04	1559.28	1392.91	1134.98	808.499	498.245
32	2038.88	1580.27	1408.40	1143.50	811.159	498.537
33	2076.58	1600.25	1423.02	1151.39	813.535	498.781
34	2113.18	1619.29	1436.81	1158.69	815.656	498.984
35	2148.72	1637.42	1449.82	1165.46	817.550	499.154
36	2183.23	1654.69	1462.10	1171.72	819.241	499.295
37	2216.72	1671.13	1473.68	1177.52	820.751	499.412
38	2249.25	1686.79	1484.60	1182.89	822.099	499.510
39	2280.82	1701.70	1494.91	1187.86	823.303	499.592
40	2311.48	1715.91	1504.63	1192.46	824.378	499.660
41	2341.24	1729.44	1513.80	1196.72	825.337	499.717
42	2370.14	1742.32	1522.45	1200.67	626.194	499.764
43	2398.19	1754.59	1530.62	1204.32	826.959	499.803
44	2425.43	1766.28	1538.32	1207.71	827.642	499.836
45	2451.87	1777.41	1545.58	1210.84	828.252	499.863
46	2477.54	1788.01	1552.44	1213.74	828.796	400.886
47	2502.47	1798.10	1558.90	1216.43	829.282	499.905
48	2526.67	1807.72	1565.00	1218.91	829.716	499.921
49	2550.17	1816.87	1570.76	1221.22	830.104	499.934
50	2572.98	1825.59	1576.19	1223.35	830.450	499.945

302   *Chapter Twelve*

to tear it down and sell the land. You hope to get $25,000 for the land at that time. Those are expectations, of course, and they may be wrong. You estimate also that you can obtain rents from your tenants that will exceed your annual costs of maintenance and operation by $15,000 per year. Those are also expectations, and they're even more uncertain. Calculate the amount you would be willing to pay for the apartment building.

You'll have to choose a rate of discount, a rate that will depend upon both the prevailing interest rate and your assessment of the probability that your estimates may turn out to be overly optimistic. The more cautious you are about assuming risk, the higher will be your rate of discount. People differ in their willingness to assume risk: risk averters use high discount rates and hence offer relatively low bids for assets, which means that they often lose them to people who are less averse to risk. Of course, the risk preferrers, while more often the successful bidders, will also end up losing their shirts more often than the risk averters.

Let's try a 12% rate of discount. Table 12A shows that the present value of a twenty-year annuity of $100 is $747 when the annuity is discounted at 12%. Multiply that by 150 and you get $112,050 as the present value of your expected rental income. But you still have to add on what you expect to get from selling the land. It's $25,000; but $25,000 twenty years from now is worth much less than that currently. Table 12B enables you to determine quickly the value of $25,000 divided by 1.12^{20}. Since $100 twenty years from now has a present value of $10.40, $25,000 twenty years from now has a present value 250 times that or $2600. $2600 plus $112,050 is $114,650. And that's what you should be willing to pay for the apartment building.[1]

Making Economic Decisions

We can put some familiar principles to work now. Notice that our calculations at no time took into account the cost of constructing the apartment building or the original price paid for the land. Those are sunk costs and hence they are irrelevant. The cost of buying land and constructing an apartment building is only relevant if it's an opportunity cost. You would want to investigate, before submitting your bid, to see whether you could put up a building with the same earning prospects for less than $114,650. If you think you can, then you will choose to build rather than buy. But that would be a future construction cost, not an historical cost. Perhaps the original builder paid $140,000 to put up the building. If he did, he won't be happy about selling for $114,650. And he will *not* sell if he reads

1. The appendix includes an article from *Fortune* on the perils of decision making in the office construction industry. It exemplifies many of the concepts explained in this chapter and earlier ones.

Table 12B PRESENT VALUES OF FUTURE AMOUNTS

Number of Years in the Future	Present Value of $100, Received the Designated Number of Years in the Future, at Various Interest Rates					
	3%	5%	6%	8%	12%	20%
1	97.0874	95.2381	94.3396	92.5926	89.2857	83.3333
2	94.2596	90.7029	88.9996	85.7339	79.7194	69.4444
3	91.5142	86.3838	83.9619	79.3832	71.1780	57.8704
4	88.8487	82.2702	79.2094	73.5030	63.5518	48.2253
5	86.2609	78.3526	74.7258	68.0583	56.7427	40.1878
6	83.7484	74.6215	70.4961	63.0170	50.6631	33.4898
7	81.3092	71.0681	66.5057	58.3490	45.2349	27.9082
8	78.9409	67.6839	62.7412	54.0269	40.3883	23.2568
9	76.6417	64.4609	59.1898	50.0249	36.0610	19.3807
10	74.4094	61.3913	55.8395	46.3193	32.1973	16.1506
11	72.2421	58.4679	52.6788	42.8883	28.7476	13.4588
12	70.1380	55.6837	49.6969	39.7114	25.6675	11.2157
13	68.0951	53.0321	46.8839	36.7698	22.9174	9.3464
14	66.1118	50.5068	44.2301	34.0461	20.4620	7.7887
15	64.1862	48.1017	41.7265	31.5242	18.2696	6.4905
16	62.3167	45.8112	39.3646	29.1890	16.3122	5.4088
17	60.5016	43.6297	37.1364	27.0269	14.5644	4.5073
18	58.7395	41.5521	35.0344	25.0249	13.0040	3.7561
19	57.0286	39.5734	33.0513	23.1712	11.6107	3.1301
20	55.3676	37.6889	31.1805	21.4548	10.3667	2.6084
21	53.7549	35.8942	29.4155	19.8656	9.2560	2.1737
22	52.1893	34.1850	27.7505	18.3941	8.2643	1.8114
23	50.6692	32.5571	26.1797	17.0315	7.3788	1.5095
24	49.1934	31.0068	24.6979	15.7699	6.5882	1.2579
25	47.7606	29.5303	23.2999	14.6018	5.8823	1.0483
26	46.3695	28.1241	21.9810	13.5202	5.2521	0.8735
27	45.0189	26.7848	20.7368	12.5187	4.6894	0.7280
28	43.7077	25.5094	19.5630	11.5914	4.1869	0.6066
29	42.4346	24.2946	18.4557	10.7328	3.7383	0.5055
30	41.1987	23.1377	17.4110	9.9377	3.3378	0.4213
31	39.9987	22.0359	16.4255	9.2016	2.9802	0.3511
32	38.8337	20.9866	15.4957	8.5200	2.6609	0.2926
33	37.7026	19.9873	14.6186	7.8889	2.3758	0.2438
34	36.6045	19.0355	13.7912	7.3045	2.1212	0.2032
35	35.5383	18.1290	13.0105	6.7635	1.8940	0.1693
36	34.5032	17.2657	12.2741	6.2625	1.6910	0.1411
37	33.4983	16.4436	11.5793	5.7986	1.5098	0.1176
38	32.5226	15.6605	10.9239	5.3690	1.3481	0.0980
39	31.5754	14.9148	10.3056	4.9713	1.2036	0.0816
40	30.6557	14.2046	9.7222	4.6031	1.0747	0.0680
41	29.7628	13.5282	9.1719	4.2621	0.9595	0.0567
42	28.8959	12.8840	8.6527	3.9464	0.8567	0.0472
43	28.0543	12.2704	8.1630	3.6541	0.7649	0.0394
44	27.2372	11.6861	7.7009	3.3834	0.6830	0.0328
45	26.4439	11.1297	7.2650	3.1328	0.6098	0.0273
46	25.6737	10.5997	6.8538	2.9007	0.5445	0.0228
47	24.9259	10.0949	6.4658	2.6859	0.4861	0.0190
48	24.1999	9.6142	6.0998	2.4869	0.4340	0.0158
49	23.4950	9.1564	5.7546	2.3027	0.3875	0.0132
50	22.8107	8.7204	5.4288	2.1321	0.3460	0.0110

the future more optimistically than you. But it is his reading of the (uncertain) future that determines what he will demand for the building, just as it is your reading of the future that determines what you're willing to pay.

Notice that the builder has lost about $26,000 *whether or not he chooses to sell.* (We're assuming now that he reads the future as you do.) He cannot avoid the loss by hanging on to the building. If he hangs on, he will simply receive $15,000 a year for twenty years and a lump sum of $25,000 at the end of that time. And the present value of those receipts is $114,650. He sustains a loss because he made a decision based upon a faulty prediction of the future: the decision to construct a building whose costs were greater in relation to subsequent revenues than he had anticipated.

Matters might have turned out differently. If net rental revenues were now expected to be $20,000 rather than $15,000 per year, the present value of the building would be $152,000 and the builder would have made a profit of $12,000. And the profit, like the loss, exists whether or not he elects to sell.

Financial commentators sometimes call such profits *paper profits,* as if an increase in the value of an asset were not real until the asset had been sold. This is very misleading. To sell an asset is always to exchange one asset for another: a building for money, for example. But is money less paperish than a building or land or shares of stock or any other asset? The answer, of course, is that it is not. Those who want to distinguish between paper profits and real profits seem to be assuming that the profit may disappear if the asset whose value increased is not quickly exchanged for money. But it is no more probable, in the estimation of most people, that the asset whose value increased will fall again in price than that it will rise still further. If one probability is generally deemed greater than the other, the *present* value of the asset will change to take account of this expectation. If the builder decides to sell at $152,000 and "take" his profit, he is only exchanging a more risky asset for a less risky one. Note what "more risky" means: It means that the future returns are more likely to be *different* from what is anticipated, *not* that they are likely to be *less.* However, in an economy subject to large and unpredictable changes in the price level, money could well be a *more* risky asset than real estate.

THE POLITICS AND ETHICS OF PROFIT

The bewildering variety of meanings assigned to the word profit is in part a reflection of the complex interrelationships that the concept must summarize. But it is also in part a result of the fact that the concept of profit arouses political and ethical passions as do few others terms in eco-

RESIDENTIAL MORTGAGE RATES

There are legal limits on the rate of interest that savings and loan institutions and mutual savings banks can pay their depositors. In 1974 they were never allowed to pay more than $6\frac{1}{2}\%$ on short term deposits, at a time when the federal government was willing to pay up to 10% interest to purchasers of government securities. Since these institutions are the major source of funds for residential mortgages, the supply of mortgage money quite understandably "dried up" in 1974. The total of deposits with these institutions, even when adjusted for changes in the purchasing power of money, had grown steadily since World War II and had more than doubled between 1960 and 1973. But in September 1974 that total was 6% *less* than it had been at the end of 1973. This was, of course, a major factor in the decline of new housing starts in 1974 and the consequent depression in the home building industry. In 1974 new housing starts averaged less than 70% of their 1973 level and less than 60% of the 1972 level.

But even if these institutions had not been subjected to legal ceilings on the amount they could pay depositors, they would have been trapped on the other end by effective ceilings on mortgage rates. Statutory ceilings were probably not as important as the simple unwillingness of home buyers to borrow at rates that would have made home mortgages fully competitive with other investment opportunities. That might have required 12% or 13% mortgage rates in 1974 when interest rates had been pulled up by expectations of close to 10% per year inflation. If prices do rise by 10% per year, then a 13% mortgage actually entails only 3% in annual interest charges because the loan will be repaid in dollars that decline 10% in value each year. Even if home buyers fully understood this relationship between the nominal and real interest rates, however, they would have been reluctant to lock themselves into long term loans when they weren't *certain* of the future course of inflation. One solution that has been proposed calls for variable interest rate mortgages, with the rates periodically adjusted up or down as the general price level and hence the value of money changes.

nomics. For one person profit is the engine of social progress and the foundation of all things true, good, and beautiful. For another person, however, it is unearned income and the consequence of exploitation. If the authors were risk averters, we might have omitted this section of chapter 12 altogether; anyone who attempts to discuss the social significance of profit is almost certain to give offense. We shall nonetheless rush in where angels fear to tread by looking at some of the additional denotations and connotations of the word *profit*.

Earned and Unearned Income

Sometimes the word is used to describe all income *not* earned by working in the current time period. This occurs, for example, when the total of the national income is divided into the wages share and the profits share. "Profits" then includes interest income and rental income as well as the more narrowly defined kind of profit we have been discussing up to this point. For many people this division of income into wages and profits corresponds closely to the categories of earned and unearned income, which correspond in turn to deserved and undeserved income. Wages are earned by one's effort and hence are justified income. But how does anyone earn the right to profits?

In the nineteenth century that question bothered some economists. One of them, Nassau Senior (1790–1864), suggested that as wages were the reward for the pain of laboring, so property income was the reward for the pain of abstaining from current consumption. Owners of capital earn income by leasing their property to society. But they only have the property available for lease because they have previously accumulated it through acts of saving. If a wage earner wants to earn interest or rent, all he must do is tighten his belt, reduce his consumption, and accumulate property through saving a regular portion of his income. Then he can enjoy property income to supplement his labor income. It is presumably painful, however, to tighten one's belt in this fashion, which is why so few people do it. Interest is the incentive and the reward for such abstinence.

This way of showing that "profits" are as fully earned and deserved as wages is just not convincing. Some few capitalists can no doubt be found today who have accumulated their wealth by scrimping and saving out of wage income, and who can hence be thought of as living now on the returns from previous sacrifices. But most saving is done by people who already have large incomes, and the concept of interest as a justified reward for painful abstinence is simply absurd when applied to most acts of saving.

Two Meanings of "Justified"

But there's another way to "justify" nonlabor income. The right to receive income from the ownership of property does in fact provide an incentive to accumulate property and to allocate it efficiently. Even "windfall gains"—the term some people apply to what we have described as increases in wealth attributable to forecasting correctly in an uncertain world—even such profits in the narrower sense can be justified. For the possibility of obtaining them encourages people to seek useful information and to assume socially unavoidable risks. The total wealth of society would be less than it is if interest, rent, and "windfall" profit were abolished.

This is a different approach to the problem of justification, however. The analogy of criminal informers may clarify the distinction. From a social point of view, the payment of rewards to informers can be justified as a way of reducing crime. From a moral point of view, however, we may be quite unwilling to grant that the informer deserves his reward even as we consent to its payment. We don't mean to imply at all that people who receive profit income are like criminal informers. Our point is rather that the meaning of justification varies with the point of view adopted, that something may be justified from the perspective of social utility and at the same time be unjustified from the perspective of personal deserts, and that the confusion of these two types of justification makes it difficult for us to agree on what we're talking about when we discuss the justice of income distribution. Some economists will insist at this point that justice is a matter of ethics and has nothing to do with economics anyway. They therefore try to confine themselves to discussions of the social consequences or the functional results of alternative systems of income distribution. But that tidy distinction breaks down in the last analysis. For one of the social consequences or functional results of any particular system for distributing income is likely to be a set of social attitudes concerning the justice of that distribution. And since those attitudes can and often do bring about changes in the system, the formation and nature of those attitudes cannot be excluded from any comprehensive study of economic systems.

Profits and Social Welfare

Some critics of profits are willing to meet the economists on the narrower issue of functions and consequences and to argue that the possibility of profits *reduces* social wealth. Their concept of profit is closely related to the second of the two sources of profit discussed earlier in this chapter: restrictions on competition. Their argument can be laid out with the aid of the analysis developed in chapters 10 and 11 and especially in figure 11A.

The possibility of profits encourages producers to seek out ways to restrict competition: through mergers, through collusion, through the purchase of resources that might otherwise be used by competitors, through the cultivation of far-reaching networks of interlocked interests, through bribery, fraud, and coercion, and of course through the control of government with its innumerable ways of hobbling competition. The consequence of all these efforts is the elimination of substitutes and the creation of market power for producers.

The degree of a firm's market power can be expressed in the elasticity of the demand curves it faces. The narrower and poorer the range of alternatives available to purchasers, the less elastic will be their demand and the greater will be the incentive for firms to restrict output. As firms restrict output to avoid spoiling their market, they refrain from producing goods whose social value as measured by the demand for them is greater than the social cost of providing them as measured by marginal opportunity cost.

An economic system actuated by the search for profits thus becomes an economic system full of unused productive capacity. It harbors an unrealized potential for the expansion of social wealth that remains unrealized so that a relatively few can protect and increase their private wealth. Profit seeking does not lead, in this analysis, to competition and greater production of desired goods, but to restrictions on competition and wasted capacity.

It is not as easy as we might wish to marshall evidence to support or refute this line of argument. For it requires comparison of what is with what might be. Enormous difficulties confront anyone who tries to measure the existing degree of market power in various industries and in the economy generally. Those difficulties are several times compounded when one asks what *would* happen if the economic system were thoroughly reorganized. The experience of other countries with alternative systems can provide some hints; but that experience can also be rejected as irrelevant by anyone who maintains that the best system has not yet been created.

The crux of the controversy, in our judgment, is the problem of information. The desire for profits does not merely provide an *incentive* to act in one way rather than another, though it certainly does that, too. More importantly, it leads to the gathering, creation, and dissemination of information, information without which inefficiency would become rampant. The profit seeker hunts diligently for the scattered and diverse bits of information that are relevant to his particular situation. His offers to buy and to sell contribute to the generation of demand and supply curves that interact to place price tags or indices of relative scarcity on resources. Those prices become further information to guide the subsequent decisions of producers and consumers as they try to increase their wealth by exploiting their particular comparative advantages. Minute changes in circumstances are in this way continually picked up, made known, and acted upon appropriately. The question is whether an economic system can be efficiently coordinated in the absence of a market system and whether an effective market system can exist in a society that severely restricts profit acquisition.

That argument pushes to the side the issue of justice, especially the justice of the income distribution that results from private ownership of property and the pursuit of profits. In the next chapter we shall probe further into the economically and politically important question of income distribution.

Once Over Lightly

Profit is a term with many meanings that lead to many different forms of economic legislation. The meanings must be sorted out if we want to understand the way in which economic systems function.

Profit can be usefully defined as total revenue minus total cost if we include all opportunity costs in our calculation of total cost.

Insofar as interest represents an opportunity cost, it must be distinguished from profit.

Interest is the difference in value between present and future goods. It is usually attached to money simply because money represents general command over present or future goods.

The rate of interest in a society is typically positive because present goods are more valuable than future goods. This reflects positive rates of time preference and the fact that goods *now* can often be employed to create more goods *later*—capital is productive.

Because economic decisions are always made *in anticipation of future costs and benefits,* they are often mistaken. The difference between generally expected and actual outcomes, due to uncertainty, is one source of profit (and loss).

The potentiality of a profit encourages risk taking and innovation on the part of those who hope to appropriate the difference between generally anticipated and actual outcomes. The way in which a society assigns profits and losses will affect people's behavior.

In the absence of uncertainty, any differences between total revenue and total (opportunity) cost would be competed away and profits would become zero—except insofar as restrictions exist on the ability to compete successfully.

Opportunities to compete are restricted by the limited availability of particular resources, which may in turn be due to nature or to social and political contrivance. Such competition-restricting scarcities are an additional source or cause of profit.

Before we decide that any particular profits are inadequate or excessive, it is important that we know what we mean by profit, how it arose, what

Profit = TR − TC (Includes Opportunity costs)

function it performed, and the consequences of adding to or subtracting from it.

Meaningful comparisons over time among different values require that future values be discounted at whatever rate of interest most adequately reflects the opportunities available to the decision maker.

The term profit is sometimes used to mean unearned income. A judgment as to whether or not particular income has been earned by its recipient depends both upon conceptions of social justice and an analysis of the functions which the possibility of profit performs. "Windfall" profits may be "justified" if the possibility of obtaining them encourages socially desirable behavior such as risk taking and the search for information. But the possibility of realizing a profit may also encourage socially undesirable behavior.

QUESTIONS FOR DISCUSSION

1. You ask your college for permission to set up a lemonade stand at the annual spring commencement and the college grants permission. After paying your bills for materials (lemons, sugar, cups, etc.) you clear $250 for an afternoon's work.

    (*a*) Did you make a $250 profit?

    (*b*) Are you likely to be given the lemonade concession again next year? What difference does it make whether or not word gets around about how much you cleared?

    (*c*) If the college next year auctions off the franchise, how much would you be willing to bid? Who will then get the profit from the lemonade stand?

2. If a district court judge enters a $300 million judgment against a corporation for violation of the antitrust statutes, do the owners of that corporation sustain a loss? What form will it take? If you believe that the judge was in error and that his decision will eventually be reversed on appeal, how could you profit from your knowledge?

3. You buy shares of common stock in two corporations. Over the next six months, the price of one falls and the price of the other rises. Which was a better buy? Which would be the better one to sell if you want cash?

4. Evaluate the following argument: "General Motors has taken advantage of its dominant position in the automobile industry and made huge profits year after year. It would be perfectly just, therefore, to impose a special tax on General Motors as a way of recovering for society some of the exorbitant profits earned in the past." Who would pay that tax?

5. In July 1971 President Allende of Chile signed a bill authorizing nationalization of the American-owned copper mines in his country. The law called for compensation to be paid to the Anaconda, Kennecott, and Cerro Companies.

(*a*) Imagine that you are the representative of one of these companies charged with responsibility for negotiating the amount of compensation to be paid. What data and arguments would you use?

(*b*) What data and arguments would you use if you were the Chilean representative in the negotiations?

(*c*) Suppose that the nationalization law is repealed and competitive bidding for the mines is allowed to occur. How will the price of the mines be determined? What difference will it make in the price if prospective owners fear another nationalization law in the future?

(*d*) Could the owners of such property *benefit* from nationalization if they were paid compensation *less* than the sum of what they originally paid for the property plus the cost of subsequent improvements? Explain.

(*e*) "Nationalization of foreign-owned industry cannot benefit a country unless that country pays a confiscatory price." Evaluate.

6. You purchase for $950 a $1000 government bond maturing one year from the date of purchase. Will you make a profit if you hold the bond to maturity? Will you make a profit if there is a sharp, general increase in prevailing interest rates a week after your purchase? What effect will this have on the price you can obtain from selling your bond in the market?

7. Humbert and Ambler are very different personalities. Humbert likes to eat, drink, and be merry and let the future care for itself. He suspects the world is liable to disintegrate in a few years anyway. Ambler is only twenty-one years old but is already planning conscientiously for his retirement years. What would you predict about their respective rates of time preference? How do people of Humbert's type benefit from the existence of people like Ambler, and vice versa?

8. What effect would you expect the rate of technological innovation in a society to have on the level of interest rates? Why?

9. The Corps of Engineers estimates that a canal between Tussle and Big Stone would save shippers $500,000 per year. The canal would cost $20 million to construct and $200,000 per year to maintain.

(*a*) Is it correct to say that the canal is a good investment in the long run because it will save society a net $300,000 per year and eventually that will come to more than the $20 million construction cost?

(*b*) About how low would the interest rate have to be to make the canal a profitable investment? (The canal would not be profitable if the interest payments ate up the saving to shippers minus maintenance costs.)

(*c*) "The advantage of having the government build the canal is that government can do things that are in the public interest while private enterprise is constrained by narrow considerations of profitability." Evaluate that argument.

10. "A wealthy society has little difficulty paying interest. But in a poor country with almost no capital, economic planners cannot afford to take interest charges into account in their calculations." What's wrong with that argument?

11. "When lenders extend credit to high risk borrowers, they must raise the interest rates they charge low risk borrowers in order to cover their losses from defaults." Do you agree?

12. What arguments can you offer to support the establishment of legal ceilings on interest rates?

13. Suppose that Congress imposes a 6% ceiling on the interest rate that may be charged for federally guaranteed mortgages. Lending institutions, meanwhile, find themselves able to obtain all the mortgage business they want at 8% interest. Will they lend at 6%? How might the interest ceiling be circumvented? If you wanted to purchase a house and were eligible for a federally guaranteed mortgage, would you want Congress to set an interest-rate ceiling on such loans?

14. Why would an agricultural economist conclude that the benefits of a government price-subsidy plus acreage-restriction program accrue largely to the owners of the land *at the time the program was started?*

15. In the spring of 1963 Fidel Castro announced a sugar production goal for 1970 of 10 million tons. As the target date approached, and it began to appear that this much publicized target might not be attained, the Cuban government transferred labor and other resources in large amounts from the production of alternative goods into the production of sugar. The goal was still missed by a large margin. How do you suppose the consequent loss was distributed? How would the profit have been distributed had this decision turned out *better* than anticipated?

16. Why do corporate officers sometimes make illegal election contributions? Does this question have any connection with the topic of the chapter?

17. When the government takes over privately owned land for a highway and pays compensation to the owners, should that compensation be based on its value in its present use, in the use to which the government will put it, or on the value of adjoining land that will increase (or decrease) in value because of the highway? What is unfair about each option?

18. Does ownership of gold or silver enable a person to protect himself against the hazards of uncertainty?

19. It has been proposed that state and local governments abolish property taxes for homeowners and turn to sales taxes or income taxes for revenue.

What effects on home prices would you predict from such a step? Who would be most likely to benefit?

20. In June 1972, the National Coalition for Land Reform asked the Secretary of the Interior to reclaim land given to the Southern Pacific Railroad in the nineteenth century. The Coalition claims the railroad was supposed to sell this land for family-sized plots at $2.50 an acre or less, or forfeit the land. What do you think would happen if the federal government now required that all such land be sold within the next year in family-sized plots and at prices not to exceed $2.50 an acre? Who would lose and who would gain?

21. You're now 20 years old and you want to start saving for your retirement at age 65. At that time you want to purchase a lifetime annuity of $20,000. The actuarial tables say that for a 65-year-old person a lifetime annuity costs the same as a 12-year annuity. You want to lay aside the same amount at the end of each year for the next 45 years and have just enough (with compounded interest) to purchase that annuity.

    (*a*) What sum will you have to save annually if the rate of interest on both your savings and the annuity is 5%?

    (*b*) What will the purchasing power of $20,000 be 45 years from now, expressed in current dollars, if inflation occurs at an average rate of 3% per year?

22. How would you want to distinguish earned from nonearned income? For what purposes would you want to make the distinction?

23. Are the profits of U.S. corporations currently earned more through coercion or through persuasion? (Definitions of terms: *Coercion:* inducing people to cooperate by reducing their options. *Persuasion:* inducing people to cooperate by expanding their options.) If you don't know how to answer the question, try thinking about the adequacy in this context of the proposed definitions for coercion and persuasion.

13

PRODUCTIVE RESOURCES AND
THE DISTRIBUTION OF INCOME

When incomes are rising, that's good; we're getting wealthier. When prices are rising, that's bad; the purchasing power of our income is falling and so we're getting poorer. It seems as if we should all cheer for higher incomes and lower prices.

DERIVED DEMAND AND MARGINAL PRODUCTIVITY

The catch is that incomes and prices are opposite sides of the same coin. The incomes of physicians are obviously a function of the prices people pay for medical care; the incomes of barbers depend on the price of haircuts. In these cases the connection is obvious because it is relatively direct. But where the connection is less obvious and direct, it is still important. The incomes of construction workers come from the prices people pay for new homes, offices, and factories, as do the incomes of construction contractors and those who supply materials to the building trades. The prices people pay for new automobiles become income for General Motors' assembly-line employees, shareholders, and managers, plus all the employees and shareholders of General Motors' many suppliers.

But don't jump to the conclusion that higher prices for a good necessarily mean larger incomes for its producers. The law of demand asserts that less will be purchased at higher prices. Higher haircut prices, to take the simplest example, might mean less rather than more income for barbers, depending on the elasticity of demand for professional haircuts. That elasticity will in turn depend on how many substitutes there are for barber shops (home clippers, longer hair, a seedy look, and so on).

The concept around which this chapter moves is *derived demand.* The central idea is that people obtain income by selling the services of the productive resources they own. The demand for productive resources is derived, of course, from the demand for the goods these resources are capable of producing. It's quite simple and fairly obvious. But it's also, to judge from the kinds of public policy recommendations one reads and hears, not very widely understood.

How would you evaluate each of the following arguments?

1. "A sizable increase in the legal minimum wage would go a long way toward reducing poverty."

2. "The ominous threat of automation is hanging over our society. We are not far from the time when a majority of the labor force will be unable to find work at all, because machines are so much more productive than people."

3. "Without unions to help him compete against large and powerful corporations, the American working man would never have been able to achieve his present economic status."

Minimum Wage Legislation

Let's look at each argument in turn. We are often told that opposition to legal minimum wages is evidence of insensitivity toward poverty. But it's not that simple. A wage is a price, the price of a productive resource. It's also the basis of a human being's income, of course; we're not denying that at all. But from the standpoint of those who hire workers and pay their wages, the wage is a price or cost. The law of demand reminds us that price and quantity purchased tend to move in opposite directions. Won't they do so also in the case of a legally imposed wage increase?

Here is the widely unrecognized consequence of raising wages by law. If the legal minimum is no higher than what employers are already paying, it has no effect. It will have an impact only if some covered employers are paying less than the legal minimum. But when these employers must raise the wage they pay, will they continue to hire as many employees?

Employers hire resources on the basis of some estimate of the probable contribution that resource will make. What will the employment of this resource add to the value of the firm's operation? The phrase economists use is *marginal productivity,* which means the additional value created by the use of the additional productive resources. If the employer wants to increase his wealth, he will only hire resources whose value to his operation is expected to exceed the additional cost he will incur by hiring that resource. It's the simple rule of chapter 10 once again: Take those actions and only those actions whose expected marginal revenue is greater than their expected marginal cost. An increase in the legal minimum wage raises the marginal cost of some employees to some employers. We can predict that some employers will consequently choose to hire fewer workers. They will lay off or not replace workers whose estimated marginal productivity is below their now higher employment cost.

Unskilled workers can consequently be hurt by a high legal minimum wage. Teenagers are also hurt by such laws, because employers often place a low estimate on the value of their contribution. Some workers will be paid the higher wage and retained; they're better off. But those who are deprived of work opportunities by the legal minimum are clearly made worse off. So it is not at all obvious that increasing the legal minimum wage reduces poverty.

employers hire fewer workers

The Fear of Automation

What are we to make of the second argument above, that machines are destroying jobs? The first question to ask is, What does it mean to say that "machines are more productive than people"? Employers aren't interested in mere physical or technical capabilities; they're interested in the relation between marginal revenues and marginal costs. A machine is more efficient than a person, and hence will be substituted for a person, only if the *value of the machine's marginal product relative to its marginal cost* is greater than the same ratio for a person. That implies, among other things, that wage rates play an important part in shaping the speed and direction of technological change in the economy.

It would be a serious mistake to suppose, for example, that automatic elevators largely replaced elevator operators in the United States over the last two decades merely because of improvements in technology. Time, energy, and money were spent to develop automatic elevators and owners of buildings installed them because of benefit-cost estimates they made, not because automatic elevators are new and shiny. In some other society where the wage rates (opportunity costs) of elevator operators are quite low, elevators run by trained operators may still be more efficient than automatic elevators.

The fear that our society or any society may run out of jobs is an odd kind of fear. A job, after all, represents an obstacle to be overcome. A society that had run out of jobs for people to do would have come very close to overcoming scarcity; and that would be something to cheer, not to fear. We are not in any such fortunate situation. As technological innovations increase the productive potential of our economy, labor resources

MARGINAL PRODUCTIVITY AND THE DEMAND FOR A RESOURCE

A simple numerical example may help you visualize the relationship between the marginal productivity of a resource and the derived demand for it. We can use the illustration employed in discussion question 16 of chapter 7.

A farmer obtains the following yields of corn from the application of fertilizer. Assume that all other inputs and costs remain the same when he changes the amount of fertilizer used. Note that the marginal values are *in between* the totals to indicate that they are the effect of *changing* from one level of fertilizer use to another. To calculate the final column we have assumed a price of $3 per bushel for corn.

Units of Fertilizer	Bushels of Corn	Marginal Corn Product	Marginal Dollar Product
0	1000		
1	1160	160	480
2	1240	80	240
3	1280	40	120
4	1300	20	60

The marginal revenue to this farmer is $480 from applying one unit of fertilizer, $240 when he applies a second unit, and so on. The marginal revenue product states the value to the farmer of using various quantities of fertilizer. It is therefore his derived demand for fertilizer: derived both from the physical productivity of fertilizer and the demand for his corn (a perfectly elastic demand at $3 per bushel).

If we assume that he can use fractional inputs, the curve below expresses his demand for fertilizer. You can read off the quantities he would demand at any price (marginal cost) for fertilizer.

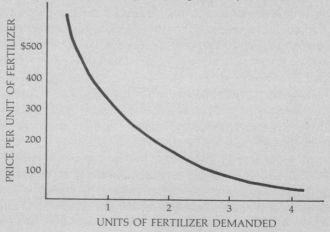

are released from some employments and made available for others. The automatic or self-service elevator made it possible for people who were formerly employed in transporting passengers up and down to do something else, to make some other and additional contribution to our total output of goods and services.

The reallocation of labor in response to changed circumstances, even though it increases the total value of society's output, does lead to a loss of wealth for some people. A rising demand for labor attracted some elevator operators into more remunerative employments and pulled up the wages of the rest. Automatic elevators were in part a response to this situation. But as they were introduced, some elevator operators found themselves pushed rather than pulled: deprived of their present jobs and compelled to accept less desirable alternatives, rather than attracted away from their present positions by better opportunities. Such people suffered, at least temporarily, a loss in wealth. They were forced to incur the cost of searching for new employment, and they were not guaranteed that the new job would be better than the old. Resistance to technological change and the fear of automation or cybernation is therefore quite understandable. Even college professors have been known to speak harshly about the introduction of such technological innovations as videotaped lectures and teaching machines.

Keep in mind, however, that prices and wages are important variables in such processes of adjustment and reallocation. If prices and wages are inflexible or change only very slowly, a larger part of the adjustment burden will be shifted onto something else.

To illustrate: Suppose that a technological breakthrough occurs in automobile production. A manufacturer named Henry Ford finds that he can produce as many automobiles as before, using half as many workers, by employing a moving assembly line. Suppose further that, at existing resource prices, the assembly-line technique cuts the cost of producing these automobiles by 25%. There will be fewer employment opportunities in automobile assembly as a result—at least at first. But if the price of the final product is then reduced, as a consequence of the reduction in cost, and if the demand for automobiles proves sufficiently elastic, there may eventually be more rather than fewer jobs available for automobile assembly workers. That is exactly what did happen. In addition, a reduction in the wages that must be paid to such workers would diminish the manufacturer's incentive to substitute machinery for direct labor; this, too, could alleviate the disemployment effect of the new technology. That has happened much more rarely.

A decline in the demand for anything results in a lesser decline in the quantity demanded if its price falls. This should be kept in mind whenever you are trying to assess the consequences of any change in technology, organization, or the composition of demand. As a matter of demonstrable

JOB PROSPECTS FOR ASTRONOMERS

A 1975 report by the National Academy of Sciences predicted that 600 new Ph.D.s in astronomy would enter the job market during the remainder of this decade to compete for only 200 openings. The report recommended that universities "reduce their production" by screening candidates more rigorously and publicizing the poor job prospects.

Attacking the problem on the demand side, the report also urged state legislatures to give high school science credits for astronomy study. If astronomy became a popular high school course, the demand for college level astronomy courses and hence the services of professional astronomers would increase.

If every college currently without an astronomer on its faculty decided to substitute an astronomer for one scientist in some other field, far more than 200 openings would appear over the next five years. The price of astronomers relative to other scientists might be an important factor in such decisions. The point is that astronomers, like most other specialized resources, have a wide range of uses into which they can be substituted if relative prices change.

fact, many prices and especially wages are "sticky," most notoriously when they are subjected to downward pressure. Such stickiness or inflexibility may have advantages, but it also has obvious disadvantages. In the early 1970s, the demand for many kinds of engineering skills fell to unexpectedly low levels. The more that the wages of engineers decline in response to such a change, the larger will be the number of job opportunities still available for engineers. Wage structures that are relatively rigid in a downward direction will leave employed engineers largely unaffected by the changed circumstances; but more engineers than otherwise will be unemployed.

Unions and Wage Rates

What has been the impact of unions on the income of the American working man? The third of the arguments given above asserts that unions help workers to compete more effectively against large corporations, and that they have thereby improved the working man's economic position. A comprehensive evaluation of unions and their impact is beyond the scope of this book. (Unions will be discussed again in chapter 16 when we take up the problems of unemployment and inflation.) But it is hard to see what insight into their effects can be acquired by someone who starts off with the assumption that workers compete against employers. Workers compete against other workers, employers against other employers. This is the competition that affects wage rates.

An employer cannot simply pay his workers the lowest wage rate his callous heart suggests because the workers have alternative opportunities, opportunities largely created by the competing offers of other employers. Similarly, no worker can successfully insist on the wage he thinks he deserves if other workers are willing to supply very similar services at lower wage rates. Workers compete against other workers, and unions are in part attempts to control *this* competition.

The implication of this is that unions improve the position of the members they represent by finding ways to restrict competition from those who are not members of the union. They may do this directly, as by securing contracts with employers that make union membership a prior condition of employment, and then limiting membership. Or they may do it indirectly. Just as a legal minimum wage excludes some people from employment opportunities, so a high wage secured by union contract (perhaps under the threat of a strike, or total withdrawal of labor services) excludes those who would be willing to work for less.

The belief that unions arose in the United States to counter the power of large corporations is unsupported by history. Unions first became powerful in this country in industries characterized by small-scale firms: construction, printing, textiles, mining. The railroads are an exception that supports the rule: it was special legislation that enabled unions to become powerful in the railroad industry. The unions that today bargain with the large corporations in steel, automobiles, and electrical machinery were originally missionary projects of the unions that bargained mostly with small employers.

A good way to guarantee confusion in thinking about all this is to begin with the assertion that labor is not a commodity. A commodity is something bought and sold, of course, and people have supposedly not been bought and sold in this country since the abolition of slavery. If any doubt remained about the status of labor, Congress allegedly cleared it away in 1914 with the ringing declaration of the Clayton Act: "The labor of a human being is not a commodity or article of commerce."

The best that can be said about such declarations is that they have no discernible relevance to any important social question. Labor services *are* offered for sale, they *are* demanded. There are prices for labor services, and these prices affect the allocation of labor and other resources. The principles that we employed earlier in talking about the pricing and purchase of consumer goods apply also to the pricing and purchase of productive resources. We saw in chapter 4 how changing prices worked to eliminate shortages and surpluses. Prices play the same kind of role in determining whether there will be shortages or surpluses of productive resources.

THE DISTRIBUTION OF INCOME AMONG PERSONS

There is nothing in the principles of supply and demand to guarantee that income will be *justly* distributed. Competition among suppliers and demanders will tend to establish prices for productive resources without regard to the health, family responsibilities, or other personal characteristics of the people who own those resources and derive income from their sale. While the market is a relatively impersonal process, the distribution of income for which the market is partly responsible is rarely regarded with dispassionate detachment.

The prices established by supply and demand are only *partly* responsible for the distribution of income, however. A more important determinant of income distribution is the initial distribution of wealth. What productive resources do people own? What can they use to secure income for themselves?

Most personal income in the United States derives from the sale of labor services. Table 13A shows the percentage of total personal income in the years 1950, 1960, and 1970 from four sources.

Well over 70% of personal income, according to these data, was earned by working. It was more than 70% even in 1950, because an undetermined

Table 13A SOURCES OF PERSONAL INCOME			
	Percentages of Total Personal Income		
Income Category	1950	1960	1970
Wages, salaries, and other labor income:	66.1%	70.5%	71.0%
Rental, dividend, and interest income:	12.0	13.1	14.4
Proprietors' income:	16.5	11.5	8.3
Transfer payments less social security taxes:	5.4	4.8	6.3

Source: Bureau of Economic Analysis. Components may not sum to 100% because of rounding.

but substantial amount of proprietors' income is actually income from the performance of labor services. This category adds together the net incomes of farmers, professional people, and unincorporated enterprises. We could safely regard half of that as labor income. Property income, then, ranged in these years somewhere between 12% and about 20%, depending on what portion of proprietors' income we attribute to the ownership of property.

If you're like most people, you'll be surprised to discover how large a percentage of total income in the United States derives from working or the rental of labor resources. But while these data are revealing, they are also misleading; for they lump together under labor income the salaries of high priced entertainers, corporation executives, retail clerks, and migrant farm workers. But it is the vast differences in the size of the labor incomes people receive that account ultimately for most of the observable inequality in the distribution of personal income.

Table 13B looks at the question of income distribution from a different angle. The first two columns show the percentages of American families and unrelated individuals with annual incomes below a certain level in the years 1950, 1960, and 1970. The level chosen is $3000 for families (two or more related individuals residing together) and $1500 for unrelated individuals (which would include people sharing a house or apartment as long as they are not related by blood, marriage, or adoption). The dollars are adjusted in value to express 1972 purchasing power. That's a very important adjustment, since a dollar in 1970 was worth less than 60% of its 1950 value.

Table 13B DISTRIBUTION OF INCOME TO
FAMILIES AND INDIVIDUALS

	Percent of Families, Less than $3000	Percent of Individuals, Less than $1500	Median Family Income	Median Individual Income
1950	20.8%	43.3%	$5757	$1877
1960	14.2	35.1	7941	2422
1970	7.9	20.7	10,617	3383

(1972 Dollars. Source: Department of Commerce, Bureau of the Census)

What do the first two columns *mean*? Do they show that poverty has been decreasing in the United States? Of course, $3000 in income for a family is hardly princely. It's the annual income that would be earned by someone working a 40-hour week for 50 weeks at an hourly wage of $1.50. But the point is that while 21% of all families had incomes below $3000 in 1950, by 1970 only 8% of American families were below that level. (Keep in mind that the figures have already been adjusted to eliminate the effects of inflation on the purchasing power of dollars.) So the problem of poverty does at least seem to have become less severe over this period.

But that raises a question. Why, if poverty was diminishing, did concern with poverty increase during this period? An important part of the answer comes from looking at the data in table 13B on median incomes. (In case you've forgotten, the median is the point in a series so chosen that half the instances are above it and half below.) In 1950, a $3000 income was 52% of the median. In 1960, however, an income with the same purchasing power was only 38% of the median, and by 1970 it had become only 28% of the median. This is significant because poverty is generally regarded as a relative, not an absolute status. A family with a $3000 income was poor in the United States in 1970 because that family had only a little more than one quarter of the average American's family income.

Relative and Absolute Poverty

We often talk about poverty as if it were an absolute condition, something that could be recognized apart from prevailing social standards. For people dying of starvation, that's no doubt the case. But no family

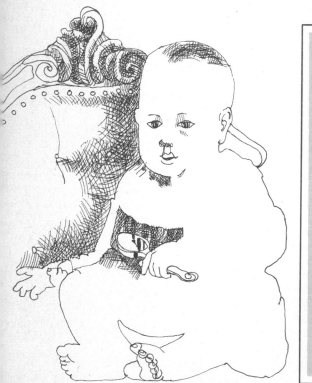

RACIAL AND SEXUAL DISCRIMINATION

A substantial amount of the inequality among those who earn their income <u>from working is related to race and sex.</u> The highest paying positions in the American economy are occupied by white males to an extent that far exceeds their representation in the total labor force. This means, of course, that the legal requirement of "equal pay for equal work," which is relatively easy to enforce, will have a limited impact on racial and sexual income differences.

The average weekly earnings of employed white males consistently exceed by a substantial margin the earnings of nonwhites and females. From 1970 to 1973, the weekly earnings of nonwhite male wage and salary workers who were fully employed averaged only 74% of the white male's earnings. It was 61% for white females, 54% for nonwhite females.

Even that understates the degree of income inequality because the unemployment rate for nonwhite males runs close to twice the white male rate. The white female rate is usually about one and one-half times the white male rate, and the unemployment rate among nonwhite females is typically between two and three times that for white males.

with an income of $3000 had to starve in the United States in 1970. Far less income than that could buy an adequately nutritious diet for a family of four. It could not, however, purchase all the commodities and services that Americans had come to consider "minimal necessities" by 1970. To be unable to attain what is considered a minimal standard in one's society is to be poor. Families with $3000 incomes were considered deprived in 1970, whereas families with the same income might not have been considered deprived in 1950 and surely would not be so considered in most other countries of the world or in the United States prior to the 1940s. We therefore cannot, according to many people, apply an absolute standard in assessing the extent of poverty in the United States today. We must look instead at the *pattern* of income distribution. Table 13C shows one common way of portraying the pattern of that distribution.

Table 13C DISTRIBUTION OF INCOME BY QUINTILES

Percent of Aggregate Income Received by Each Fifth of Families and Unrelated Individuals

Families	1950	1960	1970
Lowest Fifth	4.5%	4.9%	5.5%
Second Fifth	12.0	12.0	12.0
Third Fifth	17.4	17.6	17.4
Fourth Fifth	23.5	23.6	23.5
Highest Fifth	42.6	42.0	41.6
Unrelated Individuals			
Lowest Fifth	2.3%	2.6%	3.3%
Second Fifth	7.0	7.1	7.9
Third Fifth	13.8	13.6	13.8
Fourth Fifth	26.5	25.7	24.5
Highest Fifth	50.4	50.9	50.5

Source: Department of Commerce, Bureau of the Census.

The remarkable thing about that distributional pattern is its stability over a twenty-year period during which all sorts of economic changes occurred and median family income, adjusted for change in the price level, increased by 85%. Real incomes rose substantially, so that poorer people were able to consume more. But with the well-off getting richer at about the same rate as the less well-off, the relative position of the lowest income group did not improve significantly.

We must be careful in using and interpreting data on relative incomes. One danger lies in assuming that attention to relative rather than absolute

levels of income amounts to an endorsement of envy. "As long as the poor are better off, who cares if the rich are also better off? Only the envious!" That isn't true. Envy no doubt does play a part in shaping people's attitudes toward the distribution of income; but it is also a fact, quite apart from the problem of envy, that people learn from their society what to expect both *of* themselves and *for* themselves. People in our society are taught to perceive themselves as failures if they cannot provide for themselves and their families a minimum standard of health care, education, and comfort, a standard that is socially established and that rises as average income levels rise.[1]

A Meaningful Poverty Measure

There is, of course, no way to provide everyone with more than the average (or to keep the lowest fifth from containing 20% of all income receivers). But it may be possible to set a meaningful though relative standard for poverty incomes. The poverty line might be set at 50% of the median income, a standard argued for by the economist Victor Fuchs (and others) and therefore sometimes called the Fuchs-point. By this standard, the poverty line would be a moving average: for families, $2879 in 1950, $3971 in 1960, and $5309 in 1970—using 1972 dollars and the data of table 13B.

Agreement on the relevance of such a standard does not entail agreement on how or even whether a society should guarantee that minimum level of income to all its members. Any system for altering the distribution of income will have side effects as it changes the pattern of information and incentives that income earners confront. Suppose, for example, that every family were guaranteed by law a minimum income of $6000, with the difference between that level and earnings to be made up by a grant out of tax revenues. It would then be impossible to persuade more than a handful of people to work for less than $3.50 an hour. The consequence would be a massive economic disruption and a decline in total income that would almost certainly make it impossible to pay such grants.

---

1. They are taught this in television commercials for life insurance; "public interest" advertising over the years aimed at potential high school dropouts; textbooks used in elementary schools.

OFFICIAL CRITERIA FOR POVERTY

Here is an example of the official figures used by the federal government to determine whether a family is below the poverty line and eligible to participate in certain special programs. They were the levels in effect beginning in May 1975.

POVERTY INCOME LEVELS

	For Urban Families	For Farm Families
One member	$2590	$2200
Two members	3410	2900
Three members	4230	3600
Four members	5050	4800
Five members	5870	5000
Six members	6690	5700

During the same week in which the data above were published, the Department of Labor released its 1975 estimates of the income required for an American family of four to maintain certain budget standards. To maintain a "moderate" standard of living, a family of four had to earn $14,300 annually. The family could live at the "limited luxury" level with a $20,800 annual income. $9200 annually was required to meet the minimum standards for what the Department of Labor calls an "austere" budget. (Those are national averages. The numbers vary considerably for different cities.)

Note that the poverty line for an urban family of four is 55% of the Department's "austere" income for such a family.

The Negative Income Tax

A more feasible scheme might be a negative income tax. People now pay taxes when their earned incomes go over a certain level and larger taxes the larger their earnings. But the system doesn't provide negative tax rates for people whose incomes fall short of the minimum. A negative income tax differs in one significant way from the system just described. A flat $6000 family income guarantee as described above amounts to a 100% tax on all earned income below that level. For every additional dollar that a family earned, one dollar of its grant would be taken away—up to $6000, when presumably the current rates of income taxation would come into effect.

The negative income tax proposal, by contrast, would provide grants that vary inversely with income but by *less* than dollar for dollar. For example, families might be guaranteed incomes equal to earned income plus 25% of the difference between earnings and $6000. Table 13D shows how this would work out.

Table 13D NEGATIVE INCOME TAX		
Grant = 25% of ($6000 Minus Earned Income)		
Earned Income	Grant	Total Income
$0	$1500	$1500
2000	1000	3000
4000	500	4500
6000	0	6000
8000	0	*Less* than $8000—regular income tax rates apply

By comparing the first two columns you can see that earned income below $6000 is being taxed at a 25% rate: for every dollar that earnings increase, the grant falls by 25¢. By comparing columns 1 and 3 you see that families are able to increase their total income by 75¢ for every dollar of additional income that they earn up to $6000. Any system of income grants designed to help poor families would have to include some system like this to avoid disastrous effects on the labor market and total social product.

Conflicting Objectives

Negative income tax proposals all run into the dilemma of conflicting objectives, however. The scheme depicted in table 13D fails to move the poorest families out of poverty. A family in which no one was able to earn income would end up with a total income of only $1500. This could be corrected by establishing some higher level of grant as a base. Table 13E shows how this would work out, still using a 25% rate of tax on earned income, but with a minimum guaranteed income of $3000 as a base from which to begin.

The problem is obvious at a glance: families would still be receiving grants at earned income levels up to $12,000, and that's hardly realistic. This consequence could be avoided by raising the tax rate. Table 13F shows the consequences of a $3000 base with a 75% tax on earned income, in the form of a reduction in the size of the grant.

Table 13E   NEGATIVE INCOME TAX

Grant = $3000 Less 25% of Earned Income

Earned Income	Grant	Total Income
$0	$3000	$3000
2000	2500	4500
4000	2000	6000
6000	1500	7500
8000	1000	9000
10,000	500	10,500
12,000	0	12,000
14,000	0	*Less* than 14,000—regular income tax rates apply

The problem now is that a 75% tax rate is not likely to maintain adequate earning incentives, especially since there are costs associated with working (transportation, clothing, inability to spend one's time on other activities). These disruptive effects on the labor market and hence total income could be held down by lowering the rate to 50%. But significant disincentive effects would almost surely still exist with a 50% tax on earned incomes, and the total amount of grants to be financed out of tax revenue would remain quite large. Any negative income tax proposal will have to compromise between an adequate grant level for the most disadvantaged families and the maintenance of earning incentives, while also remaining within the bounds of fiscal feasibility. There's no way to pull every family out of poverty, maintain adequate work incentives, and avoid unacceptably high tax rates. At least there's no way to do so without some radical restructuring of the entire economic system.

Table 13F   NEGATIVE INCOME TAX

Grant = $3000 Less 75% of Earned Income

Earned Income	Grant	Total Income
$0	$3000	$3000
2000	1500	3500
4000	0	4000
6000	0	*Less* than 6000—if regular tax rates are applicable

That pessimistic conclusion does not mean there are no ways to achieve the objectives of those who want to eliminate poverty or almost all poverty without destroying the existing economic system. The first proposal we offered might be supplemented, for example, with a system of special grants to those families in which age or disability prevent any family member at all from earning income. Or we could approach the whole problem through some combination of income grants and job guarantees, with the size of the grants dependent on specific family circumstances and the willingness of able family members to accept employment.[1] But no one has yet discovered a simple and wholly satisfactory solution to the problem of family poverty. You probably suspected as much from the fact that you haven't yet heard of any such panacea.

SOURCES OF PRODUCTIVITY AND INCOME

The marginal productivity theory, as presented in this chapter, is far from a complete theory of income distribution. It asserts only that the demand for a productive resource depends upon the marginal contribution that resource is thought to be capable of making to the production of wealth, and that this demand sets a limit to the price the resource can command. One of the important questions left unanswered is *why* resources have the expected marginal productivity they do have.

Productivity as a Social Fact

In an economic system with extensive specialization, resources will tend to have higher marginal productivities than they would otherwise have. For specialization and its indispensable complement, exchange, permit resource owners to allocate their property more advantageously. Giuseppe Vibrato can enjoy a fine income from an operatic career, using the comparative advantage his voice provides while depending on other people to grow his food and make his clothing. He couldn't do that and his income would consequently be lower if he lived, for example, in a society so small that specialization could not be carried very far.

Giuseppe also benefits from the existence of very particular specialists in his society: composers, pianists, and sopranos who can play Susanna to his Figaro. How many people would pay, after all, to hear Giuseppe sing

---

1. A good basis for further discussion of these questions is Arnold H. Packer, "Employment Guarantees Should Replace the Welfare System," *Challenge*, March-April 1974, pp. 21–27. Packer is also the author of *Categorical Public Employment Guarantees: A Proposed Solution to the Poverty Problem*, published by the Joint Economic Committee of the Congress in 1973.

unaccompanied solos of his own music? It would be absurd for Giuseppe to claim that his income is solely dependent on *his voice*. Marginal productivity is a *social* product, dependent on the complementary contributions of others.

It should also be remembered that the relevant productivity is a consequence of valuations and not just of physical capacities. It isn't Giuseppe's ability to shatter a glass with his high notes but the value others place on his singing that makes his voice such a highly productive resource. Similarly, it may not be what a college graduate knows or can do that makes employers bid more for his services than for those of a high school graduate; his greater marginal productivity could be based on employers' expectations that college graduates are more likely to possess social graces, be docile, and hold conservative political views, while the cost of obtaining the degree assures that the supply of college graduates will be limited. Employers definitely do use years of schooling completed as a measure of potential productivity; this enables them to economize in their search for information about the ability of prospective employees. But it also results in some serious mistakes.

We've been talking about income inequality in this chapter in a rather broad way. By focusing on *family* incomes we've recognized that an individual who earns little income isn't necessarily poor. But we haven't paid adequate attention to the wide variety of different circumstances in which families or individuals with the *same* money income find themselves. The financial responsibilities of a retired couple, for example, will be quite different from those of a family with many children. And it may be worth noting that some people are much better than others at deriving satisfaction from what is available to them. We'll leave those issues to be filled in from your own common sense reflections. But we do want to look specifically at the issue of income distribution over the course of a lifetime, because that gets us into some important but widely neglected considerations.

Lifetime Incomes

People can and do choose lifetime income patterns. Someone who quits school to go to work at age 16 will receive more income in his early years than someone else who stays in school to age 25. But the latter person is likely to be receiving a larger income at age 45. Two people with identical incomes at age 35 could be receiving vastly different incomes at age 55 if one spends his entire income on consumption goods while the other saves a large portion of his income and invests it. In all such cases it makes more sense, if we're looking for relevant comparisons, to contrast the *lifetime* patterns of income and spending than merely to focus on the differences in income received at a particular age.

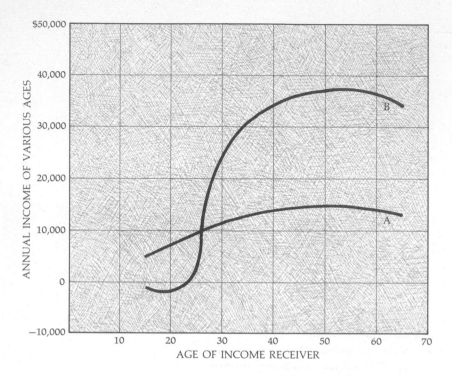

Figure 13A Lifetime incomes

Which of the two persons whose incomes are described in figure 13A has the larger total income between ages 15 and 65? Individual A quits school and goes to work at age 15. Individual B borrows to stay in school (hence the negative income for a while), doesn't reach A's level of income until age 26, but earns far more in subsequent years. To compare their incomes at age 19 would obviously be inappropriate; B is investing in knowledge, skills, or other qualities at age 19. Investment is the purchase of capital, and B is purchasing *human capital:* skills that can be used to produce future goods. Care must also be exercised in comparing their incomes at age 50 if we intend our comparisons to be relevant to the issue of justice. Individual A may have *chosen* his lower income at age 50 by electing at age 15 *not* to invest in human capital.

Discounting Expected Incomes

The area under the income curve for B is clearly greater than that under A's income curve, which suggests that B earns more over a lifetime. But this is a misleading comparison, since future income is not as valuable as present income. The relevant question is: Which expected profile would have a larger present value to the recipients at age 15 when each is making the critical choice between going to work or continuing in school? A person with a very high rate of time preference may choose the A pattern over the B pattern. Is this unknown? Don't young people often display high rates of time preference, choosing present goods over much larger amounts of future goods? An event that is ten years in the future may be so unimaginably distant to a 15-year-old that it cannot significantly affect his current decisions. And that isn't as irrational as it may appear, for life is filled with uncertainties. If individual B were to die in an automobile accident at age 21, his decision at age 15 would have been the wrong one from the standpoint of maximizing lifetime income.

We are obviously oversimplifying here by assuming that individuals have equal opportunities to choose at age 15 (they do not) and that education's only value is the contribution it makes to future income. But these simplifications help make two important points: Individuals do to some extent choose the income they will receive at different points in their lifetimes, and if we want to compare lifetime incomes we must discount them to take account of the specific years in which income is received. Let's take a very simple example.

An individual (call her Calcula) can choose at age 15 whether she wants to go to work at once and earn $10,000 for each of the next 50 years, or go to school until she's 25 at an annual cost to her of $2000 and then earn $20,000 per year to age 65. Which is the better choice if monetary income is Calcula's only concern? To find out which course Calcula will embark upon we must compare the present discounted value to her of the alternative expected income streams: $10,000 for each of the next 50 years versus a $2000 *negative* income for 10 years and $20,000 for each of the next 40 years. Let's assume that Calcula discounts future income at a rate of 8% per year.

The present value of a $10,000 annuity running for 50 years when discounted at 8% is $122,335. That can be read right off from table 12A. The second calculation is a bit more difficult. A negative annuity of $2000 for ten years has a present value of −$13,420 when discounted at 8%. A 40-year annuity of $20,000 has a present value of $238,492. But since the 40-year annuity will not begin until ten years from now, that value in turn must be discounted using table 12B. The present value of $238,492 ten years in the future is $110,468 when discounted at 8%. From this we subtract $13,420 to obtain $97,048.

The surprising result (surprising at least for people not accustomed to discounting future values) is that in the imaginary case described the present value of the decision to quit school at age 15 is about $25,000 more than the present value of the decision to remain in school. The rate of discount would have to be less than 6% before Calcula would choose more schooling over present employment. Our data were somewhat arbitrarily chosen, of course, so they don't prove that advanced education doesn't pay off in terms of monetary income. The example does provide a possible explanation, however, for the fact that so many young people with the opportunity to continue their schooling drop out, contrary to all the advice of those who show them how much more income a college graduate earns over a lifetime.

Preference and Income

The subjective rate of discount used by the decision maker is a crucial variable. If Calcula discounted the future at 20% per year in the circumstances we've described, the prospect of $70,000 per year would not be enough to keep her in school! Its present discounted value after the extra cost of the schooling has been taken into account would be less than the present discounted value of $10,000 starting at age 15. Does that surprise you? Does it help you see why so many choose to go to work rather than continue in school? Or does it only suggest how shortsighted young people often are? A 20% rate of time discount does seem rather shortsighted. But

when we compare it with the rate of interest many adults willingly pay for retail credit or consumer loans, it doesn't look all that unusual.

The analysis can be extended to another kind of choice. People can increase their future incomes by investing in property as well as in human capital. If Calcula were to drop out of school, earn $10,000 for 10 years, and invest half of that in assets yielding 8% per year, she would have about $73,000 at age 25. And that amount at 8% could buy her an added income for the next 40 years of more than $6000 per year. If she chooses instead to consume her entire income, she is simultaneously choosing a lower future income.

We aren't arguing that people choose their future incomes. We are maintaining, however, that *they do choose to some extent*. Inequalities in the income received by people in the same age brackets are in part the product of earlier decisions about the shape of the person's lifetime income stream. Less now implies more later and more now implies less later. The point is important. A society which tries to shield people from the consequences of their own decisions to discount the future at a high rate will encourage everyone to discount at an even higher rate, and to neglect investment for the future in favor of present consumption.

ECONOMIC RENT

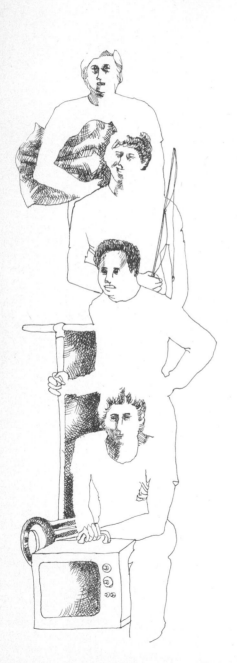

We have said that income derives from the ownership of productive resources. The quantity of productive resources anyone owns will depend upon such factors as inheritance, luck, natural abilities, earlier choices between present consumption and investment, and earlier choices among more and less risky alternatives. The price of the resources will be set by the competing offers and bids of all those who own resources and all those who want the goods the resources can produce. Between offers and bids, however, a gulf can appear, a gulf that economists refer to as *economic rent.* Most people use the word *rent* to mean the payment to a landlord for the use of his property. Economists use the word in a broader sense to mean *any return to the owner of a productive resource which is in excess of its opportunity cost.* The concept has enough important and interesting uses to justify the little time that must be spent in mastering it.

Suppose that you want to hire four neighborhood boys to help you for eight hours on Saturday with cleaning your garage. (Never mind the implication that you have an unusually large and dirty garage.) It's quite conceivable that each would be willing to work for a different hourly wage. Amos would watch cartoons all day if he weren't working, and since he's getting a little bored with the reruns anyway, he's willing to work for 50¢ an hour. Billy planned to go fishing all day, and he can't be bid away from the lake for less than 75¢ an hour. Chuck has a chance to mow lawns for $1 an hour and won't work for you for any less. Don just wants to sleep all day; but he is deeply attached to the sack and requires $1.25 an hour to give it up. You will be able to hire all four only if you offer $1.25 an hour, and if you don't discriminate, that means $1.25 an hour for each. Amos, Billy, and Chuck will consequently receive economic rent: 75¢ an hour for Amos, 50¢ for Billy, and 25¢ for Chuck, the amount by which the payment for their services exceeds the opportunity cost.

At the end of the day you will pay $40 in wages. But $12 of this does not represent a real cost from a social point of view. It is actually a mere transfer of wealth from you to Amos, Billy, and Chuck. The payment was necessary to secure the services of all four boys; and you must have valued their joint services at $40 or more, since you were willing to pay that amount. But the value of the opportunities foregone as a consequence of your garage-cleaning expedition was only $28.

If you'll check back to chapter 5 and its examination of the cost of a volunteer army, you'll see the same phenomenon illustrated. The example described in figure 5A and the accompanying discussion shows a budget outlay of $24 billion annually but a true social cost or opportunity cost of only $15 billion. Put your finger in at page 91 and check: The budget outlay is the rectangular area marked off by $8000 times 3 million volunteers. The genuine social cost is the smaller area under the supply curve which represents opportunity costs. The area above the supply curve and within the budget outlay rectangle, $9 billion, is economic rent.

How Profits Become Rents

Economic rent also appeared in chapter 12. We asked whether it would be possible for a firm to continue earning revenues in excess of total costs even after every potential competitor had learned how the firm was doing it, or in other words, whether profits could persist in the absence of uncertainty. And our answer was *yes*, if there were restrictions on the ability of others to compete. An advantageous location or a uniquely talented management might prevent other firms from competing successfully for a share of the profits and thereby eliminating the revenue-cost gap. But a firm's control of particularly productive resources would not by itself protect the firm's profits against erosion if other firms could bid for control of those resources. Suppose it becomes common knowledge in the industry that the Cagey Crockery Company is earning half a million in profits each year because its two top managers know more about crockery than Woody Hayes and Bear Bryant know about football. Cagey will then have to start raising their salaries to keep them from accepting offers from other crockery makers. Before the word gets around, they will have to be paid only the value of their managerial talents in other industries. But once the word spreads, they can command an economic rent in the crockery industry: up to half a million dollars more than they could earn in any other line of business. To hang on to its profits Cagey might have to pay its superior management team almost the full amount of those profits, since the profits would disappear if our skillful duo departed. This little tale illustrates the way in which short term profits for firms can be transformed in time into economic rents for the owners of especially productive resources.

Did we mention Woody Hayes and Bear Bryant, those incredibly successful builders of college football teams that for so many years have packed in the fans and picked off the bowl bids, swelling the revenues of the colleges that employ them? The value of their salaries plus perquisites has infuriated many a full professor, who has concluded that the relative salaries of a coach and a professor must reflect the relative value assigned by the university to football versus literature. By no means. They only reflect the relative demands of football fans and literature fans. Any English professor who can find a way for the college to sell 50,000 tickets at $8 a head to college sponsored poetry readings will soon discover that universities want him. They will bid energetically for his services, the way they now bid for successful coaches. And he will be able to do what Woody and the Bear have done: capture as economic rent a portion of the profits created for his employer by his unique abilities.

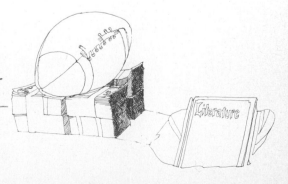

Rock and Rent

Let's look at another example of economic rent. The Salt Sellers are a popular rock group whose members love to make music together. They give 200 concerts a year, something they would be willing to do for as little as $10,000. At any lower annual wage they would choose to give up the concert tour and find some other kind of work. Thus the opportunity cost of having the Salt Sellers sing is $10,000, or about $50 a concert.

The group may nonetheless receive $5000 for every performance. Each promoter must pay this amount, not to induce the Salt Sellers to sing, but to bid them away from singing for *other* promoters. The popular demand for tickets to their performances gives rise to a demand for their services from promoters that in turn creates $4950 of economic rent for the Salt Sellers.

Do not draw the conclusion that economic rent is an unnecessary payment. In one sense it is, in another sense it is not. The $4950 is unnecessary to induce the Salt Sellers to sing. But it is necessary to induce them to sing *here* rather than *there.* Of course, the promoters might all get together and agree that it's ridiculous to pay the Salt Sellers $5000 when they would willingly work for $50. They might further agree to offer no more than $75 a night for their services. But in the absence of competitive bidding, which is eliminated by the promoter's agreement, how would it be decided where the group is to sing its annual 200 concerts? The quantity of service demanded from the Salt Sellers would far exceed the quantity supplied. If the promoters solved this problem by a lottery, they would appropriate the economic rent for themselves—or for the lucky promoters who won the lottery. Chances are excellent, however, that the unlucky promoters would find ways to violate the agreement; and if they did not, new promoters would probably appear to begin bidding for the now extremely profitable services of the Salt Sellers. But such agreements are notoriously unstable.

Rents from College Football

We can illustrate the precarious nature of such agreements by looking at college football once again. As soon as college administrators learned that there was profit to be made from intercollegiate football, they started bidding against one another for the requisite resources: quarterbacks, broken field runners, and beefy linemen. No treason to academia is asserted or suggested: a good college president raises funds, and there's nothing intrinsically more dishonorable about investing in sports enterprises than about investing in breakfast cereal stocks. Of course, the college president does not bid directly since he may not know a fair catch from a safety blitz; he hires a specialist (the way any intelligent manager does) who knows he will be well regarded and rewarded for the quality of the teams he assembles. The problem for the colleges, however, is to keep the team from appropriating all the profits in the form of economic rents.

Put most simply and crudely, if high school seniors can get competing colleges to bid against one another for their services, they will be able to appropriate in advance all the expected net income from their performances. To keep this from happening, the colleges have created the National Collegiate Athletic Association. The NCAA is a buyers' cartel. Its primary task is to prevent any college from offering more than a very low maximum salary to prospective players, and to levy financial penalties (no bowl games, no television appearances—both very lucrative) against colleges that exceed these limits. The ultimate penalty is expulsion from the cartel, which would mean no opponents, no games, and no revenue.

With competitive monetary bids to the players excluded as a way of persuading them to play for one team rather than another, colleges turn to other forms of competition. They spend more on recruiting, hiring assistant coaches by the dozens and sending these recruiters out at considerable expense to impress parents and flatter their athletic sons. Often the potential profit from able players is simply appropriated as an economic rent by able recruiters. Consistently with the law of demand, the colleges also hire *more* players than they would if they had to pay the full value of each, thereby creating pressures within the cartel for limitations on the total number of players a school can have under contract in addition to the limitation on the maximum salary each can receive. Even this doesn't work well, however. Since each college could gain from paying a little more than the maximum and thus attracting players away from colleges that adhere strictly to the rules, ways will be sought and found to sweeten the bids to prospective athletes: superior and more expensive room and board arrangements on campus, promises from wealthy alumni of good jobs after graduation, even under-the-table payments in cash or kind.

Why don't the most promising players, the ones who are being deprived of the largest economic rents by these arrangements, simply sign with an openly professional team? The answer is that the professional teams will not sign them until four years after they've entered college. The professional teams want to avoid the cost of operating their own farm system, as baseball teams must do; by agreeing not to hire a player until he has used up his college eligibility, they agree in effect not to compete with the colleges, and to let them screen, train, and audition prospective professionals. It's a satisfactory arrangement for all parties except the athletes.[1]

1. And the professional teams in most sports have their own buyers' cartels to keep the athlete from appropriating his full economic rent even after he turns pro. For a dramatic example of what can happen when these arrangements break down, review the history of the bonuses paid when there were two professional football leagues or the princely economic rent "Catfish" Hunter obtained in 1974 from baseball's New York Yankees.

But the overall arrangement has not been as satisfactory as the colleges hoped it would be, as anyone knows who follows the complaints of college administrators about the rising costs and declining revenues of football. It is just too difficult to close all the doors through which competition can erode profits. Cartel agreements, whether they're buyers' cartels to control costs or sellers' cartels to protect revenue by restricting output, are always difficult to enforce against cartel members as well as outsiders. But the government can often be of enormous help.

Protecting Economic Rents

Let's return for another look at the case of Artesian. When he earned $1048.30 in the first year after discovery of the mineral-water spring, he made a profit: an increase in Artesian's income that arose because the existence of the lucrative mineral-water spring had not been anticipated by others. But after Artesian got his business running successfully, the $1048.30, though still a profit, could also be regarded as economic rent. It was a payment for the use of the resource in excess of its opportunity cost of zero.

Competition, however, began whittling away at Artesian's rent. When he secured legal restrictions on access to the mineral-water market, Artesian was trying to keep competition from reducing or eliminating his economic rent. We very commonly observe economic rents that have been secured by means of legal restrictions on competition. This leads to both a redistribution of wealth and an inefficient allocation of resources.

The restrictions prevent resource owners from transferring their resources out of less highly valued into more highly valued employments. Suppose, for example, that no one is allowed to diagnose and treat illnesses for pay unless he has gone through four years of medical school plus two years of in-service training. This practice increases the wealth of licensed physicians. But it also results in less medical care than would otherwise be provided. Many ailments could be well taken care of by people with far less training than is required of licensed physicians. These people are denied an opportunity to pursue their comparative advantage, and society in the process is denied the benefits of increased medical care. Most physicians don't see it this way at all. They maintain that licensing is necessary to protect the public against quacks. It is probably true that legal restrictions on the practice of medicine increase the average quality of medical care *sold by physicians*. But it is quite unlikely that they increase the average quality of medical care *received by people who are ill*. That's a very important distinction.

Do you recall from chapter 11 the owner of the television sales and service center? He wanted to raise the average quality of television repair services by preventing "janitors, firemen, milkmen, and similar amateurs" from competing in the provision of these services. If he had been successful in securing the state regulation and licensing he wanted, it *might* have turned out that the average television repair job performed for a fee would be of higher quality. But he was ignoring the *additional* services that can be provided by "amateurs" who would be prevented by law from employing the skills they possess.

Or look again at the complaint of the nursing-home operator in chapter 11. He does not tell us, of course, about the protected rent that he obtains from the state system of licensing nursing homes. He directs our attention rather to the "lower standards" that would result from any relaxation of the licensing restrictions. And he is probably correct. Standards of nursing-home care probably would be lower *on average.* But a moment's thought should make it clear that higher average standards are being obtained at the cost of *less overall* nursing-home care. The patient who is effectively denied admission to *any* nursing home by the restrictive practices receives a lower, not a higher, level of care. Presumably, licensing also implies certification of minimum standards, and this can be a way to provide, at low cost, information of value to purchasers. However, certification of quality levels (for example, prime, choice, good, and so on for beef) does not require a licensing system that restricts the quantity offered. And it does not compel those who prefer less quality (at a lower price) to pay for more quality than they want.

If a union is able to enforce a high wage against an employer, it can thereby prevent him from hiring workers whose marginal productivity in his employment is greater than their opportunity cost. These workers do not "lose their jobs," since they never had the jobs in the first place. This effectively disguises an important consequence of the union's wage-setting practices. But the economic rent of the employed union members is nonetheless being obtained partially at the expense of other workers who are compelled to accept less remunerative employment.

A Defensive Conclusion

Economic analysis of the pricing of productive resources seems to generate more heat per paragraph than almost any other portion of economic theory. The explanation is not hard to find. People obtain income largely from selling the services of the productive resources they own. Competition has a tendency to push the prices of these resources toward their opportunity cost. Resource owners, however, are eager to secure rents for the resources they own, and they are often quite ingenious at enlisting the aid of the state to restrict competition and thereby protect their economic rents. It is always dressed up, of course, as protection of the public interest. Economic analysis points out the consequences of such efforts, and thereby incurs the ire of those who would prefer not to hear about these consequences. Or is it rather that they don't want *others* to hear?

Once Over Lightly

 Income is ordinarily obtained by selling the services of productive resources. The price any resource can command will be determined by the demand for the goods it produces and the marginal productivity of the resource. The marginal productivity of a resource is the additional contribution it makes to the production of wealth.

The law of demand applies to productive resources as well as to other goods. The higher the price of a particular resource, the more actively will people look for substitutes.

  The common notion that the owners of productive resources compete against the purchasers of these resources is seriously misleading. Employees, for example, do not compete against employers but against other employees and potential employers. Unionization, while it may have other goals as well, is an attempt to restrain competition *among* workers.

The marginal productivity theory of the demand for productive resources is not a complete theory of income distribution, much less a theoretical justification for any particular pattern of interpersonal distribution. Its explanation of resource pricing and use must be supplemented with an explanation of why resources are distributed among people as they are and how the larger social-economic system contributes to the establishment of particular resource potentialities.

 Resources often command prices in excess of their opportunity cost. That portion of the payment to a resource which exceeds the amount that would be required to keep the resource from migrating to its next most valuable opportunity is called *economic rent.*

Economic rent, from the overall social point of view, is a transfer of wealth rather than a genuine cost. At the same time, it is a genuine cost to the individual purchaser, who must pay the opportunity cost of the next most enthusiastic bidder. In other words, society did not give up $3 million worth of other goods when Jim "Catfish" Hunter decided in 1974 to pitch baseballs for that wage. But the team that was finally beaten out by the New York Yankee bid did lose a chance to receive that (expected) value in pitching services.

 The desire to protect economic rents lies behind many successful attempts on the part of resource owners to secure government assistance in restricting competition.

 Government actions intended to redistribute income will affect the allocation of resources.

Precise judgments about the equitability of particular patterns of inter-personal income distribution are difficult to make with confidence for many reasons, including the existence of different sized families with varying numbers of income earners, the different temporal patterns of income received over people's lifetimes, the problem of choosing between absolute and relative measures of poverty, the role that individual prefer-ences play in determining income distribution, as well as the unintended and undesired effects that redistribution may have on the allocation of time and other resources.

QUESTIONS FOR DISCUSSION

1. For many years federal minimum-wage legislation completely excluded workers in agriculture or domestic service. Yet the average wages paid to these workers ranked at the very bottom of the wages paid in the American economy. How do you explain the seeming inconsistency in this exclusion?

2. Teachers began encountering serious job shortages in the early 1970s after many years of rising demand for their services. An intensified interest in unionization has been observed. What can unionization accomplish for teachers in a highly unfavorable job market? Whom is it likely to benefit and whom will it harm?

3. "Farmers complaining that they can't get field hands now that the bracero program has been curtailed aren't sincere," said an official of the United Packinghouse Workers Union. "About one-third of the unemployed in Los Angeles are former farm workers, and the farmers could get them back if they'd make wages and working conditions attractive enough." Do you think the farmers are insincere? Could they get enough workers if they tried harder? Explain.

4. In 1940, according to the Bureau of Labor Statistics, there were 9,540,000 persons employed in agriculture. The population of the United States in 1940 was 132,122,000. In 1970 the corresponding figures were 3,462,000 farmers in a population of 205,395,000. Thus in 1940 it took one farmer to provide agricultural produce for every 14 Americans. Thirty years later one farmer could take care of almost 60 people.

    (a) What made this dramatic change possible?

    (b) What happened to the "excess" farmers? Where did they go?

    (c) What factors induced people to move out of agricultural employment?

5. Under a closed-shop arrangement, employers may only hire workers who are already union members. Under a union-shop arrangement, employers may hire whomever they please but the employees must then join the

union. What different effects would you expect these alternative arrangements to have on wages? On employment? On discrimination by the union against members of minority races? Why?

6. College professors in the United States have never had an effective union. Then why did their average wage rise spectacularly in the 1960s? How might college professors have used unionization to obtain even larger salary increases over this period? Why might some professors be interested in a law that prohibited anyone without an earned doctorate from teaching in colleges? What consequences would you predict if a few states passed such a law?

7. Do high wage rates in such strongly unionized industries as steel and automobiles pull up the general level of wages in nonunionized, lower-wage industries? If you think they do, what is the process by which this occurs? If contracts that call for high wages reduce employment opportunities in the industries that must pay these wages, where do the excluded workers find employment?

8. What will be the consequences of laws prohibiting discrimination by employers against women? (If you answer quickly, you will almost certainly answer inadequately.)

   (*a*) What will occur if employers are required to pay women equal wages for equal work but are not required to hire women? Assume in answering that employers are male chauvinists who believe women aren't as valuable employees as men.

   (*b*) What will happen if employers are forbidden to discriminate on the basis of sex in hiring, firing, promoting, or paying wages? Assume again that employers are male chauvinists. Would it be illegal under these circumstances to discriminate on the basis of height or physical strength?

   (*c*) There are (or have been until recently) many laws "protecting" women employees by limiting their hours of work, providing for mandatory rest periods, or prescribing special facilities that must be maintained for women employees. Whom do you think these laws protected? Why? Would you say that an employer subject to such laws was practicing sex discrimination when he hired men in preference to women?

   (*d*) Who do you suppose has benefited more from prejudices and resulting employment discrimination against women? Employers or male employees? Why?

9. The text's discussion of the negative income tax as a way of redistributing income stresses the conflict among the objectives of eliminating poverty, remaining within the limits of fiscal feasibility, and preserving work incentives. Could the last objective be handled separately through a work requirement imposed on all recipients of the income subsidy? What problems would such a requirement encounter?

10. What is the present value of $8000 for the next 45 years to someone who discounts the future at a 12% rate? What is the present value at 12% of $16,000 for 40 years where the income stream does not begin until 6 years in the future? Contrast the same present values using 8% and 20% rates of discount.

11. A plumbers local in Fort Lauderdale, Florida, voluntarily lowered the hourly rate for union workers on low-rise construction projects from $10.70 to $6.90 an hour (in June 1972). The $10.70 rate continued to apply to high-rise construction. The business manager of the union said this was being done to curb inflation and help home owners. Do you think it might also have been done because nonunion plumbers were available in the area at $4.50 to $5 an hour? Why do you suppose the union did not lower the rate on high-rise construction work?

12. What does baseball's reserve clause have to do with economic rent? Does it keep highly talented players from earning any rent? Why not? Do you think this is its aim? Or is its aim, as the baseball owners say, to prevent the wealthiest teams from corralling all the best players? Why do you suppose the New York Yankees were able to outbid every other team for "Catfish" Hunter's services in 1974?

13. The Department of Health, Education, and Welfare suspects that employers sometimes use education as an employment criterion because it's an indirect way to discriminate on the basis of race. (In 1973 the percentage of Blacks who had completed college was less than half the percentage of the entire population that had completed four years or more of college.) Suppose that HEW asks employers not to request information on education from applicants for nonprofessional jobs. What consequences would you predict? Do you think this would reduce employees' chances to use nonprofessional jobs as a training ground for advancement?

14. A television station whose physical facilities could be replaced for $2 million is sold for $22 million. For what was the extra $20 million a payment? What happens when the Federal Communications Commission revokes the license of a station and awards it to another ownership group?

15. If you know that a license to operate a taxicab in New York City can be purchased from an existing license holder for $80,000, what could you infer about the profitability of operating a taxicab in New York City? What actions by the city could raise or lower the market value of a license?

EXTERNALITIES AND THE MARKET

Many people have concluded in recent years that the growing problem of environmental pollution demonstrates the inadequacy of a purely economic point of view. You won't be surprised to find that position vigorously rejected here. Ecology and economics are very closely related, as a matter of fact, and in more than the common Greek stem of the words. Ecology in the narrow sense is a branch of biology that deals with the interrelations between organisms and their environment. In the broader meaning of the word, it is a point of view, an informing conviction that everything ultimately depends upon everything else. Actions prompt reactions; the reactions set the stage for all future actions. And that is also the point of view of economic theory. Economics and ecology are allies, not competitors or antagonists.

EXTERNALITIES AND PROPERTY RIGHTS:
A SURVEY OF THE PROBLEM

The economist maintains that, if pollution is a growing problem in our society, it is because we have systematically encouraged people to neglect certain costs. The problem requires for its solution that we find ways to correct this neglect. If, like Stephen Leacock's Lord Ronald, we fling ourselves upon a horse and ride madly off in all directions, we are not likely to find acceptable solutions.

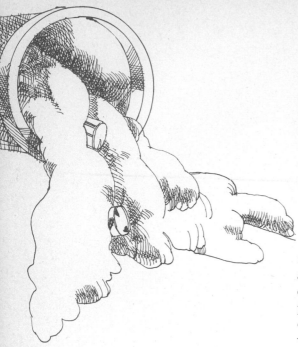

In looking at the pollution problem through the spectacles of economic theory, we shall discover that voluntary exchange and the market system do not work well under all circumstances. In this chapter and the succeeding one, we shall try to get a clear notion of just what those circumstances are, the consequences of such market failure, and the effectiveness of alternative or supplementary procedures for securing social coordination in the use of scarce resources.

Pollution Is a Cost

A good way to begin is by noticing that *pollution is a cost.* It is a cost incurred in the production of goods, and it is not essentially different from any other cost. Pollution, like all costs, represents opportunities foregone: opportunities to breathe clean air, fish or swim in sparkling streams, enjoy pleasant vistas, find solace in solitude, listen to birds sing, or eat fish without fear of mercury poisoning. All these activities are goods. They are valued opportunities that many must now forego because they have been sacrificed for the sake of other goods.

To think about pollution in this way recalls us from Utopia to the real world where there are many goods, almost all of them scarce, desired with different intensities by different people, with varying marginal costs of production. Pollution cannot be eliminated simply by banning all activities that damage the environment. The opportunity costs of doing that would be far too high to make it politically feasible, or even acceptable to anyone at all who really thought about it. What we actually want is *the optimal amount of environmental damage.* No more. But no less, either. We want to reduce the amount as long as the marginal social benefit of doing so exceeds the marginal social cost. And we want to *expand* it—heresy!—whenever the marginal social benefit of doing *that* exceeds the marginal social cost.

No one lobbies for more environmental damage, of course. But people do want a lot of goods whose production or use entails exactly that. Perhaps they *should* not want these goods, or *would* not want them if they fully knew the consequences. Those are difficult and debatable assertions. The economist makes a somewhat different assertion with considerable confidence: People *will* want less of such goods if they are themselves forced to pay more of the unpleasant consequences of having or using them.

It's just our old friend the law of demand in another set of clothes. The quantity of anything demanded decreases as its price increases. "Not so," comes that voice from the rear which has been silent through several chapters. "We are right now paying a heavy price for pollution in the form of ugliness, discomfort, destruction, and disease. But people go right on polluting in disregard of the consequences."

The voice from the rear has made a point and missed the point. The law of demand does not predict that Rod will drive his car less because Tom, Dick, and Harry must now pay more to let him do so. Rod responds to *his own costs and benefits as he perceives them.* Whether or not we decide that this is selfish and inconsiderate on the part of Rod, we had better not decide to pretend that Rod will behave otherwise or to put all our eggs in the basket of moral restraint.

Internalizing Costs

The core of the environmental problem is the increasing significance of what the economist calls *externalities.* These are *spillover costs or benefits:* consequences of action that are not taken into account by the actor and which therefore do not influence his decisions.

Individuals engage in activities for the sake of the benefits they expect to receive, after taking into account the associated costs they expect to bear. But the full costs and benefits of many activities are not confined to the actor. They may be spread out over many other people. In some instances they cannot even be traced to the activities of the people who created them. When everyone makes decisions solely on the basis of the costs he himself bears and the benefits he incurs and those decisions entail substantial additional costs or benefits to others, a serious misallocation of resources may result.

Take the case of a Los Angeles commuter. If he is seized by a vision of the public good and so leaves his car in the garage and walks, bikes, or uses public transportation to get to work, he himself bears a sizable cost. For distances are long in Los Angeles, and the public transportation system wins no prizes there. So most people prefer to drive. They thereby reduce their own travel cost substantially (time spent is a cost!) while imposing upon all other inhabitants of the Los Angeles Basin additional pollution—in such forms as engine exhaust and freeway congestion that takes the time of other motorists. Sermonizing about this is not likely to solve anything as long as each Los Angeleno continues to perceive such a large gap between the high subjective cost of "responsible" behavior and the low subjective cost of "irresponsible" behavior—especially when each one thinks that (*a*) his own sacrifice will make no noticeable difference to the community, and (*b*) his own sacrifice will not induce others to follow his lead.

The same analysis can be applied to industrial polluters. Suppose that the operation of a particular factory puts smoke and soot in the air. If the cost of installing and operating equipment to eliminate the discharge is substantial, the owner of the factory may very reasonably elect to go on polluting. He pays attention to the costs *he bears.* And he bears only a tiny portion of the total discomfort created by his factory's smoke and soot. With his air-conditioned automobile and office and his home in a distant suburb, he hardly notices it. Why should he go to a lot of expense to get rid of it?

"That's understandable but it's still wrong," says the voice from the rear, grinding out his cigarette on the classroom floor. Why did he use the floor as an ash tray? Because he was behaving in a manner analogous to the automobile driver and the factory owner. The floor is used more frequently as an ashtray as the cost of so using it diminishes *to the smoker.* People do not usually grind butts into floors that they own or must clean. Even if they rent, they will want to preserve the appearance of a floor with which they plan to continue living for a while. But when the cost of using the floor as an ashtray is borne by persons other than the smoker, he is far more likely to minimize or ignore the cost.

You may want to call that selfish behavior. It might be more helpful, however, to think of it as evidence that people have limited conceptions of self-interest. If the smoker takes into account the appearance of the room to those who will use it next; if other people's perceptions of beauty and order are important to him; if ugliness for *anyone* becomes, by an act of imaginative insight, ugliness for *him,* then the smoker has an enlarged conception of self-interest. When such a person acts in his own interest, he takes into account more of the consequences for others than are taken into account by someone with a less inclusive concept of self. The growth of such a capacity for vividly entertaining the feelings of others, or for standing in their shoes, may be the key to the advance of civilization. The late philosopher Alfred North Whitehead argued that the development of this capacity was in fact the meaning of social progress.

We can work and hope for such a world, but we had better in the meantime pay some attention to interim solutions. Every private act has social consequences; the more completely these consequences are internalized, or taken into account by actors, the more satisfactory will be the resulting allocation of resources. The spillover effects of private choices tend to become larger and more significant in an urbanized and highly industrialized society. All of which suggests that we should now give careful attention to more precise ways of *assigning responsibility* to people for the consequences of their actions.

External Benefits and Free Riders

Externalities can be positive as well as negative. When activities confer benefits on people who cannot be made to pay for the benefits they receive, we encounter the problem of *free riders.*

When Horty Kulcher planted rose bushes in his front lawn, he conferred a benefit upon all his neighbors (except those with rose fever!) for which he charged them nothing. Because he cannot get them to pay something toward the landscaping of his lot and its contribution to neighborhood beautification, his neighbors are free riders. The problem is that Horty consequently doesn't allocate enough resources to landscaping: he fails to produce aesthetic pleasures for which the community would be willing to pay if there were any low cost way to collect the payments and offer them to Horty as an inducement.

Many goods cannot easily be supplied to those who are willing to pay the price without also being supplied, to some degree at least, to others who refuse to pay the price. A less trivial example than Horty's yard is police protection. If each family had to purchase the police protection it wanted by contracting with private security organizations, the total amount of police protection in any community would tend to be insufficient *by the standards of those same people*. The value to them of additional police protection would be greater than the cost of obtaining it; and when marginal revenues or benefits exceed marginal costs, output is less than optimal. Why then wouldn't the people of the community expand their purchases? Because they would all be waiting for other families to move first, and hoping to obtain the additional police protection they themselves want as a spillover effect. For when security officers are patrolling the block to protect my neighbor's home, they are simultaneously offering increased security to my home. The problem arises from the fact that it is difficult to exclude nonpayers from obtaining some of the benefits. And when nonpayers can obtain benefits without paying, they try to do just that. They restrict their purchases and hope for a free ride.

Education provides another example. If educated people confer benefits on those around them, then the whole community gains from each person's decision to purchase more education. Conversely, the decision of parents not to purchase education for their children will inflict costs on the whole community. In such a situation people will tend to purchase less education for themselves or their children than the socially optimal amount, as they all pay attention only to the private costs and benefits of their decisions.

Or consider the problem of charity in an urbanized society. Assume that all citizens are charitably disposed and want to see more income made available to impoverished and unfortunate people. While many people derive satisfaction from knowing that they themselves contributed to a charitable cause, most people would also prefer that others assume the burden of contributing. They want to see poor people aided, but they also want to see others do the aiding. And so they will tend to behave like free riders. They will hold back somewhat on their contributions in the hope that other people will "purchase" the quantity of the good—assistance to the poor—that they desire and thus enable them to enjoy the good at a lower cost. That, of course, is why semi-coercive techniques are so widely used in successful charity campaigns.

The difficulty in all these cases is simply the mirror image of the difficulty encountered in dealing with environmental damage. Some way must be found to hold people accountable for the costs their activities generate and to make them pay for the benefits they enjoy. And that leads us into the concept of *property*.

The Definition of Property

Most Americans would say that they believe in private property. Many socialists would say that they are opposed to private property. An argument at this level of generality will produce a good deal of heat and little light. For everyone believes in *some* private property, and no one has ever discovered a way to make *all* property private. Moreover, property is often only partially private.

Property comes from the Latin *proprius,* meaning *one's own.* When is something one's own and when is it not? That isn't always as clear as you might at first suppose. Ownership usually implies the power to use something, to prevent others from using it, and to appropriate the benefits from using it. If you own an automobile, you may drive it, prosecute people who drive it without your consent, and charge your neighbor $5 a week for the privilege of riding along with you to work. But you may not drive it north on a southbound one-way street; you will not be able to prosecute successfully other drivers who splash mud on your automobile; and under certain circumstances you will be prosecuted yourself if you transport people for hire. Moreover, your right to drive your automobile when you please will be largely fictitious if the police are unable to prevent people from stealing tires, spark plugs, or entire automobiles. And of what value is your right to drive when you please if there are no roads, or the streets that you want to travel are choked with other automobiles, or there are so many drunk and reckless drivers in the community that the probability of your returning alive from a trip to the grocery store is only 80%? There are clearly many ambiguities in the concept of private property.

Private property is probably best thought of as a matter of degree. A society based on private property is one in which the power to use resources *tends* to be assigned to particular persons, along with the resulting costs and benefits, and the attendant rights *tend* to be clearly defined and effectively enforced. That is the link between property and what we called the precise assignment of responsibility. The laws and customs of societies differ enormously in their prescriptions regarding property: Which resources may be owned by particular persons? What restrictions are placed

on use? How clearly are the privileges and obligations of the owner specified? How effectively are they enforced? Statutory law and prevailing
practice may even give quite different answers to these questions, a fact
that further complicates our analysis. But the issue is a crucial one for
all its ambiguities, uncertainties, and complexities. It is intimately tied
up with the pollution problem.

Property and Pollution

Let's go back to the factory owner who is spewing black smoke into the
air. He "owns" the chimney, so he can use it as he pleases. But the smoke
leaves his chimney and passes into the atmosphere. Who owns the atmosphere? Our laws and customs have tended to answer that nobody owns
the atmosphere. So the factory owner is free to use it as a receptacle for
industrial wastes.

Such a situation seems to have been more tolerable fifty or even ten
years ago than it is today. At one time we appear to have had a working
consensus that the social advantages from allowing the atmosphere to be
used as an industrial dump were greater than the disadvantages. People
could move away from factories, or purchase residential space near the
factories at a low price if they preferred that saving to the delights of clear
air. Meanwhile factories held their costs down by discharging wastes into
the atmosphere, and this meant a greater availability of the goods that
factories produced.

But the situation has changed. The population of the United States has
increased substantially. The goods that factories produce are now available in large quantities and many people are beginning to place a lower
relative valuation on steel products and a higher relative valuation on
attractive scenery. Moreover, a little black smoke may be much more
acceptable than a lot of black smoke. When it becomes difficult to breathe,
or when people discover that beyond a certain point polluted air causes
lung disease, or when new technology reduces the cost of controlling
smoke discharges—the possibilities are almost endless—the social consensus may shift rapidly and radically. That seems to be happening now.

What is called for is renewed attention to the rules that define property.
It is not accurate to say that we must restrict property rights. One might
better argue that an extension of property rights is in order. When we
allowed the factory owner an unrestricted right to discharge soot into the
atmosphere, we denied homeowners the right to keep his soot off their
windows and curtains. A reassignment of rights in this case should not
automatically be viewed as an incursion on private property. In many
cases it could more accurately be viewed as a clarification and strength-
ening of the private-property system.

LAND-USE PLANNING

Land-use planning legislation has become a bitterly contested political issue in the last few years. In June of 1974 the U.S. House of Representatives narrowly defeated a bill, similar to one passed by the Senate in the previous year, authorizing federal funds for land-use planning. The defeated bill would have given money to the states to encourage them to plan the use of land around shopping centers, housing developments, airports, or any areas of "critical environmental concern." It was a modest bill, granting funds to states that wanted to cooperate but containing no sanctions on states that did not wish to venture into the area.

Opponents of the bill argued that it infringed on private property rights. They tended to ignore the fact that existing laws (zoning laws, for example) already abridge the rights of landowners and that some uses of land by private owners infringe on the rights of other private owners. Consider the extensive paving that often occurs as part of an area's development. This may result in rapid water runoff and the consequent flooding during rainstorms of previously dry areas lower in the watershed. Proponents of the bill, on the other hand, were generally quite vague about how they expected new land-use legislation to improve the allocation of land.

Public discussion is not likely to produce much illumination in this area when it is carried on in terms of "private property rights" versus "the public interest." For private property rights in land are a very effective way of promoting the public interest in land use *under a wide range of circumstances.* Where significant externalities exist, however, a reexamination and redefinition of property rights in land may be highly desirable—from the standpoint of land owners as well as those who do not own but are affected by the uses of land.

A lot can be accomplished by levying taxes on activities with substantial social costs in excess of their privately borne costs. The tax in effect turns the social cost into a private cost; it puts the cost on the decision maker. That is one way to *internalize externalities,* a clumsy but descriptive phrase used by economists to mean: compel decision makers to take account of the costs they inflict on others.

But the issues are enormously difficult. The property prescriptions of a society are the product of political decisions that in turn grow out of historical experience, notions of justice, predictions about consequences, and conflicting interests. They cannot be easily altered. And not *just* because interests conflict. There are social costs, which may be substantial, in altering a system of property prescriptions or enforcing new prescriptions. Nor can we always be as certain as we would like to be about the consequences of the changes we contemplate.

What Do People Really Want?

Let's go back to the automobile. Directly or indirectly, the automobile seems to be responsible for a truly astounding part of the environmental deterioration that so many now lament. Our cities have been carved up, cemented over, and stretched out to accommodate mounting masses of automobiles. Automobiles have increased isolation while diminishing solitude. They assault all our senses with fumes, noise, junkyards, collisions, and neon roadways. They gobble up nonrenewable resources. It is partly in their service that oil is spilled on the world's beaches. As a result of their proliferation, national parks during the tourist season are coming to resemble mobile-home sites. But are we willing to pay the cost of having it otherwise? There is no compelling evidence that a majority of Americans are yet willing to alter property definitions and assign to motorists the full cost of their automobile ownership and operation. Freedom to drive might as well be included in the First Amendment. Even toll roads are widely regarded as bordering on unconstitutionality. If someone threw his garbage on your lawn, you would have legal recourse. But you apparently have none when the fumes from his automobile exhaust and the noise of his engine intrude regularly upon the tranquility of your home.

So these will not be easy issues to resolve. If all this sounds terribly pessimistic, it isn't meant to sound that way at all. It is primarily intended as a reminder that perfection is an elusive goal. We are now moving in the direction of rethinking and redefining certain rights of property owners in ways more consistent with the realities of an urbanized and highly industrialized society. There is far more that can be done. But it would be a serious mistake to suppose that all Americans or even a majority of Americans are currently agreed upon just what sacrifices are worth making for the sake of specific kinds of improvement in the environment. If we assume that improvements can be made without sacrifice, or that the requisite sacrifices can be borne by all of "them" and none of "us," we are headed for severe disappointment.

We are also misleading ourselves if we thoughtlessly attribute all the evils to the operation of the market system and suppose that our problems would diminish or disappear if we only had more comprehensive planning. Pollution exists in the Soviet Union and the centrally planned economies of Eastern Europe. For them, too, clean air and water are goods but not free goods. Additional quantities of these goods can be secured only by giving up increasing quantities of alternative goods: refrigerators, grain, housing. The central planners in socialist countries must decide which of numerous competing goods to produce without even the assistance of market information: information not only about what is wanted (which they may decide to ignore), but also information on the social opportunity costs of the various courses they could pursue. There is no evidence that Comprehensive Planning as the solution to problems of the environment is anything more than a beguiling slogan.

Perhaps the most important distinction to make in thinking about these large issues of economic activity and social welfare is the distinction between market processes and property prescriptions. The marketplace is actually a shorthand term for a web of social transactions. It can be used to describe log-rolling by Congressmen, the exchange of promises for votes, or the dispensing of governmental favors as a quid for some quo, as well as to describe exchanges involving money. The concept of exchange provides a general model for thinking about social behavior in any kind

VOTING FOR THE AUTOMOBILE

How eager are Americans to improve the quality of the environment when they suspect that it means a reduction in automobile use? In November 1974, Los Angeles voters *rejected* a one percentage point increase in the 6% sales tax. The increase would have gone for the city's contribution to a mass-transit system that was scheduled to be built primarily with federal funds. By a vote of 54% to 46%, Los Angeles voters turned down a 145-mile rail system and improved bus service despite the fact that about 95% of the cost was to have been borne by the federal government.

The seven largest industrial corporations in the United States in 1974, ranked by dollar volume of sales, were in order Exxon, General Motors, Ford, Texaco, Mobil, Standard of California, and Gulf. All are obviously dependent on the automobile for the major portion of their sales. But that only begins to indicate the importance of the automobile in the U.S. economy. To understand why Americans are reluctant to vote against the automobile in any significant way you must also take account of all the other business firms, large and small, that supply products or services to automobile makers or users, and of the enormous investment of private citizens in automobiles, driveways, and two-car garages.

of political or economic system. Looked at in this way, the difference between economic systems depends not on the extent to which they rely on market processes, for they all do, but on the way in which they assign and enforce responsibility or on their system of property rights. Who has the power to control what? Who receives the benefits and who bears the costs of what actions? What are the rules? How clearly are they specified? How effectively are they enforced? How susceptible are they to change? These are the crucial questions.

ASSIGNING RESPONSIBILITY THROUGH VOLUNTARY EXCHANGE

Imagine a smoker sitting alongside a nonsmoker on a bus. There are no regulations against smoking and no separate sections for smokers and nonsmokers. The smoker ponders for a moment the expected costs and benefits of having a cigarette and decides to light up. Presumably the anticipated benefits exceeded the anticipated costs. But did he consider the cost to his neighbor? And if he had taken this cost into consideration, would he still have decided to smoke?

Suppose he asks the neighbor, "May I smoke?" and the neighbor replies, "I wish you wouldn't." We still don't know whether the benefits to the smoker exceed the combined cost to the smoker and his neighbor. "I wish you wouldn't" may express anything from a very slight distaste for the smell of cigarette smoke to a disabling allergic reaction. We also don't know the strength of the smoker's current craving for a cigarette.

But now let's suppose that the smoker does not ask. We'll assume him to be a thoroughly selfish person who pays no attention at all to anyone's pleasure or discomfort but his own. As he's about to light up, his neighbor says, "Please don't."

SMOKER:	"There's no rule against smoking."
NONSMOKER:	"It makes me cough."
SMOKER:	"That's tough. I want a smoke."
NONSMOKER:	"I'll pay you five cents not to smoke until you get off."
SMOKER:	"I'm having a nicotine fit."
NONSMOKER:	"How about ten cents?"
SMOKER:	"It's a deal."

The nonsmoker pays the smoker a dime and the smoker puts his cigarettes away. The fact that the smoker was willing to accept the bribe the nonsmoker was willing to offer shows that they are *both* better off with no smoking occurring: the smoker prefers a dime to the cigarette, the nonsmoker prefers good air to a dime.

Now let's alter the situation by assuming that no one is allowed to smoke unless he obtains his neighbor's consent.

SMOKER: "May I smoke?"
NONSMOKER: "No."
SMOKER: "I'll pay you a nickel."
NONSMOKER: "It isn't worth it."
SMOKER: "How about eight cents? That's my top offer."
NONSMOKER: "I'll take thirteen."
SMOKER: "It's not worth it."
NONSMOKER: "Then do without."

The basic difference between the two situations lies in the assignment of property rights. In the first case the smoker was assigned a right to smoke and to inflict on others the attendant costs; in the second case the nonsmoker was assigned the right to keep his air clean and to inflict on others the corresponding costs—nicotine fits, for example. The decision—smoke or not smoke—was *not affected* by the assignment of property rights. Clean air was worth thirteen cents to the nonsmoker and the cigarette was worth only eight cents to the smoker. The smoker therefore could not succeed in bribing the nonsmoker, but the nonsmoker was able to bribe the smoker. While the assignment of property rights did not affect the final decision, it did affect the distribution of wealth. When he owns the right to smoke, the smoker can obtain income from the sale of that right. And the nonsmoker must purchase the clean air he wants. With the property right assignment reversed, payments flow the other way. Of course, there's no payment because there's no exchange if the nonsmoker wants more for his clean air than the smoker is willing to pay.

Pollution, we said earlier, is a cost, a cost incurred in the production of goods. It becomes a social problem when the cost is borne by people other than the producer and there is no way for those who bear the costs to get the producer to consider them fully when making his decisions.

The Problem of Transaction Costs

Almost any action that we might take can bring costs or benefits to others. Consider the case of a young boy with a new and noisy motorcycle. He could be persuaded to trade it in for a ten-speed bicycle if he were offered a bribe equal to the total amount all the neighbors would be willing to pay for quiet evenings. But how could the bribe be collected? How could the neighbors be sure that someone else wouldn't buy a motorcycle right after they had gotten rid of the first one? How would they prevent young boys on other blocks from racing mufflerless down their street? Indeed, might the young boy they bribed just agree not to ride it on his own block, so that the neighbors purchase peace for themselves by pushing more noise into other neighborhoods? And if other blocks pursued the same course, the only discernible result might be increased wealth for all motorcycle owners and added incentive, therefore, to buy a motorcycle.

The cases of cigarettes and motorcycles illustrate a pair of important principles:

1. Externalities can be internalized if property rights are clearly assigned and effectively enforced.
2. Transaction costs set a limit upon the extent to which externalities can be internalized by the assignment of property rights.

This may sound like jargon. But think about each principle. When there was no clear assignment of property rights on the bus, there was no way for the smoker and the nonsmoker to arrive at the best solution. With the right to smoke established, however, there was a basis for negotiation and exchange: for a transaction that resulted, as it happened, in no smoking. And in greater welfare for both than if smoking had occurred!

There were costs to this transaction, however. The parties had to bargain and conclude an enforceable agreement. In the case of the motorcyclist and his neighbors, the transaction costs would be much higher, probably so high as to rule out any possibility of a satisfactory agreement.

The Pursuit of Perfection

Anyone who begins to worry about ways to internalize *all* externalities is on the path to madness. Beautiful people confer benefits upon others by their presence. Do we therefore want to induce them, through monetary payments, to spend more time than they would otherwise care to do in social circulation? Surely not. On the other hand, we *do* bribe beautiful people: They're invited to more places and treated better than surly people. It would be crass to call that bribery. But we think it's important to note that ordinary social interaction includes a lot of subtle practices for encouraging beautiful people to share their charms and surly people to keep to themselves. A parent who frowns at a whining child is inducing the child to internalize an externality: that is, to include in his benefit-cost calculations the costs that his behavior is inflicting upon others. We aren't stressing this point because we want all social interaction to be based on careful calculation. The point is rather that we do learn to discern the joys and sorrows that our behavior brings to others and we do learn to some extent to count them in with our other benefits and costs.

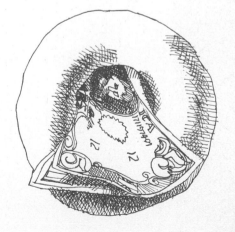

The Doughnut and the Hole

The market system quite obviously fails to internalize all externalities. But isn't that a misleading way to put the matter? We could just as accurately say that the market system manages to internalize an extraordinary number of externalities. In particular, it induces people to engage in activities that benefit others by enabling them to capture a share of those benefits for themselves. Every new or improved product or service is provided because people hope to exchange their contribution to others' welfare for something they themselves want. This doesn't deny the importance of generosity, public spirit, and serendipity. But virtue and good luck are not enough to organize an economic system. Its organization and coordination depend primarily on people's pursuit of their own advantage in situations where they are able to capture through exchange a share of the social benefits their actions create.

As for costs, they are even more nearly internalized. There are exceptions; that's why we have pollution problems. But the first step toward a resolution of these problems is to recognize as exceptions those cases where people are able to impose a substantial portion of their costs on others without securing their consent.

Measuring Costs and Benefits

The factory discharging smoke into the air would not be polluting if it secured the consent of every adversely affected party. After all, every factory inflicts costs on all the people who come to work there; this isn't a social problem because their consent is secured through the payment of "bribes." The factory "bribes" the owners of all the resources it uses to secure their consent and cooperation. But it doesn't compensate the people who bear the costs of its smokestack emissions because they do not have a clear and enforceable property right in the ambient air. By established practice, in fact, the factory owners have a property right in the air, the right to use it as a dump without charge. The question of who ought to own the air is an important one. But regardless of how that question is answered, the issue of whether or not smoke should be discharged into the air requires a comparison of social costs and social benefits.

If all the people who find themselves burdened by the smoke are willing to pay a bribe to the factory owners large enough to persuade them to clean up the air, then the discharge clearly ought to be stopped. What if the only way to stop the discharge is to shut down the factory? The factory should be shut down if the people bothered by the smoke are willing to pay the owners of all the resources involved, including employees, more than it's worth to them to keep the factory running. If they are not willing to pay that much, then the total expected benefit from its continued operation must be greater than the total expected cost, pollution included, and the factory should continue operating.

To Whom Should Property Rights Be Assigned?

This argument is subject, however, to a very important qualification. Suppose that the factory is awarded "ownership" of the air so that the people in the area must bribe the owners not to pollute. And suppose that the largest bribe they are willing to pay is $100,000. If the right to continue polluting is worth more than that to the factory owners, they will reject the bribe and continue polluting. But now suppose that we vest the property right in the residents of the area so that the factory owners must purchase the right to begin polluting. And suppose that the most the owners are willing to pay is $200,000. It is distinctly possible that the residents could refuse a $200,000 bribe even though they themselves are not willing to pay more than a $100,000 bribe. Why might this occur?

It could occur because the demand for any good depends on income. The residents would be unwilling to pay more than $100,000 because they "can't afford it." Were they wealthier, they might be willing to pay $300,000 and, even with their low incomes, they would demand that much to give up their clean air. When the property right is vested in them, their wealth is increased and they place a higher monetary value on clean air. This is an application of the concept of income elasticity of demand.[1]

There are good reasons for inclining toward the assignment of environmental rights to citizens rather than to business firms. It is not that "clean air is worth more than anything" or that "people are more important than profits." The first statement is false and the second is meaningless. The fact that business firms earn income through pollution while residents lose income through pollution does mean, however, that the income restraint is more likely to hold down the residents' bid than the bid of the business firms. In addition, the firm will usually have more ways to reduce pollution than the residents will have to escape it, and the requirement that the firm pay the bribe will induce it to search for less polluting processes. Moreover, the requirements that polluters pay the bribes (rather than be entitled to receive them) eliminates the incentives that otherwise might arise to create pollution deliberately in order to secure a reward for stopping. Nuisance actions of this kind are well known to lawyers. Finally, the relationship is not altogether symmetrical from an ethical standpoint. The case of the two passengers on the bus best illustrates what we mean. While the smoker inflicts harm on the nonsmoker by smoking, the nonsmoker does not inflict harm on the smoker by not smoking. In general, people

1. An illustration: The maximum amount someone would pay to save a leg from amputation is finite. It's limited by the person's income, so that a payment greater than some maximum would deprive him even of food. But there may be *no* amount, no matter how large, that would secure the same person's agreement to give up a leg.

who want a clean and quiet environment do impose costs on others when they are able to ban polluting activities; but they are not the "aggressors." Someone who is savoring the quiet evening breeze does not diminish the satisfaction of motorcyclists; but motorcyclists do diminish the satisfactions of breeze savorers.

In all of these cases, of course, we would also want to consider the issue of priority. Who was there first? Someone who moves in next to a long established rendering plant has less right to complain of the smell than someone who finds a rendering plant moving in next door to him. A stronger case can generally be made for the maintenance of existing and established property rights than for their reassignment.

But isn't this whole line of reasoning slightly indecent? Is it really possible to defend darkened skies and coated lungs by appealing to dollars and cents? The dollars and cents are not the point at issue. The challenge is to find some way to calculate and compare benefits and costs. Dramatic language doesn't help. That factory might be producing fertilizer that will save a million citizens of Bangladesh from starvation. Do we really want to sacrifice one million lives so that a few people can enjoy blue skies without having to move? As we said, dramatic language doesn't help. If we pretend to ourselves that every air polluting factory is doing nothing but enriching its stockholders, all of whom are already in the top 10% of income receivers, then we can dispense with cost and benefit calculations. But then we're no longer in the real world, either.

Is It Workable?

The legitimate objection to this approach arises from the transaction costs it would entail. Whether we assigned original ownership of the air to the factory or to the people in its vicinity, the cost of determining, collecting, and paying the "bribes" would be prohibitive. The fact that air pollution can spread so widely in so many different directions compounds the difficulties. But the analysis is not as far-fetched as you may suppose. This procedure can in fact be used as a way of preventing certain other kinds of pollution that can be more narrowly confined.

Suppose a firm wants to build a factory that will inflict noise upon the surrounding area up to a radius of one mile. Zoning laws are used to prevent it from locating in a settled area. (Note that the zoning decision in effect assigns to the residents of these areas the property right to a low-noise environment.) So the firm buys a roughly circular site in the country, two miles in diameter, and locates the factory in the center. What can it now do with all that buffer land?

It can sell it. Each purchaser must clearly understand that the factory will be inflicting noise on the environment. The land will then be sold to those who find that the advantage of a lower price offsets any disadvantage

PURCHASING THE AIR

Bunker Hill Company operates a lead smelter in Kellogg, Idaho. A study cosponsored by Bunker Hill and the state of Idaho in 1974 discovered that there were 29 children in 15 families living near the smelter who had more than 80 micrograms of lead per milliliters of blood. (More than 80 micrograms indicates outright lead poisoning.)

What should have been done after this discovery? Should the plant have been closed? Should it have been required to install antipollution equipment?

What in fact occurred was that Bunker Hill purchased the property of the 15 families living within the radius of contamination and helped them to relocate. The company in effect granted that the families owned the air about their residences and then purchased from them the right to use it by buying the land itself.

created by the noise. And the factory will have no neighbors except those who have consented to its noise. Any subsequent purchasers of lots in the area will also know about the factory and will have the same chance to trade more noise for a lower price. And what if the lots do *not* in fact sell for a lower price? That's evidence either that the noise is not a cost to purchasers or that there are compensating advantages. In any event, the noise emissions are not pollution; for to the extent that they are a burden on any one, the costs will have been fully internalized by the noise maker in the form of a reduced price for the lots.

There are innumerable ways in which people reduce pollution through voluntary exchange. Nonsmokers in public places try to segregate themselves from smokers, and the owners of the public places, who are interested in the patronage of nonsmokers as well as smokers, often facilitate the transaction by designating smoking and no-smoking sections. The smoke hanging over the smokers' heads is, of course, not pollution insofar as it's not a cost anyone inflicts on anyone else without his consent. People who think that commercial establishments destroy the quality of a neighborhood locate in areas where such establishments don't exist. And people who think that purely residential areas are bland and uninteresting locate in areas with shops. Both groups are reducing pollution by escaping the costs that the actions of others might impose upon them. The people who move to Manhattan because that's where the action is and the people who move to Kankakee because that's where the action is not—they are all reducing pollution.

TO WHOM SHOULD RESPONSIBILITIES BE ASSIGNED?

Here is a clearly reasoned argument from a letter to the editor of the *Wall Street Journal,* written by Beverly C. Moore, Jr., of the Corporate Accountability Research Group.

The argument that we systematically tout the benefits but ignore the costs of consumer proposals is particularly ironic to me since, as a Nader associate, cost-benefit considerations guide my own work more than anything else. I am persuaded that the cost-effectiveness of certain ad hoc safety and environmental regulations could be improved by the alternative of internalizing the social costs ("externalities") that presently escape the discipline of a market economy. If the soft drink industry were forced to compensate fully the victims of exploding bottles, if the food industry were required to account for the costs of heart disease, tooth decay, and the other consequences of improper nutrition, or if the auto industry were obliged to pay out $46 billion annually in accident costs, I suspect not only that the optimum trade-off between accident and prevention costs would be realized without supplementary government standards but also that the new economic incentives would generate technological advances which would in time substantially reduce the prevention costs.

Mr. Moore is recommending a reassignment of property rights as a way of dealing with certain potentially hazardous consumer products: the manufacturers of the products will be responsible for bearing the costs of any damages their products inflict on consumers. This would certainly create additional incentives to make the products less hazardous and stimulate technological changes to promote this end. But would his proposal move us closer to "the optimum trade-off"? Among the questions raised by his recommendation are these: (1) by what procedures would damages be evaluated and what would be the costs of administering and enforcing those procedures? and (2) (a question that enormously complicates the first question) under what circumstances would the consumer be held responsible for contributory negligence?

Take the issue of food as raised by Mr. Moore. Almost any food will damage the user's health if it is consumed in excessive amounts or without proper supplementary foods. And very few foods, including some whose nutritional value is nil, are harmful if consumed in modest quantities. A similar problem arises with automobiles. A vehicle that is very safe when driven by one motorist will be a lethal weapon in the hands of another. Automobiles could of course be made to provide passengers with far more protection under given conditions than they now provide. And if manufacturers had to pay all the medical costs of people who were hurt in their vehicles, they would make all sorts of safety changes in automobile design. But all such changes would impose higher costs of other kinds on automobile owners: higher purchase prices, higher operating costs, less comfort, and less "style," to mention just a few items that most automobile owners do seem to care about.

All this suggests that "the optimum trade-off" is not likely to be approached if *full* responsibility is assigned to manufacturers. On the contrary, Mr. Moore's proposals would surely compel careful consumers to subsidize careless ones by inducing manufacturers to produce nothing but foolproof (literally) products. Is that an optimum arrangement? How would nonsmokers and those who never smoke in bed feel about paying higher prices for less comfortable mattresses that do not burn when cigarettes are dropped on them? Would you like to see soft drinks and candy bars taken off the market because their producers don't want to pay the dental bills of teenagers who make such foods their regular breakfast and lunch diet? This is the same kind of question we encountered in chapter 8 when it was asked how a society could best economize on the costs of information gathering. It will not do so by prohibiting the parties to an exchange from voluntarily sharing those costs.

ASSIGNING RESPONSIBILITY BY SPECIAL LEGISLATION

Voluntary exchange will not be able to resolve satisfactorily all our environmental problems. One reason we'll look at later: the limited ability of future generations to bid for scarce resources. The other reason is the one we've already discussed: the transaction costs may be prohibitive. What alternatives are there when a clearer assignment of property rights and voluntary exchange cannot do the job because of high transaction costs?

Most people want to ban pollution by law. We've pointed out in many ways why that's not really a solution. And it's a fact of political life that pollution gets more knocks from environmentalists than it does from legislators. At the risk of being impaled on an ecology button we'll venture the opinion that the procrastination of legislatures isn't all bad. Where legislators have acted they have too often acted with more enthusiasm than knowledge. They have slashed at pollution because of its obvious costs with often insufficient attention to the costs of the anti-pollution regulations.

This would be a good time to review the discussion of marginal costs in chapter 6, pp. 119–23. If we hadn't thought the example was such a good one for explaining the nature and significance of marginal costs, we would have included it in this chapter to demonstrate the importance of paying attention to diminishing returns when protecting the environment. You must remember that there are innumerable ways to improve the environment, that they almost always entail costs, that the ratio of environmental improvement to cost varies from one environmental measure to another, and that for any particular environmental measure the benefit to cost ratio will tend to decline rapidly as we approach "perfection." And you always want to keep in mind the first principle of economics: There are substitutes for anything. Rising energy prices in recent years have shown how many people will even substitute other interests for ecological concerns when the relative cost to them of caring for the environment goes up.

Taxes to Control Pollution

The presence of prohibitive transaction costs will incline most economists to consider taxes rather than outright prohibitions or even quantitative regulations. We mentioned earlier that levying taxes on activities with substantial social costs in excess of their privately borne costs was one way to internalize externalities. Let's consider an example.

There are four manufacturing plants in Luvly City, and they are the sole local producers of an air pollutant which we shall call yecch. How much yecch each produces per month depends on the production process it uses. Each firm has a choice among three alternative production processes. The following table summarizes the situation:

Table 14A POLLUTION EMISSION WITH ALTERNATIVE PRODUCTION PROCESSES

	Firm A will produce	Firm B will produce	Firm C will produce	Firm D will produce	Costs for each firm
Using Process 1	500 yecch	800 yecch	1600 yecch	700 yecch	Base
Using Process 2	300 yecch	200 yecch	1200 yecch	200 yecch	Base + $2400
Using Process 3	200 yecch	50 yecch	900 yecch	150 yecch	Base + $4800

Process 1 is the cheapest production process for each firm and hence the one it will choose if pollution is no problem. If it moves to process 2, each firm increases its costs per month by $2400. If it moves to process 3, each firm increases its monthly costs by yet another $2400. Another way of interpreting the same data is to say that process 2 shows the pollution abatement attainable from a $2400 expenditure in the case of each firm, and process 3 shows the pollution abatement attainable from yet another $2400 per month expenditure.

How much yecch will be produced monthly in the absence of any concern for the environment? Each firm will choose the cheapest production process and Luvly City will sit amid 3600 yecch per month: 500 + 800 + 1600 + 700.

Now suppose we are on the City Council in Luvly City and that we have decided to reduce yecch pollution. How shall we go about it?

No yecch at all would be pleasant. But yecch reduction entails costs, so we must choose. We won't make the mistake of supposing that the costs somehow don't matter because they will fall upon the polluters. We are *all* polluters. We create pollution in the process of obtaining goods we want, and when we must curtail our pollution we can do so only by giving up some of those goods. Firm C is the biggest offender and looks like the firm to hit. But look more closely: A $2400 expenditure by firm C will reduce yecch by only 400 per month. The same expenditure at firm B would yield a 600 yecch reduction. That's 50% more yecch reduction for the dollar. Clearly a better buy. It's a more efficient choice because it gets total yecch in Luvly City down to 3000 per month at less cost. If that isn't low enough, we can reduce it to 2500 by instructing firm D to alter its production process. Firm C, the biggest polluter in the group, would be ordered to shift to process 2 only if we still wanted a further reduction in yecch emission. And we *should* want it, in our capacity as council members pursuing the *public* interest, only if we estimate that a reduction of yecch from 2500 to 2100 is worth more to the community than $2400 per month.

It isn't easy to assign dollar values to blue skies or odorless air and thus, by extension, to put a cost tag on a unit of yecch. We don't have the information we would have if there were a practical way for each citizen to express his valuations with a dollar bid. But we're being asked to assume the task as members of the City Council precisely because the transaction costs are prohibitively high. So we must make our estimate. We pass an ordinance charging (taxing) each firm $4.50 per unit of yecch emitted per month. Can you use table 14A to predict what will happen? Try it before reading on.

If they continue to use process 1, the firms will have to pay respectively $2250, $3600, $7200, and $3150 per month—for the right to continue using the air of Luvly City as a dump. That might force one or more out of busi-

ness. But we'll assume their revenues continue to be adequate in order to see what adjustments each would want to make short of shutting down operations.

The *total* tax payment is not the relevant number. Each firm can choose among alternative production processes and the corresponding alternative taxes. By shifting to process 2, firm A will reduce its tax payments by $900 (200 fewer yecch times $4.50). Since the cost of the shift is $2400, it will choose to continue with process 1. Firm B saves $2700 by shifting to process 2; it will choose to do so since the additional cost is only $2400. The tax saving for firm C is $1800 and for firm D it is $2250; they will both find it more economical to continue with process 1. The end result of the new ordinance, therefore, will be (1) a shift to process 2 by firm B and retention of process 1 by firms A, C, and D; (2) a reduction of yecch emissions to 3000 per month; (3) tax revenue for Luvly City of $13,500 per month, revenue that could perhaps be used to compensate those whose lives are made less pleasant by yecch emissions. We are ignoring the cost to the city of enforcing the ordinance; an adequate social accounting should include that.

Try your hand at calculating the consequences of other tax rates. You can demonstrate that firm D will be persuaded to shift to the more expensive but less polluting process 2 by any tax greater than $4.80. Firm C won't be induced to shift until the tax climbs to $6. Firm A will stick with process 1 unless the tax rises to $12. But after $8, firm C will shift to process 3 since doing so reduces yecch emissions by another 300; a tax saving of more than $2400 at any tax rate above $8. A tax rate of $12 (or a little more) will cut total yecch emissions to 1600: 300 + 200 + 900 + 200.

License to Pollute?

Let's be clear what we're doing by taxing yecch. We are selling firms the right to put yecch in the air. We are *not* selling them a "license to pollute," not as long as the tax adequately measures the cost to society of an additional unit of yecch. For pollution is a cost dumped on others *without their consent.* You may argue if you wish that it is the city council that's consenting, not the affected citizens. And that's a valid point. But by questioning the right of the council to speak for the citizens, you question the right of the council to intervene at all. Keep that in mind. Lots of people nonetheless object to environmental protection through taxes because they can't get beyond the notion that it "licenses pollution" or that it "allows rich polluters to go on polluting while penalizing the poor polluters."

But look again at what happened with a $4.50 tax. Firms A, C, and D paid it without reducing their emissions. Firm B cut back. *There is no evidence that any of the firms is larger or wealthier than any other.* We provided no information on this question because it isn't relevant to their responses. Each firm responds to the tax by comparing marginal costs and marginal gains.

What would have occurred had the city council adopted the much too common procedure of putting the same flat ceiling on the yecch emissions of each firm? The answer is: more yecch emissions at the same social cost or the same yecch emissions at a higher social cost. It couldn't set the maximum below 900 without driving firm C out of business. So try 900. The total cost will be $4800, and total emissions will be 2900. But the council could have reduced emissions all the way to 2500 for the same $4800 cost by persuading firms B and D to shift to process 2. (Any tax rate above $4.80 would have that consequence.)

The advantage of a properly set tax is that it internalizes externalities. It puts the costs of action on the actors and says to each, "Make your best adjustment in the light of your special circumstances." Our simplified example actually *understates* the effectiveness of this approach by assuming that there's a single, given cost of adjustment for each firm. In reality firms will usually hunt for and find lower cost techniques for reducing emissions when the tax gives them an incentive to do so. The fact that no two firms will ever have identical production processes and that the managers of a firm will have better knowledge of their own processes than any legislative body is an additional reason for choosing the tax.

On Political Obstacles

The tax approach also reduces the inevitable political problems associated with efforts to eliminate pollution. A flat ceiling tends to present firms with immediate all-or-nothing choices and to arouse intense political opposition. The firm's managers will claim that they can't meet the standards, that they will have to shut down, throw people out of work, reduce the community's tax revenues, and inflict a long parade of horrible secondary consequences on the region in which they operate. The typical response of agencies charged with administering the new regulations is then to grant a delay, during which the firm does little except lobby for another delay. If the community does not want to impose an additional financial burden on the plant, perhaps out of fear that the plant might be closed, it could grant a lump sum subsidy to the firm and *then* impose the tax.

Many people incorrectly assume that granting such a lump sum subsidy to a polluter before imposing a tax on the polluting activity would cancel out the effect of the tax. But that would only be true if the subsidy were based, as the tax would be, on the amount of the firm's pollution. No one is recommending that. A good analogy to clarify the distinction is the proposal to raise the gasoline tax and return the revenue to the public through an income tax rebate. Suppose you had to pay an additional 50¢ per gallon tax on gasoline but your income tax was reduced by $200. The additional $200 per year in spendable income would have a *slight* tendency to increase the amount of gasoline you purchase, assuming that your income elasticity of demand for gasoline is positive. But the effect on your driving habits of this increase in your income would be insignificant in comparison with the effect of the higher price for gasoline. The proposal would defeat its purpose only if the rebate were based on the quantity of gasoline purchased during the year—an absurd suggestion that no one is making.

The purpose of the lump sum subsidy would be to compensate the polluting firm for the reduction in its wealth caused by imposition of the tax. But the tax, if properly set, would still give the firm the incentive to reduce its pollution.

Perhaps nothing could make a larger contribution to the formulation of effective environmental policy than agreement on the fundamental proposition: Pollution is a cost generated by activities that produce benefits for those who undertake them, but a cost not borne by those who engage in the activities. This definition gets simultaneously at the nature of the problem and the condition of its resolution. The problem is that some people must bear costs to which they have not consented. The solution is to impose those costs on the people for whose benefit they are generated.

WHO SPEAKS FOR THE FUTURE?

And this gets us to the problem of future generations. For current activities generate costs that may in part be borne by future generations. Those who are not yet born or who are too young to make their voices heard seemingly have no opportunity to express their preferences about the current allocation of resources. Even if everyone now alive consents to the discharge of chemicals into a lake, either because it does not affect them or because they have received compensation, can we really say that no pollution is occurring? Some unborn fishermen might want to protest vigorously, and might refuse to give their consent even if offered a very large compensation—were there any way to consult them.[1] Who controls pollution on behalf of future generations?

1. And nobody ever seems to consult the fish. The authors expect to have a tough time persuading the editors to let that stand as a serious objection, further evidence of the blindly anthropocentric nature of our thinking. There were times in human history when it was considered equally absurd to assign any social value to the preferences of slaves, or serfs, or members of "inferior" races, or women. Today's certainties have a way of becoming tomorrow's insularities. [The editors read through this without blinking.]

The answer is: the present generation. Its members may or may not be effective spokesmen for future generations; but no one can deny that decisions in the present will always be made by the present generation. No one else is around. Moreover, they will make those decisions with an eye on the future, because *all* decisions are made by looking to the future. The past is sunk cost and irrelevant to decision making; it's the future that matters.

But how *distant* a future? That will depend on the rate at which people in the present discount future events. But we had better go round about if we hope to achieve clarity with respect to this intriguing, often misunderstood, and highly perplexing question. Let's detour through the issue of *conservation*.

Principles of Conservation

Some resources seem to be clearly nonrenewable. They exist in a finite amount, they cannot be recreated, and once exhausted they are gone forever. The fossil fuels are the most common example. What does it mean to practice conservation of fossil fuels on behalf of future generations? Let's see first what it *cannot* mean.

It cannot mean to use them up at such a rate that all subsequent generations will be able to utilize them at the same rate. For no matter how low the rate of current use, a finite resource will eventually be exhausted if that rate persists.

Nor can it mean not to use them at all. For a resource cannot be conserved for the *use* of future generations if it is only bequeathed to them on the condition that they not use it. But they may not use it if it is their task, also, to bequeath it to the future. An unusable resource is not a resource.

Then what *can* we mean by the conservation of nonrenewable resources? Let's shift the question and ask what we *do* mean. For we do practice conservation. We don't consume everything now without making any provision for the future. How do we decide? What criteria are used in a system where resources are privately owned? The easiest way to see what happens is to ask: What determines the rate at which the owner of a nonrenewable resource decides to mine that resource?

Allocating Production over Time

Every possible production program will yield a particular pattern of flows over time, such as 10,000 barrels each year until the oil well is depleted in 1995, or 15,000 tons of coal per month for the first year, 16,000 tons per month for the second year, and so forth. The possibilities are infinitely variable. But the resource owners are aiming ultimately at a flow of *net revenue*, and the flow of the resource is only a means to an end.

If the price of the resource is currently lower than it's expected to be five years from now, because world production relative to demand is greater today than it's expected to be in five years, then a barrel or ton of production will be expected to yield more net revenue if its production is postponed for five years than if it's undertaken now. (That assumes production costs remain the same. Changing production costs complicate the calculations but don't alter the principles.) Here is our first clue to the way conservation actually does occur. Resource owners reduce production in years of expected low prices in order to expand production in years of expected high prices. The same processes that we observed in chapter 8's discussion of speculation are working in this case.

A second principle follows immediately: Insofar as producers correctly anticipate future supply and demand conditions, they will continually adjust the rate of production to even out the pattern of resource prices over time. Thus, if the price is expected to be a great deal higher next year than this year, the owners will want to reduce sales this year in order to expand them next year; and that will raise this year's price while lowering next year's price. Once again it's simply the process of moving resources through time in response to anticipated future conditions that we examined in chapter 8.

Discounting the Future

But now comes the interesting part. With constant costs of production and no general inflation, we would expect the price of the resource to *rise each year*—assuming that it is indeed a resource whose total quantity is fixed forever and that producers correctly anticipate the future. Why? Because net revenue in the future is less highly valued than net revenue now. If the interest rate is 5%, then $100,000 this year will grow to $105,000 next year. So producers discount expected future revenue at some positive interest rate. What this means is that an expected price next year no higher than this year's price will be regarded by producers as a less advantageous price than the current one. So they will expand current production at the expense of next year's production. And their response, of course, will then reduce this year's price and raise next year's. The rate of output will continue to be adjusted in this way until next year's price is sufficiently higher than this year's to yield producers the larger net revenue they demand as a condition of delaying production for a year. How much extra net revenue they will demand and, consequently, how much higher next year's price must be and how much lower next year's output depend on the rate at which producers discount future income.

And this is the insight we're after. Resources *will* be conserved for the future as producers try to maximize the value of their expected income.

Too rapid a rate of production now would mean much higher prices at some future date, and that would offer an incentive to reduce production now in order to conserve the resource for later sale when the price is expected to be more advantageous. But this does not lead to the same rate of production year after year, because producers don't place an equal value on the same prices year after year. A future price has the same value to them as a present price only if it yields the same *discounted* income. The general conclusion now emerges: The stock of a nonrenewable resource will be gradually exhausted, with the rate of production and use declining steadily over time and the price rising steadily over time. To put it another way: We do conserve resources for the future; but remote years receive progressively less. How much less depends upon the rate at which we discount future income. At a high rate of discount we consume resources rapidly; at a low rate of discount we spread their consumption out farther into the future.

Whose Rate of Discount?

Don't conclude that the relevant rate of time discount is the rate of time preference that resource owners happen to have. It's the social rate of time discount as reflected in the prevailing interest rate that determines the distribution of production over time. The fact that a coal mine owner has a high personal rate of time preference won't induce him to mine the coal faster. If he discounts the future at a rate higher than the prevailing interest rate, he will want to *consume* his income faster than the average. But it won't be to his advantage to mine the coal faster; he will instead elect to sell the mine to obtain present income for consumption. And the highest bidder will be someone who intends to produce at the rate that maximizes the present value of expected future net income from the mine, when that net income is discounted at the prevailing, socially determined interest rate.

Now comes the sticky question. Do the private rates of time preference that create a prevailing social rate of interest yield a *justifiable* social rate of time discount? To put it simply: Do we have the right to assign a lesser importance to the satisfactions of future generations than we assign to our own satisfactions? Is that ethically defensible? However difficult it may be to implement such a goal, is the present generation not morally obligated to act as if the proper social rate of time preference were zero? In the language of economics, that's what those conservationists are calling for who want us to give to future generations the same right to share in the earth's resources that we claim for ourselves. That is why some of those who understand the way in which the market system allocates resources between present and future object to its operation.

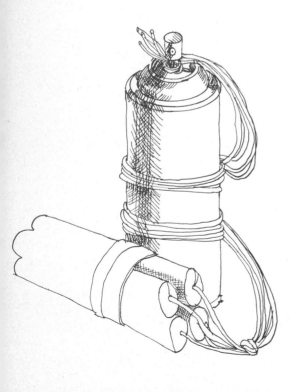

Our society is deeply divided on this issue. The clearest evidence of the division may be the polarization of opinions that so often manifests itself when we debate the probability of disastrous long-run consequences from some current practices. For example, should we stop using aerosol sprays? No one knows for certain whether they are gradually changing the earth's atmosphere or not. Our continued use of these sprays *may* have disastrous consequences for people living in the year 2100. Let's assume arbitrarily that the probability is .05: there's one chance in twenty that the sprays are a time bomb that will go off in the face of people 125 years from now, nineteen chances in twenty that they won't have any deleterious effect. Against this we have the probability of 1.0 that we will be inconvenienced by giving them up: it's a certainty, in other words. Will people faced today with those options vote to outlaw aerosol sprays?

Some will, with no hesitation. The risk is too great, they will say. The convenience of aerosol sprays is not enough to outweigh even a 5% chance of disaster. Now if that 5% probability of disaster were only one year in the future, it's hard to believe that anyone would prefer to gamble. But 125 years is a long time. None of us will be alive then, nor will anyone be alive whom we know and care for. And thus many people heavily discount that 5% probability: "It's too far off to worry about." Events in the distant future are not as vividly imagined by most of us and do not therefore have the reality of imminent events. And so we assign them a lesser importance in making present decisions. The polarization of opinion in our society on this and similar issues, with some calling for immediate and drastic action and others calling at most for further research, is compelling evidence of profound disagreement on the proper social rate of time discount.

Taking Chances with the Future

On the other hand, the greater uncertainty associated with more distant events is legitimate grounds for discounting them to some extent. A 5% probability of disaster next year really is a higher probability than a 5% probability of disaster in 125 years. That seems contradictory at first: a 5% probability is a 5% probability. But probability estimates are always based on *present knowledge*. There is a much smaller probability that we'll discover something new in the course of one year that will alter the situation favorably than that we'll make some such discovery within a 125-year span. Uncertainty about the future means that we cannot *know* what course of action is called for in the present by a zero social rate of time preference (or any other rate). And the social importance of new knowledge makes the more distant future radically uncertain. Some people are optimists because they think new scientific discoveries will rescue humanity from all the disasters now being forecast. But others criticize this optimism and call it wishful thinking. Everyone agrees that new knowledge *could* make all the difference; they disagree on whether it *will*. Only one thing is certain: No one can predict! For if new knowledge were predictable, we would already know it and it wouldn't be new knowledge. In disagreeing on whether new knowledge *will* come to save us, we are disagreeing on a question that cannot be conclusively answered.

A society that is not highly averse to risk and that is characterized by overwhelming optimism will discount future events at a high rate, spend lavishly, take chances, and leave to future generations . . . a wasteland? Perhaps. But not necessarily. For such a society is likely also to be marked by a high rate of innovation that may far more than compensate future generations for the resources consumed in the present. That society may, for example, consume the earth's fossil fuels at a frantic rate and perfect the fusion process . . . or fail to find the secret of fusion and leave its descendants impoverished.

One More Question

To all of these uncertain conclusions we must add a final question. Suppose we were to agree that the market system with private ownership of resources does not give adequate weight to the claims of future generations. What alternatives exist? Better forecasting would help. So would an improved system of futures markets. And education, especially the education that occurs as people discuss alternative values, could make important differences in the way we manage present resources. But the agency to which the critics of current procedures invariably turn is the government. If the market does not yield the best possible results, the government ought to intervene.

Is it likely, however, that government intervention will on balance move events in more desirable directions? That question has already arisen many times in this book. It will be a central question in chapters 16 to 26, as we examine the problems of recession and inflation, the system of international exchange, and the tools of fiscal and monetary policy. Talleyrand said that war was too important to be left to the generals. The economic functions of government may be too important to be left exclusively to the political scientists. Chapter 15 brings the government out from behind the curtain as it applies the economic way of thinking to the decisions that governments make.

Once Over Lightly

Pollution is an example of the problems caused by what the economist calls externalities: consequences of action that are not taken into account by decision makers because they are costs or benefits that do not accrue to the decision makers themselves.

The consequences of spillover costs (negative externalities) can be corrected if ways can be found to impose the full costs of actions on those who take them.

Spillover benefits (positive externalities) lead to a misallocation of resources by encouraging "free riders." People purchase too little of the good because they hope to receive it as a spillover benefit from the purchases of others.

A society's system of property rights is its way of assigning the responsibility for actions, both costs and benefits, to particular parties. The responsibilities people will fulfill depend upon the clarity of these assignments and the degree to which they are enforced. When responsibilities are poorly defined, people tend to behave "irresponsibly."

Voluntary exchange through a market system depends upon the clear assignment and effective enforcement of property rights. The presence of substantial externalities will prevent the market system from allocating resources efficiently.

Disagreements about environmental problems are often indicative of deeper disagreements about who should have which property rights. Improved environmental quality is not a free good, and there is a great deal of disagreement among people about who should bear its costs.

Voluntary exchange does far more than we usually realize to allocate costs and benefits to the people who choose them.

Transaction costs impose limits upon people's ability to assign responsibilities in a mutually satisfactory way through voluntary exchange.

Taxes or subsidies can be used to internalize externalities if they can be adjusted to reflect the difference between the total costs or benefits generated by an activity and the costs or benefits that accrue to those who engage in the activity.

Conservation of resources for the future occurs when people compare the value of current resource use with the expected and discounted value of future use.

People have different information and beliefs, short or long time horizons, strong or weak senses of obligation to the future, differing attitudes toward risk, and optimistic or pessimistic expectations regarding scientific and technological advance. These are some of the factors that make for widely divergent opinions in our society about the justifiable social rate of time discount.

QUESTIONS FOR DISCUSSION

1. All these questions involve some degree of incompatibility between alternative goods. How are such conflicts of interest to be resolved?

   (*a*) Do owners of motorcycles have the right to improve the operation of their vehicles by removing the mufflers?

   (*b*) Do zoning laws infringe on property rights or protect property rights?

   (*c*) Do commercial airlines have the right to interfere with your television reception by flying over your house? Should they be compelled to compensate you for the violation of your air space? What would happen if a way were found to compel commercial airlines to compensate everyone adversely affected by their operation?

   (*d*) What would you expect to occur if motorists were required to pay a tax per mile driven approximately equal to the costs their driving imposes upon all others in the society? (Assume we somehow obtained the necessary information on these costs.) Would you favor such a tax? Why or why not?

   (*e*) A large mulberry tree in your neighbor's yard provides you with welcome shade but gives him only a lot of inedible and messy mulberries. He wants to cut the tree down. Does he have the legal right to do so? Does his action affect the value of your property? Is it better from a social point of view that the tree be felled or remain standing? How might an answer be found and the better result obtained?

   (*f*) Do the owners of land along the highways have a right to erect billboards on their own private property? Who owns the view from the highway? If motorists intensely dislike billboards that despoil the countryside, could they get together and bribe farmers to remove them? What would be some of the difficulties in the way of such a solution? What arguments could be used to support this kind of approach?

2. Does an extremely bright student create any externalities for other students in her classes? Can you mention some specific external costs? Some external benefits? How could such a student be persuaded to internalize those externalities? What would that imply?

3. How many instances of significant externalities can you find on your campus? Why do they arise? How might the people who create them be brought to internalize them?

4. You have the right to live in a house and do everything with it and to it that owners usually can do *except sell it.* Is it your property? Are your actions with respect to that house likely to be different from what they would be if your ownership included the right to sell the house? In what ways?

5. You own a car and live in Lower Manhattan. In what ways are your property rights in the car limited? What consequences are these limitations likely to have for the decisions Manhattanites make with respect to cars?

6. "I know I ought to buy an umbrella, but I always lose them within two months." In what sense does this person have a weak property right? How is that affecting his decisions? Would you expect to find more or fewer umbrellas in use in a society where umbrellas are regularly stolen or mislaid than in one where they are rarely lost? Why?

7. No one "owned" the bison that roamed the Great Plains in the nineteenth century. How did this fact contribute to their near extinction?

8. Why are antique stores in large cities so often clustered together in one area? Are the owners looking for competition? Why do the location policies of antique stores differ so markedly from the location policies of grocery stores?

9. In April 1975 a federal jury in Miami ordered the seller of a radial tire to pay $2.3 million in damages to a family because of a fatal accident that followed a blowout of the tire. The tire was under a 40,000-mile warranty and blew out at 31,000 miles. The seller contended that an improper tube had been placed in the tire, that the tire was underinflated, and that the driver (who was the plaintiff in the suit) had handled the car incompetently after the blowout.

   What consequences would you predict if this decision is allowed to stand and become a precedent? Is the decision likely to promote an "optimum trade-off between accident and prevention costs"?

10. Trace out the sequence of probable consequences from the imposition of taxes on the pollutants that steel mills emit into the atmosphere. How might such taxes affect the distribution of wealth and the allocation of resources?

11. "Taxes can't control pollution. They'll just drive the little firms out of business while the big firms, who can afford to pay, go right on polluting." Do you agree?

12. What's the difference between a tax on noise emitted by cars without mufflers and a fine for not having a proper muffler?

13. What effect would an increase in the social rate of interest have on the rate at which a society consumes nonrenewable resources?

14. If the present legal owners of such nonrenewable resources as oil and coal suspect that their property will be confiscated in whole or in part within the next ten years, how will their present decisions be affected?

15. Whether or not to develop nuclear power as an energy source is a highly controversial issue in our society. Scores of experts have volunteered their testimony on both sides. Why are the experts in such fundamental disagreement?

GOVERNMENT AND THE MARKET

"Do you believe in letting free enterprise solve our economic problems or in turning them over to government?"

Most people have an answer to that question. They believe that each sector should handle those problems with which it's best equipped to deal. But very few people give much systematic thought to the differences and similarities between "free enterprise" and government, or wonder exactly why one or the other might be better able to deal with a particular problem.

"FREE ENTERPRISE" AND GOVERNMENT: SIMILARITIES AND CONTRASTS

Some of the standard contrasts don't hold up very well under close examination. For example, free enterprise is sometimes characterized as the *competitive* system. But there is competition in government, too, as every election year demonstrates. Within any government agency competition for promotion exists among employees. Competition also occurs between government agencies vying for a larger share of appropriations. The two major political parties are continually competing. The executive branch competes with the legislative, congressmen compete for committee assignments, even district judges compete with one another in the hope of an eventual appointment to a higher court.

Another alleged characteristic of the free enterprise system is its emphasis on "individualism." But very few Americans who participate in the free enterprise system do so on their own as rugged individualists. Many go to work for large corporations right after leaving school and continue as employees until retirement. Is there any significant difference between working in Baltimore as an employee of the Social Security Administration division of the Department of Health, Education, and Welfare or in Flint as an employee of the Buick division of General Motors? When Britain experimented after World War II with nationalizing, de-nationalizing, and re-nationalizing its steel industry, most of the employees (and lots of other people, too) had trouble discerning any difference. Some of the characters who frequent the halls of Congress seem far more individualistic, or at least more idiosyncratic, than the people who pass through the corridors of business.

Others would distinguish "free enterprise" from "government" by reference to the goals or motives that shape policy. But surely this is naive. The congressman who claims that "the public interest" is his objective will often have his attention riveted to the particular interests that can effect his re-election or defeat. The members of the Interstate Commerce Commission are indeed charged by law with regulating the nation's transportation system in accord with the "overall" needs of the economy; but their day-by-day decisions nonetheless reflect the tug of narrower objectives, including each member's desire to maintain and extend the influence of the commission and his own power, income, and status. The goals and motivations of the people who comprise "government" are not demonstrably different from the goals and motivations of those in "free enterprise." Moreover, the rhetoric of "the public interest" has in recent years been adopted by many business firms whose owners and managers are eager to persuade the public that social responsibility and not maximum profit is the ultimate touchstone of their decisions. Rhetoric just cannot be relied upon to give a faithful reflection of reality.

Economic Theory and Government Action

Economic theory attempts to explain the workings of the "free enterprise" system on the assumption that all participants want to advance their own interests and try to do so in a rational way. The marginal cost–marginal revenue rule that we introduced explicitly in chapter 10 but have in fact been using throughout the book is merely a formal expression of these assumptions: The way to advance one's interests is to expand each activity whose marginal revenue exceeds its marginal cost and to contract any activity where marginal cost is greater than marginal revenue. The economist does *not* assume, as we have pointed out before, that money or

REGULATION AND IMPARTIAL DECISIONS

There is only one commercial bank in Key Biscayne, Florida. In September 1973 the Comptroller of the Currency, whose office must approve all applications for national bank charters, rejected the application of a group of investors who wanted to open a second bank in Key Biscayne. The existing bank with which it would have competed was run by Charles (Bebe) Rebozo. Mr. Rebozo and another close friend of President Nixon, Robert Abplanalp, a director of the Rebozo bank, attended the public hearings in Atlanta on the application. The regional administrator for the comptroller contended that the application was turned down because the population of Key Biscayne isn't large enough to support two banks, and that one of the banks would be liable to fail.

The rejected applicants protested that they were the victims of political favoritism. That would be a difficult charge to substantiate or refute. But one might legitimately ask why a group of private investors would want to risk their money in a venture that would probably fail. Is the Comptroller of the Currency likely to be the best judge of the rate at which an area will grow and of the commercial prospects of a new bank?

When the government assumes an extensive responsibility for preventing business failures, as it does with banks, officials will understandably be reluctant to allow additional competition. The degree to which inappropriate political considerations affect their decisions will be almost impossible to determine.

material goods are the only costs and revenues (or benefits) that consumers and producers care about, or that the interests people pursue are narrow and selfish ones. Economic theory can throw light on the social consequences of *every kind* of human interest.[1] Why shouldn't it also apply to the human purposes and the social processes that control the course of government activities?

We aren't trying to expound a political philosophy here or lay out a comprehensive theory of the state. We're only asking why the principles that guide production of the privately owned *New Yorker* should be so

---

1. An interest in chaos might be the one exception. In a society where people did not value rationality, but celebrated instead the rule of caprice, accident, and purposeless action, economic theory would have almost no predictive power. Its predictive power is correspondingly greatest in those areas of social life most marked by foresight and premeditated action.

different from those that guide production of the government owned *Federal Reserve Bulletin*. And we're suggesting that they really are not so different as people commonly suppose. Governments as well as privately owned firms produce commodities and services. Governments, too, can only do that by obtaining productive resources whose opportunity cost is the value of what they would have produced in their next most valuable employment. Governments as well as privately owned firms must therefore bid for the resources they want and offer the owners of those resources adequate incentives. You'll want to note that the government can use negative as well as positive incentives: the threat of imprisonment, for example, may be a major incentive as some people decide what portion of their income to offer the Internal Revenue Service each spring. Governments even face the problem of marketing their output and of price searching, though monetary prices do play a much smaller role in the distribution of government products. But there can be no doubt that demand curves exist for government goods and that, since these goods are characteristically scarce, they must be rationed by means of some discriminatory criteria. And the people with a demand for government goods will consequently compete to satisfy those criteria, to pay the established price.

The main advantage of looking at government in this way is that it counters the tendency to think of government as a *deus ex machina:* a magical power that can resolve difficulties on command the way a playwright does so neatly in the final act of every farce. It makes us more realistic in what we expect of government. It encourages us to ask about the conditions that enable government to act effectively in any given circumstance and not just to suppose that government always gets what it wants or catches what it chases. This way of looking at government also reminds us that the immediately preceding sentence was misleading in its suggestion that government is an "it"; for government is really *many different people interacting.* Finally, this perspective on government encourages us to look for the actual marginal costs and marginal benefits that guide government actions and follow from them.

The term *free enterprise* is probably more useful to orators than to analysts. The distinguishing characteristic of any economic system, we have previously suggested, is the way it assigns responsibilities: Whom do we allow to do what? Whom do we encourage to do what? Who reaps the consequences, good or bad? A system of private property is one system for assigning responsibilities. Such a system is primarily coordinated through the voluntary exchanges to which people are led by the ratios of exchange (relative prices) they observe, with these prices continually adjusting in response to people's decisions to buy or sell. That's the social process this whole book has tried to describe. But it's far from the answer to everyone's dreams. In chapter 14 we examined the market system with an eye to the question of what enabled it to work effectively and what contributed to a less than satisfactory performance. We're really just continuing that question in this chapter, with a change in emphasis. We're still looking at social exchange and the institutional context within which it occurs. But now we are paying particular attention to government as an entity both operating within the system and operating to change the structure of the system.

The Impartial Umpire

The concept of government as Impartial Umpire has a long and honorable history. There must be rules for the ordering of any society and some procedure for securing their application and enforcement. The Latin word for rule is *regula,* and the government is usually thought of as the ultimate regulator or rule maker. The rules can be either few and general or many and detailed. Private property is one such general rule whose enforcement takes the place of many detailed rules. The clear assignment of property rights provides a basis for the ordering of society through voluntary exchange among its members with minimum interference by the umpire.

But that order becomes less satisfactory as the transaction costs of voluntary exchange increase. As the cost-to-benefit ratio of market coordination rises, hierarchical coordination becomes relatively more attractive.

We saw in chapter 9 how hierarchical coordination will be substituted for market coordination even without intervention by the "umpire"; the growth of business firms and other private organizations illustrates this process. In this chapter we want to look at some of the circumstances that give rise to a demand for "intervention by the umpire," the forms such intervention may take, and the consequences of that intervention. We've actually been doing this throughout the book, of course; "market" and "government" don't exist in separate worlds. We've examined government attempts to control prices, to redistribute income, or improve the allocation of resources through taxes on pollution. All of these presumably occurred in response to a demand for "intervention by the umpire." But we haven't yet looked systematically at what happens when the government decides to put particular private producers under detailed control or itself takes over the production of goods. That's what we want to do now.

GOVERNMENT AS REGULATOR

The standard example of a private producer under detailed governmental control is the "public utility." Why and how are public utilities "regulated"?

Let's consider a privately owned company that generates and distributes electricity. The prices such companies charge and the services they provide are usually subject to control by some government agency. Why? The usual answer is that they are "natural monopolies" and that their prices and service consequently cannot be adequately regulated by competition. Competition presupposes a number of firms that are able to provide services of roughly equivalent value. But it would be very costly to have an area served by more than one electrical utility. The cost of constructing and maintaining separate transmission systems would be almost as high for each of three or four separate companies as it would be for a single firm that served all the customers in an area. In other words, there are economies of scale in the distribution of electricity, natural gas, telephone service, or water; and these economies cannot be realized if more than one firm serves an area.[1] So governments typically award an exclusive fran-

---

1. We must be careful not to define the term *public utility* in a circular and question-begging way. The fact that a particular industry is classified as a "public utility" does not mean that it cannot be regulated by competition *if* our definition of *public utility* is the common dictionary definition: An industry providing public services and regulated by the government. It is a matter of fact, not of definition, whether the economies of scale associated with the production of a particular good make competition too costly for the government to allow it.

chise under which one firm and one firm only is allowed to sell electricity within a geographic area. With competition thus excluded by law, the government assumes the responsibility for seeing to it that the utility provides adequate service at fair prices.

We ought to recall at least in passing that a power company with an exclusive franchise is not protected from *all* competition. For there will still be substitutes for electricity in a wide range of uses. Moreover, large users have the option of generating their own electricity, and that limits the prices the power company can charge. Variations in the rates between regions will also influence location decisions by industry and thus affect the demand for electricity in the long run, both from the industries and from the population that follows industry. So electric utilities do compete for customers even though each has an exclusive franchise in the area it serves. But advocates of regulation maintain that the competition they face is not enough to prevent utilities from earning exorbitant profits at the expense of their customers. Voluntary exchange will lead to unacceptable results. The customers must be protected by government regulation.

Principles of Public Utility Regulation

The basic concept in utility regulation is that of a reasonable return on investment. The regulatory commission is supposed to approve a schedule of rates that will yield the power company a revenue sufficient to cover all its costs plus a "reasonable profit," while also making sure that the company gives fair treatment and adequate service to all its customers. But the relevant variables turn out to be exasperatingly slippery.

In the first place, the schedule of prices doesn't uniquely determine the firm's revenues because demand curves are not perfectly inelastic. That, however, is probably a minor problem; the elasticity of demand can usually be calculated with tolerable accuracy. More serious is the fact that a firm which is guaranteed a certain return beyond costs has little incentive to keep costs down. The managers of the utility may pay themselves exorbitant incomes, not in the open form of high salaries which the commission could order them to reduce, but in the disguised form of company cars, large expense allowances, thick office rugs, generous vacations, Acapulco conferences, and numerous assistants to ease their burdens of work. A firm that is not under competitive pressure to produce efficiently and hold down costs can find more than enough excuses to let costs rise. It may even include in its costs the expense of an extravagant advertising campaign designed to persuade its customers that the utility is a wholly public-spirited organization that shouldn't be harrassed by unsympathetic commissioners.

We get to the really tough questions, however, when we ask what is meant by a reasonable return. It's usually stated as some percentage on

investment. How is the commission supposed to determine the amount of the utility's investment? Is it the amount originally spent to purchase the firm's existing capital equipment? That makes sense as long as the utility was not guilty of foolish or imprudent expenditures. If inflation or deflation has occurred in the interim, the amount could be adjusted up or down by some index of the general price level. On the other hand, a case can be made for calculating the value of investment at the present replacement cost. That becomes especially tricky, though, when the firm would not want to replace existing equipment with new equipment of the same kind. How do you calculate the present replacement cost of something that's no longer being manufactured? But why would anyone want to calculate the value of investment at replacement cost rather than original cost?

Legal discussions of reasonable returns to regulated utilities have long tended to focus on the issue of fairness to past investors. That directs attention to original costs. The economist is at least as interested in the question of the attractiveness of returns to potential investors. And that directs attention to current costs. By setting prices that lead to expectations of low future revenues, the commission can make it impossible for the company to secure capital for expansion, improvement, or even the maintenance of present facilities. If demand is growing rapidly, or if the utility's equipment is becoming obsolete, or if environmental regulations require extensive changes in technology, a stingy commission can be an eventual disaster for the customers the commission is supposed to protect.

The target at which the commission wants to shoot is an expected net revenue which will attract an adequate flow of new capital. But to hit that target except by accident, the commission will have to become a forecasting agency. And if the variables were hard to fix with confidence before, they become impossible for anyone to determine now—at least in the absence of detailed and specialized information. That information may be available. The power company may have it, at least insofar as anyone could be said to "have" information on future events. Most large firms do try, though, to forecast future demand, pertinent legislative changes, technological innovations, and the state of the market for capital funds. But if the commission relies upon the company for the crucial data it uses to establish rates, is the commission or the company finally setting those rates? Why have a regulatory commission if it's only going to tell the company it may do what it thinks best?

Whom Do Regulators Represent?

There is a strong tendency for regulatory commissions gradually to adopt the point of view of the firms they regulate. Sometimes this is called the "capture" of the regulatory commission. But the military metaphor is too dramatic. Nor is it any simple matter of selling out—though commissioners have been known to accept favors that could hardly fail to affect their judgment. Commissions often adopt the point of view of the firms they regulate simply because they confront the same problems, receive the same information, and by working together come to a lot of common perceptions.

Where this does not occur at all, it is highly probable that the regulatory commission has decided to adopt an adversary position: to regard the regulated firm as the enemy whose data are always distorted and whose intentions are consistently vile. This is the attitude many people seem to expect from regulatory commissions, presumably because they themselves are convinced that nothing good can ever be expected from a utility unless its arm has been twisted by guardians of the public interest. It is by no means clear that an adversary relationship leads to better results than a cozy relationship. An adversary relationship between political regulators and electrical utilities may be especially dangerous when the demand for electricity is soaring while environmentally acceptable and low-cost ways of generating that electricity are disappearing. New York City provides an instructive case study. Complex decisions involving rate changes, service cut-offs to nonpaying customers, property taxes, rights-of-way for transmission systems, low sulphur fuels, electrostatic precipitators, the siting of new plants, and the hazards of nuclear power (there are more) are not likely to be well made when made jointly by Con Edison and politicians who see the company as a dragon and themselves as St. George.[1]

One of the possible advantages of having regulators take on at least in part a company perspective is an extension of the regulators' time horizon. The rate of time discount has a great deal to do with effective government regulation of industry. A commission is not serving the public interest if it secures low prices and good service for customers this year at the cost of a breakdown in service or very high rates a few years hence. This sort of trade-off is frequently possible in the conduct of a business. For example, the managers of a firm could allow the equipment to deteriorate and pass the cost savings on to stockholders as higher dividends. But the managers usually know that is not an effective way to win the stockholders' favor. For the market will take account of the expected decline in future earnings, the price of the stock will fall, and the owners of the firm will sustain a capital loss greater than their gain in dividends. The fact that owners pay attention to the capitalized value of expected future earnings induces managers to make provisions for the future. That's why only criminal or grossly incompetent corporate managers will exploit a privately owned enterprise for short term gains at the expense of its long term health.

---

1. The problems have been well described by Roger Starr, "Power and the People—the Case of Con Edison," *The Public Interest,* Winter 1972, pp. 75–99.

The political system has no equally effective mechanism for securing attention to the long run. Elected officials can often not afford to look beyond the next election.[1] They may discount the future, therefore, at an irresponsibly high rate. Regulatory commissions that adopt the perspective of the regulated industry will be taking a stance more in accord with the public interest insofar as they shift to a lower rate of time preference for discounting the future.

A Choice among Options

The principal question to emerge from this analysis is a simple one that surprisingly enough, almost never gets asked: What reasons do we have for believing that a regulatory commission will be willing and able to make a public utility behave more in the public interest than it would have behaved in the absence of regulation? The managers of privately owned utilities claim that they know what the public interest requires and would pursue it even in the absence of regulation. We would be wise to entertain doubts about this claim. But would we not also be wise to entertain some doubts about the ability of regulatory commissions to ensure a better performance? The most effective constraint on the behavior of privately owned utilities may not be the detailed interference of regulatory commissions, but the knowledge that the utility must keep its customers happy if it hopes to *avoid* such interference.

The fact that government regulation will probably fail to secure an ideal performance from public utilities does not imply that regulation should be abandoned. Ideal outcomes are rare, and most of life is a matter of choosing the least *un*acceptable among imperfect alternatives. But by the same argument, an imperfect performance in the absence of regulation does not imply that regulation should be instituted. The market fails to secure wholly satisfactory results under a wide range of circumstances, and public utilities present one such circumstance. The question, however, is whether regulation is likely to improve performance. In answering that question we must look at the actual rather than the ideal results of regulation. And the costs to the taxpayer of hiring regulatory commissions along with their supporting staffs must be included in our calculation of relative costs and benefits.

Moreover, the argument of chapters 11 and 13 that sellers often *want* regulation because they want restrictions on the competition they face is highly relevant here. The American Trucking Association is a loyal fan

---

1. Political parties and even the much criticized institution of the political machine might be defined as institutions that capitalize the expected value of future benefits and thereby provide politicians with additional incentives to consider the long run consequences of their decisions.

THE FUTURE OF ELECTRIC UTILITIES

Electric utilities are dependent to an unusually high degree upon their ability to borrow the funds required to finance new facilities. Business firms have basically two sources for such funds. They can generate them internally from the excess of sales revenues over costs, or they can borrow. The average nonfinancial corporation obtained 55% of such funds from internal sources in 1972, and the rest externally. Electric utilities, by contrast, generated only 31% of their funds internally and hence had to turn to lenders of one kind or another for almost 70% of the funds they required. (The source of these data is a 1974 study by Murray L. Weidenbaum, *Financing the Electric Utility Industry.*)

In recent years many electric utilities have been hard pressed to find investors who will lend on favorable terms. The reason is the prospect of low earnings. But why do potential lenders believe that electric utilities won't do well in coming years? They fear that utility regulators will either refuse to grant or be too slow in granting rate increases as utilities' costs increase. And their costs are rising rapidly. Electric utilities are like every other firm which finds that general inflation raises costs. But they have been hit especially hard by the more than proportionate rise in fuel prices because fuel costs are such a large part of an electric utility's operating costs. Another unusually large portion of utility costs is the interest paid for funds borrowed by selling bonds. Interest costs, like fuel costs, rose much more than proportionately in the early 1970s. This occurred largely because expectations of continued inflation caused lenders to demand and made borrowers willing to pay premiums to cover the expected decrease in the value of principal between borrowing and repayment time. Utility costs have also tended to rise in recent years as a result of environmental regulations.

Question: Will regulatory commissions be able and willing to grant rate increases fast enough to maintain utility earnings in the face of all these factors pushing up costs? Or will public resistance ("Didn't they just get a rate increase?") keep rates lagging behind costs so that earnings continue to deteriorate? Unless earnings improve, there will be no way for investor-owned electric utilities to maintain the quality of their service.

That apparently doesn't worry some people who respond that government will just have to take over public utilities if private enterprise can't do an adequate job. But it is precisely government that's creating the problem through its regulatory procedures. With government ownership, of course, rates can be kept low and subsidies provided out of general tax revenues. Or *is* that possible? Keep in mind that many local governments, such as New York City, require electric utilities to collect taxes, hidden within their monthly charges, because the politicians fear public response to an open increase in sales or property taxes.

Advocates of public ownership can point to data which show that public power costs residential users only two-thirds as much as private power on a nationwide average. But these are highly misleading data. For one thing, public ownership of electric utilities is far more common in areas where hydropower is abundant and generating costs consequently lower on the average. Municipally owned utilities also have access to procedures for covering their costs from other sources than rate payers. They can employ tax exempt bonds, which in effect gets them a subsidy from the federal government, and avoid altogether the payment of local taxes, which puts an additional burden on other local taxpayers. There are also laws governing the sale of power generated at federal government dams which allow municipally owned utilities to purchase at lower prices than investor-owned utilities. There is no limit to the amount of fictitious cost savings that can be created by laws which shift the burden of electricity costs from users to the general taxpayer. Such subsidies to users are particularly difficult to defend, however, in a period of increasing energy scarcity.

of the Interstate Commerce Commission and a militant opponent of those who want to dismantle the system of transportation regulation. Surely that isn't because trucking companies want to be prevented from making excessive profits at the expense of shippers. Nor do the presidents of airline companies compose letters in defense of the Civil Aeronautics Board because they think the public interest is more important than the profits of their firms.

Recall the earlier warning against concluding that an industry must be regulated because it's a public utility and then defining a public utility as an industry subject to regulation. Railroads may have been "natural monopolies" in the nineteenth century, when the Interstate Commerce Commission was created. But they certainly ceased to be that when trucks came along. The logical response to the rise of the trucking industry would have been the abolition of the ICC. The actual response was an extension of the commission's authority to the trucking industry. Why did this happen? Part of the answer is that commissions are hard to kill. Regulators benefit from the existence of regulatory commissions and are in a good position to demonstrate the essential nature of their work. They can lobby effectively, serve as the focal point for lobbying efforts by the industries that benefit from their activities, and even create problems that are often used to justify their continued operation.

WHO BENEFITS FROM REGULATION?

The American Trucking Association sends periodic news releases to its members under the heading "Truck Line." Here is a release sent out in January 1975:

One of the most effective answers to those who would eliminate or gut the time-tested regulation of transportation is provided in a "white paper" produced by the Interstate Commerce Commission. The paper, entitled "The Regulation Issue of Today," has been reprinted by ATA and a copy is enclosed.

The ICC's explanation of how regulation really works is not only a valuable primer; it is especially timely in view of the Department of Transportation's ideas on weakening the regulation of the trucking industry which you received in Truck Line 9. You can be sure your industry will face a most serious effort in Congress to put trucking at the mercy of what economists like to call "reliance on a free market system."

This booklet should be "must" reading for every motor carrier executive, even though your business experience has made you generally familiar with the advantages of regulation, and the chaos that would result from deregulation—not only to yourself but to shippers, consumers and the general economy. It will enable you to be a better-informed spokesman for regulation, and a more effective critic of those self-proclaimed experts who would dismantle the regulatory system.

The ICC's booklet can be even more effective if placed in the hands of your customers, so they can obtain a better understanding of what regulation of transportation, and the alternative, really means to them. And, hopefully, so they will add their voices to the debate which promises to rise in intensity before this issue is finally resolved by Congress. It is suggested that you order, promptly, enough copies from ATA's Public Relations Department so that the booklet can be distributed among your associates, including a supply for your salesmen so they can give them to your shippers.

GOVERNMENT AS PRODUCER

The dilemmas of regulation have persuaded many students of public utilities that outright government ownership is better than regulation. And a lot of public utilities are in fact owned by the government: the Tennessee Valley Authority, power companies in the Pacific Northwest, and municipal water and sewage systems are just a few examples. Others include police and fire departments, the national defense system, and the public schools. Let's add streets and highways, the welfare system, the national park system, and municipal departments of parks and recreation. And we might as well throw in the court system and the postal service.

Why are all of these government owned rather than privately owned and operated? It's not because they provide "essential" services: public parks are hardly more essential than food, clothing, or housing. Nor is it true that there's no other way possible. Every one of the products or services mentioned above, with the exception of national defense, is also provided by privately owned business firms. Not on a large scale in most cases—but that may only be due to their inability to compete with enterprises that are able to draw on tax funds for revenue. In the case of all the goods mentioned above, tradition plays some role: We do what we've always done even though we may have started doing it for reasons that are no longer applicable. But there are also logical reasons for looking to government as the supplier of certain kinds of goods, reasons related to the characteristics of the goods, the capabilities of markets, and the unique power of government.

The Problem of Free Riders Once Again

Suppose there were no municipal fire department so that everyone on the block had to contract with private companies for fire-fighting services. And suppose that one family in the middle of the block decided to save itself that expense. What would now happen if this family's house caught on fire? Could the fire-fighting companies under contract to protect the adjacent houses stay home and play checkers? Or would they not want to show up at the scene and at least play a little water on the houses they serve? They might even find that the best way to protect their customers would be by extinguishing the fire of a noncustomer. The upshot of the matter is that the homeowner who does *not* purchase protection increases the hazard to his neighbors, and that he will obtain some protection for which he does not pay as they attempt to control the hazard.[1] It is the spill-

---

1. People who don't rake up their leaves in the fall wait for the wind to blow them into the neighbor's yards. This "works" only if most of the neighbors behave more responsibly and rake them up before they blow back.

over effects, the externalities, that create the problem. In such a situation everyone has an incentive to look for a free ride, and the quantity of the good purchased will consequently be less than marginal cost and benefit calculations would dictate.

What special power does government possess that would enable it to provide a more adequate level of service in these cases than the market can provide? The unique power of government is the power to coerce: to eliminate the free rider problem by denying people the option of non-participation. So the government can make police and fire protection available to everyone on the block, and make everyone pay for the service in taxes. And that becomes a way of securing a quantity of the service closer to the amount people would choose to purchase if their decisions were not distorted by spillover effects and the hope of a free ride.

power to coerce
— can deny non-partisipation

Does this line of reasoning apply to all the other goods mentioned in our extended list of goods typically produced by government? It does in part. Let's look at some of the other goods mentioned.

Arguments for Government-Produced Goods

Government production of schooling and its "sale" at a very low price, for example, encourages people to purchase more education than they would want if everyone had to pay directly for the schooling consumed.

In the case of streets and highways, there does exist a low cost way of making people pay roughly in proportion to the amount that they drive. We aren't thinking of toll roads but of taxes on gasoline. Turning *every* street into a tollway would be very costly (although, as we shall see later, there may be even larger costs from *not* making some roads tollroads). But the gasoline tax does something like that indirectly. Motorists pay toward the maintenance of the roads every time they buy gasoline. By collecting all the fees and providing all the roads, the government enormously simplifies the process; it reduces the transaction costs. The solution is not completely satisfactory, since the tax is the same for someone driving on a dirt road in the country or on a city boulevard. And with different tax rates in different political jurisdictions, motorists can sometimes buy their gasoline where the tax is low and consume it where higher taxes have been used to build better roads.

Let's look at the case of a government operated welfare system. The service we're interested in is the service provided to the taxpayers who finance the system, not the service to those who receive payments under the system. We assume that the taxpayers are charitably disposed and that they obtain satisfaction from having more income made available to low income groups. But they would prefer that this aid be paid for by others. A free market system in which everyone makes voluntary purchases (that is, contributions) encounters the free rider problem. People hold back on their contributions in the hope that others will purchase the quantity of the good the free riders desire and thus enable them to enjoy it at no cost. And this is the problem that a government welfare system tries to overcome. People consent to contribute more on the condition that others will do the same; and the government enforces the "contract" by collecting "contributions" from all taxpayers.

What about parks? People can be required to pay a fee to enter a park. But in the case of municipal parks the cost of collecting the fee and excluding nonpayers would tend to be high. Moreover, parks provide some benefits for which there seems to be no way at all of making the beneficiaries pay. They delight the eyes and lift the spirits of those who pass by. They take the neighbor's children off the streets where they might break windows or upset garbage cans. National parks and wilderness areas give pleasure to many people who will never visit them, as they read about them, look at photographs, or simply savor the enjoyment that comes to some from the knowledge that wilderness exists and is being preserved. If the quantity of wilderness preserved were determined exclusively by the demand of those from whom payment could be obtained, there might be no wilderness areas at all, since the existence of a wilderness area is inconsistent with heavy use. There are some goods which we will never use but which we nonetheless would like to see kept available. Historically significant buildings are a good example. A person might want to see the boyhood home of a former president preserved and be willing to pay something to achieve this, even though he has no intention of ever visiting it. But if he never visits it, how can his contribution be collected?

The Other Side of the Coin

We have only looked at a part of the picture in each case, however; government production of goods often has other important consequences than the ones we've mentioned. And the fact that the market is unable to provide the correct amount of a good does not prove that the government will be able to provide it in a more appropriate quantity or quality.

A general problem associated with the production of goods by government is the problem of deciding on the quantity and quality to be provided. The quantity and quality of tennis rackets is governed by the willingness of players to pay the cost; the quantity and quality of tennis courts, however, has to be decided in some other way by a city that provides courts to users at no charge. Not only must the political process reach these decisions without accurate information about demand; it is also subject to some particular distortions that ought to be kept in mind.

If high income people tend to have more political influence than low income people, they may use the political process to bias the production of government goods in their own favor. They may, for example, control the location of expressways, get the city to build golf courses that few low income people will ever use, and in general secure the lion's share of public services.

The interests of the people whom the government hires to produce goods are also capable of distorting these decisions. Contractors and construction workers lobby for more public buildings, teachers for more expenditures on education, and social workers for more elaborate social services, while the "highway lobby" pursues its vision of a nation made safe for the automobile.

We may all be enemies of the public good, in fact. For even if we know that more government produced goods will necessitate higher taxes, each of us may hope that the additional goods provided for our benefit will have a greater value than the additional taxes we'll have to pay. The familiar process of log-rolling thrives on this kind of hope.

WHICH PUBLIC AGENCY IS PROTECTING THE PUBLIC?

The Food and Drug Administration in 1974 ordered Amtrak, the National Railroad Passenger Corporation, to submit a detailed plan for cleaning up its food operations. Passengers had complained of becoming ill after eating Amtrak food. When the FDA subsequently inspected Amtrak's food facilities, it found a number of unsanitary procedures. The moral of the story is that government ownership is not by itself sufficient to ensure that an enterprise will be operated in the "public interest." The "public interest" is in fact no single or simple interest. The train-riding public presumably wants sanitary food. But it also wants that food at a low price. And improved sanitation procedures have a cost that someone must bear. Where between the extremes of filth and operating room sterility is the "public interest" to be found? Although the officials of Amtrak and the FDA are all public employees, they obviously disagreed in this case on what the public interest required.

Public and Private Schools

Let's look at some of the issues that arise in conjunction with the production of particular goods. Government production of schooling has been coupled with measures that exclude competitors. People who might want to purchase education for their children from privately owned schools are forced to pay twice: once in taxes to support the public schools and again in private tuition charges. This significantly reduces the range of alternatives available and makes it easier for the schools to offer services that satisfy the producers rather than the consumers. While parents can in principle use the political process to control the quality of educational services provided by the public schools, the political process contains substantial free rider aspects of its own that reduce its effectiveness. The cost to any particular parents of fighting for improved schools will be very high in relation to any benefits they can expect to obtain for their own children from their efforts. That's why so many people are "apathetic" when urged to join the PTA or attend the meetings of the local school board. They may be thoroughly unhappy with the schools; but they also sense that they couldn't bring about the changes they want. Only people who derive satisfaction from political action itself are at all likely to expect a marginal benefit to themselves above the marginal cost of getting involved in the cause of school reform.[1]

With major spillover benefits present under either a private or a public school system, the better solution might be a more imaginative combination of the two. Children could be required to attend school for a certain number of years. This would compel parents to purchase for their children at least that quantity of education which confers significant spillover benefits on the community. But they could more easily choose between public and private schools if they were allowed to allocate their education taxes to the schools of their choice. Many proposals have been made in recent years along these lines. But they have run into questions of church-state relations, fears of racial and class segregation, and the political power of professional educators who are like everyone else in not caring much for the effects of increased competition. Any significant reforms in the American system of elementary-secondary school education will have to take account of the fact that the public schools do far more than teach (or not teach) the three Rs. They are also expected to Americanize, democ-

---

1. The cost to each voter of casting a ballot in a primary or general election is high in relation to any benefit that voter is likely to receive from the act of voting. How often does one vote make a difference, after all? So why not stay home and avoid the long line? Perfectly rational behavior of this sort by each voter could result in very small turnouts and a higher probability that the winning candidate was not the one preferred by a majority of voters. Would this justify fines for nonvoting? Remember that as the number of voters declines, the probability increases that any single voter's ballot will tip the scale. Thus some people are more likely to vote when a low turnout is predicted. In any event, nonvoters are another example of free riders, as are voters who don't take the trouble to inform themselves about the candidates in the hope that others will have done so.

ratize, homogenize, and run football teams, drill teams, baby sitting facilities, and detention camps for delinquents. But economic theory at least does not demonstrate that resources will be better allocated when all schools are owned and operated by government.

THE PRICING OF GOVERNMENT GOODS

Streets and highways provide another instructive case in the perils of jumping too quickly to conclusions. The basic argument offered above was that those who would be willing to pay for privately produced roads could not keep others from using them except at a prohibitive cost. With the facilities equally available to all, no one has an adequate incentive to pay and so roads won't be built. When everyone tries to be a free rider, everyone winds up walking.

When the government builds the roads, however, charging only the amount of the gasoline tax for their use, it contributes to the creation of problems. For one thing, road construction encourages additional driving, and we all know to what a vast range of important spillover costs this leads, especially in cities. It's certain that the gasoline tax is not enough to impose on motorists the full costs of their own decisions to drive. But we're after another point now. The gasoline tax is somewhat like a price charged for food that is based strictly on weight or volume: it doesn't discriminate accurately enough between very scarce goods and goods that aren't noticeably scarce at all. The motorist pays roughly the same tax per mile when he drives in the country or downtown, in the rush hour or at two o'clock in the morning. But the good he's consuming, road space, is not equally scarce in the country and the city or during the rush hours and off hours. Charging the same price for goods of different scarcities leads to inefficient combinations of shortages and surpluses. And government tends *not* to charge scarcity prices for the goods it produces, because government price searchers do not have an incentive to maximize net revenue.

"Free" Lunches and Long Lines

Imagine a six-lane expressway leading from the suburbs to the center of a large city. Motorists will use the expressway as long as the cost to them of doing so is less than the cost of the next best alternative. (Every valuable opportunity foregone should be included in the cost: a chance to read the newspaper while riding the bus and a serene digestive system as well as the costs more easily measured in monetary terms.) Because

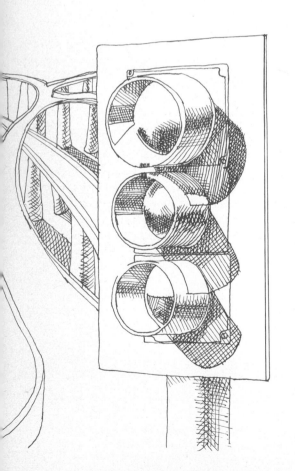

congestion raises their driving costs, drivers will avoid congested roads if there is a better alternative available. For example, a commuter who wants to go downtown during the rush hour will not take the expressway if it's so congested at that hour that he can do better (incur lower costs) via some other route. We can consequently predict that rush hour traffic will increase on the expressway until it becomes so congested that drivers find alternative routes equally attractive. More traffic than that would make the expressway a less advantageous way of going downtown, and drivers would start to desert it. Less traffic than that would make the expressway more attractive than alternative routes and pull in more drivers until the increased congestion eliminated the differential advantage. This kind of experimental searching for the most advantageous route by thousands of drivers does in fact tend to make expressways just as costly routes during the rush hour as "inferior" routes.[1]

Rationing by Congestion

But the fact that each driver who enters the expressway considers only his own costs and neglects the costs his decision inflicts on others makes this procedure a poor way to allocate rush hour space. A simplified graphical exposition will show you exactly why. The example is worth studying in some detail because it presents the economics of the rationing system often used with government produced goods: rationing by congestion.

Figure 15A shows the cost to a representative driver of a single trip downtown during the rush hour by means of the expressway (XWAY COST) or any one of a number of alternative routes (AR COST). (Ignore the other line for the moment.) We'll assume that each alternate route has the same cost and that, because there are so many of them, congestion does not increase significantly on any one of them as drivers desert the expressway. The second assumption is expressed in the fact that costs don't increase on the alternate routes as traffic moves to them from the expressway: the AR COST curve is horizontal. The XWAY COST curve rises, however, as traffic increases, to show the additional costs created by congestion. It rises in a straight line only to make the exposition simpler: In reality it would not rise at first and later on rise at an increasing rate as more traffic enters the expressway.

As each driver now searches for the lowest cost route, the flow of traffic will tend to stabilize with 5000 cars using the expressway and all other cars

1. This is the truth behind the cynicism, "Traffic expands to clog every expressway built to unclog the traffic." It is also the truth behind the observation that large cities always have serious problems. Large cities provide obvious advantages to their inhabitants. People move to the cities to enjoy the advantages. They stop moving to the cities when the problem created by so many people living in close proximity just offset the advantages.

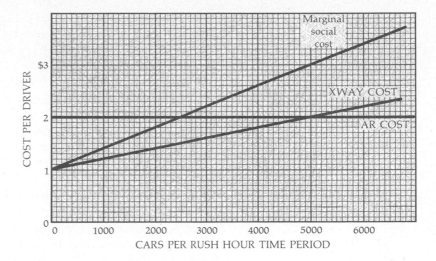

Figure 15A Cost of using expressway or alternative routes

(their number is irrelevant to our assumptions as long as the total number of cars is at least 5000) using alternate routes. And every driver will incur the same cost for a trip: $2. There cannot be a difference because any difference would induce a reallocation of traffic until the difference disappeared.

How can we show that this is a poor way to allocate rush hour space? We could compare the combined cost to the drivers of this allocation with the combined cost of other allocations. We could calculate and compare total costs with 5000 drivers on the expressway and with 4500, 4000, on down to 2000 drivers using the expressway (and everyone else using the alternative routes). But a better way is to use the marginal approach.

Suppose there are 4000 drivers already on the expressway. Each is paying $1.80. Then one more driver enters. What does *he* pay? Since the graph shows that 500 additional drivers raise the unit cost by $.10, one additional driver raises it by $.0002. The 4001st driver therefore pays $1.8002. *But so do all the other 4000 drivers.* Each must now pay an extra $.0002 to use the expressway. 4000 times $.0002 is $.80. So the 4001st driver added to total expressway costs his own $1.8002 *plus* the $.80 of extra cost his decision imposed on everyone else. The additional or marginal cost at 4000 drivers is therefore not $1.80, as the graph seems to suggest, but $2.60.

By making the same calculation at every potential level of expressway use, we obtain a curve that shows the additional cost for which one extra driver is responsible. That's the unlabeled line on figure 15A. You may now label it. Call it *marginal social cost.*

Marginal social cost on the expressway is greater than marginal social cost on alternate routes whenever expressway traffic exceeds 2500. (Since there are by definition no congestion problems on alternate routes, one additional driver adds only his own cost to total cost and marginal social cost is identical to AR COST.) It follows, therefore, that total commuting costs would be minimized if only 2500 rather than 5000 drivers used the expressway.

From the social point of view, the best pattern is found when 2500 drivers use the expressway and all the rest use alternate routes. Unfortunately, that won't happen. For each driver using an alternate route would then want to reduce his own costs by shifting to the expressway, and that would continue until 5000 cars were again clogging the expressway. What's going wrong?

The problem is that each driver consults only the costs *he* bears when choosing a route and ignores the costs his decision imposes on others. And he does so, as we shall see, because of the pricing practices pursued by the owner, the government. It's the familiar problem again of external costs, genuine social costs that decision makers do not internalize. A driver who elects to use the expressway when, let us say, 4000 cars are already using it, notes that his cost will be $1.80 versus $2.00 on alternative routes. So he enters the expressway, increasing the congestion by a tiny amount and hence raising every other expressway user's cost by a tiny amount. But when a tiny amount is multiplied by the 4000 drivers already on the expressway, the effect of his decision is no longer tiny. While one more car doesn't make a noticeable difference to anybody, it does make a noticeable difference to everybody taken together. And 1000 extra cars entering the expressway when 4000 are already on it makes a noticeable difference to both anybody *and* everybody. Each driver must now incur a $2.00 cost whereas each of the 4000 drivers could previously have gotten downtown for only $1.80.

Use your imagination to add the color of reality to this example. You shouldn't have much trouble if you've ever crawled along on an urban expressway during the rush hour, and have looked ahead to see a few additional cars come in from the entrance ramp to fill up the small gaps and bring your lane to a halt. One engineering study has shown that, with traffic moving at ten miles per hour, one additional car joining any stream for a distance of one mile adds eleven minutes to the travel time of all the other cars in the stream.[1]

Haven't you ever thought about how much you would be willing to pay to get the traffic moving? And grumbled about the people in your way who aren't in as big a hurry as you are and could just as well have taken another route or traveled at a different time? And wondered whether there

---

1. This piece of information has been taken from a fascinating study in the application of economic reasoning to social problems, *Paying for Roads: The Economics of Traffic Congestion,* by Gabriel Roth (Penguin, 1967).

could be any way of getting people to be more sensible and considerate in their times, routes, and modes of travel?

Rush hour space is most commonly rationed by congestion. Congestion or queuing (one form of congestion) turns out to be the rationing device usually employed when goods are sold below their market clearing money price. Popular national parks, for example, often become so crowded that no one enjoys them very much. Even more people would use these parks except for the fact that congestion has done what a higher price could also have done: reduce the quantity demanded. But congestion does the job by reducing the total satisfaction of all the park visitors.

Socially wasteful externalities appear in these cases because no one has both an adequate interest in rationing the scarce good efficiently and the ability to do so. Congress could authorize the Park Service to set a much higher entrance fee for admission to the Yosemite Valley or to Yellowstone during July and August. But Congress does not want to be blamed for "keeping American citizens out of their very own parks" or "reserving the parks for the exclusive use of the rich." Very few people realize that a higher price could enable citizens to *enjoy* their parks more, or stop to consider how many genuinely poor people can even afford to travel to the more popular national parks. And the government decision makers don't have the prospect of larger net revenues for themselves as an inducement to set a better price.

Scarcity Prices for Government-Produced Goods

If some users could be taken off the expressway during the rush hour and transferred to other routes, their welfare would not decline, but the welfare of those still using the expressway would increase. In the case we've been discussing, social welfare could be increased substantially if, in some fashion, every other motorist planning to use the expressway on a given day could be persuaded not to do so. Is there a way to do that? If the expressway were privately owned and hence operated to secure for its owners the largest possible net revenue, a way might be found to do exactly that. For it would be in the owners' interest to prevent an excessive deterioration, through congestion, in the quality of the service they're selling. And they could do that by setting an appropriate price for use of the expressway during rush hours.

If they set the price that maximizes their own net returns, they will set the price so as to equate marginal cost and marginal revenue. We'll assume for simplicity that additional cars using the expressway impose no costs *on the owners of the expressway* so that marginal cost *to the owners* is zero. Their marginal revenue curve will be derived from the demand curve they face. How do we find that demand curve? It will be the curve that shows the prices motorists will be willing to pay to secure the advantage, if any, of expressway use. Since that advantage depends on the extent to which the expressway has become congested, we can actually derive the rush hour demand curve from the XWAY COST curve and the AR COST curve of figure 15A. The demand curve for the expressway is the difference between the two curves at each level of use. Do you see why? Suppose the owners set the price at 80¢. Then the expressway is the lower cost route until traffic reaches 1000; after that level of congestion has been reached, it's the higher cost route with an 80¢ toll in effect. With the price at 60¢, the routes will be equally advantageous when expressway traffic reaches 2000; so 2000 "rush hour permits" will be demanded at a 60¢ toll. At any toll above $1, no one will use the expressway; at a zero toll, 5000 motorists will use it.

This demand curve is drawn in figure 15B. When we derive from it the curve showing marginal revenue, we find that marginal revenue equals marginal cost (assumed to be zero *for the owners*) at an "output" of 2500 cars. To achieve this output, the owners would want to charge a rush hour toll of 50¢ per car. (We're also ignoring the costs of toll collection.) It is no accident that this is the *same* number of cars that minimizes the total social cost of commuting. For in trying to achieve the maximum net revenue for themselves, the owners set a price that moves motorists between the two options until there is no longer anything more to be gained from further shifts. It's the same process of voluntary exchange, on the basis of perceived costs, that enables the market system to achieve an efficient allocation of resources elsewhere. The motorists are all still paying $2 to get downtown; but the wasted costs of congestion have now been converted into revenue for the expressway's owners. The cost is no longer the deadweight cost of congestion.

The waste and inefficiency of rationing through congestion is rarely observed in the case of privately produced goods because *inefficiencies create a potential for gain.* As long as the cost of the transactions that must take place to remove these inefficiencies is less than the benefits from their removal, exchanges will occur under a system of private ownership. Government production of a service will be inefficient if the service is not sold at a price that reflects its social scarcity. And because government price searchers don't have an incentive to maximize net revenue, they will less often set prices at their scarcity level.

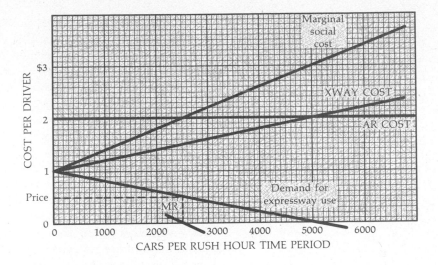

Figure 15B Setting a price for expressway use

This argument doesn't force us to the conclusion that expressways should be privately owned. It does suggest that government goods should not necessarily be priced at zero. Unfortunately, the belief that a good which is produced from tax revenues should always be offered at a zero price is widespread, and it results in some rather strange dilemmas. For example, the expressway between Dallas and Fort Worth has been a toll road ever since it was constructed. But the tolls must by law be removed when the road has earned enough revenue to cover its original construction costs. That's expected to occur in 1977. The Texas Highway Department has predicted that traffic will increase so much when the tollway becomes a freeway that the road will be severely congested during rush hours. Many current users of the expressway dread the day when it becomes a freeway. This is an instructive irony: The tolls actually increase the welfare of some who must pay the tolls to use the road. But the political process has trouble reaching the solution of tolls during rush hours. The political process might arrive at a more satisfactory solution if more people understood the economics of congestion, and therefore consented to pay the toll that would yield them the good they want: a rapid traffic flow during rush hours.

A Review of the Question

"Do you believe in letting free enterprise solve our economic problems or in turning them over to government?" That was the question with which this chapter began. Have we gotten any closer to an answer than we were when we started? Let's review.

Turning a problem over to the government means attempting to solve it through the use of different social institutions. The people who work for government are probably neither more nor less virtuous, neither wiser nor more incompetent, than those who work for privately owned enterprises. The important differences lie rather in the different kinds of information available, the different incentives decision makers confront, and the power that government has to use coercion. The unfavorable connotations of that word are reduced if we think of it as "mutual coercion mutually agreed upon," the phrase suggested by Garrett Hardin in "The Tragedy of the Commons."[1] "Mutual coercion mutually agreed upon" is a way of dealing with the externalities or spillover effects that voluntary exchange alone cannot handle and that tend to increase in more affluent, congested, and technologically advanced societies.

But government action does not make economic thinking irrelevant. Quite to the contrary, an expanded role for government in the economy seems to us to call for citizens better prepared to think in terms of marginal

---

THE BENEFICIARIES OF TAXES ON RUSH HOUR DRIVING

The private passenger automobile and public transportation are often depicted as implacable enemies. Devotees of the automobile protest stridently against any use of gasoline taxes for transit subsidies because they want the funds used to relieve congestion through building more roads and expressways. But more expressways don't seem to solve the problem; they quickly clog up as people respond by driving more. Meanwhile land acquisition costs for urban expressways are becoming almost prohibitively high.

Perhaps the solution is to finance transit subsidies from taxes placed not on gasoline but on rush hour driving. The improved traffic flow would compensate those motorists who continued to drive, the improved public transportation would compensate those whom the higher price dissuaded from driving, and the whole community would gain from less air pollution, from more conservation of petroleum, and from the better public transportation system.

The crucial task is to persuade motorists that a tax on congestion-creation is a benefit as well as a cost to those who pay it.

---

1. Hardin's much-quoted essay appeared originally in *Science*, December 13, 1968.

benefits and marginal costs, and more aware of the precise ways in which social interaction allocates scarce resources.

Once Over Lightly

The differences between "free enterprise" and government are not adequately described in such contrasts as competitive or noncompetitive, individual or social, private interest or public interest. The principles that guide decision making in the "free enterprise" sector are for the most part the same principles that guide the decisions of the individuals who act in governmental capacities.

The criterion of marginal cost–marginal benefit can be used to evaluate the efficiency of government actions. The assumption that the *people* in government will, in making decisions, pay attention to the marginal costs and benefits *that accrue to them* helps us predict the consequences of government activity.

There is very little which is humanly possible that could not be achieved through voluntary cooperation. But voluntary cooperation, especially on a large scale, often entails substantial transaction costs. Government can usefully be viewed as an institutional arrangement for accomplishing people's goals under circumstances where the costs of arranging, concluding, and enforcing voluntary exchanges are too high.

The advantage of government in securing social cooperation is its power to coerce. This power is especially effective in reducing the substantial social costs that may be associated with the "free rider" problem.

Private economic decisions do not automatically conform to the public interest merely because they have been put under government regulation. Government regulators do not have complete information and often operate with incentives and under constraints that systematically encourage decisions whose consequences are contrary to the intent of regulation.

If voluntary exchange leads to insufficient production of a good because of positive externalities, the government can expand production through subsidies to suppliers or to demanders. Subsidies to demanders are less likely to result in quality deterioration. The policy of huge government subsidies to education suppliers may be largely responsible for the low ratio of learning to schooling in our educational system.

If voluntary exchange leads to excessive production of a good or its by-products because of negative externalities, a tax on the activity to be diminished has many advantages over alternative procedures as a way of promoting more efficient resource use.

The fact that a particular good can be provided more satisfactorily by the government than by private producers does not mean the good ought to be sold at a zero price. By charging positive money prices for the goods it produces government sometimes obtains valuable information on the demand for the good and succeeds in rationing the good efficiently.

QUESTIONS FOR DISCUSSION

1. Is competition confined to market economies or at least more common and pervasive in social systems that are market coordinated rather than hierarchically coordinated?

2. When business firms lobby in the legislature on opposite sides of an issue that will affect their profits, are they competing with each other? How is this different from the activities that we usually have in mind when we think of business competition?

3. You pay your barber or stylist money to persuade him to cut your hair. Is this a bribe? What is the essential difference between this kind of payment and what we ordinarily mean by a bribe?

4.   (*a*) A legislator accepts a $5000 campaign contribution from the owner of a textile mill in his district.

   (*b*) A legislator accepts a $5000 personal gift from the owner of a textile mill in his district.

   (*c*) A legislator campaigns for election among textile workers in his distrust with a promise to work for government restrictions on textile imports.

   Is anyone taking or giving a bribe?

5. Are there economies of scale in milk distribution? Is it inefficient and wasteful to have more than one dairy deliver milk to the people living on a single block? Should dairies be assigned exclusive franchises for particular areas? Who benefits from having more than one dairy delivering milk to an area?

6. Why does the telephone company advertise despite the fact that it has exclusive franchises in the areas it services?

7. Is commercial airline service a "natural monopoly"? Why is it extensively regulated? Some people say that regulation of airlines is essential to prevent competitive practices that might reduce the safety of air travel. Would an airline be insufficiently concerned about safety if it were not regulated?

8. If there are only 2000 seats in the student section of the field house and there are about 4000 students who want to see home basketball games, how will the 2000 seats be rationed? Is there a more efficient way to ration? Why isn't it used?

9. Visualize a city half of whose citizens are green and half of whom are purple. No one objects to living next door to someone of the opposite color. But they all object to having neighbors *on both sides* of the opposite color and will move if they find themselves in that position. Will a segregated or integrated housing pattern emerge under a system of voluntary exchange? Why? If integrated housing is considered a good thing, how could it be achieved under these circumstances?
   Suppose the people in a neighborhood band together in an association that tries to enforce racial quotas. They attempt to prevent black families

from purchasing homes in areas where the black-white ratio is above the citywide average. Are they promoting segregation or integration?

10. If positive externalities create "free rider" problems to the extent suggested by the text in its analysis of government welfare programs, why do United Way campaigns work as well as they do in so many American cities? Are there elements of coercion in United Way fund drives, either in obtaining people to work on the campaign or in inducing people to contribute? What might be the advantages and disadvantages of having local government assume the welfare functions currently performed through the United Way?

11. (*a*) A common argument in support of government produced goods is that they are vital to social welfare and therefore their provision cannot safely be left to the "whims" of the marketplace. Does this explain why parks and libraries are usually municipal services while food and medical care are usually secured through the market?

(*b*) Why is the business of selling books usually handled through the market while the business of lending books is generally handled by government (public libraries)? Should libraries be provided by government because "there's no profit to be made from lending books"?

12. The court system is a good "produced" by government. Could a judicial system exist if it were not produced by government? If the judge and jury in civil suits had to be paid by the contending parties, would decisions tend more often to favor the wealthier party? Do wealthier people currently have an advantage in judicial proceedings under the government produced court system?

13. Who benefits from government production of higher education and its sale at prices below average cost? Do you think that the subsidies which states grant to students through systems of tax-supported higher education provide greater benefits to high or to low income people?

14. Would you favor a system of fines for eligible voters who fail to vote in elections?

15. You and your family enjoy camping in the national parks. You therefore urge your congressman in February to oppose a bill that would increase the fees for such camping during July and August. The following August you enter Teton National Park at 4:00 P.M. on a weekday and find that all the campsites are occupied.

(*a*) Would you now like to see a higher schedule of camping fees? Why or why not?

(*b*) Why are fees for the use of privately owned resources more likely to rise when demand increases than are fees for the use of government owned resources?

(*c*) How do varying ownership systems affect resource allocation? Why?

PRELUDE TO PART 2

In 1970 the United States economy slid into a mild recession. The total output of new goods produced in that year declined slightly from the output of 1969, and unemployment rose. What made this somewhat surprising and politically disturbing was the fact that the average level of prices paid by consumers rose 6% during 1970. In 1971 total production increased, but unemployment did too. And 1971 consumer prices were an additional 4% above 1970 prices. The word began to spread that an unprecedented malady, one that economists could not explain, had seized the economy: recession coupled with inflation.

The word that went out was incorrect. Inflation joined to rising unemployment had occurred before, in the recessions of 1958 and 1960, though the inflation in those years had been considerably less rapid. And economists were not at a total loss for an explanation. But some oversimplified notions about the causes and interrelations of recession and inflation, notions that economists had probably helped to spread, were definitely called into question by the experiences of these years. And when an even more severe recession came along in 1974 while prices were increasing at a rate greater than 10% per year, these oversimplified notions had to be abandoned. It was abundantly clear that recession and inflation were not "opposites."

Economic analysis has come in for heavy criticism in recent years, because it can offer no simple diagnosis and prescription in the face of recession coupled with rapid inflation. And insofar as economists have oversold their ability to understand and control these problems, they must accept some of the criticism. A decade ago many economists believed that they were in possession of *the* theory of inflation and recession. But events have undermined this certainty.

While there is much that economists know about these problems and even more that they are beginning to understand, the reader must be cautioned as we move into the final chapters of this book. The principles are much less settled in the area we're now approaching. Or perhaps the principles are well enough established but the appropriate ways to apply them are unclear. And that could just be a consequence of the fact that the goals for knowledge in the areas we're about to study are far more ambitious than the goals in previous chapters.

Up until now we've been studying important but small and relatively manageable problems, problems created by the way in which *particular* prices and production decisions interact. The study of inflation and recession, however, involves an examination of the *general* price level, *total* output, and employment in the economy *as a whole*. We might compare the problems studied so far to problems of how to stay warm, dry, and safe under various weather conditions; the problems we'll encounter now are more on the order of how to control the weather. That's clearly a more ambitious undertaking, and one that may require us to adopt heroic simplifications if we are not to bog down in endless details. But the more heroic the simplification, the greater the risk of oversimplification and error.

So you're invited to come along now for what will be, even more than in the preceding chapters of this book, a venture of inquiry.

We'll begin by examining some of the data economists and others use to describe and analyze employment, total output, and the price level. Then we'll take up the important topic of money. What is it? Where does it come from? What functions does it perform? In chapters 20–22 we'll present the principal theories that economists have constructed in their efforts to understand the causes of and possible remedies for inflation and recession. Chapters 23 and 24 will examine the international context of domestic economic policies. In chapters 25 and 26 we'll try to put it all together and offer some tentative conclusions about the ability of government to control unemployment and inflation. And chapter 27 will acknowledge what you will surely have suspected before then, that the formulation of economic policy requires much more than a knowledge of economics.

413

16

LABOR MARKETS,
EMPLOYMENT, AND UNEMPLOYMENT

The fear that our society or any society may run out of jobs was criticized in chapter 13. We argued there that jobs represent obstacles to be overcome, and that a society without jobs for people to perform would have come close to abolishing scarcity. Such a situation would be an occasion for rejoicing. Neither the United States nor any other contemporary society is in such a happy position.

Throughout the discussion in chapter 13, however, we left out of account a phenomenon that has puzzled and disturbed students of economic systems for more than two centuries. It used to be called the *trade cycle*, and later on the *business cycle.* Those terms began to disappear from use as economists came to have increasing doubts about the regularity of such fluctuations. The word *cycle* has connotations of predictable recurrence, connotations that may be misleading and that can be avoided by substituting a more neutral phrase, such as "fluctuations in the aggregate level of economic activity."

Whatever the fluctuations are called, there can be no doubt about their existence and importance. If those who work for wages entertain some irrational anxieties about the disappearance of job opportunities, they may also have substantial grounds for completely rational fears. Our insistence that there is no overall scarcity of jobs seems to be flatly contradicted by the experience of every industrialized nation with recessions and depressions.

In the 1930s, the study of such fluctuations, their causes and their cures, came to be called macroeconomics, from the Greek word *makros,* meaning "large." The remainder of economics was then referred to as microeconomics, from *mikros,* meaning "small." There are serious ambiguities in this use of terms, and some dangers. The beginning student ought to know that many economists would call chapters 2–15 microeconomics, and chapters 16–27 macroeconomics. You won't go far wrong if you understand macroeconomics to mean the study of fluctuations in the aggregate level of economic activity, or the study of recessions and depressions, inflation, and aggregate growth or decline.

[handwritten: macroeconomics]

Facts as Interpretations

"You can't argue with the facts," we often say. But facts aren't always as "hard" or clear as we suppose. Our experiences have to be interpreted before they become meaningful, and what we take to be "hard facts" are often in reality complex and sometimes highly questionable interpretations of events. There are many mirages in the study of social phenomena.[1]

How did you know in 1974 that the United States economy was going through a period of inflation? Inflation means a rising level of money prices. But some prices may be going up while others are not. How many prices have to rise and by how far must they rise before we have inflation? While we may rely in part on our own experience as customers, most people consult the Consumer Price Index to find out what's happening to the level of money prices. But the Consumer Price Index, as we shall see in the next chapter, is a construct of theorists and statisticians in the Department of Labor. It has been constructed on the basis of careful empirical studies and well-reasoned theories by a lot of competent and conscientious people. But it is *not* something that is simply *given* and with which one cannot argue.

[handwritten: Inflation]

How did you discover in 1974 that the economy was simultaneously entering a recession? The recognition of recession is even more difficult than the recognition of inflation. A recession generally means a declining level of production in the economy as a whole. Sometimes, however, it means only a slowdown in the rate of increase in the level of production.

---

1. There is no consensus among users of English on the distinction between "facts" and "data." But the Latin origins of the words point to a distinction that we ought to notice, whatever vocabulary we use to describe it. *Fact* comes from a word meaning "to make" (as does *factory,* a place of making). *Datum,* the singular of *data,* comes from a word which means "to give." *Data* might thus be thought of as the things given, the actual events, and *facts* as what we make of the data, our interpretation and understanding of what is given to experience. One's point of view, angle of vision, theoretical framework, and other presuppositions will help determine which "facts" emerge from the "data."

Moreover, industries and firms expand and contract production for many reasons, and they do not do so in perfect unison. Even during a deep and prolonged recession, production may be expanding in some industries or areas of the economy while it is declining in most. In the next chapter we'll introduce you to the National Income and Product Accounts, the information that most people use in deciding what is currently happening to aggregate production. We shall discover that gross national product is also a theoretical construct and not simply a "hard fact."

The most widely used measure of recession, however, and the one that arouses the greatest public concern, is the level of unemployment. This is attested to by the title of the most prominent piece of federal legislation directed toward the control of aggregate fluctuations, the Employment Act of 1946. Although this act grew out of the Full Employment Bill of 1945, it does not call for "full employment." The responsibility of the federal government under the 1946 act is to maintain "maximum employment, production, and purchasing power."

"Full employment" is an unrealistic target if one takes it literally, and a vague target if one does not. The goal of "maximum employment" escapes the charge of being unrealistic, but fares no better than "full employment," when we try to give it a clear and definite meaning. That does not imply the goal is either illusory or unimportant. It does mean that we ought to inquire carefully into the nature of employment and unemployment and examine critically the concepts we use to measure them.

THE LABOR MARKET

Let's look at some numbers provided by the Bureau of Labor Statistics in the United States Department of Labor to get an initial sense of the problems. In December 1974 the BLS sampling techniques yielded the following figures on the labor force, employment, and unemployment. We have added the Bureau of the Census estimate of 1974 population.

Population (1974 average)	211,909,000
Labor force	94,015,000
Employment	87,414,000
Unemployment	6,601,000

If 87.4 million people were employed out of a total population of 211.9 million, then 124.5 million people were *not* employed in December 1974. But unemployment totaled only 6.6 million. So there is clearly a substantial difference between being *not* employed and being *un*employed.

The Noninstitutional Population and the Labor Force

The number of those unemployed, according to BLS estimates, is the difference between the total labor force and the number employed. The question then becomes, Who is included in the labor force and who is not? Everyone under sixteen years of age or an inmate of a penal or mental institution, sanitarium, or home for the aged, infirm, or needy is automatically excluded. That eliminates from the labor force some people who are actually doing work for pay; but the omission is relatively minor. The BLS calls the group that's left the *noninstitutional population.* In December 1974 the noninstitutional population was 150,827,000, or approximately 70% of the total population.

But only 62% of the noninstitutional population was included in the labor force. By what criteria were some included and others left out? The BLS excludes from the labor force, and hence from the ranks of the officially employed or unemployed, all those who are retired, engaged in their own housework, not working while attending school, unable to work because of long-term illness, discouraged from seeking work because of personal or job-market factors, or voluntarily idle. That's a highly diverse list of criteria. Much worse, some of the criteria have extremely fuzzy edges. What's the difference between someone voluntarily idle and someone neither working nor seeking work because of discouragement growing out of personal or job market factors? What's the difference between someone seeking work (and hence in the labor force) but doing so in a half-hearted way, and someone not seeking work (and hence not in the labor force) who would be willing to take a job if the right one came along? There would seem to be an important difference between someone who retires voluntarily and someone who is retired against his wishes; but neither one is in the labor force and so neither is counted among the unemployed.

The Bureau of Labor Statistics divides the labor force into the employed and the unemployed by putting each member into one of four categories: (1) all those working for pay or working more than 15 hours a week without pay in a family-operated business, (2) those temporarily absent from

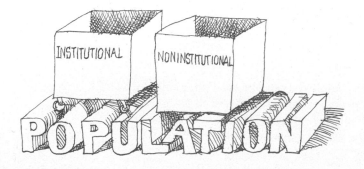

employed ⎫ official
unemployed ⎭

work because of illness, accident, strikes, or a similar cause (3) those who are not working but are waiting to be recalled after a layoff, or waiting to start a new job within 30 days, (4) those not working but actively seeking employment. Categories 1 and 2 make up the officially employed; categories 3 and 4 make up the officially unemployed.

One who is minded to quibble can always find nits to pick even in the most carefully constructed definitions. There are excellent reasons, however, for looking critically at official employment and unemployment concepts. Each month the BLS releases and the news media publicize the current unemployment rate: the total of those officially unemployed expressed as a percentage of the civilian labor force. (The civilian labor force is the total labor force minus all those in the armed forces.) The civilian labor force in December 1974 was 91,803,000. With 6,601,000 unemployed, the official unemployment rate for the month was therefore 7.2%. When that figure was published in January 1975, political pressure intensified for some kind of government action to stimulate employment. If the concepts of the labor force, the employed, and the unemployed contain serious ambiguities—as they do—the official unemployment rate can be a misleading guide and spur to action. That is why we want to look more closely at the patterns of behavior these concepts are attempting to summarize.

Think for a moment about the language of the 1946 Employment Act, which calls for policies to secure "maximum employment." Surely Congress did not mean what the words suggest if taken literally, that as many people as possible ought to be employed. The goal of the Employment Act is enough jobs to satisfy the demand of those who *want* jobs. But more people will want jobs the more attractive those jobs are, all things considered, and the more eager they are for additional income. The number of people who want jobs is not any fixed percentage of the noninstitutional population. It is rather a consequence of the options people perceive and the choices they make. The only defensible public policy toward employment is therefore one which aims at improving the range of opportunities available to the population. And that, quite obviously, is not a clear and precise target.

Economic theory is basically a theory of economizing choices. To understand the problem of employment and unemployment, therefore, we have to begin with the theory of labor market choice.

The Supply of Labor

The amount of time people supply to the labor market can be viewed as the time left over after each person reserves the amount of nonmarket time demanded. Since this nonmarket time is conventionally called leisure by labor economists, we shall use that term. Remember when it is used, however, that it includes all nonmarketed uses of time, from bird watching to sleeping, from studying advanced mathematics to following television serials, from shooting pool to soliciting funds for the March of Dimes.

leisure

The demand for leisure can be analyzed by means of the concepts introduced in chapters 2 through 5. The price of an hour's leisure, or its opportunity cost, is approximately equal to the available hourly wage rate.[1] People will choose not to be currently employed (that is, to "purchase" leisure) when they find the price of leisure sufficiently low. Putting the matter more conventionally: people will offer to supply less of their time to the labor market (purchase more leisure) the lower the wage they expect to obtain. That's just the familiar law of demand. The higher the price of any good (in this case, leisure), the more likely it is that people will choose a substitute (money income and what it will buy).

But that is only part of the picture, because the wage rate is an important component of the income on the basis of which people choose among alternative goods. The concept of income elasticity of demand reminds us that, as people's incomes change, their *demand curve* for particular goods may also change. In the case of leisure, an increase in its price which would cause people to want less entails also an increase in their incomes which may cause them to want more. Since leisure is surely not an inferior good in the technical sense (a good for which the demand decreases as income increases), the higher price of leisure may result in increased purchases of leisure. Higher wage rates, in short, may mean less time supplied to the labor market. Which effect—the substitution effect due to the change in price or the income effect, which is also due to the change in price—will control the direction of people's response to higher wage rates?

There is no consistent evidence showing that, for a given time and locale, higher wage workers do choose to work fewer hours. However, as

---

1. The equality is only approximate for several reasons. Because workers can rarely choose precisely the number of hours they want to work, they cannot equate exactly the marginal cost and the marginal benefit of leisure. Moreover, someone who supplies no labor at all to the market must be placing a marginal value on leisure that is *greater* than the available wage rate.

wage rates in the United States increased during the first half of this century, there was a notable reduction in the average number of hours worked per day and days worked per week. Apparently the demand for leisure did increase as wage income increased, and by more than enough to counter the increased opportunity cost of leisure implicit in the higher wage rates.

We must keep in mind, however, that the hours of work an individual supplies to the market will depend not only on the relative valuations placed upon rest and recreation versus money income and the goods it can purchase, but also on the value assigned to nonmarket opportunities to produce goods. Such goods might include homemade bread, a freshly painted house, or additional education. It follows that as ways are found to produce these goods more quickly in the home or more efficiently outside the home, or as the value that the culture places on household work declines, more time will be offered for sale in the labor market. One very important good produced during leisure time is information about alternative job opportunities. Searching for a better job is often a highly productive way in which to use one's leisure.

This rather awkward way of talking about wages and work has useful applications. It enables us to understand certain observable regularities in households and labor markets. For example, unemployment rates for household heads of both sexes and for married men living with their spouses are consistently lower than overall unemployment rates. These are usually people with little household income from other family members. We would therefore expect them to have a lower demand for leisure and a more inelastic demand for income. They are consequently more likely to be either working or looking for work. Because current money income is relatively more important to them than nonmarket goods, including time in which to search for a better job, they will more quickly accept job offers when they become unemployed and will less often quit jobs without having another.

Tables 16A and 16B and figures 16A through 16P present a wealth of empirical data on changing patterns of employment and unemployment in the United States economy in recent years. What we've just been talking about is illustrated in the difference between line 1 of table 16B and lines 13 and 14. Try your hand at explaining line 4 on the basis of the same principles. Why would you expect most teenagers to have a relatively high demand for leisure? What would you predict about the income elasticity of their demand for leisure and what would this imply about their response to higher wage rates? What are some of the important nonmarket opportunities to produce goods often chosen by teenagers? Why are people less likely to choose these options after age twenty, and still less likely to do so after age twenty-five? (We'll offer our own interpretations later on in this chapter.)

Table 16A EMPLOYMENT STATUS OF THE NONINSTITUTIONAL POPULATION, HOUSEHOLD DATA (Numbers in thousands)

	Employment status	Not seasonally adjusted			Seasonally adjusted					
		Apr. 1974	Mar. 1975	Apr. 1975	Apr. 1974	Dec. 1974	Jan. 1975	Feb. 1975	Mar. 1975	Apr. 1975
	TOTAL									
1	Total noninstitutional population[1]	150,283	152,646	152,840	150,283	152,020	152,230	152,445	152,646	152,840
2	Total labor force	91,736	93,593	93,564	92,567	94,015	94,284	93,709	94,027	94,457
3	Participation rate	61.0	61.3	61.2	61.6	61.8	61.9	61.5	61.6	61.8
4	Civilian noninstitutional population[1]	148,040	150,447	150,645	148,040	149,809	150,037	150,246	150,447	150,645
5	Civilian labor force	89,493	91,395	91,369	90,324	91,803	92,091	91,511	91,829	92,262
6	Participation rate	60.5	60.7	60.7	61.0	61.3	61.4	60.9	61.0	61.2
7	Employed	85,192	83,036	83,549	85,787	85,202	84,562	84,027	83,849	84,086
8	Agriculture	3,437	2,988	3,171	3,515	3,339	3,383	3,326	3,265	3,238
9	Nonagricultural industries	81,756	80,048	80,377	82,272	81,863	81,179	80,701	80,584	80,848
10	Unemployed	4,301	8,359	7,820	4,537	6,601	7,529	7,484	7,980	8,176
11	Unemployment rate	4.8	9.1	8.6	5.0	7.2	8.2	8.2	8.7	8.9
12	Not in labor force	58,547	59,053	59,276	57,716	58,006	57,946	58,735	58,618	58,383
	Males, 20 years and over									
13	Total noninstitutional population[1]	63,712	64,730	64,812	63,712	64,462	64,552	64,644	64,730	64,812
14	Total labor force	51,738	52,311	52,320	51,912	52,414	52,244	52,150	52,136	52,414
15	Participation rate	81.2	80.8	80.7	81.5	81.3	80.9	80.7	80.5	80.9
16	Civilian noninstitutional population[1]	61,897	62,997	63,080	61,897	62,690	62,824	62,911	62,997	63,080
17	Civilian labor force	49,924	50,579	50,588	50,097	50,642	50,515	50,417	50,403	50,683
18	Participation rate	80.7	80.3	80.2	80.9	80.8	80.4	80.1	80.0	80.3
19	Employed	48,104	46,612	46,901	48,341	47,961	47,490	47,288	46,990	47,123
20	Agriculture	2,508	2,310	2,401	2,506	2,451	2,422	2,475	2,421	2,399
21	Nonagricultural industries	45,596	44,302	44,500	45,835	45,510	45,068	44,813	44,569	44,724
22	Unemployed	1,820	3,966	3,688	1,756	2,681	3,025	3,129	3,413	3,560
23	Unemployment rate	3.6	7.8	7.3	3.5	5.3	6.0	6.2	6.8	7.0
24	Not in labor force	11,973	12,419	12,492	11,800	12,048	12,309	12,494	12,594	12,397
	Females, 20 years and over									
25	Civilian noninstitutional population[1]	70,139	71,266	71,358	70,139	70,961	71,061	71,167	71,266	71,358
26	Civilian labor force	31,611	32,789	32,756	31,612	21,305	32,556	32,326	32,637	32,845
27	Participation rate	45.1	46.0	45.9	45.1	45.5	45.8	45.4	45.8	46.0
28	Employed	30,159	30,073	30,145	30,033	29,992	29,932	29,719	29,877	30,007
29	Agriculture	494	374	414	541	454	524	474	443	453
30	Nonagricultural industries	29,666	29,699	29,731	29,492	29,538	29,408	29,245	29,434	29,554
31	Unemployed	1,452	2,716	2,611	1,579	2,313	2,624	2,607	2,760	2,838
32	Unemployment rate	4.6	8.3	8.0	5.0	7.2	8.1	8.1	8.5	8.6
33	Not in labor force	38,528	38,477	38,602	38,527	38,656	38,505	38,841	38,629	38,513

		Not seasonally adjusted			Seasonally adjusted					
	Employment status	Apr. 1974	Mar. 1975	Apr. 1975	Apr. 1974	Dec. 1974	Jan. 1975	Feb. 1975	Mar. 1975	Apr. 1975
	Both sexes, 16–19 years									
34	Civilian noninstitutional population[1]	16,004	16,184	16,207	16,004	16,157	16,152	16,168	16,184	16,207
35	Civilian labor force	7,958	8,027	8,025	8,615	8,856	9,020	8,768	8,789	8,734
36	Participation rate	49.7	49.6	49.5	53.8	54.8	55.8	54.2	54.3	53.9
37	Employed	6,929	6,351	6,503	7,413	7,249	7,140	7,020	6,982	6,956
38	Agriculture	435	304	357	468	434	437	377	401	386
39	Nonagricultural industries	6,494	6,047	6,146	6,945	6,815	6,703	6,643	6,581	6,570
40	Unemployed	1,029	1,677	1,522	1,202	1,607	1,880	1,748	1,807	1,778
41	Unemployment rate	12.9	20.9	19.0	14.0	18.1	20.8	19.9	20.6	20.4
42	Not in labor force	8,046	8,157	8,182	7,389	7,301	7,132	7,400	7,395	7,473
	WHITE									
43	Civilian noninstitutional population[1]	130,922	132,879	133,039	130,922	132,356	132,553	132,720	132,879	133,039
44	Civilian labor force	79,415	81,108	81,113	80,089	81,338	81,706	81,071	81,546	81,825
45	Participation rate	60.7	61.0	61.0	61.2	61.5	61.6	61.1	61.4	61.5
46	Employed	75,950	74,243	74,711	76,470	76,106	75,555	75,043	75,039	75,193
47	Unemployed	3,465	6,865	6,402	3,619	5,232	6,151	6,028	6,507	6,632
48	Unemployment rate	4.4	8.5	7.9	4.5	6.4	7.5	7.4	8.0	8.1
49	Not in labor force	51,507	51,771	51,926	50,833	51,018	50,847	51,649	51,333	51,214
	NEGRO AND OTHER RACES									
50	Civilian noninstitutional population[1]	17,118	17,568	17,606	17,118	17,452	17,484	17,527	17,568	17,606
51	Civilian labor force	10,078	10,286	10,256	10,196	10,389	10,464	10,387	10,364	10,401
52	Participation rate	58.9	58.6	58.3	59.6	59.5	59.8	59.3	59.0	59.1
53	Employed	9,242	8,792	8,837	9,296	9,090	9,057	8,989	8,893	8,886
54	Unemployed	835	1,494	1,418	900	1,299	1,407	1,398	1,471	1,515
55	Unemployment rate	8.3	14.5	13.8	8.8	12.5	13.4	13.5	14.2	14.6
56	Not in labor force	7,041	7,281	7,350	6,922	7,063	7,020	7,140	7,204	7,205

Table 16A—*continued*

Source: Bureau of Labor Statistics.

Note: Data relate to the noninstitutional population 16 years of age and over. Total noninstitutional population and total labor force include persons in the Armed Forces.

1. Seasonal variations are not present in the population figures; therefore, identical numbers appear in the unadjusted and seasonally adjusted columns. (For an explanation of seasonal adjustments, see page 471.)

Table 16B   MAJOR UNEMPLOYMENT INDICATORS, SEASONALLY ADJUSTED, HOUSEHOLD DATA

Selected categories	Number of unemployed persons (In thousands)		Unemployment rates					
	Apr. 1974	Apr. 1975	Apr. 1974	Dec. 1974	Jan. 1975	Feb. 1975	Mar. 1975	Apr. 1975
1 Total, 16 years and over	4,537	8,176	5.0	7.2	8.2	8.2	8.7	8.9
2 Males, 20 years and over	1,756	3,560	3.5	5.3	6.0	6.2	6.8	7.0
3 Females, 20 years and over	1,579	2,838	5.0	7.2	8.1	8.1	8.5	8.6
4 Both sexes, 16–19 years	1,202	1,778	14.0	18.1	20.8	19.9	20.6	20.4
5 White, total	3,619	6,632	4.5	6.4	7.5	7.4	8.0	8.1
6 Males, 20 years and over	1,431	2,912	3.2	4.7	5.5	5.6	6.2	6.4
7 Females, 20 years and over	1,262	2,333	4.6	6.5	7.7	7.6	8.0	8.2
8 Both sexes, 16–19 years	926	1,387	12.0	15.9	18.4	17.5	18.1	17.8
9 Negro and other races, total	900	1,515	8.8	12.5	13.4	13.5	14.2	14.6
10 Males, 20 years and over	327	650	6.4	9.3	10.5	11.1	11.8	12.6
11 Females, 20 years and over	300	478	7.2	10.9	11.0	10.9	11.2	11.2
12 Both sexes, 16–19 years	273	387	30.5	37.7	41.1	36.7	41.6	40.2
13 Household heads	1,593	3,194	3.0	4.6	5.2	5.4	5.8	6.0
14 Married men, spouse present	966	2,226	2.4	3.8	4.5	4.7	5.2	5.6
15 Full-time workers	3,583	6,824	4.6	6.8	7.7	7.8	8.3	8.7
16 Part-time workers	982	1,395	7.6	9.6	10.5	10.3	10.9	10.4
17 Unemployed, 15 weeks and over[1]	875	2,403	1.0	1.4	1.7	2.0	2.2	2.6
18 State insured[2]	2,118	4,494	3.3	4.8	5.5	5.9	6.4	6.8
19 Labor force time lost[3]	——	——	5.7	7.9	8.9	8.9	9.6	9.7
OCCUPATION[4]								
20 White-collar workers	1,224	2,094	2.9	4.1	4.6	4.5	4.6	4.7
21 Professional and technical	283	450	2.3	2.5	2.9	3.2	2.9	3.4
22 Managers and administrators, except farm	148	295	1.6	2.6	3.3	2.7	2.7	3.3
23 Sales workers	188	342	3.3	6.0	5.7	5.3	6.0	5.8
24 Clerical workers	605	1,007	3.9	5.4	6.3	6.2	6.6	6.2
25 Blue-collar workers	1,989	4,156	6.3	9.3	11.0	10.9	12.5	13.0
26 Craft and kindred workers	469	1,074	3.9	6.1	7.0	6.5	8.7	9.0
27 Operatives	1,033	2,248	6.9	10.7	13.1	13.3	14.1	14.9
28 Nonfarm laborers	487	834	10.3	13.0	14.3	14.1	16.2	17.2
29 Service workers	689	1,015	5.8	7.1	8.1	7.7	8.5	8.2
30 Farm workers	86	118	2.7	2.4	3.6	3.0	4.5	4.0

Table 16B—*continued*

| | Number of unemployed persons (In thousands) | | Unemployment rates | | | | | |
Selected categories	Apr. 1974	Apr. 1975	Apr. 1974	Dec. 1974	Jan. 1975	Feb. 1975	Mar. 1975	Apr. 1975
INDUSTRY[4]								
31 Nonagricultural private wage and salary workers[5]	3,422	6,582	5.2	7.7	8.7	8.8	9.3	9.8
32 Construction	449	832	9.9	14.9	15.0	15.9	18.1	19.3
33 Manufacturing	1,075	2,638	5.0	8.9	10.5	11.0	11.4	12.2
34 Durable goods	625	1,651	4.9	8.7	10.5	10.9	11.3	12.8
35 Nondurable goods.....................	450	987	5.1	9.1	10.3	11.1	11.6	11.4
36 Transportation and public utilities.....................	153	320	3.1	3.9	5.9	5.2	5.6	6.6
37 Wholesale and retail trade.....................	957	1,525	6.0	8.1	8.5	8.0	8.7	9.1
38 Finance and service industries.....................	767	1,226	4.3	5.4	6.2	6.5	6.7	6.6
39 Government workers.....................	421	569	2.9	3.2	3.4	3.6	3.9	3.8
40 Agricultural wage and salary workers.....................	112	167	7.9	7.9	10.2	8.8	12.0	12.6
VETERAN STATUS								
Males, Vietnam-era veterans[6]:								
41 20 to 34 years.....................	286	593	5.0	7.6	9.0	8.8	9.0	9.9
42 20 to 24 years.....................	114	239	9.2	15.6	19.7	17.3	17.5	22.8
43 25 to 29 years.....................	139	241	4.3	6.7	6.9	7.4	8.1	7.3
44 30 to 34 years.....................	33	113	2.7	3.7	6.1	5.9	5.2	6.8
Males, nonveterans:								
45 20 to 34 years.....................	752	1,471	5.6	8.1	8.6	9.5	10.5	10.4
46 20 to 24 years.....................	440	920	7.4	10.4	11.6	12.6	14.7	14.5
47 25 to 29 years.....................	178	284	4.7	7.2	7.2	8.6	8.5	6.9
48 30 to 34 years.....................	134	267	3.7	5.1	5.1	5.1	5.5	7.2

Source: Bureau of Labor Statistics
    1. Unemployment rate calculated as a percent of civilian labor force.
    2. Insured unemployment under State programs; unemployment rate calculated as a percent of average covered employment.
    3. Man-hours lost by the unemployed and persons on part time for economic reasons as a percent of potentially available labor force man-hours.
    4. Unemployment by occupation includes all experienced unemployed persons, whereas that by industry covers only unemployed wage and salary workers.
    5. Includes mining, not shown separately.
    6. Vietnam-era veterans are those who served after August 4, 1964.

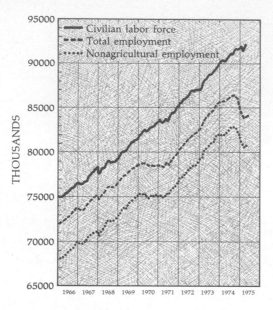

Figure 16A Labor force and employment

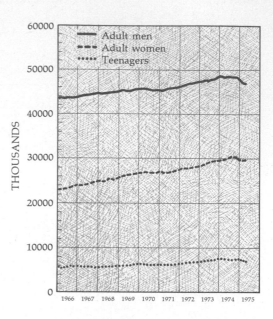

Figure 16B Total employment

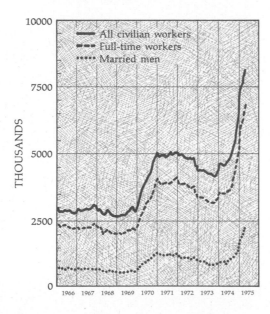

Figure 16C Unemployment

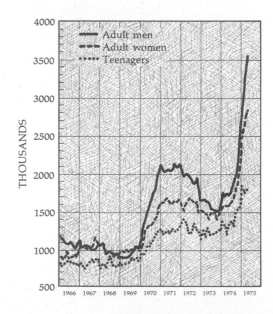

Figure 16D Unemployment

Source of figures 16A–16P: Bureau of Labor Statistics. (All data seasonally adjusted)

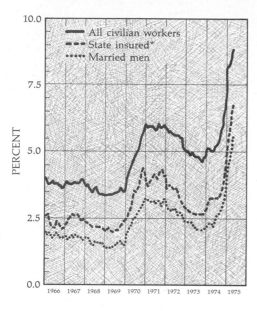

Figure 16E Unemployment rates

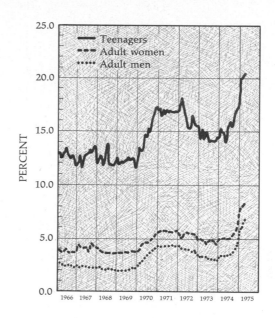

Figure 16F Unemployment rates

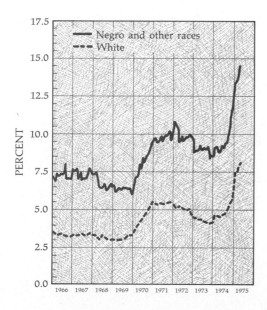

Figure 16G Unemployment rates

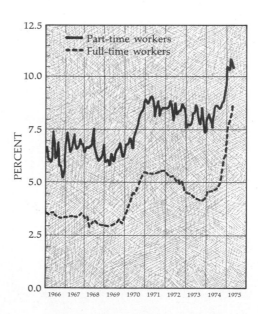

Figure 16H Unemployment rates

*State insured unemployment rate pertains to the week including the 12th of the month and represents the insured unemployed under State programs as a percent of average covered employment. The figures are derived from administrative records of unemployment insurance systems.

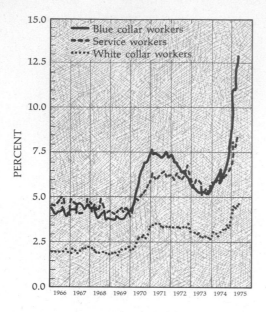

Figure 16I Unemployment rates

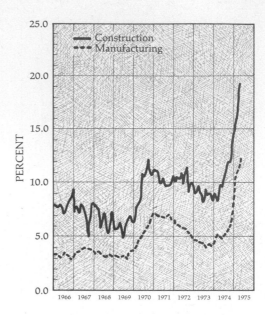

Figure 16J Unemployment rates

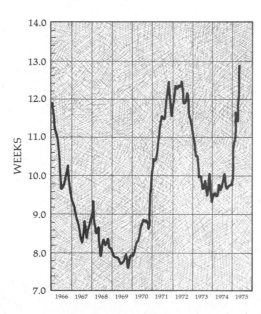

Figure 16K Average duration
of unemployment

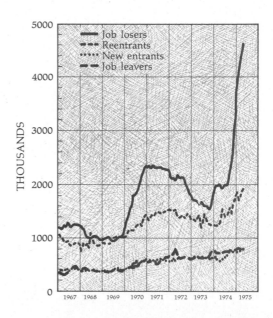

Figure 16L Unemployment by reason

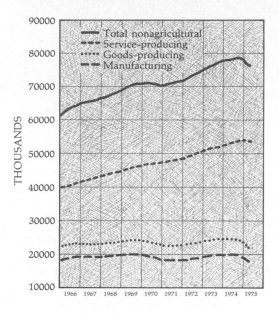

Figure 16M Employment

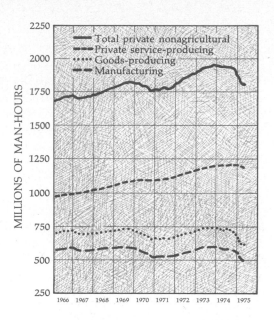

Figure 16N Man-hours worked

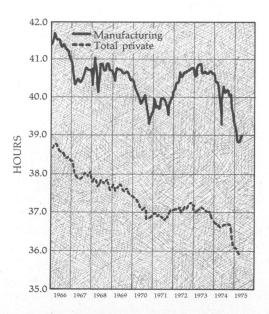

Figure 16O Average weekly hours

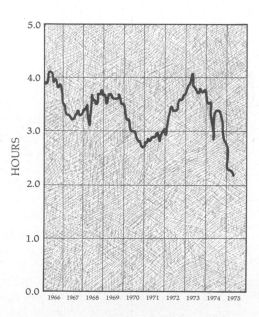

Figure 16P Average weekly overtime
hours in manufacturing

Note: Figures 16N and 16O relate to production of nonsupervisory workers; figure 16P relates to production workers. Data for the 2 most recent months are preliminary in figure 16M–16P.

The Demand for Labor

We've been focusing so far on the supply of labor market time. What about the demand for labor? Chapter 13 argued that employers will purchase productive resources as long as their expected marginal contribution to revenue is greater than the expected marginal cost. While the marginal productivity theory does not provide a complete theory of the demand for labor, it does provide important insights into the way labor markets operate. It must be used with caution, however, and with attention to the actual range of options that employers encounter. Hiring and discharging workers when wages change or when their marginal dollar product shifts is not a costless action.

An employer usually expects to incur costs in finding appropriate workers and equipping them with the skills they must have to be effective in particular positions. The costs of advertising, interviewing, testing, and filling out forms are investments that employers must make to obtain workers. Moreover, in an organization of any complexity, there are many things to be learned before workers' productivity can reach the level expected when they were hired. They may have to learn, for example, the names of associates, the formal and informal rules of social conduct, the location of specific tools and facilities, the procedures to be followed in requisitioning materials, making a sale, taking sick leave, reporting progress or trouble, replacing a light bulb, and so on. An employee who leaves after acquiring this job-specific training represents a loss to the employer of what may be a significant investment. That's why labor turnover can be quite costly and why employers often try to retain certain workers even though their marginal dollar product is expected to be temporarily below their marginal cost.

But employers have other options, too. In some circumstances they will hire on a day-by-day or even hour-by-hour basis. When the driver of a moving van arrives in town with your furniture, he will go to a labor pickup point and hire some workers for just a few hours to help him unload. Farmers may hire laborers in a similar manner. A few skilled occupations are organized so that an employer can obtain skilled workers on a short-term basis through the union hiring hall. The appropriate union certifies the qualifications of the carpenter, electrician, or plumber. The common feature in each of these cases is that the employer invests very little in finding and training workers. If employers know they can hire practically identical workers at the going wage with little cost of search or training, they may elect not to keep such workers on the payroll on the days when they cannot be used to produce revenue at least equal to their wages.

Sometimes these kinds of markets become so flexible that workers are hired for only a few minutes at a time. You hire a taxi driver and his

vehicle for only a few minutes and, unless you've traveled to a remote destination from which you intend to return very soon, you fire him and hire another for your next trip. Many consumer services are arranged on this basis. We typically think of those who provide such services as being self-employed; but they are actually being employed by the consumers of their services.

"So what does all this have to do with unemployment?" says an impatient voice from the back of the room. Suppose you were going to spend the summer working at a dude ranch in Wyoming and you didn't have room to take along your bicycle and stereo set. As a result they would be unemployed over the summer. Would you lay them off for the summer or retain them on the payroll? In other words, would you sell them before leaving and then purchase replacements in the fall? Or would you expect the transaction costs of selling and repurchasing to be greater than the opportunity cost of keeping them during the summer? For exactly the same reasons an employer may retain an employee during a period of slack business; he expects the value of the worker's marginal product to exceed the wages again in a short while and he believes it would be costly to find and train a replacement.

This provides at least a partial explanation for some of the observed employment phenomena during a recession. More highly skilled workers and those with more job-specific training have lower layoff and unemployment rates during a recession, and their unemployment rates start to rise sometime after those of other workers. It is well known that product per employee-hour tends to decline during recessions while unit labor costs rise. (See figure 16Q.) The notion of employer investment in employees explains this phenomenon.

"Involuntary" Unemployment

The Bureau of Labor Statistics maintains a statistical series on unemployment in our economy going back to 1929. The data are based on household interviews conducted in accordance with accepted sampling procedures. They recount a disturbing history.

The civilian labor force, you will recall, is defined to include everyone over the age of sixteen (over fourteen until 1947) not an inmate of an institution or in the armed forces, and either employed, actively seeking employment, or waiting to be recalled to employment. Table 16C shows in the first two columns the total number of people in the civilian labor force classified as unemployed in each year from 1929 to 1974, and the same figure expressed as a percentage of the civilian labor force. The figures are annual averages based on monthly survey data, and are given to the nearest thousand. What do they tell us?

A good place to begin asking that question is with the data for 1942–

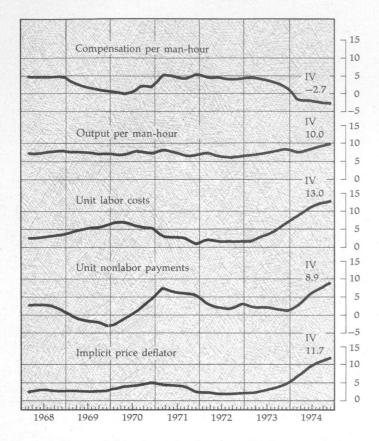

Source: *Productivity in the Private Economy, First Quarter 1975*, U.S. Department of Labor, Bureau of Labor Statistics, April 24, 1975

Figure 16Q Productivity, hourly compensation, unit costs and prices—nonfinancial corporations (percent change from same quarter a year ago)

1945, the years of World War II. No one claims that the United States had an unemployment problem during those years. Yet even in 1944, when people were being urged to leave school and take a job, to come out of retirement, to work six- and seven-day weeks, 1.2% of the labor force was classified as unemployed. Anyone who lived through those years would have trouble believing that 670,000 people could not find jobs in 1944. What was happening?

People were *looking* for work in 1944 not because they couldn't find employment, but because they wanted *better* jobs than the ones they already knew about. They were unemployed *by choice* and not involuntarily. And that leads to the somewhat controversial proposal that we shall now offer and defend: People are always unemployed by choice. Those whom the BLS statisticians count as unemployed have chosen this status because it presents, in their judgment, the best available option.

Table 16C EMPLOYMENT AND UNEMPLOYMENT, 1929–1974

Year	Unemployed (in thousands)	Percentage of Civilian Labor Force	Employed (in thousands)	Percentage of Noninstitutional Population
1929	1,550	3.2%		
1930	4,340	8.7		
1931	8,020	15.9		
1932	12,060	23.6		
1933	12,830	24.9		
1934	11,340	21.7		
1935	10,610	20.1		
1936	9,030	16.9		
1937	7,700	14.3		
1938	10,390	19.0		
1939	9,480	17.2		
1940	8,120	14.6		
1941	5,560	9.9		
1942	2,660	4.7		
1943	1,070	1.9		
1944	670	1.2		
1945	1,040	1.9		
1946	2,270	3.9		
1947	2,311	3.9	57,039	55.2%
1948	2,276	3.8	58,344	55.8
1949	3,637	5.9	57,649	54.6
1950	3,288	5.3	58,920	55.2
1951	2,055	3.3	59,962	55.7
1952	1,883	3.0	60,254	55.4
1953	1,834	2.9	61,181	55.3
1954	3,532	5.5	60,110	53.8
1955	2,852	4.4	62,171	55.1
1956	2,750	4.1	63,802	56.1
1957	2,859	4.3	64,071	55.7
1958	4,602	6.8	63,036	54.2
1959	3,740	5.5	64,630	54.8
1960	3,852	5.5	65,778	54.9
1961	4,714	6.7	65,746	54.2
1962	3,911	5.5	66,702	54.2
1963	4,070	5.7	67,762	54
1964	3,786	5.2	69,305	54.5
1965	3,366	4.5	71,088	55.0
1966	2,875	3.8	72,895	55.6
1967	2,975	3.8	74,372	55.8
1968	2,817	3.6	75,920	56.0
1969	2,831	3.5	77,902	56.5
1970	4,088	4.9	78,627	56.1
1971	4,993	5.9	79,120	55.5
1972	4,840	5.6	81,702	56.0
1973	4,304	4.9	84,409	56.9
1974	5,076	5.6	85,936	57.0

Source: Bureau of Labor Statistics. More recent data on employment and unemployment will be found in appendix 6, page 810.

Don't jump to unwarranted conclusions. We aren't supporting the notion that unemployment is due to laziness, or that everyone could find a satisfactory job if only he resolved to do so. Nothing like that is implied by the assertion that unemployment is a consequence of choice, something *chosen as the best available opportunity.* This is simply a way of thinking about unemployment that provides a more comprehensive picture than the usual notion that people can be involuntarily unemployed.

When an airplane manufacturer tells an engineer in his employ that he is being laid off at the end of the week, the engineer will make plans. Because there *are* work opportunities available, he *could* begin a new job the next day. But it is not probable that he could the very next day go to work at another job with net advantages equal to the one from which he has been laid off, or even very close. The condition of his finding a new job immediately might be a willingness to work for a small fraction of his previous wage or in some occupation that he intensely dislikes. If an engineer laid off on Friday refused to go to work on Monday as a restaurant dishwasher for $2.00 an hour (which we are now assuming to be the best option available to him for Monday), he would become officially unemployed inasmuch as he *chose* not to take the dishwashing job.

At the same time we should probably all agree that he would be foolish *not* to become officially unemployed. There are almost certainly better

opportunities not yet available because they are not yet known to him. If he takes a job that pays $4000 a year in order to avoid being counted as unemployed, he reduces his opportunities to search for a better job. The value to him of time spent searching may well be greater than $2 an hour. He may even value just fishing for a few weeks at more than $2 an hour. If he has some savings accumulated, or his wife has a good job, or he is fairly certain that another engineering position will become available shortly, voluntary unemployment could be a very sensible choice for him.

Why stress the voluntary nature of unemployment? What's the point? The point is the fundamental ambiguity, bordering on meaninglessness, of the concept of involuntary unemployment. As long as useful work remains to be done—and that covers every place and time with which we are familiar—employment opportunities exist, including opportunities for self-employment. (Notice that the official definition misleadingly counts as unemployed those persons who are working around the house while looking for more attractive opportunities elsewhere.) Of course, available opportunities may be far below the individual's expectations; they may not yield an income on which he could begin to support himself adequately; and they may—a crucial point—promise a lower marginal benefit than he anticipates from continued job searching. The possibilities are many. Choice is therefore crucial. But the concept of *involuntary* unemployment covers over the important factor of choice. That is why we have rejected it in favor of the working postulate that every unemployed person *chooses* that status. For some people, the choice will be a dismal one. But the problem for them and for society is that these people must choose among a set of very poor options; the problem is *not* that no work at all is available.

It follows, then, that 670,000 persons were unemployed on an average throughout 1944 because this number of people preferred unemployment. Why? For the most part they were out of work in order to obtain a better job. They were looking or waiting. That obviously does not make them lazy or foolish. It doesn't even make them unpatriotic. Wartime demands called for numerous reallocations of labor among jobs. The individual who was looking for a higher-paying job in 1944 can also be viewed as someone trying to move from a socially less-valued to a socially more-valued task, with the competitively determined wage reflecting social priorities.

But what of 1933? Were 13 million people voluntarily unemployed? One in every four members of the labor force? Yes, strange as that answer may sound at first. They were for the most part unhappy, frustrated, and often desperate. Something had gone radically wrong with the economic system. The value of available job opportunities had diminished spectacularly and rapidly after 1929. This was the crux of the unemployment problem. Opportunities for gainful employment were so unattractive that almost 13 million people eager for job income had no better option than to be unemployed, despite the personal and family distress that this entailed.

Once again, with all the emphasis we can muster: in defining unemployment as a consequence of choice, we are *not* assigning moral fault or minimizing the often tragic consequences of depressions. We are rather incorporating this problem, too, within the general analytical framework of economics, where action is assumed to result from choice of the best available opportunity, even in situations where the best opportunity available is a distressingly poor one.

Employment Rates and Labor Force Participation

During 1974 an average of 5.6% of the civilian labor force was unemployed, as measured by the Bureau of Labor Statistics. In 1966 the corresponding figure had been only 3.8%. May we conclude that the employment picture was more favorable in 1966 than in 1974? Let's take a closer look at the data for those years before answering.

In 1966, 57.8% of the noninstitutional population was officially included in the civilian labor force: those working, waiting to be recalled to work, or actively seeking employment. In 1974, by contrast, 60.3% of the noninstitutional population was in the civilian labor force. In other words, a considerably larger portion of the eligible population wanted jobs in 1974 than in 1966. Moreover, despite the higher unemployment rate in 1974, a larger percentage of the eligible population actually held jobs in 1974 than in 1966. The *employment* rate, defined as the percentage of the noninstitutional population holding civilian employment, was 55.6% in 1966 and 57% in 1974. It turns out that while the unemployment rate was much worse in 1974 than in 1966, the employment rate was actually higher in 1974.

Which is the more meaningful measure of the job situation? There is no simple way to answer that question. The employment rate can rise right along with the unemployment rate, which just says that the labor force is increasing faster than unemployment is increasing. That occurred between 1966 and 1974. Was it a desirable or undesirable development? Is it a good sign or a bad sign when a large percentage of the population chooses to enter the labor market? The answer depends on why they made that choice.

IS UNEMPLOYMENT VOLUNTARY OR INVOLUNTARY?

Many economists do not agree that it is useful to view all unemployment as voluntary. Some have argued that the attempt to eliminate the concept of involuntary unemployment from discussion is at best an unwarranted stretching of the meaning of words, at worst a disguised attempt to persuade people that unemployment is not a serious social problem and that public policy can therefore adopt a tolerant attitude toward it. Students encountering this mode of analysis for the first time are likely to agree: They will suspect that someone is either trying to get rid of a problem by verbal juggling or else trying subtly to insinuate that people are unemployed through their own fault. Why not conform to conventional usage and agree to call some unemployment involuntary?

But those who retain the concept of involuntary unemployment run into problems, too. First of all, how will they classify those people who are not employed and are not actively looking for work because they don't believe they could find an acceptable job? Are they involuntarily unemployed? As far as the BLS is concerned, they are not unemployed at all because they are not in the labor force. We know, however, that the BLS data understate the problem by missing all those workers who have left the labor force out of discouragement. But how shall we draw the line between those for whom not working entails severe hardship and those who feel no urgency about finding a job but nonetheless would accept employment if the right opportunity arose? We shall certainly want to draw some such line. But is there any way to do so that does not pay fundamental attention to the opportunities among which different people are *able to choose?* And that takes us back to the view that unemployment is chosen and hence voluntary.

A second difficulty is that of deciding what portion of measured unemployment shall be counted as a problem. For policy purposes, a part of the officially measured unemployment is universally regarded as voluntary: that part which reflects "normal" turnover between jobs or people in the process of "changing" jobs. The accepted term for that is *frictional unemployment.* But how is frictional unemployment to be distinguished in practice from involuntary unemployment, the unemployment that calls for corrective social policy? The standard procedure is simply to pick some percentage (2% or 3% or 4%) and to say that we have a problem whenever unemployment rises above this "unavoidable" minimum.

But with this procedure, the amount of problem unemployment is as arbitrary as the percentage figure chosen to "define" frictional

unemployment. And the unemployment problem can be eliminated (or aggravated) simply by agreement to raise (or lower) the
magic number. As a matter of historical fact, the percentage used
to "define" frictional unemployment in the United States has
drifted upward from about 2.5% or 3% in the early 1950s to 5% or
more in the mid-1970s. In other words, unemployment levels that
would have created consternation and calls for urgent action in
the 1950s are now widely accepted as appropriate targets for
policy. The concept of involuntary unemployment provides no
bulwark against complacency in the face of rising unemployment,
because it is logically linked to the concept of frictional unemployment, which in turn is little more than a fudge factor. The question remains, What is the appropriate level of frictional unemployment and why is this level to be deemed acceptable?

It seems to us far more useful to consider all unemployment as
the product of choice and to ask: Why do people choose as they
do? Why do opportunities for choice suddenly expand or decline?
Why do some people have such a terribly poor range of choices?
What can be done to enlarge and improve available opportunities,
especially for those whose choices are severely constrained?

At the very least, this way of looking at the problem does not
seem any more open to political abuse than the conventional
approach. And it is conceptually clearer, more comprehensive,
and more consistent.

In each of the imaginary cases below, people's choices are altering the
labor force participation rate. The examples were constructed to convince
you that neither entrance into nor exit from the labor force is in itself a
good thing, but that the desirability or undesirability of changes in the
labor force participation rate depends on the circumstances underlying
people's choices.

1. David Ricardo retires from his job as a stockbroker, because he
can live comfortably on his accumulated savings and he wants to
spend more time in public service.

2. Arthur Mommeter, who retired seven years ago at age 65, starts
looking for work again, because inflation has eaten up so much
of his savings.

3. Jack Daniels turns to the bottle after losing his job and refuses
even to look for work.

4. Gloria Greer, whose husband is a wealthy lawyer, takes a job after
thirteen years of marriage, because she wants something more
challenging to do than keep house for Mr. Greer.

5. Elizabeth Bennett reluctantly accepts a temporary job as a waitress when her husband's unemployment compensation runs out.

6. John London quits school and signs on with a logging crew, because he finds the forest more healthful, interesting, and profitable than college.

7. Virginia Fox enrolls in college full time, because she hasn't been able to find a good job after looking for six months.

8. Delmar Monte takes a full-time job in the cannery while attending school, because the canning company has boosted wage rates in an effort to get more help.

Employment Rates or Unemployment Rates?

A former commissioner of Labor Statistics, Geoffrey H. Moore, suggested in a recent article in the *Wall Street Journal* (May 9, 1975) that the employment rate might provide a more objective and reliable measurement of the job situation than the unemployment rate. The two variables necessary to calculate the employment rate are total civilian employment and the noninstitutional population, both of which can be objectively measured without great difficulty. The unemployment rate, by contrast, is the number waiting to be recalled or actively seeking employment divided by the civilian labor force; both of these magnitudes are difficult to measure objectively, because "actively seeking employment" is not a clear-cut status.

The fourth column of table 16C on page 433 shows the employment rate in the United States in each year since 1947. (Data prior to 1947 would not be comparable without major adjustments, because the minimum age for being counted in the noninstitutional population was raised in 1947.) Compare the two columns and ask yourself whether it makes much difference whether we consult the employment or unemployment rate in making public policy.

We'll provide one argument on each side. In March 1975 the *un*employment rate was 8.7%, worse than it had been in any recession since the years prior to World War II. But that was not nearly as great a cause for alarm as many people thought; the *em*ployment rate in the same month was 54.9%, higher than it had been in the recession years of 1949, 1954, 1958, and 1961. If the March 1975 *un*employment rate had been lowered only to 7.6%, everything else remaining unchanged, the *em*ployment rate for the month would have been at a higher level than actually prevailed in the low unemployment year of 1966.

On the other hand, the surprisingly high *em*ployment rate in March 1975 was the result of an exceptionally high rate of participation in the labor force, which may in turn have been due to the persistence of inflation and increasing unemployment. (Consult the cases above of Arthur Mommeter and Elizabeth Bennett to see how inflation and unemployment can each cause the labor force to increase.) By looking at *em*ployment rather than *un*employment rates, we may be allowing people's response to a problem to obscure the gravity of the problem.

Both arguments have merit. The wisest procedure may be to understand the concepts upon which each measurement is based and use good judgment thereafter. Neither an increase in the employment rate nor a decrease in the unemployment rate is necessarily a good thing. Economic improvement consists, as we argued in chapter 7, in an extension of the range of alternatives available to a society. The goal is more and better choices for people.

Dissecting Unemployment Data

It was a significant achievement when we were able to obtain reliable data on unemployment to substitute for casual estimates based on fragmentary evidence, estimates that provided little guidance to policymakers because they could so easily be disputed. Tables 16A and 16B and figures 16A through 16Q begin to reveal the detailed nature of the available data on unemployment. The BLS breaks the aggregates down to provide information on employment and unemployment by age, sex, and race; by selected groups such as experienced workers, household heads, married males, full and part-time workers, blue-collar workers; by duration of unemployment, from less than five weeks to more than half a year. And the Office of Manpower Administration, also in the Department of Labor, publishes extensive data on unemployment insurance programs: workers covered, claims paid, benefits exhausted. We have available a remarkably comprehensive and detailed picture of the dimensions of the unemployment problem in the United States.

But the picture, in some respects, is like a surrealist painting: vivid in detail and full of recognizable objects but somewhat disconcerting when one tries to make sense out of it.[1] The analogy must not be pressed, however, for paintings aren't required to make sense in the same way that economic data are. But what *do* the data mean? More specifically, what kind of *problem* is presented by the unemployment levels depicted?

Our concern at the moment is not with the 1930s and 1940s, but with the unemployment figures in subsequent years. What does it mean, for example, that almost 5 million people were unemployed in 1971? It does not mean, first of all, that 5 million households were without income. The

---

1. If you've never seen a painting by the late Belgian surrealist René Magritte, look him up on your next trip to the library. You may find yourself captivated by an intriguing painter. And you'll discover the force of this analogy.

average unemployment rate in 1971 for household heads was only 3.6%, and in most of these households there was income from other sources. Among married men the unemployment rate was 3.2%. On the other hand, it was 7.4% among blue-collar workers and a disturbingly high 10% among nonwhite members of the labor force. Among teenagers (16–19 years old) it was 16.9%. The aggregate figure of 5.9% obviously conceals a lot of important variation.

Let's take a look at data on duration of unemployment in 1971. The average (mean) duration was 11.3 weeks. Of the almost 5 million unemployed, about 45% were without jobs for less than five weeks. But a little more than 10% of these people were unemployed for more than half the year. Why did some go back to work quickly while others found no work for long periods of time? The figures on long-term unemployment actually understate the problem. For once a person withdraws from the labor force, he's no longer counted as unemployed. And workers who don't find employment within six months are often discouraged enough to quit looking, so that they drop out of the labor force and hence out of the unemployment figures. We referred above to the well-known phenomenon of extremely high unemployment rates among nonwhites. Does that explain why in the quarter century after 1948 labor force participation rates of nonwhite adult males dropped from 97.2% to 92% among those 35–44 years old and from 94.7% to 86.9% among those 45–54 years old? (The corresponding changes for white males were only 98% to 97% and 95.9% to 94.7%.) People who cannot find what they're looking for may eventually give up.

One more set of data will add significantly to the picture. In 1971 almost 60 million people worked at jobs covered by some kind of government-operated or -assisted system of unemployment compensation. That's slightly more than 70% of the civilian labor force. The average weekly check received by workers entitled to unemployment compensation was $54. But only 2.3 million unemployed workers, or less than half the total, received any of these benefits. The picture is again one of enormous differences, with some unemployed workers receiving benefits that, partly for tax reasons, left them almost as well off financially as when they were working, and others receiving nothing.

Clearly the unemployment problem in the United States is not a simple one. And this is the point we want to stress in asking what the BLS figures on unemployment *mean*. In using these data for policymaking purposes we must be continually aware that particular people are unemployed for very different reasons and with quite different social and personal consequences, and that no single government policy is capable of solving *the* unemployment problem because it isn't a single problem.

Largely as a result of our experience in the 1930s with prolonged, large-scale unemployment associated with low levels of private spending and huge amounts of unused productive capacity, economists and other students of economic policy have focused on the relation between unemployment and the total market demand for commodities and services. This emphasis, as we shall see in subsequent chapters, produced a great deal of theoretical and empirical work on the causes and cures of aggregate economic fluctuations. But unemployment has other causes as well, causes on which we want to reflect before launching into our analysis of aggregate demand, Keynesian economics, monetary disturbances, and fiscal and monetary policy.

Job Turnover and Labor Force Attachment

In 1971 only 46% of those listed as unemployed had lost their jobs or been laid off. The other 54% were either entering the labor force for the first time, reentering it after a period of absence, or had quit their last jobs. Moreover, job turnover has long been high in the United States. Total hirings and separations among employees in manufacturing, for example, consistently run above 4% of the labor force per month. We can

translate that loosely by saying that one out of every 25 workers in manufacturing can be expected to leave his job for some reason in the next 30 days. Unless these job leavers drop out of the labor force altogether, they will add to the unemployment totals until they go to work at a new job.

These figures suggest that much of our measured unemployment can be attributed to weak job attachment among a substantial number of workers. That thesis is supported by other evidence.

Teenage Unemployment

The unemployment rate among teenagers has long been many times higher than the national average. In part that results from the general absence in this country of programs for matching up available jobs with young people as they leave high school. High school counselors are diligent college placement officers, but they are less effective in serving those who want to go to work when they graduate or leave school. This is not to blame the counselors. They have for the most part received little encouragement or assistance from employers, parents, or the students themselves.

But there is more to the teenage unemployment picture. A large proportion of the jobs available to teenagers are simply not attractive. They don't pay much more than the legal minimum and they offer no hope of advancement. They are seen as dead-end jobs, something to be done to earn a little money but not the beginning of careers. The attractiveness of a particular job depends, of course, on the alternatives. Most teenagers have few financial obligations and many continue to live with their parents, so they can afford to quit a job and take their time about finding another. Since there are usually plenty of equally attractive (or unattractive) jobs around, they are not much deterred from quitting by the fear that they won't be able to get something just as good if they change their minds.

Moreover, many unemployed teenagers look for jobs, full or part time, while attending school, and still others only flirt with the job market because they're simultaneously flirting with the possibility of going back to school or joining the military service or maybe getting into some kind of vocational training program. The common element in all these factors is the low urgency assigned to remaining at the current job or taking another at the first opportunity.[1]

1. Martin Feldstein has suggested: "Perhaps much of the high turnover and voluntary labor force withdrawal among young non-students reflects an attempt to enjoy the same freedom and occupational irresponsibility that we take for granted in our student population of the same age." Why not? This analysis of unemployment data and their meaning owes much to Feldstein's discussion of "The Economics of the New Unemployment," based on a study he submitted to the Joint Economic Committee of the Congress in 1973 and published in *The Public Interest*, Fall 1973.

We don't mean to suggest by this analysis that teenage unemployment is not a serious social problem. We are rather trying to find out just what kind of problem it is. It is not, except in rare instances, a problem of no work to be had by those who must have income to meet their obligations. But a society that is unable to provide a substantial number of its young people with jobs they think are worth pursuing, jobs with live prospects for advancement or meaningful work, does have a serious problem. In recent years the problem may even have become more acute and widespread as college students, too, leave school and find that even a bachelor's degree no longer guarantees an attractive job offer. There is evidence that the scenario sketched above for 16–19-year-olds is beginning to be reenacted by 20–24-year-olds.

In 1971 one out of every four labor force participants listed as unemployed was a teenager; in 1973 it rose to two out of every seven. That's certainly a significant fact to keep in mind when asking about the meaning of our unemployment figures. But what about the other three out of four or five out of seven? Why are they unemployed?

ON "RETIRING" AT TWENTY OR AT SIXTY

One of the authors has done research on time and income allocation over the course of people's lifetimes. He found that an interesting pattern emerges after formal schooling is complete.

People who are more impatient than society (that is, who discount the future at a rate higher than the market rate of interest) will devote an *increasing fraction* of their time to work as they get older. They will work less when young and may not plan to retire.

People who are less impatient than society (whose internal rate of time discount is below the market rate of interest) will devote a *decreasing fraction* of their time to work as they grow older. They will work hard when young and plan for their retirement.

Is one inherently superior to the other? Yet the less impatient frequently do condemn those who are more impatient.

Abilities and Opportunities

When we begin to break down the data we discover that there are several reasonably distinct causes of unemployment among older workers, and that this diversity of causes creates different kinds of problems that will probably require for their solution quite different policy approaches.

To begin with, some workers are close to unemployable. They may have low skills, physical disabilities, emotional problems, or simply such poor work habits that few employers would want to take them on at any positive wage.

Then there are workers, again often with low skills and poor work habits, who are unwilling to accept or to remain for long at the jobs employers are willing to give them. Martin Feldstein reports on a program initiated in Boston in 1966 to provide jobs for very low-skill workers. About 15,000 were referred to employers and 70% of these received job offers. But 45% of the job offers were rejected, and half of those who did accept were no longer on the job after one month. A high proportion of these separations was initiated by the workers themselves. Many workers in this category are probably not even listed as unemployed, because they have withdrawn from the labor force. So in this case the BLS data probably understate the problem. But exactly what *is* the problem? Extravagant expectations or inadequate opportunities? Whichever alternative we elect, the situation results in poverty for a substantial number of such individuals and in many cases their dependents as well. The problem is genuine. But how should we set about solving it?

Points of View and Bias

The language of the preceding paragraph may have suggested that workers with low skills or poor work habits are themselves to blame for their situation. There are people eager to argue that a lack of ambition or personal responsibility is the root cause of a substantial amount of national unemployment. It is particularly easy for white, middle-class males to think in this fashion, and thereby to overlook the possible role of the labor market itself in creating the problem. Substantial evidence exists to support the view that hiring practices in the United States have helped to create the problem. Discrimination by employers *and fellow employees* on the basis of such factors as race and social class has tended to confine some workers to the least attractive jobs: the ones with low pay, poor prospects for advancement, little chance to acquire skills, and a low probability of permanent employment. It isn't surprising that such workers develop a weak attachment to the labor force, tend to be relatively unskilled, and display work habits that make them unattractive to employers. But what is cause and what is effect?

Social scientists are usually reluctant to enter into a discussion of "blame" or "fault." But intelligent policy formulation requires attention to causes and almost any discussion of causes, when we're looking at social phenomena, presupposes some notion of responsibility—which in practice is very difficult to distinguish from notions of credit or blame.

Because the economic way of thinking is rooted in the concept of individual choice, it tends to postulate individual responsibility for any actions that people take. This is not so much explicitly stated as presupposed. But it begs an important question: Do individuals create society? Or does society create individuals? Shall individuals or society be held responsible for the misfortunes that people encounter? That is the larger question underneath numerous contemporary public policy disputes, not just disputes over policies to deal with unemployment. It is a question, of course, that people have been debating for centuries and one that none of us is likely to resolve. We can at least be alert to the fact that the emphasis we place upon either of these poles—the individual or society—will influence our interpretation of fact and hence the policy conclusions to which we come. In such a situation there may be no better remedy than a determination to remain open to alternative points of view and to give sympathetic attention to opposing analyses.

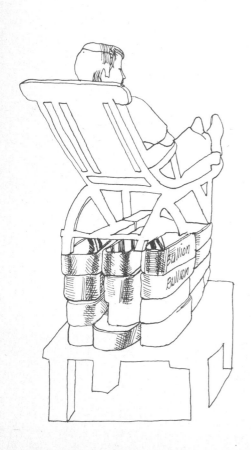

There is an additional component of our unemployment totals where individual choice is clearly involved but where the choices would not be widely regarded as intolerable. The problem—insofar as it is a problem—may have been created by our unemployment compensation system, our way of taxing wage income, the prevalence of families with more than one wage earner, and the fact that the demand for leisure tends to increase at higher income levels.

Imagine a man laid off who is eligible for unemployment compensation and whose wife is working. He loses the income from work. But he receives as compensation one-half his regular wage. Moreover, this income is not subject to income or social security taxes so that the actual reduction in his income will be considerably less than half. How eager will he be to return to work? A worker loses his eligibility for unemployment compensation if he refuses to accept a job to which he has been referred as long as that job is comparable to the one he lost; so the system doesn't provide automatic paid vacations. But it's possible to behave during a job interview in a way that reduces the probability of a job offer. The point of this analysis, in any event, is not to argue that some of the officially unemployed are goldbricking but to suggest that unemployment of limited duration is not experienced as an economic disaster by *all* those who are laid off.

Toward Clarity of Goals

So the BLS statistics on employment and unemployment require considerable dissection and interpretation before they can serve as a guide to policy. No one has ever suggested that government policy should aim at a zero unemployment rate, a target that wasn't even reached at the height of World War II. *Some* unemployment is universally accepted as necessary if workers are to be allowed freedom of choice and if the labor market is

to function as a system for reassigning workers in an economy characterized by continual change both in technology and in the composition of
demand for products. How much unemployment ought to be accepted,
not as a problem but as a condition of freedom and fluidity? The answer
can't simply be stated as a percentage. The tolerable or desirable minimum
level of unemployment should and will increase as the opportunity cost
to workers of being unemployed goes down.

Moreover, there are many among the unemployed who will not readily
find work even if the aggregate demand for labor increases. It may prove
much more difficult to devise effective and politically acceptable ways to
offer income and work to many of the unemployed than we currently
realize. So government actions aimed at creating or maintaining a high and
steadily expanding demand for labor, important as they may be, cannot
be the whole of our labor policy.

UNIONS AND THE LABOR MARKET

Where do unions fit into all of this? Economic theorists have often been
criticized for treating unions as an afterthought in their analysis of labor
markets. Part of the reason is that union goals and behavior cannot be
fitted easily into the framework of economic analysis. Because the policies
of particular unions are shaped by internal political processes as well as
by the preferences of individual workers and employers, some economists
have chosen to assign the analysis of union behavior to political scientists
and sociologists. But unions play an important role in affecting the variables with which we're concerned in this chapter, and ignoring them
entails a serious omission.

The Context of Union Policies

We must remember at the beginning that although unions *bargain* with
employers, unions are not *competing* with employers. It is more correct to
say that unions attempt to become the exclusive seller of a particular input
to the production processes of employers or that they attempt to eliminate
competition among employees. The position of unions is analogous to
that of steel producers who want to sell to automobile makers. The steel
companies do not compete against the automobile companies; they compete rather against other steel companies and against companies that
produce substitutes for steel.

A major difference between the steel companies and the United Automobile Workers, both of which are selling inputs to automobile makers,
is that the UAW must deal with conflicting interests among its current

and potential members. Higher wage rates will mean fewer employment opportunities. How shall the union compromise between the desire of some for more jobs and the desire of others for higher wages? Workers who never obtain jobs in the automobile plants because of the high wage rates negotiated by the union can perhaps be ignored by union leaders; but unemployed union members have a vote and so their interests must be considered. Executives of steel companies, by contrast, don't have to weigh the preferences of the iron ore that must wait longer in the ground before finding employment if the price of steel is raised.

The goals and practices of unions often differ systematically between the two major types of labor union that exist in the United States. *Craft unions* are those with formal apprenticeship programs that train new members in specialized and fairly clearly defined skills. Craft unions include, among others, plumbers, carpenters, pipe fitters, and electricians. Members of a craft union belong to the union organizing their craft regardless of the employer for whom they work. Because some jobs are difficult to classify by craft, some crafts are represented by more than one union. The jurisdictional disputes that subsequently arise between craft unions are further evidence that unions are not competing against employers but against those who sell substitutes for their members' productive services.

Industrial unions are organizations of all the workers in a particular industry without regard to the kind of task they perform. Sometimes industrial unions will exempt those who work at crafts for which specific craft unions exist, but at other times industrial unions will attempt to include the craft workers employed in the industries they have organized. This is another prominent source of jurisdictional disputes between unions. The United Automobile Workers, the United Steel Workers, and the United Mine Workers are examples of major industrial unions.

Because of their control over the apprenticeship programs that are the means to certification as a skilled worker, craft unions can control the supply of workers available to employers. If they can also limit employers' options for substituting other workers or capital for the services of their members, craft unions will have substantial market power. And craft union members do in fact tend to be well paid. Industrial unions, on the other hand, must accept as members whomever the industry hires. Unable effectively to limit the supply of potential employees, industrial unions are reduced to bargaining for higher wages while insisting on the seniority rights of members in order to prevent employers from substituting workers who would accept a lower wage.

The Effects of Unions

To most people it seems obvious that unions raise the income of workers. Economists aren't that sure. If fewer workers are demanded at higher wage rates and the demand for labor is elastic, the total wage bill will decline as a result of union success in bargaining for higher wages. The workers still employed in the organized crafts or industries will gain. But those excluded from employment by the higher wage rates will lose. They will be forced to accept employment elsewhere on less advantageous terms.

The question of the effect of unions on wages divides into at least three separate questions: (1) What has been their effect on the average level of money wages? (2) What has been their effect on the average level of real wages? (Insofar as prices increase as a consequence of wage increases, real wages do not increase.) (3) What has been their effect on the relative wages of unionized and nonunionized workers? Professor H. Gregg Lewis investigated the last question in a major study published in 1963, *Unionism and Relative Wages in the United States.* After examining more than twenty different industries and crafts, he concluded that, apart from periods of unusually rapid inflation, unions increased their members' wages relative to nonunion workers by at least 10%, and lowered the relative wages of nonunion workers by about 2%. He also concluded that the relative effect of unions has not been larger than 20% at any time since the late 1930s. The impact of unionism on relative wage inequality among all workers has been small, less than 6%, with the direction of the effect (toward more or less inequality) uncertain. During periods of unusually rapid inflation, the relative wages of unionized workers have lagged behind the wage increases of nonunion workers, because the length of union contracts has tended to lock members into relatively infrequent wage increases.

It also appears that the effect of unionization on the total share of national income going to labor has been small. The portion of the civilian labor force that was unionized grew from 3% to 22% between 1900 and 1945. Since then it has fluctuated between 22% and 26%, with the peak of 26% occurring in 1953. During the same period labor's share of national income has increased very slightly, from about 70% during the decade 1900–1909 to about 77% during the decade 1930–1939, and has remained fairly constant since. A slightly different measure, the ratio of wage and salary income to total nonagricultural personal income, varied between .65 and .75 during the period 1930–1974. Thus there is no evidence to show that increasing unionization has substantially enlarged the share of national income going to employees.

Many Americans believe that labor unions have been an important force in raising the income and improving the job conditions of working people, and that without them the benefits of economic growth in the United States over the last century would have been much less widely dispersed. It is difficult to separate the effects of unions from the effects of other factors, such as rising productivity, that have also been operating

Table 16D TOTAL MEMBERSHIP IN NATIONAL UNIONS AND
EMPLOYEE ASSOCIATIONS IN THE UNITED STATES, 1970

Membership and unions	Number of members	
Membership claimed by all national and international unions with headquarters in the United States...		20,690,000
Less: number outside the United States..............		1,470,000
Membership of national and international unions in the United States...		19,220,000
Add membership of locals directly affiliated with AFL-CIO...	62,000	
Add membership in single firm and local unaffiliated unions....................................	475,000	537,000
Total union membership..		19,757,000
Add membership of professional State employees associations	1,868,000	
Less: number outside the United States..............	8,000	
Add membership of municipal employee associations[1]..	235,000	
Total association membership		2,095,000
Total union and associations membership in United States...		21,852,000

Source: Bureau of Labor Statistics.

1. See Municipal Public Employees Associations (BLS Bulletin 1702, 1971). Membership adjusted to account for duplication.

to alter wages and working conditions. Unions often receive credit (or blame) for changes that would have taken place without them, though perhaps not at quite the same time or in exactly the same way. Economic theory cautions against exaggerating the impact of unions. They must pursue their objectives within the constraints imposed by the demand for labor. A higher price for any input means a smaller quantity of it will be demanded, so that unions are far from being able to redistribute income as they please.

One very important source of restraint on union power is the competition faced by the employers with whom unions bargain. Firms that are price takers cannot raise their prices to cover union-won wage increases, so that any gains must come from the returns that would otherwise have gone to the owners of other productive resources employed in the business. But over a longer period of time these resources will not be available to cooperate with unionized workers if they are not adequately compensated. The firms with whom unions bargain may go out of business or be replaced by nonunion firms. This constraint is not really avoided if the union organizes *all* the firms in an industry. These firms will still have an incentive to shift toward labor-economizing production processes, and they will still be facing competition from firms in other industries.

The possibilities for substitution in both production and consumption are enormous and extremely difficult for unions to control. Even when firms are price searchers, so that they can to some extent increase their prices to cover higher wages, the higher prices will reduce the quantity of the product demanded and hence the demand for labor to produce that product. If a union organizes an industry of price-taking firms, the union may in effect search for the optimal price for the industry's product with the same result: the higher the price, the less product sold and the fewer workers hired.

Federal Labor Legislation

When Congress passed the National Labor Relations Act (Wagner Act) in 1935, it became the official policy of the federal government to promote unionization of employees and collective bargaining. Many of the tactics previously used by employers to resist the organization of their workers or to avoid bargaining with unions over wages and working conditions were declared to be "unfair labor practices."[1] The legislation was significantly amended in 1947 (Taft-Hartley Act) to include a list of "unfair labor practices" in which unions were forbidden to engage; but the basic policy of encouraging collective bargaining was not altered. The consequences of this policy, as we have suggested, are difficult to determine with precision or confidence. The notion that employees acquire property rights in jobs for which they have been hired has undoubtedly increased job security for employed workers and reduced the extent to which workers are treated arbitrarily by employers and supervisors. The development of union-enforced grievance procedures in many industries and crafts is one major consequence of the National Labor Relations Act.

But the gains have not been made without some costs: systems of job classification and assignment that promote waste; restrictions on the power of managers to innovate; reduced opportunities for workers not fortunate enough to obtain craft certification or jobs in firms organized by powerful

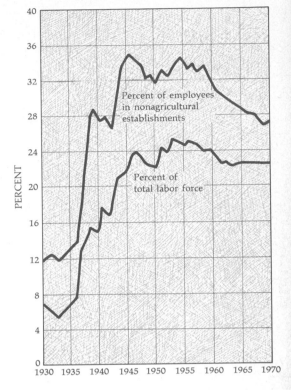

Source: Bureau of Labor Statistics.

Figure 16R Union membership as a percent of total labor force and of employees in nonagricultural establishments, 1930–70

---

1. Unions are exempt from the Sherman Act's prohibitions of combinations in restraint of trade or attempts to monopolize (unless they combine or conspire with employers). The Supreme Court ruled in 1941 that Congress could not simultaneously intend to promote collective bargaining *and* to subject unions to the Sherman Act. The Court's decision invited Congress to clarify its intentions through further legislation if this ruling was incorrect.

Table 16E SOURCES OF PERSONAL INCOME 1929–74 (in billions of dollars)

Year	Total Personal Income	Nonagricultural Personal Income	Wage and Salary Disbursements	Other Labor Income	Total Labor Income	Ratio (Total Labor to Total Personal Income)	Ratio (Total Labor to Nonagricultural Income)
1929	85.9	77.6	50.4	0.6	51.0	.594	.657
1933	47.0	43.2	29.0	0.4	29.4	.625	.681
1939	72.8	66.9	45.9	0.6	46.5	.639	.695
1940	78.3	72.3	49.8	0.7	50.5	.645	.698
1941	96.0	87.8	62.1	0.7	61.8	.644	.704
1942	122.9	111.0	82.1	0.9	83.0	.675	.748
1943	151.3	137.3	105.6	1.1	106.7	.705	.777
1944	165.3	151.2	116.9	1.5	118.4	.716	.783
1945	171.1	156.4	117.5	1.8	119.3	.697	.763
1946	178.7	161.0	112.0	1.9	113.9	.637	.707
1947	191.3	173.0	123.0	2.3	125.3	.655	.724
1948	210.2	183.4	135.3	2.7	138.0	.657	.752
1949	207.2	191.3	134.6	3.0	137.6	.664	.719
1950	227.6	210.9	146.7	3.8	150.5	.661	.714
1951	255.6	236.4	171.0	4.8	175.8	.688	.744
1952	272.5	254.1	185.1	5.3	190.4	.699	.749
1953	288.2	271.9	198.3	6.0	204.3	.709	.751
1954	290.1	274.7	196.5	6.3	202.8	.699	.738
1955	310.9	296.4	211.3	7.3	218.6	.703	.738
1956	333.0	318.5	227.8	8.4	236.2	.709	.742
1957	351.1	336.6	238.7	9.5	248.2	.707	.737
1958	361.2	344.3	239.9	9.9	249.8	.692	.726
1959	383.5	368.5	258.2	11.3	269.5	.703	.731
1960	401.0	385.2	270.8	12.0	282.8	.705	.734
1961	416.8	400.0	278.1	12.7	290.8	.698	.727
1962	442.6	425.5	296.1	13.9	310.0	.700	.729
1963	465.5	448.1	311.1	14.9	326.0	.700	.728
1964	497.5	480.9	333.7	16.6	350.3	.704	.728
1965	538.9	519.5	358.9	18.7	377.6	.701	.727
1966	587.2	566.3	394.5	20.7	415.2	.707	.733
1967	629.3	609.4	423.1	22.3	445.4	.708	.731
1968	688.9	668.8	464.9	25.4	490.3	.712	.733
1969	750.9	728.3	509.7	28.4	538.1	.717	.739
1970	808.3	784.8	542.0	32.2	574.2	.710	.732
1971	864.0	840.0	573.0	36.4	609.4	.705	.725
1972	944.9	916.5	626.8	41.7	668.5	.707	.729
1973	1055.0	1008.0	691.7	46.0	737.7	.699	.732
1974	1150.4	1108.9	751.1	51.4	802.5	.698	.724

Source: Bureau of Economic Analysis.

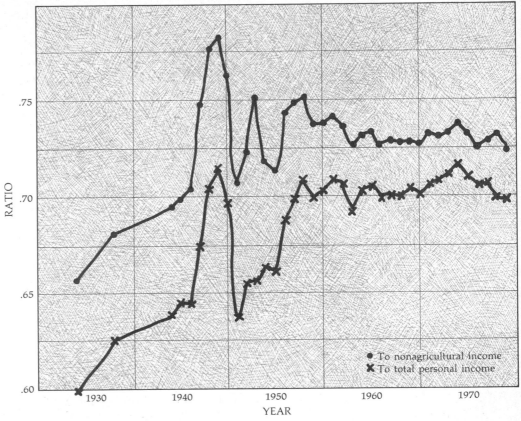

Source: Table 16E

Figure 16S Ratios of total labor income to total personal income and to nonagricultural income

industrial unions. Have unions also been responsible, as some argue, for higher unemployment rates? Or have they been, as far more people seem to believe, a major cause of inflation in the period since World War II? The last two questions relate to the topics of the following chapters. But we will not be in a good position to answer them until we have inquired more deeply into the nature and causes of fluctuations in the aggregate level of economic activity.

Once Over Lightly

The study of aggregate fluctuations in the level of economic activity, or of recessions and inflations, their causes and cures, is widely known as macroeconomics.

Macroeconomics makes extensive use of statistical series on prices, output, income, and employment. Intelligent use of this information requires understanding of the theories and concepts that have been used to construct the series.

The most widely used measure of recession and perhaps the most politically significant index of aggregate economic activity is the unemployment rate calculated each month by the Bureau of Labor Statistics.

The key concepts for understanding the unemployment rate are the noninstitutional population and the labor force. To be officially unemployed one must be in the labor force, and to be counted in the labor force one must first be included in the noninstitutional population. The noninstitutional population includes all those over sixteen years of age who are not inmates of institutions. The labor force includes all members of the noninstitutional population who are either working, absent for such reasons as illness, strikes, or accidents, waiting to resume a job or begin a new one, or actively looking for work. The official unemployment rate is the sum of the latter two categories divided by the civilian labor force (the total labor force minus members of the armed forces).

The total of those unemployed can and sometimes does rise at the same time as the total of those employed. This implies that the labor force is increasing faster than unemployment is increasing. Sometimes an increase in unemployment may even cause a further increase in unemployment by stimulating a higher rate of labor force participation.

Economic analysis of labor markets assumes that people choose whether or not to seek work and to accept or reject particular job offers by weighing the attractiveness of leisure against its opportunity cost. Leisure in this context means all nonmarket uses of time, and the opportunity cost of leisure is the wage rate that is sacrificed.

At higher wage rates, leisure becomes more expensive and so tends to be purchased less, which is to say that people supply more time to the labor market. This may be called the substitution effect of the increase in the price of leisure: people choose to substitute for leisure more of the goods that money income can buy. But an increase in the price of leisure has another important effect that tends to nudge choice in the opposite direction. An increase in the price of leisure, corresponding to an increase in the wage rate, implies an increase in income. The demand curve for leisure may shift upward to the right as income increases, so that ultimately more rather than less leisure is "purchased" when its price rises.

The demand for labor is determined by employers' estimates of the marginal contribution labor will make to revenue in particular production processes. When the cost to an employer of finding and training new workers is substantial, however, he may retain workers whose marginal dollar product is expected to be temporarily below their marginal cost.

Since people choose, by comparing the expected cost and value to them of alternative opportunities, whether or not to enter the labor force and whether or not to accept a particular job offer, employment and unemployment are the consequence of people's choices in given situations.

The employment rate is the total number of people in civilian employment divided by the noninstitutional population. For some purposes this is a better measure of the job situation than the unemployment rate, because the defining concepts can be more easily and objectively measured.

$$\frac{employed}{noninsti. pop.} = employment\ rate$$

The notion that unemployment results from people's choice of the best option available to them is consistent with empirical data on rates of labor force participation and the frequency and duration of unemployment for different categories of the population. The only defensible goal for employment policy is improvement of the range of opportunities available to people.

The aggregate level of economic activity is one factor determining job opportunities. Others include the skills and work habits of workers and the cultural practices and prejudices of employers and employees.

Labor unions attempt to control the supply of labor to employers and to limit competition for jobs among employees. Unions do not single-mindedly pursue higher wage rates, however, because this goal conflicts with the goal of more employment opportunities. Internal political processes will therefore shape the goals and behavior of particular unions.

An important distinction to make in predicting union behavior is the distinction between unions that can control entry to the occupation and those that cannot. Craft unions typically have more market power than industrial unions, because they can more directly limit the number of workers who are certified as eligible for particular jobs.

The fact that collective bargaining affects employment as well as wage rates means that unions affect the distribution of income among workers as well as the distribution between wage earners and employers or owners of other productive resources. The numerous possibilities for substitution in production and consumption when particular wages rise set closer limitations upon union power than the public commonly assumes.

QUESTIONS FOR DISCUSSION

1. Suppose that a manufacturing firm locates a plant in an economically undeveloped country and finds, as it raises its wage rates to attract additional workers, that the supply curve of labor at first rises to the right and then turns backward and rises to the left (somewhat like the right-hand parenthesis that closes this explanation).

(*a*) Explain the shape of the supply curve in terms of the demand for leisure, using the concepts of the substitution effect and the income effect of changes in the price of leisure.

(*b*) Can you think of reasons why the backward-bending portion of the supply curve might disappear over a longer period of time?

2. Is the cost to an employer of finding and training workers part of his sunk costs or of his marginal costs? What is the significance of this distinction in explaining layoff policies during a recession?

3. The questions below ask you to think critically about the relationships between the total population, the noninstitutional population, and the labor force.

(*a*) Is it desirable or undesirable for the noninstitutional population to decrease relative to the total population? Explain your answer.

(*b*) Why do you suppose that the BLS in 1947 raised the cutoff age level for inclusion in the noninstitutional population from fourteen to sixteen? Do you think it should be even higher today? Why or why not?

(*c*) What would happen to the rate of labor force participation (the total labor force as a percent of the noninstitutional population) under each of the following circumstances?

(i) Sudden, large-scale layoffs occur in major manufacturing industries.

(ii) The government puts effective pressure on employers to end sex discrimination in hiring.

(iii) Educational reforms increase the ratio of learning to teaching in the schools and also make schooling a more enjoyable experience.

(iv) The public becomes convinced that additional years of schooling are not likely to result in better job opportunities.

(v) Changes in life style occur and people move toward greater participation in family and community projects and less purchasing of commodities and services (for example, more neighborhood softball teams and less attendance at professional baseball games; more church suppers and fewer restaurant meals; neighborhood sharing of lawnmowers, washers and driers, car pools and swimming pools).

(vi) Inflation raises substantially the cost of food, clothing, and housing.

4. "Full employment" of the labor force is often said to be an important goal for government economic policy.

(*a*) What is meant by full employment of the labor force? Would you favor policies to secure *full* employment at all times?

(*b*) Why do you think it is that economic commentators tend to define employment as 96% to 97% employment of the labor force? (That is, we are deemed to have achieved full employment when the BLS data show that unemployment is down to 4% or at best 3% of the labor force.) How do they know that it should be 96% rather than 95% or even less?

(c) Are the people being counted as unemployed in a period of full employment (as defined above) voluntarily unemployed? Can you find evidence to support the claim that jobs are always available?

(d) If the BLS unemployment figure rises to 6%, are all the unemployed still to be thought of as voluntarily unemployed? Defend your answer.

5. Can there be "overfull" employment?

(a) Suppose that the vacancy rate on apartments in a large city is less than 1%. What undesirable consequences might be associated with such a full level of apartment employment? Would you enjoy moving to a city with such a low vacancy rate?

(b) If you are driving on only 80% of the automobile tires you own, is the spare tire unemployed? Would you like to be driving with your tires at "full employment"? Across the Great Salt Lake Desert?

6. Jones is a tool and die maker earning $8 an hour. He is suddenly laid off.

(a) He frequents employment agencies, reads want ads, and follows up leads on tool and die making jobs for two weeks. Is he involuntarily unemployed during this time?

(b) At the end of the two weeks he is offered a job driving a bread truck that pays $4.50 an hour. He turns it down. Is he involuntarily unemployed?

(c) He receives an offer of a job as a tool and die maker in a city 125 miles away. He turns it down because his teenage children don't want to change high schools. Is he involuntarily unemployed?

(d) After three months of searching, Jones becomes discouraged and quits looking. Is he involuntarily unemployed? Or is he no longer in the labor force?

7. Which of the following situations does *not* result in voluntary unemployment?

(a) Smith quits his job because his employer requires him to start work at 4 A.M.

(b) Smith is fired when he refuses to do something that his employer orders him to do but which he considers unethical.

(c) Would your answer be different if the act ordered by Smith's employer were also illegal?

(d) Smith is told that he can continue in his job only if he accepts a 75% cut in wages; he quits.

8. A person who is laid off from his job goes to work for himself (becomes self-employed) "producing" information about alternative job opportuni-

ties. How long he will remain self-employed in this way depends on his "productivity" (is he generating what he considers valuable information?) and the opportunity cost of this self-employment. (He'll want to continue as long as his anticipated marginal revenue exceeds anticipated marginal cost.) How will the duration of measured unemployment be affected by

(*a*) unemployment compensation?

(*b*) food stamp programs?

(*c*) persistent rumors that many large firms are beginning to hire?

(*d*) a spirit of confidence and optimism?

9. Are the hypothetical individuals who made each of the statements below voluntarily or involuntarily unemployed? How would they be classified by most people? Why would you agree or disagree with the usual classification? It is important to notice that statements such as *h* and *i* may not express different situations at all. "I don't want to work (at any job I can find)" may mean "I can't find a job (at which I want to work)."

(*a*) "I quit my job and I'm going to remain unemployed until I find a job that pays $1000 for ten hours' work a week."

(*b*) "I was laid off last month. I had a great job as marketing consultant to a franchising chain. They paid me $1000 a week for about ten hours of work. I'm going to keep looking until I find another job like that one."

(*c*) "I decided I could no longer be a part of the military-industrial complex; so I quit my job. I'm looking now for an engineer's position that doesn't require me to participate in murder, pollution, and mind-raping."

(*d*) "When Boeing laid me off, I figured I could quickly find another job in engineering. But now I don't care. I'll take any job at all that pays what I used to get."

(*e*) "I've been out of work for six months and I'm pretty desperate. I'll do anything that's legal to get food for my family. But I have an invalid wife and five small children, so I can't take any job that pays less than $100 a week."

(*f*) "I could get any one of a dozen jobs tomorrow. But I don't want to. I'm eligible for three more months of unemployment compensation, so I'm just going to take it easy until the checks run out. Oh, if something really good turned up, I'd take it, of course."

(*g*) "I could get any one of a dozen jobs tomorrow. But I don't want to. I'm eligible for three more months of unemployment compensation, so I'm just going to spend my time really looking. I'm going to use those three months to find the very best job I can possibly get."

(*h*) "I don't want to work."

(*i*) "I can't find a job."

10. Economists generally assume that business firms try to maximize profits. What do unions try to maximize? Wage rates? The wage bill (wage rates times the number employed)? Is the maximization assumption useful in the analysis of union behavior? Do you think the analysis of chapter 15 is more helpful than the analysis of chapter 10 in understanding the bargaining policies of labor unions?

11. Why is a union of textile workers in New England willing to spend money to organize textile workers in North Carolina? Why do unions fight for increases in the legal minimum wage even though all their members are being paid more than the minimum wage? Why do unions oppose exempting teenagers from coverage under the minimum-wage laws? Do you agree that each of these cases shows "the class solidarity of unionized workers"? Who would be threatened by failure to secure each of the objectives mentioned? What do these cases suggest by way of an answer to the question, With whom do unions compete?

12. Craft unions in the United States have long been notorious for discriminating against blacks. Industrial unions, on the other hand, have a record of actively supporting legislation directed against racially discriminatory practices in society? How would you explain this difference?

13. List some of the ways in which employers might hold down their wage costs in the face of a union-won increase in the wage rate. What will be the effects on employment? On the distribution of income? Why would you expect the demand for labor to prove more elastic the longer the time period over which one measures it?

14. The unemployment rate in the United States economy has tended to drift upward since World War II. That is shown in column 2 of table 16C and, we predict, the trend will continue through the decade of the 1970s. Why has this occurred? Does it represent, as some maintain, a growing inability of the economy to provide jobs? Or does it stem from changing valuations of market and nonmarket opportunities, changing family income levels, changing costs of being unemployed, and similar factors that do not necessarily represent social problems? How shall we decide on a target rate of unemployment for public policy to aim at?

TOTAL OUTPUT AND
THE PRICE LEVEL

The experience of the Great Depression lent added impetus to private efforts that had begun in the United States around 1920 to compile reliable information on the overall performance of the economy. The best-known statistical series evolving out of these efforts is the national income and product accounts compiled by the Bureau of Economic Analysis (called the Office of Business Economics until 1972) in the United States Department of Commerce. If you read only the front page of the daily newspaper, you will have heard about gross national product. This is the most comprehensive item in the Department of Commerce accounts and the one most frequently quoted. Some people watch the behavior of GNP, as it is familiarly known, with the intensity of small boys on the morning of a picnic listening to the weather report.

MEASURING TOTAL OUTPUT:
THE INCOME AND PRODUCT ACCOUNTS

What is the *gross national product?* It is *the market value of all the final goods produced in the entire economy in a year.* (The term *goods* includes both commodities and services.) In 1974 the gross national product of the United States was $1379.4 billion. That number and most of the other numbers in this chapter and the preceding one are subject to minor revisions for recent months, quarters, or years as more complete estimates become available. But the revisions very rarely entail significant changes that alter our basic conception of what has been occurring.

What does GNP attempt to measure? And what can we learn by examining its behavior over time? We shall necessarily simplify. If you don't trust simplifications, you may consult the annual National Income Issue (usually the July issue) of the *Survey of Current Business*, a publication of the Bureau of Economic Analysis, where you will find enough numbers to keep you thoroughly occupied for days.

Total Output Is Total Income

As the phrase "income and product" suggests, there are two ways to look at the statistics in the system of accounts. Calculated in one way, they measure *the value of what is produced.* On the other side of the coin, they measure the *income earned* by the producers. The value created in one year by all the productive resources of the nation will be equal to the income made available to the owners of those resources, after appropriate adjustments. The reason, of course, is that real income can come only from output and that every output constitutes income for someone. This necessary link between income and output (or product) provides part of the logical foundation for a method of analyzing aggregate fluctuations that we'll be examining in subsequent chapters.

Gross national product in 1974 was calculated at $1397.4 billion. The income made available to individuals and households in 1974, for them to spend or save, was $979.7 billion. This latter figure is labeled *disposable personal income.* (It's often referred to simply as *disposable income.*) The difference between the two arises from deductions that governments and businesses make from the total value of output before it becomes available as disposable income. Business firms retain some of the income (output) produced in order to cover wear and tear on capital equipment associated with the year's production; in addition, corporations characteristically retain a portion of their net earnings rather than pay it all out to owners. Governments levy taxes of various sorts, and this is, as everyone knows, a very large deduction from gross income. But governments and, to a much lesser extent, private firms, also pay out income to persons in what are called transfer payments. In the income and product accounts, these are income payments to persons that are *not* made in return for productive services being currently rendered; pensions, social security benefits, and welfare payments are examples. The sum of these deductions, net of the additions, roughly makes up the difference between gross national product and disposable income.

The magnitude of the difference—$1397.4 versus $979.7 billion in 1974—may prompt you to look skeptically at our previous assertion that output equals income "after appropriate adjustments." An elephant is just like a rabbit, too, "after appropriate adjustments." But the differences are also income. Taxes are income claimed by government, and the deductions made by business firms are their attempt to hang on to some income rather than pay it all out to the owners of the firms. If we think of the economy as divided into three sectors—consumers, business firms, and government—we can calculate the approximate portion of the year's output (gross national product) claimed as income by each sector. Consumers received disposable income of $979.7 billion in 1974, which was about 70% of the gross national income. Tax revenue minus government transfer payments approximated 18% of gross national product, and this we could call the net income of government. Business firms appropriated as their income the remaining 12%. (Be careful. That 12% implies nothing about the relative importance of the business sector. It is roughly the sum of undistributed corporate profits and depreciation allowances. We have called this *business income,* because it is income not at the disposal of consumers or government.)

Where Did the Output Go?

Income is desired because it permits the purchase of commodities and services. Who finally purchased the 1.4 trillion dollars worth of goods produced in 1974? A slightly different classification system may be used to answer this question. The potential purchasers of goods may be divided into consumers, government, and investors. Personal consumption expenditures by Americans in 1974 came to $876.7 billion. Federal, state, and local government purchases of goods totaled $309.2 billion. Domestic investors purchased $209.4 billion. And the remaining $2.1 billion was our net exports to foreign consumers, investors, or governments.

Investment is a key concept in economics and is defined as *the purchase of capital. Capital means goods that will be employed in the production of future commodities or services.* The distinction between an investment expenditure and a consumption expenditure will inevitably be somewhat arbitrary. An amateur tennis player purchases a racket for the sake of the future services he expects it to provide. Is the racket a consumption or an investment good? Family automobiles are also purchased for the sake of future services. A kitchen blender is an investment inasmuch as it is obtained for the sake of the goods it will produce in the future. But the income and product accounts nonetheless classify all these purchases as consumption

expenditures except when they are made by business firms. If you buy a water cooler for your patio, that's a consumption expenditure. If one is purchased for the office where you work, that's an investment expenditure. The only such purchase by households that qualifies as investment in these accounts is the purchase of new housing. Here the stream of services extends so far into the future that it seems unduly misleading to count the purchase of a new residence as consumption. But the difference between automobiles and residences is one of degree. Consumers, of course, usually don't worry about these fine accounting distinctions, and consider the purchase of a durable household good an investment. People say, quite correctly, that they "invested" in a clothes dryer, or a dining-room set, or new carpeting. That is completely consistent with our definition of investment. But accountants must make distinctions even when they are somewhat arbitrary.

The components of investment as measured by the Bureau of Economic Analysis are (*a*) residential construction, (*b*) purchases of new business structures (offices, factories, stores), (*c*) purchases of new durable equipment (machinery), and (*d*) net additions to business inventories. The last item makes sure that everything produced is counted as purchased by someone. If a business firm finds itself unable to sell all the output it has produced, it is considered to have purchased that output itself and added it, perhaps reluctantly, to inventory.

In 1974 these components of investment were calculated as follows:[1]

Residential construction	$46.0 billion
Nonresidential construction	52.0
Producers durable equipment	97.1
Addition to business inventories	14.2
	$209.4

Foreigners imported $140.2 billion of American goods in 1974 while the U.S. was importing $138.1 billion in foreign goods. So net exports (exports minus imports) took $2.1 billion of goods, the last component of gross national product. The significance of this component may vastly exceed its size; but that question will be reserved until chapter 23.

The sum of consumer, government, investor, and net foreign purchases of new goods in 1974 was $1397.4 billion, the exact amount calculated as the gross national income. To be perfectly honest, the totals will never match exactly, because there are bound to be errors and omissions in the measurement of such vast and variegated quantities as total national income and total expenditures on new goods. But since they are equal by definition, the Bureau of Economic Analysis adjusts national income with a fudge factor which it calls Statistical Discrepancy.

The Historical Record

The history of gross national product and some of its components since 1929 is summarized in table 17A. All figures represent billions of dollars, and are rounded to the nearest tenth of a billion.

As we noted earlier, recessions and depressions are marked by an increase in measured unemployment. They are also marked, as we would expect, by a decline in the rate of growth of gross national product. If you pick out from table 16C the years since World War II in which unemployment rose sharply, you will find that they are years in which gross national product either declined from the previous year (1949), remained basically unchanged (1954), or rose by a substantially smaller percentage than in the immediately preceding years (1958, 1961). The years 1970 and 1974 only *appear* to be an exception: the decline in GNP in these years is concealed by a rapid rise in prices (of which we'll say more a bit later). The decade of the 1930s has a whole sad history of its own.

1. The total is the correct figure for 1974. Components do not sum to the total because the component figures have been rounded off.

Table 17A GROSS NATIONAL PRODUCT AND COMPONENTS
(in billions of dollars)

Year	Gross National Product	Personal Consumption Expenditures	Gross Private Domestic Investment	Net Exports of Goods and Services	Government Purchases of Goods and Services	DISPOSABLE PERSONAL INCOME
1929	103.1	77.2	16.2	1.1	8.5	83.3
1930	90.4	69.9	10.3	1.0	9.2	74.5
1931	75.8	60.5	5.6	.5	9.2	64.0
1932	58.0	48.6	1.0	.4	8.1	48.7
1933	55.6	45.8	1.4	.4	8.0	45.5
1934	65.1	51.3	3.3	.6	9.8	52.4
1935	72.2	55.7	6.4	.1	10.0	58.5
1936	82.5	61.9	8.5	.1	12.0	66.3
1937	90.4	66.5	11.8	.3	11.9	71.2
1938	84.7	63.9	6.5	1.3	13.0	65.5
1939	90.5	66.8	9.3	1.1	13.3	70.3
1940	99.7	70.8	13.1	1.7	14.0	75.7
1941	124.5	80.6	17.9	1.3	24.8	92.7
1942	157.9	88.5	9.8	.0	59.6	116.9
1943	191.6	99.3	5.7	−2.0	88.6	133.5
1944	210.1	108.3	7.1	−1.8	96.5	146.3
1945	211.9	119.7	10.6	−.6	82.3	150.2
1946	208.5	143.4	30.6	7.5	27.0	160.0
1947	231.3	160.7	34.0	11.5	25.1	169.8
1948	257.6	173.6	46.0	6.4	31.6	189.1
1949	256.5	176.8	35.7	6.1	37.8	188.6
1950	284.8	191.0	54.1	1.8	37.9	206.9
1951	328.4	206.3	59.3	3.7	59.1	226.6
1952	345.5	216.7	51.9	2.2	74.7	238.3
1953	364.6	230.0	52.6	.4	81.6	252.6
1954	364.8	236.5	51.7	1.8	74.8	257.4
1955	398.0	254.4	67.4	2.0	74.2	275.3
1956	419.2	266.7	70.0	4.0	78.6	293.2
1957	441.1	281.4	67.9	5.7	86.1	308.5
1958	447.3	290.1	60.9	2.2	94.2	318.8
1959	483.7	311.2	75.3	.1	97.0	337.3
1960	503.7	325.2	74.8	4.0	99.6	350.0
1961	520.1	335.2	71.7	5.6	107.6	364.4
1962	560.3	355.1	83.0	5.1	117.1	385.3
1963	590.5	375.0	87.1	5.9	122.5	404.6
1964	632.4	401.2	94.0	8.5	128.7	438.1
1965	684.9	432.8	108.1	6.9	137.0	473.2
1966	749.9	466.3	121.4	5.3	156.8	511.9
1967	793.9	492.1	116.6	5.2	180.1	546.3
1968	864.2	536.2	126.0	2.5	199.6	591.0
1969	930.3	579.5	139.0	1.9	210.0	634.4
1970	977.1	617.6	136.3	3.6	219.5	691.7
1971	1054.9	667.1	153.7	−.2	234.2	746.4
1972	1158.0	729.0	179.3	−6.0	255.7	802.5
1973	1294.9	805.2	209.4	3.9	276.4	903.7
1974	1397.4	876.7	209.4	2.1	309.2	979.7

Source: Bureau of Economic Analysis

RECESSION OR DEPRESSION?

What's the difference between a recession and a depression? According to the tired old joke, it's a recession when your neighbor loses his job and a depression when you lose yours. There is actually no agreed upon statistical measure that precisely defines a recession or a depression. By common consent, the National Bureau of Economic Research, a private nonprofit research organization that has been measuring aggregate economic fluctuations for more than half a century, makes the "official" determination of recession. The bureau, however, does not even employ the category of depression. What is widely known as the Great Depression of the 1930s is treated by the NBER as two recessions (1929–33 and 1937–38) with associated periods of recovery.

The Structure of the Income and Product Accounts

In addition to gross national product and disposable personal income, the Bureau of Economic Analysis calculates three other measures of the nation's annual income and product flow. Because they are sometimes mentioned in the public press, they will be briefly described here.

Personal income is disposable personal income prior to the subtraction of personal taxes.

National income is a bit confusing in that the term is sometimes used to describe the entire system of accounts while also referring to one particular concept within the system. National income in the latter and narrow sense is the total income earned by owners of productive resources, or the total of wages, profits, rental income, and interest income. The BEA computes it by adding together the compensation of employees; the net income of professionals, farm proprietors, and unincorporated businesses; corporate profits; rental income earned by persons; and net interest.

Net national product is gross national product after allowances for capital consumption have been deducted. These allowances are a rough measure of the value of productive equipment used up in the process of turning out a year's goods. Consequently net national product would be a better measure of annual output than gross national product were it not for one drawback: the measurement of capital consumption allowances (or depreciation) is very rough indeed, inconsistent from year to year, and arbitrary at the outset in deciding what shall count as capital.

Given the ultimate identity in the value of income and output, or the fact that they are merely two views of the same thing, why aren't net national product and national income identical? Net national product is the nation's (net) output calculated in terms of expenditures for final products. National income is the same thing calculated by means of the receipts of those who sell the final products. Aren't these the same? They would be except for sales taxes, certain transfer payments made by business firms, some complications introduced by government business operations and subsidies, and the statistical discrepancy which equates income to output. The difference between net national product and national income, then, is primarily the amount of indirect business taxes (a somewhat more inclusive category than sales taxes as usually understood). In 1974 net national product was $1277.9 billion and national income was $1143.0, with indirect business taxes comprising 94% of the difference.

What about the relation between national income and personal or disposable personal income? That's a little more complicated but simple enough in principle. National income is the total of wages, profits, interest, and rent earned from the sale of new products. Disposable personal income is the income that actually becomes available to persons or households to spend or save. A large chunk of national income goes to taxes, especially corporate profits taxes, social security taxes, and personal income taxes. In addition, corporations retain a portion of their earnings as undistributed corporate profits. Then there are two additions to the income stream that in 1974 more than made up for the subtractions: transfer payments by business or government (but especially by government) and the net interest paid by the government and by consumers. It would take too long to explain why the BEA treats government and consumer interest payments as transfer payments rather than as contributions to national income. Unless you decide to specialize in national income accounting, you had better just accept it as one of those odd facts of classification, such as the ladybugs which entomologists say are actually beetles rather than bugs.

Table 17B presents the skeleton of the income and product accounts for selected years from 1929 through 1974 and quarterly data for 1974. Note that the quarterly data are *seasonally adjusted* totals at *annual rates.* (If the meaning of those terms is not intuitively clear, read the accompanying insert.) Undistributed corporate profits and corporate profits taxes are subtracted from national income by first subtracting the total of corporate profits and then adding dividends, since the sum of dividends, taxes, and retained earnings is the total of corporate profits. Notice that what the Bureau of Economic Analysis calls personal outlays differs from personal consumption expenditures by the total of consumer interest payments and personal transfer payments to foreigners. These last two components of personal expenditures are not regarded as purchases of final goods and hence do not enter into the expenditures that sum to the gross national product.

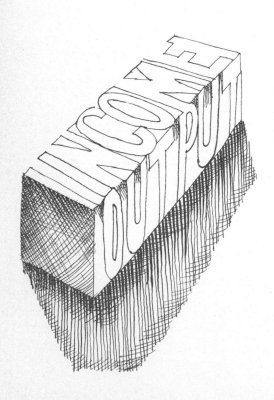

Table 17B RELATION OF GROSS NATIONAL PRODUCT, NET NATIONAL PRODUCT, NATIONAL INCOME, PERSONAL INCOME, AND DISPOSABLE PERSONAL INCOME
(in billions of dollars)

Item	1929	1933	1941	1950	1970	1971	1972	1973	1974	1974 I	1974 II	1974 III	1974 IV
Gross national product	103.1	55.6	124.5	284.8	977.1	1,054.9	1,158.0	1,294.9	1,397.4	1,358.8	1,383.8	1,416.3	1,430.9
Less: Capital consumption allowances	7.9	7.0	8.2	18.3	87.3	93.7	102.9	110.8	119.5	115.8	118.6	120.7	122.9
Equals: Net national product	95.2	48.6	116.3	266.4	889.8	961.2	1,055.1	1,184.1	1,277.9	1,243.0	1,265.2	1,295.6	1,308.0
Less: Indirect business tax and nontax liability	7.0	7.1	11.3	23.3	93.5	102.7	110.0	119.2	126.9	122.6	125.9	129.5	129.8
Business transfer payments	.6	.7	.5	.8	4.0	4.3	4.6	4.9	5.2	5.1	5.2	5.3	5.3
Statistical discrepancy	.7	.6	.4	1.5	−6.4	−2.3	−3.8	−5.0	.4	−6.3	.3	3.0	4.8
Plus: Subsidies less current surplus of government enterprises	−.1	....	.1	.2	1.7	1.1	2.3	.6	−2.9	−2.7	−3.7	−2.4	−2.7
Equals: National income	86.8	40.3	104.2	241.1	800.5	857.7	946.5	1,065.6	1,142.5	1,118.8	1,130.2	1,155.5	1,165.4
Less: Corporate profits and inventory valuation adjustment	10.5	−1.2	15.2	37.7	69.2	78.7	92.2	105.1	105.6	107.7	105.6	105.8	103.4
Contributions for social insurance	.2	.3	2.8	6.9	57.7	63.8	73.0	91.2	101.5	99.1	100.8	103.0	103.2
Excess of wage accruals over disbursements	....	....	....	....	.0	.6	.0	−.1	−.5	.0	−.6	−1.5	.0
Plus: Government transfer payments	.9	1.5	2.6	14.3	75.1	89.0	98.6	113.0	134.6	123.1	130.6	138.7	145.8
Net interest paid by government and consumers	2.5	1.6	2.2	7.2	31.0	31.2	33.0	38.3	42.3	40.8	41.9	42.7	43.6
Dividends	5.8	2.0	4.4	8.8	24.7	25.0	27.3	29.6	32.7	31.6	32.5	33.2	33.3
Business transfer payments	.6	.7	.5	.8	4.0	4.3	4.6	4.9	5.2	5.1	5.2	5.3	5.3
Equals: Personal income	85.9	47.0	96.0	227.6	808.3	864.0	944.9	1,055.0	1,150.5	1,112.5	1,134.6	1,168.2	1,186.9
Less: Personal tax and nontax payments	2.6	1.5	3.3	20.7	116.6	117.6	142.4	151.3	170.8	161.9	168.2	175.1	178.1
Equals: Disposable personal income	83.3	45.5	92.7	206.9	691.7	746.4	802.5	903.7	979.7	950.6	966.5	993.1	1,008.8

Source: Bureau of Economic Analysis

Table 17C NATIONAL INCOME
(in billions of dollars)

Item	1929	1933	1941	1950	1970	1971	1972	1973	1974	1974			
										I	II	III	IV
National Income	86.8	40.3	104.2	241.1	800.5	857.7	946.5	1,065.6	1,142.5	1,118.8	1,130.2	1,155.5	1,165.4
Compensation of employees	51.1	29.5	64.8	154.6	603.9	643.1	707.1	786.0	855.8	828.8	848.3	868.2	877.7
Wages and salaries	50.4	29.0	62.1	146.8	542.0	573.6	626.8	691.6	750.7	727.6	744.6	761.5	769.2
Private	45.5	23.9	51.9	124.4	426.9	449.5	491.4	545.1	592.4	573.8	588.3	602.5	605.1
Military	.3	.3	1.9	5.0	19.6	19.4	20.5	20.6	21.2	21.0	20.9	20.8	22.0
Government civilian	4.6	4.9	8.3	17.4	95.5	104.7	114.8	126.0	137.1	132.8	135.4	138.2	142.1
Supplements to wages and salaries	.7	.5	2.7	7.8	61.9	69.5	80.3	94.4	105.1	101.2	103.7	106.7	108.6
Employer contributions for social insurance	.1	.1	2.0	4.0	29.7	33.1	38.6	48.4	53.6	52.3	53.2	54.5	54.6
Other labor income	.6	.4	.7	3.8	32.2	36.4	41.7	46.0	51.4	48.9	50.5	52.3	54.0
Proprietors' income	15.1	5.9	17.5	37.5	66.9	69.2	75.9	96.1	93.0	98.4	89.9	92.1	91.6
Business and professional	9.0	3.3	11.1	24.0	50.0	52.0	54.9	57.6	61.2	59.3	60.7	62.3	62.5
Farm	6.2	2.6	6.4	13.5	16.9	17.2	21.0	38.5	31.8	39.1	29.1	29.8	29.1
Rental income of persons	5.4	2.0	3.5	9.4	23.9	25.2	25.9	26.1	26.5	26.4	26.3	26.6	26.8
Corporate profits and inventory valuation adjustment	10.5	− 1.2	15.2	37.7	69.2	78.7	92.2	105.1	105.6	107.7	105.6	105.8	103.4
Profits before tax	10.0	1.0	17.7	42.6	74.0	83.6	99.2	122.7	140.7	135.4	139.0	157.0	131.5
Profits tax liability	1.4	.5	7.6	17.8	34.8	37.5	41.5	49.8	55.7	52.2	55.9	62.7	52.0
Profits after tax	8.6	.4	10.1	24.9	39.3	46.1	57.7	72.9	85.0	83.2	83.1	94.3	79.5
Dividends	5.8	2.0	4.4	8.8	24.7	25.0	27.3	29.6	32.7	31.6	32.5	33.2	33.2
Undistributed Profits	2.8	− 1.6	5.7	16.0	14.6	21.1	30.3	43.3	52.4	51.6	50.5	61.1	46.2
Inventory valuation adjustment	.5	− 2.1	− 2.5	− 5.0	− 4.8	− 4.9	− 7.0	− 17.6	− 35.1	− 27.7	− 33.4	− 51.2	− 28.1
Net Interest	4.7	4.1	3.2	2.0	36.5	41.6	45.6	52.3	61.6	57.5	60.1	62.8	65.9

Table 17C shows the composition of national income (in the narrow sense) for the same years.

What Are We Actually Measuring?

The numbers in the tables of this chapter were all constructed by diligent effort and not just "discovered" in the way a child discovers crickets while aimlessly turning over rocks. They were put together by statisticians who wanted answers to certain kinds of questions and knew what they were looking for. The numerical data in the *Monthly Labor Review* or the *Survey of Current Business* represent many prior decisions about what should

SEASONAL ADJUSTMENTS

In June of each year the labor force increases more rapidly than available jobs as students seek summer employment. In December available jobs increase more rapidly than the labor force as employers look for temporary Christmas help. Measured unemployment will consequently tend to rise each June and to fall in December. The Bureau of Labor Statistics "corrects" its monthly data to compensate for such changes by means of what are called *seasonal adjustments.* The letters "S.A." accompanying monthly or quarterly economic data mean that the figures for each month or quarter have been adjusted to eliminate changes caused by seasonal fluctuations. This permits the data to show underlying trends more clearly.

Another common technique for making data easier to interpret is to state certain kinds of flows or rates of change on an *annual basis.* Quarterly data on gross national product, for example, are always presented at "seasonally adjusted annual rates"; the figures show how large GNP would be if the seasonally adjusted level in a particular quarter persisted for twelve months. Similarly, monthly changes in the Consumer Price Index are sometimes multiplied by twelve to show the rate of change on an annual basis. You're doing much the same thing when you read that you're being charged $1\frac{1}{2}\%$ per month interest on your unpaid Master Charge balance and you multiply by twelve to determine that you're paying 18% interest on an annual basis, which is the way interest rates are generally stated.

be counted, how measurements and estimates should be made, and how conflicting criteria should be employed. We'll be able to use these data more intelligently if we understand something of the way in which they're put together and what they do *not* tell us as well as what they do.

We defined gross national product as the value of all the final goods produced in the United States during a single year. In doing so we glided quickly past a fundamental question: What counts as a final good and what does not? Which commodities and services get included in the computation of GNP?

A lot of the activities carried on within families produce goods in the sense of commodities or services that satisfy wants, but the GNP statisticians ignore most of them. They count only the products sold in markets —with a few carefully chosen exceptions. If you purchase a haircut from the barber, that haircut counts in GNP; but if you get an even better hair-cut from your mother or your roommate, it adds nothing to GNP. If you drive your car everywhere and then join a health spa to get in shape, the gasoline you consume *and* the sauna you rent both make it into GNP. If you choose instead to keep in shape by selling your car and walking a lot, GNP will fall even though you're just as healthy and perhaps a lot happier. The person who enjoys working with wood may obtain intense satisfaction as well as a better bookcase by building his own, but only the wood, nails, and shellac he buys will be counted in GNP. The reason is simple: There is no satisfactory way to assign value to all the want-satisfying activities that go on in the family or that people perform for themselves or for one another without any exchange of money. So they are excluded from the calculation of GNP.

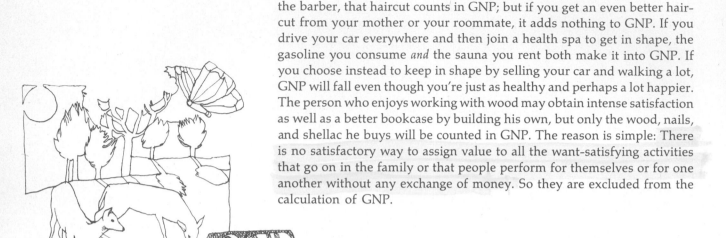

$1,397,000,000,000

Gross National Welfare?

But doesn't this reduce gross national product to a woefully inadequate measure of social welfare? That's a very odd question; but it's often asked today. It's as odd as asking whether failure to include television watching as time spent in school doesn't lead to an underestimate of learning. Both questions are misconceived, because learning is not synonymous with schooling and gross national product was never intended to be a measure of gross national welfare. The point must be stressed both to those who revere GNP far beyond its deserts and to those who want to make it worthy of such reverence by transforming it into something it simply cannot become.

The Bureau of Economic Analysis has long insisted that GNP is not a measure of social welfare and has openly advertised the limitations on what GNP purports to measure. For example, the BEA measures all commodities exchanged for money at their market prices while freely admitting that relative prices are not always reliable indicators of the contribution made by particular products to social welfare. It does not count in GNP the sale of such illegal products as heroin, but with no implication whatsoever that the legalization of heroin would add to national welfare, though it would indeed add to the gross national product. It includes only *final* goods and does not include in its calculations those intermediate goods that businesses purchase to use as inputs in the production of other goods —the steel, for example, purchased by a car manufacturer—on the grounds that this would lead to double counting. The steel will enter GNP by contributing to the final automobile. But the BEA has deliberately refused to extend the same argument to the food consumed by workers, although the food consumed by a worker is, at least in part, also an intermediate product. If someone objects that the contribution of food to welfare is exaggerated by the BEA's assumption that people eat only for pleasure, the BEA has an easy answer: It makes no such assumption and it is not even attempting to measure national welfare. The people who are today protesting that GNP doesn't measure social welfare are only agreeing with what the compilers of the data have long been saying.

In recent years, as an extension of the social welfare protest, some have begun to argue the desirability of adjustments in our methods of calculating GNP that would make it reflect changes in the quality of the environ-

NATIONAL INCOME AND "VALUE ADDED"

The total cost of any business enterprise can be thought of as the sum of its payments for the inputs it uses: goods purchased from other firms; supplies of labor, land, capital, and risk; and the services provided by government. This total for any firm will exceed its contribution to the national income or output by the amount of the first item in that list, the payments made to other firms for goods used in the production process. This portion of the firm's final output was contributed by the firms from which it purchased. If we regard taxes as the obligations of those who receive income, then the *value added* by any firm, or its specific contribution to the national income, is the total of its income payments to suppliers of labor, land, capital, and risk. And that is the definition of national income in the narrow sense. Table 17C shows the items that make up the total of these income payments by all business firms.

When indirect business taxes and capital consumption allowances (plus the few minor items discussed above and shown in table 17B) are added to national income, the total must by definition be equal to the sum of consumer, investor, government, and net foreign purchases of final goods. The statistical discrepancy takes care of any actual difference.

This provides another way of showing the conceptual identity of income and output and the reason for excluding intermediate goods from the calculation of the gross national product.

ment. One proposal would have the BEA *deduct* from gross national product the cost of expenditures undertaken to clean up the environment. The argument in this case is that GNP rises when copper is smelted to reflect the value of the copper; it should not rise still further, as now occurs, when people buy paint to cover the grime that the smelting process scatters on their houses. Another proposal would have the BEA *add* something to GNP when a smelter closes down, to reflect the added satisfaction that people now obtain from living in a less odorous environment. What these proposals have in common is dissatisfaction with the way environment-affecting activities are reflected or not reflected in the national income and product accounts. But what they also have in common is confusion about the nature and functions of these accounts. And that confusion is reflected in the opposite direction in which the two proposals move. The first wants to *subtract* from GNP the *cost* of a better environment, the second wants to *add* to GNP the *benefits* of a better environment. Let's ask a hard question of each.

Doesn't the first proposal imply that the BEA should also deduct from GNP all business expenditures that improve working conditions and all household expenditures on shrubbery and lawn fertilizer? Doesn't the second proposal imply that the BEA should add something to GNP for bright, sunny days in January and cool breezes in August? Is there any logical cut-off point once we start moving in either direction? Remember that in the absence of defensible criteria to guide our measurements, we don't know what the measurements mean. And if that's the case, what good are our new and "improved" numbers? They will manage only to make the old and unimproved numbers less reliable while fooling gullible people into believing that we know what we're doing to the environment because we have a set of numbers before us.

There is a harsh fact well known to those who toil at construction of the income and product accounts but rarely recognized by their critics: the basic data from which the accounts are constructed are largely of the type that require no philosophical judgments on the part of the data suppliers. These people provide data on actual expenditures and on dollar and cents receipts, data which they are well qualified to provide. A concept of GNP that attempted to measure changes in welfare would require the BEA to ask questions that are extraordinarily difficult even to ask and that would in practice be answered so arbitrarily as to make the data base almost meaningless. Try a little mental experiment if you want to appreciate the problem. Imagine the difficulties you would encounter if you tried to determine, through a survey questionnaire, the average *welfare* of your classmates. Think how much easier it would be to determine their average income.

The BEA statisticians and economists are not afraid of a challenge. If they decide that the failure to include some difficult-to-measure activity will significantly reduce the meaningfulness of their computations, they will attempt to measure and include it. So they do include in gross national product the food produced and consumed on farms, even though it isn't sold in the market, because failure to do so would seriously understate agricultural income. They also include the estimated rental value of owner-occupied housing because, if they did not, shifts between ownership and rental could cause misleading changes in the measure of national output. The wages and salaries that employers sometimes pay in kind (room and board, for example) are also counted, even though these goods are not sold in the market, because compensation of this kind is taken into account in wage bargaining. You may be interested to know that they do not count television programs as final commodities or services; commercial television programs enter the GNP accounts as intermediate goods—as business purchases of advertising—and are thus reflected only as a component in the total expenditures for the advertisers' products. The BEA people are aware that this means personal consumption expenditures may appear to decline when people shift from attending movies to watching television. But how much difference does it make and what would be the cost of correcting the error? The bureau's statisticians are willing to adjust their methods of computation whenever the benefits of doing so seem large enough to offset the added uncertainties from including yet another component whose value must be estimated because it is not sold in the market.

The Uses of GNP Data

If GNP doesn't measure social welfare and is a very clumsy tool for keeping track of environmental changes, of what use *are* the income and product accounts? That depends on whom you ask. Some business executives claim that they find the data useful in planning and forecasting. Governments make use of the data to anticipate tax revenues; the revenue from an income tax depends, after all, on income levels as well as on the tax rate, and the revenue from sales taxes also depends on the behavior of variables whose course is charted in the income and product accounts. Economists use the data to construct and test theories, to confirm what they already suspect, to compose multiple choice questions for college students, and simply for the comprehensive picture that a bird's-eye view can give (even if the bird happens to be color-blind and lacking in depth perception). Journalists use the data to explain to lay audiences the mysteries of prosperity and recession and no doubt on occasion to disguise essential ignorance behind an impressive array of numbers. But all intelligent users approach the data with caution.

Because of all the conventions that enter into the computation of GNP, it is not a useful device for making international comparisons, except in the hands of someone who knows a great deal about the details of national income accounting in the countries being compared. For much the same reason it ought to be used cautiously when making comparisons over long periods of time even within a single country; its focus on production for market and neglect of home production leads to an exaggerated picture of the rate of growth in output over time. Moreover, the *aggregate* character of the data will always be kept in mind by judicious users. The upward (or downward) movement of a composite does not imply anything about the direction of movement of a particular component; industries can founder and firms go bankrupt while GNP is rising smartly, just as it's possible for some firms or whole industries to prosper during a recession. And the data should *not*—we repeat—be used as an index of welfare.

A System of Welfare Indicators

No sensible person will doubt for a moment that social welfare is more important than the production of commodities and services. In fact, welfare is a concept far too important and complex to be compressed and distorted into a form suitable for packaging in the income and product accounts. The federal government officially acknowledged this in 1969, when the Department of Health, Education, and Welfare published a booklet entitled *Toward a Social Report.* The introduction is worth quoting:

> The Nation has no comprehensive set of statistics reflecting social progress or retrogression. There is no Government procedure for periodic stocktaking of the social health of the Nation. The Government makes no Social Report.
>
> We do have an Economic Report, required by statute, in which the President and his Council of Economic Advisors report to the Nation on its economic health. We also have a comprehensive set of economic indicators widely thought to be sensitive and reliable. . . .
>
> Indeed, economic indicators have become so much a part of our thinking that we have tended to equate a rising National Income with national well-being.

But this is a wholly unwarranted equation, the introduction goes on to argue, because income and disaffection *can and do* increase together. *Toward a Social Report* then suggests seven areas in which better data might be gathered and new questions asked by those who want to complement the economic indicators of the income and product accounts with a system of welfare indicators.

1. Health and illness: Are we becoming healthier while we're spending more money on medical care?

2. Social mobility: Have we made progress toward equality of opportunity?

3. Physical environment: What's happening to the settings within which we live as the average level of personal wealth continues to rise?

4. Income and poverty: How well does our society distribute economic goods among its members?

5. Public order and safety: How much do we suffer from crime and the fear of violence?

6. Learning, science, and art: How much do they contribute toward the enrichment of our lives?

7. Participation and alienation: How are we faring with respect to justice, and what is happening to our sense of community?

These questions will be far more difficult to answer than the limited and manageable questions asked by the Bureau of Economic Analysis. We think they're very much worth asking. But we don't believe that the income and product accounts are the right place to look for the answers. And we shudder whenever we hear someone talking as if those accounts do measure welfare; for money and happiness are surely not synonymous, and the production of marketable commodities and services is certainly not a satisfactory indicator of social well-being.

MEASURING CHANGES IN THE PRICE LEVEL

One more system of scorekeeping has to be introduced. All our talk about prices in preceding chapters has been about *relative* prices, or the ratios at which goods exchange for one another. Though we expressed these ratios in terms of money, we were not really interested in how much *money*, but rather in how much of *other goods*, had to be sacrificed to obtain some good in question. Thus we have so far said nothing about inflation. But inflation is an important problem and a major issue in the study of aggregate fluctuations and the struggle for economic stability.

Three Price Indices

The Bureau of Labor Statistics accumulates data on the average behavior of prices and publishes these in the form of price indices. The best known such index is the Consumer Price Index, which hits the front page of the newspapers every month during periods of substantial public concern about inflation. Another index, and one more useful for some purposes, is the Wholesale Price Index compiled by the Bureau of Labor Statistics. This is not, as the name suggests, an index of wholesale prices or the

prices paid by retailers. It is simply a measure of changes in the market prices of a long list of such basic agricultural and industrial commodities as processed foods and feeds, textile products, hides, fuels, chemicals, lumber, metals, machinery, and so on.

A third widely used index of prices is the Implicit Price Deflator for gross national product constructed by the Bureau of Economic Analysis. It reflects changes in the average prices of all new production of final goods, or all the items that contribute to the total of GNP. Table 17D summarizes all three indices from 1929 through 1974. (Note that the base year is different for the Implicit GNP Deflator.)

You can see clearly that prices fell sharply at the onset of the Great Depression. They fell slightly in the 1949 recession. But in 1954, 1958, and 1961 the consumer price index and the GNP deflator defied expectations by moving upward as employment moved downward. Inflation mixed with unemployment, a major concern after 1970, first showed its head in the 1950s.

Wars seem to promote inflation. The year 1951 shows the consequences of the Korean War; and prices began rising in the 1960s concurrently with escalation of the war in Viet Nam. While prices rose during World War II, they rose even more rapidly in the years right after the war.

The wholesale price index seems to respond more vigorously to changing conditions than does the consumer price index. It falls farther and rises faster. But look at the remarkable stability of the WPI from 1958 to 1964, when the CPI was creeping persistently upward. Was "the" price level rising in this period? It has been argued that it was not, but that the CPI was rising because consumers were shifting from commodities to services whose output could not be expanded very rapidly and whose quality improvements are more difficult to measure.

Real and Apparent Change

If prices are rising over time, figures on gross national product and its components will overstate actual increases in the output of goods from year to year. To obtain a truer picture of the expansion in the nation's output and income, GNP data must be adjusted by an index of prices. The implicit price deflators constructed by the Bureau of Economic Analysis are used to transform GNP data into dollars of constant purchasing power. Gross national product in 1958 prices for selected years from 1929 to 1960 and for each year from 1960 to 1974 is given in table 17E.

That isn't nearly as impressive as the somewhat misleading picture in table 17A. Gross national product actually fell in 1970 and 1974. The apparent increase shown in table 17A was due to inflation; the real value

	Table 17D THREE PRICE INDICES		
Year	Consumer Price Index (1967 = 100)	Wholesale Price Index (1967 = 100)	Implicit GNP Deflator (1958 = 100)
1929	51.3	49.1	50.6
1930	50.0	44.6	49.3
1931	45.6	37.6	44.8
1932	40.9	33.6	40.2
1933	38.8	34.0	39.3
1934	40.1	38.6	42.2
1935	41.1	41.3	42.6
1936	41.5	41.7	42.7
1937	43.0	44.5	44.5
1938	42.2	40.5	43.9
1939	41.6	39.8	43.2
1940	42.0	40.5	43.9
1941	44.1	45.1	47.2
1942	48.8	50.9	53.0
1943	51.8	53.3	56.8
1944	52.7	53.6	58.2
1945	53.9	54.6	59.7
1946	58.5	62.3	66.7
1947	66.9	76.5	74.6
1948	72.1	82.8	79.6
1949	71.4	78.7	79.1
1950	72.1	81.8	80.2
1951	77.8	91.1	85.6
1952	79.5	88.6	87.5
1953	80.1	87.4	88.3
1954	80.5	87.6	89.6
1955	80.2	87.8	90.9
1956	81.4	90.7	94.0
1957	84.3	93.3	97.5
1958	86.6	94.6	100.0
1959	87.3	94.8	101.7
1960	88.7	94.9	103.3
1961	89.6	94.5	104.6
1962	90.6	94.8	105.8
1963	91.7	94.5	107.2
1964	92.9	94.7	108.9
1965	94.5	96.6	110.9
1966	97.2	99.8	113.9
1967	100.0	100.0	117.6
1968	104.2	102.5	122.3
1969	109.8	106.5	128.2
1970	116.3	110.4	135.2
1971	121.3	113.9	141.4
1972	125.3	119.1	146.1
1973	133.1	134.7	154.3
1974	147.7	160.1	170.2

Source: Bureau of Labor Statistics and Bureau of Economic Analysis

Table 17E ADJUSTED GROSS NATIONAL PRODUCT

Year	Gross National Product in 1958 Prices	Percentage Change from Preceding Year *Shown*
1929	$203.6 billion	————
1933	141.5	−30.1%
1939	209.4	48.0
1944	361.3	72.5
1950	355.3	−2.7
1955	438.0	23.7
1960	487.7	11.3
1961	497.2	1.9*
1962	529.8	6.6
1963	551.0	4.0
1964	581.1	5.5
1965	617.8	6.3
1966	658.1	6.5
1967	675.2	2.6
1968	706.6	4.7
1969	725.6	2.7
1970	722.5	−0.4
1971	746.3	3.3
1972	792.5	6.2
1973	839.2	5.9
1974	821.1	−2.2

Source: Bureau of Economic Analysis
*Prior percentage changes are for periods greater than one year.

of goods produced in those years declined from the preceding year. This is consistent with what we know about the rising level of unemployment in both years and the labeling of each as a recession year.

The "Cost of Living Index"

Ordinary citizens experience inflation directly when they find that their income no longer stretches as far as it used to. They experience it indirectly when they pick up their newspapers and read that the Consumer Price Index rose 1.6 points in the past month or that it shows inflation increasing at a 14% annual rate. That's significant news for a lot of people. Household budget makers slump a little lower and think a little longer about new ways to cut corners. More than five million workers get ready for an increase in their hourly wage, because the "cost of living index" has been incorporated into many labor contracts under what are called escalator clauses: when the index of consumer prices goes up, employers increase wages. About thirty million Americans receiving Social Security can anticipate an increase in those payments, because we now use the CPI to adjust Social Security benefits. Politicians in office tremble at the news because the public expects government to prevent such things somehow. Business executives take an anxious look at their inventories and an equally anxious look at the statements being made by politicians, because they know that a rapidly rising consumer price index can lead to significant changes in both the economic and the political environment within which business operates.

An economic indicator as important as the Consumer Price Index ought to be well understood by the public. The aim of the Bureau of Labor Statistics is to provide a measure of changes in the average prices of representative goods regularly purchased by typical wage and salary earners living in cities. Don't nod too quickly. That's not quite the same as measuring *the* price level.

There's obviously no practical way to keep track of *all* prices. The BLS must use sampling procedures that it hopes will adequately portray the price movements of all those goods whose prices it's trying to summarize. But it makes no attempt to measure the prices of every kind of good. The CPI is a *consumer* price index and not an index of prices paid for raw materials or for the other intermediate goods purchased by businesses. Moreover, it's not even a measure of prices paid by *all* consumers; it tries to determine the prices paid for consumer goods by urban wage earners and clerical workers. Even that, though, is an impossible task, since no two families buy exactly the same collection of goods each month.

So the BLS must begin by deciding exactly which goods will be included in its periodic sampling of prices. More than 400 separate items are currently used to construct the CPI. Here are some of them, just to give you the flavor: restaurant meals, cinnamon rolls, liverwurst, cucumbers, pretzels, furnace repairing, sofas, baby sitting, socks, slacks, sneakers, new and used automobiles, cough syrup, psychiatric services, aerosol shaving cream, 35-millimeter color film, evening bowling fees, and funeral services. The entire list can be inspected in the statistical tables at the back of any issue of the *Monthly Labor Review*.

The Problem of Weighting

Far more items must necessarily be excluded than can be incorporated into the BLS samples. A lot of thought and investigation goes into the choice of representative goods, goods that typical families will regularly purchase and that will accurately reflect also the prices of all the goods excluded from consideration. But an even tougher decision still has to be

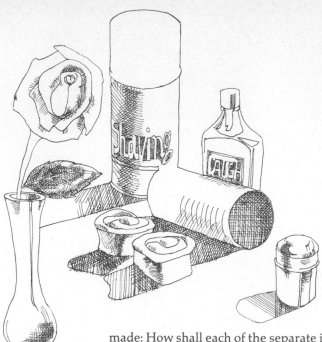

made: How shall each of the separate items be *weighted?* This is the familiar rabbit-and-horse-stew problem. The stew is not half-and-half if it contains one rabbit and one horse. Items on which consumers spend a larger percentage of their income must be weighted more heavily in the index if the composite is truly to reflect changes in the purchasing power of the consumer's dollar.

To illustrate the nature and seriousness of the weighting problem we can compare expenditure patterns in the 1930s with expenditure patterns in the 1960s. In the period 1934–36, according to a BLS survey conducted for the purpose of constructing appropriate weights, 35.4% of total consumer expenditures went for food and 8.2% for transportation. Now if food and transportation prices could be counted on always to go up or down at the same percentage rate, there would be no problem. Indeed, if all prices moved in perfect synchronization, any single item chosen at random could make up the entire price index. But that doesn't happen. So the BLS must sample the prices of many goods and must then weight them appropriately. For example, a 10% increase in food prices and a 2% increase in transportation prices doesn't average out to 6%. Since food expenditures were about 4.3 times as large as transportation expenditures, food had to be counted more than four times as heavily in constructing the average of the two. A more accurate average of the two would therefore be [4.3 (10%) + 1 (2%)] ÷ 5.3, or about 8.5%.

But expenditure patterns change over time with changing tastes, technologies, and incomes. The BLS survey for the years 1960–61 revealed that only 22.4% of consumer expenditures were for food and 13.9% for transportation. The appropriate weights had changed in one generation from approximately 4.3 to 1 to about 1.6 to 1. The same percentage increases of 10% and 2% would have yielded in the early 1960s an average price increase of [1.6 (10%) + 1 (2%)] ÷ 2.6, or only about 6.9%. That's a considerable difference.

And it makes a difference in how we interpret recent changes in the CPI. The weights used in constructing the index are based on surveys like the ones cited above. Since 1964 the BLS has used weights derived from its survey of 1960–61 expenditures. A new survey was made for the years 1972–73, but the BLS will not be able to incorporate the results into its calculation of the CPI until 1977. As a result, the impact of diverse price movements now shows up in the overall index of consumer prices in a way appropriate to the spending patterns of a decade and a half ago.

How much distortion does that introduce into the CPI? It can introduce quite a bit when prices are advancing at markedly diverse rates, as they did, for example, in 1973. Look at table 17F.

Food led the way in pushing or pulling the overall CPI up by 10.8 points, or almost 8½%, in 1973. But that means the CPI overstated actual consumer inflation during this year if consumers were purchasing *relatively* less food in 1973 than they had done in 1960–61. Since food does become a less important item in the average market basket as income rises, and since real per capita disposable income rose by more than 50% from 1960 to 1973, we can be fairly sure that the 1973 increase in the CPI overstated the amount of actual inflation.

The problem is even more difficult than this argument suggests, however. The fixed weights of the CPI are relative *physical quantities* in the base period. That means in effect that the BLS calculates the index by comparing 1967 prices times 1967 quantities-purchased with current prices times *1967 quantities-purchased.* Notice that current prices are not multiplied by current quantities but by the quantities purchased in the base period when relative prices may have been markedly different. That can cause serious distortions when prices change in a highly diverse way because, as the law of demand asserts, consumers alter the quantities of various goods purchased when their relative prices change. The CPI thus reflected the 1973 increase in beef prices as if those increases prompted no reduc-

	All Items	Food	Housing	Apparel and Upkeep	Transportation	Health and Recreation
Table 17F CONSUMER PRICE INDICES (1967 = 100)						
January, 1973	127.7	128.6	131.4	123.0	121.0	127.8
December, 1973	138.5	151.3	140.6	130.5	126.7	133.0

tions at all in the amount of beef purchased. Similarly, fuel oil and coal prices rose 45% in the twelve months following December 1972; but the overall CPI ignored the possibility (certainty?) that people responded to such a dramatic price increase by reducing their consumption of fuel oil and coal.

THE WEIGHTING GAME

The easiest way to see the effect of weighting decisions on a price index (or any index) is to work through an example.

In the year 1710 the typical consumer on Crusoe's Isle consumed 0.8 liters of ale and 1.0 kilo of bread per day. The price of ale was 5 clams per liter and the price of bread was 6 clams per kilo. In 1715 ale sold for 4 clams per liter and bread for 8 clams per kilo. The consumer price index in 1715, with 1710 prices and weights as the base, was

$$CPI = \left(\frac{(4 \times 0.8) + (8 \times 1.0)}{(5 \times 0.8) + (6 \times 1.0)}\right)100 = \left(\frac{11.2}{10}\right)100 = 112$$

This is the way in which the Bureau of Labor Statistics calculates the Consumer Price Index.

But with ale cheaper and bread more expensive in 1715, consumers would probably substitute ale for bread. Suppose that in 1715 the typical consumer bought 1.0 liter of ale and 0.9 kilos of bread per day. If we use 1715 weights to calculate the price index, we get

$$CPI = \left(\frac{(4 \times 1.0) + (8 \times 0.9)}{(5 \times 1.0) + (6 \times 0.9)}\right)100 = \left(\frac{11.2}{10.4}\right)100 = 107.7$$

The first index overstates the impact of the price changes because it fails to take account of substitution. A person whose income in 1710 was 100 clams would be *better off* in 1715 with an income of 112 clams. The income of 112 clams would still allow the original purchases of 0.8 liters of ale and 1.0 kilo of bread; but by substituting, the consumer could be better off.

The index with 1715 weights understates the impact. The typical consumer with an income of 107.7 clams in 1715 could have purchased the ale and bread actually bought in 1715 for only 100 clams in 1710. But at 1710 prices he would have chosen a different mix; and 107.7 clams is not enough to make him as well off in 1715 as he would have been with 100 clams in 1710.

The Problem of Quality Changes

The diligent statisticians at the BLS have still other problems to worry about. One is how to take account of *quality* changes. Some are comparatively simple to handle. Specific improvements in the quality of automobiles are treated as increases in quantity and are valued at their estimated cost. That makes sense. A car with an automatic starter is not more expensive than one that has to be cranked just because it costs more; it *is* more; it's a different product. There are plenty of problems even in this to tax the ingenuity of the BLS people. For example, are seat belts an improvement in quality for the person who refuses to wear them? Tastes differ, and quality is inseparable from considerations of taste. But the problems with automobiles at least seem manageable.

Less manageable is a problem like this one: When the cost of a hospital room goes up from $30 to $50 a day, is that a genuine price increase if at the same time improved drugs or other medical procedures reduce the

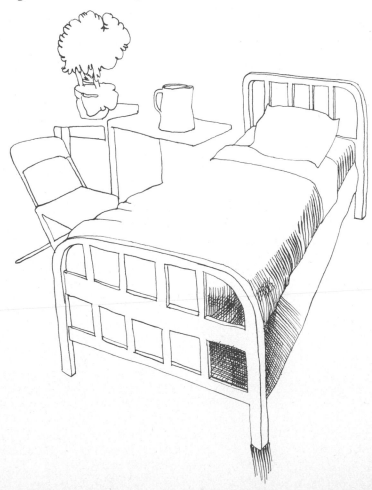

hospital stay from six days to three days? The cost of health (and that's the consumer good most of us are after; few people go to the hospital for a vacation) would have *decreased* in this case from $180 to $150.

Or try this one. One of the authors thinks that the best movies being made today are far more enjoyable than the best movies made a decade ago. The price of movie tickets has also gone up over the decade. But how much more expensive is movie *entertainment*? Three times as much entertainment for twice the money is a price reduction, isn't it? Some economists have argued that the CPI, because of its inability to take quality improvements adequately into account, overstates increases in the price level by 1% to $1\frac{1}{2}$% per year.

Decomposing the GNP Deflator

The Bureau of Economic Analysis confronts most of the same problems in constructing the GNP deflator, and so it is subject to many of the same limitations as the consumer price index. We see how misleading an aggregate index of this type can be if we compare the changes within a set of price indices during the period 1958 to 1964. Contrast the following percentage changes over those years:

7.3%	Consumer price index, all items
8.9	GNP deflator, total
7.4	GNP deflator, personal consumption expenditures
.4	GNP deflator, personal consumption expenditures on durable goods
4.9	GNP deflator, personal consumption expenditures on nondurable goods
13.1	GNP deflator, personal consumption expenditures on services
7.6	GNP deflator, total investment expenditures
15.7	GNP deflator, government purchases of goods
7.1	GNP deflator, total private sector
28.4	GNP deflator, total government sector

It would appear that "the" price level rose from 1958 to 1964 largely because the price of services and of general government operations, which are dominated by services, increased substantially. Does this have any implications for policy? Should we have concluded that the apparent inflation of those years was an illusion? If a family shifts from eating beef to eating lobster, their "cost of living" increases because they are paying higher prices for food; but we would not want to attribute this to inflation. If a large part of the public shifts from beef to lobster, they will similarly pay higher prices for food. But in addition they will do what one family by itself could not do: raise further the price of lobster relative to beef, because the quantity of lobster supplied cannot easily be increased in response to a larger demand. This shift in the public's eating preferences will consequently raise "the" price level.

There just is no satisfactory answer to the question, What is *really* happening to *the* price level? Every price index is a theoretical construct subject to misinterpretation by anyone who doesn't know how it was constructed. We'll provide one further example that will also give us a chance to look briefly at the other price index presented in table 17D, the Wholesale Price Index.

Inflation and the Wholesale Price Index

Suppose we agree that the economy experiences *real* inflation when the total quantity of goods demanded at current prices is greater than the total quantity supplied. That definition is consistent with the analysis of price behavior presented in chapter 4. If the definition is to be empirically useful, however, we must find a gauge which will register any gaps between aggregate demand and aggregate supply. Is the Wholesale Price Index a good candidate for the job? This is an index of changes in the average prices of basic agricultural and industrial commodities. It seems reasonable to assume that these prices will be especially sensitive to changes in the relation between aggregate demand and aggregate supply, because the commodities enter into so many different production processes and because their prices are established by the bids and offers of numerous users and producers. If we accept this hypothesis and look at the behavior of the WPI from 1958 to 1964, we can conclude that there was no genuine inflation during these years. The index varied only within the narrow range of 94.5 to 94.9.

But a sensitive gauge is not always a reliable gauge. The Wholesale Price Index rose 38% from January 1973 to December 1974, almost certainly overstating by a considerable amount the degree of overall inflation during this period. The WPI often magnifies the effects of changes in its components, because they enter as inputs into the production of other components. Consider the effect of fuel prices, for example. The composite index of prices for coal, coke, gas, electricity, crude petroleum, and refined petroleum products increased 87% from January 1973 to December 1974, largely because the Organization of Petroleum Exporting Countries became a successful cartel during this period. That directly raised the price of petroleum, which in turn caused the price of refined petroleum products to increase, which in turn created a greater demand for substitute fuels whose production could not be quickly accelerated so that their prices also rose, which boosted the cost of farm products, chemicals, metal products, and other commodities also entering into the Wholesale Price Index.

Our most sensitive measure of discrepancies between aggregate demand and aggregate supply under some circumstances may become our most unreliable measure under other circumstances, suggesting once again that "hard facts" are not good substitutes for informed judgment. But informed judgment presupposes an ability to see the larger picture and the way in which events relate to one another. That's the job of theory. We must now turn our attention to the theoretical frameworks that economists have constructed for analyzing the phenomena of recession and inflation.

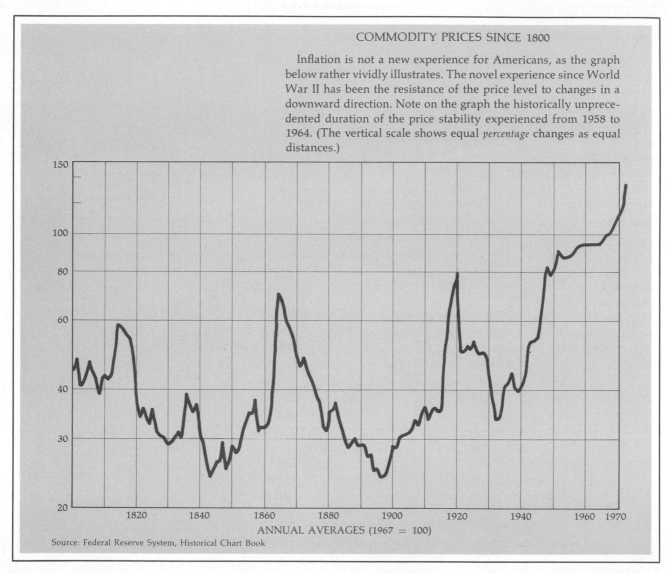

COMMODITY PRICES SINCE 1800

Inflation is not a new experience for Americans, as the graph below rather vividly illustrates. The novel experience since World War II has been the resistance of the price level to changes in a downward direction. Note on the graph the historically unprecedented duration of the price stability experienced from 1958 to 1964. (The vertical scale shows equal *percentage* changes as equal distances.)

ANNUAL AVERAGES (1967 = 100)

Source: Federal Reserve System, Historical Chart Book

Once Over Lightly

The income and product accounts compiled by the Bureau of Economic Analysis are our most comprehensive measure of aggregate economic activity.

Gross national product is the market value of all the final goods produced in a year. It is calculated by adding together the purchases of final goods by domestic consumers, investors, and governments plus the net purchases of foreigners (their purchases of our goods minus our purchases of theirs).

Gross national product can also be calculated by summing the value added to production by each business firm. This will be the total of each firm's before-tax payments to suppliers of labor, land, capital, and risk (*national income* in the narrow sense) plus indirect business taxes and a few other minor items (*net national product*) and capital consumption allowances. The value of gross national product as calculated through value added would equal exactly the value as calculated through total expenditures if it were possible to measure all the components without error.

Final goods produced but not purchased during a year are considered to have been purchased by the firms that produced them; they are additions to inventory, which is one of the components of investment. This seemingly minor point is singled out for review because, as we shall see in chapter 20, many economists believe that unintended changes in business inventories are a key factor in the understanding of aggregate fluctuations.

Disposable personal income can be calculated from national income by subtracting corporate profits taxes, social insurance taxes, personal taxes, and undistributed corporate profits and adding government and business transfer payments to persons, interest paid by government, and the net interest paid by consumers. What the Bureau of Economic Analysis calls *personal income* is disposable income before the subtraction of personal taxes.

The income and product accounts are not intended to be, and should not be, used as a measure of gross national welfare. A great deal of important goods production that contributes to social welfare (home and family production, for example) is not included in gross national product; and many of the costs of production that reduce social welfare (environmental pollution, for example) are also not taken into account.

The principal indices used to measure changes in the price level are the Consumer Price Index and the Wholesale Price Index constructed by the Bureau of Labor Statistics and the Implicit GNP Deflator constructed by the Bureau of Economic Analysis.

Difficult problems of selection, sampling, and weighting must be resolved if an index is to reflect in a reliable way changes in the purchasing power of money or the average money price of goods. It is probably not possible to construct a single index that will satisfactorily measure changes in *the* price level.

Real, as distinct from nominal, changes in income or output are calculated by dividing data on national product in current dollar terms by an index of the price level.

QUESTIONS FOR DISCUSSION

1. Can a society's output increase faster than its income? Can its income increase faster than its output?

2. Suppose that every American family had a counterfeiting operation in the back room and added $40 per week to family income by printing four ten-dollar bills each week. Would this increase national income without a corresponding increase in national output?

3. Why would it be misleading for the Bureau of Economic Analysis to include transfer payments in its calculation of national income? Why would it be misleading for the BEA *not* to include transfer payments in its calculation of personal income? (Hint: Question 3 is related to questions 1 and 2.)

4. BEA statisticians strive to avoid double counting in their calculations of gross national product. Why would there be double counting if the total output of wheat and the total output of bread in a given year were both included in gross national product? Do you understand how double counting is avoided by *not* counting sales of intermediate products *or* by counting only the *value added* by producers?

5. List some ways in which increased *inefficiency* could cause gross national product to rise. Are there any goods contributing to the total of gross national product whose rising output clearly reflects *reduced* welfare?

6. Are government purchases of commodities and services consumption expenditures or investment expenditures? They must be one or the other. Why do you suppose the Bureau of Economic Analysis groups them separately?

7. Why must total expenditures for final goods by consumers, investors, and government and the net purchases of foreigners necessarily equal gross national product? What if some of the year's output is not sold?

8. If it could be shown that a rising gross national product promoted a rising level of anxiety, tension, and conflict in the population, would you favor deducting these psychological costs to obtain the true value of gross national product? How would you do it?

9. Would you favor including the services of housewives in the calculation of gross national product? What arguments could be given for doing so? Are there any good reasons for continuing to exclude these services from the calculation of GNP?

10. As an economy industrializes, a larger percentage of its population tends to enter the labor force as conventionally measured. Less production occurs in the home for family use and a larger proportion of total product passes through the marketplace. What does this imply about the usefulness of GNP data in industrializing societies? Will estimates of per capita income derived from GNP data tend to overstate or understate improvement over time?

11. To be certain that you understand the relation between nominal GNP, real GNP, and the price level, try deriving either the level of GNP in current dollars (table 17A), the level of GNP in 1958 dollars (table 17E), or the Implicit GNP Deflator (table 17D) from the other two for any given year.

12. How much better off financially was a person in 1967 than in 1953 if his income increased over that period by 50%? Use the data of the Consumer Price Index to answer. Do you think your answer overestimates or underestimates the real improvement in the person's living level. Why?

13. Suppose that in 1960 the price of a man's white dress shirt was $5 and the price of a colored dress shirt was $6, and in 1970 the price of a white shirt was $6 and the price of a colored shirt was $8. If 80% of the dress shirts purchased by American males were white and 20% were colored, what was the percentage increase in the price of dress shirts? Would your answer be different if in 1970 80% of the shirts purchased were colored and 20% were white?

14. From 1967 to 1973 the price of cornflakes increased $4\frac{1}{2}$%, the price of refined sugar 25%, milk 27%, eggs 60%, and bacon 61%. What happened over this period to the price of breakfast?

15. From 1967 to 1973 the average price of a visit to a physician's office rose 39.5%. During the same period the average price of prescription antibiotics decreased 28.9%. Did the price of medical care rise or fall? Why might some families find that the net result was a decrease in the price of medical care while others experienced a net increase? What changes in medical care practices might be induced by these divergent price movements?

18

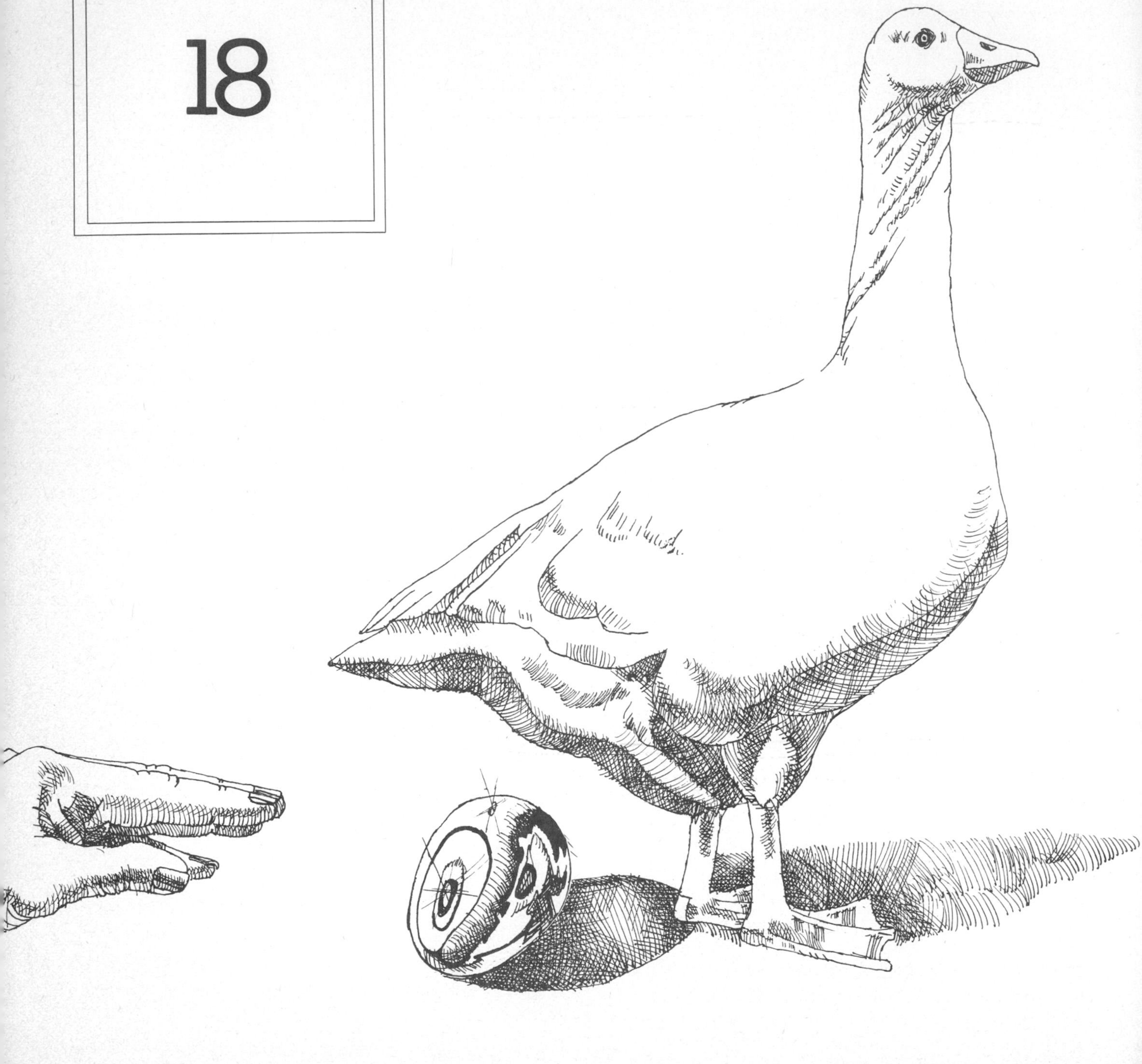

MONEY AND THE BANKING SYSTEM

The time has come to talk about *money*. You probably didn't even notice that we have come this far without discussing it. The previous chapters, after all, were replete with dollar signs, and dollars are money. But the dollar referred to earlier was simply a conventional unit for discussing relative values, a common denominator that enabled us to compare and add apples and oranges, convenient transportation and unpolluted air, goods in the hand and goods in the bush, the services of engineers and the gains from exchange.

THE USE OF MONEY

One important function of money in a social system is to provide such a unit for accounting. We might have used such other common denominators as bread or human labor. We could have stated the prices of gasoline and sugar in terms of the number of standard loaves for which a gallon of one and a pound of the other would exchange. Or we could have expressed the gross national product as the equivalent of so many hours of "average" labor time. The fact that we don't actually exchange something doesn't prevent us from using it to express comparative or total values. Prices are sometimes expressed in "mills" even though we don't use coins with a value of $\frac{1}{10}$ cent. Similarly British merchants often state prices in "guineas," coins that have not been issued in England since 1813. Both mills and guineas illustrate this accounting function of money.

A Medium of Exchange

We're all accustomed to thinking and talking about prices in terms of dollars, because dollars are what we use in the process of exchanging one good for another. We have had a lot of practice in translating the prices of diverse commodities and services into dollar terms. Money functions effectively as a unit of accounting because of all the experience we've had with its function as a medium of exchange.

A "medium of exchange" is just what the words say: a middle-thing used in the process of exchanging one good for another. The alternative to employing a medium of exchange is barter: exchanging the goods at our command directly for the goods we want to obtain.

The advantages of using money rather than a barter system are enormous. The cost of exchanging would be far greater, and social wealth as a consequence far less, if there were no money to facilitate the process. In an economic system limited to barter, people would have to spend an inordinate amount of time searching for others with whom they could advantageously exchange. A violin maker would have to find a grocer, a haberdasher, an electrical utility, and a glue supplier, among many others, all willing to accept violins in return for the goods they handle. All that time devoted to searching would be time unavailable for violin making, and the production of violins would fall. Aware of the high costs of exchanging, people would increasingly try to produce goods for their own use to avoid the necessity of searching out others from whom they could buy and to whom they could sell. In a society confined to barter, specialization would decline dramatically. And that means, of course, that people would lose the benefits that accrue from the systematic and widespread exploitation of comparative advantage. The evolution of some kind of money system in almost every known society, even when conditions were extremely unfavorable for it, is eloquent testimony to the advantages of having a generally accepted medium of exchange. R. A. Radford's essay in the appendix on "The Economic Organization of a P.O.W. Camp" shows how quickly cigarettes became the accepted medium of exchange when the prisoners started trading.

If money is that important, why hasn't it been introduced earlier? There are several reasons. First of all, we took its existence for granted until now and just assumed you wouldn't notice. Second, the existence or non-existence of money does not, by and large, affect the concepts we were using in the first fifteen chapters. In fact, we several times urged you to ignore money, to pretend it wasn't there. The important concept of opportunity cost, a major unifying thread in the economic way of thinking, goes beyond the *monetary* notion that first comes to mind when people think about costs. Obsession with money and monetary values can easily

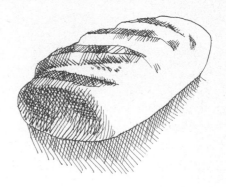

obscure understanding of the way the economy functions and of the real costs of economic activities. That's why economists in the nineteenth century sometimes spoke of money as a *veil* that had to be pushed aside before one could see clearly the nature of economic relationships. A vivid illustration of what they meant is provided by the story (perhaps only a legend) of the business executive called to Washington during World War II to help organize military production. Informed one morning that a key defense plant had burned to the ground, he shrugged it off with the comment, "It was insured, wasn't it?" But money from an insurance company does not produce synthetic rubber or "secrete steel rails."[1] Thus a preoccupation with monetary values can sometimes obscure the real forces responsible for the creation of wealth.

Monetary Complications   *Inflation*

We have already encountered one problem, however, that cannot be talked about without introducing money specifically. And that is the problem of inflation. For inflation means a decline in the value of money relative to all other goods or, in more familiar terms, a rise in the money price of goods generally. If you immediately start applying the concepts of economic reasoning to the issue of inflation, you will suspect that a decline in the price (or purchasing power) of money occurs for the same reason that a decline occurs in the price of parsnips or pocket calculators: the supply has increased relative to the demand. And you will be right on target.

But while money is like other goods in many ways, it also has some peculiar characteristics that make it a unique good. Fluctuations in the price of parsnips pose major problems for parsnip growers and minor problems for those who buy them. Fluctuations in the price of money, however, are fluctuations in the measuring rod of economic decision makers that make decisions more difficult and uncertain. Money, as it turns out, is more than the lubricant of the economic system, the coordinator of exchange that adds to our wealth through its power to extend specialization. It can grease the skids as well as oil the economic system.

Many of the difficulties created by money arise from the fact that it is *not* exchanged for goods the moment it's received. If it were, we would in effect have a barter system. The violin maker who wants to eat sells his product to the violinists he can find when he finds them, and *holds* the money he receives—at least until he can get to the grocery store. That might be fifteen minutes later if he's very hungry; or it might be a week later, a month later, a year later. If those nineteenth century economists

1. Clarence E. Ayres relates the story in *The Theory of Economic Progress*, first published in 1944.

to whom we referred a moment ago had examined more closely the implications of the fact that people do hold money for periods of time before they spend it, they might more easily have seen that money is not a mere veil to be pushed aside if one wishes to view the functioning of the economic system. Money is a part of that functioning, and it can become a cause of its malfunctioning.

Liquidity and the Demand for Money

"Nobody desires money for its own sake," we often say, "but only for the sake of what it can buy." King Midas is supposedly the exception that proves the rule: he was a fool. It's quite true that we accept money in exchange for the goods we have to offer because we intend to use the money to purchase other goods we want. But we do not, as a matter of fact, immediately exchange the money we acquire for some other goods. We hold money, for longer or shorter periods of time, and wait for the right opportunity or for the arrival of some future obligation. If we could not do this, money would actually have no value as a medium of exchange. Money is useful to the violin maker because it enables him to sell his products whenever and wherever he finds a would-be fiddler, and then wait until the opportune occasion to purchase corned beef or pay his electric bill. It follows from this that normal people, and not just King Midas, have a *demand for money*. We want money to hold and not just to spend. The fact is that when we acquire money we rarely know exactly how or when we will spend it. We simply add the money to our stock of assets and wait.

The special advantage of money as an asset to hold, or as one of many forms in which we can store wealth, is its *liquidity*. Money is the most liquid asset. That's what qualifies it to be called money. The more liquid something is, the more moneylike it is. When an asset is completely liquid, it has attained the zenith of moneyness.

What do we mean by liquidity? *The liquidity of an asset depends on the cost of exchanging it for other assets.* An asset that can be exchanged for any other asset at a zero cost is a completely liquid asset. The Federal Reserve note in your wallet is an excellent example. It's an asset you can give in exchange for a great variety of other things you might want because sellers of every sort are willing to accept it without question and at face value. An asset that could not be exchanged at all because no one else would be willing to give anything in exchange for it would be a completely illiquid asset. (Your toothbrush?) In Seattle, a Canadian dollar may be as liquid an asset as a U.S. Federal Reserve note. Farther south, away from the border, its liquidity declines, until merchants refuse to accept Canadian money altogether. If you own a government savings bond, you can exchange it for other assets, but first you'll have to incur the cost of a trip to the bank where you exchange the bond for currency. So government savings bonds are liquid assets, but they're not as liquid as Federal Reserve notes. Are they money? Just how liquid does an asset have to be to qualify as money? That turns out to be a difficult question and competent people disagree on the answer. We'll have to come back to it. In this world of continuous variables and every shade of grey, assets will rarely hit either end of the liquid-illiquid continuum. Most assets are somewhat liquid. The point to remember is that an asset becomes more moneylike, or liquid, as the cost of exchanging it for other assets approaches zero.

Liquidity – cost of exchange approaches zero.

The concept of liquidity is important in the economist's way of looking at the world. To be liquid is to have a greater range of choices, better opportunities, and hence more wealth. Your wealth, by which we always mean the range of options available to you, depends (among other things) upon the precise forms in which you're currently holding the goods you own, or, in the useful jargon of finance, upon the *composition of your asset portfolio*. Suppose, for example, that you're in a strange city with a checkbook but no currency and you're hungry. The restaurant signs saying "No Checks Accepted" establish that you are at the moment not as wealthy as you would be with twenty dollars less in your checking account and twenty dollars more in your wallet.

The Cost of Liquidity

Liquidity is valuable and so people have a demand for liquidity. But that's only one part of the picture. In order to possess liquidity you must typically sacrifice other advantages. For example, if you're keeping a sizeable amount in your checking account in order to have it immediately available for purchases you might want to make, you're sacrificing the interest you could earn from having that amount in a savings account. So the opportunity cost of liquidity sets limits to the quantity of liquidity people will demand. The demand curve for liquidity, like all properly behaved demand curves in economics, slopes downward to the right.

cost for liquidity.

The concept of a demand for money often puzzles people; and that, along with the importance of the concept, explains why we're trying to help you think it through carefully. Do not confuse the demand for money with the desire for income. Income is a flow; money is a stock. Your income is the stream of assets coming into your possession, measured per week or month or year, and most people understandably would like it to be larger. Your demand for money expresses the *form* in which you prefer to hold the assets currently in your possession.

Think about it in terms of your own experience. *You* have a demand for liquidity. You probably hold some fraction of your wealth, pitifully small though your total wealth may be, in the form of currency or a checking account. These assets yield you no physiological nutrition, no comfort when reclining, no transportation service, and not even any

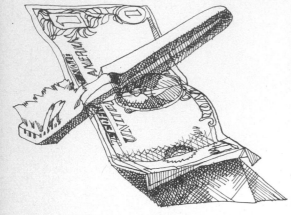

interest income. Why don't you, upon acquiring money, immediately exchange it for something that can minister to your wants? The answer is that one of your wants is for liquidity. Currency in the wallet and a balance in the checking account give you room to maneuver. When you have a supply of these highly liquid assets, you are more free to take advantage of opportunities that present themselves. You are better equipped to handle emergencies, which might take the form of a sudden yen for new bell-bottoms, a threat by the telephone company to cut off your service, or an unexpected chance to attend a concert.

The cost of liquidity is the value of whatever you sacrifice by being liquid. So you don't keep *all* of your monthly allowance in the form of money until the next allowance comes in; but you do try to keep *some*. You are guided in part by the relative liquidity of other assets you possess. If you know that you can sell your record collection in a pinch, you will regard it as a contribution toward your overall liquidity and reduce somewhat your demand to hold money, the almost completely liquid asset. Your ability to borrow is also an important asset and one that may significantly affect your demand for money; if you can exchange your creditworthiness for money at a low cost, your creditworthiness is a highly liquid asset.

Your demand for money and other liquid assets will clearly vary with circumstances. If your monthly income is so small that every dollar you hold in reserve entails the sacrifice of something important to you, you will hold little money on the average. If your immediate future seems secure and well provided for because the college functions capably in loco parentis, you will feel less desire for liquidity. Reckless souls despise liquidity; cautious ones crave it. If the future begins to look more uncertain, then, other things remaining equal, your demand for liquidity will increase. "More uncertain" doesn't necessarily mean more threatening. This uncertainty refers to the good opportunities that may unpredictably come your way as well as to the misfortunes that may strike.

 Many economists believe that the public's demand for money or demand for liquidity is an important key to the understanding of aggregate economic stability. We'll be working with the concept in detail in chapter 22, but a brief summary at this point may prove helpful. The quantity of money people will want to hold is going to depend on their current and expected income; the larger their income the more money they will usually want to hold. It will also depend on their reading of the future; the more uncertain the future the more money they will want to hold. And it will depend on the opportunity cost of holding money; the larger the return they can expect from holding alternative assets, such as government bonds or shares in a mutual fund, the smaller the quantity of money they will want to hold.

BANKS AND THE CREATION OF MONEY

Enough of the demand for money. The time has come to talk about the stuff itself. What do we use in the United States as our medium of exchange? Where does it come from? Who decides how much there shall be? Our principal task in the remainder of this chapter and in chapter 19 will be to explain the interactions of private and governmental decision makers that create the supply of money.

When most people think about money they think immediately of green pieces of paper, called Federal Reserve notes, and coins of various sizes and colors. Economists lump these all together and call them currency. But what else do we use as a medium of exchange?

currency

Bank Deposits Are Money

The most widely used medium of exchange is not currency but *demand deposit* credits in commercial banks, usually called checking accounts. These are deposits that can be withdrawn or transferred at the pleasure of the depositor or "on demand." Savings accounts are called *time deposits* because banks may legally require advance notification of withdrawal.

checking accounts

Many students have trouble at first in seeing that demand deposits really are money. They themselves may handle all their transactions by means of currency; when they receive a check, they "cash" it—that is, they obtain currency for the check and spend the currency. But student habits are not typical of the transaction procedures of business firms, government units, and households. The overwhelming majority of exchanges, measured in dollar value, use demand deposits as the medium of exchange. A purchaser instructs his bank to transfer ownership of a portion of his deposit to the seller: he writes a check, in other words. The seller typically deposits the check instead of cashing it: she instructs her own bank to collect the sum whose transfer was ordered by the check writer. No currency at all changes hands. The bank in which the check is deposited makes an entry in its books; the bank on which the check is written makes an equal but opposite entry in its books.

It isn't hard to imagine a situation in which demand deposits are the *only* medium of exchange. As credit cards become more common, people will carry less currency and pay for more of their purchases with monthly checks. Couldn't *all* transactions be handled in this way? It would be possible, although inconvenient in some cases. But currency *could* disappear from existence without any reduction in our use of money as a medium of exchange.[1]

1. Credit cards are *not* a medium of exchange but a way of *postponing* payment for a purchase.

Currency plus demand deposits. Is that all? Suppose someone asked, "How much money do you have?" You would calculate the currency in your possession. Having read this far you would then add the balance in your checking account. Should you also add what you have in your savings account? You can get it out quickly or transfer it to your checking account. It's available for spending, even though savings accounts cannot be used directly as a medium of exchange. But then what of the deposit you have in a savings and loan institution? You could also convert that amount into ready cash. And why not also the government bonds you own? They can be cashed too. How far shall we go in calculating how much money you have? Your automobile could also be converted into currency or a demand deposit. Is it, therefore, money?

Notice what we've done now. We have subtly shifted the definition of money from "the commonly employed medium of exchange" to "liquid assets." If we adhered strictly to the definition of money as a medium of exchange, we would want to define the money supply in the United States as the *total of currency in circulation plus demand deposits at commercial banks.* For that is what we use to pay for almost all our purchases. To avoid double counting we must include only the currency that is in circulation and not the amount in bank vaults. Thus when someone deposits a $20 bill in his checking account, the money supply does not change. The demand deposit component rises by $20, but currency in circulation falls by $20. If we continued to count as money the currency now in the bank's possession, we would come to the highly misleading conclusion that deposits or withdrawals of currency from checking accounts change the quantity of the exchange medium held by the community. But they don't; they only change the *form* in which it is held. After you've written a check for "cash," you still have exactly as much money as before, and so does everyone else.

How Do We Want to Define the Money Supply?

But do we want to define money strictly as that which actually functions as the common medium of exchange? What we're really looking for in these chapters is an explanation of aggregate demand or total expenditures. As we shall see, that will depend in part upon the amount of money people are holding relative to the quantities of other assets that they own or would like to acquire. The more money people possess, other things being equal, the more likely they are to surrender some portion of it in exchange for an alternate asset when an attractive opportunity presents itself. Now it is quite clear that most people do not just look at their present stock of currency and demand deposits in deciding how much money they have. Savings held in commercial banks as time deposits

and savings held in such nonbank thrift institutions as savings and loan associations would be regarded by most people as "available cash." So shouldn't we include these deposits in our working definition of the money supply?

There is just no completely satisfactory way to decide what should go into the calculation of the money supply and what should be excluded. The central bankers of the United States, the managers of the Federal Reserve System, calculate the money supply in at least three ways and publish three sets of figures as M_1, M_2, and M_3.

M_1 is demand deposits plus currency in circulation.

M_2 is M_1 plus time deposits in commercial banks—those banks which provide checking account service as well as accepting the deposits of savers, making loans, selling money orders, and so on.

M_3 is M_2 plus deposits in mutual savings banks and savings and loan associations—sometimes called nonbank thrift institutions.

The table below gives you some notion of the magnitude of the money stock by each of these measures. Since the money supply can and does fluctuate considerably from day to day, figures are usually expressed as averages over such periods of time as a month or a quarter. The numbers below are in billions of dollars and give the average of daily figures throughout the last month of three recent years.

$$M_1 = \text{demand deposits} + \text{currency}$$
$$M_2 = M_1 + \text{time deposits}$$
$$M_3 = M_2 + \text{deposits in thrift inst.}$$

Table 18A	MONEY SUPPLY IN BILLIONS OF DOLLARS		
	M_1	M_2	M_3
1967	186.9	349.6	532.6
1970	221.5	425.3	642.8
1973	271.5	572.2	895.3

Source: Board of Governors, Federal Reserve System

Whichever definition of the money supply we choose, they have all increased significantly since 1967. Moreover, the percentage rates of increase have varied considerably, both among the three measures of the money stock and from year to year within each measure.

But what difference does any of it make? Is there some correct level for the money supply or some ideal rate at which it ought to grow over time? These are important questions. Before you can make sense of the various answers that economists have given to them, however, you must understand something about how money is created and destroyed. What are the forces in both the private and the government sectors of the economy that interact to determine changes in the size of the money stock?

What Determines the Size of the Money Supply?

We can begin with what you know already or can figure out from what has been said. Individuals can directly change the relative sizes of these money stock measures by transferring funds from their checking accounts to their savings accounts or to a savings and loan association and back again. They can also, according to their preferences, hold their share of M_1 in the form of a demand deposit or as currency. The Fed (the common collective term for the Federal Reserve Banks) supplies whatever

amount of currency the public chooses to hold, and takes it back again whenever the public no longer wishes to hold it. Hence an increase in the public's net preference for currency over time deposits, perhaps at Christmas time or during the vacation season, will increase M_1. But since M_1's gain is M_2's loss and M_2 includes M_1, that would not bring about directly a change in the total of M_2.

The reason for mentioning all of this is that such changes in the composition of the public's money holdings have potentially significant indirect effects. Insofar as these preference shifts are seasonal and predictable, they pose no serious problem to the nation's monetary managers. There is mounting evidence, however, that the public is becoming more adept at shifting about among liquid and near-liquid assets and that this is making it more difficult for the Fed to control the supply of money with adequate precision. The issue is one to which we shall return.

The Crucial Role of Bank Loans

But none of this explains how it's possible for M_3 to increase. In December 1973, M_3 was 70% larger than it had been in 1967, as a consequence of a 45% rise in currency and demand deposits, an 85% increase in time deposits, and a 50% jump in deposits with nonbank thrift institutions. Where did all this additional money come from? The basic answer is that it came about through a net expansion of commercial bank loans. For *the money supply increases when commercial banks make loans to their customers and decreases when customers repay the loans they obtained from commercial banks.* That's the short of the story. The long of it is a bit more complicated but not really difficult to grasp.

Suppose your application for a loan of $500 from the First National Bank is approved. The lending officer will make out a deposit slip in your name for $500, initial it in some appropriate way, and hand it to a teller who will then credit your checking account with an additional $500. Demand deposits will have risen by $500. The money supply will be larger by that amount.

Where did the $500 come from? The bank *created* the $500 to lend you. Out of thin air? Not really. But the raw material isn't as important at this point as the fact that the bank really did create new money in making you a loan.

But what if you don't have a checking account at First National? Then the bank can open one and start you off with a $500 balance. But suppose you don't want a demand deposit—you want the money? Slips! A demand deposit *is* money. You can use the demand deposit to buy whatever it is you borrowed for. All right; but what if you decide to withdraw your $500 right away in $20 bills? Fine. The teller will accommodate you. The total of demand deposits will fall by $500, but the total of currency in circulation will increase by $500. The bank takes the currency from its vault, where it is *not* money, and gives it to you, whereupon it becomes currency held by the nonbank public or currency in circulation and hence *is* money.

Does it all seem too simple? Why don't banks keep on doing that indefinitely? It seems just like having your own money machine in the basement. We'll see in a moment that banks are limited in their ability to make loans and thus add to the money supply. But first let's see how the money supply is increased.

One year later your note comes due. In the interim you've built up your money balance to be able to pay off the loan on time. You have $500 (plus the interest due, which we neglect for present purposes) either in your checking account or in your cookie jar. If it's in the cookie jar, you turn it over to the bank on the due date and money in circulation drops by $500. Note again that currency counts as money when and only when it is held outside the banking system.

If, as is more likely, you have the $500 in your checking account, you write a check for that amount to the bank. The bank subtracts $500 from your demand deposit balance. The money supply goes down by $500.

If you have grasped this simple process, you now understand how money is created and destroyed and the way in which the stock of money expands and contracts. But you must still be wondering what has been left out. Surely private, commercial bankers cannot create money without constraint. And you are right; they cannot. First of all, the bankers must find people willing to borrow on the terms at which the banks are willing to lend. Second, each bank operates within the constraint imposed by its reserves. This is the constraint that banking authorities use to control bank lending and hence the process of money creation. Every bank is legally required to hold reserves in forms specified by law. A bank may make new loans, and thus create money, only when it has reserves greater than the minimum amount it is legally obligated to hold. And the Fed has the power to increase or decrease the reserves of the banking system.

The Central Bank

The Federal Reserve Banks constitute the central bank of the United States, created by an act of Congress in 1913. Although technically owned by the commercial banks that are members of the Federal Reserve System, the Fed is in fact a government agency. Its board of governors in Washington is appointed by the president of the United States with the consent of the Senate. And the board effectively controls the policies of the twelve Federal Reserve Banks. We *seem* to have twelve central banks, but this is only an appearance; it is a legacy from the days when much of the country harbored a populist suspicion of Easterners, Wall Streeters, and men in striped pants with cutaway coats. These suspicions were allayed by scattering Federal Reserve Banks around the country. But the Fed has actually been a single bank (with branches) at least since the legislative changes enacted by Congress in the 1930s. The power of any one of the twelve Banks depends pretty much on the influence it is able to exert, which in turn depends on the quality of its executive officers and its research staff.

Many of the commercial banks in the United States are not subject to the rules of the Federal Reserve System. Banks holding charters from the federal government have the right to put the word "National" in their name and the obligation to join the Federal Reserve System. But many banks hold state government charters; they are permitted but not required to join the Fed. If they choose *not* to join, they operate in accordance with state definitions of reserves and state-established legal reserve minima. Although less than half of all the commercial banks in the United States belong to the Federal Reserve System, member banks have more than three-fourths of the total assets and liabilities of the entire commercial banking system. We're going to simplify this account by pretending that *all* banks are subject to the rules and regulations of the Fed. Since the Fed indirectly but powerfully influences the position of all banks and not just those subject to its direct regulation, this assumption won't give a seriously misleading picture. In the next chapter, when we examine the processes of monetary management, we'll ask about the possible significance of the fact that the percentage of banks holding membership in the Fed has slowly decreased in recent years.

Bank Reserves as Constraints on the Money Supply

Because of its power to fix legal reserve requirements for member banks (within wide limits set by Congress) and its power to expand or contract the dollar volume of reserves, the Fed controls the lending activities of the commercial banking system and thus the process of money creation. Reserve requirements differ for time deposits and demand deposits; moreover, the legal reserve requirement on demand deposits currently varies between 8% and 17½%, depending on the size of a particular bank's total demand deposit liabilities. Under Fed regulations that became effective in 1975, a bank with $500 million in demand deposits must hold reserves equal to 8% of the first $2 million, 10½% of the next $8 million, 12½% of the next $90 million, 13½% of the next $300 million, and 17½% of all demand deposit liabilities over $400 million. (Note that demand deposits are bank *liabilities*; your bank owes you the amount in your checking account.) The Fed also decides what may count as legal reserves. Since 1960 it has been the banks' vault cash plus the deposits the commercial

banks themselves have at the Federal Reserve Bank of their district. To
see what all this has to do with changes in the money supply, we'll move
in for a close-up look at the First National Bank of Anywhere.

Suppose that the First National Bank has demand deposit liabilities of
$90 million and legal reserves of $12 million. (We ignore the complicating
but for our purposes irrelevant calculations that would be necessary if we
took account of other liabilities and the reserves held against them.) With
a little pencil work you can quickly calculate that First National has $1
million of reserves beyond its legal requirements. Against the first $2
million of those deposits it must hold an 8% reserve, or $.16 million;
against the next $8 million it must hold a 10½% reserve, or $.84 million;
and against the remaining $80 million it must hold a 12½% reserve, or $10
million. With $12 million in actual reserves and only $11 million legally
required, First National has excess legal reserves of $1 million. And excess
reserves are what banks can lend. So First National will be able to make
new loans of $1 million if it can find acceptable borrowers. Let's assume it
does so and watch what happens as a result.

First National extends the loans by creating new demand deposits for
its borrowers. After the loans have been made, then, First has $91 million
in demand deposit liabilities and an unchanged $12 million of reserves.
Since with a marginal reserve requirement of 12½% only $.08 million of
additional reserves must be held against the additional $1 million in liabil-
ities, the bank will still have excess legal reserves of $.92 million. But the
bank cannot expect those new liabilities to remain on deposit. The loans
were presumably taken out to finance expenditures. So the borrowers will
write checks against the new deposits, payable to customers of other banks
for the most part, and First National will lose reserves. To keep the example
neat, we'll assume that the $1 million just borrowed is all paid out by the
borrowers to people who maintain accounts in other banks. Recipients
of the checks deposit them in their own banks; these banks send the checks
to the Fed for clearance; the Fed subtracts the amount of the checks from
the recipient deposit of First National and adds it to the reserve deposits of
the recipient banks; the checks are then forwarded to First National, which
deducts the amounts from the demand deposit balance of the payers. At
the end of this process, First National will again have $90 million in
demand deposit liabilities but now only $11 million in legal reserves.

By this process First National has converted its excess legal reserves into
an addition to the stock of money. The new money has left First National
and now exists as new demand deposits in other banks. But First National
has acquired additional earning assets in the form of new loans, which
was its purpose in making the loans.

It should be clear from this brief account that excess reserves and a
demand for bank loans on the part of eligible borrowers are the two factors

jointly controlling the expansion of the money supply. The Fed can therefore facilitate the growth of the money supply either by reducing the legal reserve requirements or by increasing the dollar volume of reserves. The latter is in fact the Fed's regular operating lever in money management. We'll describe and evaluate the process in the next chapter. Postponing the question of how reserves originate, we now want to trace out what happens when reserves increase.

The Effect of Changes in Bank Reserves

Go back to the case of First National. We started the bank out with $1 million in excess legal reserves. (The word *legal* is important. If a bank's managers want to hold more reserves than the law requires, the entire amount of the legal excess will not in fact be "excess" and will not be available for new loans.) Suppose those reserves had just been created by the Fed because it wanted to expand the supply of money. We traced through the process by which the lending of the reserves added $1 million to the stock of money. But that won't be the end of the matter. A one-dollar change in reserves tends to cause a change in the money stock of *several* dollars. That's why bank reserves are sometimes called "high-power money."

To see why this is so, look at the new position of the banks in which that freshly created money was deposited. They jointly acquired $1 million in additional demand deposits *plus* $1 million in additional reserves. Remember that when the Fed cleared the checks, it transferred $1 million in reserves from the account of First National to the accounts of the recipient banks. So these recipient banks acquired, dollar for dollar, new reserves to match their new demand deposits.

But under a fractional-reserve banking system (where reserves need only be some fraction of deposits), new deposits plus matching new reserves create excess legal reserves. Just to keep matters simple, assume that all the deposits flow to banks in the $10–$100 million deposit category so that they are all subject to a $12\frac{1}{2}\%$ legal reserve requirement. These banks will consequently find themselves with $.875 million in excess legal reserves. If they don't want to hold the reserves and can find acceptable borrowers, they can now make new loans in that amount and thereby create an additional $.875 million of new money. But this still isn't the end, because the banks in which this newly created money is deposited will now acquire excess legal reserves: $.875 million of new demand deposits plus $.875 million of new reserves amounts to a $765,625 addition to excess legal reserves (if the applicable reserve requirement is still $12\frac{1}{2}\%$). The whole process can thus repeat itself again.

CHECK-CLEARING SERVICES

The use of demand deposits as a medium of exchange is greatly facilitated by the check-clearing services the Federal Reserve Banks provide. When an Amarillo, Texas, reader instructs his bank to pay $6.95 to Chess Fanatics Magazine and sends those instructions, in the guise of a check, to the magazine's office in Raleigh, North Carolina, how does the magazine collect? It certainly won't have a representative stop by the Amarillo bank to pick up the amount due. Instead it will deposit the check in its own bank, receive a $6.95 addition to its demand deposits, and let the bank worry about collecting from Amarillo. The Raleigh bank will collect by sending the check to the Federal Reserve Bank of Richmond, Virginia, which will credit it with a $6.95 addition to its reserve account. The Richmond Federal Reserve Bank will in turn send the check to the Federal Reserve Bank of Dallas, which will deduct $6.95 from the reserve account of the Amarillo bank and send it the check. When the check gets back to Amarillo, the chess fanatic will have $6.95 deducted from his account. And the canceled check will be sent to him in his monthly statement. The Federal Reserve Bank of Dallas remits $6.95 to the Federal Reserve Bank of Richmond through the Interdistrict Settlement Fund.

The Fed does not operate the only check-clearing services in the country. Banks often collect local checks through local clearing houses, and sometimes they even collect by sending the check directly to the bank on which it was drawn. The settlement of most checks drawn on member banks, however, is made through the balances the banks maintain with the Federal Reserve Bank of their district.

All checks collected and cleared through the Federal Reserve Banks must be paid in full by the banks on which they were drawn, without deduction of a fee or charge. A handful of banks still collect a fee for clearing checks and are hence ineligible to participate in the Fed's clearing system.

Although the cost of collecting and clearing checks is a substantial part of Fed expenses, the Federal Reserve Banks supply this service at no charge.

The "Money Multiplier"

The essential point is a simple one which should not get lost in the arithmetic. When the Fed (or any other factor) adds one dollar to bank reserves, it enables the commercial banking system to create several dol-

lars of additional money. Exactly how many additional dollars depends
on the applicable reserve requirement and the extent to which the newly
created money is shifted out of demand deposits. Some portion of newly
created demand deposits tends to be withdrawn into circulating currency.
Currency in circulation is no longer vault cash and is not included in bank
reserves. And this leakage of reserves reduces the value of the "money
multiplier."

To illustrate: if all banks were subject to a $12\frac{1}{2}\%$ marginal-reserve
requirement, if all legal excess reserves were loaned out, and there were
no leakage of currency into circulation (and no transfers from demand
deposits into time deposits), then $1 of new reserves would lead to
the creation of $8 in additional money. Why exactly $8? Because
$1 + (.875) + (.875)(.875) + (.875)^3 \ldots$, the expansion path of the money
creation process, ultimately approaches $1 \times 1/.125$, or 8.

The actual money multiplier is much less than this, running in recent
years between 2 and 3. A multiplier of 2.5 would result from a combination of an average applicable reserve requirement of 15% and a 25%
leakage of currency into circulation. The latter would occur if the public
withdrew $1 in currency for every $4 added to the money stock, and this
is close to actual practice in recent years. Of course, whether the money
multiplier is 2 or 8 or anything in between, the expansion process depends
on the ability of banks to locate eligible borrowers. So expansion takes
time; it doesn't occur instantaneously. That's another point to which
we'll return in chapter 19.

This entire discussion has been carried on in terms of excess reserves,
additional loans, and more money. It also works in reverse. When reserves
are reduced by an action of the Fed (or anyone else), the power of banks
to lend is contracted. When a bank's reserves fall below the legal minimum, it reduces its rate of new loans below the rate at which the old loans
are being repaid, in order to acquire additional reserves. If the entire
banking system is doing this, the result is a net contraction of loans and
hence a reduction in the money supply. Eventually, through the acquisition by the commercial banks of additional currency and the reduction of
demand deposits as the public repays loans, the legal minimum reserve-
to-deposit ratio will be reached. Then the process of contraction will stop.

How We Got This Way

Does it bother you that privately owned banks have the power to create
money? A power that the Constitution of the United States assigns to
Congress? It all came about because few people understood exactly what
was happening when it began. The Constitution speaks only of the power
to *coin* money, because almost everyone thought in 1790 that gold and
silver coins would be the dominant component of the money supply. By

THE MECHANICS OF MONEY CREATION

The mysterious character of money creation through bank lending diminishes when we describe it in terms of changes in the assets and liabilities of commercial banks. We can more easily focus on the elementary mechanics of the process if we adopt a few simplifying assumptions:

1. The entire commercial banking system is a single bank.
2. The bank maintains only the minimum reserves required by law.
3. There is no leakage of currency from the banks into circulation as demand deposits increase, and no transfer of demand deposits into time deposits.
4. The legal reserve requirement on all demand deposits is 20%.

We assume that Universal Bank has zero excess reserves at the outset and that, in accordance with the conventions of accounting, its total assets are equal to its total liabilities including net worth. To start the process moving, we'll have a prospector walk into one of the branches of Universal Bank with $10,000 worth of gold. He turns the gold over to the bank and receives in return a $10,000 demand deposit. Universal Bank sends the gold to the Federal Reserve Bank of its district and receives in return a $10,000 additional credit to its reserve account. The bank's balance sheet then looks like this:

Assets		Liabilities
Original assets	$700,000,000,000	$700,000,000,000 Original liabilities
Reserve account +	10,000	10,000 Prospector's demand deposit

Because Universal Bank need maintain only $2000 in reserves against $10,000 in demand deposits, it now has $8000 in excess reserves. It lends this amount to Avery by creating a demand deposit, and receives in return Avery's IOU. Avery writes a check for $8000 to Barnes, who deposits the check in the bank. The balance sheet will now look like this:

Assets		Liabilities
Original assets	$700,000,000,000	$700,000,000,000 Original liabilities
Reserve account +	10,000	10,000 Prospector's demand deposit
Avery's IOU	8,000	8,000 Barnes's demand deposit

Notice that *no reserves have been lost* even though the bank loaned out its excess reserves; the banking *system* does not lose reserves when deposits are transferred from one bank to another. Universal Bank still has the $10,000 in its reserve account; but with $18,000 in additional demand deposits it must now earmark $3600 as required reserves. That leaves $6400 in excess reserves which can be loaned to Clyde by giving him a demand deposit in that amount. When Clyde writes a $6400 check to Darrell and Darrell deposits the check, the balance sheet looks like this:

Assets	Liabilities
Original assets $700,000,000,000	$700,000,000,000 Original liabilities
Reserve account + 10,000	10,000 Prospector's demand deposit
Avery's IOU 8,000	8,000 Barnes's demand deposit
Clyde's IOU 6,400	6,400 Darrell's demand deposit

The bank will now have $24,400 in new demand deposits, against which it is required to hold $4880 in reserves. So $5120 in excess reserves will be available for lending.

If we continued to trace out in this way the growth in Universal Bank's assets and liabilities as it acquired additional IOUs and created additional demand deposits, each successive item would be 80% of the preceding item. The cumulative total of $10,000 + .8(\$10,000) + $.8^2(\$10,000)$ + $.8^3(\$10,000)$ + $\cdots$ + $.8^n(\$10,000)$ approaches $50,000 as n approaches infinity. The total will get very close to $50,000 while n is still quite small: ten repetitions of the process described above will bring the total to $45,705, and when n reaches twenty the total will be over $49,500.

Each additional dollar of reserves that enters the banking system enables Universal Bank ultimately to add $5 to the total money supply when the legal reserve requirement is 20%. The legal constraint on the banking system's ability to expand deposits on the basis of new reserves is given by the formula $1/R$, where R is the reserve requirement. Any other factor that also uses reserves, such as currency withdrawals, will reduce the value of the "multiplier" by increasing the denominator in the formula. Thus if the legal reserve requirement were 15% and the public always held $1 in currency for every $4 it held in demand deposits, the banking system would be able to create $2.50 in deposits for every $1 of new reserves. With the required reserve and currency holdings both stated as a percentage of demand deposits, the formula becomes: $1/(.15 + .25) = 1/.4 = 2.5$.

the time we fully realized that commercial banks could be money creators as important as the Mint or the Bureau of Engraving, we had accumulated enough experience with the system to let it continue. More importantly, perhaps, we weren't at all sure what to put in its place. The complex banking and monetary systems of the industrialized world were not based

BANK CREATION OF CURRENCY

Students are often surprised to learn that commercial banks, which are privately owned institutions operated for profit, create most of the money used as the medium of exchange in the United States. The suspicion that this just cannot be the case may account in part for their resistance to the notion that demand deposits are *really* money.

But for most of our nation's history the federal government has not even been the exclusive supplier of *currency*. Before the Civil War, the principal suppliers of paper money were privately owned banks that printed and distributed their own banknotes. Moreover, these banks were not chartered or controlled by the federal government. They were for the most part chartered by state governments and controlled in their note issues by the willingness of the public to accept the notes. These notes were usually promises to pay gold to the bearer on demand, which the banks issued in the process of extending loans. If the public had confidence in a bank's willingness and ability to redeem its obligations on demand, the notes might circulate indefinitely. If the public lost confidence in a bank, however, note holders would rush to demand redemption. If the bank did not have enough gold to meet its obligations, it would be forced to suspend redemption. Since few people would want to accept the notes of a bank that had suspended redemption, the value of the notes in circulation would fall to a fraction of their face value.

The currency system of the United States before the Civil War was consequently a bewildering variety of banknotes exchanging at uncertain and fluctuating percentages of their face value. In 1863, in an effort to bring greater order out of this chaos, the federal government established a national banking system. National banks were required to invest one-third of their capital in government bonds and were authorized to issue banknotes in an amount up to 90% of the market value of these bonds. (Creating support for the government bond market was probably the government's principal goal at this time.) These notes, called national banknotes, were printed for the banks by the Bureau of Engraving in order to give the currency a uniform appearance. Moreover, each national bank was required to accept the notes issued by other national banks at par. When relatively few banks elected to take out national charters, the federal government in 1865 imposed a 10% tax on state banknotes. This drove state banknotes out of circulation and created a much more uniform currency throughout the nation.

But by the end of the Civil War demand deposits had become more important than currency as a medium of exchange. And so the state banks were not driven out of business. They continued to make loans, but by creating demand deposits rather than by issuing banknotes.

on the principles described in this chapter and the next. On the contrary, these principles were discovered by examination of the processes that had already evolved. Bankers had created the system long before economists, government officials, or *bankers themselves* understood it.

If you wonder how it was possible for a functioning social institution to be created by people who did not understand it, then you're too much a rationalist to be a good historian. Comprehensive social institutions rarely develop in accordance with anyone's plan; they are much more likely to evolve out of step-by-step adjustments to unanticipated changes in circumstances. We must hurry on to add that the banking-monetary system that evolved in the United States often functioned badly, creating speculative booms, inflations, financial panics, bankruptcies, and recessions in a continuing succession, in addition to providing a medium of exchange and a credit mechanism to finance economic expansion.

Do we know enough now to control the banking-monetary system of the country and to ensure that the growth of the money supply keeps in even step with the expanding demand for money and credit, so that money lubricates without disrupting production and exchange? The next chapter carries us into that question.

Once Over Lightly

Money is a social institution that increases wealth by lowering costs of exchange. Low costs of exchange enable people to specialize more fully in accordance with their comparative advantages.

Money is used as the standard unit of accounting in comparing relative values because we have all had experience in using it as a medium of exchange.

Money could not function as a medium of exchange if it did not also function as a store of value over time. People accept money in return for other goods because they know they can hold the money and use it later to obtain the goods they want. But the fact that people can at low cost hold more or less money introduces additional uncertainty and complications into the functioning of an economic system.

An asset is moneylike to the degree that it is liquid. The liquidity of any asset depends on the cost of exchanging it for other assets. An asset that can be exchanged for other assets at zero cost is completely liquid.

The demand for liquidity (or the demand for money to hold) expresses people's desire to have a greater range of choices, more opportunities, and consequently additional wealth. The quantity of money people wish to hold will depend upon their income, their reading of the future, and the opportunity cost of holding money. The opportunity cost of holding money is the value of what is given up by not holding alternative assets.

Because liquidity is a matter of degree, there is no sharp line of distinction between the assets that are money and those that are not. Federal Reserve notes and coins are clearly part of the money supply. Demand deposits are also without any question part of the money supply. Time deposits cannot be used directly as a medium of exchange but are highly liquid; whether or not they should be counted in the money supply is more difficult to determine. Deposits in nonbank thrift institutions raise the same question. Since many other assets are also highly liquid, the decision on exactly what to include in the definition of the money supply must depend on an analysis of current practices and the uses to which the definition will be put.

The money supply increases when commercial banks make loans to their customers and decreases when customers repay the loans.

Banks can make new loans and thereby expand the stock of money when they hold reserves in excess of the minimum amounts established by the banking authorities.

The Federal Reserve Banks attempt to control changes in the stock of money by increasing or decreasing legal reserve minimums and by adding to or subtracting from the total of commercial bank reserves.

Under a system where banks must hold as reserves only a fraction of their total deposits, every one dollar change in reserves leads to a greater than one dollar change in deposits. The relation between changes in reserves and changes in the money supply will be governed primarily by legal reserve ratios, the extent to which the public withdraws additional currency from the banks as bank deposits increase, and the willingness of banks and borrowers to negotiate additional loans.

QUESTIONS FOR DISCUSSION

1. Would your existence be more or less secure if we had a barter economy rather than one using money? Why would we all be poorer if we had to rely exclusively on barter? Is a very poor person subject to 5% fluctuations in his income more or less secure than a wealthy person subject to 50% fluctuations in his income?

2. Can you think of any ways in which emphasis on money obscures the real workings and effects of economic events? What about an argument that the government of India could attack poverty by printing more rupees and distributing them to the poorest people?

3. How much money do you hold, on the average, over the course of a typical month? What would induce you to increase that amount? How could you do this? (Do not confuse money with income.)

4. Name some liquid assets that you own. Rank them in order of liquidity. What criterion are you using to determine relative liquidity?

5. You plan to buy a bicycle this year as soon as you've saved enough money. You have about half the amount saved when you read that bicycle prices are expected to rise considerably in coming months. What might you do? How would this affect your liquidity? Suppose that you have saved the entire purchase price, and then you read that overproduction of bicycles will probably result in large price decreases in coming months. What might you do, and how will your decision affect your liquidity?

6. Shares of common stock listed on a major exchange can be sold quickly—that is, exchanged for other assets. Are shares of stock as liquid as money? Why might a person hold part of his wealth in common stocks and part in money? Why might he shift the composition of his portfolio in order to hold more of one asset and less of the other?

7. Suppose everyone came to believe that prices were going to rise sharply in the next month or so. How would this belief affect their demand for money balances? How would it affect their demand for goods other than money? What effect would this likely have on the prices of goods other than money? What effect would it likely have on the price of money? (The price of money is the rate at which it exchanges for goods, just as the price of other goods is the rate at which they exchange for money.)

8. Money gets a lot of attention but tends to have a bad press. Are the authors of the following statements talking about money as we have defined it, or are they using money as a synonym or symbol for something else? What is that "something else" in each case in which you conclude that money is not really the subject of discussion?

   (a) "The love of money is the root of all evil." (Often misquoted as "Money is the root of all evil.")

   (b) "Health is . . . a blessing that money cannot buy."

   (c) "Don't marry for money."

   (d) "Well, fancy giving money to the government! Might as well have put it down the drain."

   (e) "Hath a dog money? Is it possible a cur can lend three thousand ducats?"

   (f) "If this be not love, it is madness, and then it is pardonable. Nay, yet a more certain sign than all this: I give thee my money."

   (g) "Wine maketh merry; but money answereth all things."

   (h) "Words are the tokens current and accepted for conceits, as moneys are for values."

   (i) "Money speaks a language all nations understand."

9. If you were to ask someone how much money he has in the bank, he might not distinguish in answering between his checking account balance and his savings account balance. Why would economists want to distinguish between the two?

10. At any moment in time, some already printed Federal Reserve notes will be in (*a*) the wallets of the public, (*b*) the vaults and tills of commercial banks, and (*c*) the vaults of Federal Reserve Banks. How does each enter into or otherwise affect the total money supply?

11. People cannot spend the deposits they hold in commercial bank savings accounts or savings and loan institutions without first withdrawing the funds, that is, converting them into currency or demand deposits. But since they are able to do that at almost no cost, these deposits are assets almost as liquid as checking account balances.

    (*a*) Does it follow that total spending ought to be more closely correlated with M_3 than with M_1?

    (*b*) What does a faster rate of increase in M_3 than in M_1 suggest about the public's spending *intentions?*

    (*c*) If electronic funds transfer systems lower the cost of spending savings deposits to the current cost of spending checking deposits, what effect would you expect to observe in the relative sizes of M_1, M_2, and M_3?

12. If bankers can create money, why can't you? Is it against the law for you to create an accepted medium of exchange? Can you think of a situation in which you might succeed in creating a little money? (Hint: Demand deposits, which serve as money, are liabilities of commercial banks; suppose your promissory notes were considered in the community as "good as gold"?)

13. If money is created by bank lending, is it also created by the lending of savings and loan associations, credit unions, and consumer credit companies? What is the difference?

14. Use the information provided in the text to test your understanding of the relationship between bank reserves and money creation.

    (*a*) Fog National Bank has $1 billion in demand deposit liabilities. How many dollars must it legally hold as reserves against these deposits? Do you get an answer of $157.75 million?

    (*b*) Suppose Fog Bank has $160 million in reserves. If we ignore time deposits and the reserves which they require, how large are the bank's excess legal reserves?

    (*c*) If the managers of Fog Bank prefer to maintain $2 million of reserves in addition to the minimum legal requirement, how large are Fog Bank's *excess* reserves?

    (*d*) Fog Bank loans its excess reserves of $250,000 to the Lovers Lanes Company for the purchase of new pin-setting equipment. When the equipment supplier deposits the $250,000 check in the River National Bank, which has total demand deposit liabilities of $200 million, what effect does this have on the River Bank's excess legal reserves?

(*e*) River Bank extends a new loan of $216,250 to a silver processor who uses it to purchase silver from a mine in Two Cushion, Montana. The Two Cushion Bank, where the check is deposited, has total demand deposit liabilities of $7 million. How much will the deposit add to the bank's excess legal reserves?

(*f*) The silver mine in Two Cushion uses all the money received to pay its employees. None of the miners maintains a bank account. They all cash their weekly checks and use currency to handle their purchases. What will happen to the Two Cushion Bank's excess legal reserves right after payday?

(*g*) If all the merchants in Two Cushion use the local bank, what will happen to the bank's liabilities and reserves over the course of the week?

15. How does a withdrawal of currency from checking accounts affect the money supply? How does it affect a bank's reserves? How does it affect excess legal reserves? What effect might this have subsequently on the money supply?

19

THE FEDERAL RESERVE
AND THE MONETARY SYSTEM

The money supply increases as commercial banks acquire new earning assets by lending out their excess reserves. That was the theme of the last half of chapter 18. It raises a long list of questions.

Where do reserves come from? What are the controls on the system? How does the Fed, as the nation's central bank and, by act of Congress, the manager of the monetary system, exercise its authority? How well does it do so? What are its goals? Are the goals it pursues the goals it ought to pursue? Does it have the power to achieve the goals it sets? If you have definitive answers to all those questions when you've read this chapter, you'll know more than the authors or anyone else we're aware of. But at least when you've finished you should have a better idea of where the troublesome questions are and some insight into the interesting life of a central banker.

BANK RESERVES AND THE MONEY SUPPLY

Bank reserves. What are they? Where do they come from? The *Federal Reserve Bulletin,* a monthly publication of the Fed, regularly lists all the Factors Supplying Reserve Funds. But the *Federal Reserve Bulletin* regularly prints more than almost anyone would want to know. The important thing is to understand the principal factors that contribute to *changes* in reserve funds. The best approach is to think it through rather than look it up.

Any one bank can add to its reserves by attracting deposits from other banks. If you want to close your checking account in First National and open an account in Second National, the easiest way is to write a check and deposit it in your new account. When the Fed clearinghouse gets the check, it will subtract the amount of your balance from the reserve account of First and credit it to the reserve account of Second. Similarly, one bank acquires reserves from other banks as its current depositors receive and deposit payments from the customers of other banks. But none of this alters the *total* reserves of the banking system.[1]

The system as a whole will acquire or lose reserves as the public reduces or expands its holdings of currency. Currency that goes into circulation reduces vault cash. If the banks replenish their vault cash by obtaining more Federal Reserve notes, the Fed deducts the value of the notes from the banks' reserve accounts.

Another source of fluctuations in total system reserves is *float.* It takes time for checks to move through the banking system, from the bank of deposit in Des Moines, let us say, to the Federal Reserve Bank in Chicago, then to the Federal Reserve Bank in San Francisco, and finally to the bank in Sacramento on which the check was originally drawn. The Chicago FRB may credit the reserve account of the Des Moines bank before the San Francisco FRB gets around to debiting the reserve account of the Sacramento bank. In the interim, total bank reserves will have grown. *Float* is the term applied to the portion of bank reserves that results from the double counting of uncollected checks. The total can and does vary considerably, due to transportation tie-ups, long holiday weekends, or other seasonal factors. The Fed must estimate and predict the amount of float in bank reserves if it wants to exercise a precise control over those reserves; uncompensated changes in float can lead to sharp expansions and contractions of bank lending.[2]

The United States Treasury is all by itself a potential bull in the china shop. The flow of funds through Treasury hands, as you well know, is enormous; it is also bunchy rather than smooth and steady, with receipts heavily concentrated around tax due dates and those times when the Treasury is selling large issues of government bonds. The Treasury uses the Federal Reserve as its banker, so that a check drawn on a commercial bank and deposited by the Internal Revenue Service draws reserves out of commercial bank reserve accounts. The Treasury tries to compensate by depositing some of the funds received back into its Tax and Loan

1. Because bank deposits are subject to different reserve requirements, such a shuffling could alter the pattern of excess reserves and thus expand or contract the banking system's ability to lend.

2. Individuals who write checks on nonexistent balances shortly before payday knowing that the checks will take several days to reach their bank are creating float for their own use

Accounts at major commercial banks. The goal is to keep the bull quiet in the china shop: the Treasury, in consultation with the money managers at the Fed, tries to exert a neutral effect on reserves so that they can be more easily controlled by those who are supposed to be in charge.

Another factor affecting reserves is foreign exchange, an important topic that we'll have to postpone to chapter 23. It's enough for now if you think about what happens when the authors send £40 to the journal *Economica* in England for permission to reprint "The Economics of a P.O.W. Camp"—a bargain at that price as you'll surely agree. Their joint bank account falls by about $95 and an English account rises by £40. Our bank owes us less and some English bank owes *Economica* more. How was the English bank persuaded to add £40 to its obligations? It received compensation. From whom? From our bank, to balance the $95 by which it reduced its liabilities to us. The details don't have to concern us further. But it should be clear that the transaction requires, at some step, the transfer of reserves out of the account of an American bank into the account of a British bank. Foreign exchange, as we'll see later on, can be a highly unsettling force on a domestic monetary system.

Controlling Reserves for Policy Purposes

So far the play has been *Hamlet* without the prince of Denmark. The time has come to introduce the Fed, the central character, and its tools of monetary management. The most powerful tool and the one that sets the stage for the rest is its authority to establish legal reserve requirements. The Fed has been sliding those percentages around quite a bit in recent years; but its aim has been more to adjust certain relationships between banks than to stimulate or contract bank lending.[1] Changes in reserve requirements are generally viewed by Fed officials as blunt weapons, not suitable for the delicate surgery that monetary management usually requires. They prefer to take the reserve requirements as the framework and alter the volume of reserves.

How is that done? The briefest explanation is that the Fed creates and destroys reserves in the same way that commercial banks create and destroy money: by increasing and reducing their loans.

The Fed can extend a loan to a commercial bank directly. This is the second tool it uses to affect bank lending activity. It does so by crediting the bank's reserve account and taking in return the bank's IOU or someone else's IOU (a government bond, for example) that happens to be in

---

1. Recall the paragraphs at the end of chapter 18 on the trial and error evolution of the United States banking system. Variations in reserve requirements for different banks often make sense only if you're familiar with history.

the bank's portfolio—just as a commercial bank lends to its customers by creating a deposit balance in return for an IOU. This directly increases commercial bank reserves. The interest rate at which such loans are made is called the *discount rate.* It's a financial-page celebrity, because many people look upon it as a sign of current Fed policy. It is probably more of a symbol than a genuine rationing device, since the Fed is selective about the banks to which it will loan. Official Fed policy is to accommodate special circumstances rather than loan to any bank willing to pay the rate, and to behave more like a Dutch uncle than a profit-seeking lender. But that's what most people look for from a central bank.

The third and principal technique that the Fed employs to control reserves is the purchase and sale of U.S. government securities. This is also a way of increasing or reducing its loans, either to the United States Treasury when the Fed buys newly issued securities, or to previous purchasers and holders of these securities. The Fed currently holds a portfolio of government securities approaching a value of $100 billion. When it increases its holdings by purchasing securities through dealers in government bonds, it writes checks for the amount of the purchases on its own credit. These checks are deposited in commercial banks. When the banks forward the checks to their Federal Reserve Bank, they are credited with additions to their reserve balances.

In short, the acquisition by the Fed of new earning assets (which is the same thing as the extension of credit to someone, whether commercial banks, the government, or holders of government bonds) tends to increase commercial bank reserves by that amount. And this, as we have seen, enables commercial banks to increase their own loans and thereby the money supply.

The entire process is reversible, of course. The Fed can withdraw credit from member banks or sell some of the government securities already in its asset portfolio. This results in a reduction of commercial bank reserves. For example, when the Fed sells a $1000 government bond, the bond winds up in the hands of someone who pays the bond dealer with a check. But the dealer in turn pays the Fed with a check, and the amount of the check is deducted from the reserve account of the bank on which it is drawn. That wipes out a portion of the total reserves of the banking system.

The Open Market Committee

Federal Reserve purchases and sales of government securities, with the intent of changing commercial bank reserves and thereby affecting the money supply, are called *open market operations.* This is the principal working tool of monetary management. A special committee, made up of the seven members of the board of governors and five of the twelve Reserve Bank presidents, sits as the Open Market Committee and continuously determines the direction of monetary policy. The question of the effectiveness with which the Open Market Committee and the Federal Reserve System manage the money supply has long been debated by both friends and critics of the Fed and by both economists and politicians.

There are two main questions. One concerns the determination of policy. Does the Fed set appropriate goals? The other concerns the execution of policy. Does the Fed do an effective job of achieving the goals it sets for itself? The questions are related, of course, because intelligent policy formulation presupposes a realistic assessment of technical capabilities. The football coach who orders a passing strategy when his team is two touchdowns behind in the fourth quarter is making a poor policy decision if his quarterback has a rubber arm and all his receivers have butterfingers. Textbook accounts are often like football plays on the blackboard; both of them tend to gloss over problems of execution. We must not simply assume that the Open Market Committee automatically does Good, or even that it succeeds all the time in achieving what it sets out to do.

What Can the Fed Actually Control?

In reality, the Fed has no direct control over the money supply. This should be clear from our description of the process by which money is created and destroyed in the United States. The Fed holds the money supply on a leash, and a somewhat elastic leash at that. It can let out the leash—that is, pump additional reserves into the banking system—but exactly how or when this will affect the money supply depends on the responses of the commercial banks and their customers. If they aren't straining at the leash, eager to make new loans, the leash may simply go slack when the Fed extends it: the new reserves will not be fully used to make additional loans and thus create additional money. The years from 1929 to 1939 provide the best example. During that period, the *total* reserves of member banks increased from \$2.4 billion to \$11.5 billion, while their *required* reserves increased only from \$2.35 billion to \$6.5 billion. In short, member banks in 1929 tended to hold only the reserves required by law; they turned the rest of their reserves into earning assets, and hence into money, by lending them out. But in 1939, banks retained reserves far beyond the legal requirement. Almost 45% of the reserves held by member banks at the end of 1939 were over and above the minimum requirements set by the rules and regulations of the Fed. From the standpoint of the cautious and conservative banking community, those legally uncommitted reserves were not *excess* reserves. The very low interest rates on low-risk assets gave bankers little incentive to acquire them. They preferred to hold the reserves and hope for better opportunities.

One must be careful about deriving generalizations from the experi-

THROUGH THE BALANCE SHEET LOOKING GLASS

You will acquire a surer grasp of the basic principles of monetary management if you trace through the effects of various actions both on the consolidated balance sheets of the Federal Reserve Banks and on the balance sheet of the Universal Bank (the single bank we introduced in the last chapter to represent the entire commercial banking system).

The number preceding each entry on the balance sheets corresponds to the number assigned to the action as described below. Notice that after each action has been completed the equality between assets and liabilities will have been maintained on each balance sheet.

1. The Fed buys $1000 worth of new securities from the Treasury.
2. The government purchases $1000 worth of rubber cement from the Sanford Ink Company.
3. The Fed sells $500 worth of government bonds, through a bond dealer, to the Sanford Ink Company.
4. Sanford withdraws $100 in currency for the petty cash drawer.
5. Universal Bank replenishes its vault cash by obtaining $100 of additional Federal Reserve notes.
6. The Fed loans Universal Bank $400 and takes as collateral prime commercial paper held by Universal Bank.
7. Universal Bank has acquired through all these steps $800 in additional legal reserves and $400 in additional demand deposits. If the legal reserve requirement is 20%, it has $720 in excess legal reserves. It loans $720 to International Business Machines.
8. IBM pays $720 in taxes due to the federal government.
9. The government transfers $720 from its account at the Fed to its Tax and Loan Account at Universal Bank.
10. The government purchases $720 worth of rubber bands from Elasto, Inc., with a check drawn on its Tax and Loan Account. (We would merely be retracing the preceding step if we had the government transfer the funds back to its Fed account before making the purchase.)
11. Universal Bank repays its $400 loan from the Fed.
12. The Fed lowers the legal reserve requirement to 20%. (There are no entries on the balance sheet corresponding to this action. Why not? What consequences would you predict?)

| FEDERAL RESERVE BANKS | | UNIVERSAL BANK | |
Assets	Liabilities	Assets	Liabilities
(1) + $1000 government bonds	(1) + $1000 Treasury deposits		
	(2) − $1000 Treasury deposits	(2) + $1000 reserve account	(2) + $1000 Sanford demand deposits
	(2) + $1000 UB reserve account		
(3) − $500 government bonds	(3) − $500 UB reserve account	(3) − $500 reserve account	(3) − $500 Sanford demand deposits
		(4) − $100 vault cash	(4) − $100 Sanford demand deposits
	(5) + $100 Federal Reserve notes outstanding	(5) + $100 vault cash	
	(5) − $100 UB reserve account	(5) − $100 reserve account	
(6) + $400 commercial paper	(6) + $400 UB reserve account	(6) + $400 reserve account	
		(6) − $400 commercial paper	
		(7) + $720 IBM IOU	(7) + $720 IBM demand deposits
	(8) + $720 Treasury deposits	(8) − $720 reserve account	(8) − $720 IBM demand deposits
	(8) − $720 UB reserve account		
	(9) − $720 Treasury deposits	(9) + $720 reserve account	(9) + $720 Treasury deposits
	(9) + $720 UB reserve account		
			(10) − $720 Treasury deposits
			(10) + $720 Elasto demand deposits
		(11) − $400 reserve account	
(11) − $400 commercial paper	(11) − $400 UB reserve account	(11) + $400 commercial paper	

ences of the 1930s. Banks in the Federal Reserve System have not allowed their excess legal reserves to increase beyond 4% of their total reserves since the end of the Korean war. And during the last decade the ratio of excess legal to total reserves has hung in the one-half of 1% to 2% range while trending downward. Since excess legal reserves represent foregone earning opportunities for banks, we should expect the banks to be

straining continuously against the leash—barring the kind of crisis of confidence that seems to have paralyzed a lot of economic activity in the 1930s. But even a little slack and small fluctuations in banks' holdings of excess reserves are enough to blunt the edge of Fed attempts to control the money supply with precision.

The leash analogy suggests that reducing the money supply may be easier than increasing it. After all, you can rein a dog in against his will (think of a Pekingese, not a Great Dane), even though you can't make him leave your side just by giving him more rope. There is some validity in the analogy. But the leash of monetary control is, as we said earlier, a somewhat elastic one, so that even contractionary policy is less precise than people at the Fed would prefer. By shifting the composition of their assets and liabilities in response to Fed pressure, the commercial banks can resist efforts to bring down the money supply. For example, banks might persuade some of their checking account customers to transfer a portion of their demand deposit balances into time deposits, on which the legal reserve requirement is much lower. That wouldn't increase the reserves of the bank, but it would increase the excess reserves by reducing the amount of legally required reserves.

The public itself has a large number of ways in which it can frustrate the intentions of the nation's money managers at the Fed. Of course, no one sets out obstinately to deflect the course of monetary policy; single individuals, and even single institutions, probably couldn't succeed in such an undertaking, anyway. But people do respond to changing circumstances in ways calculated to secure their own best advantage. Suppose, for example, that interest rates rise rapidly, as they did in 1973 and, after a brief fall, again in 1974. This could well reduce people's willingness to hold money in the form of demand deposits, on which banks are legally prohibited from paying interest. If a substantial quantity of demand deposits is shifted into savings accounts, M_1 will fall. But that won't be the end of the matter. Since time deposits are subject to a significantly lower reserve requirement, the transfer of funds out of demand deposits will increase the excess reserves and hence the lending power of the commercial banks. As new loans subsequently increase, M_1 will rise once more. In short, a widespread decision to reduce demand deposits and build up time deposits is capable of causing the total of demand *and* time deposits to increase. And such decisions might be made simultaneously by many people in response to changing conditions that the Fed itself brought about.

Federal Reserve data reveal clearly that M_1 and M_2 are not rigidly connected. And neither is rigidly connected to the variables over which the Fed has direct control: reserves and reserve requirements. We really should not be surprised to discover that the Fed often sets targets for itself that it subsequently misses by a large margin.

Returning to our leash analogy: Further complications arise from the fact that the dog on one end of the leash isn't always in sight of his master on the other end. The Fed obtains regular and reasonably accurate data on the money supply from member banks, but banks outside the system report much less frequently on the amount of their deposits. The Fed has to make estimates, therefore, and those estimates sometimes turn out to be wrong by a wide margin. The simple way to handle this problem would be to require all commercial banks to join the Federal Reserve System. Officials at the Fed are alarmed by the trend of recent years for state-chartered banks to leave the system and for new banks to enter business without joining. The proportion of total deposits in member banks fell from 86% to 77% between 1947 and 1974 and could go considerably lower if more banks decide that they prefer state to federal reserve requirements.

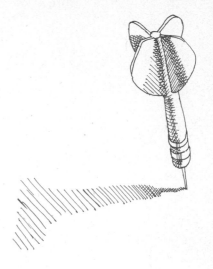

But the Fed will encounter serious political obstacles if it tries to tighten up its control by getting Congress to require Federal Reserve membership for all commercial banks. The nonmember banks will obviously lobby against such a move, and they can expect support from a number of sources. There are people who think that the Fed is incompetent and should have its power curtailed; others think that the Fed is really controlled by the banking interests it's supposed to regulate and should therefore be given no additional authority. Then there are the state banking officials who don't want to lose their functions or their jobs and can be counted on to employ the rhetoric of states' rights in defense of the present dual system. Whether the United States Constitution settles this question depends on how one interprets the power to "coin money." The authors of the Constitution did not even foresee the importance of banknotes and had no inkling at all of the role that commercial bank deposits would eventually play in the economy as the most important component of the money supply. Had they anticipated this development, they might have reserved to Congress and agencies of its creation the exclusive right to charter and regulate banks. But since they did not, and since the present dual system has a long history, the Fed will not find it easy to persuade Congress that all banks should be required to join the Federal Reserve System or at least be bound by its rules. And so the leash may become even longer and more elastic in the years ahead.

What Is the Target and Where Is It?

The execution of monetary policy is also made difficult by the fact that open market operations are designed to adjust to a moving target when no one can be quite sure at the moment of adjustment exactly where it is or which way it's moving. Worse than that, the target is typically several targets, and they may be moving in different directions. That calls to mind the problem raised earlier: What exactly do we mean by the money

TECHNOLOGY AND THE MONEY SUPPLY

In 1974 First Federal Savings and Loan of Lincoln, Nebraska, concluded an agreement with a local supermarket chain that established the nation's first system of electronic branch banks. Any customer of the Hinky Dinky supermarket chain who also maintained an account with First Federal could pay for his groceries without currency, check, or credit card. The grocery clerk used a small computer terminal to transfer the amount of the purchases from the customer's account into the account that Hinky Dinky maintained at First Federal.

Such electronic branches have been proliferating ever since. A few commercial banks have stepped gingerly into electronic funds transfer systems; but savings and loan associations have been scrambling to get in. The reason is simple. S and L's are not allowed to provide checking account service; electronic funds transfer systems enable them partly to bypass that constraint. By establishing a terminal at the point of sale, they can provide a service much like a checking account, and in some ways even superior. And they can thereby attract a portion of the deposits that now go into checking accounts at commercial banks.

If government regulatory authorities do not intervene (and they are under great pressure to do so), electronic funds transfer might in a few years take over much of the work currently done by demand deposits. If savings and loan associations provide the service, the public will begin to deposit in them a larger percentage of funds that now go into demand deposits. And so deposits in nonbank thrift institutions will increasingly include highly active money. If commercial banks provide the service, they will probably allow consumers to transfer funds from time deposits.

All of this will tend to change the relation between aggregate expenditures and M_1, M_2, and M_3, and will compel economists and monetary officials to reformulate their definitions of the money supply and of the targets at which monetary policy ought to aim.

supply? Should the Fed try to control only M_1, demand deposits and currency held by the nonbank public? Or should the object of its control be M_2 or possibly M_3?[1] The case for concentrating on M_1 is that M_1 is the

1. Fed officials have in recent years begun to suggest that still more comprehensive measures of the money supply than M_3 might be the appropriate gauge for policymakers to watch, and two-digit subscripts for M have started to appear in their discussions.

actual medium of exchange in the economy; it is what we use in making expenditures, and aggregate expenditures ought to be the Fed's real concern. If aggregate expenditures exceed the capacity of the economic system to produce goods at the current prices, prices will be bid up and inflation will result. But if aggregate expenditures fall short of productive capacity at current prices, output may fall and the economy may slide into a recession. However, aggregate spending could well be more closely correlated with M_2 or M_3 if spending depends significantly on liquidity and people view *all* deposits in financial institutions as liquid wealth. On which measure should the Fed focus?

One way to answer that question might be to compare each measure of the money stock with the total of expenditures for that year and see which measure is most closely correlated with expenditures. That's what we've done in table 19A.

The dollar figures are the money supply *in December of the preceding year.* Thus money supply data for December 1959 are listed with 1960, on the assumption that the stock of money most likely to influence 1960 spending is the stock at the outset of the year. This seems more plausible than using the average money stock over the course of 1960.

The second column under each measure of the money stock shows the

Table 19A

Year	M$_1$ Money stock	M$_1$ % change	M$_1$ GNP/ money stock	M$_2$ Money stock	M$_2$ % change	M$_2$ GNP/ money stock	M$_3$ Money stock	M$_3$ % change	M$_3$ GNP/ money stock
1960	$143.4		3.51	$210.9		2.39	$299.4		1.68
1961	144.2	.56%	3.61	217.1	2.94%	2.40	314.4	5.01%	1.65
1962	148.7	3.12	3.77	228.6	5.30	2.45	336.5	7.03	1.67
1963	150.9	1.48	3.91	242.8	6.21	2.43	362.9	7.85	1.63
1964	156.5	3.71	4.04	258.9	6.63	2.44	393.2	8.35	1.61
1965	163.7	4.60	4.18	277.1	7.03	2.47	426.3	8.42	1.61
1966	171.3	4.64	4.38	301.3	8.73	2.49	462.6	8.52	1.62
1967	175.4	2.39	4.53	317.8	5.48	2.50	485.2	4.89	1.64
1968	186.9	6.56	4.62	349.6	10.01	2.47	532.6	9.77	1.62
1969	201.7	7.92	4.61	382.3	9.35	2.43	576.8	8.30	1.61
1970	208.7	3.47	4.68	392.2	2.59	2.49	593.5	2.90	1.65
1971	221.4	6.09	4.76	425.3	8.44	2.48	642.8	8.31	1.64
1972	235.3	6.28	4.92	473.1	11.24	2.45	727.9	13.24	1.59
1973	255.8	8.71	5.06	525.7	11.12	2.46	823.2	13.09	1.57
1974	271.5	6.14	5.15	572.2	8.85	2.44	895.3	8.76	1.56

Sources: Board of Governors of the Federal Reserve System; Bureau of Economic Analysis

different rates at which each increased, from year to year. The figures show the percentage increase over the preceding year. Thus M_1 increased .56% from 1960 to 1961. (More accurately, as explained in the last paragraph, this was the percentage increase from December 1959 through December 1960.)

The numbers in the third column under each measure show gross national product for the year divided by the money stock. We divided the money supply into GNP to obtain the numbers we're finally after, on the assumption that GNP is a good proxy for total expenditures. There are, as you know from chapter 17, many expenditures that do not enter into the calculation of gross national product, but it's reasonable to suppose that total expenditures from year to year vary proportionately with GNP.

What do the data show? The relation between the stock of money and total expenditures is reasonably stable from year to year, no matter which concept of money we use. The ratio of GNP to M_1 has been rising over time, but it has been rising fairly steadily. The ratio of GNP to M_3 has not moved from year to year by more than 4%, the amount by which it fell from 1971 to 1972. But M_2 shows the most stable relationship to GNP since 1960. The maximum deviations from the average value of 2.45 were a minus 2.5% (1960) and a plus 2% (1967).

The Velocity of Money Circulation

It will be easier to talk about this ratio if we give it a name. Fortunately, it already has a name. Those who study the relationship between the money supply and aggregate spending call it the *velocity of money circulation* or just *velocity.* (It is sometimes called *income velocity,* because it is the velocity with which money circulates relative to expenditures for goods included

in the calculation of GNP.) It is the average number of times each unit of money changed hands to accommodate total spending on GNP.

The economic meaning of the velocity numbers becomes clearer if we look at them in a slightly different way. In 1972, for example, the public held currency, demand deposits, and time deposits equal in total to $\frac{1}{2.45}$ or 41% of total expenditures on GNP. In 1973, when M_2 was more than $50 billion greater than in the preceding year, it was still about 41% of GNP. Another increase of almost $50 billion in M_2 in 1974 failed to bring any substantial change in that percentage: it continued to be 41% of GNP. It certainly would appear that the public prefers to hold currency plus demand and time deposits equal to about 41% of expenditures on GNP. Despite the sharply different percentage rates at which M_2 has increased from year to year since 1960 (ranging from $2\frac{1}{2}$% to $11\frac{1}{4}$%), the public's holdings of M_2 have varied only between 40% and 42% of GNP.

Does it follow from all of this that the Fed can control the rate at which gross national product grows by controlling the rate of growth in M_2? Have we perhaps found a key to stabilization policy in this stable relationship between M_2 and GNP? Matters are unfortunately not that simple, as later chapters will show. But several questions can be raised at this point even though we are not yet in a position to answer them adequately. In the first place, would M_2 and GNP continue to be so closely correlated if the Fed set out consciously to use one as a means of controlling the other? We could have more confidence in the *future* stability of that relationship if we had a satisfactory theoretical explanation for it. In the absence of such a theoretical explanation we have nothing but an historical correlation; and in human affairs we cannot always be certain that the future will be like the past. One of our subsequent tasks will be to examine a possible reason for the relationship between total expenditures and the stock of

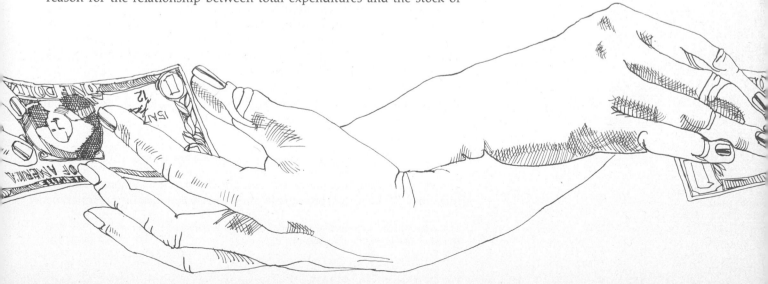

money and to see how much confidence we're entitled to have in the stock of money as an instrument for controlling total spending.

But a more serious dilemma presents itself when we think about the composition of GNP. GNP is equal to real output *times* the price level. An increase in GNP can therefore occur as a result of a decline in the level of production and an increase in prices. That's exactly what did occur from 1973 to 1974. Gross national product rose by 8%, but it did so because a 10.3% increase in prices more than made up for a 2.2% decline in real output. Inflation is hardly compensation for recession. The ability to control the rate of growth in GNP will only be socially useful if it entails the ability to affect *separately* the rate of real growth and the rate of change in the price level.[1]

The third critical question concerns the technical and political constraints on the Fed's ability to manipulate M_2 or any other variable it sets out to control. It's a gross oversimplification to suppose that the Fed has a monetary brake and a monetary accelerator with which it adjusts the money supply as easily and surely as you slow down and speed up your car in traffic. Monetary management may be more like driving a balky mule train which sometimes refuses to go and sometimes won't stop going even when firmly ordered to halt. Let's take a closer look.

FORMULATING AND EXECUTING POLICY

The problems of policy formulation facing the Open Market Committee arise from several sources. The first is uncertainty about the current state of the economy. What's happening to gross national product, employment, prices, exports and imports? It's not enough to have information about what *has* happened—such information is never wholly accurate anyway, and it always arrives with a time lag. If policy is to be effective in countering undesirable trends, policymakers must make good predictions about what *will* happen. The point is obvious and should not have to be mentioned; unfortunately, the obvious is often easy to overlook, and stabilization policy is much too frequently discussed on the assumption that policymakers possess infallible crystal balls.

Political Constraints on Monetary Policy

A second set of problems arises from the fact that the monetary authorities are under continual pressure to pursue goals that may be incompatible

---

1. Appendix 6 at the end of this book presents a statistical history of the 1974–1975 recession which vividly illustrates this dilemma.

with one another. One such goal is the maintenance of an "orderly market" for government bonds. The phrase is in quotation marks because at times in the past it has really meant making sure that the Treasury can sell new securities when it wants to without depressing the price of government bonds. Deficit spending by the federal government requires the Treasury to bid for funds against other borrowers, often on such a large scale that the borrowing exerts significant upward pressure on interest rates. The Fed, therefore, assumes responsibility for what it calls "even keel" operations whenever the Treasury is engaged in sizeable offerings of new debt. The Fed supplies additional reserves to the banking system at such times to help insure that the Treasury will find purchasers for its bonds without raising interest rates very much and squeezing out other borrowers. This goal can conflict with the Fed's aim of controlling bank reserves to achieve stability of prices and production.

The Fed is also under continual political pressure to keep interest rates down. Down to what? That's rarely made clear. But lower interest rates are better than higher ones in the eyes of a lot of people with considerable political influence. The view persists in some circles that high interest rates benefit bankers at the expense of small business firms, veterans and others who wish to buy homes, and "little people" generally. Who would choose to side with the bankers in such an unequal conflict of interests? Tight money; credit scarcity; bad times for the building industry and the many people (from construction workers, contractors, and materials suppliers through realtors to current and potential homeowners) whose fortunes are tied up with that industry; a falling stock-market average; reduced spending; more unemployment—these are all in the package of associated ills that people point to as evidence that the Fed is pursuing an unduly restrictive monetary policy. And rising interest rates are the most visible indicator, the flashing red light which supposedly signals that the Fed is "putting the economy through the wringer" or creating a "credit crunch." The popularity of such metaphors is itself vivid evidence of the public attitude toward restrictive monetary policy.

Opposition to high interest rates (where "high" often means no more than "higher than they once were") reflects in part an inability to see the necessity of rationing. This is coupled to some extent with hostility toward rationing by means of higher prices, an attitude we've encountered previously. But in the case of interest rates the problem is compounded by the apparently widespread belief that high interest rates arise from a scarcity of money. And money, of course, is only scarce if the monetary authorities decide to make it scarce.

But high interest rates can be attributed to a tight money policy only under special circumstances. In 1973 and 1974, for example, when the prime rate (the rate banks charge on their most secure loans) shot up to

BOND PRICES AND INTEREST RATES

If a bond that will pay $1000 upon maturity ten years from now can be purchased for $558.40, the effective interest rate on that bond is 6%. Table 12B shows that $1000 to be received in ten years has a present value of $558.40 if the interest rate is 6%.

Suppose that the Fed owns a large number of these bonds and begins to sell heavily. The price of the bonds will fall, just as the price of wheat falls when the supply increases relative to the demand. If the price of the bonds fell all the way to $463.19, the effective interest rate would become 8%. If, on the other hand, the Fed began a large-scale purchasing operation that pulled the price of the bonds up to $613.91, the interest rate would decline to 5%. (Check those results in table 12B.)

Note that the effective interest rate on a marketable security which promises a fixed amount of money does not depend upon what is printed on the bond or what was promised by the original seller. It depends upon the price of the bond in relation to its maturity date.

Does this mean that if you want to buy government bonds but avoid risk you had better purchase nonmarketable securities? Not at all. Suppose you paid $55.84 for a nonmarketable bond which promises to pay $100 in ten years. You will receive 6% interest if you hold the bond to maturity. But if interest rates rise the next day to 8%, you will have lost out on an additional 2% per year by locking yourself in for ten years. If you had purchased a marketable security instead, its price would have fallen to $46.32. The difference of $9.52 is the present value of the additional 2% interest that you just missed out on. Interest is lost in one way, capital value is lost in the other way.

The federal government does allow purchasers of nonmarketable securities to sell their bonds back to the government prior to maturity ("cash" them) for the original principal plus accumulated interest. But the interest accumulates during the first years at less than a 6% rate, so that purchasers of these bonds incur a financial penalty if they fail to hold them to maturity. Bond purchasers can choose their risks, but they cannot avoid them.

record levels, reaching 12% in July of 1974 and staying at that level into October, the cause was definitely *not* tight money. The cause was the experience of inflation and the general expectation of continued inflation. Many financial commentators nevertheless continued to equate high interest rates with tight money and to take the 12% prime rate as incontrovertible evidence that the Fed was "strangling" the economy by "choking off" the supply of money and credit. (Note the metaphors once again.)

Nominal and Real Interest Rates

It may well be that the Fed did not allow sufficient growth in the money stock in 1973 and 1974. The point here is only that interest rates in 1974 were *not* evidence of this fact. We must look closely at the relation between monetary policy and interest rates if we are to avoid the fundamental error that many financial commentators committed in 1974 by using the prime rate (and other interest rates) as evidence of tight money. When the Fed increases the supply of money, the demand remaining constant, elementary supply and demand analysis tells us that the price of money will fall. That's correct. *But interest is not the price of money!* Confusion multiplies like mosquitoes in a mountain thaw when we think of interest as the price of money. Interest rates can be thought of as the price of *credit*; but the price of *money* is the value of money or its purchasing power. Just as the price of strawberries is measured by the amount of money for which strawberries exchange, so the price of money is the amount of strawberries for which money will exchange, or the amount of pipe wrenches, baked beans, book ends, for which it exchanges. .

When the Fed increases bank reserves as part of an easier money policy, banks are enabled to expand their lending. Credit becomes easier to obtain and interest rates consequently do tend to move downward. Another way of looking at it is to note that the Fed increases bank reserves by purchasing large quantities of government securities in the bond market. This tends to raise the price of the bonds; and since bond prices are inversely related to their interest yields, we can say that it reduces the interest rate on government bonds. To the extent that government bonds and other interest-paying assets are substitutes, the purchase operations of the Fed push all interest rates down. The two ways of viewing the matter are complementary and lead to the same conclusion: easier money leads to lower interest rates. At least momentarily.

But we must push the analysis further. What happens to the new money created by the Fed when it purchased those bonds and by the commercial banking system when it used the addition to bank reserves to make new loans? The increase in the money supply tends to increase aggregate demand. If the demand for credit from investors, local governments, and consumers expands when aggregate demand grows, that will tend to pull interest rates back up. The net effect after a longer period of time cannot easily be predicted. More importantly, if the expansionary monetary policy leads to an excessive rate of increase in aggregate demand, prices will start to rise. And *the expectation of rising prices will cause interest rates to rise.* Why? Because if prices are expected to increase by 10% per year, lenders will demand an additional 10% in interest as compensation for the anticipated decrease in the value or purchasing power (the *price*) of money. And borrowers with the same expectation of inflation will consent to pay the additional 10% because they anticipate repaying the loan with depreciated dollars. The *nominal* interest rate will then exceed the *real* interest rate by 10%. And it is the nominal rate to which critics were pointing in 1974 when they complained about exorbitant interest rates.

From January 1973 to January 1974, consumer prices rose 9.9% and wholesale prices rose 17.4%. From January 1974 to July 1974, when the prime rate first hit 12%, consumer prices continued to increase at an annual rate of approximately 10% and wholesale prices went up at almost 20% on an annual basis. What would you say were "reasonable" expectations in July of 1974 about the future behavior of prices and the value of money? A 12% prime rate was hardly surprising. The real rate buried at the bottom of that nominal rate may have been as low as 2%.

The irony of all this and the acute policy dilemma it poses for the Fed became exceptionally clear in early 1975, when interest rates were falling but critics complained that they were not falling rapidly enough and called for a faster rate of growth in the money supply to get interest rates down more quickly. The basic facts—the rate of growth in the money supply and the movement of interest rates—were not at issue. The federal funds rate, which is the rate at which banks borrow reserves from one another and a key indicator of interest rate levels in the Fed's thinking, had fallen from 13.5% to 6% between July, 1974 and March, 1975. The total of currency and demand deposits (M_1) had risen at an annual rate of about 2% over this same period. All parties agreed to those facts. Even more interestingly, there was a remarkable consensus among economists inside and outside the Fed that the 2% rate of growth in M_1 was definitely too slow. But the commentators were offering two contradictory analyses in March of 1975. One group was saying that the Fed could and should push interest rates down more rapidly by accelerating the rate of growth in the money supply. The other group maintained that nominal interest rates might in fact rise if the Fed increased the rate of growth in the money supply—even though this group also wanted a faster rate of money growth. In other words, one group was saying to the monetary managers: "Increase the money supply until interest rates go down far enough." And the other was saying: "Increase the money supply but ignore interest rates which might well rise as you do so."

A fuller discussion of exactly how monetary policy affects spending and how both are related to interest rates must be reserved for subsequent chapters. The point here is only that opinions differ and that the Fed is consequently under pressure to control *several* variables whose *joint* control may be beyond its capabilities. The size of the money stock, however defined, is one target at which the Fed is asked to aim; the level and structure of interest rates is an alternative target urged upon the Fed. If changes in interest rates were always tightly correlated with changes in the money stock, it would make little difference at which target the Fed chose to aim. But as we have just seen, the relationship between interest rates and changes in the supply of money is obscure and extremely difficult to predict. By concentrating on the stabilization of interest rates, the Fed may destabilize the rate of growth in the money stock. By concentrating on a stable rate of growth in the money stock, it may allow or even cause fluctuations in interest rates.

The published record of the Open Market Committee's policy directives reveals that through most of the 1960s and to a lesser extent in the 1970s, open market operations were conducted on the assumption that the Fed could and should exercise control over interest rates. Those two convictions began to be less firmly held in the late 1960s, and the focus of the committee's studies and directives came increasingly to be monetary aggregates: bank reserves and outstanding currency, which together are called the *monetary base,* and the stock of money measured by M_1 and M_2. But the published reports of the Committee continue to reveal uncertainty about the most appropriate strategy for economic stabilization.

Steady and Erratic Monetary Growth

Some critics of the Fed believe that this uncertainty is a major cause of the Fed's poor stabilization record over the years. How poor that record has been is, of course, a subject of debate. But one part of the record is clear. The money stock has grown over the years in fits and starts and not in the smooth way recommended by those who believe that fluctuations in the money supply are a major cause of fluctuations in real output. Figure 19A shows what the critics are complaining about. It graphs the annual percentage changes in M_1 and M_2 that were presented in table 19A. To provide a more complete picture, we also show the average federal funds rate in each year as an indicator of the level of interest rates.

Was money a stabilizing or a destabilizing force over this period? Could better monetary policy have produced less inflation over this period? A lower average unemployment rate? Even if the answers to the last two questions are affirmative, does the Fed have the technical capacity and the political independence to design a "better" monetary policy? The issue of political constraints will be considered again after we have examined alternative views of the causes and cures of inflation and recession. But we do want to look more closely at technical problems in monetary management before going on.

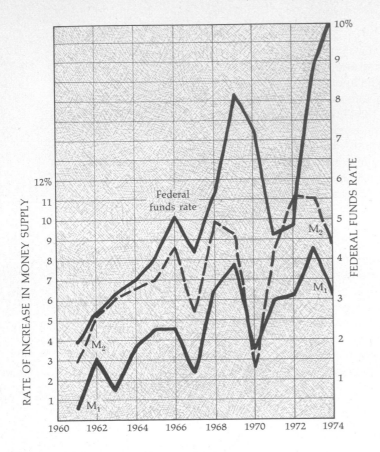

Figure 19A Percentage increase from year to year in M_1 and M_2 and annual average federal funds rate

The Conduct of Open Market Operations

Open market operations are the Fed's day-to-day tool of monetary management. Let's assume that the Open Market Committee has reached a consensus on policy. What happens next?

The real action begins with a domestic policy directive issued to the "Trading Desk" at the New York Federal Reserve Bank. "Trading Desk" is the insiders' jargon for the office of Manager of the System Open Market Account. It is located in the New York Bank because New York City is the center of the country's financial markets. Directives to the Trading Desk are released to the public about 45 days after they're issued, at which time they make extremely dull reading.[1] The assumption behind this procedure is that the public has a right to know what the Fed is up to, but that

1. Prior to April 1975, release was postponed for approximately 90 days.

MONETARY BASE

The *monetary base* is the term used to describe the total of member bank deposits with the Federal Reserve plus currency held by the public and in the vaults of commercial banks (with certain minor adjustments). The monetary base is the variable that the central bankers can most directly affect in their efforts to control the nation's stock of money and, through that, the level of total private spending. As the chart below indicates, however, ability to control the monetary base is not enough to secure accurate control over the money stock, because the relationship between them can and does vary. Note the slight downward drift in the "multiplier" for M_1 and the pronounced upward drift during this period in the "multiplier" for M_2.

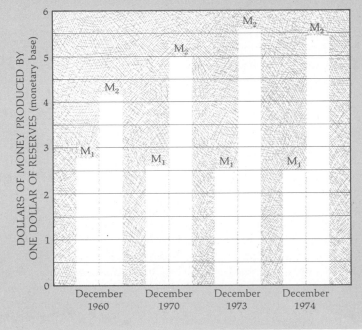

speculation would complicate the Fed's task if the public found out what the Fed was doing before it had finished doing it. Perhaps the Fed prefers not to announce a policy target in advance for fear of embarrassment if it misses.

The directives are drafted by the Open Market Committee at its monthly meeting, after staff reports have been made and the state of the economy, especially of the financial sector, has been discussed. The Trading Desk might be told, for example, to maintain about the prevailing restrictive money market conditions, to keep the annual rate of growth of M_1 between 3% and 7% and M_2 between $4\frac{1}{2}$% and $7\frac{1}{2}$%, to allow the weekly average federal funds rate to vary in an orderly fashion from as low as 7% to as high as $7\frac{1}{2}$%, and to take account all the while of developments in domestic and international financial markets. The Trading Desk may ask for further instructions if these directives turn out to be inconsistent or to raise unforeseen difficulties. The Desk politely does not mention the fact that the directives are always somewhat fuzzy. But monetary management has elements of art as well as science; and this is precisely the point: it may be better to be fuzzy than lucidly wrong.

In executing the directives of the Open Market Committee, the Trading Desk draws upon the voluminous data available to the Fed on monetary aggregates, interest rates of many kinds, bank reserve positions, foreign exchange markets, and the like. But yesterday's data are really useful only insofar as they provide clues to the course of such future events as *tomorrow's* bank reserve positions. So the Trading Desk constructs daily projections and always compares yesterday's forecast of this morning's events with this morning's reality in the hope that this will be a check on the accuracy of this morning's forecast of tomorrow's events that is going to guide this afternoon's open market operations. (The complexity of that sentence is a symbol for the reality it describes.)

Then there are the many factors outside the control of the Trading Desk that affect bank reserves. These factors were discussed at the beginning of this chapter: changes in the public's demand for currency, changes in United States holding of gold and foreign currencies, changes in Treasury balances, changes in float. These must all be countered if the Trading Desk is to exercise control over total bank reserves; but they can only be countered effectively if they are predicted correctly.

So a lot of looking, thinking, conferring, estimating, and projecting goes on each morning before the Trading Desk can transform a policy directive into concrete action for a particular afternoon. The actual open market operations are relatively simple, although they require a fair amount of coordination. Suppose that the Trading Desk decides to sell $200 million in short term government bonds. It contacts the twenty or so government security dealers with which it does business and asks them to obtain bids. Their detailed knowledge of the market enables them to provide within a few minutes firm bids for specific quantities of securities at specific prices. The Trading Desk then chooses the best offers and within half an hour has surrendered title to $200 million of government bonds and received in return checks for $200 million. When the amount of these checks is subtracted from the reserve accounts of the commercial banks on which they are drawn, the Fed will have reduced bank reserves as well as the aggregate stock of money. It will also have applied pressure toward a further reduction in the money supply, since each dollar of reserves under the fractional reserve system is the basis for several dollars of demand deposit liabilities. And all of this will make it a little harder for potential borrowers to obtain bank credit.

But *how much pressure* will this action finally exert on the total banking system and ultimately on the level of spending? That pressure depends on the responses of investors, consumers, local governments, holders of financial assets, and of course commercial bankers. The courses of action they subsequently pursue will be determined by the way they assess the net advantages of many options. Expectations are of crucial importance. A reduction in interest rates will not stimulate spending on capital projects by those who take them as a sign of even lower rates in the near future. Moreover, people are more likely to borrow and spend if their outlook is optimistic. While the actions of the Fed have some effect on private economic forecasts, they hardly control them. In a period of low confidence, a great deal of monetary ease may be unable to induce much additional borrowing and spending. Or the easy money policy may have to be continued for a long time before it counters the prevailing state of pessimism. The danger then is that the ample bank reserves created to spur expansion will be too ample for a period of optimism, and that total spending will generate inflation before the Fed can reverse its policies. A critical question for monetary policy, and one that extensive empirical inquiry has not been able to answer satisfactorily, is the question of the time lag between a monetary action and its effects, from first wave to final ripple.

The design and execution of monetary policy is still a difficult and uncertain art. Scientific knowledge in this area will probably progress slowly enough to keep the life of central bankers interesting for a good while yet.

MUST MONEY HAVE "BACKING"?

Throughout our description of money and the banking system we have treated reserves as constraints upon the power of banks to make loans and thus to expand the money supply. This seems to have little or nothing to do with the concept of a *reserve* fund—something that can be drawn upon in an emergency. But legal reserves do not in fact perform a significant reserve function. The reserve requirement is today primarily a control lever that enables the monetary authorities to adjust the stock of money in the hands of the public.

Financial Panics and Monetary Instability

There was a time when bank reserves were thought to be important because they would enable banks to satisfy their depositors' demand for gold or currency. Thus a bank was expected to keep in its vaults gold and currency equal to a certain percent of its liabilities as insurance against the possibility that depositors might suddenly want to make heavy withdrawals. This system did not work well at all. In normal times a bank would be holding large reserves seemingly to no good purpose. But in times of panic, when people began to fear that banks might be unable to meet depositors' demands for cash, even very large reserves were likely to prove inadequate. Banks tried to provide additional protection for themselves without holding a lot of idle, nonearning assets by maintaining deposits in other banks. Interest could be earned on these deposits, but they could also be withdrawn on demand to satisfy an unexpected increase in depositors' demand for gold or currency. However, this was no real solution when the public began to lose confidence in the banking system generally. The New York banks where such interbank deposits were concentrated could not meet the demands on them when these demands started coming in from everywhere simultaneously.

The whole system was like a house of cards. A rumor of trouble at a big bank could create panic among smaller banks holding deposits there. If they rushed to withdraw their deposits, the big bank would find itself with insufficient reserves. If the word spread that some prominent bank might be unable to cover its liabilities, people would become suspicious of other banks and the panic would spread. When banks could not redeem their liabilities, they had to suspend their operations. Each bank closing added to the public's anxiety and made additional runs more likely. Meanwhile, banks would attempt to strengthen their reserve positions in the face of the panic by calling and curtailing loans and by selling liquid assets. At such a time everyone seemed to be demanding gold and currency: depositors who wanted to withdraw their money; banks faced with demands for currency and gold from depositors; business firms called upon to repay promissory notes or denied an extension of existing loans. And as everyone tried to sell off other financial assets to obtain gold or currency, the price of these assets fell. Commercial banks that consequently found the dollar value of the assets they held falling below the value of their liabilities went bankrupt and had to close their doors. This wiped out the money held by customers as deposits in those banks and reduced the money supply. With the stock of money thus reduced and the economy in the throes of a liquidity crisis, the demand for new commodities and services also fell and precipitated a recession.

That pattern of events was repeated for the last time between 1929 and 1933. Currency in circulation rose from $3.6 billion in 1929 to $4.8 billion in 1933, but demand deposits fell from $22.8 billion to $15 billion, reducing the total money supply from $26.4 billion to $19.8 billion: a 25% reduction in the money supply! It isn't surprising that consumer and investor expenditures on new goods was cut almost in half between 1929 and 1933, from $93.4 billion to $47.2 billion.

A More Stable Banking System

But there hasn't been a financial panic in the United States now for more than forty years. Why not? What has changed? The answer has nothing to do with the level of bank reserves. Bank customers no longer rush to withdraw their deposits on every rumor of financial trouble, because their deposits are now insured by the Federal Deposit Insurance Corporation. If a bank closes, for whatever reason, its depositors can expect reimbursement within a few days. When the FDIC was established in 1935, some critics argued that the premiums it charged banks to insure their deposits were far too low, and that it would go broke trying to pay off depositors when banks closed their doors. But the very existence of the FDIC ended the phenomenon of bank runs; and in the absence of runs, banks no longer failed the way they formerly did. The FDIC premiums have thus proved more than adequate. And the institution of the FDIC has turned out to be probably the single most stabilizing reform of the 1930s.

Some credit must also go to improved procedures at the Fed since the 1930s. The Fed now understands clearly that it has the responsibility to provide short term liquidity to the banking system, without regard to the amounts banks happen to be holding as reserves. Thus a bank today can meet any demand for currency, however large, by obtaining additional currency from the Fed. If the bank were to use up its entire reserve balance, the Fed would simply lend the bank additional reserves, taking as collateral some of the IOUs in the asset portfolio of the borrowing bank. Banks are granted access to this "discount privilege" whenever they have a legitimate demand for additional reserves; and this has made the whole banking and monetary system more responsive to changing conditions and more resistant to crises and temporary dislocations.

Every now and then prophets rise up to announce in Sunday supplements and somber tones that the economy is on the verge of another 1929. We don't think you should take them too seriously. Even if the federal government were not as strongly committed as it is to the maintenance of high employment and even if we had learned nothing at all about how to deal with depressions, another collapse like that of the 1930s would be most unlikely. For the banking and monetary system of the United States is today securely buttressed against the kind of collapse that did so much to aggravate fluctuations prior to the thirties and that contributed heavily to the depth and duration of the Great Depression.

What about Gold?

But hasn't something important been left out of all this? If reserves aren't really reserves, what is it that provides *backing* for money? Doesn't money have to have some kind of backing? And where does gold fit into the picture?

The conviction that money must have "backing" if it is to have value raises an interesting question. What stands behind the backing to give *it* value? And behind the backing of the backing? But the whole set of questions is misdirected. In economics, value is the consequence of scarcity. And scarcity is the result of demand plus limited availability. It is clear enough why there exists a demand for money: it can be used to obtain all sorts of other things that people want, which is to say that it is accepted as a medium of exchange. The other part of the picture, limited availability, is taken care of more or less well by the monetary managers.

A commercial bank is solvent not because it has adequate reserves to back up its deposit liabilities, but because it owns assets at least equal in value to its liabilities. When First National makes a $1000 loan by creating a new demand deposit, this $1000 increase in the liabilities of First National is matched by a $1000 increase in its assets. The new asset is the IOU it obtains in return for the loan. A bank stays *solvent* by acquiring good quality assets in return for the loans it makes. Its *liquidity* is protected by the FDIC and by the Fed, which stands ready to discount the bank's eligible assets and provide additional reserves to meet either increased withdrawals of currency or adverse check clearing balances.

But what about the Federal Reserve Banks? We saw that the Fed can create additional money as well as additional bank reserves simply by writing checks on its own credit. Do these checks have any "backing"? Not in the sense most people have in mind when they ask the question. Until rather recently, federal law did require that the Fed maintain reserves equal to a certain percentage of its liabilities. The Fed's liabilities are primarily the sums deposited at the various Reserve Banks by member commercial banks, by foreign institutions, and by the Treasury, plus all outstanding Federal Reserve notes. The old law required the Fed to hold gold or certificates of gold ownership as reserves. But to what purpose? The reserves were not available to anyone on demand, and the statement on old Federal Reserve notes that they could be "redeemed in lawful money" at any Federal Reserve Bank was meaningless: anyone turning notes in for redemption would simply be given new notes. So the statement was finally removed from the face of the notes at about the same time that Congress agreed to drop the pretense that the Fed must itself be required to hold reserves.

The Fed's liabilities, like those of commercial banks, are balanced by

BANK SOLVENCY AND BANK LIQUIDITY

Here is a simplified balance sheet for the Thawville National Bank:

Assets		Liabilities	
Land, buildings, equipment	$300,000	$320,000	Stock shares issued
Vault cash	4,000	160,000	Demand deposits
Reserve account	32,000	200,000	Time deposits
Commercial IOUs	315,000	20,000	Net worth
Government securities	49,000		
Total assets	$700,000	$700,000	Total liabilities plus net worth

The bank is solvent. Its net worth (assets minus liabilities) is $20,000. But is the bank adequately liquid? Suppose that the largest employer in Thawville unexpectedly moves to Eyota and transfers $60,000 in demand deposits to the Eyota Bank. The Thawville Bank will have to meet a sudden $60,000 adverse clearing balance, a sum greater than its entire reserve account. It will find itself insufficiently liquid.

Can the Fed help out? It could loan the Thawville Bank enough reserves to cover its liquidity deficit. Suppose it loaned the $28,000 difference between the Thawville Bank's present reserve account and the demand made on that account by the Eyota Bank. Assets would decline by $32,000 as the bank's reserve account went to zero. But liabilities would also decline by $32,000: a $60,000 decrease in demand deposits minus a $28,000 increase in the Thawville Bank's indebtedness to the Fed. The bank would still be solvent.

The Thawville Bank would find itself in debt to the Fed by more than $28,000, however. The $4000 it still retains as vault cash will not be an adequate legal reserve against its remaining $100,000 in demand deposits and $200,000 in time deposits. Suppose that the minimum reserve requirement on those deposit totals is $25,000; then the Thawville Bank has a reserve deficiency of $21,000. When we add the previous $28,000 to the $21,000 reserve account deficit, the Thawville Bank owes the Fed a total of $49,000. We can think of the Fed as adding $21,000 to the bank's assets by crediting its reserve account with the amount of the deficiency; the Thawville Bank balances this by adding a further $21,000 to its liabilities to the Fed. The bank continues to be both solvent and adequately liquid.

How can the bank eliminate its indebtedness to the Fed? If it sells to other banks its entire holding of government securities, it will acquire from them $49,000 in additional reserves. That will be balanced by a $49,000 loss in earning assets. The bank is still both solvent and liquid.

Now suppose that demand and time deposits in the Thawville Bank fall further as income drops in town and both people and businesses move away. If the Fed refuses to help, the Thawville bank could experience a liquidity problem. It might run out of reserves before it had satisfied depositors' demands for currency and the demands of other banks for reserves to settle negative clearing balances.

If the Thawville Bank tried to maintain its liquidity (satisfy promptly the demands being made upon it for currency and reserves) by selling commercial IOUs to other banks, it might threaten its solvency. If the other banks were unwilling to accept these IOUs except at substantial discounts from the values at which the Thawville Bank is carrying them on its books, the total value of its assets might fall considerably. The bank's liquidity problems would have pushed it toward insolvency.

The Fed protects the solvency of the banking system by helping banks maintain adequate liquidity. If banks are forced to sell earning assets to acquire liquid assets quickly, they may be forced into insolvency through a decline in the value of their asset portfolio. This would be especially likely if an economywide demand for increased liquidity caused the demand for income-earning financial assets to fall just when banks were forced to sell large quantities of these assets.

We have greatly simplified the analysis by ignoring the effect of all this on the largest component of the bank's liabilities, the value of its stock. Net worth and stockholders' equity are in practice inseparable. The market value of the bank's stock could fall all the way to zero as the value of its assets declined, thereby maintaining the balance between assets and liabilities and staving off bankruptcy. Stockholder losses have always been a buffer that partially protected depositors against losses due to bank insolvencies. The risk to bank stockholders is much less now that the Fed works so diligently at maintaining the liquidity of individual banks, even when their problems are attributable to mismanagement.

assets, not by reserves. When the Fed increases its liabilities either by issuing additional Federal Reserve notes or by adding to the amounts in commercial bank accounts, it acquires matching additions to its assets, usually in the form of government securities or high grade commercial IOUs. A commercial bank can become insolvent if the value of the financial assets it owns falls so far that it cannot satisfy the demands for payment of its creditors. Can the Fed become insolvent in the same way? It's hard even to imagine how that might occur. The liabilities of the Fed are the sums on deposit with it and outstanding currency. Suppose these creditors demand payment. What could that even mean? Federal Reserve notes are "legal tender for all debts, public and private"; the Fed can pay off its "debts" by handing the creditor freshly printed "debts," which it can have printed at practically no cost.

A lot of popular thinking on the subject of money is still in the grip of vague notions about "backing" for money, of "ultimate" assets somehow "standing behind" the money we use in everyday transactions. These ideas are probably a heritage from the days of the gold standard. But the United States is not on the gold standard (or any other standard). American citizens have not had the privilege of redeeming their money in gold since the 1930s, and the last vestige of any real gold standard disappeared in the 1970s, when the United States abandoned its commitment to redeem in gold the dollar holdings of foreign central banks. If this fact causes you to doubt the value of your currency or checking account, you can easily shore up your faith by "selling" your money to others. You will find that they are willing to take it and to give you other valuable assets in exchange.

Governments and the Value of Money

The critical factor in preserving the value of money is its limited availability and confidence that the supply will continue to be limited. Nature has made gold relatively rare. It's up to the Fed to keep Federal Reserve notes and demand deposits relatively rare. But some people have more confidence in the reliability of Nature than in the reliability of central bankers and governments. That is why some intelligent and well-informed people would like to see us return to a genuine gold standard, under which currency could be exchanged for gold at some fixed ratio. It is *not* because they think that money must have backing, but because they distrust governmental money managers. If the government were required to maintain the convertibility of demand deposits into currency and currency into gold at predetermined exchange ratios, the limited availability of gold would severely restrict the government's power to increase the money supply.

As a matter of fact, governments have often, especially in wartime, created additional money as a way of financing expenditures without the painful necessity of openly levying taxes. The consequence has usually been inflation, which is a more concealed but hardly a more equitable way for the government to finance its expenditures. Urging a return to the gold standard would seem to be a counsel of despair, however. A government so irresponsible that it must be reined in by gold would be most unlikely to adopt a gold standard or to keep the reins on when they

LESSONS FROM A BANK FAILURE

At the end of 1973 the Franklin National Bank of New York was ranked as the nation's twentieth largest bank and had total deposits of more than $3.7 billion. The spectacular failure of Franklin National in 1974 stirred up memories of the early 1930s, when numerous bank failures contributed to the paralysis of private spending. But the case of Franklin National demonstrates the significant differences between the banking system in the 1930s and in the 1970s.

First, because depositors were insured against loss, they did not initiate a run on the bank when rumors of its mismanagement began to circulate early in 1974. Second, Franklin National *was* mismanaged. Franklin's downfall was not triggered by the state of the economy, something beyond Franklin's control, but by foolish speculation in foreign exchange, apparently motivated by managerial megalomania. Finally, the determination of government monetary managers and banking authorities to assume responsibility was clearly demonstrated. They may even have been *too* eager to assume responsibility and to rescue the bank's owners from the consequences of mismanagement. One could easily infer from the Franklin case that the most rational policy in bank management is a high risk policy, because any profits will go to the bank's owners and drastic losses will be absorbed by protective agencies of the federal government. The Fed ended up lending Franklin $1.7 billion in 1974 to prevent its collapse. And the loan was assumed by the Federal Deposit Insurance Corporation in October 1974, after Franklin had failed. That may have been unwise, but it certainly wasn't a do-nothing policy.

irritated. The problem of irresponsible government is a weighty one; but we cannot believe that the problem could be solved by a return to the gold standard.

Consideration of that issue does, however, raise the question of government spending, taxation, and deficits. The canons of financial orthodoxy long decreed that a government must *balance its budget.* The failure to do so was regarded as a clear sign of irresponsibility, and persistence in such a course was seen as a guarantee of eventual economic disaster. That view was challenged head-on in the 1930s by the argument that government deficits, under the proper circumstances, were a powerful tool for the creation of prosperity. A new way of thinking about the interrelations

GOVERNMENTS OLD AND NEW

Could we solve the problem of irresponsible government management of the money supply by returning to a metallic standard and using as our monetary base some commodity whose quantity is firmly restricted by nature? That was the practice in 1776 when Adam Smith wrote the following:

In every country of the world, I believe, the avarice and injustice of princes and sovereign states, abusing the confidence of their subjects, have by degrees diminished the real quantity of metal which had been originally contained in their coins. . . . By means of those operations the princes and sovereign states which performed them were enabled, in appearance, to pay their debts and to fulfill their engagements with a smaller quantity of silver than would otherwise have been requisite. It was indeed in appearance only; for their creditors were really defrauded of a part of what was due to them. All other debtors in the state were allowed the same privilege, and might pay with the same nominal sum of the new and debased coin whatever they had borrowed in the old. Such operations, therefore, have always proved favorable to the debtor and ruinous to the creditor, and have sometimes produced a greater and more universal revolution in the fortunes of private persons than could have been occasioned by a very great public calamity.

Where there is a will on the part of sovereigns, a way is usually found.

between income, expenditure, deficits, money, and interest rates evolved—a way of thinking often referred to as "the Keynesian revolution." That's the subject to which we now turn.

Once Over Lightly

Commercial bank reserves are the primary lever that the Fed uses in its efforts to control the money supply.

The Fed can control bank lending and money creation by altering legal reserve requirements or by altering the dollar volume of bank reserves.

The Fed increases the volume of commercial bank reserves by extending credit. It reduces reserves by withdrawing credit previously supplied.

The Fed extends credit directly to a commercial bank by adding to its reserve account and taking as collateral notes or securities in the bank's asset portfolio. The rate of interest on such loans is called the discount rate.

The Fed changes bank reserves more indirectly by purchasing government securities or by selling securities from its large portfolio. If it purchases newly issued securities, it pays for them by crediting the Treasury's account. When the Treasury draws on this account to make payments to the public, the Fed credit becomes reserves in the commercial banking system. When the Fed purchases previously issued government securities from the public, it pays by means of checks drawn on its own credit, which become bank reserves when deposited.

The purchase and sale by the Fed of government securities as a means of controlling the money supply or otherwise influencing financial markets is called open market operations. Open market operations are the Fed's principal working tool in the conduct of monetary policy.

There are major disagreements among competent authorities about the conduct of open market operations. These disagreements reflect differences of opinion both about the proper goals for monetary policy to pursue and about the targets at which it should aim in pursuit of these goals. Such differences of opinion have been difficult to resolve, because the chain of causal sequences with which the Fed must be concerned is long and uncertain at many points: from data gathering to policy discussions to Trading Desk operations to reserve changes to movements in monetary aggregates and money market conditions to total spending. And at the last there remains uncertainty about the way changes in total spending will separately affect output and the price level.

A key concept for understanding the relation between the money supply and levels of economic activity is the velocity of money circulation. This is the average number of times each unit of money changes hands over a period of time. Velocity declines when the public chooses to hold larger money balances and rises when the public chooses to reduce its money holdings relative to its income or expenditures.

Reserves do not function today as backing for money but as constraints upon bank credit expansion and money creation. The value of money depends not upon its backing, but upon its acceptability as a medium of exchange. The monetary managers maintain the acceptability of money by restricting its quantity.

The Fed contributes to monetary stability by helping the banks maintain liquidity under changing circumstances. Improved Fed procedures for maintaining liquidity at desired levels and the establishment of the Federal Deposit Insurance Corporation have made the banking and monetary system of the United States far more stable than it was prior to the 1930s.

QUESTIONS FOR DISCUSSION

1. To an employee, a bank is a place, people, and activities. But to an economist, banks are often nothing but assets and liabilities in motion. Simplified asset and liability statements are given below for the Federal Reserve System and the Commercial Banking System, each viewed as a single composite bank.

FEDERAL RESERVE SYSTEM		COMMERCIAL BANK SYSTEM	
Assets	Liabilities	Assets	Liabilities
_____	_____	_____	_____
_____	_____	_____	_____
_____	_____	_____	_____
_____	_____	_____	_____

(a) Insert each of the following dollar amounts (in billions) into the appropriate place or places. (Don't worry about the fact that assets aren't equal to liabilities; these are only partial statements of bank positions.)

$80 U.S. government securities owned by the Fed
 55 U.S. government securities owned by commercial banks
 3 U.S. Treasury deposits with the Fed
215 Demand deposits owned by the public
 8 Federal Reserve notes in commercial bank vaults
200 IOUs of customers who have borrowed from commercial banks
 2 Member bank borrowings from the Fed
 30 Member bank reserves on deposit with the Fed
 65 Federal Reserve notes in the hands of the public
 4 Treasury tax and loan accounts at commercial banks

(b) How large is M_1?

(c) The public decides to increase its holding of currency to $70 billion by reducing demand deposits to $210 billion. How might this additional currency be supplied, and how would that affect the asset and liability components above?

(d) What would be the effects of a Fed purchase of $2 billion in government securities from the commercial banks? What would be the effects of a purchase from the nonbanking public?

(e) Trace through the effects on various assets and liabilities if the Treasury borrows an additional $5 billion from the Fed and subsequently spends that amount for goods purchased from the public. What difference would it make if the Treasury borrowed from the commercial banks?

(f) What would be the effect if the Treasury borrowed from the Fed and just kept the borrowed funds idle in its account at the Fed? Suppose it kept the borrowed funds idle in its tax and loan accounts with the commercial banks?

(*g*) Where else could the Treasury go to borrow? What effects would you expect on the bank asset and liability statements if the Treasury spent money after borrowing it from the nonbank public?

2. If the Treasury were to sell bonds to the Fed and then purchase goods and services with the proceeds, the money supply would increase. If resources in the economy were already fully employed, where would the goods and services purchased by the government come from? What would happen to prices? Do you agree that "inflation is a tax"?

3. Many people worry about the size of the national debt. (We'll examine that concern in chapter 21.) The marketable debt of the United States government (the savings bonds that many individuals own are not marketable, because they cannot be bought and sold) currently stands at around $300 billion. Suppose the Fed, a government agency, bought up all the outstanding marketable government securities, so that—in a sense—the government owed the debt only to itself. How could this be done? What would happen as a result?

4. You're the manager of a commercial bank, and you want to increase your bank's excess legal reserves. Perhaps you currently have *negative* excess reserves—in which case your bank is borrowing from the Fed, and the Fed may be putting pressure on you to remove that debt. Or you may simply believe that your bank would be in a more advantageous position with a somewhat higher level of reserves. What policies could you pursue to reach your objective? What effects would these policies have on the banking and monetary system?

5. Why does the Fed use open market operations as its principal tool of monetary management rather than changes in legal reserve requirements?

6. Why might the Fed find it easier to expand the money supply in a period of prosperity than in a period of falling output and rising unemployment?

7. There were 14,338 commercial banks in the United States as of June 30, 1974. One-third of these, or 4695, were national banks and therefore required to maintain membership in the Federal Reserve System. Only 1068, or one-ninth, of all state banks chose membership in the System. That was down from one-sixth of all state banks ten years earlier. Do you think membership should be required for all banks? How would you assess the political chances for such a proposal?

8. The only practicable way to calculate the velocity of money circulation is to divide a measure of the money stock into some measure of total expenditures.

(*a*) Test your understanding of the velocity concept by thinking up some way by which it could be measured more directly.

(*b*) Suppose you kept track for one year of your daily holdings of currency and demand deposits. How could you obtain from these data a measure of your own personal contribution to the velocity of money circulation?

9. Examine the data in appendix 6 at the end of the book to see the difference between the rate of change in the money supply and the rate of change in real, as distinct from nominal, output and income. What was the percentage change in M_2 from the first quarter to the fourth quarter of 1974? The percentage change in nominal GNP? The percentage change in GNP when measured in dollars of constant value?

10. When are interest rates "too high"? Why is it difficult for the Fed to control the level of interest rates?

11. The text asserts that in the spring of 1975, most economic commentators were urging the Fed to increase the rate of growth in the money stock. As long as they agreed in this policy recommendation, why would it matter whether they disagreed over the effect this would have on interest rates?

12. Does figure 19A provide any evidence on the question of how interest rates respond to changing rates of increase in the money stock?

13. Why is it important to know not only how large an impact a change in the money stock will have on spending but also *when* this impact will occur?

14. If it is not essential to the value of money that it have "backing" of some kind, why do so many people believe otherwise?

15. What changes in the attitudes of commercial bank managers toward risk and in bank operating procedures would you expect to observe when the government assumes a substantial responsibility for preventing bank failures? Who is likely to gain and who is likely to lose as a result of such changes in bank operations?

16. "Nature has made gold rare but people have made it scarce." Explain.

20

THE KEYNESIAN REVOLUTION
AND INCOME-EXPENDITURES ANALYSIS

John Maynard Keynes was born in 1883 and died in 1946. In between he made a modest fortune in the stock market, married a prima ballerina, edited the official journal of the Royal Economic Society, composed brilliant biographical sketches, served as a Treasury representative at the Versailles peace conference, resigned that position to write a scathing attack on the treaty and its architects, was raised to the peerage as Lord Keynes, and helped design the international monetary system that was put into effect after World War II. He did a great deal more as well, for he was a brilliant, versatile, and energetic man. Almost twenty years after his death he achieved the cover of *Time* magazine, not for any of these accomplishments but because of a book on money that he had published in 1930 and a second book written out of dissatisfaction with the first one. The second and far more famous book was *The General Theory of Employment, Interest and Money*.

ORIGINS OF THE GENERAL THEORY

The *General Theory*, published in 1936 is by common agreement an obscure and in large part badly written book. The lucid and vivid prose of Keynes's biographical essays breaks through only occasionally in this, his best-known work and probably the single most influential economics book of the century. "What the *General Theory* Means" was a topic for numerous essays and symposia after 1936, evidence both that its meaning was deemed important and that few were certain just what the meaning was. Books and articles on what Keynes *really* meant are still appearing four decades after publication of the *General Theory.*

Sometimes we see more readily what a person is trying to assert if we understand what it is he's rejecting. Keynes was convinced that the economic analysis in which he had been trained was incapable of diagnosing and prescribing a cure for depressions because its approach to the question actually assumed the problem away.

Disequilibrium and Equilibrium

What do we observe in a period of depression or recession? Workers are unable to find jobs because employers are not hiring because products cannot be sold. There is an imbalance, it would appear, between quantities demanded and quantities supplied. A surplus exists or, in the language of the nineteenth century economists, an excess of supply.

The economist's solution to a surplus is a lower price. If workers cannot find jobs, it's because they're holding out for a wage that's above their marginal productivity; at some lower wage, all those who want work will be able to find it. If producers cannot sell their entire output, it's again because they're asking too high a price; useful goods can always be sold at a sufficiently low price. It's a matter of supply and demand. A recession is simply a temporary disequilibrium. It will come to an end when prices and wages move to their equilibrium or market-clearing levels.

But there is a difficulty that the traditional curves of supply and demand conceal. They overlook the question of the *path* to equilibrium. Figure 20A shows a supply curve and two demand curves. If for some reason demand falls from D_1 to D_2, the price will presumably move from p_1 to p_2. *But it won't jump there instantaneously.* Not even in the most competitive markets will a new equilibrium price be reached without a *process* requiring time and including step-by-step adjustments.

Through what process will the new equilibrium price of p_2 be reached? Let's make the reasonable assumption that suppliers continue for a while to ask p_1 when the demand falls to D_2. How would they even know the demand had fallen, after all, until they had tried for a time to sell at p_1 and found themselves unable to locate purchasers? But with demand at D_2 and the price still at p_1, the quantity purchased will be q_2. The difference between q_1 and q_2 is the surplus in the hands of sellers and is an unintended and unwanted addition to suppliers' inventories. Eventually this surplus will lead to price cutting and a movement toward the new equilibrium, where the price will be p_2, and the quantity q_3 will be both demanded and supplied. Or will it?

Usually, we just assume in the supply-demand analysis of competitive markets an instantaneous jump to the new equilibrium after a change in one of the curves. But when we do so, we're overlooking the actual process of adjustment and everything that might occur as a consequence of this time-consuming process. What occurs in the case just described? For one thing, the gross income of suppliers is immediately reduced by the difference between $q_1 \times p_1$ and $q_2 \times p_1$. With their incomes unexpectedly reduced, suppliers (who are also demanders) may be compelled to reduce their own demands for goods. As they do so, they shift the demand curves for other products downward to the left, creating for other suppliers the same situation they themselves encountered. Moreover, as producers now find themselves with unintended additions to their inventories, they will curtail production until inventories have been reduced. This reduces the incomes of employees as it increases unemployment. As the adjustment process follows the same course in one market after another, declining incomes and declining demand may spread cumulatively through the economy.

Now go back to figure 20A. With demand falling generally, the new equilibrium of p_2 and q_3 *may never be reached.* Before the price can reach p_2, demand may fall even further as a consequence of the general, economy-wide decline in sales, output, employment, and income.

This is all much too simple of course, but it is surely no more so than the assumption that prices shift instantaneously to new market-clearing levels whenever demand falls. The simple description above at least calls attention to the fact that production, marketing, the receipt of income, spending, and price changes all occur in a world characterized by uncertainty, so that buyers and sellers, whether of goods or labor, must *search* for a new equilibrium. This inevitably takes time. And so there will always be a period of disequilibrium before any new equilibrium is reached. And that raises the questions which bothered Keynes.

How long will it take to reach a new equilibrium after the original one has been disturbed by a decline in demand? What prevents the reduced incomes during the disequilibrium period from causing a further and cumulative fall in demand? And why do we assume that the new equilibrium will be unaffected by what happens during the disequilibrium?

Assuming the Problem Away

In the *General Theory*, Keynes wanted to replace the "classical" concept of the equilibrating process because it was not a process at all. Its *assumption* of perfect information guaranteed that all markets would always be in equilibrium *and implied that unemployment or excess supply was impossible.*

No economic theorist prior to Keynes or since his time has actually

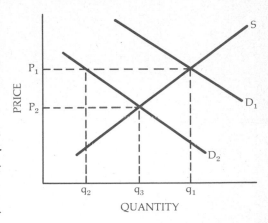

Figure 20A Paths toward equilibrium

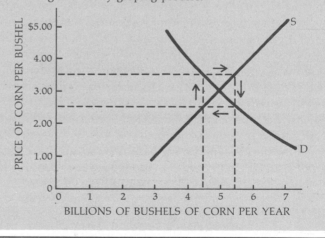

SEARCHING FOR "EQUILIBRIUM"

A popular sequence in the old silent comedy films had the hero trying to balance a kitchen table by sawing a little off one leg, then another, then still another, always removing a bit too much and trying to correct it on another leg until he wound up with a coffee table. That's an illustration of how a final equilibrium can be altered by the process of reaching equilibrium.

Here's another simple example drawn from agriculture. The equilibrium price in the graph below would seem to be $3. But planting decisions are made in anticipation of prices that may not be realized. Suppose that the quantity of corn planted depends on *last year's* price, while the quantity demanded depends on *this year's* price. In Year One, drought and blight reduce the intended crop of 5 billion bushels to an actual harvest of 4.5 billion. The price in Year One therefore becomes $3.50. Looking at that price in Year Two, farmers plant for a harvest of 5.5 billion bushels. When they hit their target, the price falls to $2.50. So in Year Three farmers plant less corn (and more soybeans or sorghum). In Year Three, the price rises as a result to $3.50.

In a world of uncertainty, where the "right" decision depends upon correctly guessing what others are doing concurrently, "equilibrium" may never be reached. Or it may only be approached after a long and costly groping process.

thought that unemployment is impossible or that equilibrium reoccurs instantaneously whenever it's disturbed. But Keynes believed that the equilibrium-oriented and essentially timeless analysis which dominated economists' thinking prevented them from formulating an adequate theory of changes in total output and income. They had no theory of recessions, for the ruling theory assumed them away. The challenge he set himself in the *General Theory* was to "escape from habitual modes of thought and expression" and from old ideas "which ramify, for those brought up as most of us have been, into every corner of our minds." He wanted to construct a theory that would explain the phenomenon of recession by taking into account the consequences of uncertainty and the processes of adjustment over time. That was the origin of *income-expenditures analysis.*

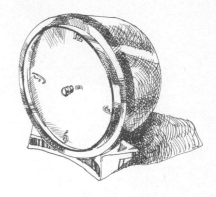

INCOME-EXPENDITURES ANALYSIS: AN INTRODUCTION

Keynes employed two new concepts to express his ideas in simple theoretical form. One was the *propensity to consume* (now more often called the *consumption function*); the other was the *multiplier.*

(propensity to consume)
consumption function
multiplier

The Consumption Function

We can best approach income-expenditures analysis by asking what determines consumers' demand for goods. The answer is: far more factors than we can begin to enumerate; but one of these factors is surely consumer income. Keynes maintained that if we deal with *all* consumers together, we can confidently expect to observe a stable relation between aggregate income and aggregate consumption. He called this relation the *propensity to consume.* Moreover, we can confidently state the normal shape of this function, he argued, on the basis of introspection and everyday facts of experience: People increase or decrease their consumption as their income increases or decreases, but not by as much as the change in their income. Let's see to what conclusions this leads.

(consumption function)
— *aggregate income and aggregate consumption, relationship between.*

Picture first a very simple economic system without government, foreign trade, or investment. All demand is therefore consumer demand, and all the income generated by production goes to consumers. Because production responds to demand, consumption expenditure determines output. The economy can be viewed as the simple system of circulation shown in figure 20B. Consumption expenditures are exchanged for consumer goods in the lower loop. In the upper loop, income is provided to consumers in exchange for productive services. The system is in equilibrium when the value of the flows in the top loop equals the value of the flows in the bottom loop. For an inequality in either direction must lead to changes in the rates of flow. If the income that producers pay for productive services exceeds the expenditures consumers make for goods, producers won't be able to pay as much income to consumers in the next round of circulation. If expenditures exceed income, on the other hand, income will increase as

(circular flow)

Figure 20B The economy as a <u>circular flow system</u>

producers expand output and purchase more productive services to do so. <u>Only when the flows exactly match each other is there no incentive toward change.</u>

The Multiplier

What happens now if something occurs to jar the system away from equilibrium? <u>Let's suppose that consumption expenditures decline be-cause consumers suddenly decide to hold on to a portion of their income.</u> <u>Fewer goods will now flow to consumers.</u> But producers will subsequently find themselves holding excess inventories of goods and <u>they will curtail production. As a result they will be purchasing fewer productive services from consumers, and so income will decline.</u>

But the concept of the consumption function asserts that consumption expenditure varies in the same direction as income. And so consumption expenditure will experience a further decline. Producers will consequently reduce output again, which will further reduce consumer income; this will again reduce consumption expenditure, and reduced consumption expenditures will again lower production.

Where will the process stop? On the assumption Keynes made about the *shape* of the consumption function, the process will not continue indefinitely. Recall that consumption increases or decreases as income increases or decreases, *but by a smaller amount.* Suppose that for every $1 change in income, consumption demand changes by 75¢. We can then predict that an initial reduction in demand will lead eventually to a reduction in income and consumption four times as large. The multiplier in this case is four.

factor that keeps equilibrium or depression from continuing down

The Marginal Propensity to Consume and the Multiplier

The multiplier is the ratio between the eventual change in income and the initial change in demand that caused income to change. How do we know it would have a value of four in the circumstances just described? The logic is exactly the same as that used with the "money multiplier" in chapter 18, relating changes in the money stock to changes in bank reserves. Assume an initial decline in consumption of $64. Income will fall by $64 as a result. Consumption will then fall again by (.75)$64, or $48, reducing income by another $48. This will cause a reduction of consumption by (.75)$48, or $36. The cumulative total of all the successive declines in income will be:

$$\$64 + (.75)\$64 + (.75)^2\$64 + (.75)^3\$64 + (.75)^4\$64 + \cdots + (.75)^n\$64$$

or

$$\$64 + \$48 + \$36 + \$27 + \$20.25 + \$15.1875 + \$11.390625 + \cdots$$

which approaches a total of $64[1/(1 − .75)] as n becomes infinitely large. Since $1/(1 − .75)$ is 4, the multiplier will be 4 when the marginal propensity to consume is .75. The *marginal propensity to consume* is the term Keynes applied to *the ratio of the change in consumption expenditure to the change in income.*

By means of these two concepts—the propensity to consume and the multiplier—Keynes linked aggregate demand and aggregate supply in a different kind of equilibrium analysis. In doing so he provided a theoretical framework that could explain both (1) the cumulative character of economic downturns and revivals and (2) why a decline or an upturn, once begun, did not continue indefinitely.

SAVING AND INVESTMENT: THE PUZZLE

But hasn't something crucial been overlooked? When income is constant and consumption declines, as we assumed at the beginning in the simple case just described, something else must immediately rise by the same amount. Income not spent for consumption goods is income saved. What happened, we might ask, to that initial increase in unspent income or saving? Did it just sit idly in cookie jars, checking accounts, or savings deposits? Did it have no effect at all on the multiplier process and the movement of the economic system to its new equilibrium between aggregate demand and aggregate supply?

Investment and Saving Before the General Theory

Economists have always known that a portion of consumer income is saved and not spent for consumption goods. But they have also known that consumption is not the total of all expenditures for new goods. Even leaving out, as we shall continue to do in this chapter, government and international trade, the public also purchases *investment* goods. Part of the demand for new production is a demand for capital goods.

As we pointed out in chapter 17, the distinction between capital goods and consumer goods cannot be drawn precisely. Capital goods are defined as produced goods used to produce future goods. But that actually describes every useful good that gets produced. In the national income and product accounts, however, a clear distinction is drawn. Capital goods include (1) producers' durable equipment; (2) producers' buildings; (3) producers' inventories, from stockpiled raw materials through goods in process to goods completed but not yet sold; and (4) residences. The last is added to what is otherwise an exclusively producers' list because the purchase of a house results in a flow of services extending far into the future. The income and product accounts classify government expenditures separately, largely to avoid the difficult problem of distinguishing those government expenditures that are investment from those which should be classified as consumption. However the distinction is finally drawn, it's a useful one. And it's necessary as a complement to the distinction between consumption and saving.

Why, we might ask, would anyone choose to save a portion of his income rather than use it to obtain goods that will provide present satisfaction? The answer is that people are to some extent future-oriented and want to provide for future satisfaction. That can be done by saving: by not consuming the entire amount of current income. If savings are effectively invested, the stream of future satisfactions will be larger than it would be if savings were merely allowed to accumulate in the form of unused money hoards. As long as there are investment opportunities available that offer the prospect of a positive net return, it makes little sense to save and not invest. Many of the "classical" economists whom Keynes criticized were so convinced of the absurdity of saving and not investing that they *identified* saving with investment. "No one saves but to invest." "The portion of income that is saved purchases labor and commodities just as surely as that which is said to be spent." "No one was ever so absurd as to assume that saving will be hoarded." And notice what this implies. A decline in consumption will not trigger any cumulative decline in output and income, because a decline in consumption is a rise in saving, saving is always invested, and investment expenditure must therefore rise by just enough to compensate for the decline in consumption expenditure.

Did the "Classical" Analysis Make Sense?

At first glance all this seems an affront to common sense. People *do* sometimes save without investing, and surely without investing right away. Some saving *does* get hoarded, for short periods of time at least. Income that is saved may be placed in a bank savings account to accumulate interest, but until it is borrowed by someone who wants to spend it, it will *not* purchase "labor and commodities." In what world were the authors of those statements living?

Their problem was the habit of analyzing the phenomena of saving and investment in that timeless world without uncertainty that we criticized earlier, a world in which any imbalance between supply and demand produces an instantaneous change in relative prices and all markets are cleared. They reasoned that if the quantity of savings supplied is greater than the quantity demanded by investors, the two quantities will be brought to equality through some combination of changes in the rate of interest and changes in relative prices.

The following argument tries to present their case in a simple way. Consumption plus saving by definition equals income; and income measures the supply of output at market prices. Consumption plus investment is the demand for output at current prices. If consumption plus saving is greater than consumption plus investment, the quantity of goods being supplied is greater than the quantity being demanded *at current prices;* and so the price level will fall. Not all prices will fall; but the prices of the particular goods in oversupply will fall, causing the average of all prices to decline, until the quantity demanded just equals the quantity supplied.

The trouble with this argument is that it assumes the problem out of existence. It postulates a system of prices so flexible and rapid in its adjustments that everything produced will always be sold. If that were the case, real output and income would never have to make any adjustments in the face of a declining demand. The problem, however, is to understand why real output and income *do* fall; a theory that explains why they will *not* fall is hardly what we're looking for.

When we examine the actual processes of producer adjustment to an inadequate demand, we observe something quite different. Suppose that producers anticipate total sales of $500 billion; they consequently produce $500 billion of goods and generate $500 billion in income. Consumption

EQUALITIES, IDENTITIES, AND
EQUILIBRIUM CONDITIONS

The equality between saving and investment that plays such a central role in income expenditures analysis can be a source of confusion if the different kinds of equality are not carefully distinguished.

Actual saving and actual investment are equal in our model by definition of the terms we're using:

total output = total income
total output = consumption purchases
+ investment purchases
total income = consumption purchases + saving

Necessarily, then:

investment purchases = saving

All four of the equalities listed above are identities, which means that the equality is entailed by the definitions of the terms. The equality sign in such cases is often written with three lines rather than two to indicate that the terms are equal by definition. We don't look at any empirical data to see whether total output really does equal total income; if the data we're using provide different totals, we assume that errors occurred in measurement.

The definitions used in the model are not arbitrary, however. They rest upon some real-world relationships. Individuals and societies will either use their current income for current consumption or reserve it for the future, which means that they will either consume their income or save it. They will utilize current output either to provide current services or to provide services in the future, which means that they will either consume it or invest it. The definitional equality or identity between saving and investment rests upon the recognition that saving and investment are different sides of the same phenomenon, namely, the income or output that is not currently consumed but assigned instead to future use.

The classifications used in national income accounting similarly reflect the fact that investment is constrained by the supply of saving and that all saving is invested in some fashion. Even income converted into currency and placed under the mattress has, from the standpoint of the mattress stuffer, been invested. He has refrained from present consumption in order to have money available in the future. He has therefore made an investment, even though it earns a zero rate of return if the purchasing power of money does not change, and a negative rate of return if inflation occurs.

The equality between *intended* saving and *intended* investment is not an identity. It is a *condition of equilibrium.* Think of two wash tubs with a connecting tube at the bottom. Will the water levels in the two tubs necessarily be equal? Not always. If an additional bucket of water is poured quickly into the tub on the right, the water level will be higher there than in the other tub. But water

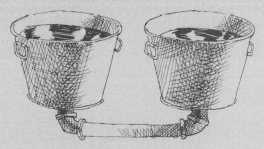

will immediately begin flowing through the tube from the tub on the right to the tub on the left and will continue flowing until the levels are again equal. We can say, then, that equality of the water levels is an equilibrium condition, because if the water levels are not equal they will change in both tubs until they are equal.

The equality between intended saving and intended investment is similarly an equilibrium condition, because if they are not equal intended saving will adjust until it is equal to intended investment. In the case of the tubs, the divergence in pressure is the equalizing or equilibrating mechanism. In the case of intended saving and investment, changes in income push intended saving toward equality with intended investment.

was expected to be $450 billion, and investment expenditures were expected to absorb the remaining $50 billion of output. But consumers for some reason cut back their expenditures to $440 billion and thereby automatically increased their savings to $60 billion. Since it is altogether unlikely that investors will want to purchase those undemanded $10 billion of consumer goods, producers will find themselves holding $10 billion of *unintended inventories.* Additions to inventory are one component of total investment, so total investment will in fact be equal to saving at $60 billion. But $10 billion of that is *unintended investment.* And it will have an effect on future output and income. Producers will curtail production, laying off workers and reducing their demand for other resources, in an effort to bring their inventories down closer to the preferred level.

The classical economists had another argument to fall back upon. The interest rate, as we pointed out in chapter 12, expresses the relative values of present and future goods. At lower interest rates, future goods become

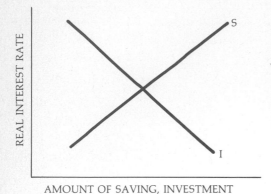

Figure 20C The "classical" theory of interest-rate determination

REAL INTEREST RATE

S

I

AMOUNT OF SAVING, INVESTMENT

more valuable relative to goods for present consumption. That's just another way of saying that the demand for capital goods increases as the interest rate falls, or that the rate of investment expenditure varies inversely with the rate of interest. But interest is also the return on saving and the rate of saving varies directly with the rate of interest. If intended saving increases by $10 billion with no increase in intended investment, the interest rate will fall. As it does so, savers will choose to save less, and investors will want to spend more. The interest rate will continue falling until the intentions of savers and investors are brought into balance.

If we reject the hypothesis that the "classical" economists were utterly foolish, we must conclude that when they identified saving with investment they were asserting what would be true *at equilibrium.* By assuming that adjustments from a disequilibrium to an equilibrium position occur through instantaneous price adjustments or, what comes to the same thing, by ignoring the processes of adjustment, they could assert that saving must always equal investment.

An Alternate Perspective

Keynes's attack upon this way of looking at the question took two forms: (1) a different theory of interest, and (2) a different description of the process by which saving and investment are brought into balance. Once again, his attempts at theoretical reformulation stemmed from his recognition of the fundamental importance of uncertainty, of lags and resistances in the processes of adjustment to equilibrium, and of the factors that can intervene to shift an equilibrium position before it is reached.

The Theory of Interest

The preceding discussion of the interest rate was cast in terms of the supply of and demand for *loanable funds.* We can place the interest rate on the vertical axis, the dollar amounts of saving and investment on the horizontal axis. The willingness of income receivers to save, and to save more at higher and less at lower interest rates, yields a supply curve sloping upward to the right. The demand for those funds from potential investors will slope downward to the right, because capital goods are more valuable at lower interest rates. The market interest rate is then determined by the intersection of supply and demand curves.

Keynes had a number of objections to that way of viewing the matter. He doubted that saving depended in any stable or predictable way on the rate of interest. Surely the interest rate was not as important a determinant of the rate of saving as was income. Remember that an increase in people's desire to save is a reduction in consumption, that a decline in consumption reduces income, and that the multiplier process can greatly magnify the effect that such a change will have on income. Any effect that changes in the interest rate might have on saving could easily be swamped by changes in income. And was the level of aggregate saving positively correlated with the interest rate even when considered in isolation? Some might save more at the prospect of a higher return, but others might save less, since at a higher rate of interest a given future income could be obtained from a smaller nest egg. All in all, the interest-saving connection was an extremely weak link in the classical argument.

As for investment, Keynes agreed that it would increase at lower interest rates. But investment also depended, and depended more fundamentally, on the state of investors' expectations. And that, in his judgment, was one of the most volatile and unstable elements in the economic system. It depended not only upon the careful calculation of expected returns from various branches of production, but also upon speculative fancies and the general state of business confidence. "In estimating the prospects of investment," Keynes wrote, "we must have regard, therefore, to the nerves and hysteria and even the digestions and reactions to the weather of those upon whose spontaneous activity it largely depends." In a period of dismal expectations, such as might be brought on by the prospect of recession, even a zero interest rate might not be low enough to maintain an adequate level of investment. Figure 20D expresses the situation Keynes had in mind.

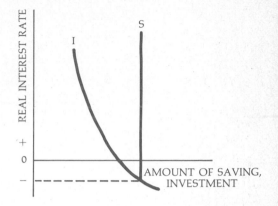

Figure 20D "Equilibrium" at a *negative* interest rate

A Monetary Theory of Interest

With the link between the interest rate and saving and investment decisions thus radically weakened if not severed altogether, Keynes required an alternate explanation of the forces determining the rate of interest. What he proposed was a monetary theory of interest. The rate of interest was determined by the relationship between the supply of *money* and the demand for *money*. The quantity of money the public wanted to hold varied inversely with the interest rate. Money is demanded, we know, because liquidity is valuable. But at higher interest rates, the opportunity cost of surrendering liquidity tends to be overcome by the opportunity cost of holding onto money (losing the return from ownership of interest-bearing assets). The monetary authorities can control the rate of interest, Keynes argued, by adjusting the stock of money along the public's demand curve for money, as in figure 20E.

Saving and Investment: Intentions versus Outcomes

But the major thrust of Keynes's counterproposal was his alternative explanation of the process by which aggregate saving and investment are equated. His explanation was constructed by means of the two new concepts already introduced: the marginal propensity to consume (along with its complement, the marginal propensity to save) and the multiplier.

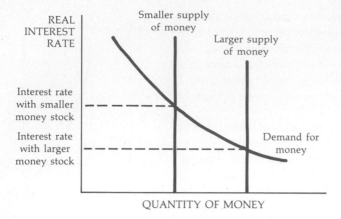

REAL INTEREST RATE

Smaller supply of money

Larger supply of money

Interest rate with smaller money stock

Interest rate with larger money stock

Demand for money

QUANTITY OF MONEY

Figure 20E Keynes's "monetary" theory of interest-rate determination

We can visualize the process Keynes had in mind by expanding the circular flow diagram of figure 20B. We'll now ignore the flow of real goods (the productive services and consumer goods) to concentrate on the flow of income and consumption expenditures to which each of the real flows is equivalent. We then add a savings flow and another expenditure flow, the flow of investment spending. Figure 20F presents the expanded model.

Consumption and saving both depend upon income. Investment depends upon expectations and the rate of interest. For the system to be in equilibrium, the flow of intended saving must equal the flow of intended investment. Why? Because if intended investment is more than intended saving, then consumption plus investment (aggregate demand) will be greater than aggregate income (consumption plus saving). That will lead to an increase in production, which will increase income. Income will continue rising in this fashion until the larger income has caused intended saving to increase by enough to match the intentions of investors.

If intended investment were to be less than intended saving initially, then aggregate demand would fall short of current output, and income would decline as production was curtailed. Income would continue falling until the smaller income had caused intended saving to decrease by enough to match intended investment.

It may help if you think of a partially filled bathtub with the drain and the faucet both open. The water level will rise as long as the faucet (intended investment) injects water faster than the drain releases it; the water level will fall as long as the size of the drain opening (intended saving) releases water faster than the faucet injects it. "Equilibrium" (no further change in the water level) will require that the rate of injection be equal to the rate of leakage. A bathtub equilibrium could occur with the water at any level in the tub between empty and overflowing the sides.

A Graphic Model of the Saving-Investment-Income Relationship

Perhaps the easiest way to grasp the Keynesian model of the saving-investment-income relationship is by means of a graph like figure 20G. S represents the propensity to save, or savings function. It shows intended saving as a function of income, represented by the letter Y. (Why the letter Y? It's simply a tradition that Keynes originated. The letter I had been appropriated by *investment*.) I represents intended investment, which is assumed in this simple case *not* to vary with income. The equilibrium level of Y will be $800 billion, because that is the only level of Y that allows intended saving to be equal to intended investment.

Let's use figure 20G to calculate the new equilibrium level of Y if intended investment decreases by $20 billion. If line I is redrawn $20 billion lower, it intersects line S where Y is $720 billion. So the equilibrium level of income would be $720 billion rather than $800 billion if intended investment were $80 billion rather than $100 billion.

Figure 20F Circular flow of income and expenditures

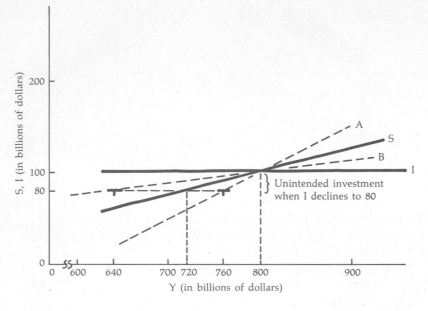

Figure 20G The *intentions*
of savers and investors
determine Y

The Marginal Propensity to Save and the Multiplier

The multiplier in figure 20G must be 4, because an initial spending change of $20 billion caused an ultimate change in income of $80 billion. The value of the multiplier quite obviously depends on the *slope* of the line S. If S had the steeper slope of the broken line A, Y would fall only to $760 billion in response to a $20 billion decline in intended investment, and the multiplier would be 2. If S had the flatter slope of the broken line B, the multiplier would be 8: a $20 billion decrease in intended investment would cause a $160 billion decline in income.

The slope of the line S is the ratio of the change in saving to the change in income. And this defines the *marginal propensity to save.* We saw earlier that the *marginal propensity to consume* determined the multiplier; the marginal propensity to save is simply its complement. The marginal propensity to save plus the marginal propensity to consume necessarily equals one, because additional income must be either saved or consumed by the definitions we're using. The multiplier will in fact be the inverse of the marginal propensity to save: one divided by the marginal propensity to save.[1]

1. Since MPC + MPS = 1, MPS = 1 − MPC. The multiplier is 1/(1 − MPC), which is the same as 1/MPS.

INCOME-EXPENDITURES ANALYSIS
AND THE INCOME AND PRODUCT ACCOUNTS

Which item or items in the income and product accounts, presented in chapter 17, corresponds to Y, which we are calling total income or output? Since we are assuming in this chapter that all saving is done by household consumers, we are ignoring undistributed corporate profits and capital consumption allowances. But if we ignore the setting aside of income to cover depreciation of capital (which is saving), we must also ignore the expenditure of that income to replace or restore capital equipment (which is investment). Investment was defined above as the total of producers' expenditures for new buildings and equipment, expenditures for new residential buildings, and changes in business inventories. That is more accurately known as *gross* investment. *Net* investment is the same total minus capital consumption allowances. Under these assumptions and with government expenditures left out of the picture, the sum of consumption expenditures and net investment is *net national product*.

In the absence of government there are no taxes or transfer payments, and net national product becomes identical with disposable income. Since disposable income is equal to consumption expenditures plus saving, net national product also equals consumption plus saving. In summary:

$$\text{consumption} + \text{(net) investment} = \text{net national product}$$
$$\text{net national product} = \text{disposable income}$$
$$\text{disposable income} = \text{consumption} + \text{saving}$$
$$\text{(net) investment} = \text{saving}$$

Actual saving and *actual* investment must be equal. But *intended* saving and *intended* investment may differ from each other. The income and product accounts do not, of course, register intentions; they only show what has actually occurred. They do, however, measure the variables that form the crucial relationships in income-expenditures analysis: consumption and saving in relation to disposable income, and changes in business inventories in relation to output and expenditures.

Implications of the Keynesian Model

All this is mechanics, however; what we want to understand is the significance of the approach Keynes proposed as an alternative to the saving-investment relationship. He rejected the view that if savers elect to increase their rate of saving or investors decide to reduce their rate of investment, interest rates and other prices will change to bring actual saving and investment into equality and thereby prevent the recession that would have occurred if total demand had fallen short of total output and income.

Instead, Keynes argued, an attempt by savers to save more or by investors to spend less *causes a recession,* and it is the recession that brings the desires of savers and investors into balance. Any gap between savers' plans and investors' plans will translate itself into a cumulative change in income that will continue until saving has been adjusted to investment.

Go back to figure 20G and the original equilibrium with Y at $800 billion. Then assume that income receivers decide to be more thrifty and to save something more than the $100 billion they're currently laying aside out of income. Suppose they collectively decide to save $120 billion. That would be shown on figure 20G by shifting the S curve upward so that saving is $120 billion rather than $100 billion when Y is $800 billion. If we assume that the *marginal* propensity to save (the slope of the savings function) remains unchanged, and draw the new S curve, it will intersect I where Y is $720 billion.

What has happened? The attempt by savers to save more than the $100 billion investors were willing to invest caused a recession. It initially created $20 billion of unintended investment in the form of undesired additions to business inventories. That in turn caused a reduction in output and hence in income. When the recession had reduced income to $720 billion, savers were indeed saving a larger percentage of their income—their original intention. But the income out of which they were saving had fallen by so much that the total amount of saving was no greater than before. It was still equal to the total of original intended investment.

Aggregate Demand and Total Output

All of this can be expressed by means of an alternative statement of the condition for an aggregate equilibrium: consumption expenditures plus intended investment expenditures must equal total output or income.

Consumption plus *actual* investment must always be the same as total output. Consumption plus investment purchases cannot be *less* than output, because any unsold output becomes investment; it is considered to have been purchased by its producer as an addition, willing or unwilling, to inventory. Could consumption plus investment be *greater* than output? There is obviously no way to purchase more of this year's output than was produced this year, but it is certainly possible for consumers and investors to purchase everything produced this year plus some of the output left over from previous years. If this occurs, however, inventories are being reduced, and a decline in inventories is *negative* investment. The amount by which the total of consumer and investor purchases might exceed current output will necessarily be equal to the amount by which net inventories are reduced this year, or the amount of negative investment that occurs. When this negative investment is subtracted from total investor purchases, consumption plus investment will necessarily equal total output.

Intended investment and consumption are another matter, however. If consumption plus intended investment is less than total output, some unintended investment or unintended addition to inventories has occurred. Producers will respond by reducing output, just as they would have wanted to increase output if unexpectedly large purchases had reduced their inventories below desired levels. A reduction in output reduces income and causes consumption to fall. As a result, consumption plus intended investment will once again fall short of total output, and this will prompt further production cutbacks. The multiplier process will continue in this fashion until actual output has fallen to the level of consumption plus intended investment.

We can use the same kind of graphical analysis as in figure 20G to present this version of the equilibrating process. Since income minus saving is by definition equal to consumption, we can derive the corresponding consumption function from the saving function of figure 20G. It is labeled C in figure 20H. We've drawn a line through the graph to mark off all those points at which expenditures on the vertical axis equal income on the horizontal axis. The vertical distance between the consumption function and this reference line shows the level of saving at each level of income.

The investment function has been added to the consumption function to show aggregate demand at various levels of income. It lies $100 billion above the consumption function and is labeled C + I. The equilibrium level of income emerges as $800 billion, because that is the only level at which consumption plus intended investment will equal total output or income.

If consumers now decide to spend $680 billion rather than $700 billion (or to save $120 billion rather than $100 billion), the consumption function and hence the C + I line will shift downward by $20 billion. The result will be a new equilibrium at $720 billion. At this level of income, and only at this level of income, consumption plus intended investment will equal output. The $20 billion change in expenditures causes a change of $80 billion in income; the multiplier is 4. Notice that saving will not be at the originally intended level of $120 billion. The decline in income will have altered the intentions of consumer-savers so that they now want to save only $100 billion.

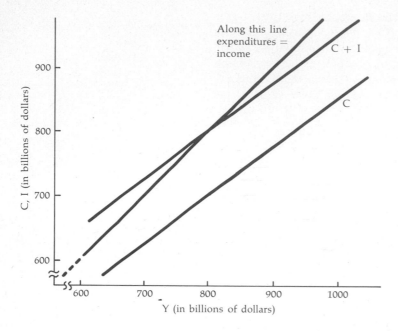

Along this line expenditures = income

C + I

C

Figure 20H The *intentions* of consumers and investors determine Y

Each way of stating the equilibrium condition, as $S = I$ or as $C + I = Y$, has some advantages. The formula that intended saving must equal intended investment focuses attention on a crucial contention of income-expenditures analysis: equality between intended saving and intended investment will not be brought about by adjustments in interest rates and relative prices, but by changes in total income and output. The fact that any inequality between intended saving and intended investment is evidence of a disequilibrium does not prove, as the classical theorists maintained, that recessions will quickly correct themselves. On the contrary, Keynes argued, it is recession itself that brings about the new equilibrium. We chose this way of introducing income-expenditures analysis in order to focus on the difference between the Keynesian position and the older point of view.

The alternative way of putting it, that consumption plus intended investment must equal total output, has the advantage of being easier to grasp intuitively. Everyone understands that production decisions respond to demand. If buyers do not want to purchase everything that has been produced, producers reduce output; if buyers want to purchase more than has been produced, producers find it in their interest to expand output. Production is undertaken in anticipation of demand, and rises or falls as realized or actual demand exceeds or falls short of expected demand.

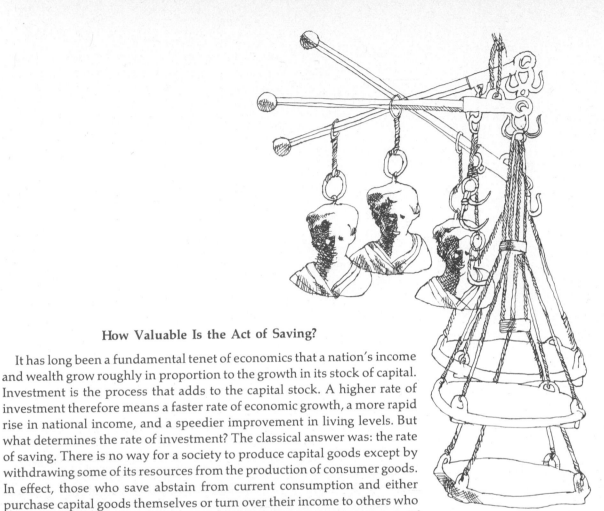

How Valuable Is the Act of Saving?

It has long been a fundamental tenet of economics that a nation's income and wealth grow roughly in proportion to the growth in its stock of capital. Investment is the process that adds to the capital stock. A higher rate of investment therefore means a faster rate of economic growth, a more rapid rise in national income, and a speedier improvement in living levels. But what determines the rate of investment? The classical answer was: the rate of saving. There is no way for a society to produce capital goods except by withdrawing some of its resources from the production of consumer goods. In effect, those who save abstain from current consumption and either purchase capital goods themselves or turn over their income to others who purchase capital goods. Without saving there can be no investment. (If investment is financed by borrowing from abroad, foreigners must do the saving.) The incentive to save must, therefore, be preserved and extended, according to the classical argument, because it is the root cause of social progress.

In the concluding chapter of the *General Theory,* Keynes speculated on the social consequences toward which acceptance of his theory might lead. He thought it might well reduce society's traditional reluctance to interfere with the distribution of income. This reluctance was largely based on the argument of the preceding paragraph plus the assumption that wealthy people save a larger percentage of their income than poor people do. Any attempt to improve the lot of the poor by redistributing income from the rich therefore runs the risk of eventually making the whole society poorer.

The surer route to improving the lot of the poor lay through the encouragement of saving. And that argued against any redistribution of income in the direction of greater equality.

The "Paradox of Thrift"

Keynes's theory cast doubt upon this line of reasoning by suggesting that the desire to save might actually retard investment and economic growth. At least in industrially developed and affluent societies, an increase in "thrift" would reduce aggregate demand and so lower the actual rate of investment and hence the rate of economic growth. This argument came to be known as the paradox of thrift.

To illustrate the operation of the paradox, let's revise the graph of figure 20G. Instead of assuming that intended investment is constant, let's assume that it varies directly with income. Investment decisions depend upon expectations of profit; these expectations are formed in part by expectations of growth in total income; and changes in current income may be regarded by investors as a clue to future income levels. Let's assume, therefore, that investment spending increases or decreases as income increases or decreases, and by an amount equal to $\frac{1}{8}$ of the change in Y.

In figure 20I, the curves of saving and investment determine the equilibrium level of Y at $800 billion. Note that the marginal propensity to save is still $\frac{1}{4}$, but that the marginal propensity to invest is now $\frac{1}{8}$ rather than zero (as in Figure 20G). Now we introduce an increase in thriftiness, just as we did before: the public decides to save $120 billion rather than just $100 billion out of an income of $800 billion. We show that decision by raising the curve S $20 billion all along its length. The two curves will now intersect where Y is $640 billion. At the new equilibrium level of income, saving and investment will, of course, be equal; but they will have fallen by $20 billion. An increase in the desire to save actually caused a decline in both saving and investment. This is the paradox of thrift.

What happened? The rise in the savings function triggered a cumulative decline in income. But with intended investment spending also dependent upon the level of income, that decline pulled down investment; and the decline in intended investment then added its own impact to the cumulative process that savers had initiated. In this kind of world, a concern for maintaining the incentive to save would seem to be absurd. The situation calls for an increase in spending, not in saving. A higher level of saving will appear of its own accord as income rises if some way can be found to stimulate spending and thus the level of income and output.

But now we've begun to discuss the policy implications of the *General Theory*. Before we can do that, we must introduce government spending and taxes into the income-expenditures model.

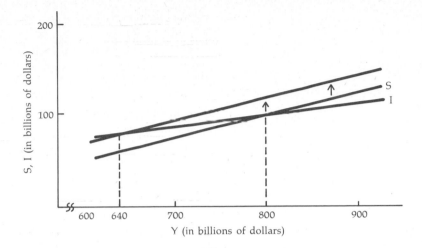

Once Over Lightly

When conditions of demand or supply change, business firms and sellers of productive resources do not immediately make perfect adjustments. Because information is a scarce good in an uncertain world, they must search for the pattern of resource allocation that will be most advantageous under the altered circumstances. This takes time and entails learning through mistakes.

Traditional equilibrium analysis has usually abstracted from time and uncertainty by assuming that demanders and suppliers instantly and faultlessly adjust their behavior when change occurs. In such a world, recessions would be impossible. Prices would always be at market clearing levels and all resources would always be employed to their best advantage.

Income-expenditures analysis provides an alternative way of viewing adjustments between aggregate demand and supply, based on the concepts of the consumption function and the multiplier.

If expenditures for new goods unexpectedly decline so that producers are unable to sell at current prices as much as they had planned to sell, producers accumulate unwanted inventories. Their response is not to cut prices but rather to reduce output in an attempt to bring inventories back down to desired levels. But when output is reduced, the incomes of producers fall. Keynes postulated a consumption function according to which consumption changes as income changes but by less than the change in income. And so consumption also declines when output is cut back.

This decline in consumption leads to further disappointments for sellers, who again find themselves with excessive inventories of goods. They reduce production further, which reduces incomes once more, which causes an additional decline in consumption expenditures.

The multiplier in income-expenditures analysis is the ratio between the eventual change in income and the original change in expenditures that triggered it. The value of the multiplier depends upon the rate at which consumption changes as income changes, or upon the marginal propensity to consume (change in consumption divided by change in income). The eventual change in income will be equal to the initial change in expenditures times $1/(1 - MPC)$, where MPC is the marginal propensity to consume. Since the marginal propensity to consume plus the marginal propensity to save equals one, the multiplier can also be stated as $1/MPS$.

In a simple model from which government activities and business saving are excluded, consumption plus (net) investment equals net national product. Consumption plus saving equals disposable income, which, in the absence of business saving, taxes, and government transfer payments, is also equal to net national product. Saving and investment therefore *must be equal.* But this is only true of *actual* or *realized* saving and investment. *Intended* saving can be quite different from *intended* investment.

The "classical" theory assumed that any divergence between intended saving and intended investment would cause changes in the rate of interest and in relative prices that would bring the plans of savers and investors back into balance. The Keynesian theory asserted that, in an uncertain world, interest rates and relative prices would not perform this equilibrating task, or, at least, would not perform it quickly enough to forestall the operation of an alternative equilibrating mechanism. Under this mechanism, the rate of production changes in response to any divergence between intended saving and intended investment. This causes a change in income, which in turn causes savers to revise their intentions. Income and output continue to fall (or rise) until the economy is in aggregate equilibrium, or until intended saving is equal to intended investment.

In the "classical" view of things, saving was what made investment possible. In the Keynesian view, investment also makes saving possible. The critical problem in a developed and affluent economy, Keynes suggested, is not that of providing incentives to savers so that investment can take place and economic growth can continue. The problem is more likely to be one of providing incentives to investors so that the level of output and income can be maintained and recession avoided.

QUESTIONS FOR DISCUSSION

1. Can an economy be at equilibrium if much of its industrial capacity is standing idle and a large percentage of its labor force is unemployed? Is that a question about fact or a disguised argument about the proper way to use the concept of equilibrium?

2. Suppose that demand for the goods listed below turns out to be less than producers anticipated, so that the goods already produced cannot all be sold at current prices. What consequences would you predict in the case of each good? Would prices or production levels be likely to fall first? How long will the sequence of adjustments take?

   (*a*) automobiles

   (*b*) beef cattle

   (*c*) secondary school teachers

3. Is it true, as Keynes assumed in describing the consumption function, that people increase their consumption as their income increases, but not by as much as the increase in their income? Does consumption in one period (a month, for example) depend upon income in that particular period? Would you expect a salesman receiving a highly variable monthly income to vary his consumption as his income varies?

4. Explain in your own words what is meant by the "multiplier." How does the multiplier depend upon the consumption function? If every increase in spending increases income, and every increase in income increases spending, wouldn't the ultimate effect of any initial change in spending be infinitely large? Why not?

5. The text presents two theories of the interest rate. One explains the interest rate as a product of the supply of and the demand for loanable funds, the other as a product of the supply of and the demand for money.

   (*a*) What is the difference between loanable funds and money?

   (*b*) Do the two theories have significantly different implications?

6. If saving suddenly and unexpectedly increases, unintended investment will rise by enough to keep actual saving and investment equal.

   (*a*) What form does this unintended investment take?

   (*b*) What further consequences will this unintended investment have?

   (*c*) Suppose that saving suddenly and unexpectedly *decreased.* Would that be capable of creating a temporary inequality between saving and investment? Explain what might occur.

7. (*a*) How are the marginal propensity to consume and the marginal propensity to save related?

   (*b*) How is each related to the multiplier in income-expenditures analysis?

8. Does investment depend upon saving? Can investment occur if there has been no saving? What are the real differences between the older view that investment could only be maintained by maintaining saving and Keynes's view that a high rate of investment was a precondition for a high rate of saving?

9. Does the "paradox of thrift" imply that saving is an antisocial act and consumption an act that benefits society?

10. Increase your familiarity with the graphic analysis employed in figures 20G, 20H, and 20I and the interrelationships these graphs try to summarize by answering the following questions.

In figure 20G:

(*a*) What would be the new equilibrium level of Y if intended investment increased to $130 billion?

(*b*) What would be the value of the multiplier?

(*c*) If $800 billion is the full employment level of Y, could Y increase by such a large percentage? How?

(*d*) Equilibrium occurs when *intended* saving and *intended* investment are equal. How might such a sudden and unexpected 30% increase in investment force *actual* saving to be larger for a period of time than the amount of income which savers *want* to hold out of consumption? (Hint: How would investors obtain command over the capital goods they want to accumulate?)

In Figure 20I:

(*a*) What is the value of the multiplier?

(*b*) Why is it larger than indicated by the formula for deriving the multiplier from the marginal propensity to consume?

In Figure 20H:

(*a*) What is the level of saving when income is $640 billion? When it is $800 billion?

(*b*) What is the numerical slope of the consumption function? How is it related to the slope of the saving function graphed in figure 20G?

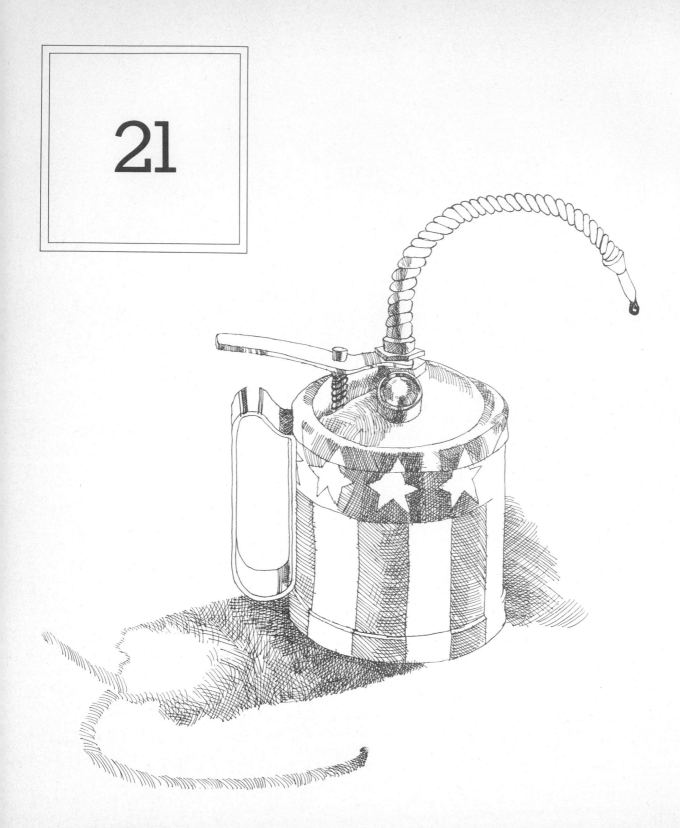

21

INCOME–EXPENDITURES ANALYSIS
AND FISCAL POLICY

To the classical economists whom Keynes criticized, the ability of an economic system to produce goods and provide jobs was determined by its stock of capital. As saving increased, investment could be increased, the stock of capital enlarged, and employment opportunities expanded. Keynes did not deny that argument, but he did deny its relevance to the economy in which he lived. The modern problem, as he saw it, was to make fuller use of already existing capacity. Increasing the capacity of the economy was a problem of secondary importance. An increased propensity to save would not expand employment. On the contrary, it would be an added threat to full employment because it would be a more difficult challenge for investment to fulfill. The *actual* level of output and employment was determined by the willingness of investors to spend all that the public wanted to save. Recessions came about because the propensity to save in conditions of relatively full employment was greater than the demand for new capital.

Moreover, the demand for capital, Keynes believed, was highly unstable. Some of the arguments he put forward on behalf of that thesis are no longer convincing, but the thesis is inherently plausible and it can be supported with historical data. Investment spending is typically oriented to a more distant future than is consumption spending. Changing expectations about the course of future events will therefore have a larger impact on current investment decisions than on consumption decisions. Investment expenditures also tend to be highly postponable. One can make do with present buildings and equipment for a while *or* take advantage of favorable circumstances to acquire new buildings and equipment ahead of schedule.

Investment spending is therefore more likely to be "bunched" than is spending on consumer goods and especially on nondurable goods.

When the unpredictability and instability of investment spending is inserted into the income-expenditures model of chapter 20, the implica-

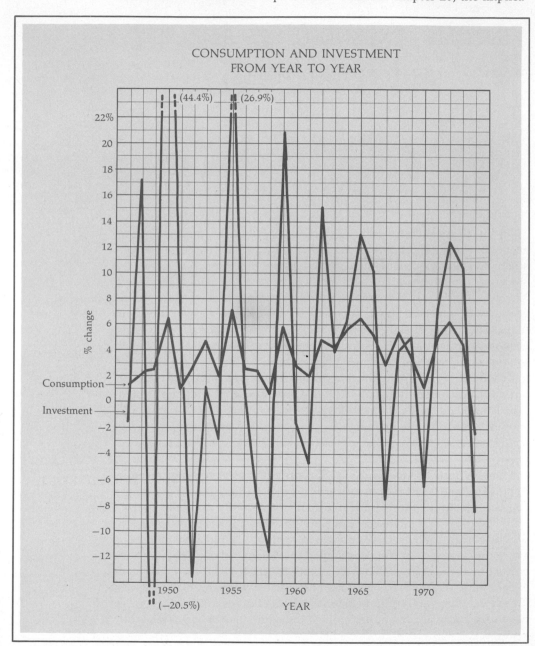

tions are disturbing. Income and output are not likely to increase steadily over time as society adds to its stock of capital equipment. On the contrary, the economy will be exposed to periodic increases and decreases in the rate of investment spending that will be transformed through the multiplier into large fluctuations in the level of income. Moreover, what is lost in the downturns will not be recovered in the upturns. A downturn leads to idle resources—high unemployment in the labor force and unused physical facilities. The output thus lost is gone forever and includes any additions it might have made to future productivity. But the waste of potential output is of lesser importance than the suffering that a downturn imposes upon the workers who lose their jobs and upon new entrants to the labor force who cannot find adequate employment opportunities during a recession. A subsequent upturn will not make up for what has been lost.

Nor may we take for granted that every upturn will be an unmixed blessing. If spurts in investment spending trigger a cumulative expansion that carries aggregate demand beyond the economic system's productive capabilities, prices will rise and the economy will undergo inflation. The policy question to which Keynes was addressing himself—and those who knew him have testified that he never devised a theoretical concept without having in mind a policy application—was whether the economy must submit itself to an endless recurrence of expansions and contractions. Were there ways to correct or compensate for the destabilizing effects of private investment decisions?

The focus in this chapter will be upon fiscal policy and its potential applications to the problem of recessions. Keynes did not believe that fiscal policy was only applicable in periods of recession or that it was the only stabilization tool the government had. But income-expenditures analysis was developed in the depths of the Great Depression and was based largely upon reflections on the problems of recession and unemployment. Its instantaneous success among large numbers of economists was unquestionably related to its apparent applicability to those particular problems, whose urgency in the 1930s would be hard to exaggerate. And it did in fact lead to a preoccupation with fiscal policy, at least among economists, that pushed alternative or supplementary stabilization policies off the stage for almost a quarter century.

THE GOVERNMENT BUDGET
IN AN INCOME-EXPENDITURES MODEL

Fiscal policy is budget policy. Every organization or individual with a budget has a budget policy: a way of managing receipts and disbursements to achieve certain goals. In the narrower sense in which the term is now usually employed, however, *fiscal policy means specifically the employment by the federal government of expenditures and taxes to influence the aggregate level of economic activity.*

We can incorporate the government's budget into income-expenditures analysis in either of two ways. One is to regard taxes as a leakage similar to saving, and disbursements as an injection similar to investment, and rewrite the equilibrium condition as follows: Intended saving plus taxes must equal the total of intended investment plus disbursements by government. (This must include federal, state, and local governments.) Or we can add government purchases of final goods to the purchases of consumers and investors and restate the equilibrium condition: Total output or income must equal the sum of consumption expenditures, intended investment, and government purchases of commodities and services.

A Formal Model

Ordinary language is a very clumsy tool when we try to provide even the simplest summary description of the interrelationships among all our variables once government has been introduced into the picture. Taxes create a difference between net national product and the disposable income on which consumption and saving decisions depend, so that the marginal propensities to consume or save will now have to be expressed as functions of income after taxes. Since taxes will themselves vary with the level of economic activity, they ought to be expressed as a function of income *taxes* rather than as some constant amount. If we allow investment expenditures to vary with income, as we did in Figure 20I and the accompanying discussion, we have another variable that can't be treated as a constant in our analysis. A further complication arises if we want to treat government transfer payments separately from other expenditures; and we probably

ought to do that because transfer payments do not create a direct demand for output as do government expenditures for commodities and services.

Algebra was created for just such situations. Because the algebra used will be of the most elementary kind, the letters, numbers, and equations which follow should not intimidate anyone. We'll use algebra to put the picture together and to discover the principal implications of the theory. A few minutes spent in mastering the relationships that the equations describe will enable you to think about and discuss the issues of stabilization policy far more surely and confidently.

Step one: Let's define all the symbols we'll be using:

Y = total income or total output
C = the consumption function
S = the saving function
I = the investment function
G = government expenditures for commodities and services
  (government transfer payments are not included)
Tx = taxes
Tr = government transfer payments (payments not made for services currently being rendered: unemployment compensation, social security benefits, general welfare assistance, veterans' benefits, *etc.*)
$Yd = Y - Tx + Tr$ = disposable income
  (also $C + S$, by definition)

Step two: We set down the conditions for an equilibrium. What we want to do with all these letters is put them together to see how the equilibrium level of total income is determined and how changes in one variable will change others. We can state the equilibrium condition in either of two ways:

1. $Y = C + I + G$
     (aggregate output or income = aggregate intended expenditures)

2. $S + Tx = I + G + Tr$
     (intended deductions from the income-expenditures flow = intended injections into the income-expenditures flow)

Step three: If we now assign appropriate numerical values, we can solve for the equilibrium value of Y. But we won't want to run through the entire set of equations each time we change a number, so we shall first solve for Y in a general form. Consumption expenditures will be some constant amount plus the marginal propensity to consume times disposable income. We'll treat intended investment, government purchases, and transfer payments as constants. And taxes will be assumed to vary with total income.

Letting c_o represent the constant amount in the consumption function and c_m the marginal propensity to consume, $C = c_o + c_m Yd$. If t stands for the tax rate, $Tx = tY$. We can now proceed as follows:

$$Y = C + I + G$$
$$Y = (c_o + c_m Yd) + I + G$$
$$Y = c_o + c_m(Y - Tx + Tr) + I + G$$
$$Y = c_o + c_m(Y - tY + Tr) + I + G$$
$$Y = c_o + c_m Y - c_m tY + c_m Tr + I + G$$
$$Y - c_m Y + c_m tY = c_o + c_m Tr + I + G$$
$$(1 - c_m + c_m t)Y = c_o + c_m Tr + I + G$$
$$Y = \left(\frac{1}{1 - c_m + c_m t}\right)(c_o + c_m Tr + I + G)$$

Let's try it out with some numerical values, all representing billions of dollars. Assume that investors want to spend 140 while government purchases 300 of commodities and services and disburses 100 in transfer payments. Let taxes be .25Y and let the consumption function be 120 + .8Yd. Then

$$\frac{1}{1 - c_m + c_m t} = \frac{1}{1 - .8 + .2} = \frac{1}{.4} = 2.5$$

and

$$Y = 2.5(120 + 80 + 140 + 300)$$
$$Y = 2.5(640)$$
$$Y = 1600$$

We can now calculate the equilibrium level of disposable income and of consumption expenditures:

$$Yd = 1600 - 400 + 100 + 1300$$

And so, at equilibrium

$$C = 120 + .8(1300) = 1160$$

Checking our results, we find that Y does equal the total of C, I, and G:

$$1600 = 1160 + 140 + 300$$

Are our results consistent with the alternative equilibrium condition, that saving plus taxes be equal to the total of intended investment, government purchases, and transfers? If

$$C = 120 + .8(1300)$$

then

$$S = -120 + .2(1300)$$
$$S = 140$$

The equilibrium condition is

$$S + Tx = I + G + Tr$$

Inserting the values already obtained, we get

$$140 + 400 = 140 + 300 + 100$$
$$540 = 540$$

There are two ways to get hung up in the mechanics of all these equations. One is to be intimidated by the algebra. The other is to become proficient with the algebra and forget that it is intended as a simplified description of the interactions that determine total output and income. Master the algebra to clear the way. Then you'll be ready to consider the potential implications of all this for policymaking.

The Government Budget and Full Employment

All we know about that $1600 billion income is that it's the equilibrium level under the conditions given. But is that level of income and output consistent with full employment and price stability?

As we know from chapter 16, full employment is extraordinarily hard to define in a way that is neither meaningless nor misleading. As a first approximation, however, let's just assume that we know what we mean by full employment, that we can measure it satisfactorily, and that it's achieved with total income and output at a $1600 billion level. Any increase in aggregate demand that pulled income above that level would therefore cause inflation. The *nominal* value of income—its value measured in current dollars—would increase. But if we assume that *real* output and income cannot be increased beyond the full employment level, any increase in nominal income above $1600 billion would mean that the price level had gone up.[1]

If aggregate demand falls short of $1600 billion, on the other hand, unemployment will appear. What would occur, under these circumstances, if a sudden wave of pessimistic expectations swept the economy and intended investment fell by $16 billion? It isn't necessary to run through all the calculations again. We can see at a glance that with I equal to $124 billion instead of $140 billion

$$Y = 2.5(624)$$

Y will consequently decline from $1600 billion to $1560 billion. How will that affect the other variables that are dependent on the level of income?

---

1. Since full employment, however defined, is a matter of degree, we should not expect the price level to remain completely stable as income approaches the full employment level, or anticipate *no* increases in real output after that point has been reached.

Taxes will decline to $390 billion. Disposable income will therefore decline to $1270 billion. Consumption will fall to $1136 billion, and saving to $134 billion.

Let's compare the original values and the new values of all the variables.

	Original Value	New Value
I	140	124
Y	1600	1560
Yd	1300	1270
C	1160	1136
S	140	134
G	300	300
Tx	400	390
Tr	100	100

Saving, you should notice, is no longer equal to investment. But with government in the picture, it does not have to be equal to investment. The total of saving plus taxes must be equal to the total of investment and government expenditures plus transfer payments. And it is. When Y = $1560 billion the government is running a deficit of $10 billion, and this compensates for the $10 billion by which saving exceeds investment. The total of government expenditures and transfer payments is $10 billion more than tax revenue.

Most of us have learned to think of deficits as Bad Things and evidence that someone is trying to live beyond his means. But note what would happen in our model if the government tried to get rid of the deficit. Any increase in tax rates will reduce disposable income and hence consumption, driving total income even further below the full employment level. A decrease in government expenditures will also reduce aggregate demand and trigger further declines in total income. And as income falls, tax revenues will also decline.

Suppose the government reduced its expenditures by $10 billion in response to the budget deficit. Total income would then fall to $1535. And the budget would still be in deficit, because tax receipts would have fallen to $383.75 billion. The reduction in government spending would only have reduced the deficit from $10 billion to $6.25 billion. The cost of this reduction in the deficit would be a further $25 billion loss in output.

It might be instructive to figure out by how much the government would have to reduce its expenditures to achieve a balanced budget under the circumstances of our model. For the system to be in equilibrium with a balanced budget, saving would have to equal the $124 billion of intended investment. Setting saving equal to investment and solving for the equilibrium value of Y, we obtain the following:

$$S = I$$
$$-120 + .2Yd = 124$$
$$-120 + .2(Y - .25Y + 100) = 124$$
$$-120 + .2Y - .05Y + 20 = 124$$
$$.15Y = 224$$
$$Y = 1493\tfrac{1}{3}$$
$$Yd = 1493\tfrac{1}{3} - 373\tfrac{1}{3} + 100 = 1220$$
$$C = 120 + .8(1220) = 1096$$

Since I = 124 and the sum of C, I, and G must be $1493\tfrac{1}{3}$, the government would have to reduce its expenditures to $273\tfrac{1}{3}$ billion in order to balance the budget. But it would thereby cause a further reduction of $41\tfrac{2}{3}$ billion in output and the increase in unemployment that would go along with it.

Changing Attitudes toward the "Balanced Budget"

Would any government behave in such a fashion? Probably no longer. And that is some evidence of the extent to which the income-expenditures approach to government budgeting has influenced the thinking of contemporary policymakers. Federal government receipts fell by almost a billion dollars between the 1957 and 1959 fiscal years because of the 1958 recession. They had been expected to rise, and expenditures had been budgeted in anticipation of a continuing increase in tax revenues. With expenditures increasing on schedule—even a little ahead of schedule because of the additional outlays for transfer payments that a recession causes—the government budget slipped deeply into the red. The $13 billion deficit in the 1959 fiscal year was the largest peacetime deficit ever incurred. But despite President Eisenhower's numerous past expressions of devotion to the ideal of a balanced budget, no serious efforts were made by his administration to raise taxes or reduce expenditures.

In 1932, by contrast, in the depths of the Great Depression, Franklin D. Roosevelt campaigned for the presidency by promising to balance the budget. Throughout his first administration, during which unemployment ranged from 17% to 25% of the labor force, he repeatedly tried to reduce government expenditures and persistently proposed new taxes. His primary goal in proposing tax increases may not have been a balanced budget; he seems to have been at least as interested in increasing the taxes on large incomes as in acquiring additional revenue. But the contrast with contemporary practice is striking nonetheless.

In 1975, with the economy again in the throes of recession and the budget deeply in the red, a Republican administration reputed to favor a balanced budget actually called for tax decreases that would add to the size of the deficit.

WHAT DO WE MEAN BY A "BALANCED BUDGET"?

The budget is balanced when expenditures match income. That seems clear enough. But is it really? Think about each of the following cases. In which of them are you engaged in "deficit spending"?

1. You spend $20 per day even though your income on six days of the week is zero and you receive $140 on Friday. Are you running a surplus on Friday and a deficit the other six days of the week? It's obvious that no one balances his budget except with reference to some period of time. But what is the relevant period?

2. You're a salesman whose monthly income fluctuates between $600 and $1000. You nonetheless maintain your expenditures at $800 per month. Are you alternating between deficits and surpluses or are you balancing your budget? Would it make sense to say that you won't know until later whether you've been balancing your budget?

3. You will receive $10,000 next year when the legal formalities are completed on your rich uncle's will. Are you running a deficit if you borrow money in order to increase your expenditures this year? Would your answer change if you aren't certain that his bequest to you will survive a legal test?

4. You borrow money at age twenty-five to buy a house. Are you "living beyond your means"? How would you go about answering that question?

5. By borrowing money now at 6% interest you can purchase an education that will probably double your income for many years in the future. Are you "running in the red"? Is it ever profitable to "run in the red"?

Each of these three administrations displayed a different attitude toward the phenomenon of a budget thrown into deficit by a recession. In the 1930s there was a strong emphasis on bringing the budget back into balance. In the 1950s the approach was to take no action and thus to accept the deficit brought on by recession. In the 1970s the budget was viewed as an active tool for achieving recovery, and an even larger deficit was deliberately courted. In each decade the government had a fiscal policy. But the progression from Roosevelt through Eisenhower to Ford shows the growing influence of income-expenditures analysis on the formulation of that policy.

The Full Employment Budget

Income-expenditures analysis has clearly taught economists and politicians to look at the government budget in a different way. The thought of a deficit is no longer entertained with the same horror it once aroused among students of public finance. And the older definition of a deficit as simply an excess of government expenditures over receipts has lost ground to such newer concepts as the *full employment deficit or surplus.*

The *full employment budget* is the budget that would be in effect if the economy were operating at full employment. The concept is a useful one despite the fact that it rests inevitably on somewhat arbitrary definitions of full employment and on debatable projections of revenue and expenditures. But we do know that tax revenues and, to a lesser extent, transfer payments vary with the level of economic activity. A budget deficit incurred while the economy is operating below capacity might well turn into a surplus at full employment, without any changes at all in tax rates or spending programs.

The only budget that ought to be balanced, many economists now argue, is the full employment budget. In other words, the government should set tax rates that will yield just enough revenue to cover expenditures when the economy is operating at full employment. A downturn will then cause a deficit but the deficit should be ignored. And a boom will yield a surplus, which also ought to be ignored. Such deficits and surpluses will then function as automatic stabilizers. Deficits will compensate in part for declines in private spending, even without deliberate policy actions. And surpluses will serve as an automatic brake on total spending when it rises so rapidly that inflation threatens.

COUNTERCYCLICAL FISCAL POLICY

All of this describes a rather passive use of fiscal policy. Can it be used more aggressively to control or offset fluctuations in aggregate demand? In our model, there is a great difference between the consequences of not taking any action to reduce deficits and the consequences of deliberately creating or adding to a deficit during a recession.

By drawing conclusions from a simple algebraic model we run the risk of slighting the political and technical difficulties that confront budget planners, including all the difficulties associated with uncertainty about the future. But we ought to master the simple mechanics before introducing the qualifications. So let's go back to the model we've developed and ask what size changes in the government budget would restore the economy to full employment.

An Activist Fiscal Policy

The recession was brought on by a $16 billion decline in investment. A $16 billion increase in government expenditures in our example would exactly compensate for that decline. At the new equilibrium induced by the expansion of government spending, total income, disposable income, consumption, and saving will all be restored to their previous levels. Saving will therefore be $16 billion more than investment. But government "saving" will be negative: taxes will be $400 billion, government outlays for goods and transfer payments will be $416 billion, and the $16 billion deficit will compensate for the gap between private saving and investment.

The full employment equilibrium could also be restored by reducing taxes or increasing transfer payments. Suppose the government increases transfer payments by $16 billion instead of increasing its own purchases of goods by $16 billion. That won't be enough. By the assumptions of our model, aggregate demand does not increase by the full amount of any increase in transfer payments. Only .8 of any increase in disposable income goes toward increasing expenditures, while the other .2 flows into saving. While a $16 billion increase in government expenditures *directly* increases the demand for output by that amount, a $16 billion increase in disposable income leads to only a $12.8 billion initial increase in demand. And an initial expenditure increase of $12.8 billion would only bring total income up to $1592 billion after completion of the multiplier process.[1] To restore Y to its full employment level, the government would have to raise transfer payments by $20 billion. As .8 of that, or $16 billion, went toward an increase in consumption, Y would rise via the multiplier process to $1600 billion. The deficit would therefore be somewhat larger than if the government restored the system to full employment via an increase in its own purchases of goods.

We've been looking at changes in the level of transfer payments as the fiscal policy alternative to changes in government expenditures for commodities and services. The alternative usually talked about, and the one chosen in 1975, was changes in *taxes*. But the same analysis applies. The government could pay the transfers to taxpayers in the form of a $16 billion rebate. Taxes would then become 25% of Y minus $16 billion. It makes a good deal of difference, politically and otherwise, whether the government

---

1. The effective multiplier for any change in expenditures in our model is 2.5. You can see that at once by looking at the solution of the model and noting that Y changes by $\frac{1}{4}$, or 2.5, dollars for every one-dollar change in I or G. The formal value of the effective multiplier in this model is

$$\frac{1}{1 - c_m + c_m t}$$

This expresses the fact that the impact of a change in income on consumption is reduced in the model by both the marginal tax rate *and* the marginal propensity to save.

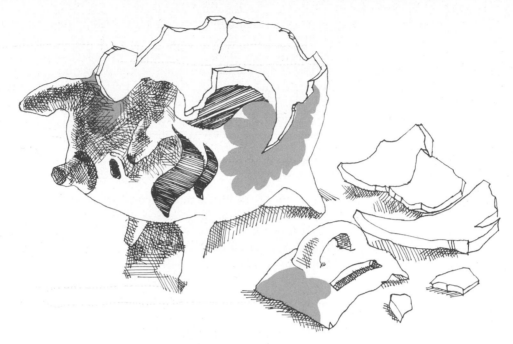

offers rebates to taxpayers or increases its payments to veterans, the unemployed, those on welfare, or retired people receiving social security. But in our simplified model the consequences will be the same either way. And our point here is simply that a change in transfer payments or tax receipts is a less powerful weapon for altering total income than a change in government purchases.[1]

This does not imply that government expenditure increases are preferable to tax cuts when the government wants to expand national income. It implies only that expenditure increases of a given amount are more *powerful* in our model than tax decreases in the same amount. And it explains the objection some economists voiced to President Nixon's 1971 proposal to stimulate the economy by cutting taxes while reducing government expenditures by an equal amount. These economists argued, on the basis of a model similar to the one we're using, that the net effect of the combined actions would be negative. They invoked the concept of the *balanced budget multiplier.* This concept, based on the reasoning we've just gone through, asserts that a change in expenditures coupled with a change in tax receipts of the same amount causes total income to move in the direc-

---

1. We presented the argument in terms of transfer payments because in our model taxes are not a set amount but a function of Y. The analysis would become more complex than seems worthwhile if we tried to determine the tax *rate* change that would yield a specified *receipts* change.

tion of the expenditure change. Thus a $20 billion decrease in tax receipts joined to a $20 billion decrease in government spending would reduce income in our model by $10 billion. For while the tax cut prompts $16 billion of additional consumption, the reduction in government spending lowers demand by $20 billion. The initial impact on aggregate demand is consequently a net decrease of $4 billion. With an effective multiplier of 2.5, as in our model, that becomes a $10 billion reduction in national income when the new equilibrium is reached.

Great Expectations

Income-expenditures analysis achieved rapid acceptance among economists after 1936 largely because it described the dynamics of aggregate fluctuations in a way that also suggested the cure. If recessions are the result of an increased desire to save not matched by a desire to invest, or a fall in investment spending decisions when the public isn't willing to shift its consumption function upward, why not have the government counteract the change through a *compensatory* fiscal policy? It seems quite simple and it would appear to be in everyone's best interest. What stands in the way except the ignorance of the public and politicians? Could more courses in economic principles wipe out recessions the way vaccination has wiped out smallpox? One of the authors grew up during the Great Depression and still remembers vividly the sense of relief with which he discovered fiscal policy in his first economics course. Depressions were not inevitable! The government now knew how to cure them!

But does the economy actually work in the way our model describes it? Or have too many important relationships been omitted? We know, for example, that saving and consumption decisions do not depend exclusively on current income as the consumption function assumes. People often maintain an accustomed level of spending by borrowing when current income declines and by adding to their saving when it rises. Consumption spending can also be affected by expectations of *future* income. How reliable is the multiplier process when we take these factors into account? As for investment spending, it's not only a variable subject to sudden and unexpected changes; it is sometimes fickle enough to respond perversely to the very government actions designed to correct for its misbehavior. To what extent will this invalidate our analysis? And what about the money supply? When we discussed money in chapters 18 and 19, we took for granted that changes in the size of the money stock had some effect on total demand. Can we safely ignore those effects?

We're raising questions now that economists could not even begin to answer until quite recently. And since the answers have only recently begun to be formulated, they're still incomplete and tentative. The problem has been that the effectiveness of fiscal policy as an active tool for economic stabilization could not be tested until those who had political power were willing to try it. That may not have occurred even yet, and it certainly did not occur in this country prior to the 1960s.

Inconclusive Results

Income-expenditures analysis captured the economics profession (or a majority of the profession—some never surrendered) long before it won a sympathetic hearing from any American president or from more than a handful of legislators. Income-expenditures analysis was incorporated into introductory economics texts shortly after World War II, in a move pioneered by the subsequent Nobel prizewinner Paul Samuelson. In his text it became "the modern theory of national income determination." But Keynes didn't make the cover of *Time* that year—or the next. He made it in 1965, one year after Congress enacted and the president signed a tax-reduction bill that had been advocated on the basis of income-expenditures analysis.

Economists don't have an economy of their own to experiment with; they have to rely on the one all the rest of us use. Experiments to test a theory in the social sciences are often not possible until legislators have been persuaded that the theory is a sound one, and it's hard to persuade them in the absence of controlled experiments. Such experiments may never be possible because of our reluctance or inability to employ adequate controls. So it shouldn't surprise you that the reliability of fiscal policy as a stabilization tool is still very much disputed.

In the absence of controlled experiments, economists have fallen back on "thought experiments" and such tests as history happened to provide. The "thought experiments" consisted of thinking through the possibilities and searching for plausible relationships. The *General Theory* was one such grand exercise in experimental thinking.

But an economic theory is better tested by its applicability to events. In the absence of governments willing to run tests, economists interested in the income-expenditures approach looked for verification of its insights in such events as World War II. And many found there a convincing confirmation of the theory.

Empirical Tests?

Throughout the decade of the 1930s the federal government ran deficits that were much too small in the view of those who wanted a major and decisive government stimulus to aggregate demand. But even those modest deficits were largely offset by the surpluses of state and local governments.

World War II changed all that. The total government deficit rose from $.7 billion in 1940 to $3.8 billion in 1941 and then to $31.4, $44.1, $51.8, and $39.5 billion from 1942 through 1945. Real gross national product (in 1958 dollars) rose from $227 billion in 1940 to $361 billion in 1944—a 60% increase in just four years—before declining to $355 billion in 1945. Unemployment in 1940 was 14.6% of the labor force; in subsequent years it fell to 9.9%, 4.7%, 1.9%, and 1.2% in 1944 before rising to 1.9% in 1945.

One of the most interesting pieces of data from this period is the course of personal consumption expenditures. Government purchases expanded enormously during the war, from $36 billion in 1940 to a peak of $182 billion in 1944. But despite this huge government drain on the economy's productive capabilities, personal consumption expenditures also managed to rise between 1940 and 1944. Once the economic system had been prodded into action, it was able to provide 10% more consumer goods while satisfying the extraordinary demands of wartime.

This "experiment in fiscal policy" meant little to those unfamiliar with income-expenditures analysis. Most Americans were convinced in 1945 that the surfeit of jobs was due solely to the huge demand for military goods and the fact that $11\frac{1}{2}$ million workers were in the armed forces (more than $\frac{1}{6}$ of the entire 1944 labor force and 20% of the prewar labor force). They expected the return of unemployment lines and depression when the war ended. But for economists learning to think about the economy in the framework of income-expenditures analysis, the wartime experience demonstrated the effectiveness of fiscal policy. It would have been better, they argued, if the government had paid people during the 1930s to dig holes and fill them in again rather than allow massive unemployment to continue. The income received from such wasted effort would have increased consumption spending, created a larger demand for useful output, and provided additional jobs and income. Of course, it would have been better for the government to pay these people to do useful work. But useless work that stimulated incomes and spending would have been less wasteful in the end than tolerating unemployment and idle resources.

The wartime experience had been a demonstration of the paradox that income-expenditures analysis tried to resolve. The stimulus given to the economy by government deficits had enabled the nation to maintain and even raise real per capita consumption while producing vast amounts of war materials and lending $11\frac{1}{2}$ million members of the labor force to military service.

But the demonstration was most convincing to those who had already been largely persuaded by the logic of the argument. The test was hardly a conclusive proof of the effectiveness of countercyclical fiscal policy. Even if one granted that massive increases in government expenditure, especially when financed by borrowing rather than taxation, were capable of ending a deep and prolonged depression, one might doubt that fiscal policy was in general an effective tool for eliminating aggregate fluctuations.

Many supporters of income-expenditures analysis have therefore appealed to the postwar experience as further evidence in support of their thesis that countercyclical fiscal policy works. It can be shown that recessions have been neither prolonged nor very deep since World War II. The 1974–75 recession broke all postwar records but fell far short of what had happened in the 1930s. But can this record be attributed to the operations of fiscal policy? We would first have to establish that fiscal policy was systematically used as a stabilization tool.

Has Countercyclical Fiscal Policy Really Been Tried?

Neither President Truman nor President Eisenhower seems to have been firmly persuaded that fiscal policy was an appropriate and useful stabilization tool. President Kennedy had studied income-expenditures analysis at Harvard, and he chose as his economic advisers some of the more eminent advocates of that approach to the understanding and control of economic fluctuations. But even Kennedy's public pronouncements on the subject of government expenditures and taxation reveal something less than a total commitment to countercyclical fiscal policy. That may reflect his assessment of popular and Congressional devotion to balanced budgets more than his own views. But if that was the case, then Congressional support for a conscious and deliberate countercyclical use of fiscal policy was not yet present even in the early 1960s. The notion that the federal budget ought to be balanced in each and every fiscal year could hardly be held by someone who accepted countercyclical fiscal policy as an appropriate tool in government efforts at stabilization. The fact that many members of Congress apparently still held this view in the 1960s casts considerable doubt on the argument that the federal government was systematically employing the policy.

Did the tide finally turn in 1964? *Time* magazine obviously thought so. But anyone who looks closely at the Congressional debates preceding the tax cuts and at pollsters' sampling of public opinion in 1964 might retain doubts. The public thought taxes were definitely too high and favored reductions. The argument of the president's economic advisors that high tax rates were imposing "fiscal drag" on the economy was especially appealing. But none of this is convincing evidence that the public or Congress was eager to adopt countercyclical fiscal policy. We know only that they were willing to be told that a tax cut was a good thing for the whole economy and not just for them personally, and a good thing in the long run as well as right now.

The question here is not whether countercyclical fiscal policy *works.* The

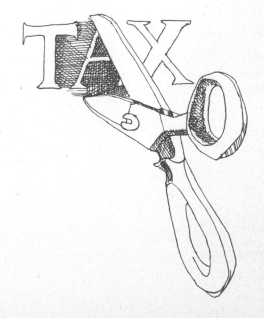

question is whether it has ever been *tried.* If doubt can still remain on the second question it will be very hard indeed to muster convincing empirical evidence for or against the more important first question. The lack of consensus among economists on the effectiveness of fiscal policy as a stabilization tool should not be surprising.

We'll return to the question of fiscal policy and its effects in subsequent chapters, after we've taken another look at the role money might play in determining the level of economic activity, and after we've brought the

---

PUMP PRIMING

Income-expenditures analysis suggests that the incentives to private investors in the 1930s were not sufficient to secure a level of investment expenditure consistent with high output and employment and that government spending filled the gap in the early 1940s. But why did private investment spending increase after the war and remain high? Why wasn't continued deficit spending by the government necessary to prevent the return of depression?

Income-expenditures analysis does not answer this question, because it offers no explanation for the level of intended investment. Keynes said that investment decisions are based on profit expectations and that these expectations are in large part governed by psychological factors. He provided no systematic theory that would explain why intended investment was so low in the 1930s and so much higher after World War II.

It may be that under appropriate circumstances deficit spending has a "pump priming" effect. By raising the aggregate level of economic activity it may stimulate greater optimism and thereby a revival of investor confidence. Once fiscal policy had primed the pump in this fashion, it might be able to withdraw and again allow private spending decisions to determine the level of output and employment.

Can fiscal policy induce a *self-sustaining* expansion of economic activity? Income-expenditures analysis makes no assertions about the effectiveness or ineffectiveness of pump priming. For that reason it does not explain the marked difference between prewar and postwar investment levels. This is an important issue. But given our enormous ignorance about the way in which mass expectations form and reform, it's an issue on which we can say very little beyond what the "classical" economists said: that a "return of confidence" is essential to economic recovery.

rest of the world into the picture. But all this talk about government surpluses and deficits has brought another issue to the fore.

THE NATIONAL DEBT

Conversations about deficit spending versus balanced budgets always come around eventually to the question of the national debt. This looms so large (if rather vaguely) in the public mind as a serious problem that Congress has placed a legal ceiling on the debt. It's an odd sort of ceiling, much like the ceiling in an elevator going up; the President periodically asks that it be raised and Congress always cooperates. But the existence of a statutory ceiling, even a flexible one, at least persuades people that someone has an eye on the problem.

What kind of problem is it? How large can the debt grow before we encounter disaster? Surely the government can't go on indefinitely living beyond its means, can it? When will the debt have to be repaid? And *how?*

Direct questions deserve direct answers. Very few knowledgeable people worry about the national debt or consider it much of a problem. It could probably grow to several times its present size without presenting any unmanageable difficulties. The federal government can, if it chooses, live beyond its means indefinitely. The debt doesn't ever have to be repaid. The question of how to retire the debt is academic in view of the fact that it will probably never be retired.

Nothing in that paragraph should alarm you or arouse the suspicion that the government is a welsher. No debtor has to pay back his creditors as long as the creditors don't demand repayment. And the individuals and institutions to whom the federal government is indebted are not holding government bonds out of either patriotism or necessity, but out of concern for their own financial welfare. They purchased the bonds because they decided the best thing they could do with their money was to lend it to the government. Moreover, should they change their minds, they would find that the federal government cheerfully redeems certain bonds on demand and that for the remainder there exists an active market through which some other party can easily be found to take the bonds and return the original purchaser's principal.

Refinancing the Debt

Despite the fact that bonds regularly fall due, requiring the federal government to repay the principal, the debt is never retired. For the government secures the funds to repay the principal basically by selling more

bonds. As long as it can find purchasers, the government faces no problems. And finding purchasers isn't difficult. If a particular issue of new bonds doesn't sell, that means the Treasury Department has been stingy in setting the yield. A slightly lower price for the bonds, which comes to the same thing as a slightly higher interest rate, will bring a surge of additional offers to purchase.[1]

You could do the same thing if you enjoyed an adequate credit rating, and many private firms and individuals do. They borrow for a set term and then extend the loan when it falls due. In effect they are paying the interest and borrowing the funds to repay the principal. Lenders are glad to cooperate because they earn their income by lending; the repayment of principal is a nuisance which requires the lender to find a new borrower, and why should the lender want to go to that trouble if the borrower is a good risk and the lender has little fear of default on the loan?

The federal government enjoys a uniquely high credit rating among lenders. Lenders do not request an audit of the government's books, demand collateral, raise embarrassing questions about the efficiency with which the government manages its business, or insist upon evidence that the government is going to start living within its means. For they know that the federal government has the power to collect revenue by coercion and, even more importantly, that it has the power to print money. State and local governments can and do default on their obligations at times; so do some of the largest corporations when their revenues fall short of expectations. But the federal government in such a fix could simply create the money with which to pay its debts. In a pinch it can always count on the cooperation of the Federal Reserve Banks. This power makes the bonds of the federal government uniquely safe and guarantees that buyers can be found at the right price.

Are we to conclude, then, that the national debt is neither a problem nor a burden? That would be going too far. What happens to the debt does make a difference.

Dangers in a Growing Debt

In the first place, *increases* in the debt mean that the government is injecting more into the income stream than it is taking out. If the economy is operating close to capacity, deficit financing may be inflationary. Of course, if the economy is in a depression, an increase in the debt may be the demand stimulus that restores prosperity. It is thus not the absolute size of the debt so much as the direction in which it is changing that ought

1. If a bond maturing one year from now with a value at maturity of $2700 can be purchased for $2500, the yield or effective interest rate on that bond is 8%: a $200 return on $2500. The return is greater than 8% at prices below $2500, less than 8% at prices above $2500.

to be carefully watched. That, of course, is the central argument of fiscal policy advocates.

But the effect of debt increases on aggregate demand is not the only effect. Government borrowing pulls resources away from private into public uses. While taxation has the same effect, taxes have a greater political impact, and expenditures undertaken out of tax revenues therefore tend to be scrutinized more critically than expenditures financed through borrowing. Whether this is a point for or against government borrowing depends upon how one evaluates the relative importance of public and private spending. Some students of American society maintain that we spend far too much on goods for private consumption (automobiles, houses, filet mignon) and far too little on the goods whose provision is largely left to government (education, public parks, national defense). But there are others who maintain just as insistently that government expenditure promotes social welfare less efficiently than private expenditure. However you stand on that issue, the ability to increase expenditures without increasing taxes almost certainly enables governments to spend more than they otherwise would.

The Burden of the Debt

The often heard argument that deficit financing pushes the burden of present expenditures onto our descendants is almost wholly mistaken. The debt we pass on to future generations is for the most part matched by the bonds we bequeath them. If we leave them assets as well as liabilities, we leave them no net burden of indebtedness.

When you stop to think about it, you realize that current expenditures, however they are *financed,* require the use of current real resources. Wars, for example, can be *financed* by borrowing, but they must be *fought* by drawing upon the current population and using the productive capabilities of the current economy. Highways, schools, and dams, regardless of how these projects are financed, all require for their construction the use of current resources that are consequently not available to provide other goods for the current generation. In fact, deficit financing may well make future generations better off. If the borrowed funds are wisely used in the construction of projects that will yield large future services, the current generation is sacrificing the present enjoyment of real resources in order to provide a larger real income to later generations. We are benefiting right now from past government expenditures on schools, roads, public buildings, parks, dams, irrigation projects, and other public investment in the form of a larger output of privately produced commodities and services.

There is one partial exception to all this. If a government borrows from *foreigners* to finance current expenditures, then it is attempting to use the currrent resources of foreigners rather than its own citizens. And future generations will be left with the obligation to repay that borrowing by giving up some of their resources to foreign bondholders. Of course, if the projects for which the government borrows are good investments, they will augment the real income of future generations by more than enough to repay the resources originally borrowed from abroad. We see again that the wisdom of the project for which the borrowing is undertaken is more important than the mere fact that the expenditure is financed by borrowing. And this agrees with everything we know about private spending and borrowing. A business firm or a household will gain from going into debt whenever the project financed by borrowing increases the flow of future goods (income) by more than it increases the stream of future payments on principal and interest.

Numbers and Alarums

This discussion of the national debt has stayed away from actual numbers, because the principles are more important than the numbers, however dramatic the latter can sometimes be made to appear. Some people are apparently thrilled in a terrifying sort of way by the news that if Alexander the Great had started to spend money after the Battle of Issus at the rate of $400 a minute, he would not yet today have spent a sum equal to the total of our public debt. But what does that *mean?* Do we gain a relevant sense of proportion from such numbers? Or are they like estimating the relative importance of mosquitoes and elephants by figuring out how many mosquitoes would have to be put on a scale to balance one elephant?

The interest paid by the federal government annually on the national debt may be a more meaningful measure of its significance, because the interest is the "carrying charge" on the debt. It is currently close to 2% of the gross national product. That's a substantial sum, but it hardly spells fiscal ruin. Another way to put the debt into perspective is to note that in 1945, at the end of World War II, it was approximately equal to the gross national product. Thirty years later the debt was more than twice as large, but it was less than 40% of the value of our annual output.

In short, the national debt is not a major problem. If you've been worrying about it in a vaguely fearful way, we encourage you to discard your anxieties or transfer them to some social problem more deserving of your concern.

Once Over Lightly

Fiscal policy is the use by the federal government of expenditures and taxes to influence the aggregate level of economic activity.

Income-expenditures analysis asserts that government expenditures which exceed or fall short of government income have the same effect on the aggregate economy as gaps between intended investment and intended saving. Aggregate equilibrium exists when intended saving plus tax receipts equals intended investment plus government disbursements for the purchase of goods and for transfer payments. An alternative statement of the equilibrium condition is that intended investment purchases plus consumption and government purchases must equal total output or income.

A change in tax receipts or transfer payments will have a smaller effect on output and income than a change in government goods purchases of the same amount as long as the marginal propensity to consume is less than one.

Insofar as the aggregate level of economic activity affects the balance between government receipts and disbursements, fluctuations in output and income will create deficits and surpluses that will in turn affect the level of income and output. The government could allow recessions to create budget deficits and allow booms to create surpluses without taking any action to close these gaps. That would be one kind of fiscal policy. The government could also move to close these gaps or to widen them in response to recessions and booms. By trying to close the gaps or keep the budget balanced the government would be lending additional impetus to the forces that had generated the recession or boom. By widening the gaps the government would be attempting to introduce a larger counterforce to private spending decisions than will come about automatically as tax receipts and transfer payments change with the level of economic activity.

Economists do not know how powerful or precise an instrument fiscal policy is for the stabilization of economic activity. Part of the reason is the impossibility of adequately controlled experiments. Another reason is the unwillingness of Congress and the president, at least until very recently, to use fiscal policy deliberately and systematically as a stabilization tool.

The size of the national debt is not a good argument against deficit spending. The debt is today a far smaller percentage of the gross national product than it was right after World War II. The government can refinance the debt indefinitely as it falls due and could probably carry a considerably larger debt without serious difficulty.

Changes in the size of the debt are more important than its mere total, because changes represent deficits or surpluses that affect the aggregate level of economic activity.

The wisdom of increasing the national debt should be determined by examining the probable effects on aggregate economic activity and the social productivity of the projects for which borrowing occurs.

An economy viewed as a whole does not shift the burden of current expenditures onto future generations merely by borrowing to finance those expenditures. The real costs of any project are the opportunities foregone by using real resources in one way rather than another. Any expenditure that increases the net value of the future flow of goods benefits those who will live in the future regardless of how that expenditure is financed.

QUESTIONS FOR DISCUSSION

1. When the federal government purchases buildings, airplanes, or the services of economists:

    (a) What are the real costs?

    (b) How is it determined who will bear the real costs?

    (c) If all purchases were financed out of personal income taxes, would the real costs be borne by citizens in proportion to the taxes they pay?

    (d) What differences would you predict in the distribution of the real costs if the purchases were financed by borrowing?

2. Will your answers to the questions above depend on whether the economy is at full employment? Will the particular goods the government is purchasing and the level of employment in the industries producing or using those goods make a difference in your answers?

3. The economy moves into a recession and federal government tax revenues fall, creating a budget deficit. The government can raise taxes and/or reduce expenditures to bring the budget back into balance; maintain present tax *rates* and previously planned expenditures and accept the deficit; or reduce taxes and/or increase expenditures, creating an even larger deficit.

    (a) Which approach would you recommend, and why?

    (b) What arguments might be raised against the approach you recommend?

    (c) Which approach would you *least* want to recommend? Why?

4. If the government decreased spending on highways by $5 billion and simultaneously increased spending on energy development by $5 billion, would the equilibrium level of Y be affected? What actual effects on the level of unemployment would you expect?

5. Assume that Congress and the president want to cut taxes by $5 billion to stimulate the economy in a period of recession. Does it matter whether they cut personal income taxes or corporate income taxes? Whether the cuts in personal income taxes are concentrated among low-income groups or more widely distributed? In what ways does it matter?

6. Suppose the unemployment rate is 8% and economic statisticians tell the government that 2 of those 8 percentage points are a direct result of sharply reduced purchases of new automobiles. Discuss the advantages and disadvantages in such a situation of offering a tax rebate to purchasers of new automobiles equal to 10% of the manufacturers' suggested retail price. Is a dollar of tax reduction offered in this way likely to reduce unemployment more than a dollar of personal income tax reduction? Are the longer run effects on unemployment likely to be different from the short run effects?

7. During the depression of the 1930s, increases in federal government expenditures were often accompanied by promises (threats?) of future tax increases to hold down the size of the budget deficit. Do you think this policy had any effect on investment spending?

8. Use the data in Table 17A to discuss the real costs of the 300% increase in government purchases from 1941 to 1944.

9. "The size of the national debt is not as important as the size of changes in the debt." Evaluate that assertion.

10. What would be the consequences of a systematic effort by the federal government to retire the national debt over a period of 20 years?

11. Federal government expenditures for national defense, when expressed in dollars of 1975 purchasing power, have averaged just about $100 billion per year from 1966 through 1975. Suppose that world peace were somehow miraculously declared and that the government abolished the national defense budget. What consequences would you predict for the economy? Do you think this would trigger a major depression? Why or why not? What fiscal policies would you recommend to accompany this disappearance of all national defense expenditures?

12. When a corporation successfully sells additional bonds it goes more deeply into debt. Is this evidence that the corporation is failing or succeeding? How well do analogies from the area of business indebtedness apply to questions of government indebtedness? Where do such analogies present a misleading picture, and why?

22

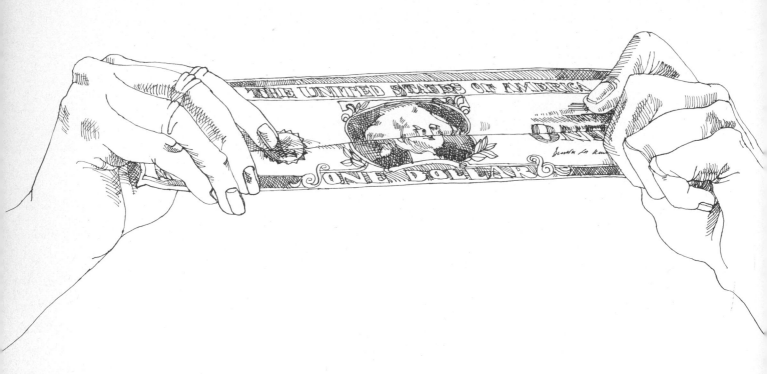

INFLATION AND THE REVIVAL
OF MONETARY POLICY

Ten years after its publication Keynes's *General Theory of Employment,*
Interest and Money had become the general theory that interest and money
have little to do with employment. We'll sidestep the question of whether
this was the intent of Keynes or the work of disciples more Keynesian than
their mentor. Either way, it happened. The role that monetary policy might
play in preventing undesirable movements in economic aggregates was
pushed to the side by economists more interested in the applications of
fiscal policy. The United States consistently had a monetary policy during
these years, just as it had a fiscal policy long before economists concluded
that the government budget might make a contribution toward economic
stabilization. But the majority of economists paid little attention to monetary policy in the 1940s and 1950s or assigned it the role of minor assistant
to fiscal policy.

MONEY IN INCOME-EXPENDITURES ANALYSIS

The expenditures that make up aggregate demand are almost entirely
monetary expenditures. But this does not necessarily mean that the quantity of money affects those expenditures. In the first fifteen chapters of this
book we repeatedly examined transactions that involved money without
asking whether it made any difference that they occurred through a
medium of exchange rather than by barter. The same kind of abstraction
from money might work in analyzing aggregate fluctuations.

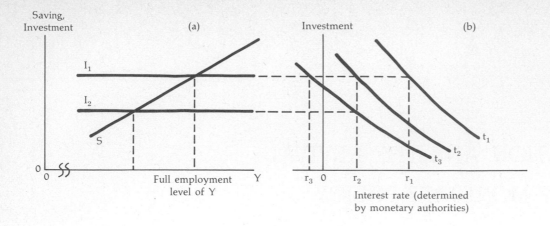

Figure 22A Interest rates and full employment

Keynes was himself extremely interested in the properties of money and the peculiar effects it might have on economic decisions; the title of his book is sufficient evidence of that. But he nonetheless contributed in two ways to the decline of interest in money and monetary policy. First, he constructed an analytical model that *could* be used without necessarily bringing in money. And second, he expressed his skepticism about the effectiveness of monetary policy as an antirecession tool.

Money, Interest Rates, and Investment

How was money incorporated into the *General Theory?* We can answer that question with the help of Figure 22A. Graph (a) presents the aggregate propensity to save (S) and the propensity to invest (I_1, I_2) in a hypothetical economy. The intersection of these curves determines the equilibrium level of total income (Y).

Graph (b) shows the relationship between the quantity of investment and the interest rate with different states of investor confidence. If confidence declines, the curve will shift downward and to the left, from t_1 to t_2 to t_3. Less investment will take place at any particular rate of interest the further "southwest" the curve lies.

According to Keynes, the monetary authorities set the interest rate when they determine the size of the money stock. Suppose they set the interest rate at the level r_1 in graph (b). This will determine how much investment investors are willing to undertake, given their expectations of profit from particular projects and the general state of confidence. The curves t_1, t_2, and t_3 all slope downward to the right because investment opportunities with the prospect of low yields will only be undertaken if the opportunity cost of doing so—the rate of interest—is also low. At higher interest rates, projects promising lower yields are squeezed out. With the interest rate at r_1 and the level of confidence shown by t_1, just the right amount of investment occurs: I_1 and S intersect at the full employment level of Y.

Now suppose a wave of pessimism sweeps over the economy and investors' expectations sink. Each potential investment project is now viewed as offering either the prospect of a lower net return or a smaller probability of the previously expected return. Either way, the curve relating investment and the interest rate will fall downward and to the left. If it falls to the position shown by curve t_2, the monetary authorities might be able to maintain full employment by increasing the money supply enough to reduce the interest rate to r_2.

But if the curve falls to t_3, nothing short of a negative interest rate, r_3, would be able to maintain investment at the level necessary for full employment. If r_2 turns out to be the practical limit below which monetary authorities cannot reduce the interest rate (and Keynes thought there was such a floor under the interest rate), then investment will be at the level shown by I_2, and the economy will move to an equilibrium at less than full employment.

In the analysis of figure 22A, monetary policy does have the power to affect aggregate demand through its effect on interest rates and thus on investment. That power will be limited, however, by the sensitivity of investment to changes in the rate of interest. And it may disappear altogether in the face of a major collapse in investor confidence. In the *General Theory*, Keynes expressed skepticism about monetary policy's usefulness, because he feared that investment was far more responsive to psychological moods and speculative swings than to any practicable changes in the rate of interest. Investment decisions would be dominated by shifts in the curves (t_1, t_2, t_3), with interest rates playing a relatively minor role. Most users of income-expenditures analysis were willing to follow this lead in the years immediately following World War II. And so they looked to fiscal policy as the government's effective weapon in the battle against unemployment.[1]

THE EQUATION OF EXCHANGE

The notion that monetary policy affects total expenditures only through the interest rate was a novel idea in the 1930s. An older tradition in economics, going back at least to the economist-philosophers John Locke and David Hume, asserted a much more direct and powerful influence of money upon total spending. This older theory of money had been used primarily to explain the relationship between the money supply and the price level. It was called the *quantity theory of money*.

1. Or did they conclude that monetary policy was ineffective because they were so caught up in the potentialities of fiscal policy? The actual causal connections between policy preferences, choice of theories, and empirical conclusions are not always as clear and straightforward as we would like them to be. We all sometimes reason from conclusions to facts.

The Money Supply and the Price Level

The quantity theory developed out of an interest in the effect that gold imports had on a country's price level in an age when the domestic money supply was closely linked to a nation's monetary gold stock. But the usefulness of the theory does not depend on the particular way in which a country's money supply is determined. In its simplest form, the quantity theory asserts that the price level will vary in proportion to changes in the quantity of money. A doubling of the money supply will double the average of all prices. Halving the money supply will halve the price level. Stated so baldly and boldly, the theory had at least this virtue: it warned statesmen against the folly of supposing that the national income could be increased simply by acquiring more money. The wealth of nations, as Adam Smith pointed out, depended upon their ability to produce want-satisfying goods. A greater quantity of money was of no value to a country if it only altered the rate of exchange between those goods and money, or the price level.

But stated so baldly and boldly, the theory is also wrong. The price level will not always change in direct proportion to changes in the money supply. There are two other possibilities. One is that the change in the money supply will bring about changes in the rate at which real goods are produced. In that case prices will not change by the same percentage as the money supply. The other possibility is that money may be circulated more or less rapidly as its quantity changes. This will again break the direct proportionality of changes in the price level and changes in the money supply.

The possibilities are contained in a simple formula usually known as the *equation of exchange:*

$$MV = PQ$$

M represents the stock of money; V is the velocity of circulation or the average number of times each unit of money changes hands during the period under study; P is the price level; and Q is an index of the real transactions occurring during the period, or the quantity of goods exchanged by means of money.

P times Q is therefore the dollar value of all goods sold for money. M times V is the dollar value of all monetary expenditures for the purchase of goods. And so MV is actually equal to PQ by definition. The equation is an identity and could be written: $MV \equiv PQ$.

You encountered the equation of exchange, even though you weren't introduced at the time, in chapter 19. While discussing the Fed's procedures for exercising control over the money supply, we asked *which measure* of the money stock was the most important one to control. If the goal of the Fed is to control aggregate demand, then the measure on which to focus would be the measure most closely linked to total expenditures. So we ran a little test, the results of which are shown in table 19A. We took gross national product in current dollars as our measure of total expenditures during a year, and let the size of the money stock in the preceding December represent the quantity of money available to finance those expenditures. Dividing GNP by each measure of the money stock gave us a numerical measurement of the relation between changes in each measure of M and changes in total expenditures. And we pointed out at the time that this number had a name: the velocity of money circulation.

Because GNP does not take *all* money-goods exchanges into account, the velocities we calculated were actually the velocities of circulation only for expenditures on goods included in the calculation of the gross national product. But GNP is a good proxy for total expenditures as well as the best measure we have for changes in the value of total output and income. We'll therefore follow the standard practice of using GNP as a synonym for PQ.

By means of these definitions we can now assign an empirical meaning to the four terms in the equation of exchange:

M = the stock of money, measured by M_1, M_2, or M_3

P = the price level, measured by the GNP deflator
(presented in table 17D)

Q = the quantity of goods produced, measured by dividing the GNP deflator into the value of GNP in current dollars
(presented in table 17E)

V = the velocity of money circulation, measured by dividing the money stock into PQ, or GNP in current dollars

With the aid of these definitions, let's inquire more closely into the meaning and implications of the quantity theory of money.

What Can Happen When the Stock of Money Changes?

The economists who asserted that the price level would always change in proportion to any change in the quantity of money were implicitly maintaining that V and Q are not affected by changes in the money supply. Money does not circulate more or less rapidly when its quantity alters, they were assuming, and the volume of production does not change when the money supply increases or decreases. No one today defends that simple statement of the quantity theory, and probably no economist ever did mean to defend it as an exact description of reality. But it was useful as a defensive weapon against those who might identify money with wealth and think they could achieve prosperity merely by expanding the supply of money.

An alternative possibility is to hold that V always varies inversely with M so as to maintain a constant volume of money expenditures when the money supply changes. If this were the case, the size of the money stock would be a matter of no consequence at all. The public would simply circulate money more or less rapidly, as its quantity declined or rose, in order to continue spending at its preferred rate. Neither the price level nor the volume of production would respond to changes in the money supply. That proposition is also too extreme ever to have been held as an exact description of a monetary economy. But it was useful to economists who wanted to argue that increases in the money supply were not an effective way to restore prosperity in a recession. In periods of particularly deep or prolonged depression, it might be that any increases in the money stock would simply increase idle money balances. Even that proposition has not been tested, however, because there were no really massive injections of money into the economy in the 1930s.

Let's consider one additional possibility. Suppose that V does not change when M changes, so that increases or decreases in M bring about proportionate increases or decreases in the product of P and Q. How will the effects be distributed between P and Q? This is an extremely important question for anyone who holds that the stock of money does affect the total volume of expenditures. If the economy is already operating at "full employment," then Q cannot increase. If we admit that "full employment" is a somewhat fuzzy concept, we might want to say that Q cannot increase very much or very rapidly when the economy is already operating at high employment. Large increases in the money supply would then have their principal impact on P, and would cause inflation. This is still assuming that V is constant when M increases. The economists who used the simple version of the quantity theory were actually assuming both the constancy of V and an economy operating continuously at "full employment." If, on the other hand, the economy is running well below the "full employment" level, an increase in M when V is constant might cause an increase in Q, and an increase in P, or some combination of the two. If the increase in M primarily affected Q in such a case, "full employment" might be restored in periods of recession through increases in the money supply.

How Stable Is Velocity?

It should be clear from all of this that the importance of money, and hence the potential effectiveness of monetary policy, depends on the actual behavior of V when M changes and the actual separate responses of P and Q under the conditions that exist at the time.

What do we know about the actual behavior of V? One of the factors contributing to the eventual revival of interest in monetary policy after World War II was a wealth of empirical studies demonstrating the relative stability of V. Although those studies were far more comprehensive and detailed than the data presented in table 19A, the velocity numbers in that

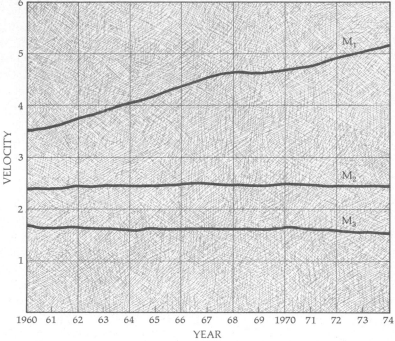

Source: Table 19A

table provide a good enough picture for our purposes. Figure 22B charts the course of velocity from 1960 to 1974. The velocity of M_1 has tended to rise since 1960, but at a fairly steady rate. The velocity of M_2 has fluctuated slightly and shown no long-term tendency to increase or decrease. The velocity of M_3 has fluctuated just a little more than M_2 while drifting almost imperceptibly downward.

If changes in the money stock are in fact closely correlated with changes in PQ, may we conclude the PQ can be controlled by controlling the money supply? We raised the same question briefly in chapter 19 and pointed out three objections to that conclusion. Let's review them. One is the difficulty in separating the effects upon P and upon Q. In a period of inflation we want to restrain P but not Q. In a period of recession we want to expand Q but not P. Can monetary policy do that? The ability to affect the course of P *times* Q is not enough.

Another objection has to do with the difficulties inherent in managing the money supply. We discussed that problem at length in chapter 19. The monetary authorities have not found it easy to select appropriate targets or to hit the targets they choose.

The third objection is the one we want to consider now. In the social sciences a historical correlation is rarely acceptable evidence of a causal

Figure 22B Velocity of money circulation, 1970–74
(GNP ÷ money stock
in preceding December)

connection. We might find a strong negative correlation over time between new housing starts and the rate of change in the price of medical services; but we would be reluctant to conclude that the direct manipulation of one will control the other. We would demand a theoretical explanation. If we were then told that general inflation raises the price of medical services and also creates the expectation of continuing inflation, which in turn slows down residential construction by raising interest rates, we might be satisfied that the correlation is not mere coincidence. But we would not then try to stimulate the home building industry by putting price controls on doctors and hospitals.

THE DEMAND FOR MONEY BALANCES

Is there an adequate theoretical explanation for the stability of V? We can best answer that question by using the little device employed in chapter 19 when we first called attention to the velocity concept. Instead of writing the equation of exchange as $MV = PQ$, we write: $M = (1/V)PQ$. While the equations are mathematically equivalent, the latter form makes more behavioral sense. People don't think about the velocity with which they want to circulate money and then take steps to reach their preferred velocity. But people do think about their money balances. They think about them in relation to their anticipated expenditures, and they take actions designed to move their money balances toward the levels they prefer. The public's total stock of money balances is $1/V$ expressed as a fraction of PQ, which is the volume of current expenditures.

It follows that V will be stable if the public does not quickly or easily change its demand for money, or, more specifically, its preferred ratio between money balances and current expenditures.

Actual and Preferred Money Balances

The public as a whole must hold the entire money supply, because it isn't counted as money unless it *is* being held by the public. So total money balances will always be identical to M (regardless of which measure of M we use). But *actual* money balances may not be equal to *preferred* money balances. If the monetary authorities were to increase the money supply at a time when the public was satisfied with its current money holdings, some people would necessarily find themselves holding larger money balances than they preferred to hold. So they would take steps to reduce their money balances back to the preferred level. And if the Fed were to reduce the money supply when people were holding their preferred amounts of money, they would try to raise their balances back up to the previous level.

We issued this caution before, but it may be worth mentioning again: Do not confuse the concepts of money and income. Money is a stock; income is a flow. When we talk about people's preferences for money balances, we are not talking about their attitude toward income. The preference for money balances is the same thing as the demand for money. And the demand for money is the demand for liquidity, not for more income. When someone says that Local 13 of the United Federation of Dingleworkers is "demanding more money," that translates in our terminology into a demand for more income, in the form of higher wages. People can increase their incomes without increasing the amount of their money holdings if they simply step up their spending by the amount of the increase in income. Or they can increase their money holdings in the face of a decreasing income if they are willing to reduce their expenditures by more than the decline in their income. An increase in the demand for money always means an increased desire to hold money balances *in preference to alternative assets.* Thus a person who increases his money balances is not necessarily wealthier than he was before; he simply holds more wealth than before in the form of money rather than in such nonmoney forms as refrigerators or corporate bonds.

Nominal and Real Money Balances

It is the connection between *actual* money balances and *preferred* balances that explains how changes in the money supply affect the economy. But to see how it works you must distinguish between *nominal* and *real* money balances. A person's *real* money balance is the command over other goods that those dollars provide. You might feel secure with $200 in your checking account. But if the price level doubled, that money balance wouldn't be as comfortable. You would have to hold $400 in your *nominal* balance to maintain the level of your *real* balance. People's preferences are for *real* balances; they're concerned, in other words, about the value or purchasing power of those balances. It's true that people may be fooled for a while into supposing that their real balances haven't declined when the price level rises; but they tend to discover the truth and make adjustments. A rising price level, by reducing the purchasing power of money, lowers real balances even though nominal balances haven't changed. On the other hand, a falling price level, other things remaining equal, raises real balances.

Effects of Changes in the Supply of Money

What will happen if the Fed increases the money stock at a time when the public is holding the amount of money it prefers to hold? People will find themselves holding more money than they want to hold. So they will spend some. They will shift the composition of their asset portfolio by exchanging money for other goods. The public *as a whole* cannot get rid of money in this way, because one person's surrender of money for an alternative good must be some other person's acquisition of precisely that amount of money. But the *attempt* on the part of people to reduce their money balances has several kinds of effects that will finally bring actual balances into equality with preferred balances.

One effect will be on the prices of goods. With people more eager than before to acquire goods for money, the price of goods will be bid up. That's inflation: an increase in P.

If the enhanced bidding for goods doesn't raise their price, it must mean that the supply of goods has increased. That's an expansion of production: an increase in Q.

Now if the demand for money balances is a demand for *real* balances, then the rise in P or Q or both will eventually cause the quantity of nominal money balances demanded to increase. It will continue increasing as long as PQ is increasing; PQ will keep increasing as long as the public keeps increasing its demand for goods; and the public will keep increasing its demand for goods as long as its actual money balances are greater than its preferred balances.

Does that seem much too complicated to remember? Then don't try to remember it. Think it through. The average amount of money you want to hold over some period of time will depend on your anticipated expenditures during that time. If the dollar amount of your anticipated expenditures goes up, you will probably want to hold more money on average or to maintain the size of your *real* balances by increasing your *nominal* balances. The point of this whole account is that when the Fed allows more money to be created than the public wants to hold at the time, the attempt to reduce those now excessive balances leads to an increased demand for goods, and hence to either higher prices or expanded output or both. That's an increase in PQ. If you're a representative member of the public, your "share" of PQ will rise, so you'll want to hold more money than you did before. It's all quite logical. PQ rises in response to the increased supply of money until the quantity demanded is equal to the larger quantity now being supplied.

The Demand for Money in the Equation of Exchange

The key to the whole process is the presumed relationship between the quantity of money demanded by the public and PQ. If the public wants to hold money balances equal to $(\frac{1}{5})$PQ, the public in effect wants V to be 5. Suppose that P is 1.00 (100% of the base year), Q is $1350 billion, the public wants to hold money balances equal to $(\frac{1}{5})$PQ, and M (we'll use M_1) is $270 billion. The quantity of money being demanded is equal to the quantity supplied. Then the Fed increases M to $300 billion. The public still wants to hold only $270 billion, and so people try to buy more goods with their extra money holdings. This bids up the prices of goods and/or stimulates additional production. Until PQ has increased to $1500 billion, the public will be holding more money than it wants to hold and as a consequence will be taking actions that raise the level of PQ. Equilibrium will be reached when—and this is only one of the many possible combinations, of course—the price level has risen 10% and real GNP has increased to $1364 billion.

Will this same process work in reverse? What would we expect to occur if the Fed decreased the money supply to $250 billion in the initial circumstances described above? With GNP at $1350 and the public demanding money balances equal to $\frac{1}{5}$ of that amount, people will find themselves holding less money than they prefer to hold. And so they will reduce their demand for goods in an effort to restore their money balances. As a consequence, P may fall and Q will probably fall. If PQ falls to $1250 billion, equilibrium will be restored with the quantity of money now available, $250 billion, equal to the quantity demanded, $(\frac{1}{5})$$1250 billion.

If the demand for money $(\frac{1}{V})$ is constant, changes in the stock of money (M) will lead to proportionate changes in nominal gross national product (PQ). But two qualifications to this analysis must be mentioned.

Hyperinflation and Velocity

If the monetary authorities were to increase the money stock so rapidly that almost everyone came to expect large increases in the price level, the demand for money would almost certainly fall. Money would then be an asset whose future value relative to other assets was expected to decline rapidly. People would therefore want to exchange money for other goods before this happened. Money would become like the Old Maid card that all players try to pass on as soon as they can, and the velocity of circulation would rise. That's what occurred in the German hyperinflation of the 1920s.

A continuing rapid rate of growth in the money supply caused prices to rise; the continuing inflation created expectations of further inflation; these expectations prompted an increase in V and an even more rapid inflation; the falling real value of money induced the monetary authorities to make even more nominal money available; inflationary expectations increased still further and prompted an ever greater reluctance to hold money, until finally people quit work early in the day to spend their money income before it had become almost worthless. In such a situation, *where no one wants to hold money, money is useless;* the monetary system disintegrates, and exchange must occur through the cumbersome processes of barter.

Interest Rates and Velocity

That is one qualification to the generalization that changes in M will induce proportionate changes in PQ. The second qualification is less

PARALLELS AND CONTRASTS

Recall that the equilibrium condition in income expenditures analysis is equality between intended saving and intended investment. In monetary analysis the condition of equilibrium is equality between actual money balances and preferred money balances. We can translate the latter condition as an equality between the quantity of money supplied by the monetary authorities and the quantity of money demanded by the public. The parallel with income-expenditures analysis emerges more clearly if we paraphrase that statement in turn and make it an equality between the quantity of money the monetary authorities intend to supply and the quantity the public intends to hold.

In income-expenditures analysis any divergence between savers' and investors' intentions causes changes in Y, which in turn cause savers to adjust their intentions. In monetary analysis any divergence between the intentions of the monetary authorities and the public causes changes in PQ, which in turn cause the public to adjust the quantity of nominal money it wants to hold.

The equilibrating factors are respectively changes in Y and changes in PQ. Because Y and PQ both represent the level of total output in current dollars or the nominal value of total income, it is changes in the level of the gross or the net national product that bring about equilibrium in both analyses.

But income-expenditures analysis and monetary analysis are not simply alternative ways of saying the same thing. One directs attention to consumer and investor spending intentions and suggests that they are not significantly dependent on the size of the money stock. The other directs attention to changes in the stock of money as the critical factor influencing spending intentions. Income-expenditures analysis assumes the stability of the consumption function. Monetary analysis assumes the stability of velocity. The predictive power and hence the relative usefulness of each theory will depend largely upon the actual stability of these relationships: the relationship between changes in income and changes in consumption in the case of income-expenditures analysis, and the relationship between changes in the money supply and changes in total nominal output in the case of monetary analysis.

drastic. Suppose we ask *why* the public would want to hold money balances equal to $\frac{1}{5}$ of anticipated expenditures rather than, say, $\frac{1}{4}$ or $\frac{1}{6}$. The general answer is that the public is balancing the marginal benefits against the marginal costs of holding additional money. The benefits are the expanded opportunities that liquidity offers. One of the costs is the income foregone by keeping assets in the form of currency or checking deposits rather than in forms that yield interest. It follows, then, that at higher interest rates the quantity of money demanded for any volume of anticipated expenditures would be less than when interest rates are low.

This suggests our second qualification to the assertion that changes in M will induce proportionate changes in PQ. Go back to the numerical example employed a few paragraphs earlier. The public initially wants to hold money balances equal to $(\frac{1}{5})$PQ. If PQ is $1350 billion and M is $270 billion, the quantity of money demanded equals the quantity supplied. When the Fed increases M to $300 billion, the public finds itself holding more money than it wants to hold and consequently begins exchanging money for other assets. But those other assets don't have to be such goods as suitcases and porterhouse steaks, which are included in the gross national product. They could also be financial assets like government bonds or corporate securities.

An increased demand for financial assets will bid up their price and thereby reduce their percentage yield. (A security whose ownership yields $10 per year is returning 8% when its price is $125, but only 6% if its price rises to $167.) Declining rates of return on securities mean declining interest rates and hence a lower opportunity cost of holding money. As a result, the public might now be willing to hold money balances equal to some larger percentage of anticipated expenditures.

Assume just for purposes of illustration that the prevailing rate of return on financial assets does fall as a result of the $30 billion increase in the money supply, and that the public consequently decides it's now willing to hold money balances equal to $\frac{1}{4.8}$ of anticipated expenditures. In that case the new equilibrium would occur with a smaller increase in PQ; PQ would increase to only $1440 billion rather than to $1500 billion. That could be achieved through some such combination as a 6% increase in the price level and a rise in real GNP to about $1358 billion.

The important lesson to be drawn from these qualifications is that we do not have good grounds for concluding that V is a constant or that it will not change in response to changes in M. But the money supply will be an important variable to control, and monetary policy can be effective even if that stringent condition is not satisfied. It is enough for V to be *stable* and *predictable*. Empirical studies of the U.S. economy strongly indicate that the demand for money *is* stable and predictable within the range of economic experiences since World War II.

Summing Up

The thread of the argument has now twisted through some fairly unfamiliar terrain. We hope the thread hasn't broken in your hand and that the unfamiliar now appears less strange than it did when the argument began. What we've been after in this chapter is an answer to the question, *What difference does money make?* How much does money matter when we're concerned with fluctuations in income and output, the level of employment, or the price level? Whatever effects money might have, how do these effects make themselves felt?

The chapter began with a short account of the modest role assigned to money in the framework of income-expenditures analysis. The short account was symbolic of the short shrift usually given to money after World War II, when income-expenditures analysis was riding high and most economists had their eyes fixed hopefully on fiscal policy. But in the 1950s interest in monetary policy and its possible contributions to stabilization efforts began to grow, and economists started to think once more about the role that money played in economic transactions. In the second and third parts of this chapter, we tried to give you a working grasp of contemporary monetary theory by using the equation of exchange and the concept of a demand for money balances. Above all we wanted you to understand the economic meaning of the velocity concept and to see that the way in which money matters is crucially dependent on the stability of money velocity.

THE QUESTION OF INFLATION

The revival of interest in monetary theory that this chapter has reflected came about in part because money *had* been neglected after the 1930s and the Keynesian revolution, and a neglected topic is certain to be cultivated after a while if there are lots of people looking for soil to till. But there was an additional explanation for the renewal of interest in money. The Great Depression failed to return and postwar recessions turned out to be surprisingly mild and shortlived. Instead of the anticipated depression, the United States and most other industrialized nations found themselves battling persistent inflation. And while the impotence of monetary policy against recession was a dogma for many disciples of Keynes, there was much less reason to believe it was powerless to combat inflation.

Monetary policy might also be the only game in town. The low taxes and high expenditures that fiscal policy prescribed against recessions were more feasible politically than the higher taxes and reduced expenditures for which inflation called. If Congress was unwilling or unable to practice enough budgetary restraint to prevent inflation, that task might have to be assigned entirely to monetary policy. As income-expenditures analysis and fiscal policy were developed to deal with depression, so the refurbished quantity theory of money and monetary policy gained adherents partly because it promised it could do something about inflation.

How well monetary policy has done, how well it might do, and the possible costs of using it are questions we'll return to when we try to put all the policy pieces together in chapters 25 and 26. There are important reasons, as we shall see, for deferring those questions until we've brought international exchange into our picture. But if we aren't yet ready to evaluate solutions, we can at least take the time now to look more closely at the nature of the problem.

The Effects of Inflation

Why *is* inflation a social evil? It's hard to get people to take that question seriously in a period of fairly rapid inflation, when every pronouncement by politicians, union leaders, business executives, and television commercials begins with the *assumption* that it's a grave evil and asks only what must be done to stop it.

"In an inflation everything becomes more expensive. And that's obviously bad, isn't it?" It would indeed be bad if it were true; but it isn't true. If the price of *everything* increases in equal proportion, then in *real* terms *nothing* has become more expensive. Note carefully that "everything" includes the services of wage-and-salary workers and every kind of financial asset from mortgages through bank deposits to the "entitlements" of people drawing pensions or social security benefits. Of course, all prices do not increase in equal proportion during an inflation, and so some goods do become more expensive in real terms. But it is a logical corollary that other goods must then become less expensive in real terms. A large part of the social problem, as we shall see, is the tendency of goods to rise in price at different rates during a period of inflation. But unless this has other effects that we haven't yet mentioned, the losses must exactly balance the gains. A pure inflation does not in itself make a society as a whole worse off.

Supply Inflation and Demand Inflation

Pure inflation? The word *pure* should make you suspicious, just as the words *always* and *never* ought to do in questions on a true-false test. By a pure inflation we mean a rise in the average price level not caused by any changes in conditions of supply but brought about entirely by changes in demand. Both kinds of change can cause such an index of the price level as the Consumer or Wholesale Price Index or the GNP deflator to rise. But they ought to be distinguished conceptually. Extensive crop failures will cause food prices to rise. Hurricane damage will raise the price of housing in the affected area. Airplane hijackings will raise the price of air travel if the airlines are compelled to hire security guards. The exhaustion of scarce mineral resources will raise the prices of all goods subsequently produced with resources less suited to the task. Work rules or trade regulations that

reduce efficiency will cause higher prices. These are all examples of price increases originating from the supply side. In each case, the ratio of output to input was reduced and there was a consequent reduction in welfare.

When prices rise with the conditions of supply unchanged, however, they can only be rising because the monetary demand has increased. And that is what we mean by a pure inflation. A pure inflation is a decrease in the value of money relative to all other goods, with no change induced by altered supply conditions in the values of those other goods relative to one another.

CHANGES IN THE COMPOSITION OF DEMAND

Even with total monetary demand in an economy constant, the composition of that demand will be changing continually. Tennis will suddenly catch on with the public, for example, and the demand for rackets, balls, nets, and related equipment will rise, while the demand for other goods declines. Will this affect overall price indices? It may.

If the production of a particular good cannot be increased quickly when the demand for it increases, the good's price will rise. And it may well rise by more than the fall in price of goods whose demand has decreased, resulting in a net increase in the level of measured prices. In general, the more inelastic the supply curves of goods for which demand is increasing, the greater will be the upward pressure exerted on price indices by changes in the composition of demand. Should this be called inflation? Does it qualify as "pure inflation"? There are grounds for answering either way. But however we label it, we will want to distinguish increases in the measured price level due to changes in the composition of demand from changes due to an increase in the total of monetary demand. Their causes are different, their effects are different, and they will yield to different remedies.

From 1958 through 1964, when the Wholesale Price Index was holding steady, the Consumer Price Index was creeping up by about 1% per year. The latter may have been due to the fact that consumers were shifting their expenditures more toward services and other goods whose production could only be increased at sharply higher costs.

We cannot tell merely from looking at a price index to what extent the rise in price of a particular good was due to changes in supply conditions and how much was due to monetary demand. The rise in food prices from 1967 to the present must be attributed in part to each; but sorting out the effect of government acreage restrictions and bad weather from the consequences of an increased money demand is a difficult task. The distinction must be made, however, because the causes and consequences are different. We might say, in fact, that price increases originating on the supply side are evidence of the problem of increased scarcity. There is less of what we want than there was before. But price increases resulting from increased money demand are evidence only of increased money demand. A pure inflation in and of itself makes no one work harder and forces no one to curtail consumption. Its effect is like that of going from measurement in yards to measurement in feet.

The Redistribution of Wealth

How does inflation (and we mean from now on price increases due entirely to increased money demand) create social problems? What problems does it cause? In the first place, it redistributes wealth and income. For when aggregate money demand increases, all prices will not increase in the same proportion and at the same time. Some prices are set for only short periods of time and can move up quickly in response to increased demand: examples are the prices of farm products and many of the raw materials used in industrial production. Other prices, like those at a retail grocery chain, are revised less frequently and so respond less quickly to demand. Commercial and residential rents are usually set by contract and often cannot be changed for long periods; although there are ways for landlords to compel a reopening of the contract and negotiate a higher rental, these procedures entail additional costs to the landlord. Wages and salaries are typically established by agreements that are supposed to extend over longer periods of time; these agreements can also be renegotiated during the contract period, and some will even contain formal clauses calling for renegotiation if certain conditions change. But wages and salaries tend to be less quickly responsive to increased money demand than retail prices and somewhat more responsive than rental prices. There are many prices that cannot be raised quickly, because to raise them requires the consent of a regulatory body that may move with glacial speed: railroads, airlines, gas and electric utilities, and telephone companies all complain of their inability to respond quickly enough to an increased money demand. Then there are creditors who have made long-term loans and cannot raise the payments they regularly receive for that service until the loan matures, perhaps twenty-five years in the future. On the other hand, consider the happy position of the federal government, selling us national defense and a variety of social services and charging a price (the personal income tax) that not only increases, but increases at a progressive rate as monetary demand increases. The net result of all this is that inflation redistributes income.

Prices that respond more slowly to increased demand don't necessarily increase less; sometimes they just take longer to get where they're going. But that still means that income is redistributed during the transitional period. Compare the prices of food and of clothing, relatively quick responders, with the price of rental housing, a slow responder, during and after the sharp inflation at the onset of the Korean War. Table 22A shows the percentage increases from the preceding year for each.

Table 22A PRICE INCREASES FROM PRECEDING YEAR			
	Food	Rent	Clothing
1951	+11.1%	+4.0%	+9.0%
1952	+1.8%	+4.1%	−0.9%
1953	−1.5%	+5.4%	−0.8%
1954	−0.2%	+3.6%	−0.1%

Source: Bureau of Labor Statistics

But that's ancient history to those who weren't born until after 1954. Let's compare some differential rates of price increase for the protracted inflationary period from 1967 to 1973. (We'll examine inflation since 1973 separately because it tells a somewhat different tale.) Table 22B gives the percentage increases from average price levels in 1967 to average levels in 1973. Plus signs are superfluous in this table: there were no decreases.

Compare these with another significant set of figures. The mean hourly wage of production or nonsupervisory workers in private, nonagricultural industries increased over the same period by 46.5%. Per capita disposable income increased by 52.6%. The statement often made in this period that inflation was eating into the average American's take home pay and reducing his real income is simply untrue. *Real* per capita disposable income rose 20.3% between 1967 and 1973. The mean *real* hourly earnings of production workers rose 10.1% and their *real* spendable weekly earnings rose 4.6%. Part of the difference between these last two figures, by the way, can be attributed to the higher personal income and social security taxes paid in 1973. They averaged 10.7% of gross weekly earnings in 1967 but 12.3% of 1973 earnings.

Who is hurt by inflation, then? Not necessarily the average American worker celebrated in speech and story along every campaign trail in the land.[1] Sharpen up your sense of melodrama on the news that landlords and holders of mortgages are among the chief victims of inflation!

The income redistribution effects of inflation depend heavily, however,

---

1. Remember, though, that the mean, like all averages, conceals differences. All workers did not fare equally well.

Table 22B	PRICE INCREASES FROM 1967 TO 1973					
Food	Rent	Clothing	Medical care	Transportation	Fuel oil and Coal	Gas and Electricity
41.4%	24.2%	26.8%	37.7%	23.8%	36.0%	26.4%

Source: Bureau of Labor Statistics

on how rapidly the inflation occurs and how well it has been anticipated. From January, 1973 to July 1974, the consumer price index rose 16.1%. Over this same period the average hourly wage of production workers increased only 11.9%, and the *real* hourly wage fell by 3.3%. Other available evidence supports the thesis suggested by these data. When prices are increasing slowly, workers can keep pace, but they fall behind when the inflation rate steps up. Landlords also suffered, by the way, as rental rates on housing increased only 7% over this period, or by less than half as much as the average of all items included in the consumer price index. (You're wrong if you think we're ridiculing landlords. Our intention is to call into question the strange but widely shared belief that owners of rental housing are all wealthy, and that they can usually gouge additional rent from tenants at the twirl of a moustache.)

Victims and Beneficiaries

Data on average hourly wages, per capita income, or rental prices conceal a lot of internal differences, of course. And differences are the heart of the problem. Inflation redistributes income because some sellers can raise their prices more quickly in response to a demand increase than can others. During inflationary periods, people whose income derives from prices that increase more slowly than the average surrender purchasing power to people deriving income from prices that increase more rapidly. They quite understandably resent inflation and insist that the government do something about it.

These victims of inflation find political allies, interestingly enough, among many of the beneficiaries of inflation. The political significance of inflation and the strength of popular pressure on government to control it (or at least seem to be controlling it) can only be appreciated if one understands why the beneficiaries of inflation so often join in denouncing it. The principal reason is that they think they too are victims.

Someone who receives a 10% salary increase almost inevitably regards the raise as completely merited, only just, perhaps long overdue. The fact that 8 of those 10 percentage points may reflect nothing but an increase or an anticipated increase in the price of the worker's product is not something that can be readily observed. So it's overlooked. If prices then rise by

FARM PRICES AND FOOD PRICES

The relation between the prices consumers pay for food and the prices farmers receive for their products has enormous political importance. The public generally regards rising food prices as a great evil, but farmers and their political allies become deeply disturbed when prices for agricultural products decline. Over long periods of time, these two indices do tend to move together. But over shorter periods, they can and often do move quite diversely, as the table below shows. And during a period when prices at the store are rising while prices at the farm are declining, the volume of political protest rises rapidly. Silence usually reigns, however, when food prices are lagging behind the rate of increase in farm prices.

	Food in the Consumer Price Index	Farm Products in the Wholesale Price Index		Food in the Consumer Price Index	Farm Products in the Wholesale Price Index
1960	88.0	97.2	July 1973	140.9	173.3
1961	89.1	96.3	Aug	149.4	213.3
1962	89.9	98.0	Sept	148.3	200.4
1963	91.2	94.6	Oct	148.4	188.4
1964	92.4	94.6	Nov	150.0	184.0
1965	94.4	98.7	Dec	151.3	187.2
1966	99.1	105.9	Jan 1974	153.7	202.6
1967	100.0	100.0	Feb	157.6	205.6
1968	103.6	102.5	Mar	159.1	197.0
1969	108.9	109.1	Apr	158.6	186.2
1970	114.9	111.0	May	159.7	180.8
1971	118.4	112.9	June	160.3	168.6
1972	123.5	125.0			
1973	141.4	176.3			

Notice that over the first six months of 1974, the index of food prices rose at an *annual* rate of about $8\frac{1}{2}$%, while the index of farm product prices fell at an *annual* rate of about 40%. That is a sure formula for political unrest, despite the fact that farm product prices in June 1974 were 68.6% above their 1967 level, while food prices were only 60.3% higher than they had been in the index base year.

6% during the same period because of the same increase in aggregate demand that accounted for 8 of the 10 percentage points in his last raise, the worker will not rejoice in the fact that he gained from inflation. Instead he will complain that inflation has eaten up 60% of his last raise, and start thinking about ways to restore his loss through another salary increase. We all tend to regard increases in our own money income as our just desert. Increases in the general price level, however, are bad and should be prevented. But prices are not only costs. Looked at from the other side, they're the components of income. We just don't tie the two together.

Inflation is almost universally unpopular, even with the beneficiaries of its redistribution effects, because of the myopia and self-centeredness that causes most of us to regard increases in our own incomes as fully justified and increases in the prices we must pay as a failure in the system. Government will receive no credit, obviously, for getting me what I deserve and have fully earned; but it will be blamed for creating or tolerating a situation in which others are able to rob me of my gains through higher prices.

Effects on Production

Illusion thus plays a major role in making inflation unpopular and creating pressure on governments to do something about it. But the costs of inflation to a society as a whole are not *completely* illusory. Imagine a situation in which the various state governments controlled the standards for weights and measures. Suppose further that the officials in most states had come to the conclusion that the only way to effect a shift to the metric system was to sneak it over on people by gradually expanding the inch until it had become one thirty-sixth of a meter. So at periodic but unpredictable intervals, the officials of various states would announce for their jurisdictions an official increase in the length of the inch—"never enough to notice," as they might say, but enough to push the inch over ten years from its present length of .0254 meters to the desired length of .0277/9 meters.

Where would the costs of such a procedure show up? In resources devoted to guessing the timing and rate of changes and insuring against the consequences of mistakes; in resources spent on coordinating decisions among states with inches of temporarily varying length; in resources employed to fit tools conforming to older specifications to products made to newer specifications; in resources wasted on the correction of mistakes arising from the increased uncertainty and the complexity of the coordinating task. The real costs of inflation to a society are like the costs just described.

It is sometimes said that inflation is merely a change in the "length" of

the measuring instrument. Let that be true; it does not follow that inflation has no real costs. An elastic measuring instrument is a serious problem whenever decisions have to be coordinated over space and time. A grave danger arising from the experience of inflation is that people will devote so many resources to dealing with the inflation that production will decline substantially.

PRICES SUBJECT TO CHANGE

When prices are rising rapidly, catalogs quickly become out of date. And companies that sell heavily through catalogs run into problems. Because customers often become angry when told after ordering a good that it is only available at a price higher than the one listed in the catalog, companies prefer to stand by their catalog prices. But if prices rise by 10% per year, a company that issues its catalogs annually may take a severe beating on goods sold shortly before its new catalog is issued. One solution is putting catalogs out more frequently. Another is to issue smaller, special catalogs at various times throughout the year. But either solution raises the firm's cost of doing business.

Acceleration and Hyperinflation

In a hyperinflation, such as some countries have experienced as a result of wars and as Germany experienced in a spectacular way from 1921 to 1923, the measuring instrument becomes worthless. The purchasing power of money becomes so unpredictable that money is no longer useful, barter replaces monetary exchange, inefficiencies multiply, and production finally collapses. But inflation of the kind experienced in recent years in the United States is a much different thing from the German inflation of the 1920s, when prices rose more than *60 billion percent* in a single year. The German experience stands as a warning, however, and raises the question whether inflation can be contained once it gets beyond a certain rate. The economy can adjust to creeping inflation and occasional gallops; we've done it successfully ever since the 1930s. But our past success in containing inflation may have been due in large part to the fact that inflation was not expected to *continue* at any considerable rate. Once inflationary expectations become general, and everyone tries to keep up by getting ahead, won't the rate of inflation tend to increase? And finally reach hyperinflation levels?

That certainly *can* occur. Suppose that everyone anticipates regular and large future price increases. That means they expect the value of money to fall relative to the value of other assets. A rational plan of action for someone with these expectations is to hold money balances to a minimum. But this increases the money demand for goods, raises their prices farther and faster, and creates aggravated expectations of inflation that further reduce the demand to hold money. At the limit, where desired money balances are zero, the velocity of money circulation is infinite. M times V is a very large and inflationary money demand indeed when the value of V is infinity.

Living with Inflation

On the other hand, quite a few countries have lived with rates of inflation in recent years well beyond anything we've experienced and without moving toward hyperinflation and economic collapse. The annual rate of change in the Brazilian price level from 1952 through 1973 was about 30% and went up and down from rates near 10% to rates of almost 100% over the course of a single year. And Brazil has survived. It has done so in part by extensive use of what is called *indexing.* A familiar example of indexing in this country is the escalator clause in wage contracts that calls for automatic wage adjustments when the price index changes. Social security benefits are also indexed by law to prevent their real value from declining as prices rise. We could go much farther in this direction. *All* wages, salaries, rents, and pensions could be indexed. Congress could also adjust the progressive income tax so that higher rates come into play only when *real* income rises. The rate schedules used by public utilities could easily be indexed. So could many kinds of financial assets. The federal government might provide a simple, safe hedge against inflation to the unsophisticated saver of modest means by selling bonds whose value changes with the Consumer Price Index.

The Brazilian indexing system seems at least to have prevented much of the income redistribution that inflation normally causes. And it may have promoted efficiency by reducing uncertainty for investors. But with the gradual extension of the system so that it compensates more fully and more quickly for all increases in the price level, Brazil may now be on the verge of building inflationary expectations so solidly into the economy that inflation will start feeding on itself. For example, an increase in the price level will call for higher wages, the money supply will have to be increased to pay the higher wages, and the larger money supply will pull prices up even faster. It's a way of living with inflation that is full of difficulties and dangers.

Inflation and Social Stability

And how well *has* Brazil survived? Contemporary Brazil is no one's model of a free and democratic society. We can only speculate about the extent to which the social tensions generated by inflation contributed to the social disorder that in turn produced a military dictatorship in 1964. But it is a fact that the annual rate of inflation rose rapidly in the early sixties, from 40% to 55% to 80% per year in 1963, and on up to an annual rate of 150% in March of 1964. Then production collapsed and a military government seized power. And it was this military government that cut through complexities and conflicting interests to establish an indexing system. It is not obvious what the experience of Brazil has to teach us.

Political freedom and democracy rest in any society upon a substantial social consensus. People must believe that they are net beneficiaries of the "system," of the kinds of interaction that the political and social structure allows and encourages. When people come to believe that they are more the victims than the members of a society, they withdraw their allegiance and desert the consensus. And the alternative to government by consensus is government by force. The point of this excursion into political philosophy is that inflation generates a widespread sense of injustice, even—as we argued earlier—among its beneficiaries. If rapid inflation fosters social instability, it may be a serious threat to political freedom and democratic rule.

Once Over Lightly

Economists interested in income-expenditures analysis tended to neglect money and monetary policy after the appearance of Keynes's *General Theory*. They argued that the supply of money affects the level of economic activity primarily through its effect on interest rates and their effect in turn on investment expenditures, and that this effect is of minor importance in countering the impact that expectations have on investment.

Interest in money and monetary policy revived as the fear of depression diminished in the 1950s and concern about inflation increased. New inquiries into the importance of money were grounded in the equation of exchange, $MV = PQ$, which expresses the identity between the stock of money times its velocity of circulation and the average price of goods times the quantity of goods exchanged.

The effect that changes in the supply of money will have on the level of aggregate economic activity depends on the behavior of velocity. The velocity of money circulation when inverted becomes the quantity of money demanded expressed as a fraction of PQ. Changes in M will therefore have predictable effects on PQ insofar as the demand for money is stable and predictable.

If M (the quantity of money supplied) and PQ/V (the quantity of money demanded) are not equal, then the public will want to hold some different quantity of money from the amount the monetary authorities have made available. The public's efforts to increase or decrease its money balances will lead to a decrease or increase in the demand for goods (Q) and a consequent decrease or increase in PQ. This can occur through changes in real output, changes in prices, or both. Since the demand for money balances is a demand for real balances, the quantity of nominal money demanded will increase or decrease with PQ until it equals the quantity of nominal money available to hold. In this way, changes in PQ become the equilibrating mechanism that brings the preferred level of money balances into equality with the actual level of money balances, or M.

Changes in M may themselves cause the quantity of money demanded to change in the same direction and reduce the impact of changes in M on PQ. This occurs through the effect of money-supply changes on interest rates. The opportunity cost of holding money will increase if interest rates rise as a consequence of restrictive monetary policy, and so the public will want to hold somewhat smaller money balances (that is, V will increase). Larger money balances will be desired if interest rates decline in response to an increase in the supply of money (V will decrease).

Inflation should not be thought of as an increase in the price of everything, but rather as an increase in the price of everything *relative to money*. But if *everything* actually increased in price relative to money, inflation would be a very minor problem. Inflation is a social problem in large part because prices of goods rise at different rates and thereby redistribute income and wealth.

Inflation is politically unpopular because those who gain from inflation often mistakenly assume that they have been harmed by it. They blame inflation for increases in the money price of goods they purchase but fail to credit inflation adequately for increases in the money price of goods they sell.

Inflation is capable of reducing aggregate real output by increasing the real costs of coordinating economic decisions.

While there are ways to reduce the wealth-redistributing effects of inflation, there may be none that are both politically feasible and unlikely to accelerate the inflation.

QUESTIONS FOR DISCUSSION

1. How do interest rates affect investment spending?

    (*a*) How do higher interest rates affect residential construction?

    (*b*) "Shall we maintain production and allow our inventories of unsold goods to rise, or should we shut down production until we've managed to sell off most of the finished goods now in the warehouses?" How might the level of interest rates enter into this decision?

(c) An electric utility postpones construction of a new generating plant because the market price of its bonds is disappointingly low. How does this illustrate the investment–interest rate relationship?

(d) A corporation plans to begin a huge capital expansion program and use proceeds from a sale of new stock to finance the program. But common stock prices decline and the firm postpones the stock sale and the investment program it was intended to finance. Does that have anything to do with interest rates?

(e) "Higher interest rates don't deter any business firm that has a profitable use for the money. If we can make 30% on an investment, we're going to invest whether we can borrow at 3% or have to pay 12%." Evaluate.

(f) "The higher the interest rate I can get, the more I'm going to invest. Investment increases as interest rates rise." Is that right? Reconcile these sentences with the text's analysis of the investment–interest rate relationship.

2. *Can* the monetary authorities raise or lower interest rates by decreasing or increasing the money supply? What limitations exist on their ability to do this?

3. Is a negative interest rate an absurd conception? Can you cite any negative (real!) interest rates in recent years? What was the real rate of interest earned on $100 in a 5% savings account during 1974, when the price level rose 12%. If you were a business executive able to borrow short term money from the bank at 8%, would your decision on whether or not to go ahead with the loan be affected by your expectations regarding the behavior of prices in the coming year?

4. "A recession occurs when MV is less than PQ." Evaluate that assertion.

5. If V is constant, will an increase in M be more likely to raise P or Q? What are some of the factors that might determine the relative impact on P or Q? Would it make any difference whether the increase in M came about because of Treasury borrowing or because of private borrowing?

6. If P rises while M remains constant, what happens to real money balances? If people were holding their preferred level of real balances prior to the increase in the price level, what actions might they take to restore the level of their real balances? Can inflation occurring simultaneously with a zero rate of growth in the money supply cause a recession?

7. "We cannot predict the effect of a change in the rate of growth in the money stock on the velocity of circulation unless we know how it affects people's expectations regarding *future* changes in the price level." Evaluate that argument.

8. Suppose the Fed substantially increases the reserves of commercial banks and the banks use these additional reserves to add more government securities to their portfolio of earning assets. How will this affect the yield on government securities? Why will it tend also to affect the yield on corporate bonds and mortgages?

9. Numerous public opinion surveys in 1974 and 1975 revealed that the majority of Americans regarded inflation as a more serious threat than unemployment.

    (*a*) Does this imply that the majority of Americans would prefer unemployment with stable prices to being employed in a time of rising prices?

    (*b*) If the management of a firm allowed employees to vote on whether the firm should lay off 10% of the employees or reduce wage rates by 5%, how do you think they would vote? Do you think it would matter whether the workers laid off were to be the ones with the least seniority or were to be chosen by a lottery?

10. If inflation redistributes income and wealth, there will be gainers as well as losers. Which classes and categories of people are most likely to gain from an inflation? Which are most likely to lose? What difference does it make how well the inflation is anticipated?

11. Supply and demand conditions in the market for college professors have changed markedly from the 1960s to the 1970s. Is it easy for college administrators to lower salaries when supply increases and demand decreases? What reaction would you expect from professors who were told that market conditions call for a 7% reduction in their annual salary? What reaction would you expect from them if they were told that the budget will not allow for any salary increases this year although the Consumer Price Index has risen 14% since last year? Does inflation ease the process of making relative price and wage adjustments?

12. Some people argue that the complexity of federal tax laws generates significant social waste. It encourages the extensive use of valuable resources (accountants, lawyers) in searching for loopholes and prompts people toward inefficient activities that are profitable because of tax law quirks. Does inflation generate similar kinds of waste?

13. Secretary of the Treasury William Simon told the House Ways and Means Committee in 1975 that there was no subtler and surer means of overturning the existing basis of society than to "debauch the currency," that is, create continuing inflation. (Mr. Simon cited Keynes and Lenin in support of this position.) Do you agree?

THE ECONOMICS AND POLITICS
OF INTERNATIONAL TRADE

No introductory textbook known to us contains a separate chapter on inter*state* economics. But inter*national economics* has its own section in almost every text, its own courses in departmental curricula, and its own specialists working in business, government, and universities. Why is this?

The answer is that specialization and exchange, the social processes that economics attempts to explain, often encounter peculiar difficulties when they are conducted across national boundaries. Unique problems of coordination arise in international exchange. International economics tries to explain the origin of these problems and the consequences of the varied ways in which individuals and national governments deal with them.

NATIONALISM AND INTERNATIONAL TRADE

The statement is often made that nationalism is obsolete in this era of jet planes, space travel, radio-television communication, and nuclear weapons. If obsolete means *no longer appropriate,* the statement may be correct. But if it means *no longer in existence,* the statement is demonstrably false. National governments still erect barriers to trade at their boundaries, still pursue domestic policies that presuppose restrictions on exchange with other nations, and still try to solve domestic problems by treating foreigners as enemies rather than as potential partners in mutually advantageous specialization. We may regret this but we cannot afford to ignore it.

637

These two chapters on the international economy are inserted here, prior to our final look at the economics and politics of stabilization policies, because to a large and growing extent domestic stabilization policies are not likely to succeed unless they take account of international repercussions. In one sense national governments have always known this. The assumption that domestic prosperity can be achieved by managing foreign trade in appropriate ways is as old as the nation-state itself. In another sense, however, national governments have been insufficiently attentive to international repercussions. They have too frequently assumed that other nations would remain passive in the face of economic aggression, and they have underestimated the ingenuity of those with an interest in circumventing international barriers to voluntary exchange.

An effective stabilization policy for the United States economy today must be constructed in an international context. In the past few chapters we have disregarded the effects of international trade on total output and income, focusing exclusively on the domestic determinants of the money supply and the price level. This was a seriously misleading omission that we must now begin to correct.

How Important Is the International Trade Sector?

In table 17A, we say that net U.S. exports constituted one of the four components making up the aggregate demand for gross national product. Because the numbers in the net exports column were relatively small, neglecting them may not have seemed a serious omission. But there's a lot of activity hiding behind those small numbers and the activity has been increasing in recent years. The value of United States exports in 1974, as measured by the Bureau of Economic Analysis, was $140.2 billion. By subtracting the $138.1 billion worth of imports, we arrived at the seemingly insignificant total of $2.1 billion for *net* exports. But $140 billion is 10% of the gross national product. A substantial share of domestic production occurs, in other words, in response to foreign demand. And a moment's thought should make it clear that, if all foreign trade suddenly stopped, the decline in our imports would not compensate for the loss of export markets. It's true that $138 billion is almost as much as $140 billion; but the *composition* of our demand for imports is vastly different from the composition of foreign demand for our exports. A disruption of international trade could therefore have disastrous effects on gross national product and employment, even though the little number showing "net exports" hardly budged.

We said that international trade has become increasingly important in recent years. The trend is apparent from table 23A, which shows U.S. exports as a percentage of gross national product in recent years. The increase is partly a statistical illusion. The Bureau of Economic Analysis has improved its procedures for keeping track of exports and imports. But this only means the percentages for earlier years were understated. The important fact is that exports are now about 10% of the entire output of the economy.

Table 23A

Year	U.S. Exports (in billions of dollars)	Exports as % of GNP
1950	$13.8	4.8%
1954	17.8	4.9
1958	23.1	5.2
1962	30.3	5.4
1966	43.4	5.8
1970	62.9	6.4
1974	140.2	10.0

Source: Bureau of Economic Analysis

How Independent Are National Economies?

There is another way to point up the dangers in ignoring international trade. From 1958 to 1964, consumer prices in the United States rose at an average annual rate of 1.2%. From 1971 to 1973, they rose at a rate of 4.8% per year, four times as rapidly as in the 1958–1964 period. What was happening during these same periods in some of the countries with which the United States traded extensively? Table 23B compares the rates of increase in the consumer price level in ten countries.

In each country, consumer prices rose significantly faster in the 1971–73 period than they had in 1958–64. In every case but one, the annual rate of increase was between 3.5 and 5.8 percentage points greater in the later period. That seems odd at first glance. Each country has its own central bank, its own government budget, and its own institutional structures for price and wage setting; yet consumer prices changed in a strikingly similar way. This looks like a remarkable coincidence only until we realize that domestic price levels are affected significantly by international exchange.

Does any other assumption really make sense, though? We don't expect prices in Arizona to diverge significantly from those in Louisiana, despite the considerable geographic and cultural differences between the two states. Paris is closer to Boston than Honolulu is. Why then should we expect the same forces to determine income and price levels in Hawaii and Massachusetts but not in Massachusetts and France?

Table 23B	INCREASES IN CONSUMER PRICES (annual rates of change)	
	1958–64	1971–73
United States	1.2%	4.8%
Canada	1.3	6.2
United Kingdom	2.4	8.2
Germany	2.2	6.3
Japan	4.8	8.3
France	4.3	6.3
Italy	4.2	8.1
Switzerland	2.2	7.7
Netherlands	2.7	7.9
Belgium	1.7	6.2

Sources: Bureau of Labor Statistics, International Monetary Fund, Organization for Economic Cooperation and Development. Data compiled by Research Department, Federal Reserve Bank of St. Louis.

National Currencies and National Interests

One reason to expect differences might be the fact that France and the United States use different currencies. And this does indeed turn out to be a central issue. If every society in the world used the same medium of exchange, the chapters on international exchange in economics textbooks could be very short. They might even be left out altogether. But almost every nation has its own kind of money. As a result, exchanges between the citizens, business firms, or governments of different nations require an extra step: the buyer's money must be exchanged for the seller's money before the transaction can be completed. This gives rise to special problems. More importantly, it provides an opportunity for the *creation* of special problems, with governments usually functioning as the creative agents.

Why don't all nations use the same medium of exchange as the separate states do in this country? How did *national* monetary systems come into existence, and why do they persist?

The ideal would seem to be a single world monetary unit. Is that impossible? The world is presently moving toward universal adoption of the metric system. Why not a universal money as well? Think how inconvenient it would be if every state in this country had its own medium of exchange. Interstate transactions would always require foreign exchange purchases, an added nuisance and an added uncertainty as well. Producers buying or shipping out of state would have to pay attention to fluctuations in exchange rates, since a substantial change that went unnoticed could mean a large loss on a purchase of supplies or a contracted sale. There would probably be far less interstate trade and consequently less opportunity to gain from the varying comparative advantages of each state. One of the reasons economic growth has occurred more rapidly in the United States than in the separate nations of Europe is the larger market in this country to which producers can sell and within which buyers can choose. Adam Smith, perceptive as usual, noted that division of labor—what we would now call the exploitation of comparative advantages—was the principal source of increases in the wealth of nations and that the division of labor was limited by the extent of the market.

But hoping for a unified world monetary system is probably putting the cart in front of the horse. If the peoples of the world woke up tomorrow and found themselves all using the same medium of exchange, they would be no less nationalistic than they are now. They would presumably still want to secure gains for their country at the expense of other countries, and they would still be in the grip of those popular mythologies which insist that buying at home benefits the home economy. Their governments would continue interfering in various ways with international trade. Moreover, policymakers would probably discover before long that having a separate national money makes it easier to interfere with foreign trade and to pursue independent economic policies. And so secessions from the world system would probably begin rather quickly. The point is that, while one money would help to create one world, it also presupposes one world. And that isn't where we are at the three-quarter mark in the twentieth century.

The Evolution of National Monetary Systems

The world has to some extent always had a unified monetary system. Certain metals, especially gold and silver, have functioned for thousands of years as universally accepted mediums of exchange. How did they come to acquire such wide acceptance? The answer lies in some combination of rareness, distinctiveness, beauty, malleability, and high ratio of weight to volume. These characteristics helped assure that the medium of exchange would be scarce, easily recognized, divisible into convenient units, portable, and hard to counterfeit, all of which are characteristics of a successful money. Contemporary national monetary units evolved from gold and silver, or *specie* money.

specie money ✗

There were many reasons for this evolution. To begin with, specie provides a much more convenient money when it has been minted into coins of a certified weight. And government was a logical candidate for the job of minting and certifying. By putting a little less metal into the coin than was indicated by its stamped value, the government could even earn

seigniorage

revenue from this service. The term for the difference between the coined value of the metal and its bullion value is seigniorage. As long as the seigniorage did not exceed the additional convenience value of having coins rather than bullion, the coins would circulate at their stamped value rather than their lower bullion value.

Governments pressed for revenue often yielded to the temptation to reduce the amount of metal in their coins beyond this limit. (We quoted Adam Smith on the subject in chapter 19.) This policy worked most effectively as a revenue-gathering device when coins minted elsewhere and offering a higher ratio of bullion value to stamped value could be excluded or otherwise discriminated against.[1] And so national governments acquired a special interest in coins of their own minting and gradually assumed for themselves the exclusive legal right to coin specie within their own borders. This created a system of predominantly national coins and was a significant step toward separate national monetary systems.

Another major step was taken with the evolution of paper money. Paper money originated as receipts for specie in storage. People owning large quantities of gold, for example, might want to store it with the local goldsmith, who had facilities for keeping gold secure. Later on, when they wanted to make a payment, they could hand over the receipt rather than go to the trouble of withdrawing the actual gold. If the goldsmith who had issued the receipt was thoroughly reliable, his receipt might be retained by the new holder and used again by him as a means of payment. When goldsmiths discovered that their receipts were circulating as money so that only a fraction of the gold in their vaults would ever be needed at one time to redeem outstanding receipts, they began to lend some of the gold left in their care. The easiest way to lend was by giving the borrower a receipt rather than the actual gold. If the receipt circulated and was not presented for redemption, the gold remained on deposit and might be loaned again. And now we have described the origin of money creation through the lending of reserves, as well as the origin of paper money.

As goldsmiths turned into banks and gold receipts into banknotes promising to pay specie on demand, paper money came to be denominated in national monetary units rather than in specie weight: 50 *dollars* of gold, for example, rather than 2.5 *ounces* of gold. This step toward the nationalization of paper money was carried further as national governments first tried to

---

1. One way for a government to discriminate in favor of its own coinage is to make it *legal tender* and to accept no other coins in payment of taxes. Money is legal tender whenever creditors must accept it in payment of debts or lose any further legal claim on the debtor who "tenders" (offers) it. Federal Reserve notes display the sentence, "This note is legal tender for all debts, public and private." A loan company might refuse to accept your check when your loan falls due and continue charging you interest. But the company could not refuse your tender of Federal Reserve notes and legally collect further interest.

regulate, then began to issue, and finally claimed the exclusive right to print paper money.

As long as all paper money was redeemable in gold at a fixed rate, each nation's paper money had a fixed value relative to that of every other nation. If a twenty-dollar Federal Reserve note can be exchanged for 1 ounce of gold and a twenty-pound Bank of England note for 5 ounces of gold, then 1 British pound will exchange for 5 American dollars. Banknotes that promised to pay gold to the bearer on demand did not always fulfill their promises, of course. We described briefly in chapter 18 the vicissitudes of privately issued banknotes in this country. Government-issued notes that were not redeemable in specie would also fluctuate in value, introducing shifting and uncertain disparities between the price of goods in *gold* dollars and the price of the same goods in *paper* dollars. When governments obtained effective control of paper-money issue, however, a new possibility appeared. A note that promised 20 dollars in gold promised 1 ounce of gold *only if the value of a dollar was* $\frac{1}{20}$ *ounce of gold.* Could governments possibly change the gold value of the dollar (or the pound or the franc) to achieve certain policy objectives?

The fact is that anyone with sufficient control over supplies of gold and paper dollars can set the value of each in terms of the other through buying gold with dollars whenever the price of gold falls and selling gold for dollars whenever it rises. This is called *pegging* the dollar to gold or, alternatively, pegging gold to the dollar. National governments concluded in this century that they did have the power to peg their currencies and thereby to fix the rate at which their monetary units exchanged for the monetary units of other nations. And that conclusion was another major step toward the nationalization of the international economy.

EXCHANGE RATES: CAUSES AND CONSEQUENCES

Any description of the evolution of national monetary systems runs the risk of exaggerating the power of national governments. We noted at the beginning of this chapter that governments have persistently underestimated the ingenuity of those whose interests conflicted with the goals the government was pursuing through its international policies. No government has ever been able to peg its monetary unit to gold or to anything else in an arbitrary way. The dollar value of gold and the gold value of the dollar are prices; and prices affect behavior, which in turn affects prices.

Let's suppose that the U.S. government pegs the dollar at $\frac{1}{35}$ ounce of gold and the German government pegs the mark at $\frac{1}{140}$ ounce of gold.

(The exposition will be much simpler if we assume there are only two nations in the world; the principles are the same for any number of nations.) What will now occur?

To begin with, Americans will now be able to purchase 4 marks for 1 dollar and Germans will be able to purchase 1 dollar for 4 marks. The two currencies are linked to each other through their common link to gold. The exchange rate between dollars and marks is 1 dollar = 4 marks.[1]

The important fact is that this exchange rate determines the price to Americans of German goods and the price to Germans of American goods. A Volkswagen, for example, that carries a factory price tag of 10,000 marks will carry also an implicit price of 2500 dollars. If the exchange rate were 1 dollar for 5 marks, a 10,000-mark price would be a 2000-dollar price. Meanwhile, a factory price tag of 3000 dollars on a Chevrolet would be read by Germans as 12,000 marks if the exchange rate is 1 dollar for 4 marks. At a rate of 1 for 5, the Chevrolet, though its factory price remained unchanged, would seem to a German to have gone up in price to 15,000 marks.

Demand and Supply

It follows that the attractiveness of foreign goods will depend on the exchange rate and on the price levels in each country. A devaluation of the dollar relative to gold will raise the dollar price of the mark, lower the mark price of the dollar, cause German goods to look less attractive to Americans, and cause American goods to look more attractive to Germans.[2] German imports (equals American exports) would consequently tend to increase and American imports (equals German exports) would tend to decrease.

The "demand for marks" curve in figure 23A says that, at prevailing price levels in the two countries, Americans will demand 12 million marks to purchase 12 million marks worth of German goods. At 40¢ per mark they will demand 10 million marks, at 50¢ they will demand 8 million, at 25¢ they will demand 16 million. It just so happens that in each case Americans will be supplying 4 million dollars: $33\frac{1}{3}$¢ × 12 million, 40¢ × 10 million, 50¢ × 8 million, 25¢ × 16 million all equal 4 million dollars. (The

1. The post–World War II system under which the mark was pegged directly to the dollar will be discussed in the next chapter.

2. Students are often confused by the fact that a devaluation sometimes looks at first glance like a revaluation (the word always implies an *upward* revaluation). You have to think about it for a moment to see that, when the mark goes from 25 cents to 30 cents, this is a decline in the value of the dollar and an increase in the value of the mark. The British pound was *devalued* in 1967 when it was changed from $2.80 to $2.40. The value of the dollar *increased*, relative to the pound.

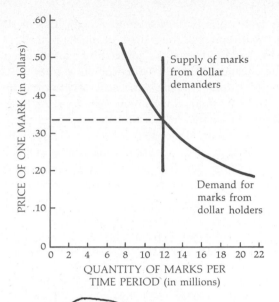

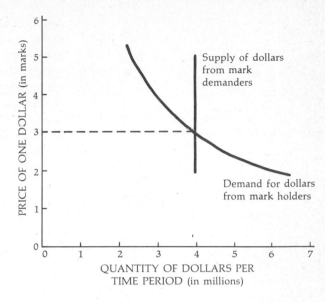

demand for marks is *unit elastic.* On the right side of figure 23A we have drawn the supply curve of dollars, consistently with the demand curve for dollars, as a vertical line at 4 million dollars.

The supply curve for marks (on the left graph) shows that Germans will offer 12 million marks to obtain dollars at every price of marks within the range shown. That translates into the "demand for dollars" curve shown on the right graph: 3 million dollars demanded at a price of 4 marks per dollar, 4 million dollars at a price of 3 marks, 6 million dollars at a price of 2 marks. (The unit elasticity of the two demand curves, which yields vertical supply curves in each case, is another expositional simplification and not an empirical assertion.)

The same conclusion emerges from either graph. The gold price of the dollar and of the mark must be set so that 1 dollar exchanges for 3 marks. At any other exchange rate, given the price levels in each country, the quantities of each currency demanded and supplied will not match.

Figure 23A At any exchange rate other than 3 marks = 1 dollar, there will be either a surplus of dollars (= shortage of marks) or a shortage of dollars (= surplus of marks)

Undervalued and Overvalued Currencies

What will happen if the German government nonetheless pegs the gold price of the mark at $\frac{1}{140}$ ounce of gold while the dollar is pegged at $\frac{1}{35}$ ounce of gold, so that the exchange rate is 4 marks for 1 dollar? Figure 23A tells us that 16 million marks will be demanded while only 12 million marks are supplied, which is equivalent to saying that 3 million dollars will be demanded and 4 million dollars supplied.

The American banks that handle foreign-exchange transactions will consequently find themselves running out of marks and the German banks will find themselves accumulating mounting quantities of dollars. The American banks will replenish their stock of marks by selling dollars to the government for gold and using the gold to buy marks from the German government. The German banks will reduce their unwanted dollar accumulations by selling the dollars to the American government for gold and selling the gold to the German government for marks. As long as Americans can keep acquiring marks in this way and Germans can continue to sell unwanted dollar accumulations, the exchange rate will remain at 1 dollar = 4 marks and the dollar-mark market will be in disequilibrium.

A "disequilibrium" implies that something now happening cannot continue indefinitely. The critical factor is the gold flow.

1. The United States will be continuously selling gold to Germany and reducing its stock of monetary gold.
2. The U.S. government (or the central bank) will be draining dollars out of private holdings and reducing the size of the money stock in the United States.
3. The German government will be continuously accumulating gold and adding to its monetary gold stock.
4. The German government will be pouring marks into private holdings and increasing the size of the money stock in Germany.
5. Because the dollars lost in the United States and the marks created in Germany respectively reduce and increase commercial bank reserves, a further contraction of the U.S. money supply and expansion of the German money supply will ensue.

What happens next cannot be predicted unless we know what policies the U.S. and German governments choose to follow in such a situation. One prediction can be made with confidence, however: people in the United States will begin talking about the "balance of payments deficit." For rather odd reasons to which we'll come, people in Germany are less likely to begin talking about a "balance of payments surplus."

THE BALANCE OF PAYMENTS

Any price that fails to equate the quantity demanded with the quantity supplied will result in either shortages or surpluses. Where will shortages or surpluses in international exchange show up? According to the conventional wisdom they reveal themselves in the *balance of payments*. But it would be far more accurate to say that they are *concealed* by the balance of payments. To understand why this is so, you must first acquire a little knowledge about balance of payments accounting.

Credits and Debits

Balance of payments accounting is an attempt to keep track of one country's international transactions by dividing them into transactions that earn foreign exchange, called credits, and transactions that use up foreign exchange, called debits. If you keep this basic definition in mind you should have no trouble deciding under which column to list a particular item.

Exports are credit items in the balance of payments. Foreigners who want to purchase our products must ultimately pay dollars to the American sellers. This results either in the reacquisition by Americans of dollars previously held by foreigners, in the acquisition of foreign currency that is used to purchase dollars, or in the acquisition of some other medium of international exchange that can be used to purchase dollars. U.S. imports simply reverse this flow. To purchase the products of some other country, we must either turn over previously acquired holdings of that country's currency, obtain some by giving up dollars in exchange, or use up our stocks of some other accepted international exchange medium to obtain the required currency.

That's all there is to the balance of payments if we define exports and imports broadly enough. Imports, for example, must include not only commodities like magnesium and tape recorders, but also services like the Geneva hotel room used by an American tourist or the entertainment provided in Fort Worth by an English rock group. Payment for these services entails the using up of foreign exchange and so they are debit items in the U.S. balance of payments.

What about gold? Gold sales or exports are credit items, just like any other exports; gold purchases or imports are debit items. Gold sales are a way of acquiring foreign exchange just as are sales of wheat. Momentary confusion may arise from the fact that gold is itself considered a medium of international exchange. Treat it like any other commodity, however, and you'll get it into the correct column.

We must also include under imports the "purchase" of whatever it is we obtain when our government extends foreign aid, or when Americans send money to relatives in Europe. If it seems inappropriate to think of either activity as "importing," the fact remains that any payments made to foreigners by the United States government, private organizations, or individuals use up foreign exchange and must therefore be classified as debits. These payments may in turn be used to purchase American exports (sometimes that's a condition of the grant); if so, the export is a credit item, but the gift, grant, pension, or other remittance that made it possible goes under the debit column. By the same token, gifts to us by foreigners or payments made to Americans by Lloyds of London in settlement of insurance claims are credit items in our balance of payments. And the sizable income we receive each year as a return on our overseas investments goes into the credit column, because it is a source of foreign exchange earnings for the United States.

Accounting for Foreign Investment

What about the original acts of investing? Capital flows can be treated like commodities and services if attention is focused on the stock, bond, or other evidence of indebtedness that changes hands. Thus foreign investment by Americans amounts to importing IOUs, and investment by foreigners in the United States is a U.S. export of IOUs. If this way of describing the matter strikes you as strained, you can keep the effects of foreign investment clear by concentrating on the definition of credits and debits. Investment by Americans in the French economy is a debit item in our balance of payments, because Americans must purchase French francs to buy an interest in French companies. And Britons buying shares of General Motors contribute to the credit side of our balance of payments, because they must obtain dollars to complete the purchase.

There is an alternative way of looking at foreign investment that sometimes proves useful. We can regard international investment as the acquisition of *claims.* Anything that increases our claims on foreigners or decreases their claims on us is a debit item in our balance of payments. Anything that decreases our claims on foreigners or increases their claims on us is a credit item. Don't try to memorize that; just use the definition of credits and debits: We acquire claims on foreigners by extending them loans, whether long-term or short-term. That requires us to use up foreign exchange, so it's a debit item. When such loans are repaid, foreigners reduce our claims on them by giving us foreign exchange and this is a credit in our balance of payments. The usefulness of this somewhat strange way of describing the matter will emerge when we try to puzzle out the meaning of a balance of payments deficit or surplus. The point is that if a substantial part of our credit items consists of loans from foreigners, we are enlarging the total of foreign claims against us; we are going more deeply into debt. That isn't necessarily bad. But short-term debts that might have to be repaid suddenly are a cause of concern to some students of the balance of payments.

The pieces of the puzzle have all been laid out. Suppose that we now sum the values of all the debits in the course of a year, then of all the credits, and find that they are not equal. We conclude in such a case that we made a mistake in record keeping. Errors and omissions are inevitable, of course, when one is trying to keep track of *all* international transactions.

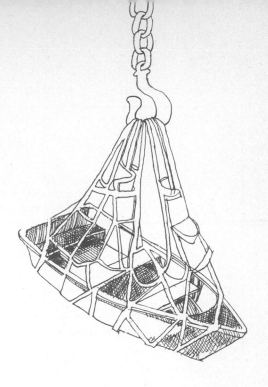

The value of some transactions can only be guessed at (as when the balance of payments accountants tacked on $40 million in the 1920s for imports of bootleg liquor). And the value of many perfectly legal transactions is estimated from incomplete records, inaccurate data, and partial samples. So measured credits and debits never do turn out to be precisely equal in balance of payments statements. The keepers of the accounts rise to the occasion by adding the difference to the smaller of the two totals and labeling it Net Errors and Omissions.

Credits Always Equal Debits

The Errors and Omissions component in the balance of payments has been embarrassingly large in recent years, hitting a record $10 billion in 1971—one-quarter the size of all our measured merchandise exports. But that isn't our concern at the moment. The significant fact for our purposes is that the Bureau of Economic Analysis always inserts whatever fudge factor is required to make the credits and the debits equal. *For the balance of payments always and necessarily balances.* It is constructed in accordance with the rules of double-entry bookkeeping, which specify that each transaction must be entered on the ledger twice, once as a debit and once as a credit. Let's see how this works out.

Suppose that Germany exported 100 boats to America, and that this was the only international transaction of the year by either country. The German accountants would enter the value of the boats as a credit in their balance of payments because it's a merchandise export. The American accountants would enter it as a debit under merchandise imports. It appears at first that, in both countries, the balance of payments is out of balance for the year; Germany will have a credit surplus, America a debit surplus. But not actually. The rules of double-entry bookkeeping decree that the boats must be "paid for" in some fashion. In the unlikely event that Germany gave them away, the German accountants would balance the credit item (so many marks worth of boats) with a debit item: a gift, or grant, or unilateral transfer of the same mark value as the boats. If, as usually occurs in such cases, Germany sold the boats but America hasn't yet paid for them, the German accountants balance the credit with a debit item called foreign loans: Germany imported IOUs to balance the export of boats. And in America the accountants balance the debit item created by importing boats with a credit item reflecting an export of IOUs just sufficient to purchase the boats. That makes excellent sense. Anything that hasn't yet been paid for (and wasn't a gift) has been sold on credit. The seller has in effect made a loan to the buyer; the seller has imported an IOU, or acquired a new claim on the importing country.

You might be a little surprised to discover that the balance of payments

U.S. BALANCE OF PAYMENTS SUMMARY

Balance of payments accounting is a complex and continuously changing science. You won't understand everything in this summary. But the authors don't, either, so you probably shouldn't worry about it. All figures are in millions of dollars.

Line	Credits (+), debits (−)	1971	1972	1973
1	Merchandise trade balance[1]	−2,722	−6,986	471
2	Exports	42,754	48,768	70,277
3	Imports	−45,476	−55,754	−69,806
4	Military transactions, net	−2,908	−3,604	−2,266
5	Travel and transportation, net	−2,341	−3,055	−2,710
6	Investment income, net[2]	5,021	4,526	5,291
7	U.S. direct investments abroad[2]	6,385	6,925	9,415
8	Other U.S. investments abroad	3,444	3,494	4,569
9	Foreign investments in the United States[2]	−4,809	−5,893	−8,693
10	Other services net[2]	2,781	3,110	3,540
11	**Balance on goods and services**[3]	**−170**	**−6,009**	**4,327**
12	Remittances, pensions, and other transfers	−1,604	−1,624	−1,943
13	**Balance on goods, services, and remittances**	**−1,774**	**−7,634**	**2,383**
14	U.S. Government grants (excluding military)	−2,043	−2,173	−1,933
15	**Balance on current account**	**−3,817**	**−9,807**	**450**
16	U.S. Government capital flows excluding nonscheduled repayments, net[4]	−2,111	−1,705	−2,938
17	Nonscheduled repayments of U.S. Government assets	227	137	289
18	U.S. Government nonliquid liabilities to other than foreign official reserve agencies	−478	238	1,111
19	Long-term private capital flows, net	−4,381	−98	62
20	U.S. direct investments abroad	−4,943	−3,517	−4,872
21	Foreign direct investments in the United States	−115	383	2,537
22	Foreign securities	−966	−654	−807
23	U.S. securities other than Treasury issues	2,289	4,507	4,051
24	Other, reported by U.S. banks	−862	−1,158	−647
25	Other, reported by U.S. nonbanking concerns	216	341	−200
26	**Balance on current account and long-term capital**[4]	**−10,559**	**−11,235**	**−1,026**
27	Nonliquid short-term private capital flows, net	−2,347	−1,541	−4,276
28	Claims reported by U.S. banks	−1,802	−1,457	−3,940
29	Claims reported by U.S. nonbanking concerns	−530	−305	−1,240
30	Liabilities reported by U.S. nonbanking concerns	−15	221	904
31	Allocation of Special Drawing Rights (SDR's)	717	710	....
32	Errors and omissions, net	−9,776	−1,790	−2,303

Line	Credits (+), debits (−)	1971	1972	1973
33	**Net liquidity balance**	−21,965	−13,856	−7,606
34	Liquid private capital flows, net	−7,788	3,502	2,302
35	Liquid claims	−1,097	−1,247	−1,944
36	Reported by U.S. banks	−566	−742	−1,103
37	Reported by U.S. nonbanking concerns	−531	−505	−841
38	Liquid liabilities—	−6,691	4,749	4,246
39	Foreign commercial banks	−6,908	3,716	2,952
40	International and regional organizations	682	104	377
41	Other foreigners	−465	929	887
42	**Official reserve transactions balance, financed by changes in—**	−29,753	−10,354	−5,304
43	Liquid liabilities to foreign official agencies	27,615	9,734	4,452
44	Other readily marketable liabilities to foreign official agencies[5]	−551	399	1,118
45	Nonliquid liabilities to foreign official reserve agencies reported by U.S. Govt.	341	189	−475
46	U.S. official reserve assets, net	2,348	32	209
47	Gold	866	547	....
48	SDR's	−249	−703	9
49	Convertible currencies	381	35	233
50	Gold tranche position in IMF	1,350	153	−33
	Memoranda:			
51	Transfers under military grant programs (excluded from lines 2, 4, and 14)	3,204	4,189	2,772
52	Reinvested earnings of foreign incorporated affiliates of U.S. firms (excluded from lines 7 and 20)	3,157	4,521	....
53	Reinvested earnings of U.S. incorporated affiliates of foreign firms (excluded from lines 9 and 21)	498	548	....
	Balances excluding allocations of SDR's:			
54	Net liquidity	−22,682	−14,566	−7,606
55	Official reserve transactions	−30,470	−11,064	−5,304

Notes to table

1. Adjusted to balance of payments basis; excludes exports under U.S. military agency sales contracts, and imports of U.S. military agencies.

2. Fees and royalties from U.S. direct investments abroad or from foreign direct investments in the United States are excluded from investment income and included in "Other services."

3. Includes special military shipments to Israel that are excluded from the "net exports of goods and services" in the national income and product (GNP) accounts of the United States.

4. Includes some short-term U.S. Govt. assets.

5. Includes changes in long-term liabilities reported by banks in the United States and in investments by foreign official agencies in debt securities of U.S. federally sponsored agencies and U.S. corporations.

Note.—Data are from U.S. Department of Commerce, Bureau of Economic Analysis. Details may not add to totals because of rounding.

always and necessarily balances. Time and again one hears that we *must* do this, or we *cannot* do that, "because of the balance of payments." The implication is that its balance is precarious, and that we are in danger of disastrously losing our equilibrium. But patriotism is the last refuge of a scoundrel, as Samuel Johnson suggested; and the balance of payments has often been the last refuge of Dr. Johnson's patriots. Special-interest groups looking for favors look also for a way to wrap themselves in the balance of payments. A little clarity on the significance of the balance of payments can therefore go a long way toward locating the public interest amid the confusing claims of competing partial interests.

The Ambiguity of Equilibrium

No one who understands balance of payments accounting is ever worried that the balance of payments won't balance. But many people do worry about the *way* it balances. In essence, they disapprove of some events that contributed to the balance. It isn't always easy to determine *why* they disapprove. An extraordinary amount of foggy rhetoric surrounds most discussions of the balance of payments. Some of the rhetoric is disguised political pleading and is therefore purposely foggy. But what one person fears and calls a disequilibrium in the balance of payments will often be recommended by another as a good policy for avoiding or curing a disequilibrium.

What was it that informed people had in mind in the 1960s when they started to worry about America's continuing balance of payments "deficits"? Where did such deficits show up? We know they could not appear as an excess of debits over credits; that would be Errors and Omissions and not a deficit. Where did they appear? One place was in the item for gold exports. Net sales of gold by the United States steadily reduced the Treasury's gold stock from $22.86 billion in 1957 to $10.89 billion in 1968. But why call that a deficit? Because, according to those who saw gold exports as evidence of disequilibrium in the balance of payments, a country cannot continue indefinitely to pay for its imports by drawing down its gold stock.

That's true, of course. But neither can a country continue indefinitely to pay for its imports by drawing down its stock of mineral resources. Nonetheless, no one regards Venezuelan oil exports or Rhodesian chrome exports as evidence of a deficit in those countries' balance of payments. Why single out gold for special treatment? We'll return to that question.

The other major piece of evidence pointed to by those who argued that the United States was running a deficit in its balance of payments was the rising total of short-term claims on the United States in the hands of foreigners. This large and growing total was evidence, they said, that we

were paying for our imports by persuading foreigners to extend us short-term loans. That was also true. But why was it evidence of a deficit? Why wasn't it simply viewed as part of the exchange-obtaining or credit transactions that balanced our exchange-using or debit transactions? The answer, once again, was that we could not expect to continue on such a course indefinitely. Sooner or later foreigners would presumably decide that they held enough claims against us, refuse to extend further credit, and start calling for payment on the claims already held.

One response to this argument is, So what? If foreigners won't lend us the means to buy their goods, we'll either find other means or stop buying. The United States imported a lot of IOUs in the 1950s in payment for our merchandise exports. When we were no longer willing to lend, we reduced our exports. And if foreigners decide to reduce their holdings of claims on the United States, we'll simply pay them off when the claims come due.

But could we do this? By what means can we pay off foreign claims on the United States? Suppose German commercial banks are holding $10 billion on deposit in New York banks or as dollar deposits in foreign branches of U.S. banks. These are claims on the United States; they are liabilities owed to German banks by U.S. banks. How were they acquired? Let's assume that the deposits were accumulated as Americans purchased Volkswagens and other imports from Germany. To buy German goods, we must pay with marks. The German banks made this possible by accepting the dollars from Americans and turning over an equivalent value in marks to the German exporters. By hanging on to those dollars and not asking the United States to redeem them with marks, gold, or some other acceptable foreign currency (or wheat, computers, or Chevrolets), the German banks were lending us the foreign exchange with which to import German goods.

Suppose now that they want to "liquidate" these claims. The deposits are payable on demand, and the German banks demand payment, just as you do when you write a check against your account in a commercial bank. The U.S. banks will meet the demand—but with *dollars,* of course, since their liabilities are denominated in dollars and not in marks, gold, or Chevrolets. The German banks will have to obtain the marks they want in exchange for dollars by turning the dollars over to the Central Bank of Germany. The net result of these transactions from the U.S. point of view is that the $10 billion formerly owed by U.S. banks to German commercial banks is now owed to the German Central Bank. If it's willing to hold the dollars, all is well. But if it's not, it had the right until recently to ask the U.S. Treasury to take the dollars off its hands for an equivalent value in gold. Until 1971, the Treasury Department was committed to redeeming dollars in gold at $35 an ounce for any central bank holding dollars but preferring gold.

That brings us back to the first symptom of a "deficit": gold sales. An increase in short-term foreign claims on the United States could not continue indefinitely, because they were potential claims on our stock of gold. Not only is that stock finite; in the 1960s it shrank while the total of potential claims against it swelled, so that the U.S. Treasury could no longer exchange gold for all the foreign-owned dollars. A disastrous run on U.S. gold reserves seemed imminent.

But why would that be "disastrous"? Suppose we simply paid gold to the official agencies authorized to exchange dollars for gold until our gold stock was exhausted and then announced that we had no more to sell. That wouldn't be dishonest; we would have honored our commitment as long as we could and quit only when there was no longer any way to continue. Unsatisfied holders of dollars could then choose either to continue holding the dollars or to exchange them for some other asset: commodities and services produced in the United States, for example, or income-earning securities such as U.S. government bonds or shares in American corporations. Where is the "disaster" in any of this?

We must push the analysis one step farther. The willingness of German banks to accept dollars (from American importers) and pay out marks (to German exporters) maintained a balance between the quantities of each currency demanded and supplied. If they had not acted in this way, the efforts of Americans to purchase a greater value of marks than Germans were willing to purchase of dollars would have led to further U.S. gold exports to Germany.

The Hidden Agenda: No Change in the Exchange Rate

Why were the German commercial banks willing to go on accepting dollars at the official rate of exchange even though supply and demand were calling for a lower exchange rate for dollars? The answer is that they knew they could obtain marks for the dollars at the official rate from their own Central Bank. The Central Bank, in turn, continued paying at this rate because that was the rate at which its dollar holdings would be converted by the U.S. Treasury, into either marks or an equivalent value in gold. The linchpin of the system was the willingness and ability of the U.S. Treasury to continue paying gold for dollars at the predetermined rate. If it stopped doing that, supply and demand would take over. The dollar would presumably depreciate and the mark would appreciate. And that was the "disastrous" consequence that so many feared and for which we've been searching in the last few paragraphs.

The whole business is complicated by the fact that the German Central Bank (and some other central banks) went on accumulating dollars even after they knew that the U.S. Treasury could not redeem them in gold. They cooperated by not exercising an option they had, because they did not want to precipitate "disaster."

Is there a voice from the back of the room willing to wonder out loud what's so "disastrous" about a change in the dollar-mark exchange rate? If relative prices, including exchange rates, do not reflect conditions of demand and supply, shouldn't we expect them to change? Aren't price changes the way to correct a disequilibrium?

When Is the Solution the Problem?

Those who believe that exchange rates should be fixed and unvarying will naturally reject the argument that a new rate of exchange can be a solution to the *disequilibrium.* As far as they're concerned it's like calling the death of the patient a cure for cancer. They will rather urge special government policies to reduce the pressure. They might point out that the supply of dollars is something the U.S. government controls, and that the simplest way for any supplier to keep the price of his product from depreciating is to stop supplying so much. That makes excellent sense, but it is often a difficult counsel for governments to accept. The U.S. government chose instead to impose additional taxes on imports, create new restrictions on the travel of Americans abroad, enact legal limitations on foreign investment by Americans, and utter all sorts of threats and promises to American corporations doing business abroad. The aim of each such policy was to deter people from engaging in activities that increase the demand for marks and thereby increase the pressure for an appreciation in the mark's value (which equals a depreciation of the dollar.)

But could any or all of these policies eliminate the disequilibrium? Those who see such government interference with voluntary international exchange as *evidence* of disequilibrium will certainly not agree that controls can *end* the disequilibrium. Consider an example from earlier chapters. If a city imposes rent controls because municipal officials believe that rising rents mean disequilibrium in the rental housing market, these officials will soon find themselves compelled to write and administer detailed codes of conduct governing landlord-tenant relations. They will regard such codes and other accompaniments of rent control, like long waiting lists, as necessary to achieve equilibrium. Opponents of rent control, who define equilibrium as rough equality between quantity demanded and quantity supplied *without* codes or waiting lists will point to the queues and codes as evidence of disequilibrium and to rising rents as the solution. The fascinating part of all this is that one group's solution is the other group's evidence of disequilibrium. That happens in many areas of economic life, but it happens most frequently and confusingly in the area of international exchange, where the concept of a balance of payments equilibrium is widely used but extraordinarily difficult to define in a satisfactory way.

Equilibrium always turns out to mean a balance among the *appropriate* factors. The concept is therefore a source of confusion whenever the criteria

of appropriateness cannot be agreed upon. In the rent-control case, for example, the controlled price becomes an equilibrium price as soon as one includes in the total price such nonmonetary costs as the inconveniences of queuing up. But economists usually agree in such cases to exclude nonmonetary costs as "inappropriate" to their concept of equilibrium. When we apply the concept, however, to the sum of all the international transactions engaged in by a nation's inhabitants, we run the risk of obscuring more than we clarify. Experts simply do not agree on how to measure the deficit or surplus in a nation's balance of payments, or even whether *any* definition can be adequately defended. The consequence is a variety of definitions with *disguised political intent.* We're not implying any malice or attempt to deceive on the part of those who define the balance in a particular way. But the fact remains that by defining the balance on the hidden assumption that particular objectives must be achieved, one can too easily sidestep the task of defending the appropriateness of those objectives.

Remember the warning at the outset of this chapter. International economic policies often pursue poorly defined and inconsistent goals. A concept as vague and ambiguous as "balance of payments equilibrium" makes it all the harder to decide what we're actually doing and what we really want to achieve.

NATIONAL GOALS AND FOREIGN TRADE POLICY

We're ready now to return to the question we left unanswered at the end of the section on Undervalued and Overvalued Currencies in order to discuss the uses and abuses of the balance of payments concept. What will happen when the exchange rate between two currencies is inconsistent with the demand for each currency? It depends upon the policies the governments are pursuing.

The Rules of the International Gold Standard

It was the task of the monetary authorities under the gold standard system to choose an initial gold value for their currency that would reflect the currency's actual purchasing power relative to other currencies. This, it was assumed, would balance the international demands for each currency and prevent the consequences enumerated at the end of the section on Exchange Rates.

But the purchasing power of a currency depends on price levels at home and abroad, and price levels change. Varying rates of inflation or deflation as well as differing rates of economic growth continuously threatened to

ON THE IDENTIFICATION OF DEFICITS

The *Survey of Current Business* celebrated its fiftieth birthday in 1971 with a special anniversary issue. A long list of distinguished economists was invited to submit papers commenting on the contributions to knowledge made over the years by the *Survey's* various statistical series (*The Economic Accounts of the United States: Retrospect and Prospect*, July 1971). A number chose to focus on balance of payments data and the meaning of a "deficit." The director of the Bureau of Economic Analysis, George Jaszi, reviewed the reviews at the end of the volume. He had this to say about the problem of defining a balance of payments deficit:

> With differences only in their degree of emphasis, our contributors point out that the payments balance cannot be represented by a single figure and that the presentation of a wide variety of balances is more conducive to the analysis of our balance of payments position. Ideally, perhaps no balance should be published at all. . . .
>
> Several factors seem to conspire to make the definition of payments balance an impossible task. The very notion of a dynamic balance of payments equilibrium is elusive, and balance of payments adjustment theory is torn by internal dissent. To make matters worse, even the view that ex post [actual] magnitudes can be used as though they were ex ante [intended] is allowed to infiltrate. In the realm of the GNP accounts, short shrift would be given to a fifth column which spread the view that the presence of expansionary or deflationary tendencies would be visible in an imbalance between [actual] saving and investment in the saving-investment account.
>
> Having witnessed over the years many attempts to define and redefine a payments balance—attempts whose only visible progression was circular—I have often felt that all definitions of a payments balance should be abolished, with a fine shout of "a plague on all your houses."

create over- or undervalued currencies and thus to trigger the kind of gold flow described above. The easy solution would seem to be regular adjustments in the price at which the various monetary authorities exchanged their currencies for gold. The "rules of the game" under the old gold standard frowned on that method of adjustment, however. For a country experiencing inflation relative to other countries to devalue its currency by raising the price of gold was to endorse that inflation. The sound, orthodox procedure called for the monetary authorities to resist the inflation by maintaining the price of gold. What was then supposed to occur?

Changes in the Domestic Price Level

When gold began to be exported from a country because inflation had caused its currency to be overvalued, that country's money supply and commercial bank reserves would decline. As the reserve losses forced banks to reduce their lending, the money supply would contract still further. The countries with undervalued currencies would import gold and their bank reserves and money supply would consequently rise. The price level was assumed to be a function of the money supply. In terms of the equation of exchange in chapter 22, P was thought to be determined by M, because V and Q were assumed to be fixed by nonmonetary forces or, at the very least, to be relatively stable. Deflation would consequently occur in countries with overvalued currencies, inflation in those with undervalued currencies, and both would continue until purchasing powers were again at parity. Thus domestic price level changes that were out of step with price level changes in other countries were supposed to be self-correcting. If all nations followed the rules of the game, gold flows and consequent changes in the size of money stocks would continuously adjust each price level to all others. Despite the use of different currencies, then, the economic systems of nations on the gold standard would be closely linked in a unified international economy.

In actual practice the system never worked that smoothly or automatically. Monetary authorities could and did intervene, either to aid or to inhibit the working of the adjustment mechanism. They might aid it by taking independent action to restrict bank lending and raise interest rates as soon as they detected a decline in the nation's gold reserves. On the other hand, they might choose to neutralize the gold outflow by supplying new reserves to the banking system to compensate for the reserves lost when gold was exported. The domestic money supply and price level would not decline in that case. *Supportive* actions by domestic monetary authorities presumably improved the functioning of the adjustment mechanism. But there were often good reasons, as they saw it, to *counter* the adjustment mechanism by supplying new reserves to the banking system when gold was exported, and by siphoning off the additions to reserves that came with gold imports. Nations were reluctant to accept the domestic inflation that was called for to correct an international undervaluation of their currencies. And they were even more reluctant to accept deflation as a cure for an overvalued currency when deflation turned out to be associated with falling output and rising unemployment.

Changes in Output and Employment

The theory of the international gold standard prescribed painless adjustments in domestic price levels as the cure for inappropriate rates of exchange between different currencies. But the adjustments were not in fact painless. Changes in M were not confined in their effects to changes in P; they also affected Q. The international gold standard collapsed in the 1930s, after stumbling attempts to restore it following World War I, because governments were not willing to subject their economies to disruptions originating in the rest of the world. In fact, they began to look upon exports and imports as variables that could be adjusted to achieve national goals rather than as autonomous forces to which domestic policy must conform.

The policies of the 1930s can be explained with the aid of the income-expenditures model. That model makes national income and output dependent on aggregate demand, defined now as the sum of consumption, investment, and government expenditures *plus* net exports (exports minus imports). We'll use PQ rather than Y in the model so that we can distinguish price level changes from changes in real output and associated changes in employment. The basic equation is

$$PQ = C + I + G + Ex - Im$$

A decline in aggregate demand, whatever its source, need not cause a fall in real output and employment if prices are sufficiently flexible. And price flexibility was widely assumed by economic analysts prior to the 1930s. But prices do not in fact adjust all that easily and quickly to decreases in demand. Firms that are not price takers as defined in chapter 9 (and most are not) set their prices initially on the basis of money costs previously incurred and anticipated demand; they tend to resist price reductions when demand falls short of expectations. At best, therefore, prices will fall only after some time has elapsed; and during that time unsold inventories will mount and production will be curtailed. This is the essence of a recession when it occurs in many industries simultaneously.

A government facing the onset of a recession and looking at this model might choose to counter the decline in aggregate demand with actions designed to increase exports or decrease imports. Policymakers in the early 1930s were not thinking in terms of this model because it hadn't yet been developed. But they didn't have to. There was a more immediate force that impelled them to look at the international sector for a possible policy tool: the interests of particular producers who could marshall strong political support. "Everybody knows" that imports destroy the jobs of American workers. In a period of high unemployment, therefore, producer lobbying for protection against foreign competition becomes almost impossible for politicians to resist. Taxes on imports are consequently raised and quotas are imposed. There are also many ways in which a government can subsidize exports and many arguments by which sellers seek to justify such subsidies. All those arguments become more persuasive in a recession.

In terms of the model, each nation tried to increase exports and decrease imports in order to raise PQ and reduce unemployment. In effect, each nation wanted to cut back on its employment of foreign workers and get other nations to hire more of its own labor force. There was obviously no way such a policy could work for every country. Exports as well as imports consequently declined for everyone. Each country was in effect trying to "export" its unemployment problem. But the principal result was a decline in the total of international trade, further economic disruption, and a loss of the gains from specialization.

Tariffs or quotas on imports and subsidies to exporters were one set of techniques in this abortive policy. Another was deliberate devaluation. Recall the way in which exchange rates between currencies affect the prices perceived by foreigners. The prices of exports become more attractive when a country's currency depreciates, while the prices of imports rise to discourage import purchases. A single country or a few countries can at least temporarily increase net exports in this way; but they cannot all do so simultaneously. The international monetary system turned chaotic as governments competed to manipulate the links among currencies in the hope of stimulating their net exports. The gold standard broke down and international trade increasingly had to be conducted through clumsy and inefficient barter negotiations.

It is obvious in retrospect that these policies were ineffective and even perverse. They could not stimulate aggregate demand in one country without depressing it in another. But they could and did reduce real income by inhibiting the gains from international specialization and trade during the 1930s. One source of the problem was a worldwide depression for which governments were desperately seeking remedies. Since the use of fiscal or monetary policy as correctives was not well understood, governments grasped at whatever straws they found. And in a depression, as we have seen, special interests will make the straws of trade intervention look politically attractive.

But another source of the problem seemed to be the international monetary system itself. The gold standard appeared to be too rigid in a period of major economic distrubances. When countries tried to make it more flexible by altering the gold price of their currencies, the system broke down completely.

This background enables us better to understand the directions in which the international monetary system evolved after World War II. We'll examine the rise of that system and the causes of its decline in the next chapter. Before we do so, however, let's take a look at some of the popular misconceptions about international trade that helped shape the self-defeating policies of the 1930s and that, unfortunately, still command wide allegiance today.

COMPARATIVE ADVANTAGE AND INTERNATIONAL TRADE

Popular thinking hangs on tenaciously to the notion that some countries may be able to produce almost everything at a lower cost. If wages in Japan or Mexico or Italy are lower than in the United States, won't Japanese, Mexican, and Italian manufacturers be able to produce just about anything more cheaply than U.S. manufacturers can do it? How can the United States compete with countries that tolerate wage rates, even for skilled workers, below our legal minimum? In Japan, Mexico, and Italy, however, you could find workers arguing that they can't compete with America's low cost techniques of mass production. And the suspicion arises that something is wrong with the argument.

Opportunity Cost and Comparative Advantage

The basic flaw in such arguments is the neglect of opportunity cost. It is *logically* impossible for one country to be more efficient than another in the production of everything. And that becomes apparent as soon as you remember to calculate efficiency as a ratio between what is produced and what is consequently *not* produced. The real cost of producing anything is the value of what is given up in order to produce it. Calculations in dollars, yen, pesos, and lira all too easily obscure these real costs of production.

The fundamental principle guiding international trade is the familiar principle of comparative advantage, first stated explicitly in chapter 7: Don't do anything yourself if you can persuade someone else to do it for you at a lower cost. To be persuasive, simply offer in exchange something that you can in turn produce at a lower cost. But that refers to *opportunity costs.*

Suppose that two television sets of identical quality cost respectively $300 and 90,000 yen to produce in the United States and Japan. Which cost is lower? We obviously can't know until we find out the relative value of dollars and yen. If 300 yen exchange for $1, then the costs of production are the same. If $1 will buy 310 yen, then the Japanese set is cheaper, because the cost of the Japanese set would be about $290, or 90,000 divided by 310. If we make the comparison in Japanese currency, the U.S. set would cost 93,000 yen. The U.S. sets would be cheaper, on the other hand, if $1 were worth anything less than 300 yen.

During 1971 the average price of a yen to Americans was about .29 cents ($.0029). In 1973, however, a yen cost .37 cents. That's a substantial difference. A Japanese television set costing 90,000 yen would have cost $261 dollars in 1971 but $333 in 1973. We obviously can't make meaningful cost comparisons between countries unless we know the rates of exchange between their currencies. At *some* exchange rate, all prices in one country could indeed be higher or lower than in some other country. But the problem then would not be rooted in low wage rates or efficient techniques of mass production. It would simply reflect an inappropriate exchange rate.

But what is an *appropriate* exchange rate? We argued earlier that it's a rate which equates the quantities of a country's currency that are internationally demanded and supplied. Let's try to tie that in now with the important principle of comparative advantage. We'll work with a simple problem involving two countries which each produce only four goods. Once the basic principles are clear, the conclusions can be applied to as many countries and goods as you please. The table below lists the domestic prices for all four goods in the United States and in Japan. We'll assume that those relative prices reflect opportunity costs within each country, and that the units refer to goods of identical quality.

Prices per Unit
(identical quantity and quality)

	United States	Japan
textiles (x yards)	$20	4,500 yen
meat (y pounds)	40	13,500
grain (z bushels)	30	10,500
radios (one set)	50	14,400

Forget about the exchange rate between dollars and yen. Assume, if you wish, that the United States and Japan do not yet trade. The question we want to ask is: Which country produces which goods at a lower cost than the other? If those are the only goods produced in each country and their relative prices reflect relative opportunity costs, can you decide which country is the more efficient (lower-cost) producer of each good?

All we can do with the data we have is determine the *relative* costs of any two goods in one country *relative* to the other country. But we require no more, because that is the meaning of comparative advantage.

Because meat costs 3 times as much to produce as textiles cost to produce in Japan but only 2 times as much in the United States, Japan has a comparative advantage over the United States in the production of textiles relative to meat. It follows logically that the United States then has a comparative advantage over Japan in meat production relative to textiles.

Between textiles and grain, the comparative advantage in textiles lies with Japan and so the comparative advantage in grain must lie with the

United States. The proof again is the fact that in Japan grain costs $2\frac{1}{3}$ times as much to produce as textiles and in the United States only $1\frac{1}{2}$ times as much.

Between textiles and radios, Japan again has a comparative advantage in the production of textiles and so the United States must have the comparative advantage in radio production.

How about meat and radios? The United States produces radios at $1\frac{1}{4}$ times the cost of meat and Japan at only $1\frac{1}{15}$ times the cost of meat. So Japan has the comparative advantage in radios and the United States in meat. Contrast this with the preceding case to be sure you grasp the point. Japan has a comparative advantage relative to the United States in radios *if the comparison is with meat.* If the comparison is with textiles, the United States has the comparative advantage in radio production.

To finish off the list of possible comparisons: Between meat and grain, Japan has the comparative advantage in meat and so the United States has the comparative advantage in grain. Between grain and radios, the United States has the comparative advantage in grain, which means that Japan has the comparative advantage in radios.

Prices as Indices of Comparative Advantage

A student could lose his mind doing this. The data are hard to keep straight and the conclusions are even harder to express verbally in any simple way. If this is the meaning of comparative advantage, how could it possibly guide efficient decision making? It takes an advanced degree in crossword puzzles just to figure out who has a comparative advantage in what relative to which relative to whom. Fortunately for us all, prices very neatly sum up all the information any decision maker has to have. By looking at relative prices and the exchange rate, any producer or purchaser can obtain at a single glance the essence of the results that we just ground out so laboriously.

If the exchange rate is 300 yen = \$1, textiles and radios are cheaper in Japan and meat and grain are cheaper in the United States. The table below shows all prices in yen.

Prices in Yen
(300 yen = \$1)

	United States	Japan
textiles (x yards)	6,000	4,500
meat (y pounds)	12,000	13,500
grain (z bushels)	9,000	10,500
radios (one set)	15,000	14,400

If the exchange rate is 280 yen = \$1, only textiles are cheaper in Japan. The table again shows all prices in yen.

Prices in Yen
(280 yen = $1)

	United States	Japan
textiles (x yards)	5,600	4,500
meat (y pounds)	11,200	13,500
grain (z bushels)	8,400	10,500
radios (one set)	14,000	14,400

The yen price of a dollar would have to fall below 225 yen to make even textiles cheaper in the United States. *But then Japan and the United States could not trade at all.* The yen would be so overvalued at that rate that there would be no dollar demand for yen and hence no dollars available for Japanese to use in purchasing the cheaper American goods. That exchange rate would turn the United States and Japan into isolated economies unable to take advantage of one another's relative efficiencies. Japanese consumers could not benefit from the relatively abundant supply of land in the United States that is presumably the explanation for America's comparative advantage in meat and grain production; and American consumers could not benefit from the relatively abundant supply of labor that makes textiles and radios cheaper to produce in Japan.

If any trade at all is to occur, the exchange rate must be between 225 yen = $1 and 350 yen = $1. (We're ignoring the effect of transportation costs, which would further narrow the permissible range.) Exactly where it settles down within that range will depend upon the strength of the demands for each good, the ability of each country to expand production, and what happens to relative opportunity costs as production patterns change in response to international trade.

One illustration will be enough to make the point. Suppose the rate starts out at 300 yen = $1. Americans then find Japanese radios cheaper than domestically produced radios ($48 versus $50). If a huge American demand for radios causes an expansion of the radio industry in Japan, and that expansion requires the use of resources not as well suited to radio production, the marginal opportunity cost and hence the price of Japanese radios will rise. It couldn't rise above 15,000 yen, because at that price the U.S. demand would disappear. But the prices of other goods in both countries would also be changing in response to the reallocation of productive resources that trade had brought about and the consequent changes in marginal costs. The possibilities are endless.

Perhaps you were beginning to fear that this example would be endless too. But it's important to see how *relative prices reveal comparative advantages* in international trade and what real opportunity costs of production lie behind those prices.

The Fear of Imports

The principle of comparative advantage took a distant back seat in the early 1930s, when the industrial countries of the world watched domestic production and employment tumble. Everyone knew that imports replaced domestically produced goods and that domestic production increased when exports increased. Reversing the decline in domestic production was the priority item on each country's agenda. Restricting imports while subsidizing exports seemed a straightforward approach toward that goal. And for reasons that we have examined, it was an approach with political appeal.

The argument that imports destroy jobs has the seductive appeal of a half-truth. When Americans buy Japanese radios they do not buy as many domestically made radios. An increase in radio imports can therefore lead to production cutbacks and layoffs in the domestic radio industry. So the owners and employees of radio manufacturing firms have an obvious interest in restricting imports. And when they go to Congress to request taxes or quotas on radio imports, they have a handy slogan with which to claim that such protection is good for the country: It protects American jobs. The popular appeal of that slogan will be especially strong in any period when unemployment is increasing and there is a recession in the economy.

But the argument is highly misleading. In the first place, jobs are created by the production of exports as well as by the production of goods that compete with imports. And how can American firms continue to sell abroad if foreign firms are not allowed to sell in the United States?

Secondly, jobs should not automatically be treated as goods. Some jobs no doubt are intrinsically satisfying and worth doing for themselves without regard to the commodities or services that result. But that's certainly rare. The justification for jobs is generally the income they provide for workers and the corresponding benefit to others in the form of useful goods. The "protect American jobs" argument ignores the gains in real income that come from specialization. If the Japanese can make better radios and sell them at lower prices than American manufacturers can do, Americans ought to produce other products and buy their radios from Japan. The attempt to justify the protection of less efficient producers on the grounds that this will preserve jobs runs quickly into absurdity. Why not push the argument further and produce domestically all the coffee we consume? American soil, climate, and geography are not as well suited for the production of coffee trees as are large areas of Brazil and Colombia; but think of all the jobs we could create by building and operating huge greenhouses in which we try to duplicate the favorable growing conditions in those countries. And why stop with goods currently imported? Think of

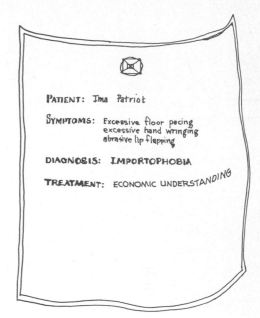

PATIENT: Ima Patriot

SYMPTOMS: Excessive floor pacing
excessive hand wringing
abrasive lip flapping

DIAGNOSIS: IMPORTOPHOBIA

TREATMENT: ECONOMIC UNDERSTANDING

how many new jobs we could create by outlawing the use of automated equipment in the telephone industry or by requiring street sweepers to use toothbrushes in their work.

Producer Interests and the National Interest

For two centuries economists have argued along these lines against the proponents of restrictions on imports, but they have not had much success. A French pamphleteer-economist named Frédéric Bastiat (1801–1850) wrote a witty satire in 1845 in the form of a petition by the French candlemakers for protection against the unfair competition of the sun. Their request to the Chamber of Deputies for legislation that would protect the jobs of candlemakers by prohibiting windows brilliantly exposes the absurdity of protectionist logic. Bastiat's satire has been reprinted numerous times, but the arguments he ridiculed do not disappear.

Part of the explanation must be found in the resistance of special-interest groups to mere logic. People are readily persuaded by arguments in which they want to believe, but have difficulty understanding arguments that run counter to their interests. And the political process almost guarantees that the group that stands to benefit from restrictions on international trade will have a louder voice in policy formation than the larger group that stands to lose.

The beneficiaries of tariffs or quotas on radio imports are the owners and employees of American firms manufacturing radios. They know precisely what their interest requires; they keep themselves informed about changes and prospective changes in economic or political circumstances that might affect their interests in any way; and their interest in the specific issue of U.S. importation of Japanese radios is substantial enough to justify lobbying for their cause.

Those who are harmed by restrictions are potential purchasers of radios, the owners and employees of firms producing goods for export, and the owners and employees of the Japanese radio firms. Each individual in the first two groups has such a small interest in the outcome of policy discussions regarding radio imports that he isn't likely even to notice that such discussions are taking place, and he is even less likely to invest his time or energy in lobbying for that interest. It's not that domestic radio buyers lose less than the domestic radio producers gain but rather that the losses are spread over many millions of people while the gains are concentrated among relatively few. The larger interest does not acquire proportionate political influence because it costs too much to organize that interest and give it effective expression. This is the same phenomenon we encountered in our earlier discussion of externalities, and it explains why special interests so often defeat the "public interest."

The third group harmed by import restrictions—the Japanese producers —have a sufficiently concentrated interest; but as foreigners, they lack political influence. The upshot of the matter is that the jobs and income of people producing import-competitive goods are often protected by their governments despite the fact that their gains are less than the losses incurred by those who are less effectively represented in the political process.

This explanation for the popularity of governmental restrictions on imports may be unduly cynical. There can be little doubt that many Americans, including some who are actually harmed by protective tariffs and import quotas, genuinely believe that this country can, at least under certain circumstances, be damaged by imports. Let's examine the arguments they use.

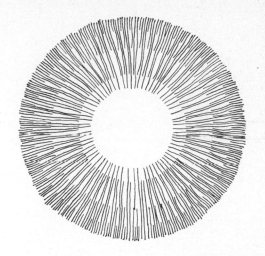

Arguments for Protection

The national security argument comes first. If we don't restrict the import of Japanese radios, our radio making industry may be destroyed. Then what would we do for radios in the event of war with Japan or even war with some other country that results in a cutoff of our Japanese trade? Maybe we could do without radios for the duration. But don't radio makers possess special skills that might be essential in wartime? Can we afford not to have an available pool of human skills and specialized equipment that can readily be adapted in a national emergency to the production of sophisticated military hardware? The basic argument can be applied with modest changes to almost any industry one might mention. Even the candle manufacturing industry included "high essentiality of labor and materials under war conditions" in a 1951 brief filed with the Senate Finance Committee on behalf of protection against candle imports. (What would we do, after all, if the lights went out in wartime?) The national security argument is not *logically* fallacious. But the fact that the argument can so easily be extended to any imports whatsoever should at least make us wary. How large a price should we be willing to pay in reduced real income for how large a gain in military self-sufficiency? And is this a genuine gain in national security? Can't the economic strength and hence the military security of a country actually be reduced by excessive efforts toward self-sufficiency? How often are these questions seriously asked before the national security is invoked to justify a new tariff or quota?

Another logically valid argument for protection goes by the name of the "infant industry" argument. It may take some time for an industry to develop the special skills, experience, and other resources that would make it efficient. If established foreign producers are allowed to sell freely in the American market, they may be able to keep domestic firms from developing. The argument assumes that American firms are less efficient

ENERGY INDEPENDENCE

Should the United States try to become independent of all foreign energy sources by 1980?

Both independence and interdependence have real costs, but in a period of national alarm about the threats other nations might pose to our security and well-being we are likely to underestimate the cost of independence.

Any and every import creates a degree of dependence on foreign suppliers, and dependence entails increased vulnerability. There is more to the matter than this, however. The dependence runs both ways, since those from whom we import also import from us. So long as it is in their interest to buy from us, it will be in their interest to sell to us.

Moreover, the pursuit of invulnerability through independence is a costly route to take. No one can predict with confidence how much more we will pay for energy between now and 1980 and afterward, because the cost will depend, to mention just some obvious factors, upon technological developments, the amount of attention given to environmental concerns, and the encouragement or discouragement that nuclear power receives. But the costs will be considerable, and the political difficulties that President Ford's energy independence program was encountering in 1975 suggest the public may find the price too high.

Is the public too nearsighted to discern the genuine public interest? If direct costs are the only consideration, the public's alleged myopia may actually be the better long-run perspective. A *certain* increase in *present and future* costs to preclude a *possible* increase in *future* costs does not automatically sound like a good bargain.

How much would we save in future costs after 1980 if we went ahead with our energy independence program and our worst fears were realized? What is the probability that our worst fears will in fact be realized? What is the present value of these additional costs multiplied by their probability when discounted at an appropriate rate of interest? And is that sum greater than the sum of the discounted costs we will incur by pushing ahead toward energy independence?

But there are also indirect costs that ought to enter the calculations. What will be the effect on the environment, on life styles, or on other nations through the example we set if the United States does or does not increase present energy costs and reduce energy consumption? The economic calculus can help us find the answers, but it is no substitute for hard thought and informed discussion about the goals we want to pursue.

in their infancy but would become more efficient than foreign competitors if they were given protection while they matured. Alexander Hamilton, the first U.S. Secretary of the Treasury, used this argument in an effort to persuade Congress that some protection against imports was in the national interest. He also argued, though, that outright subsidies were preferable to other forms of protection, because subsidies were clearly visible and could more easily be removed once they had served their purpose. That part of Hamilton's argument has not been popular with the advocates of protection, who understandably prefer a subsidy disguised as a tax on imports. But it's hard to imagine how the infant-industry argument could possibly be appropriate in the United States today. Do we have any infant industries? We have *new* industries appearing all the time. But for the purposes of this argument an infant industry is a new domestic industry competing for survival among *well-established* foreign industries. Examples are hard to find. And even if examples can be located, the argument will only apply if the infant shows promise of maturing quickly into an adolescent who can more than make it on his own. He must *more* than make it if he is to compensate society for the cost of supporting him during his infancy. All things considered, the infant-industry argument probably has no applicability to the United States today. It is an intellectual curiosity that probably hangs around only as a strategic diaper for gray-bearded but anemic "infants."

Are there other good arguments for protection? A legitimate but limited argument can be constructed from the costs of change. The closing or curtailment of an industry unable to meet foreign competition entails losses for its owners and employees. The losses will be greater the more narrowly specialized are the human and property resources displaced by competition. Is there a case for protection under such circumstances? Notice that the argument can be applied to the case of an industry hurt by domestic as well as foreign competition. Domestic competitors have political influence, of course, and are therefore harder to exclude by special legislation. Nonetheless, if resources were attracted into an industry because of existing tariff protection, it may be unfair to jerk that protection away suddenly. So there is a case for the maintenance of prior and long-continued restrictions on imports, or at least a case for their reduction (in the interest of efficiency) at a slow rate (in the interest of equity). Equity considerations, along with political realities, may also suggest a policy of transitional subsidies designed to reduce the loss to workers and owners or to help them move into new opportunities. But this argument cannot support the introduction of new or additional restrictions against imports.

Uncommon Sense: Comparative Advantage

Since there is no limit to the number of bad arguments that can be constructed in support of restrictions on imports, it would be an exercise in futility to attempt to anticipate and refute each one. The fact that there is at least a kernel of truth in most such arguments complicates the task of analyzing them. The truth must be winnowed from the chaff which surrounds it before the limitations of its applicability can be discussed. Nothing would contribute more toward raising the quality of public discussion in this area than a firm grasp of the principle of comparative advantage.

The principle of comparative advantage shows why and how exchange creates wealth. It keeps insisting that the cost of a transaction is the value of what is given up and the benefit is the value of what is obtained, and that it is nonsense to suppose a country can grow wealthy by exporting more than it imports. The principle of comparative advantage destroys the claim that one country may be more efficient than another in the production of *everything.* The logical impossibility of this premise is apparent from the very definition of efficiency as a ratio between the value of what is produced and the value of what is consequently *not* produced, or between the value of the goods obtained and the value of the goods that had to be sacrificed to obtain them. By focusing on the real factors involved in production and trade, the principle of comparative advantage disperses the fog that creeps in when trade policy is discussed exclusively in monetary terms.

"But then we'd be losing dollars!" So? Dollars cost almost nothing to produce. If other countries want to trade transistor radios for dollars, that's a marvelous swap from our point of view. And that's actually what occurred for about fifteen years under the new international monetary system created after World War II.

Once Over Lightly

As long as goods and financial assets can be exchanged across national boundaries, international trade will affect national levels and patterns of output, employment, prices, and income distribution. Increasing international trade makes the coordination of domestic and international policies more urgent. The increasing determination of national governments to manage their domestic economies may simultaneously make it more difficult.

An international monetary system, like any monetary system, reduces the cost of transactions and so facilitates specialization and improves efficiency. But the world money supply is composed of many different moneys, often exchanging for one another at uncertain and unpredictable rates.

The exchange rates between currencies and domestic prices in each country are variables that mutually determine one another. The reduction of a currency's price in foreign exchange will increase the total quantity of domestic goods demanded, both by making that country's exports cheaper to foreigners and by making imports more expensive to its own residents.

A government that pegs the rate of exchange for its currency at a level that does not equate the quantity of its currency demanded with the quantity supplied will lose or accumulate international reserve assets. The government will call this a disequilibrium in its balance of payments only if it does not *want* to lose or accumulate such assets.

The balance of payments must always balance, because it measures international transactions that are always assumed to entail something of value received for anything given up. The term *deficit* or *surplus* is applied to balancing items of which someone disapproves or to actions affecting the composition of the accounts of which someone disapproves. The disapproval rests upon predictions of undesired consequences.

The loss or accumulation of international reserve assets affects the level of domestic bank reserves and the money supply. This in turn may affect price levels, or levels of output and employment or both.

Governments that try simultaneously to manage their foreign exports and imports and their domestic price and output levels often find this to be a difficult balancing act. Harmonizing such policies is especially difficult when other governments are pursuing parallel but conflicting policies.

A major source of inconsistency in national policies is the desire of governments to satisfy political pressures from producers who want both an expansion of export markets and protection against import competition.

International efficiency is promoted when international exchange is governed by relative opportunity costs or the principle of comparative advantage. Inappropriate exchange rates, import tariffs or quotas, and export subsidies can conceal or distort relative opportunity costs. Nationalist sentiment and the disproportionate political influence of producers tend to keep the principle of comparative advantage from regulating international trade as effectively as it regulates domestic trade.

QUESTIONS FOR DISCUSSION

1. In order to take advantage of lower production costs, a Massachusetts textile manufacturer builds a factory in North Carolina and a United States television maker opens an assembly plant in Mexico.

    (a) In what ways is the action by the television firm different from the action by the textile firm?

    (b) Is either action contrary to the national interest?

    (c) Is either action likely to encounter effective political opposition?

2. The table below shows consumer price indices for four countries from 1970 to 1974.

Year	United States	Canada	France	Germany
1970	100.0	100.0	100.0	100.0
1971	104.3	102.9	105.5	105.3
1972	107.7	107.8	111.7	111.1
1973	114.4	116.0	119.9	118.8
1974	127.0	127.9	135.5	126.8

Do you think the similar patterns between the United States and Canada and between France and Germany are mere coincidence?

3. What would be the consequence for Volkswagen sales in the United States of a depreciation in the mark relative to the dollar? How would this affect the profitability of sales to the United States by the Volkswagen Company? Would you expect the longer term effects to differ from the short run effects?

4. How are the supply curves of figure 23A related to the demand curves? What would the supply curves look like if the demand curves fell more steeply? If they fell less steeply?

5. 1971 and 1972 were years in which there was widespread concern about the "deficit" in the U.S. balance of payments. Where would you locate the "deficits" in the balance of payments summaries for those years?

6. One of the steps taken by the U.S. government in the 1960s to correct the "balance of payments problem" was to restrict foreign investment by U.S. firms and banks. How would such a program, if it had been effective, have influenced U.S. debits and credits? Would the longer term consequences be different from the short run consequences?

7. If the value of Iran's merchandise imports is 20% greater than the value of its merchandise exports, does Iran have a deficit in its balance of payments—

    (a) If the difference is covered by twenty-year loans?

    (b) If the difference is covered by one-year loans?

    (c) If the difference is covered by selling gold from the national treasury?

    (d) If the difference is covered by selling newly mined gold?

    (e) If merchandise imports are 400% greater than merchandise exports *excluding petroleum,* and the difference is made up by selling newly extracted "black gold"?

8. Why do so many Americans believe that this country would be endangered by Arab ownership of "essential" U.S. industries and also believe that American owners of foreign industries pose no threat to the national security of those countries? Why are U.S.-owned foreign enterprises thought to be at the mercy of foreign governments, while the United States is at the mercy of foreigners owning U.S. enterprises?

9. How do U.S. imports reduce the domestic money supply? How can the Fed prevent this from occurring? What would be the consequences of such "neutralization" actions by the monetary authorities?

10. Why cannot one country have a comparative advantage over another country in the production of everything if the first country has excellent natural resources, a huge capital stock, a highly skilled labor force, and ingenious technicians and managers, while the second country is poor in all four areas?

11. What evidence exists to support the view that Japan has a comparative advantage over against the United States in the production of small automobiles? How would you account for this comparative advantage? How would you explain the fact that the United States seems in general to have a comparative advantage in the production of large automobiles but a comparative disadvantage in the production of smaller ones?

12. How does the theory of external benefits and "free riders" presented in chapters 14 and 15 help explain why the legislative influence of producers is generally greater than that of consumers?

13. Suppose that a Canadian firm appeals for protection against imports from the United States using the infant industry argument. It offers data showing that it can currently produce and sell widgets for $10, that American producers can sell them in Canada for $8, and that if American competitors are excluded from the Canadian market, the firm will develop greater efficiency and after ten years of protection be able to sell widgets for $7. It therefore proposes what is in effect a $2 per widget tax on Canadian consumers for ten years in return for a $1 benefit in perpetuity.

    (a) Would that be a good bargain for Canadian consumers if the facts are as stated? (You must use tables 12A and 12B to answer.)

    (b) How did you choose the discount rate to use in calculating your answer?

    (c) If the protection were granted, do you think it would be eliminated at the end of ten years? What arguments would be used to support its continuance?

    (d) Do you think the efficiency of the Canadian firm is as likely to increase when it is protected from foreign competition as when it is not?

    (e) Why do so many Americans believe that competition is not altogether desirable when it comes from foreign producers?

24

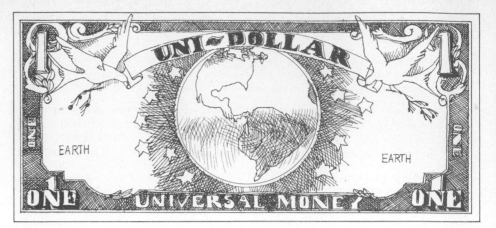

THE CHANGING
INTERNATIONAL MONETARY SYSTEM

The principles of the international monetary system and the prerequisites for international monetary order may have been better understood a decade ago than they are now. Events have moved faster than theories in recent years, and new truths have not yet firmly established themselves as successors to the old truths that practice has called into question.

THE SYSTEM OF BRETTON WOODS

The statesmen who gathered at Bretton Woods, New Hampshire, in 1944 to design a new system for linking the world's currencies could hardly doubt the power of nationalism. They knew that a successful world monetary system would have to leave each government free, within wide limits, to pursue its own chosen domestic policies. But the participants in the Bretton Woods monetary conferences were also internationalists, and they hoped to devise a system under which national sovereignty could coexist with international cooperation.

John Maynard Keynes was a leading participant in those conferences. He was convinced, as were most other participants in the negotiations, that national governments had the power to influence domestic levels of income and employment. They expected that power to be used against any recurrence of depression. Their task, therefore, was to devise a system of international currency links that could maintain itself and function effectively in the face of divergent national economic policies.

The twin concepts of *links* and *liquidity* will help us appreciate the nature of the problems they saw themselves facing.

Maintaining Fixed Exchange Rates

The demand for particular currencies from holders of other currencies varies continuously, even over short periods of time, in response to continuously shifting patterns of relative prices and production within countries. Moreover, levels of prices and production will shift over time as a result of changes in demand, in technology, in resource availability, and also in government fiscal and monetary policies. It was feared that if supply and demand were allowed to determine exchange rates without any official intervention, the rates would fluctuate unpredictably and seriously hamper international exchange by making it too uncertain and risky. Fluctuating exchange rates were regarded as unsatisfactory international monetary links.

If official monetary institutions, such as central banks, are to peg exchange rates at a steady level, they must possess an adequate stock of acceptable international reserves. An exchange rate is pegged by selling a currency when its value starts to rise and buying when it starts to decline. But what could a central bank use to buy its own currency? It would have to be an asset that was acceptable to the other countries from whom the currency was being purchased. Gold was one such reserve asset. A stock of monetary gold would give a central bank liquidity with which to maintain a stable price for its currency in the face of temporary downward pressure. Was there enough monetary gold around to provide every central bank with sufficient liquidity to prevent its currency from fluctuating in value? Perhaps there was not. Of course, the value of the physical gold stock could have been increased simply by raising the price of gold in terms of the dollar and other currencies. As we shall see, however, there was strong resistance to taking that step. Moreover, the bulk of the world's monetary gold stock was in the United States by the end of World War II, so that the gold in other nations seemed to many clearly insufficient to permit monetary authorities to maintain their currency's price by pegging.

International Reserve Currencies

But gold is not the only reserve asset that might be used. The international reserves available to a central bank for pegging operations will include, besides its monetary gold stock, its holdings of "sound" foreign currencies. When is a foreign currency "sound"? It is sound when everyone believes that the currency is not going to depreciate in the foreseeable future. And why would they believe that? They would believe it if they were convinced that the country issuing the currency was willing and able to pursue policies that would prevent depreciation. And what causes or prevents depreciation? Depreciation results from a country's inability to export at prevailing exchange rates as much as it wants to import, and from its inability in such a situation to stem the depreciation by selling gold or other reserve assets. A country currently balancing its trade accounts by importing short-term liquid assets and also holding a huge stock of reserve assets therefore possesses a sound currency par excellence.

Sound as a Dollar

And now we have described the U.S. dollar as it appeared at the end of World War II. The U.S. gold stock was over $20 billion in 1946 and had climbed to almost $25 billion by 1949—certainly enough, it seemed, to maintain the price of the dollar even in the face of prolonged pressures toward depreciation. But no pressure appeared imminent. U.S. exports were in heavy demand and the war-ravaged economies of Europe seemingly would, for some time, have little to offer in return. Inflation in the United States could alter this picture; but there was no reason to believe this country would experience inflation at a greater rate than the rest of the world, and substantial reason to believe its productive capacity would do a better job than anyone else's of keeping the supply of goods in step with the demand. So the dollar after World War II was "as good as gold." It was *better* than gold, in fact, because a nation's gold reserves earned no interest. But a country that chose to hold its international reserves in the form of dollars could earn a return on those reserves by depositing them in U.S. banks or by purchasing U.S. government securities that could be quickly and costlessly converted into dollar deposits.

The Dollar as International Currency

That's how it came about that the Western world moved toward a dollar-gold standard after World War II. The United States pegged the dollar to gold at a price of $35 per ounce. Other countries then pegged their currency to the dollar. The United States held its international reserves primarily in the form of gold. Other countries might hold gold too; but they could also hold as reserves dollar deposits and assets such as U.S. government securities that were convertible into dollar deposits. These deposits were in turn convertible into gold on demand by foreign monetary authorities.[1]

1. We are unjustly ignoring in this discussion the pound sterling. During the era of the classical gold standard, London was the financial center of the world. The Bank of England maintained pound-gold convertibility, and the pound was the major international reserve asset. After World War II, nations that maintained close and extensive trading relations with the United Kingdom resumed the practice of holding sterling balances as reserves. Not until 1954 did the total of sterling in international reserves fall below the total of dollars. But the decline of sterling as an international reserve occurred steadily; it fell from 40% of all official reserves in 1948 to a little more than 5% by 1971.

Under this system the dollar performed on the international level all the functions typically performed by a domestic currency. It was an international medium of exchange: French imports from Sweden, for example, could be paid for by transferring ownership of dollar deposits. Dollars were held not only by central banks that wanted international reserves, but also by private citizens of foreign countries. They often preferred to accumulate dollar assets rather than their own currency, because they believed that the dollar was less likely to depreciate through inflation. It was also the international unit of accounting and was employed in practice to measure the value of international transactions. And the dollar was the world's intervention currency, because the monetary authorities of different nations purchased and sold dollars in order to maintain the value of their currencies in the foreign exchange market.

How Much Liquidity?

A major difference between such a dollar-gold system and a gold-only system is the larger stock of international reserve assets that the former provides. Why is that important? The monetary authorities of any country want liquidity for reasons similar to those discussed in chapter 18, where we described the demand for liquidity. The future is uncertain. They want to be able to handle unforeseen contingencies. Unexpected developments might push a country's imports far beyond its exports for a temporary but protracted period. This could be handled without depreciation by dipping into the reserves. With inadequate reserves, depreciation might be avoidable only by curtailing imports that were important to that country's economic development, military security, or political stability. How much liquidity was desirable?

Just as there's no rule of thumb for deciding how large any individual's money balances ought to be, there's no rule of thumb for choosing the appropriate amount of international liquidity. But the world's monetary gold stock was relatively fixed.[1] And there seemed to be no law of nature decreeing that the amount of heavy yellow metal in the world, at its current price, had to be equal to the amount that all countries collectively wanted to hold as reserves. The supply of monetary gold, at the fixed rates of exchange between gold and various currencies, might be insufficient to satisfy the international demand for liquidity. Wasn't that likely, in fact? Just as an individual's preferred level of money holdings is a function of his regular income and expenditures, so a nation's preferred level of reserve holdings could be expected to depend on the total of its imports and exports. An expansion of world trade would presumably require an

---

1. It was *relatively* fixed because gold could be attracted from the ground or private hoards, and could also disappear into private hoards or into industrial and ornamental uses.

expansion of reserve assets if the trading world was not to encounter a persistent liquidity shortage. And liquidity shortages threatened free trade and stable exchange rates.

How so? A nation with inadequate reserves could not weather temporary import surpluses. Even minor dislocations, due perhaps to a poor harvest or a development boom, could quickly deplete the reserves and compel a choice between accepting a lower exchange rate or some combination of import restrictions and export subsidies. Either choice conjured up memories of the 1930s. Adequate reserves were therefore desirable as insurance against a return to the thoroughly discredited policies of the thirties. The dollar-gold system met the demand for an increased supply of international reserves and pleased those who thought that gold by itself provided insufficient international liquidity.

The International Monetary Fund

The architects of the postwar international monetary system designed an additional stabilizing feature for the system in the form of the International Monetary Fund. The IMF was designed to be the central bank of the central banks, or the monetary authorities' monetary authority. Assigned to headquarters in Washington, D.C., in deference to the dominant position of the United States in international finance, the IMF was supposed to increase the liquidity of the international monetary system by lending reserves to countries that were experiencing temporary pressures toward depreciation. The IMF would tide them over until the emergency had passed and they could again begin earning through exports enough foreign exchange to pay for their imports. The loans were made out of sums deposited with the IMF for that purpose by member countries, but principally by the United States. The loans were for short periods and were intended to cover only temporary exchange shortages. A nation was expected to get its affairs in order during this period of grace, and the IMF was not above nagging when it thought a government might be abusing the grace it had received.

What Is "Irresponsible"?

Let's pause for breath. You can test your comprehension at this point by thinking about ways in which such grace could be abused. To begin with, we know that a country runs into trouble when it can't export enough IOUs (that is, borrow enough) to make up the difference between its merchandise and service exports and everything it's trying to import. Why might that be occurring?

A government could be purchasing goods from abroad in blithe disregard of its eventual ability to produce enough goods to pay for them. It could be doing that to build up its military strength, to promote an economic development program, or in response to any of the innumerable pressures toward increased expenditures experienced by governments subject to popular will. It's analogous to a consumer on a credit binge, who prefers not to think about the relation between his future income and his coming monthly payments.

Or a government might be spending more than it's collecting in taxes and financing the deficit by adding to the money supply. This causes domestic inflation, and inflation makes foreign goods look more attractive to importers and exports less attractive to foreigners.

Both examples show a government trying to live beyond its means—that is, beyond its ability to finance current expenditures out of current taxes or domestic borrowing. And that's what the IMF would complain about when warning that its line of credit was temporary and nagging a country to set its house in order. Nagging, as you might suspect, has never been an effective tool of international diplomacy. But nagging by a banker carries a sanction: the possibility of no more credit. And without IMF credit, the country would be unable to continue living beyond its means. It would be forced to change its ways.

Or would it? The offending government sometimes responded by imposing import restrictions or interfering in other ways with the free flow of international trade, the very event the IMF was supposed to make unnecessary. Or it suddenly devalued its currency, another violation of the IMF's code of good conduct. It would announce one morning that the pound sterling (or franc, lira, escudo, peseta) would now be exchanged for $2\frac{2}{5}$ dollars rather than the $2\frac{4}{5}$ dollars offered yesterday. With this one move it could make its exports cheaper to foreigners and imports more expensive to its own citizens—*if* other countries did not respond by devaluing their own currencies proportionately. This last possibility was the one that made the IMF nervous. Devaluations to promote exports and curtail imports were reminiscent of the 1930s. Moreover, they broke the link among currencies whose maintenance was the primary goal of the entire system. A wave of devaluations, or even the fear of a wave of devaluations, would introduce all the uncertainties of freely fluctuating rates. They would upset the planning of exporters and importers, encourage purely speculative purchases and sales, and generally interfere with the development of stable patterns of trade and specialization. What could be done?

The Best Laid Schemes

The inevitability of *some* devaluations and revaluations (remember that the term *revaluation* is reserved for *upward* revaluations) was generally recognized. The rules of the IMF therefore provided for limited exchange-rate adjustments, after consultation with the IMF, when the international value of a country's currency was seriously out of line with its domestic value. And this procedure, the Bretton Woods conferees hoped, would correct the excessive rigidity of the old gold standard. The new system was built to bend so that it would not break.

But the system never worked as it had been designed to do. The tendency for currencies to appreciate or depreciate away from the official rates proved the rule rather than the exception in the quarter century after World War II. Economic development moved in many different directions, at vastly different speeds, and with diverse and unpredictable effects on production and price levels. Governments were simply not willing to let their domestic policies be dictated by the need to maintain a fixed rate of exchange between their currency, the dollar, and the other currencies pegged to the dollar. The flexibility of the new system still wasn't sufficient, because the world itself was changing rapidly and because national governments insisted upon far more freedom to maneuver than most observers had anticipated.

England probably tried harder than any other nation to follow the rules of international responsibility. She wanted the pound sterling to be a sound currency and not one that fluctuated in value or displayed a persistent tendency to depreciate. And so England pursued contractionary monetary and fiscal policies whenever the pound started to depreciate because Britons were trying to purchase abroad more than they were selling. The results, in the opinion of critical observers, were "stop-and-go policies" that disrupted domestic production but could not prevent depreciation of the pound. Evidence mounted steadily that stop-and-go policies designed to secure exchange rate stability reduced real incomes, added to unemployment, slowed down economic growth, aggravated social conflicts of interest, and ultimately failed to prevent domestic inflation.

Recall the "classical" mechanism by which a balance was supposed to be maintained by each nation between its credits and debits. Rising debits would reduce the domestic money supply, pull down domestic prices, stimulate exports, and discourage imports. Nations with rising credits would experience domestic inflation and its twin consequences of expanding imports and shrinking exports. In this manner a balance was supposed to be automatically maintained. There is surprisingly little evidence, however, that prices actually moved enough to achieve the desired results. The results may have appeared nonetheless because a different mechanism was at work. Nations losing international reserves would indeed experience a monetary contraction, often because the monetary authorities induced it as a way of raising interest rates and encouraging foreign deposits in domestic banks to build up international reserves. But all this was more likely, as it turned out, to cause recession than deflation. The nation would experience a fall in Q rather than P. In a recession, however, imports fall sharply. And they rise sharply in nations experiencing an

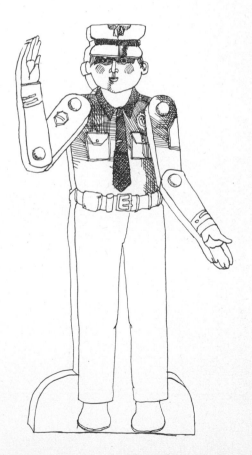

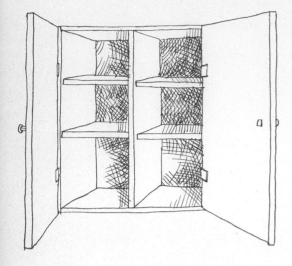

economic boom brought about by the easy money and low interest rates that an inflow of international reserves either causes or permits. So the cure largely worked, to the extent it worked at all, by giving the patient a disease (recession or inflation) worse than the one for which the cure was designed (balance of payments "disequilibrium").

On top of all this, it is not universally conceded that the new flexible-fixed exchange rate system actually succeeded in reducing uncertainty and promoting a more efficient international allocation of resources. The exchange rates were not in fact fixed, as proved by periodic devaluations and revaluations. They did not, it is true, fluctuate from week to week except within the very narrow limits permitted by the peg. But because they were not free to move regularly in response to changing conditions of supply and demand, their movements were large and abrupt when they finally did occur. The certainty of international traders and investors regarding day-to-day exchange rates was accompanied by longer term uncertainty. It is not clear that the former certainty did more to promote trade than the latter uncertainty did to inhibit and distort it. On the other hand, it isn't clear that either form of uncertainty had significant effects. The largest impact of the "flexibly fixed" exchange rate system may have been on the domestic policies of the countries that more or less faithfully paid homage to it.

THE ROLE AND FATE OF THE DOLLAR

This description and evaluation of the dollar-gold standard in the quarter century following World War II has so far slighted the principal actor in the drama, the dollar. It was the dollar and U.S. policy that sustained the Bretton Woods system in its early years and finally brought about its disintegration in 1971. The international monetary system at this writing and the direction of its probable evolution can best be understood by looking at the history of the dollar as the world's reserve currency.

The "Dollar Shortage"

A nation obviously cannot build up and hold dollar reserves unless it finds ways to acquire dollars. How *did* the countries on the dollar-gold standard acquire supplies of dollars after 1945? Since dollars originate in the United States, they can only be obtained through direct or indirect transactions with the United States. Let's review the kinds of transactions that supply dollars to the rest of the world.

United States imports are one. But U.S. exports exceeded imports in every year from 1946 to 1970 by amounts ranging from $310 million in 1959 to $11.6 billion in the reconstruction year of 1947. And exports use

up the dollars that our imports supply. So the exchange of merchandise and services made a negative net contribution toward supplying the world with dollar reserves.

Another source of dollars was U.S. government grants, pension payments, private gifts, and other "unilateral transfers." From 1946 to 1970 the annual total of such transfers never fell below $2.2 billion and in 1949 hit a peak of $5.6 billion. To this total can be added the expenditures made abroad by the government for military purposes. After the Korean war these expenditures climbed from $2 billion in 1952 to almost $5 billion at the end of the 1960s.

But against all this must be set the payments other countries made to the United States as a return on its foreign investments. The income-earning foreign investments of American citizens and corporations grew rapidly during the quarter century we're examining and by the late 1960s they were receiving net investment income of around $6 billion a year.

From 1946 to 1957, the net outflow of U.S. dollars from all the transactions we have mentioned was *negative*. Over $17 billion more dollars were *earned* for the United States through all these transactions than were *supplied*. This was made up by extensive foreign investment, both by the U.S. government and by private organizations and individuals, short term and long term, direct and portfolio.[1] But the net amount was not enough, from the standpoint of some critics, to provide adequate international reserves and liquidity for the nations on the gold-dollar standard. That was what lay behind much of the talk (up to 1957) about "the dollar shortage." Unable to earn enough dollars to build up their reserves to a satisfactory level, other countries found themselves quickly in a bind whenever their export earnings dipped or their import payments rose. Without a supply of dollars, monetary authorities in other countries could not maintain their currencies at the established exchange ratios. They had no choice then, unless they wanted to swallow the bitter medicine of deflation or, more probably, recession, except to impose controls on international transactions or to devalue. And either course was contrary to the intent of the system.

Not Enough Liquidity?

Some students of the problem came to the conclusion that the periodic devaluations, controls, and half-hearted attempts to take the classical "cure" which plagued the world economy after World War II could only be eliminated by finding an additional source of international liquidity. One way to do that would be to increase the price of gold. The stock of

---

1. Direct investment occurs when a U.S. company expands the capital invested in overseas operations that it controls. Portfolio investment is the purchase of securities in foreign firms that are not controlled, simply as a way of acquiring additional income-earning assets. The distinction is fuzzy at the edges.

gold, though relatively constant in physical terms, could easily be increased in value terms through a decision by the United States to raise its dollar price. If the United States had announced in the late 1940s that it would henceforth pay $70 rather than $35 for an ounce of gold, the world's stock of monetary gold would have been doubled by a stroke of the pen. It would probably have more than doubled, since the higher price would have stimulated additional gold production and persuaded private holders to sell at least a portion of their hoards to the monetary authorities.

Or Not Enough Self-Discipline?

Why wasn't this recommendation adopted? The primary reason was probably the belief that a shortage of liquidity was not the actual problem. Particular countries were chronically running out of reserves because they were unwilling to discipline themselves and live within their means. There was no dollar shortage; there was only a widespread desire by countries to spend more than they earned. An increase in the overall supply of reserves would have alleviated their problems only temporarily and given them an excuse to continue on their undisciplined courses. The danger of any rise in the price of gold was the additional latitude and incentive it provided for inflation. The same reasoning was applied to the proposal put forward in the 1950s that the IMF act as a genuine central bank and create new international reserves on its own credit, much as the Fed creates reserves for commercial banks in the United States. The objections to these proposals go to the heart of the perplexing issue that has dogged our steps throughout these past two chapters. Let's deal with it through a series of questions.

The Fundamental Questions

1. When a government incurs a budget deficit, is it doing so to stimulate output and employment? Or is it doing so because it cannot or will not collect the taxes required to support its expenditures?

2. Does the deficit stimulate real output, or does it pull up the price level? If it does both, when does it do which? Are the effects even separable? If they're separable in principle, are they separable in actual practice? Do we know enough to be able to cut off stimulus after it has had its major effect on output and employment, and before it starts to cause inflation? Is it possible, given institutional and political realities, that fiscal or monetary stimulus is regularly required for "full" employment *and* that it inevitably causes some inflation?

3. If the last question is answered affirmatively, a critical question arises: What is the desirable tradeoff between high employment and price stability? How much of one ought to be sacrificed for the sake of the other?

SHORTAGES OF MONEY

Complaints about a shortage of money go as far back into history as commerce itself. Seventeenth and eighteenth century thinking about the sources of national prosperity frequently focused on the importance of an ample money supply and ways to secure it. An obsession with money was perhaps the chief characteristic of economics in the "age of mercantilism." One of the American colonists' objections to British economic policy was its alleged tendency to drain specie from the colonies and leave them with an inadequate money supply. William Jennings Bryan campaigned for president in the 1890s proclaiming, "You shall not crucify mankind upon a cross of gold"; he and his followers demanded the monetization of silver because they wanted a larger supply of money.

Those whose livelihood depends upon their ability to sell goods for money are understandably tempted to identify hard times with a shortage of money. But a shortage can always be eliminated, as we saw in chapter 2, by an increase in price. Why weren't shortages of money handled in this way?

The problem is that the price of money is its general purchasing power. An increase in the price of money is therefore a fall in the general price level. And to many people that was the problem, not the solution. They did not want to see the prices of the goods they sold fall. Falling prices were to them evidence of the problem: a shortage of money.

Deflation, like inflation, redistributes income and wealth and antagonizes those it harms. But it is also associated with recession and rising unemployment if prices resist the downward push of a declining monetary demand. The "hard times" that popular thinking identified with "money shortage" were therefore not entirely a product of the merchant's obsession with monetary demand; people were correctly associating money shortage with deteriorating economic opportunities.

4. And this question leads in turn to another: how much attention should governments pay to the international repercussions of domestic policies? Is it irresponsible or is it sensible for a government to select its policies with attention to the domestic economy and let the exchange rate fend for itself? And if a government does accept an obligation to maintain the international value of its currency, to whom is that obligation owed? Is it owed to other countries? To its own exporters, importers, and investors

in foreign enterprises? To its own citizens who dislike inflation and for whom government attention to the exchange rate is a discipline against the chronic temptations of governments to follow inflationary policies?

These questions were not answered during the discussions of the 1950s and they have still not been answered conclusively to this day. The quest for an international monetary system that will enable nations to behave responsibly toward one another is still impeded by disagreements regarding the wisdom of particular domestic policies.

But the United States had its own reasons for not wanting to increase the price of gold in the 1950s and they probably tipped the scale. In the first place, an increase in the dollar price of gold is a devaluation of the dollar, at least with respect to gold. And a devaluation of the dollar seemed to be an abandonment of the U.S. commitment to maintain a constant value for the dollar in terms of gold. Nations that were holding dollars rather than gold reserves would be penalized for their participation in the dollar reserve system. The beneficiaries would be individuals hoarding gold (illegal for Americans from the 1930s until 1975, but not illegal in other countries); nations that had turned up their noses at the dollar by exchanging dollars for gold; the Soviet Union, which had a gold stock of unknown but considerable size; and the Union of South Africa, which was the world's leading gold producer. None of these was thought to be a particularly worthy recipient of the windfall gains that would accrue from an increase in the price of gold. To increase the dollar price of gold in the absence of urgent reasons seemed like raising the wages of wickedness.

From Shortage to Surplus

As so often happens, however, events outran discussion. The problem changed while everyone was still arguing about its nature and solution. In the late 1950s the U.S. gold stock began to flow overseas into the reserves of other nations and foreign holdings of dollars steadily increased. Conferences on the dollar shortage had not yet adjourned before some began to worry about the threat of a dollar surplus. What had happened?

In the first place, the nations of Western Europe and Japan had largely recovered from the devastation of World War II. They were increasingly able to do without imports from the United States and to compete with the United States for export markets.

Moreover, some of them—most notably France—resented the privileged position of the dollar in the international monetary system and saw no reason, now that they were again economically strong, why they ought to accept the dollar as an international reserve asset. Certain economic advantages accrue to a country able to get its currency accepted as an international reserve asset. In effect it is able to purchase goods from abroad on credit at low or even zero interest rates. The exporting nation holds the payment received as a reserve instead of using it to claim in turn commodities and services from the importing nation.

There was a great deal of American resentment against France when the French monetary authorities under de Gaulle began purchasing gold from the United States with the dollars they acquired. But France had a special incentive to redeem dollars in gold: some of those dollars had been acquired through the purchase by U.S. corporations of controlling interests in French firms. The French resented that and doubly resented the suggestion that they should themselves finance the takeovers by agreeing to hold the dollars spent for the purchase of their own corporations.

Whatever the root causes, the mounting dollar "surplus" reflected an attempt on the part of the United States to import more from other nations than we were exporting to them. Our merchandise and service exports continued to exceed imports until 1971, and our net income from foreign investments continued to grow; but the margin was not large enough to cover net new foreign investment by the United States (imports of securities) plus the total of our foreign grants and overseas military expenditures. And so the dollar came to be viewed as an *overvalued* currency. This means that the quantity of dollars demanded at existing rates of exchange fell short of the quantity we were supplying in the absence of continuing intervention by monetary authorities to shore up the demand.

The Unique Status of the Dollar

Other countries in such a situation could and did devalue their currencies to make their exports temporarily more attractive to others and imports less attractive to their own citizens. But that wasn't a readily available option for the United States, because we did not control the rate of exchange between the dollar and other currencies. The dollar was pegged only to gold; the rate at which it exchanged *for other currencies* was determined by the rate at which those currencies were pegged by their governments to the dollar. All we could have done, then, was devalue the dollar relative to gold. Unless this prompted other countries to revalue their currencies with respect to the dollar, such a devaluation would have no effect. One of the costs associated with being the issuer of a reserve currency is that the issuing nation gives up a large measure of control over the rate at which its currency will exchange for others.

If the dollar was overvalued, some other currencies had to be undervalued. Why weren't the monetary authorities in those countries willing to revalue their currencies upward and thus accomplish the dollar devaluation we could not effect on our own? Part of the answer is contained in the politics of protection discussed in the last chapter. The undervaluation of the German mark and the Japanese yen meant that producers in these countries had a competitive advantage in selling their goods abroad. It also

meant that German and Japanese consumers paid higher prices for the goods they imported, but the voice of consumers is rarely as influential as that of producers in shaping a government's international trade policy. The German and Japanese governments "cooperated" diligently to maintain the value of the dollar by accumulating and holding short-term claims against the United States. Thus they kept their own currencies undervalued and maintained their competitive advantage in exports.

With the burden of adjusting to the "disequilibrium" thus thrown back upon the United States, we tried a variety of measures to reduce the flow of dollars abroad. At one time or another we raised the cost to American tourists of bringing back foreign merchandise, placed a tax on borrowing by foreign corporations in the United States, restricted foreign lending by U.S. banks, imposed first voluntary and later mandatory controls on direct investment abroad by U.S. corporations, recalled the dependents of American servicemen stationed overseas, threatened to impose quotas unless particular countries "voluntarily" curtailed their exports to us, and in a variety of smaller ways tried to discourage imports and encourage exports. Meanwhile we began lecturing other nations on their obligation to assume a fair share of the expenditures we were making abroad for military security in Europe and economic development in poor countries.

Away from Gold

In 1968, with the outward flow of dollars continuing, we announced to the world that we would henceforth redeem dollars in gold *only* for foreign central banks. The real significance of this declaration was its clear implication that our continued readiness to redeem dollars for central banks depended on their sparing use of the privilege. So a "two-tier" market for gold was officially established. The United States bought from and sold (very little!) gold to central banks at $35, and private purchasers paid whatever supply and demand might dictate. The subsequent rise in the free market price of gold, to almost $200 an ounce at one point, excited speculators, grabbed headlines, displeased jewelers, delighted gold producers and owners of stock in gold companies, troubled dentists and their patients, and confirmed prophecies of all those who had said that gold was grossly undervalued at $35 an ounce. But it did not seriously affect the world monetary system. The world monetary system had moved farther from any meaningful kind of gold standard than most people suspected. Gold was on its way to becoming just another good.

In August of 1971, by presidential decree, the Treasury Department suspended "temporarily" the convertibility of dollars into gold "except in amounts and conditions determined to be in the interest of monetary stability, and in the best interests of the United States." The world was officially off the dollar-gold standard. The president's speech announcing this policy indicated that it was a response to "speculators" who were "attacking" the dollar. But that's a lot like saying that a divorce is caused by the judge who enters the decree. The plain fact was that the United States no longer wished to live with the situation in which it found itself.

THE FUTURE OF THE INTERNATIONAL MONETARY SYSTEM

If the world was off the dollar-gold standard after 1971, what standard was it on? For awhile after the suspension of the dollar's convertibility into gold, no one was quite sure. Foreign countries continued to peg their currencies to the dollar at the previous rates. But they now knew that if these rates resulted in a net inflow of dollars, they could not count on the United States to convert the dollars into gold. Two of their options were to continue pegging their currencies at the old rate and accumulate undesired dollar balances that were likely to decline in value, or to revalue their currencies by paying less for dollars, thus making their own goods more expensive and American goods less expensive.

Floating Exchange Rates

There was a third option. The monetary authorities in those countries could simply stop purchasing dollars. When their citizens acquired dollars in international exchange, they would have to turn elsewhere than to the central bank in order to turn those dollars into domestic currency. By taking that option, monetary authorities would give up the attempt to peg the rate of exchange between their currencies and the dollar, and allow it to find its own level in the market. The ideal of fixed exchange rates yields to a system of *free* or *flexible* or *floating* exchange rates. Apparently any label will do as long as it begins with the letter *f*, but *floating* has come to be the preferred term. It has also since 1971 come to be the preferred option.

When the United States suspended the convertibility of the dollar and other countries more or less reluctantly gave up the effort to maintain an established rate of exchange between their currencies and the dollar, some experts announced the breakdown of the international monetary system and the appearance of a world monetary crisis. They called for emergency conferences to create a new system that would restore order before the flow of trade and exchange broke down in chaos.

But other experts rejoiced in the disappearance of the old system. The first group's crisis was the second group's solution. Those who held the

latter view had long argued that the real problems in the international monetary system arose from that system itself and specifically from the attempt to maintain fixed exchange rates. The chronic balance-of-payments deficits and surpluses that worried so many governments were simply the consequence of their refusal to let exchange rates float with changing conditions of supply and demand. It was not a problem to be managed but a problem arising out of the attempt to manage. In international economics, as we commented earlier, solutions are often problems and problems are solutions, depending upon one's perspective and objectives.

Prior to 1971 there was extensive support among academic economists for a movement toward floating exchange rates. These economists argued that government attempts to fix the rates had demonstrably failed. Such attempts did not in fact make it easier for international traders and investors to predict the future. On the contrary, as price controls of any sort inevitably do, they led governments into all sorts of trade and exchange restrictions. And they did not subject domestic policy to any "balance of payments discipline," because countries were always willing to devalue anyway when attention to the balance of payments might threaten cherished domestic objectives. In short, fixed exchange rates offered the worst of all possible worlds: increased uncertainty in the name of greater stability, restrictions on trade for the sake of free trade, and a "discipline" that inhibited flexibility and allowed irresponsibility.

Outside of academic circles, however, and especially among the economists working for central banks, floating exchange rates were regarded as unworkable if desirable and undesirable even if workable. They would indeed increase uncertainty for foreign traders and investors, it was argued. But they would also create additional uncertainty for domestic producers and investors because a change in exchange rates could quickly and radically change the potential profitability of industries producing exports or goods that competed with imports. Moreover, governments were not likely to remain passive when a sudden depreciation in the currency of a major trading country led to an unexpected surge of imports or threatened established export markets. They were far more likely to retaliate with trade and exchange controls that would eventually lead to a breakdown of international exchange similar to the one that occurred in in the 1930s. And though the discipline of the balance of payments had not compelled governments to pursue noninflationary policies, their fiscal and monetary policies had generally been less expansionary and inflationary than they would have been under a system where floating exchange rates removed any reason to be concerned with the balance of payments.

It may be worth observing that the proponents of fixed rates often spoke about the "academic" (that is, unrealistic) nature of the floating rate proposals offered from the ivory tower vantage point of a university setting.

THE "PETRODOLLAR CRISIS"

There are fads and fashions in popular crises, and 1975 was a banner year for the "petrodollar crisis." *Petrodollar* was the new word coined in 1974 for the monetary payments made by oil-importing countries to the members of the Organization of Petroleum Exporting Countries. Why were petrodollars an object of concern?

The export earnings of OPEC countries more than quadrupled from 1973 to 1974 because of higher oil prices. There was obviously no way in which these countries, most of them with quite small populations, could increase their imports proportionately in a short period of time. That meant they were going to accumulate large and growing stocks of such monetary assets as marks, pounds, yen, francs, gold, and dollars, which were the preferred medium of exchange for oil imports. The Banque de Bruxelles estimated, for example, that Saudi Arabia and Iran collectively increased their oil revenues from $8.8 billion in 1973 to $47.6 billion in 1974. But their combined international spending in 1974 was only $16.1 billion. (The data were reported in the *Wall Street Journal* of December 30, 1974.) The total OPEC surplus for 1974 was estimated at $60 billion. What was going to happen to that surplus or to the "overhang of petrodollars" as some ominously called it?

Well, what *could* happen? The OPEC countries will presumably want to loan their surplus. But to whom, on what terms, and for what purposes? Financial transactions by OPEC countries have so far been veiled in just enough secrecy to aggravate the anxiety of those who fear that petrodollars will soon disrupt the whole international monetary system. One fear is that the substantial funds deposited in international banks (and subsequently loaned to borrowers) might be recalled suddenly. Banks cannot pay interest on deposits unless they can lend on the basis of those deposits. But they cannot grant borrowers the long-term loans they want if OPEC countries insist that their deposits always be available on short notice.

One solution is for potential borrowers of the surplus to seduce OPEC countries into long-term commitments by offering a higher rate of return. That has clearly been happening. But long-term investments encounter another problem: the suspicion of foreign investment. Americans for some reason don't like the idea of Arabs buying (that is, investing in) Miami hotels, Iowa farms, or Lockheed Aircraft, and Germans are upset to learn that Kuwait has purchased a piece of Daimler-Benz, the manufacturer of Mercedes automobiles.

There is a fine irony in the thought of Saudi Arabian owners of

American hotels worrying about shrinking profit margins caused
by rising utility bills that result from the higher price of Arab oil,
or of Kuwaiti investors lamenting Daimler-Benz losses attributable to the reduced demand for automobiles brought about by
rising gasoline prices.

We might do well to remember that international investment
creates international communities of interest. That can't be altogether bad in a world threatened by international suspicion and
hostility. What better way is there to persuade the Arab nations
to understand and sympathize with our interests than to have
them purchase a large piece of those interests?

And the academic economists occasionally noted that the fixed rate system
provided a lot of gainful employment for central bank economists and
required them to attend frequent conferences in such pleasant or exotic
places as Geneva and Nairobi.

Some of the evidence is now in. Floating rates *do* work. The majority of
the world's countries, however, do not let their currencies float freely. They
try to keep them more or less closely related to some other, major currency.
The dollar is only one such currency; the pound sterling, the French franc,
and the mark have their own set of satellite currencies. Even the major currencies are not always allowed to float freely. Governments intervene to
practice what has come to be called a "dirty float" and do not keep their
hands off to achieve a "clean float." Don't conclude that "dirty" necessarily
means naughty. The new head of the International Monetary Fund, presumably a spokesman for virtue, told an IMF conference in Nairobi in
September of 1973 that he welcomed central bank intervention in currency
markets as a way of reducing "gyrations" and pushing currencies toward
their true "underlying value."

Where Are We Headed?

How can the beginning student of economics hope to decide which is
the best monetary system for the world when the experts disagree? Perhaps
it isn't that important to decide. This chapter has tried to show that events
have their own logic in international economics. We shall nonetheless
attempt a concluding summary and a timorous glance into the future.

Gold is gone as *the* international reserve asset. It will always have value
because it has other uses than as a medium of exchange. And as long as
people "believe in gold" or think of it as the safest investment in a period
of inflation or uncertainty, the demand for it and consequently its price

FOREIGN EXCHANGE RATES IN RECENT YEARS

(In cents per unit of foreign currency)

Period	Australia (dollar)	Austria (schilling)	Belgium (franc)	Canada (dollar)	Denmark (krone)	France (franc)	Germany (Deutsche mark)	India (rupee)	Ireland (pound)	Italy (lira)	Japan (yen)
1971	113.61	4.0009	2.0598	99.021	13.508	18.148	28.768	13.338	244.42	.16174	.28779
1972	119.23	4.3228	2.2716	100.937	14.384	19.825	31.364	13.246	250.08	.17132	.32995
1973	141.94	5.1649	2.5761	99.977	16.603	22.536	37.758	12.071	245.10	.17192	.36915
1974	143.89	5.3564	2.5713	102.257	16.442	20.805	38.723	12.460	234.03	.15372	.34302
1974—Jan	148.23	4.8318	2.3329	100.859	14.981	19.905	35.529	11.854	222.40	.15433	.33559
Feb	148.50	5.0022	2.4358	102.398	15.570	20.187	36.844	12.131	227.49	.15275	.34367
Mar	148.55	5.1605	2.5040	102.877	16.031	20.742	38.211	12.415	234.06	.15687	.35454
Apr	148.41	5.3345	2.5686	103.356	16.496	20.541	39.594	12.711	238.86	.15720	.36001
May	148.44	5.5655	2.6559	103.916	17.012	20.540	40.635	12.841	241.37	.15808	.35847
June	148.34	5.5085	2.6366	103.481	16.754	20.408	39.603	12.735	239.02	.15379	.35340
July	147.99	5.4973	2.6378	102.424	16.858	20.984	39.174	12.759	238.96	.15522	.34372
Aug	148.24	5.3909	2.5815	102.053	16.547	20.912	38.197	12.525	234.56	.15269	.33082
Sept	144.87	5.2975	2.5364	101.384	16.111	20.831	37.580	12.316	231.65	.15103	.33439
Oct	130.92	5.4068	2.5939	101.727	16.592	21.131	38.571	12.416	233.30	.14992	.33404
Nov	131.10	5.5511	2.6529	101.280	16.997	21.384	39.836	12.397	232.50	.14996	.33325
Dec	131.72	5.7176	2.7158	101.192	17.315	22.109	40.816	12.352	232.94	.15179	.33288

Period	Malaysia (dollar)	Mexico (peso)	Netherlands (guilder)	New Zealand (dollar)	Norway (krone)	Portugal (escudo)	South Africa (rand)	Spain (peseta)	Sweden (krona)	Switzerland (franc)	United Kingdom (pound)
1971	32.989	8.0056	28.650	113.71	14.205	3.5456	140.29	1.4383	19.592	24.325	244.42
1972	35.610	8.0000	31.153	119.35	15.180	3.7023	129.43	1.5559	21.022	26.193	250.08
1973	40.988	8.0000	35.977	136.04	17.406	4.1080	143.88	1.7178	22.970	31.700	245.10
1974	41.682	8.0000	37.267	140.02	18.119	3.9506	146.98	1.7337	22.563	33.688	234.03
1974—Jan	40.094	8.0000	34.009	139.08	16.739	3.7195	148.66	1.7205	20.781	29.727	222.40
Feb	40.489	8.0000	35.349	140.31	17.351	3.8567	148.76	1.6933	21.373	31.494	227.49
Mar	41.152	8.0000	36.354	143.40	17.734	3.9519	148.88	1.6927	21.915	32.490	234.06
Apr	41.959	8.0000	37.416	145.12	18.170	4.0232	148.85	1.7080	22.730	33.044	238.86
May	42.155	8.0000	38.509	146.07	18.771	4.1036	148.78	1.7409	23.388	34.288	241.37
June	41.586	8.0000	37.757	145.29	18.410	4.0160	148.86	1.7450	22.885	33.449	239.02
July	41.471	8.0000	38.043	145.15	18.519	3.9886	149.73	1.7525	22.861	33.739	238.96
Aug	42.780	8.0000	37.419	143.73	18.246	3.9277	146.83	1.7466	22.597	33.509	234.56
Sept	41.443	8.0000	36.870	139.64	17.993	3.8565	142.69	1.7339	22.333	33.371	231.65
Oct	41.560	8.0000	37.639	129.95	18.165	3.9246	142.75	1.7422	22.683	34.528	233.29
Nov	43.075	8.0000	38.438	130.42	18.404	3.9911	143.88	1.7522	23.175	36.384	232.52
Dec	42.431	8.0000	39.331	130.56	18.873	4.0400	144.70	1.7716	23.897	38.442	232.94

Source: *Federal Reserve Bulletin*

may remain near current levels. (The policy of South Africa toward gold production will have a lot to do with the future price of gold.) And gold will probably continue to serve as a benchmark of some sort in international exchange. The values of at least some assets will continue to be stated in a particular weight of gold even though the assets are not freely convertible into gold. But the world will not return to a real gold standard in which the value of currencies is maintained by keeping them directly or indirectly convertible into gold.

Neither are we likely to see a return to the dollar-gold standard or to a system where any single currency functions as the dominant medium of international exchange, principal reserve asset, universal unit of international accounting, and pivot to which other currencies are pegged. Countries whose currencies might be candidates for the role will likely decline such an extensive honor to avoid the limitations that the role imposes on independent policy formation. And other countries will be reluctant to concede the honor, because they regard it more as a privilege than a burden.

The Social Character of Money

What kind of system might evolve, then, to provide links between separate monetary systems and adequate international liquidity? The safest prediction is that it will indeed evolve, and not be created by a conference either of world bankers or academic economists. For money is a social phenomenon, not just an artifact of commercial banks, monetary authorities, and financial experts. The indispensable prerequisite for an international money is that it be almost universally accepted throughout the world as a medium of exchange. What gives money universal acceptability? Nothing other than the fact that it is universally accepted! Acceptability requires use, in other words, and use presupposes acceptability. This isn't arguing in a circle. It is simply taking note of the fact that nothing has ever come to function successfully as money except by coming gradually to be used and accepted in a particular society. Social use and not legal declarations creates a monetary system. Consider the easygoing acceptance of Canadian money in northern border areas of the United States. Or ask yourself how checking accounts came to be the major component of the money supply in this country.

This analysis rules out, at least for the foreseeable future, a single world currency used in all countries alike. That's the system used to facilitate "international" exchange among the fifty states. But the social foundation for such a reform does not exist throughout the world. Even Canada and the United States have separate (though strikingly similar) currencies, evidence that Canadians and Canadian interests are at least somewhat different from the people and interests to the south. Separate currencies reflect both a measure of social distance and a determination to preserve that distance. The United States could easily supply a stock of money adequate for all of North America. But Canadians and Mexicans would see in such a move evidence of a U.S. desire to take them over and destroy their separate identities. A single monetary system promotes economic integration. The governments of Canada and Mexico would probably be reluctant to sacrifice the additional bit of independence that the *absence* of a common money provides.

Special Drawing Rights

The future of SDRs should be viewed in this light. SDR stands for Special Drawing Rights on the International Monetary Fund, sometimes referred to as "paper gold." We mentioned earlier, in discussing the international demand for liquidity, the proposal that the IMF create international money in the way that national central banks create domestic money. There is no logical reason why this could not be done. And SDRs currently exist, in quite limited quantities. They are credits that nations have with the IMF that can be transferred to other nations in settlement of international claims. But the total value of SDRs is fairly small at the present time and cannot be expanded in the absence of international agreement on the method of expansion. Anything more than a limited agreement for a limited expansion of SDRs will be difficult to achieve. If the IMF functions successfully in the years ahead and gains increasing trust and cooperation from member nations, it will increasingly be regarded as "everybody's" central bank and may be authorized to issue large quantities of additional SDRs. But for the IMF to function successfully and acquire that kind of trust and cooperation, it will first have to be viewed as "everybody's" central bank and not as the creature of the developed Western nations or of the United States. That in turn presupposes an evolution toward internationalist attitudes and sentiment far beyond what we currently observe.

No gold standard. No dollar or sterling standard. No SDR standard. No single currency for the world. Toward what system *are* we likely to move, then? Probably toward one not very different from the system which evolved after 1971. The rates at which currencies exchange for one another will be set by underlying forces of supply and demand with regular nudges in this direction or that from the monetary authorities and an occasional sharp jolt. Now that the pins have fallen out of the old fixed exchange rate system, it will be extraordinarily difficult to reconstruct it or build a new one. Governments have come to prize their freedom to cut the cloth of domestic economic policy to the pattern they choose; the system of fixed exchange rates required that governments tailor domestic policy to fit the shape of the international economy. That may or may not have been a valuable discipline; but external discipline is no more appreciated by governments than it is by college students.

A second reason why we should not expect to see the reemergence of a fixed exchange rate system is that its construction would require extensive international cooperation. Sufficiently close cooperation among the nations of the world is unlikely at the present time. Not only are there conflicting interests that would have to be resolved before a working agreement could be reached; there is also no consensus on what went wrong with the old system and what should have or even could have been done to save it. The

SDRs: SPECIAL DRAWING RIGHTS

The International Monetary Fund created Special Drawing Rights (SDRs) in 1969 as a new international reserve asset that the IMF could issue whenever it thought a growth in global reserves was desirable. Countries were obligated to supply their own currencies, up to a certain limit, in return for SDRs tendered by other countries—although this requirement was only imposed on countries with strong reserve positions. The IMF intended to create SDRs and credit them to the account of a country with a serious reserve shortage; that country would then use them to obtain a defined amount of currency from other participating countries. By imposing *obligations* to accept SDRs, the IMF itself designated them as inferior reserve assets.

What is the value of one SDR? It was set originally at the dollar's par value in gold: 1 SDR = 1 dollar = $\frac{1}{35}$ ounce of gold. But the United States subsequently devalued the dollar relative to gold, and 1 SDR rose to $1.08571; 1 SDR rose to $1.20635 with the second devaluation of the dollar.

Since July 1974, the value of the SDR has rested on a weighted average of the exchange rates of 16 IMF member countries. The weights vary from 33% for the U.S. dollar and 12.5% for the German mark down to 1% each for the Austrian schilling and South African rand. That makes the SDR a highly stable reserve asset. Its value will rise or fall roughly in proportion to the average rise or fall in the prices of the principal currencies for which it exchanges. It was this stability that prompted OPEC nations in 1975 to shift from the dollar to the SDR in quoting oil prices.

During the single month of February 1975, the average daily value of the SDR fluctuated between $1.231342 and $1.2613187. That's a $2\frac{1}{2}$% variation within just a few weeks and the SDR doesn't seem to be very stable. But think about it again. Was it the SDR or the dollar that was fluctuating in value? If the yardstick is continually varying in length, the item being measured will *seem* to change its length.

Since the SDR's value is now a weighted average of the value of the principal international currencies against which SDRs exchange, it makes more sense to think of the SDR as the yardstick and assign the variation to the dollar. There is, of course, no absolute standard of value in economics. But SDRs may be the most satisfactory yardstick we have. They are certainly more satisfactory than gold, whose purchasing power in terms of national currencies or real goods has varied enormously in recent years. The notion that gold is *the* standard is a powerful prejudice that is difficult to shake, despite the fact that the purchasing power of gold can easily be manipulated by the governments of the Soviet Union and South Africa.

United States has blamed the nations that deliberately maintained under-valued currencies, discriminated against our exports, and refused in general to shoulder their share of the world's burdens. Other nations have blamed the United States for trying to hang on to the benefits of having the world's key reserve currency without being willing to accept the costs. Those costs are primarily the acceptance of fiscal and monetary restraint to staunch an outward flow of international reserves even when such restraint threatens to reduce domestic output and employment.

Both criticisms overlook a major dilemma confronting any reserve currency. There is a slippery relationship between its supply and its demand. Supply and demand analysis would yield few useful predictions if changes in the supply of some commodity regularly triggered changes in the demand for it. But that happens with reserve currencies. The United States supplied dollars to the world by making expenditures abroad. Those dollars became international reserves insofar as countries retained some portion of the expenditures in the form of short-term claims on the United States. But by the conventional measure, this is a *deficit* in the U.S. balance of payments. And deficits are signs of economic weakness. Here is the paradox: The dollar is in strong demand when it is regarded as sound. An increased supply of dollars to meet a strong demand is interpreted, however, as a sign of weakness, and reduces the foreign demand to hold dollars. Perhaps this is why the dollar shortage turned so suddenly to a dollar surplus in the late fifties. The line between shortage and surplus may be a razor's edge on which a currency can only be balanced by skilled and strenuous acrobatics.

International Policies in National Contexts

If the requisite skill coupled with the requisite will to recreate and maintain a world system of fixed exchange rates does not exist, a system of floating rates, either dirty or clean, is the alternative. We have already noted the alleged advantage of such a system: It puts the burden of adjustment to changing international trade patterns upon international exchange rates, thereby insulates the domestic economy from the effects of international disturbances, and enables domestic policymakers to ignore the balance of payments. That sounds good, but it may be neither wholly true nor wholly a blessing.

A change in a country's foreign exchange rate *does* affect the domestic economy. A depreciation, for example, makes imports more expensive and so drives up the prices people must pay. It also increases the foreign demand for exports, which pulls up prices and puts additional upward pressure on the domestic price level. Since depreciation is usually the consequence of *prior* inflation, the fact that it causes *further* inflation should at least be grounds for caution. If prices were as flexible downward as they are upward, the inflationary pressures in the countries with depreciating currencies might be countered by deflationary pressures in the countries whose currencies are appreciating. But if most prices are strongly resistant to downward pressure, as many insist they are, all relative price adjustments must be upward adjustments. Floating exchange rates could then be a system for the international transmission of inflation. To what extent have floating exchange rates been responsible for the worldwide inflation of the past few years? Some critics have assigned them a major share of the blame.

In addition to the inflationary threat they pose, they create substantial price uncertainty for exporting industries and industries that compete extensively with imports. This increases investor and producer uncertainty and may aggravate income and employment instability. An American firm that had just invested heavily in a new bicycle-manufacturing plant could be badly hurt by a sudden depreciation of the pound that made British bicycles temporarily much cheaper than its own. If this starts to occur, will nations be willing to let the international economy run itself? Or will they once again pick up the weapons of import restrictions, export subsidies, and controls on capital movements? The use of these weapons reduces global welfare by preventing resources from being allocated in accord with comparative advantage. But neither the principle of comparative advantage nor the concept of global welfare has ever won a national election. The international economy, and consequently the international monetary system, will continue to be subservient to national economic goals as long as nationalism controls the policies of governments.

Perhaps the difficult questions are finally not questions of the best institutional arrangements for ordering an international economic system. These may be mere technical questions that reasonably intelligent and informed people could answer to almost everyone's satisfaction *if* national governments stopped pursuing domestic policies that interfere with *any* international order. This last statement doesn't necessarily imply that national governments are villainous. But the overriding fact is that international policies are developed in the context of national economic policies. Governments today have programs by means of which they try to control economic growth, fluctuations in production, unemployment, price levels, and the distribution of income. And the realities of democratic politics decree that those programs take precedence over the maintenance of a stable international economic system. Four passengers in a single automobile will never agree on the best way to get where they're going if they disagree about where they ought to be going.

Perhaps when we acquire a better understanding of the effects of fiscal

EURO-DOLLARS AND OTHER STRANGE BEASTS

Some of the most complex issues in international monetary economics are issues created by the use of bank deposits denominated in foreign currencies. No one is quite sure about the size of these deposits, the way in which they expand or shrink, or how they can be controlled in the interest of domestic and international monetary stability.

Suppose that a German citizen purchased a painting by Jasper Johns from a New York dealer and paid for it with a check for 180,000 marks drawn on a Hamburg bank. If the dealer then deposited the check in First National City Bank, his balance would rise by about $75,000. (The exchange rate is assumed to be 2.4 marks to the dollar.) First National could offset the $75,000 increase in its liabilities if it sold the marks for that amount of dollars.

But suppose that the dealer prefers to hold marks because he thinks marks are less likely to depreciate than dollars. And he persuades First National to maintain its liability to him *in marks.* He would then be the owner of a checking account denominated in a foreign currency. He could spend those marks by writing checks against that account. If there are other Americans who would prefer marks to dollars, these "Americo-marks" could function as money in the United States. They would constitute a genuine addition to the stock of assets that can be used directly as a medium of exchange.

"Americo-marks" are not in fact a medium of exchange in the United States. But Euro-dollars *are* an important component of the money supply in Europe. Some of those European bank deposits denominated in dollars did not even originate in U.S. payments to Europeans. They were created by the same kind of money-creation-through-lending that we described in chapter 18. Insofar as dollar loans by European banks to Europeans are redeposited in European banks that offer dollar-denominated accounts to their customers, the only limit on the Euro-dollar "money multiplier" will be the reserve ratio the banks collectively wish to, or are required to, maintain.

The Euro-dollar is a vivid symbol of the international nature of the monetary economy and one more reminder of the dangers and difficulties inherent in managing a national economy as if it were isolated from the rest of the world.

and monetary policies and of other government techniques for influencing economic activity, we shall be in a better position to construct a satisfactory international system. But that may require a more comprehensive understanding of economic systems than the science of economics by itself can provide. Some even argue that it would require a reorientation of our basic approach to the organization of economic systems. Those are some of the issues with which we'll be wrestling in the concluding chapters of this book.

Once Over Lightly

The new international monetary system that was formulated at Bretton Woods in 1944 and that survived roughly (in both senses) until 1971 was designed to secure both flexibility and stability in international exchange and to harmonize national independence with international interdependence.

Fixed exchange rates were the goal. Other nations pegged their currencies to the dollar and the United States pegged the dollar to gold.

Divergent rates of inflation and economic growth, shifts in demand and technological change, and differences in policy targets and procedures for hitting those targets created constant pressure for exchange-rate adjustments under the Bretton Woods system. Insofar as nations altered their exchange rates, the system failed to provide stability. Insofar as they imposed restrictions on international trade or domestic production to maintain their exchange rates, the system failed to provide adequate flexibility.

The system invited extensive recriminations. The United States was blamed first for importing too little and creating a dollar shortage, then for importing too much and cheapening the principal international reserve currency. Other countries were blamed for irresponsibly trying to live beyond their means or for irresponsibly seeking competitive export advantages by maintaining undervalued currencies. Through all of this, people nonetheless found ways to expand the volume of international trade.

The system collapsed when neither the United States nor other countries could or would take steps to achieve a balance between the quantity of dollars demanded and the quantity of dollars supplied internationally. The United States severed the last official gold-dollar link in 1971 and other countries reclaimed their right to peg or not peg their currencies as they saw fit.

The system of floating exchange rates that ensued has apparently not yet introduced so much uncertainty as to create new restrictions, legal or voluntary, on trade. It has reduced the frequency of "balance of payments crises" by making nations, and especially central bankers, less anxious (or at least less vociferously anxious) about movements in exchange rates.

The system may also have contributed to the international transmission of inflation by removing an incentive for national governments to practice monetary restraint.

It will be difficult and perhaps impossible in the foreseeable future to create a new international monetary system because of the difficulties in the way of achieving consensus among national governments. But so long as international trade in goods and securities continues, and even continues to grow, a functioning international monetary system exists.

The most serious problem facing national governments today may not be the creation of an international exchange system, but the reconciliation of inconsistent domestic and international policy objectives.

QUESTIONS FOR DISCUSSION

1. Does the United States today have a single currency and a completely unified monetary system? Are exchange rates between Georgia and Alabama fixed or floating? Can you think of circumstances where money acceptable as a medium of exchange in one geographic region must be converted into another form of money (at some cost) before it can be used in other regions? How do people who travel extensively in the United States avoid both the risk of carrying large quantities of universally accepted money and the inconvenience of not having a money that is generally acceptable where they're traveling?

2. In 1860, there were about 1500 state chartered banks in the United States, each issuing its own paper money in a variety of different types. These bank notes were promises to pay specie on demand to the bearer of the note; they were therefore liabilities of the issuing banks. There was no homogeneous paper money that was accepted everywhere.

    (a) What kinds of problems would you expect to find under such a system?

    (b) Did the different regions of the country have fixed exchange rates?

    (c) Could "balance of payments deficits" occur under such a system?

    (d) Would you expect such a system to reduce or intensify interregional conflicts of interest?

3. As one way of paying for the Civil War, the federal government in 1862 began issuing non-interest-bearing notes that were not redeemable in specie. The federal government simultaneously refused to accept "greenbacks," as they came to be called, in payment of taxes.

    (a) What would you expect to occur in such a situation?

    (b) In July 1864, the New York money market was offering about $40 in gold for $100 in greenbacks. What does this imply about prices of goods in the United States at the time? If you were to ask a seller of clothing what price he was charging, how would he answer?

4. Per capita currency in circulation in the United States increased by almost 20% from 1870 to 1895. Does this prove that the claims of a money shortage made by William Jennings Bryan and his followers in the 1896 presidential campaign were mistaken?

5. A farmer plants corn in May expecting to purchase dollars in October when he harvests his crop. How does he protect himself against an unanticipated increase in the price of dollars (equals depreciation in the price of corn)? Is the same kind of protection possible for British producers of Scotch whiskey who contract to sell a certain quantity to the United States for a certain number of future dollars and want to protect themselves against a depreciation of the dollar relative to the pound?

6. If someone bought gold in 1944 at $35 an ounce and sold it in 1974 at $175 an ounce, how much "profit" did he earn? What was the annual percentage return on his investment over this period? (Table 12B will tell you approximately what interest rate equates $35 now with $175 available 30 years in the future.) Would he have done better by purchasing shares in a mutual fund that paid 8% compound interest in dividends plus appreciated value? (Hint: At 8%, a dollar 30 years from now has a present value of less than 10¢.)

7. In the late 1960s, the Fed tried to keep short-term interest rates up in order to "protect the U.S. balance of payments." How could this affect the balance of payments? The Fed simultaneously tried to keep long term interest rates low to encourage investment and economic growth. Where is the line between the short term and the long term? Can the "line" be crossed?

8. How would you expect a recession to affect a country's imports of merchandise, services, and securities?

9. Explain what Charles de Gaulle meant when he rejected U.S. complaints about French purchases of gold in the 1960s by stating that France could not be expected to finance an American takeover of French industry.

10. "Floating exchange rates free a nation to pursue the domestic policies it prefers." Is that true?

11. "Money is accepted because it's acceptable." Is that an empty platitude or an important truth?

12. How will the acceptability of SDRs be affected by the decision of OPEC governments to quote petroleum prices in SDRs rather than dollars? Will this make petroleum more expensive or less expensive to United States buyers? Explain your answer.

13. SDRs are credits created by the International Monetary Fund. How should the IMF decide how many such credits to create and to which countries' accounts they ought to be credited? Some people have suggested that since SDRs are new money, they should be given initially to the poorer countries.

Do you agree? Would this be a costless way of aiding less developed countries?

14. Is it harmful to U.S. prestige when the dollar depreciates? Why do you suppose that governments usually express more official alarm over depreciation than over appreciation of their currencies?

15. Assume that you are the manager of the German Central Bank and that you are confronted with the problem presented at the end of the section on Exchange Rates in chapter 23. The mark is undervalued relative to the dollar so that your bank is continuously acquiring additions to its gold stock and adding marks to the domestic money supply.

   (*a*) Why will this tend to cause domestic inflation?

   (*b*) What effect will the domestic inflation have on the flow of gold?

   (*c*) What steps might you take (other than revaluing the mark) to prevent the undervaluation of the mark from causing inflation?

   (*d*) If you call in the owners of the Volkswagen Corporation and ask them whether you should revalue the mark, what do you think they would say?

   (*e*) If a Chevrolet costs 4000 dollars, a Volkswagen costs 12,000 marks, and the dollar-mark exchange rate is 1 for 4, what is the Chevrolet-Volkswagen exchange rate? (What percentage of a Chevrolet will a Volkswagen purchase and how many Volkswagens will a Chevrolet purchase?) Who would gain from a revaluation of the mark? Who would lose?

   (*f*) What might the elasticities of demand for internationally traded goods have to do with your answer to the last question?

16. The governments of Lower Slobbovia and Upper Elysium each ran $5-billion budget deficits last year, which they financed by selling bonds to their central banks. Imagine that you are the IMF representative assigned to deal with each country and that they appeal to you for a loan to help them with balance-of-payments difficulties they're beginning to encounter. Construct some plausible dialogues that might ensue.

17. Every Federal Reserve note shows the name of the Federal Reserve Bank that issued it. Check the notes in the possession of members of the class to see where they were issued.

   (*a*) How did notes from outside the Federal Reserve district in which you live come into the possession of people in the class?

   (*b*) What would occur if the Federal Reserve Bank of Boston drastically curtailed its issue of Federal Reserve notes and the Bank of San Francisco substantially increased its issue while all other Reserve Banks maintained their present policies? How would you expect this to affect the distribution of Federal Reserve notes by the bank of issue? How do you think this policy would change the pattern of notes held by students in your class after a period of one year? (The little map which follows may help you make reasonable guesses.)

(c) What would occur if the monetary authorities in the United States sharply increased the rate of money production while monetary authorities in Germany sharply decreased the rate of money production? Would you expect the same consequences as in part b of this question? Why or why not?

(d) The data below show the compounded annual rates of change in the money supply of ten industrialized countries on which the Federal Reserve Bank of St. Louis publishes a quarterly scorecard.

	% change, 1st quarter 1970 to 4th quarter 1972	% change, 4th quarter 1972 to 4th quarter 1974
Belgium	10.9%	9.6%
Canada	12.5	9.3
France	12.2	11.0
Germany	12.2	5.7
Italy	21.8	18.2*
Japan	24.6	14.4
Netherlands	16.2	4.8
Switzerland	12.8	−0.9
United Kingdom	14.2	5.2*
United States	6.9	5.8

(*through 3d quarter 1974)

Those data certainly do not provide a definitive answer to part c of this question. But they do provide a license to speculate. What do they suggest to you?

(e) If U.S. monetary authorities create new money at a faster rate than Americans want to add to their money holdings, by what processes might some of that money flow to other countries? How might we manage to make use of money created in other countries if U.S. monetary authorities increased the domestic supply less rapidly than the demand was growing?

25

FISCAL AND MONETARY POLICY
The management of aggregate demand

Beginning students of economics sometimes get the impression that fluctuations in the aggregate level of economic activity could be easily controlled if we simply made up our minds to do so. Unemployment and inflation both *seem* to be consequences of inappropriate levels of aggregate demand. Since the government can change the level of aggregate demand by means of fiscal or monetary policy, it would appear that government has the power to stop inflation and reduce unemployment. Some therefore conclude that the failure to control aggregate fluctuations is evidence of the stupidity or wickedness of politicians or of the political influence wielded by reactionary special-interest groups.

THE GENIE CONCEPTION OF GOVERNMENT

"If current demand is inadequate or excessive, let the government use its powers to alter aggregate demand and bring it to the appropriate level." It sounds so simple and sensible. But it isn't necessarily sensible, because it isn't simple at all. Who knows the current level of aggregate demand, the appropriate level, and the actions that will move aggregate demand from the wrong to the right level? Who knows all the unintended side effects of such actions, and how to prevent the undesirable and bring about all the desired side effects? Who knows the length of the time lags between a fiscal or monetary policy action and its impact on spending, prices, output, and employment? And what good will it do to know if one lacks the power to compel action? In a democracy power is shared by many people with different perspectives and ideals and conflicting interests. Among these human beings who are neither omniscient, omnipotent, nor wholly impartial we must regrettably include Federal Reserve officials, members of the House and Senate, officers of the federal administration up to and including the chief executive, and even the professional economists who serve on their research staffs, function as their council of advisers, or offer outside criticism.

Solutions by Assumption

A strange thing often happens when social scientists try to construct policy proposals. They suggest a solution to problems in their area of competence and assume that problems in other areas either don't exist or can be resolved with no difficulty. A psychologist, for example, may look at the growing incidence of "mental illness," attribute it to the way children are reared in our society, and recommend new socialization patterns as the solution. But a sociologist disturbed by some of the consequences of the ways Americans rear their children will attribute our patterns of socialization to psychological problems and urge us to adjust our attitudes. The psychologist ignores the problems of social interaction and the sociologist ignores the problems of motivation and character structure.

Economic reformers make this mistake when they assume that government is a *deus ex machina:* that it need only be invoked and instructed and, like Aladdin's marvelous genie, it will faithfully do as it is told. They are assuming in such cases that the problem the political scientist wrestles with —getting governments to behave efficiently and equitably—has already been solved. This Genie Conception of government enables economists to get around the difficulties arising from the fact that political institutions are controlled by people. And that doesn't mean The People—another dangerous abstraction—but people like us, who are often ignorant and shortsighted and sometimes even guilty of defining the public interest in suspiciously self-serving ways.

No economist would construct policy proposals on the assumptions that producers and sellers put the public interest ahead of their own interests, have all the information they want, and cannot be prevented by their suppliers, employers, or customers from doing whatever they deem best. To do that would be to ignore the very questions economists try to answer. Noneconomists frequently argue today that pressing social problems like pollution should be handled through the acceptance by business firms of their "social responsibilities." It's undoubtedly true that a lot of problems would diminish or disappear if business executives always acted in the public interest. But will they *want to,* will they *know how to,* and will they *be able to?* Economists realize that to assume an affirmative answer in each case is to ignore the problems of the economic order. We must be careful not to adopt in the political sphere a conception of human interests and capabilities that we would recognize as absurd if adopted in the economic sphere. In short, we must be on our guard throughout this chapter against the Genie Conception of government.

FISCAL AND MONETARY POLICY IN USE

The preceding chapters have introduced you to two tools for the management of aggregate demand: fiscal policy and monetary policy. How much difference does it make which one is chosen? Is one more effective than the other? Do they have different side effects that make one a more appropriate tool than the other? Or does it depend on the circumstances? Is there a proper mix of the two or different mixes appropriate for different circumstances? While there is a considerable consensus among economists today on these questions, major areas of disagreement still remain. More importantly, perhaps, the debate between advocates of fiscal policy and advocates of monetary policy has been joined by those who believe that either policy is likely to be too much and by a growing number who find both together inadequate. The making of stabilization policy is still far from a settled science.

The Rise of Eclecticism

It has only been within the last decade that monetary policy has achieved anything like equal status with fiscal policy in the thinking of economists. The impotence of monetary policy as a means of restoring prosperity seemed to many to have been adequately demonstrated in the Great Depression when the Fed relaxed the controls over money creation but could not stir a revival of bank lending and private spending. The power of fiscal policy had seemingly been just as clearly demonstrated by the "fiscal experiment" of 1940–44. When the urgencies of war finally overcame concern for a balanced budget and the federal government began spending profusely, private spending also revived. For reasons that are not altogether clear, private consumption and investment were able to take up the slack when government expenditures fell sharply after the war.

Monetary policy inched its way back into esteem through a concurrence of events that we've already mentioned. One was the unexpected mildness of recessions in the postwar period and the persistence of inflation. Inflation was a problem against which monetary policy was *not* considered powerless and on which the monetary managers were able to practice their stabilization skills. Related to this was increasing recognition of the possibility that monetary policy, though perhaps impotent at the depth of a severe depression, might well be effective as an expansionary tool in mild recessions. Another reason for the revival of monetary policy was the research done during this period by economists convinced that changes in the money supply had a more predictable impact on total spending than the advocates of fiscal policy believed.

Today most economists prefer to think of themselves as eclectics, willing to use fiscal *or* monetary policy rather than debate their respective merits. This may be evidence of an admirable open-mindedness. It may also be simple prudence in the face of the difficulties encountered when one tries to measure the effects of either policy. These difficulties are compounded by the fact that fiscal policies will usually have monetary repercussions whether or not they're intended. A fan of fiscal policy can then credit his preferred tools, while the fan of monetary policy attributes the effects to the changes that the fiscal action induced in monetary conditions.

Monetary Responses to Fiscal Policies

Why does fiscal policy inevitably have an impact on the monetary sector? Consider the case of a government decision to provide a fiscal stimulus by cutting taxes while increasing expenditures. The Treasury must obtain money in order to spend. There are basically two ways to get it. The Treasury can either have new money created, or it can borrow from the stock of already existing money. Whichever course is chosen, the fiscal actions will have monetary effects. Let's try to sort out the possibilities.

The Treasury does not create new money on its own. As we saw in chapters 18 and 19, the creation of additional money comes about through credit expansion by commercial banks and the Fed. We can therefore set the problem up in terms of the three sources from which the Treasury may borrow: the Fed, commercial banks, or the nonbank public.

Suppose the Treasury borrows from the Fed in order to secure the funds to finance expenditures not covered by taxes. The Fed in effect gives the Treasury additional deposits in exchange for government securities. When the Treasury then spends these deposits, they flow into the bank accounts or currency holdings of defense contractors, welfare recipients, military personnel, or whoever is on the receiving end of the expenditures. The money supply consequently increases.

These new deposits are also new reserves for the commercial banking system. Banks will therefore find their lending power increased. If they can locate eligible borrowers, the commercial banks will, by expanding their loans, create a further addition to the money supply.

It follows that the money supply could increase by the entire amount of the deficit, even though the Fed directly financed only a portion of the deficit. A $50-billion deficit, for example, could be handled through some combination like a Fed purchase of $15 billion in new government securities and commercial bank purchases of $35 billion. The Fed purchase, by supplying new reserves to the banking system, enables the commercial banks to acquire additional government securities by creating new demand deposits.

Now suppose that the Fed wants to prevent the growth in the money supply that would result from increased Treasury borrowing. Insofar as the Fed is successful, the Treasury will be forced to compete with other borrowers for use of the existing money stock. Unless there are idle funds around, interest rates will consequently rise until the higher cost of borrowing squeezes out the excess demand. The net effect, then, will be an expansion of government spending and a compensating reduction of private spending. But this defeats the original purpose of the government's policy; an increase in government spending that is exactly matched by a decrease in private spending provides no stimulus to *total* expenditures.

There's one other possibility. Suppose the public is holding large money balances because consumers and investors are fearful of the future. They might be persuaded to exchange those balances for government securities. That would give the Treasury the money it wants without an increase in the measured money stock. More spending would then occur with no increase in M because the public had been persuaded to exchange money for government bonds and the government then spent the money. In effect,

V would have increased. But is any of this very likely except in a period of deep depression? Perhaps in the 1930s public confidence was so low that deficit spending could tap large idle money balances. But that doesn't seem to describe the situation at any time in the past three decades.

The conclusion is a simple one. Deficit spending by the government affects the monetary sector. It results in some combination of an enlarged money stock and higher interest rates. If the Fed tries to prevent public expenditures from crowding out private expenditures by making more credit available when the Treasury is borrowing, it causes a growth in the money supply. But if the Fed tries to prevent an increase in the money supply, it will force private borrowers to bid against the Treasury for the limited supply of credit. Fiscal policy is inseparable from monetary policy.

Is monetary policy equally inseparable from fiscal policy? The link is not as close in the other direction. Government spending uses money but more money can be created and spent independently of any changes in the government budget. It doesn't follow, however, that fiscal policy cannot be a useful aid to monetary policy. Remember that the Fed does not directly control the size of the money stock. It can increase the available reserves of the banking system, but it cannot force anyone to borrow and thereby convert free reserves into money. Government borrowing and expenditure is one way to increase the money supply. And in a period of low confidence, when consumers and investors don't want to borrow, fiscal policy might be the only practical way to make monetary policy effective.

All of this has one very important implication. The sometimes vehement debate in recent years over the respective roles of fiscal and monetary policy in causing inflation was largely a debate over a non-issue. The federal government ran very large deficits in the 1968, 1971, 1972, and 1973 fiscal years, spending about $85 billion altogether in these four years beyond what it collected in taxes. To ask whether this would have caused inflation if the Fed had not simultaneously allowed a rapid expansion in the money supply is a pointless question. An expansion of the money supply was necessary if the mounting federal expenditures were not to crowd out private spending.

Fiscal Policy: Scalpel or Axe?

It is more useful to ask why the federal government ran such large deficits. And the answer isn't hard to find. The government was committed to military and domestic programs that entailed an expansion of budget outlays beyond the rate at which Congress was willing to raise taxes. But it's a bit more complicated than this suggests. Tax rates were in fact increased in 1968 as a result of which federal government budget receipts rose 30% from 1967 to 1969. Expenditures increased by only 15% over this period, and the federal budget, measured through the income and product accounts, showed an $8 billion surplus in 1969. But something unexpected happened. The percentage of disposable income that consumers saved fell from 7.4% in 1967 to only 6% in 1969. Consumers were apparently unwilling to reduce their expenditures in the face of what they saw as a temporary increase in taxes. They cut their saving instead, so aggregate private demand did not fall as much as Congress had anticipated. Investment spending also failed to slow down. It increased by 8% in 1968 and 10% in 1969. (From 1966 to 1967 it had *declined* by 4%, and it fell by 2% from 1969 to 1970). In short, we cannot simply blame Congress and the president for a cowardly refusal to raise taxes to match mounting expenditures. Private spending didn't respond as sensitively to tax rate changes as many had expected.

In defending our political leaders against the charge of fiscal irresponsibility, we have also called attention to a potential weakness in fiscal policy as a tool for aggregate demand management. In the income-expenditures model of chapter 21, consumption expenditures were treated as a stable function of after-tax income. We could also have made investment depend on tax rates, because it undoubtedly does; but we took the simpler route and assumed that changes in taxes had no effect on investment expenditures. The crucial question, however, is whether investment spending is a stable and predictable function of tax rates. The evidence strongly suggests that we do not know how to predict the short term effect of changes in taxes on private spending. A large enough increase in taxes will certainly reduce private spending, and a sufficiently large tax reduction is bound to increase it. But we'll have to have a far more precise knowledge than that if we hope to use tax changes as a way of preventing undesired movements in aggregate demand.

The Importance Once Again of Uncertainty

Perhaps we must go back to Keynes and his reminder that economic decisions are made over time and in the presence of uncertainty. Substantial unemployment could arise and persist, Keynes argued, because changed conditions do not immediately create a new equilibrium. Consumer and producer responses to one another are hesitant, groping, and often erroneous. They don't cease to be hesitant, groping, and erroneous simply because the government is trying to control aggregate demand. The unpredictability of the government's actions may even increase the frequency and severity of errors in the private sector.

One of the small group of people who discussed the ideas of the *General Theory* prior to their publication, the distinguished British economist Joan Robinson, has protested vigorously in recent years against the tendency to use Keynesian notions and to forget the insight on which they were based. The essence of Keynes's problem, she has pointed out, was uncertainty.

"The main point of the *General Theory* was to break out of the cocoon of equilibrium and consider the nature of life lived in time—the difference between yesterday and tomorrow. Here and now, the past is irrevocable and the future is unknown." But this was apparently "too great a shock," she added sarcastically, and "orthodoxy managed to wind it up in a cocoon again."[1] It would certainly be a very unKeynesian use of Keynes to substitute our equilibrium models for reality and assume that the effects of fiscal policy *or* monetary policy can be predicted with precision.

Let's take a systematic look at the information problems any successful program of aggregate demand management must solve. Policy making today can take advantage of the vast strides we have made in recent years in the accumulation of statistical data on the economy's performance. But information of this sort will always be approximate. It just isn't possible to summarize in both an accurate and a useful way a diverse and multifaceted economic system the size of ours. When we say, then, that "unemployment has risen from 5.2% to 5.4%," we mean that the summary indicator constructed by the Bureau of Labor Statistics from sample data shows a rise *last month* in measured unemployment. By itself that indicator does not tell us who the unemployed are, why they've become unemployed, what the net costs to them of unemployment are, where unemployment is rising and where it's declining, how many people have left the labor force as a result of discouragement, how many have entered to compensate for family income lost through another person's unemployment, or the distribution of unemployment by duration. Additional information is available on each of these questions. But where is the line between too little information to tell us what's happening and too much information for us to see what's going on?[2] New techniques for gathering and processing information can help, but they aren't the complete answer. The first rule for computer-assisted analysts is still the GIGO principle: Garbage In, Garbage Out.

Moreover, all the information available will be dated. It will summarize the situation in the past. That past will be a more-or-less recent past depending upon the speed with which accurate data can be assembled. It's quite fast for data on the monetary system because of legal requirements for regular and accurate reporting by banks, but it is much slower and more inaccurate for data on gross national product or international trade. But even very recent and reliable data aren't enough. Since any policy

---

1. The quotations are from a lecture delivered by Joan Robinson before the American Economic Association and printed in the *American Economic Review,* May 1972, pp. 1–10.

2. Executives in large organizations are dependent upon subordinates to feed them adequate information. It isn't as often recognized, however, that an executive's power to make effective decisions also depends upon the willingness and ability of subordinates to *screen out* less useful data.

actions will impinge on future situations, the challenge is to obtain estimates on future data by extrapolating from the past. And this requires that theorizing accompany the data. If unemployment has gone up by two-tenths of one per cent in each of the last three months, shall we choose a policy on the assumption that it's bound to continue? Or shall we assume that what goes up must come down? Either assumption would be naive; theorizing of considerable sophistication is required to extrapolate economic data effectively.

Predicting the Consequences of Policy Actions

What we really want to know, however, is what will happen *if various policy actions are taken.* What will be the direct and indirect effects of the actions, and how long will they take to make themselves felt? How long does it take for a purchase of government securities by the Fed to result in an increased demand for consumption and investment goods? How much of the impact will come almost at once, perhaps as a reaction to the mere news of an easier monetary policy? How will the rest of the impact be distributed over time? Fiscal actions raise the same questions. The actual multiplier effect of a change in government expenditures or taxes can't be determined by arithmetic manipulations of various marginal propensities, because we don't really know the future values of those propensities. Public attitudes toward tax and expenditure changes may bring about a shift in spending or saving plans and the size of the relevant multiplier when the policy action is announced. And the distribution of the multiplier effects over time is a crucial piece of information if stabilization policy is not to become destabilization policy.

Knowledge about the time lags between monetary or fiscal actions and their effects has been extremely hard to obtain. There is no way to deduce the distribution of lags from pure theory; we have to rely on empirical measurements. But how are we going to sort out the effects of a particular fiscal or monetary stimulus from the effects of all the other forces at work in the economy? Perhaps we could sort them out if we could run a dozen experiments over the course of a quarter century, or divide the economy at the Mississippi River, set up a blockade to keep the effects from leaking back and forth, and then give the injection to the West while using the East as the control group. Even these heroic measures would yield unreliable knowledge, however, because the lags might well be growing longer or shorter over the years. It's quite possible that in trying to measure the time lag between a fiscal or monetary action and its effects we're trying to measure the length of something that has no standard length. At best it's like trying to measure the length of an earthworm. Unless you kill it, how do you measure the length of a wiggling worm that makes itself longer and shorter in response to your measurement efforts?

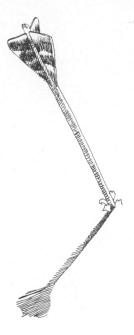

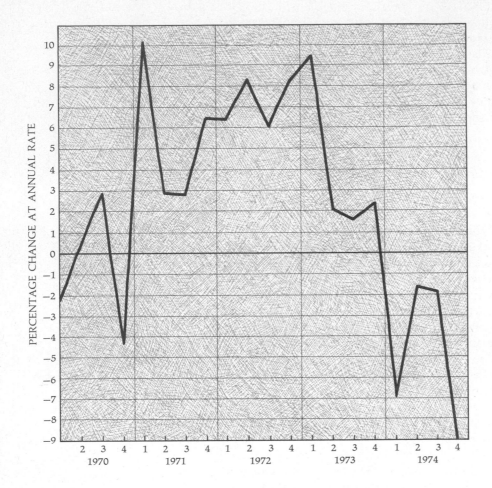

Figure 25A Quarterly changes in real gross national product

How much difference does all this make? Try your hand with figure 25A to see how much difference it *might* make. The graph shows percentage changes (at an annual rate) from quarter to quarter in real gross national product from the first quarter of 1970 to the final quarter of 1974. The average annual growth rate for real GNP over the past twenty years has been close to 4%, so you may use 4% as a benchmark.

If you had been National Stabilization Czar in the third quarter of 1970, would you have wanted to step on the fiscal-monetary brake, press on the accelerator, or just coast? (Remember that you can't see ahead!) Would you have changed your mind when the fourth quarter data came in? How would you have felt about your fourth quarter stabilization actions when you finally saw the data for the first quarter of 1971?

Or look at the record of real GNP from the third quarter of 1971 through the first quarter of 1973. Would you have been worrying at the start of 1973 about an unsustainable boom and the danger of future inflation? Especially if you also saw that the implicit price deflator had risen 5% on an annual basis since the last quarter of 1972? If you came to the reasonable conclusion that some restraint was in order at this time and stepped on the fiscal-monetary brake, you might have been encouraging contraction in a period when private spending was undergoing its own contraction. And if there is a 15 month time lag before the principal effects of fiscal-monetary actions are absorbed, you might have guaranteed a sharp and prolonged recession.

Fiscal or Monetary Policy

In order to focus on some of the problems that must be faced in any attempt at demand management, we have been looking at fiscal and monetary policy as if they were simply alternative ways of accomplishing the same ends. But fiscal and monetary policy are by no means perfect substitutes, and many economists doubt that they are really close substitutes at all. The differences, real or alleged, have to do with direct effects, indirect or side effects, and political constraints.

Direct Effects

We have already encountered the argument that monetary policy is of little use in combating a recession. That argument is less widely held today than it once was. It stays around largely as a result of the belief that in a deep and prolonged depression an expansion of bank reserves would probably not increase private spending significantly. Fiscal policy would have to be employed under those circumstances to turn the reserves into money and get the money into circulation. The effectiveness of monetary policy in *holding down* aggregate demand during a period of inflation is generally accepted, however.

What about the direct effects of fiscal policy? Here there is considerable disagreement among economists. The argument has been advanced in recent years that the level of real income and output is not significantly affected by increases in government expenditure. This represents a dramatic dissent from what was generally accepted only ten years ago and it is even now a minority position. Those who argue this position maintain that if the government increases expenditures relative to taxes without simultaneously increasing the money supply, the primary effect will be to crowd out private spending. The government will have to reduce the money holdings of the public in order to obtain the funds for its expenditures, and the public will respond by reducing expenditures relative to income in an effort to restore its money balances.

Another way of looking at the matter is to note that when the government tries to increase expenditures relative to tax receipts, it will be increasing the demand for a fixed supply of loanable funds. This will raise interest rates, and less private spending will occur when interest rates rise.

Two arguments may be weaker than one, however. If interest rates rise in response to increased government borrowing, the quantity of money the public wants to hold will decrease. Recall from chapter 22 that the demand for money balances is a negative function of the interest rate, because the interest rate is part of the opportunity cost of holding money. Some net increase in total spending should probably be expected, then, when the government borrows from the nonbank public in order to spend.

But this probably doesn't get at the important issues. The advocates of fiscal policy can point out that deficit spending is called for at times when the reluctance of the public to borrow and spend is keeping the money supply too low. It is therefore unrealistic to analyze the effects of fiscal policy on the assumption that no increase occurs in the stock of money. Those who question the effectiveness of fiscal policy, on the other hand, may be making an equally important but quite different point. Deficit spending in recent years has not in fact been financed to any significant extent out of bank reserves that were legally available for money creation but could not actually be loaned because the private demand for credit had collapsed. And when there are no excess bank reserves for the Treasury to tap, then an increase in government expenditure (relative to taxation) will either crowd out private spending *or* cause an inflationary increase in the money supply. Total money demand may rise in such a case, but without a corresponding increase in real output. That results in inflation.

If this is an accurate representation of the argument, the competing claims are compatible. One side is pointing to the effectiveness of fiscal policy in a major recession; the opposite side is warning against the inflationary potential of deficit spending at all other times.

Indirect Effects

What about the indirect effects of fiscal and monetary policy? Assume that either one is capable of providing a sedative or a stimulus to economic activity when sedative or stimulus is the appropriate medicine. Are there side effects that might incline us to choose one over the other?

A lot of attention has been directed to the effect of monetary policy on interest rates and to the consequences of interest rate changes. We must be careful about the assertions we make here, for it is not simply true that easier money means lower interest rates and tighter money means higher rates. The immediate effects and the later effects of monetary policy on interest rates, especially if we're looking at nominal rates, tend to be in opposite directions. But it's nonetheless true that an active monetary policy can cause interest rates to change. And that can have unsettling and inequitable effects.

Discriminatory Effects of Monetary Policy

Some sectors of the economy are unusually sensitive to interest rate changes. State and local government capital projects may have to be halted when interest rates rise. But the standard example is residential construction. Fluctuating interest rates can cause alternating boom and recession in the construction industry and impose large costs on the people who work in that industry.

Another way in which monetary policy may create inequities is through its effects on bond prices. A rise in interest rates causes a fall in the market price of bonds. Suppose that a university has invested its September tuition receipts in government bonds and intends to sell the bonds as it requires cash to finance expenditures. It would sustain a loss if Fed policy caused short term rates to rise sharply just before the university had to sell its securities to obtain cash.

Some have also argued that tight money discriminates against small business firms because larger firms get preferred treatment from banks when credit is tight, can more easily raise money from nonbank sources, and are able to generate funds internally.

A great deal of concern was expressed in the 1960s about the effects of interest rates on the U.S. balance of payments. The foreign demand for dollars depends in part on the interest rate foreigners can obtain by holding dollars, relative to what they can obtain from holding other currencies. Higher interest rates in the United States therefore attract an additional supply of foreign exchange (or, what comes to the same thing, they maintain the foreign demand for dollars). The Fed was consequently under pressure in the 1960s to keep interest rates high as a way of "protecting the balance of payments." This restricted the Fed's ability to pursue other objectives through monetary policy. The movement to floating exchange rates described in the last chapter has enabled the Fed to pay less attention to the international repercussions of its actions.

Another argument asserts that economic growth depends in the long run on the rate of investment and that the rate of investment varies inversely with the average level of interest rates. Suppose that the government uses monetary policy as the preferred instrument for contracting aggregate demand and fiscal policy when it wants to provide a stimulus to output and employment. A side effect would supposedly be higher average interest rates, less investment, smaller increases in the capital stock, and less growth in the productive potential of the economy.

Effects of Government Spending

The argument that by using fiscal policy to stimulate spending and monetary policy to restrain spending we are reducing the rate of investment rests, however, upon the questionable assumption that the government is not purchasing capital goods when it spends. A sizable percentage of total government spending does go, however, toward the purchase of capital. Schools, dams, highways, and public buildings of many kinds are all capital. By allowing the government to control a larger portion of total spending, we may in fact be *increasing* the investment-to-consumption ratio and thus increasing the rate at which the nation's productive potential expands. Since government investment decisions are not based on the same criteria as private investment decisions, we have no good way to decide whether the rate at which future output expands is increased or decreased by more government spending and less private spending. How do we compare the additional services produced by an expanded Smithsonian Institution with the services that would have been produced if the funds had gone instead to residential construction? And who will be courageous enough to divide military expenditures into consumption and investment and to estimate what part of the latter is profitable rather than wasteful investment?

Some people think our inability to answer questions like these is in itself a strong argument against growth of the government sector. And one side effect of fiscal policy is certainly its tendency to promote such growth. Fiscal policy is in theory a contractionary or expansionary tool. In practice, however, it is primarily a weapon for promoting expansion, because it's so much easier politically to reduce taxes and raise expenditures than to reverse the procedure. A society committed to the use of fiscal policy will consequently tend to find itself steadily enlarging the government sector of the economy.

Has that been happening in recent years? Table 25A provides some data on the relative size of the government sector. The first column in table 25A shows *total government* purchases of commodities and services as a percentage of gross national product. The second column shows *federal* government purchases as a percentage of GNP. The third column takes account of the increasing importance of transfer payments by presenting total government *receipts* as a percentage of GNP.

Year	Table 25A GOVERNMENT ACTIVITIES AS A PERCENTAGE OF GNP		
	Total Government Purchases	Federal Government Purchases	Total Government Receipts
1929	8.2%	1.3%	11.0%
1939	14.7	5.6	17.0
1949	14.7	7.8	21.8
1959	20.0	11.1	26.8
1969	22.6	10.6	31.9

Source: Bureau of Economic Analysis

THE PERILS OF FINE-TUNING

There is something slightly absurd about the belief that the federal government can use its budget as a stabilization tool when almost all observers agree that Congress no longer has effective control over the budget. The spending programs of the federal government are so many and so complex that no one in Congress or the Executive Branch can even begin to evaluate all of them for the purpose of determining annual appropriations. Next year's budget begins, as a result, by taking this year's budget for granted and adding on. Once a program finds a home in the budget, it is almost impossible to evict. Its beneficiaries form a knowledgeable and determined lobby for its continuance and no one on Capitol Hill will have the time, energy, or interest to accumulate the evidence that could justify its removal. What's the use of knocking yourself out just to cut $3 million from the budget when $3 million is only .001% of the total? And why make the effort when the only certain outcome for the legislator who does is the perpetual enmity of those whose appropriations are challenged?

Grand Designs

The emphasis on side effects serves as a useful reminder that "aggregate demand" is a broad abstraction. The social impact of any expansion or contraction on total spending depends upon what is being purchased or not purchased. Government expenditures stimulate the production of particular goods, not goods in general, and any expansion of government spending relative to private spending increases the relative size of the

public sector. Demand can be expanded through fiscal policy without enlarging the public sector if taxes are cut; but this, too, will affect the *composition* of output in a manner dependent upon which taxes are reduced. A tax credit given to businesses for investment in plant and equipment will increase the rate of capital formation more than will a reduction in the personal income tax. One of the practical difficulties confronted by fiscal policy is precisely this need to choose from among competing claimants. Any change in the pattern of taxes or government expenditures will be a matter for political bargaining, because it will inevitably affect the distribution of income. It will also affect future economic development because it alters the ratio of consumption to investment.

Some economists have viewed these side effects as more of an opportunity than a difficulty. Since either fiscal policy or monetary policy is capable of providing as much expansion or contraction in aggregate demand as we're likely to want, they argue that we should choose our mix by first choosing the side effects we prefer. It has been suggested, for example, that if we want rapid economic growth, we could pursue an easy money policy with plenty of credit at low interest rates for potential investors, and counter the inflationary consequences with a high rate of taxation on consumption expenditures. There was a period in the 1960s when the more enthusiastic students of aggregate demand management were cheering a three-cornered dance. The Fed was to keep short term interest rates high to attract foreign bank deposits and protect the balance of payments and to keep long term rates low to encourage investment. Meanwhile recession and inflation would be prevented by deft manipulation of the federal budget.

Scanty Information

The truth is, however, that we don't begin to have the detailed knowledge that such delicate operations would require. How long could investment and consumption expenditures be "twisted" in the manner just described before reduced consumer spending brought a halt to further investment? How would different industries be affected, and with what consequences? Presumably such an approach would reduce output in consumer goods industries and expand it in investment goods industries. How quickly would workers released from automobile assembly lines find jobs producing machine tools? When the policy changed again, would they find their way back? How much would unemployment increase and for how long in response to these policy-initiated changes in the composition of aggregate demand? It's all slightly reminiscent of the tenth grader who just dissected his first crayfish and wants to move right on to heart transplants.

WHAT DO AVERAGES AND AGGREGATES CONCEAL?

The graph below provides a picture of the diversity contained within the movement of economic aggregates. The lines graph selected components of the Federal Reserve Board of Governors' Index of Industrial Production. The average level of production in each industrial category is stated as a percentage of 1967 production levels. The heavy line charts the *total* index of industrial production. (The monthly data given for 1974 are seasonally adjusted.)

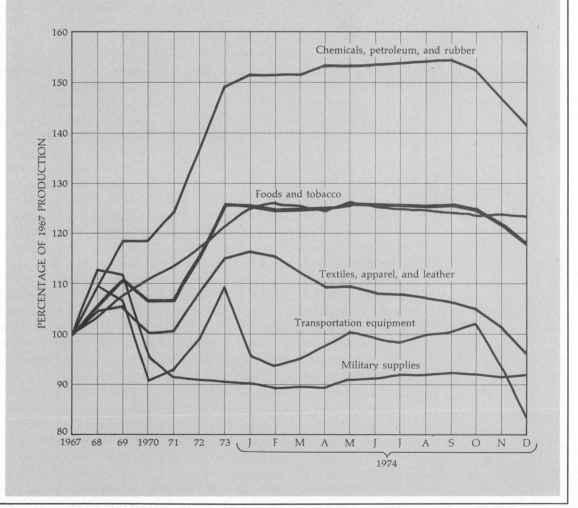

Political Constraints and Problems of Timing

Much of the optimism of the 1960s with regard to the potentialities of demand management stemmed from a failure to give proper weight to political constraints. The Genie Conception of government entered into the recommendations of economists when they assumed that nothing was required to improve policy except further economic research. Once the experts had found the best policy, putting it into effect would be no problem at all.

But fiscal policy in particular is clearly subject to major constraints imposed by the political process. A change in federal government expenditures or taxes requires action by the House of Representatives and the Senate, with committee meetings before and often after, and a presidential signature at the end. That takes *time* and timing is crucial in effective countercyclical policy. The discussions will be complicated and prolonged by the fact that, even if Congress agrees quickly on the desirability of changing expenditures or taxes by a particular amount, it would still have to decide *whose* taxes and *which* expenditures will be changed. Conflicting interests will be involved and alternative theories about the expansionary or contractionary effects of a particular action will enter the debate. Meanwhile some members of Congress will certainly decide that an important tax or expenditure bill provides an opportunity to eliminate the depletion allowance for oil producers, give a bonus to retired people on social security, prop up the housing industry with a special subsidy, or take a slap at multinational corporations—to mention only those concerns that managed to achieve expression in the March 1975 "antirecessionary" tax bill.

The more in a hurry Congress and the president are, the more likely they are to produce fiscal policy actions that no competent and impartial observer will be able to defend. The imperative of haste tends to enhance the power of the less responsible elements who are willing to enforce their demands by threatening to block any action at all. But due deliberation, the careful assessment of alternatives, and the weighing of probable short- and long-term outcomes may require so much time that the moment for action passes before any action is taken. The 1974–75 recession probably began late in 1973. Congress passed an antirecessionary tax cut at the end of March in 1975, and it was even at that late date a tax bill filled with evidence of undue haste. Only six months prior to the tax cut, the word from the White House was still WIN (Whip *Inflation* Now). Could we find better evidence of the lag between the appearance and the recognition of a problem?

Advocates of stabilization through fiscal policy who are not mesmerized by the Genie Conception of government have long been aware of these difficulties. They know that the protracted discussions that precede any

Congressional action on taxes and expenditures can easily make fiscal policy unworkable: action may not be possible until the time for it has passed. They have consequently looked around for ways to speed up the process. One proposal recommended by some economists and urged by President Kennedy was that Congress authorize unilateral action by the president. Appropriations for particular projects could be approved by Congress, put on the shelf, and taken off whenever the president and his advisers decided that the stimulus of increased government expenditures was called for. Congress could also authorize the president to increase or decrease tax rates within narrow limits when aggregate demand seemed excessive or inadequate.

This proposal doesn't exactly assume a genie; it's more like trying to create one. If you're wondering why Congress never acted on such a "sensible" recommendation, think for a moment about the political power that a president would command if he could unilaterally determine the timing of tax decreases and the placement of expenditure projects. Do you recall the furor that erupted in the early 1970s when a president tried to "impound" appropriations on the grounds that they would add to the deficit and increase the rate of inflation? We are not likely soon to sanction such actions by even the most trusted of leaders. And that means discretionary fiscal policy will continue to be a largely unusable weapon against fluctuations in total spending.

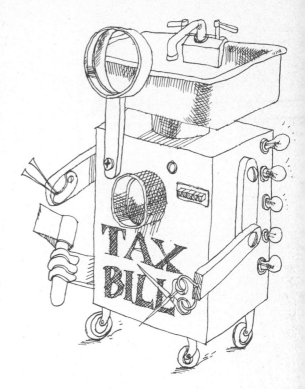

Democratic Monetary Policy?

If fiscal policy is subject to such stringent political constraints and if monetary policy is an alternate way to bring about changes in aggregate demand, should the government rely on monetary policy to promote stabilization? The question raises important issues in political philosophy. Isn't it a virtue of fiscal policy in a democratic society that it requires political consent and cannot be practiced, as monetary policy can, by a small group of experts insulated from the pressures of public opinion? On the other hand, might it not be a good thing to insulate aggregate demand management from irrelevant and uninformed pressures? Still, who is to say which pressures are irrelevant? And what are the implications for democracy of policies that take advantage of public ignorance? Wouldn't it be better in the long run to educate the public than to run policies behind the back of Congress?

You can't expect educators to take a stand against education and we won't. But the educational task, difficult enough already, will be even more difficult if the experts themselves don't know exactly *how* fiscal policy and monetary policy work, singly as well as jointly, to affect aggregate demand.

Is It Better to Have Tried and Failed?

It has become increasingly obvious in recent years that we do not have the knowledge that would be required to steer the economy on a steady course of full employment and price stability. But are we better off than we would have been if we hadn't tried? Many economists now agree that *fine-tuning,* as it is called, has been oversold, that we have been much too optimistic about our ability to reduce aggregate fluctuations through demand management. A smaller number go farther and argue that the attempt to stabilize has actually increased both unemployment and inflation.

How could this occur? The key element in their argument is the relation between unemployment and uncertainty. Unemployment occurs largely because mistakes have been made that must subsequently be acknowledged and corrected. Anything that increases uncertainty for economic decision makers increases the probability of mistakes and hence the frequency with which resources must be reallocated. And that will increase the average level of unemployment. The question then becomes: Have the behavior of the federal budget and the behavior of the money supply in recent years made the future more predictable? Or have they increased the uncertainties confronting economic decision makers?

Stabilizing Factors

We cannot jump from the fact that there have been no major recessions since the 1930s to the conclusion that the net effect of government stabilization efforts was greater stability. Other factors have been at work. We earlier discussed the importance of the Federal Deposit Insurance Corporation in eliminating the phenomenon of bank runs and the supporting role of the Fed as the guarantor of short-run liquidity to the banking system. Between them they have eliminated the panics that once swept regularly through the financial sector; and with financial panics a thing of the past, the economy has not again had to go through anything even remotely approaching the 25% contraction in the money supply experienced between 1929 and 1933.

Another stabilizing factor seems to have been the tendency for personal consumption expenditures since World War II to maintain their own steady rate of increase despite fluctuations in GNP. From 1948 to the recession year of 1949, for example, real GNP remained nearly constant, but personal consumption expenditures increased 2.7%. From 1953 to 1954, while GNP was falling 1.4%, consumption was rising 2%. From 1957 to 1958, GNP fell 1.1%, but consumption increased .7%. Some of this can be credited to the partial insulation of disposable personal income from fluctuations in GNP. In the three years cited above, disposable personal income (in real terms once more) increased more rapidly than GNP, rising

.4%, 1%, and .9%. One insulator is our system of progressive taxes on personal and corporate income, which automatically reduces tax receipts as GNP falls and reduces those receipts by more than the percentage fall in GNP. Another insulator is the fact that government transfer payments rise when GNP falls and fall when it rises. We spoke of these earlier as automatic fiscal stabilizers. The point here is that they operated even in the absence of efforts to fine-tune the economy, and might well have been responsible for the mildness of postwar recessions.

Destabilizing Factors

If personal consumption expenditures have been a steady and stabilizing component of aggregate demand, investment expenditures have not. You can go back to table 17A or, even better, to the graph on page 584, to see just how unstable private investment spending has been. But how much of this was due to changes originating in the government sector? Changing tax regulations, especially those affecting investment, shifts in the degree of monetary ease or tightness, and huge swings in the government budget from deficit to surplus and back to deficit *may* have been compensatory forces. But they may also have caused some of the fluctuations in investment. We've already mentioned the way in which money market conditions, affected by fiscal and monetary actions, tend to destabilize the housing industry. What about the policy of shifting between tax surcharges to dampen inflation and special tax credits for investment spending to promote employment? Since there is usually considerable discretion about the timing of investment expenditures, government policy reversals may themselves be largely responsible for the large fluctuations in private investment from year to year.

But it's most important that we probe beneath the surface of such aggregates as consumption, investment, and government purchases. For the changing composition as well as the changing level of these totals affects the unemployment rate. A very large part of the 1974 unemployment was the consequence of changes in the demand for automobiles. And a rise in consumer spending is not certain to return that demand to earlier levels. There is something disturbing about a government that officially encourages us to burn less gasoline (to conserve energy) and to buy more cars (to restore prosperity) and simultaneously claims to be responsible for *stabilizing* employment. Can we really depend on the stabilization skills of an agent so adept at keeping its right hand from finding out what its left hand is doing?

Before asking what the government might do to *reduce* unemployment in a particular industry, we might want to ask whether the government has done anything to *raise* unemployment. The supply of people with doctoral degrees in the sciences is today greater than the number of available jobs in large part because the government began subsidizing the education of scientists fifteen years ago and continued to do so even after surpluses had started to appear. When the government makes a decision to send men to the moon, to produce a particular military plane, to restrict oil imports, to subsidize a giant railroad system, to enforce high standards of job safety in industry, to become self-sufficient in energy by 1980, to encourage home ownership with government subsidized loans, to enlarge steel-making capacity by granting special tax refunds for investment—all examples are actual decisions the federal government has made—it signals labor and other resources to move in specific directions. It tells people to change their places of residence, to acquire certain knowledge and skills, and to sink resources into particular projects. Any subsequent slackening of government intentions or shift in emphasis announces that these resource movements were partly mistaken and creates unemployment.

Good timing is at the heart of effective countercyclical policy and good timing is difficult to achieve for all the reasons we've mentioned. Moreover, the mere probability of government intervention coupled with uncertainty about the nature and timing of that intervention makes the future more difficult to predict. And any sudden change in government policy, even though it may stabilize *aggregate* demand, will create additional unemployment for a period of time while particular industries are adjusting to the change. We certainly know now in the mid-seventies that a high and rising level of aggregate demand is consistent with falling demand in particular areas and temporary increases in unemployment.

The Case for an Automatic Pilot

Increases in the unemployment rate are political signals, however, for an expansion of aggregate demand. But that expansion may well be inflationary if the unemployment is due to something other than a deficiency of aggregate demand. We can sketch an instructive scenario in which the government's attempts to fine-tune the economy upset a lot of private economic calculations, the adjustments people make add to the official unemployment rate, government responds by increasing aggregate demand, this causes the price level to begin rising, and attempts to stop the inflation aggravate unemployment. Some economists are today persuaded that this has in fact occurred and that government could consequently make its most effective contribution toward eliminating aggregate fluctuations by not trying so hard to eliminate all fluctuations. A graceful elephant *could* succeed in stabilizing a small boat on a rough sea by shifting its weight with delicacy and perfect timing. Some of the passengers might nonetheless prefer that the elephant sit as still as possible.

"Automaticity" is the policy goal of economists who doubt the practicality of discretionary demand management. They want the Fed to maintain a steady hand on the money stock and either hold it constant or cause it to increase by some definite, known, and uniform rate. As for fiscal policy, they want only as much of it as comes about automatically, without the discretionary intervention of Congress or the Executive Branch. When an economic downturn begins, tax receipts will automatically fall because corporate and personal incomes are declining and government outlays will increase because government transfer payments rise when the aggregate level of economic activity declines. These automatic stabilizers presumably function in the manner of mechanical governors and dampen oscillations in the economy. The proponents of automaticity argue that any additional discretionary policy actions are more likely to aggravate than reduce instability because discretionary actions are so hard to time appropriately and because anticipation of them creates additional uncertainty for private decision makers.

The contemporary case for an automatic pilot is not identical with the view that dominated economic thinking prior to the 1930s and the publication of Keynes's *General Theory.* The older view was that government should actually retrench in a recession and cut its expenditures and increase tax rates if that was necessary to preserve a balanced budget. A balanced budget, in turn, was viewed as the test of responsible government and the one surest indicator to the business community of the government's determination to maintain or restore "confidence." And confidence was seen as the key to recovery. That view, though still influential in the 1930s, has very few supporters today. But note that such a policy, if adopted, would also be a discretionary policy, not an automatic one. It would be equally capable of aggravating instability because of faulty estimates, errors in timing, and the additional uncertainties created for decision makers.

Automatic versus Discretionary Policy

There are automatic monetary stabilizers as well as automatic fiscal stabilizers in the economic system. A boom will eventually run against rising interest rates and credit rationing if the monetary managers don't feed the boom by pumping new reserves into the banking system. During a period of economic decline, lending terms tend to improve and this will encourage some potential investors. But the monetary managers have in fact behaved perversely a good part of the time, the leading opponents of monetary fine-tuning argue. For one thing, they have paid too much attention to interest rates and, by attempting to stabilize interest rates, they have caused the money supply to grow erratically. This in turn has fostered an irregular rate of growth in gross national product, higher unemployment, and then inflationary rates of expansion in the money stock in response to the rise in unemployment.

THE DANGERS IN PICTURESQUE ARGUMENTS

Debates between the proponents of discretionary stabilization policy and purely automatic policy are often conducted by means of analogies and metaphors. The elephant-in-the-boat example used in the text is an argument by analogy and, like all such arguments, can provide only an illustration and never a proof. Here is an analogy commonly used by the advocates of discretionary policy:

It's true that automobile accidents are occasionally caused by a driver's misguided efforts to avoid an accident. But will anyone seriously claim that we would have fewer accidents if drivers were forbidden to engage in defensive maneuvering?

But is driving an automobile really analogous to fine-tuning an economy? Or is it an altogether different kind of task? The argument by analogy begs that question.

Sometimes the analogy is less clearly stated and hence the extent to which the argument rests upon analogy is harder to recognize.

Consider this statement: "History provides no support for the notion that our economy is inherently stable. On the contrary, experience shows that blind reliance on self-correcting tendencies leads to serious trouble."

Hidden in that line of reasoning is the assumption that the economy is like an object without eyes. But economic decisions are made by human beings who do have eyes and who make conscious decisions. Isn't the real question one of *whose* eyes and *whose* decisions can best be relied upon? Do the many eyes of individual consumers, investors, and producers enable them to make better decisions than will be made by government economic managers who will necessarily have less information? The metaphor begs that question.

The argument against discretionary fiscal and monetary policy is hard to evaluate because of the difficulties in devising experimental tests. In the absence of convincing empirical evidence, economists behave like anyone else and take their positions on the basis of theoretical predilections and political preferences. General skepticism about the ability of government to solve social problems and admiration for the way in which free-market processes do the job make an economist more receptive to evidence that discretionary demand management has done more harm than good. Those who are less satisfied with the performance of the market system find a touch of absurdity in the notion that policymakers should have their hands tied, and are quite unimpressed by the evidence that discretionary policy has been destabilizing in its net effects.

Suppose we were to ask both the advocates and the opponents of discretionary demand management how their views had been affected by international economic developments in the 1970s. We could single out, as international developments that might have compelled changes in their thinking about stabilization policies, the unanticipated shortfalls in world grain production that boosted average crop prices more than 100% from 1970 to 1974; the equally unexpected successes of the OPEC cartel that had so much to do with the doubling of fuel prices over the same period; revolutions and counterrevolutions in Chile, Southeast Asia, and elsewhere; the breakdown of the fixed exchange rate system; and the simultaneous acceleration of money stock growth rates and inflation rates in industrialized countries. A much more chaotic world economy now seems to be intruding consistently upon the relatively stable and predictable economic universe to which business decision makers in the United States had become accustomed. Drought, revolution, industrial development, or shifts in the direction of economic planning anywhere in the world will in the future much more than in the past affect the demand for U.S. goods and the availability of the imports upon which our gross national product increasingly depends. What does all this imply for domestic policymakers charged with pursuing full employment and price stability?

The advocates of discretionary fiscal-monetary policy might reply that aggregate demand managers will have to play a major role in cushioning the effects of such external disturbances. Stable growth for the U.S. economy in a highly unstable world will require frequent monetary and fiscal actions of a compensatory nature. The economy may have been able to stay on a fairly steady course in the 1950s and 1960s without a great deal of active assistance from fiscal or monetary policy. But, as the inflations and recessions of the 1970s have already demonstrated, that is far less likely in the future.

What might the opponents of discretionary stabilization policy say in response to the same question? They might reply that international developments in this decade have further demonstrated the impossibility of achieving economic stability by manipulating aggregate demand. Increasing interdependence among national economies means that effective economic decision making now requires more information of a broader nature than it has ever required before and increased flexibility of response. Statistical data on economic aggregates are the kind of information available to fiscal and monetary managers, but are not the kind of information that successful economic coordination requires. If we did not know how to stabilize the economy in the relatively placid context of the 1950s and 1960s, we certainly do not know how to stabilize it now. The most important task for government may be to avoid throwing its considerable weight around in ways that increase uncertainty and aggravate instability.

What Are the Unanswered Questions?

Disagreement among economists about the relative effectiveness of fiscal and of monetary policy or about the desirability and dangers of attempting to fine-tune the economy with the tools of demand management is evidence of the unsettled state of economic knowledge. While much has been learned since the 1930s, many fundamental questions are still unresolved.

One such question is the relative utility of income-expenditures and monetary analyses. $Y = C + I + G$ and $MV = PQ$ aren't contradictory theories, of course; they both assert that aggregate demand determines the nominal level of total income or the national product measured in current dollars. Both theories can be extended, and have been extended, to take account of variables that the other theory deems important. But they are competitive theories nonetheless. One theory calls attention to consumption and investment as the components of private demand; the other passes over these components to focus on money as the medium of demand. Implicit in any economist's choice of one equation over the other as an analytical framework are judgments on unsettled questions such as these:

1. How stable is the demand for money in the short run and in the long run?
2. How stable is the relation between consumption and disposable income?
3. How does monetary policy affect the nominal interest rate quoted by lenders and the real interest rate that results from subtracting expectations of future inflation?
4. How do interest rates affect consumption and investment spending?
5. How do increased government expenditures affect consumption and investment spending directly (by perhaps displacing them) and indirectly (by stimulating them)?
6. What are the principal factors responsible for fluctuations in aggregate investment?
7. How long are the lags between policy actions and their effect on spending decisions?
8. How closely are unemployment rates and rates of inflation linked to changes in aggregate demand?
9. How are output and employment fluctuations in one country transmitted to other countries?

10. How much control do monetary managers have over the money supply when banks, corporations, and individual citizens have learned how to transfer financial assets and liabilities so quickly and almost costlessly from one nation to another?

One can hope that further empirical inquiry and theoretical discussion will eventually resolve these questions and others that may prove equally important. But that would not necessarily end all controversy. Underneath these and, indeed, *most* significant controversies in economics lies a much broader question and one far more difficult to answer: *How effectively does the market function to allocate resources?* How flexible are prices and how quickly do resources move in response to a decrease in demand in one area and an increase in another? If prices are inflexible and especially if they are inflexible in a downward direction, if resources respond sluggishly to changes in demand conditions, or if powerful economic interests are more *controlling of* than *controlled by* supply and demand, then even the most adroit management of aggregate demand will have little chance of promoting full employment and price stability.

Does the market work well enough to give fiscal policy *or* monetary policy a reasonable chance to succeed? We'll examine that question in the next chapter and discover how very far it takes us beyond the questions for which economists have any satisfactory answers.

FLEXIBILITY AND FINE-TUNING: A LOGICAL PUZZLE

Is there an inconsistency in the argument for fine-tuning?

The case for fine-tuning assumes that the economy is flexible enough to channel a dose of stimulus into slack sectors without unduly expanding demand in those sectors that are already operating close to capacity. It assumes, for example, that a tax cut or an increase in the money stock to counter the recession developing in 1974 would have had much greater effects on the automobile and housing industries than on nondurable consumer goods industries, and that its impact on construction activity would be greatest in those geographic areas where building trades unemployment was highest.

But if the economy was not flexible enough to prevent the unemployment level from rising to 9% in the spring of 1975, would it have been flexible enough to channel aggregate demand stimulus into those sectors where it's most wanted?

Once Over Lightly

The <u>potential effectiveness of fiscal or monetary policy</u> as tools by which government might stabilize the <u>aggregate level</u> of economic activity depends on the effectiveness of political processes as well as the knowledge and skills of economic advisers.

The separate impacts of fiscal policy and monetary policy are very difficult to determine, because fiscal policy inevitably affects the monetary sector and monetary policy actions are often accompanied by fiscal policy actions.

Because government deficits must be financed in some way, they will tend to cause either an increase in the money stock or increased competition for available funds, higher interest rates, and a partial displacement of private spending. The latter is the potential "crowding out" of private expenditures by government expenditures.

Fiscal policy depends on changes in federal government expenditures and tax receipts, and both of these are subject to major political constraints. Proposals for making fiscal policy a more flexible tool by granting to the president a limited authority to alter expenditures and taxes will encounter political resistance to any reduction in the power of Congress over the budget.

The tidy equilibrium models of economists in which there are no data problems and no time lags of uncertain length present a misleadingly simple picture of the difficulties that fiscal or monetary policy encounter in practice. The information that policymakers can have will be both dated and inaccurate.

One of the most important obstacles to the use of fiscal or monetary policy as stabilization tools is our lack of reliable information on the time lag between a policy action and its consequences.

Neither fiscal policy nor monetary policy is neutral in its effects on the composition of output and the distribution of income. These side effects may become reasons for choosing or not choosing a particular policy.

Fiscal or monetary policy may be able to alter the level of aggregate demand but nonetheless be unable to alter it with sufficient precision to reduce aggregate fluctuations.

Attempts to stabilize could actually be destabilizing. The greater our ignorance or misinformation about the time lags inherent in aggregate demand management, the greater is the probability that stabilization policy will be destabilizing.

The economic system contains a number of automatic stabilizers that come into operation in the absence of any decisions by government and partially offset expansions and contractions in aggregate demand. The effectiveness of these stabilizers is a disputed issue. The stabilizers range from automatic changes in tax receipts as GNP changes, through movements in interest rates as private demand for credit changes, to movements in prices and wages in response to conditions of excess or inadequate demand.

Some economists are sufficiently impressed by the destabilizing potential of discretionary policy to argue that exclusive reliance on automatic stabilizers will yield better results than will attempts to fine-tune the economy.

Inadequate knowledge about important behavioral relationships and continuing theoretical disagreements continue to impede the development of a consensus among economists on the effectiveness of aggregate demand management. A good deal of controversy is rooted in disagreement about how effectively the market system allocates resources.

QUESTIONS FOR DISCUSSION

1. What gives rise to "social problems"? What special advantages might government have for dealing with "social problems"? Choose some particular social problem that you think government is uniquely qualified to solve, and then reflect on the assumptions you're making about the workings of government.

2. Some observers claim to find evidence that from the 1930s to the 1960s Americans believed strongly in the ability of government to solve social problems (poverty, crime, urban decay, mental health, unequal education, racial and sexual discrimination, health care), but that the late 1960s and the 1970s have seen a growing disillusionment in this area. What evidence can you present for or against this thesis?

3. Would most of our economic problems disappear if business firms operated more on the basis of the public interest rather than private interests? Is the proposal that business behave in a more socially responsible way a useful proposal? Substitute "government officials" for "business firms" and examine the same question.

4. When did the Great Depression end? Why did it end? How do you know?

5. Examine the thesis that the federal budget deficits for the 1976 and 1977 fiscal years did or did not significantly "crowd out" private expenditures.

6. Senator Hubert Humphrey said shortly after the March 1975 tax cuts that "common sense" told him federal borrowing would not raise interest rates and crowd out private borrowers. "To a large extent this credit market question takes care of itself," he said. "Private demands for credit go down when unemployment is high. This makes room in the credit market for government demand, which goes up." Do you agree?

7. Can you think of any experiment by which we might test the proposition that fiscal policy affects total spending regardless of what is happening to the money supply?

8. Does monetary policy require assistance from fiscal policy to be effective?

9. Suppose we knew that an increase in the budget deficit or in the growth rate of the money stock would have 95% of its impact by the end of two years, 55% of its impact within one year, and 20% within six months. Would that knowledge solve the timing problems associated with aggregate demand management?

10. "An increase or decrease in government spending will usually entail an offsetting decrease or increase in private spending." Under what circumstances would you expect that statement to be true? Why? Under what circumstances would you expect that statement to be false? Why?

11. "An easy money policy is good for the housing industry in the short run but bad in the long run." Evaluate that argument.

12. What are some of the ways in which monetary policy can affect the flow of international payments?

13. In 1974, government purchased 22% of the goods in the gross national product, and the private sector purchased the other 78%. The 78% that went to the private sector was divided between consumption and investment expenditures; consumption took 81% and investment 19%.

    (*a*) Do you think the government spent more than 19% of its share on investment goods?

    (*b*) State and local governments purchased 62% of the goods absorbed by the government sector, and the federal government 38%. Would you classify the $70 billion spent by state and local governments on education as a consumption or an investment expenditure?

14. Would you favor the proposal, mentioned in the text, to give the president authority to change tax rates or to authorize expenditures on his own (within Congressionally designated limits) as a way of making fiscal policy more flexible? Why or why not?

15. Can discretionary monetary policy improve upon the automatic monetary stabilizers that would be operative if the Fed simply increased bank reserves at a steady rate? Under what circumstances would discretionary policy be destabilizing in its effects? Under what circumstances would it reenforce the operation of the automatic stabilizers?

16. Would you expect to find a relationship between an informed person's attitude toward attempts at fine-tuning and his reactions to the following judgments? Explain why.

(*a*) "The article by Hayek in the appendix on the problem of knowledge exaggerates both the difficulty of obtaining useful information and the effectiveness of the market in generating and disseminating such information."

(*b*) "The government must establish procedures for national economic planning if we are to avoid the kinds of economic crises experienced in the early 1970s."

(*c*) "The market does not work as it used to. Competition no longer sets prices or allocates resources in the U.S. economy. Most of that is done by organized interest groups with substantial market power."

(*d*) "The U.S. economy displays an absurd social imbalance. Privately purchased goods are produced in abundance, while public sector goods such as education must be content with the leavings."

(*e*) "Power tends to corrupt and absolute power corrupts absolutely."

26

INFLATION, UNEMPLOYMENT, AND THE POLITICALIZATION OF THE ECONOMY

Nothing contributed as much to the public's sudden disillusionment with economists in the early 1970s as the appearance of rapid inflation combined with high and rising unemployment. This wasn't supposed to happen, according to the public's notion of what economists were teaching, because inflation and recession are opposites.

INFLATION *VERSUS* UNEMPLOYMENT

Inflation and recession are not actually opposites, of course. The opposite of inflation is deflation, which is a falling rather than a rising price level. There is no generally accepted term for the opposite of recession, but *boom* comes close. It is a period of increasing output and employment mixed possibly, but not necessarily, with rising prices. But if inflation and recession aren't opposite in the strict sense, they have been considered opposites in the sense of sunshine and rain: the two are not expected to occur at the same time.

It's clear that the general public was surprised in 1970 when unemployment rose to 6.2% in the month of December, despite the fact that the consumer price index had gone up throughout the year at an average annual rate of 7%. The spectacular show was still to come, however. Unemployment rose during 1974 from 5.2% in January to 7.2% in December, while the Consumer Price Index added the phrase "double-digit inflation" to our vocabulary of jargon by rising 11%.

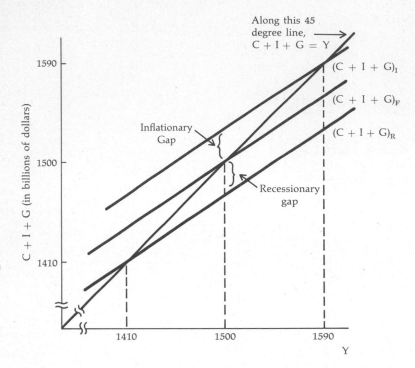

Along this 45
degree line,
$C + I + G = Y$

$(C + I + G)_I$

$(C + I + G)_F$

$(C + I + G)_R$

Inflationary
Gap

Recessionary
gap

1590

1500

1410

C + I + G (in billions of dollars)

1410   1500   1590

Y

Figure 26A Implications of
income-expenditures analysis

Inflationary and Recessionary Gaps

Professional economists weren't as embarrassed by all this as some journalists and television commentators, perhaps too eager to proclaim a crisis, claimed they were. But it is true that the economics textbooks had for some years been analyzing inflation and recession as if they resulted from opposite forces and therefore could not occur simultaneously. Income-expenditures analysis was especially vulnerable on this score, with its concept of a full employment level of aggregate demand below which involuntary unemployment appeared and above which the price level rose. Graphs like the one in figure 26A were often used by economists to present the implications of income-expenditures analysis.

The sum of the components of aggregate demand is on the vertical axis and total income or output is on the horizontal axis. At equilibrium, $C + I + G$ will be equal to Y. The 45 degree line, because it marks off all the points in the graph at which $C + I + G$ does equal Y, shows all possible equilibrium positions. Since consumption increases as income increases, on Keynes's assumptions, but by less than the increase in income, the total of C, I, and G will increase as Y increases, but at a slower rate. The three aggregate demand curves are drawn with a slope of less than one (actually $\frac{2}{3}$) in order to show this relation between total expenditure and income. All this is merely an extension of the graphical analysis introduced in chapter 20 (see especially figure 20H on page 574).

If the intentions of consumers, investors, and the government are as shown by $(C + I + G)_F$ in figure 26A, the equilibrium level of Y will be $1500 billion. You can readily see from the graph that, at any higher level of Y, $(C + I + G)_F$ would be less than Y and so, by the logic of the process described in chapter 20, Y would fall. At any lower level of Y, $C + I + G$ would be greater than Y, and Y would rise.

Assume that $1500 is the full employment level of Y. Then, by definition, there will be excessive unemployment if aggregate demand generates only a $1410 billion level of Y. This would occur if the intentions of consumers, investors, and the government were as shown by $(C + I + G)_R$. If, on the other hand, aggregate spending plans were as shown by $(C + I + G)_I$, so that Y rose to $1590 billion, the economy would undergo inflation.

The vertical difference between $(C + I + G)_F$ and $(C + I + G)_R$ was called a recessionary gap; it's the amount by which aggregate demand falls short of what it would have to be to get the economy to full employment. The vertical difference between $(C + I + G)_F$ and $(C + I + G)_I$ is an inflationary gap; it's the amount by which aggregate demand exceeds the ability of the economy to supply new goods at stable prices.

INFLATION *WITH* UNEMPLOYMENT

This way of setting up the problem leaves the impression that inflation cannot occur when a recessionary gap exists and recession cannot occur in the presence of an inflationary gap. Inflation and unemployment in this analysis are opposites. They are caused, respectively, by an excessive level or an inadequate level of aggregate demand, and we should not expect to observe both at the same time. Moreover, the way to deal with inflation is to "close" the inflationary gap. Recession calls for closing the recessionary gap. Inflation *plus* recession then calls for . . . some other way of looking at the problem.

Bottlenecks, Full Employment, and Inflation

The standard textbook analysis that we've been summarizing actually did allow for the possibility of *some* inflation before a recessionary gap had been fully closed (or before full employment was reached) and the appearance of *some* unemployment before an inflationary gap had been completely closed (or increases in the price level brought to a halt). Figure 26B presents that analysis by extending figure 26A.

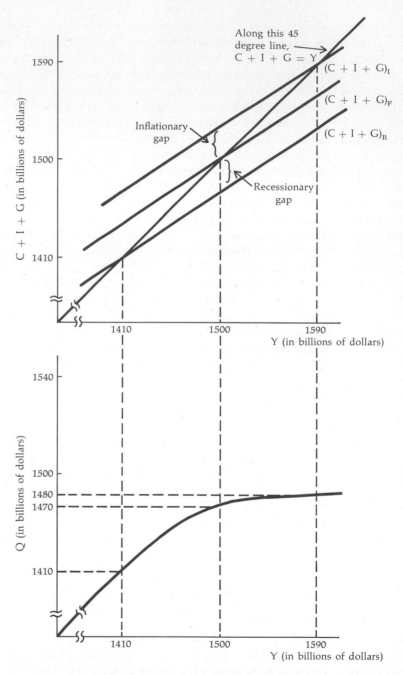

Figure 26B Extension of figure 26A

The level of employment actually depends on real output Q rather than nominal output or income Y (which equals $P \times Q$). Increases or decreases in Y ordinarily entail increases or decreases in Q. But when the economy is operating near the full employment level, increases in Q (real output) are hard to obtain. Bottlenecks of various sorts appear, and some prices rise even though resources are not fully employed. This is shown on the lower graph of figure 26B by the curve, the slope of which increases at a decreasing rate as Y gets close to $1500 billion. Beyond the full employent level of Y, Q can be increased only with great difficulty, and increases in Y result in very small increases in Q.

Since $Y = PQ$, $P = Y/Q$. The price level, in other words, is the ratio of nominal to real income. The economy cannot be brought from a $1410 billion level to the full employment equilibrium of $1500 billion without some increase in the price level. On the graph, this is an increase from the price level 1410/1410 to the price level 1500/1470 or a 2% increase in the price level. If aggregate demand rose to $(C + I + G)_I$, the equilibrium level of Y would be $1590 billion but real income would only be $1480 billion. This would entail an additional 5% increase in the price level.

This, in outline, is the analysis behind the argument, familiar long before 1970, that inflation and unemployment not only *could* coexist but were even *likely* to be found together. The conclusion of this exercise was that acceptance of a certain amount of inflation is the price society must pay to achieve "full employment." If the economy depicted in figure 26B is to be spared *completely* from inflation, then Y cannot be allowed to increase beyond about $1425 billion. Above that level, Q cannot keep pace with Y and inflation begins. But unemployment will be high—the graph doesn't tell us *how* high—if Y is only $1425 billion. Society must therefore choose between less unemployment and less inflation; within a certain range, at least, one cannot be reduced without increasing the other.

This line of analysis has considerable political importance. If the zealous pursuit of full employment causes inflation and if inflation cannot be stopped without creating unemployment, policymakers face a dilemma. But the dilemma is more complex than this simplified analysis suggests. Let's look at the matter more closely.

Full Employment, Search Costs, and Inflation

It's plausible to assume that when expansionary fiscal policy or monetary policy increases aggregate demand from $(C + I + G)_R$ to $(C + I + G)_F$, some inflation will occur before equilibrium is reached at $1500 billion. Resources must be *attracted* back into employment by a bidding process that is quite likely to mean some increase in the average of all prices. But

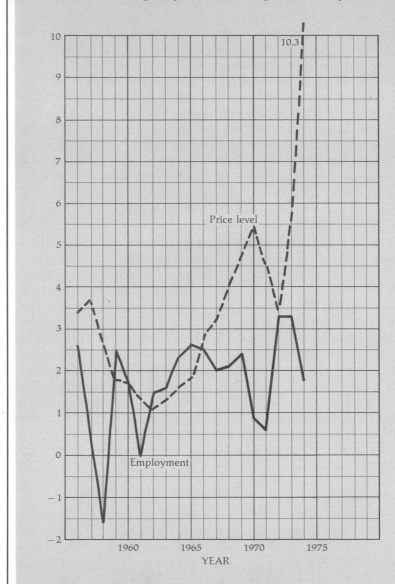

EMPLOYMENT AND INFLATION

Percentage change from year to year in total civilian employment and in the implicit price deflator for gross national product.

will the price level *continue* rising after the new equilibrium has been reached? Once resources are again fully employed, no further bidding up of prices or wages would seem to be required. The inflation associated with the movement to full employment could be a consequence of this *movement* and not of the full employment. An increase in the price level may have to be accepted to *restore* full employment, but once full employment has been reached, there is less reason to expect prices to continue rising.

But that is too simple a view of the matter. An economy "in aggregate equilibrium" will still contain a great deal of internal movement. Some industries will be growing and others declining. New production techniques, changes in the composition of demand, and entry into and exit from the labor force continue even when the economy is at a "full employment equilibrium." Resources will still have to be attracted into the expanding sectors through the offer of better employment terms. If prices and wages would fall slightly in declining industries and rise slightly in expanding industries, this continual reallocation of resources could take place with no increase in the average level of prices. If, however, prices and wages are quite rigid in a downward direction, all the price-wage adjustments needed to secure a reallocation of resources will have to be upward adjustments. Prices will then rise in expanding industries while remaining constant in declining industries, and the net effect will be an increase in the price level.

Downward adjustments of prices and wages are less likely to occur the closer the economy is to full employment. Why is this? Suppose that a college faced with declining enrollments tries to reduce faculty salaries. If the faculty members who are offered lower salaries believe that they can easily find other jobs that are just as good, they aren't likely to accept the reductions. If, on the other hand, they suspect that alternative employment opportunities will be hard to find, they will at least think twice before turning down the college's offer and looking for a different job. Anyone who followed the news closely during the 1974–75 recession could read about many cases where employees accepted wage reductions as an alternative to employment cutbacks. The employees would surely have been more reluctant to accept reductions (in some cases employees even initiated them) if they had thought that there were good employment opportunities elsewhere.

Remember that employers and employees do not have perfect information. They must search for what they want and incur the costs of that search. In a period of high employment, the cost of finding a new job will on average be lower for employees; they will therefore be more ready to give up a job when they think the wage is unsatisfactory and begin searching for another. So employers will find it more difficult to reduce wages.

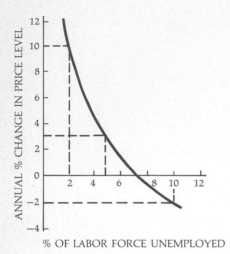

Figure 26C Phillips curve

Search costs for employers, however, are higher in periods of full employment. And so employers will offer wages higher than they might otherwise be willing to offer in order to avoid extending the costly search for the new employees they want.

The same argument applies to prices in product markets. When the economy is operating close to its capacity, excess supplies are generally hard to find and buyers will pay higher prices rather than search for alternative sources of supply. In a period of high unemployment and substantial excess capacity, sellers will be shaving prices because buyers are hard to find.

The identical conclusion emerges however we look at it. Full employment fosters an upward creep in prices and wages; substantial unemployment and excess capacity encourages a downward drift in prices and wages.

The Phillips Curve: Use and Abuse

In 1958 a British economist named A. W. Phillips published a study on "The Relationship between Unemployment and the Rate of Change of Money Wage Rates in the United Kingdom, 1861–1957" and invented the "Phillips curve." Phillips showed that there was a stable relation during the period he studied between the unemployment rate and the rate at which the average money wage increased. Unemployment was greater when money wage rates were increasing more slowly and fell in periods when money wage rates were rising rapidly. That seems thoroughly plausible. During periods of high demand for labor, employers will tend to bid up wage rates to obtain and keep the employees they want. In periods of high unemployment, employers will not have to bid so energetically for labor, and wage rates will increase less. But the argument was subsequently extended by others to suggest that unemployment might be reduced by allowing an inflationary rate of increase in money wages and, by extension, in the average of all prices. The Phillips curve of this latter argument purports to show that there is a trade-off between inflation and unemployment, so that less of one can be obtained by accepting more of the other. Figure 26C offers an illustration.

The Phillips curve as drawn above suggests that unemployment can be lowered to 2% of the labor force by accepting 10% inflation per year; that 2% annual *deflation* can be achieved by accepting a 10% unemployment rate; and that 5% unemployment can be obtained with 3% annual inflation.

At first glance this may seem to be only an illustration of the argument we've been making about the relation between upward creeping prices and wages and the level at which the economy is operating. But it actually implies much more than we've contended, and its implications may be seriously misleading. It does *not* follow either from the argument we've presented or from A. W. Phillips' data that policymakers have a menu like the one in figure 26C from which they can simply choose their preferred combination of inflation and unemployment.

The problem is that an attempt on the part of fiscal and monetary authorities to *use* the curve will cause it to *shift*. Suppose that the unemployment rate has been 5% for some time and that prices have been rising at an annual rate of 3%. The government consults the Phillips curve and decides to reduce unemployment to 3% by raising the inflation rate to 7%. It adopts a more expansionary fiscal or monetary policy, prices and wages rise at a faster rate, and unemployment falls toward 3%. The key question now is whether unemployment can be *maintained* at this lower level without *further* accelerating the rate of inflation.

Can Inflation Lower the Unemployment Rate Permanently?

To answer this question we must ask *why* unemployment would decline in the first place. In reasoning through the unemployment-inflation relationship, we argued that price and wage movements were a response to tightness or slackness in markets. In other words, the level of employment was the cause and price-wage movement the effect. We cannot simply assume that because full employment causes inflation, inflation will bring about full employment. When there is a big crowd at the basketball game, the gymnasium temperature rises because of the body heat; but the athletic department cannot make a crowd come to watch a losing basketball team by overheating the gymnasium.

Nonetheless, the policy of deliberately stepping up inflation probably would lower the unemployment rate—temporarily. People are unemployed because they don't find the job opportunities of which they're aware sufficiently attractive. If the level of real wages could somehow be increased across the board, all employment opportunities would become more attractive. Employment would therefore increase *except* for the fact that employers will demand less labor at higher real wage rates. However, when money wages and prices advance together, as they do in a general inflation, real wages don't actually increase. But *workers think they have increased,* and that will be enough to lower the unemployment rate.

A policy of deliberate inflation makes job opportunities *seem* more attractive by raising the *money* wage rate offers of employers. And this is how inflation reduces unemployment. But the higher wage rate offers are only *seemingly* more attractive. *Real* wage rates do not rise; only money wage rates rise. As long as potential employees don't realize that the job opportunities they're now accepting are in reality no better than the opportunities they previously rejected, employment will indeed rise. Employment will fall back down to its previous level, however, when employees discover what's happening and realize that inflation is creating the illusion of more attractive wage offers. As they discover that they've been "tricked,"

employment will decline again and the Phillips curve will now pass through the point of 7% inflation, but with unemployment back at its previous level of 5%. The curve will have shifted upward. No permanent reduction in unemployment will have occurred, but the economy will be undergoing more rapid inflation.

A deliberate policy of pursuing lower unemployment by creating a higher rate of inflation calls for *continually increasing* the inflation rate so that workers continually *expect* less than the actual rate of inflation. In this way they can be made continually to overestimate the real value of the money wages they are being offered. We must either continually increase the rate of inflation or assume that employees pay exclusive attention to money wage rates and never consider real wage rates. This is a superficially plausible assumption; we know that few employees consult the most recent changes in the Consumer Price Index before deciding whether a wage offer is adequate. They look at *money* wage rates, in other words. But they also learn after a while that their wages buy less and adjust their perception of the wage rate's real value. An extreme example will make the point. In 1956, workers stood in line for jobs at manufacturing firms offering $2 an hour. In 1976, manufacturers can find almost no one who will accept employment at that wage. Employees *do* know, even if they've never heard of price indices, that $2 is a much lower hourly wage today than it was twenty years ago.

Policy cannot be constructed on the assumption that workers will be permanently fooled; people do learn from experience. And the simultaneous existence of high unemployment with very rapid inflation in the early 1970s ought to be sufficient evidence that people *have* learned. When they begin to assume continued inflation, they no longer suffer from the illusion that money wages and real wages are the same thing.

But now suppose that the government discerns the error of its ways and regrets its policy initiative. Unemployment is back at the old 5% level but inflation is now progressing at 7% per year. The government therefore decides to reverse its policy and get inflation down to 3% again. So it eases up on the fiscal-monetary stimulus it's been applying. Monetary demand will now stop increasing so rapidly, producers will be unable to sell at the prices they had anticipated, inventories will mount, production will be curtailed, and unemployment will rise. Eventually sellers will learn not to expect such a rapid rise in prices, they will adjust downward the prices they ask and the prices they offer to pay for inputs, sales will revive, inventories will decline, production will start up again, and unemployment will fall. But that won't all happen within a week or even a month. The higher unemployment that will result from an attempt to slow down the rate of inflation will be temporary; but temporary can be a long time. The cost of letting inflation get out of hand may be very high indeed.

Conclusions and Implications

Let's try to summarize the conclusions that have emerged so far from our examination of the relationship between inflation and unemployment.

1. A movement from a situation of low employment to one of high or "full" employment will generally be accompanied by a rising price level. Increased demand will bid up some prices and wages even before "full" employment is achieved.

2. Increases in aggregate demand when the economy is already operating in the vicinity of "full" employment will have their principal impact on the price-wage level. Modest and temporary increases in real output and employment may result, but most of the rise in Y will be in P rather than in Q.

3. An economy operating in the vicinity of "full" employment tends to experience creeping inflation. By lowering search costs for sellers of both products and labor and raising search costs for buyers, "full" employment promotes an upward drift in the terms of price and wage bargains.

4. The unemployment rate is affected by *changes* in the rate of inflation. An unanticipated increase in the inflation rate tends to reduce unemployment; and an unanticipated decrease in the inflation rate tends to increase unemployment. But a constant rate of inflation, because it's presumably fully anticipated, probably has no effect on the unemployment rate.

There are some important policy lessons tucked away in those four conclusions for anyone who dislikes both high unemployment rates *and* inflation.

1. Avoid recessions if you want to avoid inflation because the process of recovery from a recession usually entails inflation.

2. Try not to let inflation get started if you want to prevent high unemployment because slowing down the rate of inflation will ordinarily cause unemployment to increase.

3. Creeping inflation is probably the price that a society must pay for all the gains that accrue from continuous operation at or near the economy's capacity.

4. The Phillips curve is a dangerous concept if it encourages the illusion that a permanently lower unemployment rate can be "purchased" by accepting a higher rate of inflation.

Lessons 3 and 4 are not contradictory. Lesson 3 merely acknowledges the fact that upward price adjustments will dominate downward adjustments and lead to a slow upward drift in the price level when the economic system is operating with very little slack. It warns, you might say, against the pursuit of perfection. Lesson 4 warns against confusing cause and effect and assuming that since high employment generates inflation, more inflation will generate higher employment.

WHAT UNEMPLOYMENT RATE IS ACCEPTABLE?

When is the unemployment rate "too high"? If there is an unavoidable minimum of "frictional" unemployment, how can we decide whether it is 2%, 6%, or something else? Is there a *natural* rate of unemployment?

Appendix 4 at the end of the book presents an article on office space in New York City that suggests a way of thinking about this question. There will always be *some* vacant office space in New York. A zero vacancy rate is neither possible nor desirable. Firms will continually be moving into and out of the city or looking for office space more suitable to their changed circumstances. Newly constructed space will not be rented immediately and vacated space will stand empty for at least a short interval. If the vacancy rate were to fall to 1%, firms looking for space would have difficulty finding it. We would expect to hear complaints about the "tightness" of the market, to observe rising rents as firms competed for the office space they wanted, and to see an increase in the rate of office building construction as developers came to anticipate larger profits from providing new space.

A 10% vacancy rate would produce the opposite results. Owners of office buildings would complain about the "glutted" market, rents would decline as owners competed for occupants, and the rate of new construction would slow down.

If we were to observe no net tendency for rents to rise or decline, no tendency for the rate of new construction to accelerate or slow down, and no greater incidence of complaints from owners about "gluts" than from tenants about the "tight" market, we could conclude that the vacancy rate was at its "natural" level.

Could we argue in an analogous way that the unemployment rate is at its "natural" level when we observe no net tendency for wage rates to rise or decline, no tendency for the rate of labor-force participation to increase or decrease, and about as many complaints from workers that "there are no jobs" as complaints from employers that "you can't get help"? Since the volume of complaints would be hard to tabulate, we might substitute something like the number of job seekers registered with state employment agencies and the number of job vacancies listed by employers.

This approach will unfortunately not enable us to decide with confidence whether the unemployment rate at any time is excessive or merely at its "natural" and acceptable level. But it does clarify the problem somewhat and indicate the kind of data at which we might look to decide whether or not the current unemployment rate should be a matter for concern.

The Bureau of Labor Statistics divides the unemployed into job losers, job leavers, those who are reentering the labor force after an absence, and new entrants into the labor force. We can compare each with a category of office space. Job losers correspond to offices that are empty because tenants choose to leave. Job leavers correspond to offices that are empty because tenants have been evicted. (Note that landlords often "evict" tenants by demanding a higher rent.) Reentrants correspond to offices that had previously been withdrawn from the market because the owners did not expect to receive rental income equal to maintenance costs but are now again being offered for rent. New entrants can be divided into two groups. Young people entering the labor force for the first time correspond to newly constructed space. Older people who have not previously held jobs because other family members earned an adequate income but who have now been pulled into the labor force either by declining family income or by more attractive job offers correspond to older space being offered for rent for the first time. A firm may decide, for example, to sublet a portion of the space it had previously reserved for its own purposes, either because business has fallen off or because high rental prices have persuaded its managers that more can be earned by renting out the space than by using it for the firm's own operations.

All of this suggests that a wide variety of economic, political, or cultural changes could cause the "natural" unemployment rate to increase or decrease. Do you agree that each of the following would *increase* the "natural" rate of unemployment?

(*a*) Employer discrimination against women diminishes and more women consequently begin looking for jobs in the labor market.

(*b*) Blacks come to believe that job prospects have improved, perhaps as a result of antidiscrimination legislation, and some who had stopped looking for work out of discouragement reenter the labor force.

(*c*) Unemployment compensation benefits are increased and extended so that the cost of remaining unemployed while searching for a better job declines.

(*d*) Young people come to believe that they should not select a career course until they have experimented with a variety of jobs.

(*e*) Family incomes rise significantly faster than per capita incomes.

Lessons 1 and 2 are of doubtful value if we don't know *how* to avoid recessions or increases in the rate of inflation. A fiscal-monetary activist might extract from them a recommendation for fine-tuning. A fiscal-monetary passivist, on the other hand, will argue that the attempt to fine-tune is a principal cause of recession and inflation, and will see in these lessons a case for restraint in the practice of demand management. The issue of fine-tuning versus automatic controls was discussed in chapter 25. One conclusion to which we came then was that a satisfactory conclusion is unlikely until we know a great deal more about the way individual decision makers adjust to change when the future is uncertain.

Would a sure recipe for rapid inflation coupled with high unemployment be of any use? Could it serve as a warning to policymakers? Let the government run continual large deficits and finance them by creating new money with Fed purchases of government securities. The accompanying expenditure programs should change often and unpredictably. Tax policy should also change often and unpredictably. Credits granted for new investment should be followed by surtaxes on capital purchases. Then policy should move back to investment tax credits. Periodic threats to raise corporate income taxes will also help if the threats can be made credible. Price controls should be imposed to create shortages that may compel some firms to shut down; the controls should be removed before the public learns to adjust to them, however, and then reimposed after a while. The government should also pass legislation imposing detailed but unenforceable controls on job safety procedures and emission of pollutants and then rescind the legislation long after its unworkability has become apparent. Impose and remove, in as unpredictable a way as possible, import quotas, tariffs, taxes, other controls on foreign investment, and export subsidies. (Anyone can add his own ingredients as soon as he understands the formula.) Increase monetary demand well beyond the rate at which real output can increase while introducing as much uncertainty as possible into the situations confronted by consumers, investors, employees, and employers. Rapid inflation and high unemployment are guaranteed to occur simultaneously.

PRICE AND WAGE CONTROLS

Arthur F. Burns is a distinguished economist who became chairman of the board of governors of the Federal Reserve System in 1970. Along with most other economists, Burns had long maintained that the key to a stable price level is monetary and fiscal restraint on the part of government and not wage or price controls. But when he found himself in charge of imposing an important part of that restraint, Burns changed the direction of his thinking. His public speeches reveal the evolution of his thought.[1] Burns reluctantly concluded that labor and product markets did not function well enough for fiscal and monetary policy to be effective. Strong unions and business firms with substantial market power were able to raise wages and prices in the absence of any increases in demand. Confronted with this situation, monetary and fiscal authorities had to choose between causing unemployment by refusing to expand total demand or increasing the rate of inflation by underwriting the wage and price increases.

Market Power, Unemployment, and Inflation

To understand Burns's reasoning, suppose that a significant number of wage rates are set by collective bargaining, and that unions have the ability to obtain money wage increases in excess of productivity increases. This would mean that unions (or some unions) can obtain for their members a money wage that is above the value of labor's marginal productivity. Another way of putting it is to say that the unions can persuade some employers to pay workers a money wage greater than the current value of the marginal worker's *net* contribution to the firm's revenue.

Because marginal workers now add more to the costs than to the revenue of the firm, employers adjust by reducing the number of workers they hire. They may not actually lay anyone off; instead they will just refrain from replacing workers as they retire or quit. The result is a reduction in the number of jobs available and an increase in measured unemployment. If employers raise their prices to recover the higher labor costs, they won't be able to sell as much at higher prices and the reduced sales will eventually lead to employment cutbacks. Even if union members realize that higher money wages mean fewer jobs, a majority may vote for the wage increase in the belief that they themselves will be protected by seniority; they risk the jobs of *other* employees who have less seniority.

---

1. A comprehensive but succinct summary of Burns's opinions on the possibilities and difficulties of demand management is contained in the appendix. It's valuable to study the views of a powerful policymaker who has substantial freedom from political constraints and is an excellent economist and a lucid writer.

Rising unemployment caused by this kind of market power puts the government under pressure to adopt an expansionary fiscal or monetary policy. When it does so, the price level rises. The rise in the price of everything else will reduce the *relative* price of the good whose sales had fallen, its sales will expand once more, and employment in that industry will be restored. In the event that employers are price takers and lack the market power to pass the wage increase along to buyers, the increase in the price of *all* goods does the job for them. The real wage is consequently reduced and employment is restored to its initial level. The upshot of the matter is that the use of excessive market power creates unemployment problems and that the government is forced to cause inflation to deal with the unemployment problems.

How did we get into such a bind? Is there a way out? Burns has pointed to three principal causes of the problem. They are strong unions; business firms selling in insufficiently competitive markets; and innumerable government regulations that tolerate, encourage, and even require practices that raise costs and reduce efficiency. In the last category Burns includes subsidies to farmers, legal restrictions on entry into various trades or professions, import quotas and tariffs, the federal minimum wage law (especially in its application to teenagers), aspects of our welfare programs, price maintenance laws, and the failure to enforce antitrust legislation. The solution is structural reforms directed toward increasing competition and thereby making wages and prices more responsive to forces of supply and demand.[1]

But reforms of that sort can't be implemented quickly. The active participation of government in the creation of the problems suggests that such reforms will only be possible, if they're possible at all, after a long campaign of public education. In the meantime we shall have to make do with second-best policies. Some legal controls on prices and wages may be necessary if we are to avoid confronting the nation's fiscal-monetary managers with the unpleasant choice between accepting unemployment of causing inflation.

Defensible and Indefensible Arguments for Controls

The general public has never had much trouble believing that inflation is the result of irresponsible behavior on the part of sellers, whether of products or of labor services. The public looks for villains when things go wrong and seems to find them among the business firms that announce price increases and the union leaders who call for wage hikes. An excessive rate of increase in monetary demand is a force too abstract and impersonal

1. Keep in mind that union strength, corporate market power, and anticompetitive government regulations *must be increasing* if the problem to which Burns calls attention is growing worse.

"DEMAND-PULL" AND "COST-PUSH" INFLATION

If the monetary demand for goods increases faster than additional goods can be produced, prices will be bid up. This is the usual way in which inflation occurs. But the average of all prices might also rise because some sellers are able to raise their prices in the absence of any increase in demand. This is sometimes called *cost-push* inflation to distinguish it from the traditional *demand-pull* inflation. But cost-push inflation usually requires assistance from demand-pull. The market power of sellers is unlikely to cause persistent inflation unless the monetary managers cooperate.

We can use the equation of exchange, $MV = PQ$, to consider the possibilities. Let's suppose that there is a competitive sector of the economy where individual sellers of products and of labor have no power to raise their prices or wages and where they do not combine to achieve this power. And let's suppose that the remainder of the economy is a "monopolistic" sector (with "monopolistic" enclosed in quotation marks to remind you that it's a word with almost as many meanings as it has users). Goods produced in the competitive sector are represented by Q_c, goods produced in the "monopolistic" sector by Q_m. Now $Q_c + Q_m = Q$, and if P_c and P_m represent respectively the average prices of goods produced in each sector, then $P_c Q_c + P_m Q_m = PQ$. We rewrite the equation of exchange as

$$MV = P_c Q_c + P_m Q_m$$

What will occur if the government regulators, powerful labor unions, or giant corporations allegedly responsible for the existence of a "monopolistic" sector raise P_m in the absence of any increase in the demand for Q_m?

The law of demand tells us that when P_m rises, Q_m will fall. The more elastic the demand for Q_m, the larger will be the decline in Q_m and the consequent increase in unemployment in the "monopolistic" sector. But output and employment might also decrease in the competitive sector. If the demand for Q_m is inelastic, people will spend more income than before in purchasing a smaller quantity of these higher-priced goods, less income will consequently be left for the purchase of competitively produced goods, and so the demand for Q_c will decrease. The more resistant prices in the competitive sector are to downward pressure, the larger will be the resulting decline in Q_c and decline in employment in the competitive sector.

The maintenance of previous levels of output and employment in the face of a rise in P_m requires, therefore, an increase in MV. V would increase when the "monopolistic" sector raises its prices only if the increase in P_m somehow induced the public to prefer smaller money balances. It is difficult to imagine why or how that would occur. If the demand for money balances does *not* decrease, an increase in MV requires a larger stock of money. And so the responsibility passes to the monetary managers. M will have to be increased if a rise in the unemployment rate is to be prevented.

Whether we choose to call the resulting rise in the average of all prices a cost-push or a demand-pull inflation and whether we put the blame on the "monopolists" or the money managers is less important than that we understand the process by which this kind of inflation might occur. Of course, a model of how it *might* occur is no evidence that it *has* occurred. How much power "monopolists"—unions, corporations, or government agencies—actually have to raise prices in this manner is a difficult empirical question. And regardless of how much power they have, the problem will not have grown worse in recent years unless their power has been increasing. That, too, is a disputed empirical question.

to be a good candidate for villain, and so corporations and unions tend to be blamed for inflation even when wages and prices are clearly being pulled up by excess demand and not being pushed up by market power. That's why the imposition of wage and price controls during a period of inflation usually encounters, at least initially, an overwhelmingly favorable response from the public. A case in point is the wage-price freeze announced in August 1971.

The popularity of wage and price controls as a way of dealing with inflation makes it all the more urgent that the public understand the mechanisms of inflation. The argument made by Arthur Burns and many other economists is a defensible one. It calls for controls on those wages and prices that are not adequately controlled by competition, so that the fiscal and monetary authorities can pursue noninflationary policies. And it looks forward to structural reforms that would eliminate the restrictive practices that made the controls necessary.

This is an argument vastly different from the one that calls for controls to keep wages and prices from rising *after* the fiscal or monetary authorities have expanded aggregate demand at a more rapid rate than the rate at which real output can be increased, or after some disaster (war, oil embargoes, crop failures) has reduced the level of real output. In such circumstances, controls are worse than useless. They suspend the rationing system by which scarce goods are allocated among competing claimants. This means that the goods have to be allocated by other criteria. Buyers will get in line early, cultivate contacts, try to negotiate special agreements, or offer illegal monetary inducements to get around the maximum price.

The incentive to hoard goods increases, because goods are undervalued at their legal prices and because buyers cannot be sure of obtaining supplies in the future. This further aggravates the scarcity. Producers have less incentive to expand output and maintain quality. Production will fall further as manufacturers find themselves unable to obtain particular inputs that have disappeared from suppliers' inventories. They may even have to suspend production and lay workers off. Export controls will be instituted to keep other countries from taking advantage of the controlled prices. Bartering will creep into the supply system and not only decrease efficiency but also raise cries of inequity from those producers who have nothing of value to offer their suppliers. Items such as paper bags, shoe heels, plastic syringes, and lawn fertilizer will unexpectedly disappear from retail shelves as shortages multiply and breed further shortages. Relative prices will not be able to change in response to changing relative scarcities, and the structure of prices will start to give misleading signals to resource users. In short, suppression of the price system suspends the mechanism of economic coordination and leads to inequities, inefficiencies, and disruptions of production that only worsen the imbalance between demand and supply.

Imposing price controls in the face of an inflation caused by too many dollars chasing too few goods aggravates the problem by reducing the supply of goods and diminishing the incentive of demanders to economize in their use. And this is true whether the imbalance was caused by an excessive creation of dollars or a deficient creation of goods. Moreover, it diverts the attention of the public from the actual causes of the inflation and the proper remedies. Of course, a government whose fiscal and monetary policies have fueled an inflation will be only too happy to encourage the public's belief that private avarice is the root of the problem, that public-spirited self-restraint on the part of citizens is the ultimate answer, and that the rascals who have no public spirit must be controlled by law. Congress will rarely admit that its own spending habits are the cause of any ills.

What Can We Learn from Wartime Price and Wage Controls?

The wage and price controls of World War II are sometimes brought forward as evidence that controls can in fact be effective in preventing excess demand from pulling up prices. But this argument ignores some important facts. For one, it overlooks the public's willingness to put up with shortages and tolerate inequities when they are viewed as temporary necessities. Above all, it overlooks the alternative rationing system created by the federal government during World War II to allocate scarce goods among competing claimants. It ignores the complex point system, the books of ration stamps, the special gasoline coupons, the priority allocations, and the army of controllers that were all required to make the system work as well as it did. It overlooks the role of wartime patriotism in securing the voluntary cooperation that kept the system functioning for several years and closes its eyes to the illegal and semilegal evasions that sometimes helped the system work by enabling people to circumvent it. And when the controls were removed after the war, the excess demand dammed up behind them poured out to raise prices 33% between 1945 and 1948.

The public must learn to distinguish carefully between arguments for limited controls in selected situations where competition is an ineffective regulating force and across-the-board controls imposed to prevent excess money demand from raising prices. The latter is a recipe for disaster. The former may be an effective way to deal with a difficult economic and political problem.

But even limited wage and price controls are going to pose major difficulties. On whom will they be imposed, and how will this be determined? Who will decide when adjustments are called for and what criteria will they employ? Whatever the economic rationale, will the political system be adequate to such a task? It is essential to note that Arthur Burns assigns much of the blame for the decline of competition to government policies. Is it realistic to expect the same government to undo its own work? Regulatory agencies like the Interstate Commerce Commission and the Civil Aeronautics Board that have long taken their function to be the prevention of competition will not suddenly revise their thinking and procedures. State legislators who bow to industry lobbies and create legal cartel arrangements aren't likely to acquire new wisdom or courage any time soon. Anticompetitive laws in the areas of agriculture, labor, and international trade continue to command a Congressional majority. Who will mind the sheep when the shepherds have such a taste for mutton?

INCOMES POLICY

A phrase sometimes used in place of "wage and price controls" to describe the kind of approach recommended by Burns is *incomes policy*. It's an apt phrase, because it calls attention to the origins of the problem and the inherent difficulty of resolving it. If costs are in fact pushed up in the absence of demand increases, it is the result of people's pursuit of higher incomes. They want a larger share. Workers want higher wages, property owners want larger returns on their investment, and business executives want larger rewards for making their firms' revenues increase faster than costs. They all pursue their objectives by trying to raise certain prices relative to others. This poses no problem if competition adequately constrains them. But where economic interests are able to combine or collude, they may be successful in enlarging their share of the pie. Or they may simply offset one another and leave everyone's share unchanged while jacking up the price level in the course of the struggle.

Controls and Income Distribution

If the government tries to control the prices that these groups are able to set it implicitly makes a judgment on *how income ought to be distributed.* By referring to such a program as an incomes policy we are at least calling attention to the scope and importance of the problem being tackled. And it's a problem that looks more formidable the longer it's examined.

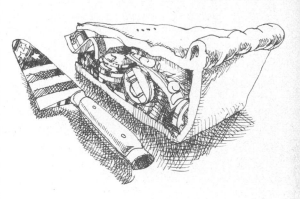

The problem is that the sum of the dollar claims people make on the national income invariably comes to much more than 100% of the dollar value of the national income. To put it crudely, there aren't many people who believe they deserve less than the average and a lot of people who claim more than the average. So what's new? There may be nothing new in the situation if you confine your attention to Western nations and the other nations and cultures descended from Europe. But within these societies the demand by individuals and groups for a larger share of the social product has generally been kept in check by the similar demands of others, and the market has functioned as the adjudicator of competing claims. The market was never a completely "free" market; groups that were able to use political processes to influence market outcomes did so. Two hundred years ago the American Revolution came about in part as the consequence of conflict among such powerful economic interests; each was bent on using the state to improve and protect its own economic opportunities.

The Organizational Revolution

But in the twentieth century two new elements may have appeared. Interest groups are now more effectively organized into labor unions, farm federations, corporations, and professional and trade associations. They are consequently better able to protect their members against the adverse consequences of competition. The economist Kenneth Boulding has called this "the organizational revolution" in a book with that title. As each group pursues its own interests by reducing competition, the market ceases to be an effective regulator of economic activity. The invisible hand that Adam Smith saw leading people to promote the public interest while intending only to pursue their private interests depends upon the existence of competition. In an economy dominated by power blocs, the pursuit of private interests may destroy the public interest.

Rejection of the Market

A second development that some observers see is a decline in the perceived legitimacy of market outcomes. By this we mean that fewer people are now prepared to accept market processes as fundamentally just. Perhaps this is related to the first factor mentioned. If people believe that the economy is not governed by "fair competition" but by "special interests," they will not give their consent to the way income is distributed. They will rather try to use the political process to shape the economic process more into line with their own perceptions of fairness.

If this analysis is correct, then governments will not be able to use incomes policy to rein in conflicting interests because *it is incomes policy over which the interests are conflicting.* A particular criterion of fairness cannot be used to settle a dispute over the appropriateness of that criterion. The Genie Conception of government conceals this dilemma. We may be able to see that the economic system does not work as it should and to outline government policies that would improve its performance. But the same forces responsible for the unsatisfactory performance of the economy will block the adoption of the political policies being recommended. It is painfully reminiscent of the fable about the mice who wanted to protect themselves against cats by putting a bell on each cat. If cats let themselves be belled by mice, however, mice would have no reason to want bells on cats.

THE POLITICALIZATION OF THE ECONOMY

Throughout most of this book we have assumed that people want for themselves more of the commodities and services that the economy can provide. From chapter 16 on we have supposed that everyone prefers higher to lower unemployment rates and price stability to inflation. The analysis of economic practices and policies is much easier when we know what the goals are and can take certain shared social purposes for granted. When the goals themselves are in dispute, however, it is difficult to find a vantage point from which to gain perspective.

Economists are no more adept than anyone else at resolving disagreements that involve conflicting goals. The science of economics has nonetheless been able to make analytical advances in the face of conflicting social interests by tying itself closely to the analysis of market processses and outcomes. Markets are just exchange networks. And voluntary exchange is a process by which people who have conflicting interests achieve agreement. It's a limited agreement; but it's enough to enable people with conflicting interests to cooperate in ways that make each participant better off. Anyone who is not made better off simply doesn't exchange. To secure the cooperation of others in improving our own positions, we must find ways to improve their positions, too. Economists view the market as a vast computer into which all preferences are registered, in which all contradictory intentions are accommodated, and from which a particular mixture of output emerges and is distributed. By sticking closely to the analysis of market processes, economists have been able to incorporate conflicting goals and interests into their analyses *without judging among them.* No vantage point above the fray is required to interpret what's going on.

Economic Decisions and Political Judgments

When the members of a society begin to object to the market process itself, however, and when one of the goals becomes the transformation of the system for accommodating conflicting purposes, the economist's task grows immensely more difficult. And that is the situation we have today. What we have called the politicalization of the economy is in large part an attempt to change the rules of the game. The market system itself is in question.

The most fundamental objection to the market process is that, while it may enable all participants to better their conditions, it takes for granted the initial distribution of the resources on the basis of which people exchange. The justice and therefore the political acceptability of market outcomes depends on the justice of the positions from which everyone begins. In very poor societies it makes a great deal of sense to ignore the distribution of wealth in order to concentrate on increasing the total amount available. This is especially sensible if the growth of national income entails increases in income for those at the bottom of the ladder. And this has in fact been the historical tendency in market-organized economies. But more total income becomes relatively less important as a society becomes more affluent, and questions about the way the income is distributed start to take on increasing significance.

A closely related objection to the market process has to do with the appropriate tradeoff between marketable commodities and services on the one hand and less tangible goods such as serenity, beauty, or community on the other. In a society with an abundance of marketable goods, the marginal cost of paying attention to their marginal cost may seem too high to justify the effort. And an economic system that works by focusing attention on these costs may increasingly seem to reflect an irrational attachment to rationality.

The link between all this and the pursuit of full employment and price stability should be obvious. Economic policymakers will be hard-pressed to achieve these goals, not only because we lack an adequate knowledge of money velocities, expenditure multipliers, and time lags, but also because full employment and price stability are not the only goals we're pursuing. We have turned increasingly in this century to government as the appropriate agency to regulate the economy in the interest of a better society. If the results have often been disappointing, it may be because we have thoughtlessly adopted the Genie Conception of government and have paid too little attention to the actual consequences of well-intentioned proposals. But it may also be because we have given too little thought to the question of what we mean by "a better society."

Once Over Lightly

Recession and inflation are not simple alternatives between which policymakers can choose. The fact that low rates of unemployment are historically associated with periods of rising prices does not mean that policymakers can always reduce unemployment by causing or tolerating inflation.

In a period of recovery from a recession, the price level may begin rising before total output and employment regain prerecession levels. This is especially likely if increased demand raises some wages and prices and others are resistant to downward pressure.

Halting or slowing down the rate of inflation may cause a recession. If sellers of products and labor anticipate continued inflation, they will hold out for higher prices and wages than they would otherwise ask. If the expected inflation does not materialize, they will be unable to sell as much as they had anticipated selling. High unemployment rates and accumulations of unwanted inventories will continue until events have taught sellers to revise their expectations and lower their price and wage demands.

An economy that is continuously operating close to capacity tends to create sellers' markets. In such markets, search costs are low for sellers and high for buyers. Sellers consequently tend to hold out longer against lowering their prices, buyers tend more quickly to accept prices higher than they had anticipated, and price and wage levels creep upward.

Unemployment levels might be lowered temporarily and output levels temporarily increased by an acceleration in the rate of inflation. This will occur if sellers of labor and products mistakenly assume that they are being offered better terms. But employment and output levels will decline again as sellers of labor learn that *real* wages have not increased and sellers of products learn that costs have increased along with prices. Only a constantly accelerating inflation can maintain the illusion of better terms and keep employment and output at these higher levels.

Price and wage controls that are imposed when aggregate demand exceeds the ability of the economy to produce at current prices create shortages, inefficient resource allocation, and disruptions in production.

They cannot solve the problem of inflation caused by excessive monetary demand, but they can make the problem worse.

Sellers of labor and products who are sufficiently well organized to raise wages and prices in the absence of any increase in monetary demand will reduce the quantity of labor demanded and increase unemployment. If the government responds by increasing monetary demand, it will be able to prevent the increase in unemployment by causing inflation. Some economists believe that labor unions, large corporations, and government regulations are reducing competition in many sectors of the economy and thereby confronting aggregate demand managers with the unpleasant necessity of choosing between the acceptance of unemployment and the acceptance of inflation. They therefore argue for controls on those wages and prices that are not, in their estimation, adequately controlled by competition.

The imposition of such controls entails a prior decision by government as to which groups will not be allowed to use their political or market power to increase their incomes. In the absence of a political consensus on how income *ought* to be distributed, the government will probably be unable to formulate and enforce such an incomes policy.

Most goods are scarce; they can only be obtained by sacrificing other goods. This may also be true for the goods of high employment and stable prices. It is possible that some of the goals we are pursuing through political processes will make high employment and price stability impossible to achieve.

QUESTIONS FOR DISCUSSION

1.   (a) Why is the price level likely to rise faster the lower the level of unemployment in the economy?

    (b) Does raising the unemployment rate slow down inflation? How so? How long does it take?

2.   (a) Is aggregate demand inadequate if there is a shortage of automotive mechanics and a surplus of secondary school teachers?

    (b) Can substantial unemployment exist at a time when listed job vacancies exceed total unemployment?

3.   "There is no danger that a government deficit will cause inflation when unemployment stands at 8% of the civilian labor force." Do you agree?

4.   How and why does the attempt to lower the permanent rate of unemployment by deliberately causing inflation depend upon an illusion?

5. "The basic cause of an excessively high unemployment rate is uncertainty." Explain whether you agree or disagree with this statement and why.

6. Would you expect a different effect on employment from the imposition of a temporary quota against imports than from the imposition of a quota that is expected to be permanent? Why?

7. If union-won wage increases add to unemployment and the Fed then expands the money supply to reduce the unemployment rate, who is the villain responsible for inflation?

8. If it is socially irresponsible for sellers to raise their prices in periods of inflation, why did the government raise the price of the annual *Economic Report of the President* from $3.05 in 1974 to $3.25 in 1975?

9. Is it socially responsible for the Civil Aeronautics Board to raise the prices of airline travel but socially irresponsible for food processors to raise the prices of frozen vegetables?

10. Make up two lists of prices and wages. One should contain specific prices and wages that in your judgment *are not* adequately controlled by competition and the other should contain specific wages and prices that you think *are* adequately controlled by competition. What criteria will you use? What evidence do you have to support your lists?

11. Is it unjust for money wage rates to rise less rapidly than prices? Is it unjust for some money wage rates to rise faster and others more slowly than prices? Can you think of some wage and salary rates that *ought to* rise less rapidly than prices? On what basis would you answer this question?

12. "A teacher of chemistry should not be paid more than a teacher of history simply because the demand for chemistry teachers is greater relative to the supply. Teachers are not commodities. They are professional persons with family responsibilities who are providing essential public services." Do you agree with that statement? Under what circumstances do you think its principles are most likely to find acceptance?

13. Why does it take so much more effort and involve so much more conflict for the faculty of a college to agree on a revision of the curriculum they are "selling" to students than for the managers of department stores to decide on the mixture of goods they will offer for sale?

14. Is it possible to control inflation by having a panel of experts pass on all proposed wage and price increases? Should such panels include an equal number of business, labor, and consumer representatives.

15. "Because government is not limited by private profit, it can often accomplish what private interests cannot accomplish." Discuss.

ECONOMICS AND THE GOOD SOCIETY

Why is there so much disagreement about economic policies among intelligent and well-informed people who are genuinely looking for the public interest and not simply advocating their own narrow interests? Why is it so much more difficult to achieve consensus on the best way to manage the economy than on the best way to put people on the moon? Are economic interrelationships that much more complex than the relationships that had to be mastered to achieve a successful lunar landing?

FACTS AND VALUES

Economists have often pointed out, as a way of answering these questions, that disagreements over economic policy stem from two different kinds of disagreement. There is disagreement about *what is* and disagreement about *what ought to be.* Science can supposedly answer questions of the first type, because they only require attention to facts and logical reasoning. But when we disagree about what ought to be or about the goals of economic policy, we are in the realm of ethics. And we do not have any way of resolving ethical disagreements. They are ultimately judgments of value; and ultimate value judgments cannot finally be proved or disproved.

There is something unsatisfactory about this way of setting up the problem, however. In the first place, the science of economics is not completely independent of economists' value judgments. Our theories are not

based exclusively on observation and the rules of logic; the value judgments of scientists often shape their choice of theories, both in the physical sciences and more obviously in the social sciences. In the second place, disagreements about what ought to be often *can* be resolved by closer attention to fact and logic. Perhaps there is no way of resolving disagreement on *ultimate* values. But when is a value ultimate? How many of our important ethical disagreements are actually rooted in ultimate and therefore unresolvable differences?

One very important reason why people disagree about goals is that they disagree on what is possible. One group may recommend a policy because its members assign a high priority to achieving greater economic equality. Another group may oppose the policy because its members place a high value on individual freedom of choice. But each group may believe that its goal can be achieved without any substantial sacrifice of the other goal and make its policy recommendations on this assumption. For example, people who want laws against racial and sexual discrimination by employers rarely believe that the administration of these laws will infringe in any significant way on individual freedom. Opponents of such legislation, on the other hand, often do not see how it can be made effective unless those charged with administering the law are granted the power to make essentially arbitrary decisions. The real disagreement may consequently not be about the relative importance of equality and freedom but about the problems likely to be encountered in administering ambiguous laws. Even the fundamental (or seemingly fundamental) disagreements that characterize debates between "capitalists" and "socialists" may be largely of this kind.

Surprisingly little of the disagreement over economic policy turns out to be purely disagreement about goals. Far more commonly, a policy will be recommended by one group but opposed by another because the two groups expect different consequences from its adoption. This does not mean that we could easily reach consensus if we all looked at the consequences of the proposals we're recommending. It does mean, however, that we have much to learn by paying closer attention to the criticisms of others. Every action has unintended and often undesirable consequences. But someone strongly committed to the goal an action is designed to achieve will be less capable of perceiving or appreciating these consequences than someone else whose primary commitment is to different goals.

The authors of this book do not believe, therefore, that strong convictions have no proper role in economic policy discussions or that economists ought to or even can keep value judgments out of their analysis. But this danger is much less than the danger that people will refuse to let their goals be affected by criticism. It is much too easy to become totally convinced of the justice of one's goals and to treat all criticism as evidence of bad faith. But the best and the worst social goals can only be sought by employing fallible policies that may in the end do more harm than good despite the purity of intention behind them. The full consequences of the economic policies we adopt will never be known with certainty. But economics can suggest answers even for a society beginning to question its goals, because economics is a way of thinking that clarifies the consequences of social action.

THE ECONOMIST'S PERSPECTIVE

An answer presupposes a question, however, and the answers we discover are products of the questions we ask. A great deal therefore depends on where we begin, the point of view we adopt, what we assume before we start, and the concepts that we use to organize our thinking and questioning. Thomas Kuhn, an influential philosopher of science, has argued that all scientific activity is rooted in some *paradigm*. By this he means a set of working assumptions that guide inquiry by posing certain questions and ignoring others. Every scientific theory reveals something at the same time that it conceals something else. What does the economic way of thinking reveal? And what does it conceal?

The economic way of thinking employs such concepts as demand, opportunity cost, marginal effects, and comparative advantage to *order* familiar phenomena. The economist knows very little about the real world that is not better known by businessmen, engineers, and others who make things happen. What he does know *is how things fit together*. The concepts of economics enable us to make better sense out of what we observe and to think more consistently and coherently about a wide range of interrelated phenomena.

This turns out in practice to be a largely negative kind of knowledge. Perhaps you detected, as you read through the chapters of this book, a greater emphasis on what *should not* than on what *should* be done. But negative conclusions are important, and they may be especially important in an area like economics. The economist Frank Knight used to defend the heavily negative character of economic reasoning with a quotation: "It ain't ignorance that does the most damage; it's knowin' so derned much that ain't so."

Too many people "know" how to solve pressing social problems. Their mental picture of the economic universe is a simple one in which intentions can easily be realized and the only obstacle to a better society is therefore a lack of good intentions. How many times have we encountered grand solutions to vexing social problems prefaced with the words "All we need to do is . . ."? But social actions have consequences that run far beyond those that can be easily predicted or foreseen. Restricting textile imports into the United States, for example, does, for the present at least, protect the jobs and income of textile producers; that's clear enough. But it takes a tutored eye to notice that this will shift even more income away from other Americans by raising textile prices, reducing American export opportunities, and in general inhibiting the exploitation of comparative advantage. Again, it is easy to see that rent controls hold down the money payments that tenants must make to landlords. But how many advocates of such controls are aware of the alternative payments that tenants will have to make, of the new forms of discrimination that will replace discrimination on the basis of money price, and of the short- and long-run effects upon the supply of rental housing?

Nonetheless, people easily become impatient with those who warn against the inadvisability of actions that will make matters worse and propose no solutions of their own. In a society such as ours, accustomed to the almost miraculous accomplishments of science and technology, the demand for "doing something" tends to exceed by a wide margin the supply of genuine solutions to social problems. We have probably erred in assuming that social problems can be handled in the same way that we manage technological problems. We know that conflicting interests create hard problems for social policymakers. We still underestimate the difficulties in the way of bringing about planned social change because we underestimate the complexity of social systems, of the networks of interaction through which behavior is coordinated in a society and people are induced to cooperate in the achievement of their goals.

Economists and the Market System

This argument is closely related to the accusation that the economic way of thinking contains an implicit bias in favor of capitalism, competition, and free exchange. The accusation is substantially true. Many economists have been and are socialists, of course; many have had serious misgivings about the consequences of unrestricted competition; and economists are by no means unanimously in favor of completely free exchange. But the critics who accuse economics of this kind of ideological bias are really talking about a predisposition of thought; they are not denying that there are exceptions. And they have a point.

Economics developed in the late eighteenth and early nineteenth centuries largely out of efforts to understand the self-regulating aspects of economic systems. In the face of a widespread belief, amounting almost to a commonsense conviction, that political regulation was indispensable to an adequately functioning economy, economists assumed the task of expounding the alternative thesis. As they examined in ever greater detail and depth the interactions among the innumerable decisions that make up an economic system, they evolved a body of theory stressing the cooperative aspects of free exchange. The economist's way of thinking has tended to reveal the order and the coordination that lie beneath the seeming chaos of an unplanned and unregulated economy. The elements of conflict, disorder, and disruption that are also found in every economic system have tended to be regarded by the economist more as disturbing factors than as objects of his primary interest.

On top of all this, economic theory often treats proposals for reform of the economic system rather unkindly. It is not that economists are themselves uninterested in reform or that they are the paid lackeys of the privileged classes. But economic theory, by revealing the inter-dependence of decisions, calls attention to the unexamined consequences of proposals for change. "It won't work out that way" is the economist's standard response to many well-intentioned policy proposals. Realism is not necessarily conservatism, but it often appears to be quite similar. And there *is* a sense in which knowledge does promote conservatism. Even physicists have been accused of hopeless conservatism by would-be inventors of perpetual-motion machines.

Individualism and Economic Analysis

Another indictment frequently leveled against economics accuses it of an excessively individualistic point of view. The critics object that economists conceive of society as nothing but a collection of individuals pursuing their own interests. And that's quite true in one sense. The fundamental concepts of economics refer to choice as the basis of all economizing activity; and the only choices about which we can think and talk meaningfully are the subjective evaluations of individuals. So the economic way of thinking is deeply colored by "methodological individualism," a procedure that makes individual choice the basic unit of analysis and tries to explain all social occurrences by reference to the preferences of individuals.

But is this a flaw or a strength? No one seriously believes that "the good" can be simply identified with "what individuals happen to prefer." As a working assumption, however, this may be less dangerous than unexamined concepts of the social welfare, the national interest, or the good of society. The economist is occupationally conditioned to wonder about the composition of such aggregates as "social," "national," and "public" and to suspect all aggregates until they have been broken down into the costs and benefits that individuals experience. That's a healthy suspicion, and probably a strength rather than a limitation of the economic way of thinking.

It's associated, however, with some additional modes of thinking that may not be equally defensible. One is a reluctance to inquire into the origins of the values that individuals happen to hold. Our choices as individuals are certainly conditioned by our socialization, and no one who has given serious attention to the question will deny that our socialization sometimes serves us badly. There is consequently much to be said for looking critically at the way in which values are formed in our society and at how and why individuals come to hold the preferences that guide their choices. Since the tools of economic analysis are not well suited for this kind of inquiry, the writings of economists contain almost nothing on the origin of preferences. And that often leaves the impression, whether intended or not, that economists consider the preferences of individuals to be *beyond criticism.*

Consensus and Cooperation

There is an additional reason why economists may be relatively disinterested in the criticism of individual values. They know that social cooperation is often possible among people even when their values diverge widely. The economic way of thinking spells out the workings of the market system, a remarkably effective means of securing cooperation without agreement. This may well be the most important difference between economic and political processes. While the political process works through the establishment of consensus, the economic or market process allows more room for individuals to go their own separate ways and even to help one another attain goals of which they mutually disapprove.

Think for a moment about *books.* Books not only reflect particular values; they also *teach* values. Sometimes openly, sometimes covertly, sometimes without the authors even being aware of it, books inculcate attitudes toward family, sex, religion, politics, or authority. Even a determined effort to avoid value judgments teaches values; although the authors may claim that it teaches openness and tolerance, their critics can often justifiably claim that it teaches skepticism and ethical relativism. *Books are controversial.* But with the market controlling the publication of books, everyone can be relatively satisfied. People will buy and read what they prefer and largely ignore the rest. Moreover, the lumberjack who belongs to the John Birch Society will cut down trees to make paper for the printing of communist pamphlets and the militant trade unionist will set type for a book attacking labor unions. When the production and distribution of books becomes subject to the political process, however, this easy method of accommodation is not available. A consensus on values must be reached before decisions can be made. Bitter, violent, and prolonged controversy erupted in Kanawha County, West Virginia, in 1974 when people began to criticize the textbooks used in elementary and secondary public schools. They claimed that their children were being indoctrinated in alien

values. The Kanawha County case showed both how difficult it may be to reach a consensus on values and what can occur when political decisions are made in the absence of consensus.

The questions raised in West Virginia proved bitterly divisive not because they touched upon ultimate human concerns but because these concerns had to be reconciled through the political process. The differences in value and belief were surely no broader or deeper than some of the differences among people of various religious persuasions; the former might even be viewed as an aspect of the latter differences as they existed in West Virginia in 1974. But we do not have public churches in this country and we do have public schools. People can choose the church they prefer and ignore the rest; they cannot easily choose for their children the kind of public school they prefer. The point is that conflicting values can peaceably coexist within a market or economic system and they cannot peaceably coexist within a political system.

This does not prove that we should prohibit public schools as we have prohibited state churches. Some disagreements on value questions may have to be faced and a resolution attempted despite the difficulty of the task. The 1954 Supreme Court decision on racial segregation forced this nation into a discussion of values that still continues and from which we have learned a great deal and grown in ways that no one could have predicted a quarter century ago. That decision also opened the way to greater discord and violence, however; and these are signs of the distance we must still traverse in reaching a consensus on the ethical significance of racial differences.

"Basic Values" or "Mere Tastes"?

But could a society such as ours hold together if value consensus were the precondition for *all* social cooperation? Is it not one of the strengths of the market system that it can tolerate an extraordinary range of value differences? To put it bluntly, the market system permits individuals to pursue all kinds of tasteless, inane, elitist, immoral, and useless goals and to do so with the cooperation of some of the very people who think those goals are contemptible.

Economists, as analysts of the market system, object only to the use of such adjectives as tasteless or contemptible. In the market system and in economic analysis, all judgments, from the most thoroughly reasoned and deeply felt to the most capricious and trivial, become "tastes and preferences." And *de gustibus non est disputandum*: one does not argue about tastes. Or is it that one *should* not argue about tastes? At least one does not *have to* argue about tastes under a market system. So why go looking for trouble?

"Quantity of pleasure being equal," the utilitarian philosopher Jeremy

Bentham once asserted, "pushpin [a children's game] is as good as poetry." While economists have often felt repelled by the philistinism of that remark, they have also tended to view it as a position preferable to most efforts to impose one's preferences upon others. And they have supported the market system in part because it offers a way by which society can minimize the need to legislate values.

Economics and Ethics

There is another sense in which economics has been accused of excessive individualism. The economic way of thinking is often said to *endorse* self-seeking activities and to place a stamp of approval upon the pursuit of one's own interests and the neglect of the public interest. The basic assumption of economic theory—that individuals do in fact pursue their own interests in a rational way—is sometimes hard to distinguish from the belief that everyone *ought* to look out for himself first and foremost. Adam Smith said that an individual who pursued his own interest frequently promoted the interests of society more effectively than when he consciously aimed at the public good. This may be true. But it is dangerous as a principle of ethics and this is what it has sometimes become in the hands of Adam Smith's descendants. In a subtle way it suggests that the person who tends most narrowly to his own business and never thinks about anyone's welfare but his own is really more ethical than the person who occupies himself with social causes.

But Adam Smith wrote a book entitled *The Theory of Moral Sentiments* before he wrote *The Wealth of Nations.* In the earlier book he maintained that sympathy, a feeling for others through "putting ourselves in their situations," was the effective cement of society. The ideas in *The Wealth of Nations* presuppose the ideas in *The Theory of Moral Sentiments.* Economic theory presupposes a social bond. The pursuit of one's own interests that Adam Smith recommended presupposes at least some sympathetic inclusion of the welfare of others in one's own interests. In short, a free society, in which people may behave as they please, is only possible if there are some ways in which it does not in fact please people to behave. The economic way of thinking can ignore the important role that consideration for others plays in the functioning of an economic system only if such consideration is a dominant feature of social life.

Economics and Rationality

We argued explicitly in chapter 15 that economic theory can explain the social consequences flowing from the pursuit of *every kind* of human interest as long as people are rational. If people are not interested in rationality, the predictive power of economics diminishes rapidly. Rationality here means concern for the relationship between ends and means, the attitude of calculation and planning, and purposive behavior. Frank Knight once described economic theory as "an abstract rationale of all conduct which is rational at all, and a rationale of all social relations arising through the organization of rational activity." Rationality in this sense is what Wordsworth had in mind when he wrote:

> . . . high Heaven rejects the lore
> Of nicely-calculated less or more.

Wordsworth could speak for "high Heaven" only by virtue of his poetic license. But he gave effective expression to the feelings that many people have toward a social order in which cost-benefit analysis is the ruling principle, and toward a science of society that explains all behavior in terms of marginal costs and benefits. The romantic doctrine of Wordsworth is dangerous. It too easily becomes a glorification of impulse and a rejection of intelligence, and leads to attitudes that will not create great poetry *or* engineering triumphs. But it is possible that we have become so preoccupied with technique and with means toward ends that we have lost our capacity to discover and nurture worthwhile goals. Perhaps we do tend to view everything as a potential input, a mere means to an end, and to treat other people and finally ourselves as no more than economic resources. Has a too narrowly conceived rationality become an obsession in our society and crowded out such alternative perspectives on life as the contemplative, the aesthetic, and the playful? Some critics maintain that the economic way of thinking encourages our already excessive compulsion to use, control, and dominate in a society that would gain far more from learning to be open, nonmanipulative, and receptive toward the surrounding world.

The sociologist Daniel Bell, who is an opponent neither of rationality nor of economics, has written: "The economizing mode—the exact calculation of monetary costs and returns—has been an efficient organizer of production, but at the expense of . . . the treating of men as 'things' within the sphere of production." Economists use two defenses against this argument. One is that they only describe; they do not prescribe. The other is that the economic way of thinking only treats people as things in the hands of those who are unwilling to view them as anything more. A good example is the economic valuation of human life. Who can place a money value on a life? But if the economist can show that certain social policies implicitly value human life at *less than* its worth as a productive machine, then surely those policies ought to be changed.

But to escape from tradition is never easy. And the tradition in which economists were reared does tend to regard consumable things as "goods" and all else as resources, things that can be used in the production of goods. Thus labor becomes a resource and abilities become human capital. There is nothing in the *logic* of economics that precludes us from viewing work as a social activity that can and should have value for itself. But there is a great deal in the *history* of economics that makes it difficult for economists to do so. This may be a very important limitation in a world where more things yield progressively less additional satisfaction as they simultaneously become more difficult to produce, and where the process of creating may soon be more valuable than its product.

Economics and Civilization

John Maynard Keynes once proposed a toast to economists, "the keepers of the possibility of civilization." The possibility of civilization—that is all. The efficient allocation of resources enlarges the realm of possibility; but it does not by itself guarantee the progress of civilization. A well-coordinated and smoothly functioning economic system gives individuals more opportunity to choose; it does not guarantee that they will choose well. The economic way of thinking, especially in a democracy, is an important preliminary. It is extremely important; but it is only preliminary.

Economists are for the most part ready to admit that the concepts they employ sometimes distort the reality they study. And they are willing to submit their analyses and conclusions to the test of rational criticism. But some point of view is indispensable to any inquiry, in the physical sciences as well as the social sciences. A completely open mind is a completely empty mind, and empty minds learn nothing. If the economic way of thinking sometimes leads to distortions, to misplaced emphasis, or even to outright error, the appropriate corrective is rational criticism. The application of that corrective has frequently altered the conclusions of economic science in the past. It will probably continue to do so in the future.

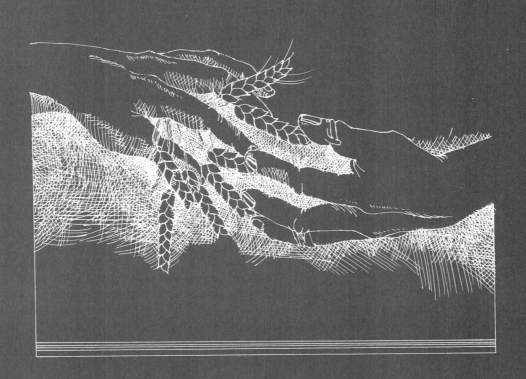

appendix 1

THE USE OF KNOWLEDGE IN SOCIETY

F. A. HAYEK

I

What is the problem we wish to solve when we try to construct a rational economic order?

On certain familiar assumptions the answer is simple enough. *If* we possess all the relevant information, *if* we can start out from a given system of preferences and *if* we command complete knowledge of available means, the problem which remains is purely one of logic. That is, the answer to the question of what is the best use of the available means is implicit in our assumptions. The conditions which the solution of this optimum problem must satisfy have been fully worked out and can be stated best in mathematical form: put at their briefest, they are that the marginal rates of substitution between any two commodities or factors must be the same in all their different uses.

This, however, is emphatically *not* the economic problem which society faces. And the economic calculus which we have developed to solve this logical problem, though an important step toward the solution of the economic problem of society, does not yet provide an answer to it. The reason for this is that the "data" from which the economic calculus starts are never for the whole society "given" to a single mind which could work out the implications, and can never be so given.

The peculiar character of the problem of a rational economic order is determined precisely by the fact that the knowledge of the circumstances of which we must make use never exists in concentrated or integrated form, but solely as the dispersed bits of incomplete and frequently contradictory knowledge which all the separate individuals possess.

Reprinted by permission of the author and the American Economic Association from *American Economic Review,* September 1945.

The economic problem of society is thus not merely a problem of how to allocate "given" resources—if "given" is taken to mean given to a single mind which deliberately solves the problem set by these "data." It is rather a problem of how to secure the best use of resources known to any of the members of society, for ends whose relative importance only these individuals know. Or, to put it briefly, it is a problem of the utilization of knowledge not given to anyone in its totality.

This character of the fundamental problem has, I am afraid, been rather obscured than illuminated by many of the recent refinements of economic theory, particularly by many of the uses made of mathematics. Though the problem with which I want primarily to deal in this paper is the problem of a rational economic organization, I shall in its course be led again and again to point to its close connections with certain methodological questions. Many of the points I wish to make are indeed conclusions toward which diverse paths of reasoning have unexpectedly converged. But as I now see these problems, this is no accident. It seems to me that many of the current disputes with regard to both economic theory and economic policy have their common origin in a misconception about the nature of the economic problem of society. This misconception in turn is due to an erroneous transfer to social phenomena of the habits of thought we have developed in dealing with the phenomena of nature.

II

In ordinary language we describe by the word "planning" the complex of interrelated decisions about the allocation of our available resources. All economic activity is in this sense planning; and in any society in which many people collaborate, this planning, whoever does it, will in some measure have to be based on knowledge which, in the first instance, is not given to the planner but to somebody else, which somehow will have to be conveyed to the planner. The various ways in which the knowledge on which people base their plans is communicated to them is the crucial problem for any theory explaining the economic process. And the problem of what is the best way of utilizing knowledge initially dispersed among all the people is at least one of the main problems of economic policy—or of designing an efficient economic system.

The answer to this question is closely connected with that other question which arises here, that of *who* is to do the planning. It is about this question that all the dispute about "economic planning" centers. This is not a dispute about whether planning is to be done or not. It is a dispute as to whether planning is to be done centrally, by one authority for the whole economic system, or is to be divided among many individuals. Planning in the specific sense in which the term is used in contemporary controversy necessarily means central planning—direction of the whole economic system according to one unified plan. Competition, on the other hand, means decentralized planning by many separate persons. The half-way house between the two, about which many people talk but which few like when they see it, is the delegation of planning to organized industries, or, in other words, monopoly.

Which of these systems is likely to be more efficient depends mainly on the question under which of them we can expect that fuller use will be made of the existing knowledge. And this, in turn, depends on whether we are more likely to succeed in putting at the disposal of a single central authority all the knowledge which ought to be used but which is initially dispersed among many different individuals, or in conveying to the individuals such additional knowledge as they need in order to enable them to fit their plans in with those of others.

III

It will at once be evident that on this point the position will be different with respect to different kinds of knowledge; and the answer to our question will therefore largely turn on the relative importance of the different kinds of knowledge; those more likely to be at the disposal of particular individuals and those which we should with greater confidence expect to find in the possession of an authority made up of suitably chosen experts. If it is today so widely assumed that the latter will be in a better position, this is because one kind of knowledge, namely, scientific knowledge, occupies now so prominent a place in public imagination that we tend to forget that it is not the only kind that is relevant. It may be admitted that, so far as scientific knowledge is concerned, a body of suitably chosen experts may be in the best position to command all the best knowledge available—though this is of course merely shifting the difficulty to the problem of selecting the experts. What I wish to point out is that, even assuming that this problem can be readily solved, it is only a small part of the wider problem.

Today it is almost heresy to suggest that scientific knowledge is not the sum of all knowledge. But a little reflection will show that there is beyond question a body of very important but unorganized knowledge which cannot possibly be called scientific in the sense of knowledge of general rules: the knowledge of the particular circumstances of time and place. It is with respect to this that practically every individual has some advantage over all others in that he possesses unique information of which beneficial use might be made, but of which use can be made only if the decisions depending on it are left to him or are made with his active coöperation. We need to remember only how much we have to learn in any occupation after we have completed our theoretical training, how big a part of our working life we spend learning particular jobs, and how valuable an asset in all walks of life is knowledge of people, of local conditions, and special circumstances. To know of and put to use a machine not fully employed, or somebody's skill which could be better utilized, or to be aware of a surplus stock which can be drawn upon during an interruption of supplies, is socially quite as useful as the knowledge of better alternative techniques. And the shipper who earns his living from using otherwise empty or half-filled journeys of tramp-steamers, or the estate agent whose whole knowledge is almost exclusively one of temporary opportunities, or the *arbitrageur* who gains from local differences of commodity prices, are all performing eminently useful functions based on special knowledge of circumstances of the fleeting moment not known to others.

It is a curious fact that this sort of knowledge should today be generally regarded with a kind of contempt, and that anyone who by such knowledge gains an advantage over somebody better equipped with theoretical or technical knowledge is thought to have acted almost disreputably. To gain an advantage from better knowledge of facilities of communication or transport is sometimes regarded as almost dishonest, although it is quite as important that society make use of the best opportunities in this respect as in using the latest scientific discoveries. This prejudice has in a considerable measure affected the attitude toward commerce in general compared with that toward production. Even economists who regard themselves as definitely above the crude materialist fallacies of the past constantly commit the same mistake where activities directed toward the acquisition of such practical knowledge are concerned—apparently because in their scheme of things all such knowledge is supposed to be "given." The common idea now seems to be that all such knowledge should as a matter of course be readily at the command of everybody, and the reproach of irrationality leveled against the existing economic order is frequently based on the fact that it is not so available. This view disregards the fact that the method by which such knowledge can be made as widely available as possible is precisely the problem to which we have to find an answer.

IV

If it is fashionable today to minimize the importance of the knowledge of the particular circumstances of time and place, this is closely connected with the smaller importance which is now attached to change as such. Indeed, there are few points on which the assumptions made (usually only implicitly) by the "planners" differ from those of their opponents as much as with regard to the significance and frequency of changes which will make substantial alterations of production plans necessary. Of course, if detailed economic plans could be laid down for fairly long periods in advance and then closely adhered to, so that no further economic decisions of importance would be required, the task of drawing up a comprehensive plan governing all economic activity would appear much less formidable.

It is, perhaps, worth stressing that economic problems arise always and only in consequence of change. So long as things continue as before, or at least as they were expected to, there arise no new problems requiring a decision, no need to form a new plan. The belief that changes, or at least day-to-day adjustments, have become less important in modern times implies the contention that economic problems also have become less important. This belief in the decreasing importance of change is, for that reason, usually held by the same people who argue that the importance of economic considerations has been driven into the background by the growing importance of technological knowledge.

Is it true that, with the elaborate apparatus of modern production, economic decisions are required only at long inter-

vals, as when a new factory is to be erected or a new process to be introduced? Is it true that, once a plant has been built, the rest is all more or less mechanical, determined by the character of the plant, and leaving little to be changed in adapting to the ever-changing circumstances of the moment?

The fairly widespread belief in the affirmative is not, so far as I can ascertain, borne out by the practical experience of the business man. In a competitive industry at any rate—and such an industry alone can serve as a test—the task of keeping cost from rising requires constant struggle, absorbing a great part of the energy of the manager. How easy it is for an inefficient manager to dissipate the differentials on which profitability rests, and that it is possible, with the same technical facilities, to produce with a great variety of costs, are among the commonplaces of business experience which do not seem to be equally familiar in the study of the economist. The very strength of the desire, constantly voiced by producers and engineers, to be able to proceed untrammeled by considerations of money costs, is eloquent testimony to the extent to which these factors enter into their daily work.

One reason why economists are increasingly apt to forget about the constant small changes which make up the whole economic picture is probably their growing preoccupation with statistical aggregates, which show a very much greater stability than the movements of the detail. The comparative stability of the aggregates cannot, however, be accounted for —as the statisticians seem occasionally to be inclined to do— by the "law of large numbers" or the mutual compensation of random changes. The number of elements with which we have to deal is not large enough for such accidental forces to produce stability. The continuous flow of goods and services is maintained by constant deliberate adjustments, by new dispositions made every day in the light of circumstances not known the day before, by B stepping in at once when A fails to deliver. Even the large and highly mechanized plant keeps going largely because of an environment upon which it can draw for all sorts of unexpected needs; tiles for its roof, stationery for its forms, and all the thousand and one kinds of equipment in which it cannot be self-contained and which the plans for the operation of the plant require to be readily available in the market.

This is, perhaps, also the point where I should briefly mention the fact that the sort of knowledge with which I have been concerned is knowledge of the kind which by its nature cannot enter into statistics and therefore cannot be conveyed to any central authority in statistical form. The statistics which such a central authority would have to use would have to be arrived at precisely by abstracting from minor differences between the things, by lumping together, as resources of one kind, items which differ as regards location, quality, and other particulars, in a way which may be very significant for the specific decision. It follows from this that central planning based on statistical information by its nature cannot take direct account of these circumstances of time and place, and that the central planner will have to find some way or other in which the decisions depending on them can be left to the "man on the spot."

V

If we can agree that the economic problem of society is mainly one of rapid adaptation to changes in the particular circumstances of time and place, it would seem to follow that the ultimate decisions must be left to the people who are familiar with these circumstances, who know directly of the relevant changes and of the resources immediately available to meet them. We cannot expect that this problem will be solved by first communicating all this knowledge to a central board which, after integrating *all* knowledge, issues its orders. We must solve it by some form of decentralization. But this answers only part of our problem. We need decentralization because only thus can we ensure that the knowledge of the particular circumstances of time and place will be promptly used. But the "man on the spot" cannot decide solely on the basis of his limited but intimate knowledge of the facts of his immediate surroundings. There still remains the problem of communicating to him such further information as he needs to fit his decisions into the whole pattern of changes of the larger economic system.

How much knowledge does he need to do so successfully? Which of the events which happen beyond the horizon of his immediate knowledge are of relevance to his immediate decision, and how much of them need he know?

There is hardly anything that happens anywhere in the world that *might* not have an effect on the decision he ought to make. But he need not know of these events as such, nor of *all* their effects. It does not matter for him *why* at the particular moment more screws of one size than of another are wanted, *why* paper bags are more readily available than canvas bags, or *why* skilled labor, or particular machine tools, have for the moment become more difficult to acquire. All that is significant for him is *how much more or less* difficult to procure they have become compared with other things with which he is also concerned, or how much more or less ur-

gently wanted are the alternative things he produces or uses. It is always a question of the relative importance of the particular things with which he is concerned, and the causes which alter their relative importance are of no interest to him beyond the effect on those concrete things of his own environment.

It is in this connection that what I have called the economic calculus proper helps us, at least by analogy, to see how this problem can be solved, and in fact is being solved, by the price system. Even the single controlling mind, in possession of all the data for some small, self-contained economic system, would not—every time some small adjustment in the allocation of resources had to be made—go explicitly through all the relations between ends and means which might possibly be affected. It is indeed the great contribution of the pure logic of choice that it has demonstrated conclusively that even such a single mind could solve this kind of problem only by constructing and constantly using rates of equivalence (or "values," or "marginal rates of substitution"), *i.e.*, by attaching to each kind of scarce resource a numerical index which cannot be derived from any property possessed by that particular thing, but which reflects, or in which is condensed, its significance in view of the whole means-end structure. In any small change he will have to consider only these quantitative indices (or "values") in which all the relevant information is concentrated; and by adjusting the quantities one by one, he can appropriately rearrange his dispositions without having to solve the whole puzzle *ab initio*, or without needing at any stage to survey it at once in all its ramifications.

Fundamentally, in a system where the knowledge of the relevant facts is dispersed among many people, prices can act to coördinate the separate actions of different people in the same way as subjective values help the individual to coördinate the parts of his plan. It is worth contemplating for a moment a very simple and commonplace instance of the action of the price system to see what precisely it accomplishes. Assume that somewhere in the world a new opportunity for the use of some raw material, say tin, has arisen, or that one of the sources of supply of tin has been eliminated. It does not matter for our purpose—and it is very significant that it does not matter—which of these two causes has made tin more scarce. All that the users of tin need to know is that some of the tin they used to consume is now more profitably employed elsewhere, and that in consequence they must economize tin. There is no need for the great majority of them even to know where the more urgent need has arisen, or in favor of what other needs they ought to husband the supply. If only some of them know directly of the new demand, and switch resources over to it, and if the people who are aware of the new gap thus created in turn fill it from still other sources, the effect will rapidly spread throughout the whole economic system and influence not only all the uses of tin, but also those of its substitutes and the substitutes of these substitutes, the supply of all the things made of tin, and their substitutes, and so on; and all this without the great majority of those instrumental in bringing about these substitutions knowing anything at all about the original cause of these changes. The whole acts as one market, not because any of its members survey the whole field, but because their limited individual fields of vision sufficiently overlap so that through many intermediaries the relevant information is communicated to all. The mere fact that there is one price for any commodity—or rather that local prices are connected in a manner determined by the cost of transport, etc.—brings about the solution which (it is just conceptually possible) might have been arrived at by one single mind possessing all the information which is in fact dispersed among all the people involved in the process.

VI

We must look at the price system as such a mechanism for communicating information if we want to understand its real function—a function which, of course, it fulfills less perfectly as prices grow more rigid. (Even when quoted prices have become quite rigid, however, the forces which would operate through changes in price still operate to a considerable extent through changes in the other terms of the contract.) The most significant fact about this system is the economy of knowledge with which it operates, or how little the individual participants need to know in order to be able to take the right action. In abbreviated form, by a kind of symbol, only the most essential information is passed on, and passed on only to those concerned. It is more than a metaphor to describe the price system as a kind of machinery for registering change, or a system of telecommunications which enables individual producers to watch merely the movement of a few pointers, as an engineer might watch the hands of a few dials, in order to adjust their activities to changes of which they may never know more than is reflected in the price movement.

Of course, these adjustments are probably never "perfect" in the sense in which the economist conceives of them in his equilibrium analysis. But I fear that our theoretical habits of approaching the problem with the assumption of more or less perfect knowledge on the part of almost eveyone has made us somewhat blind to the true function of the price mechanism and led us to apply rather misleading standards in judging its efficiency. The marvel is that in a case like that of a scarcity of one raw material, without an order being issued, without more than perhaps a handful of people knowing the cause, tens of thousands of people whose identity could not be ascertained by months of investigation, are made to use the material or its products more sparingly; *i.e.,* they move in the right direction. This is enough of a marvel even if, in a constantly changing world, not all will hit it off so perfectly that their profit rates will always be maintained at the same constant or "normal" level.

I have deliberately used the word "marvel" to shock the reader out of the complacency with which we often take the working of this mechanism for granted. I am convinced that if it were the result of deliberate human design, and if the people guided by the price changes understood that their decisions have significance far beyond their immediate aim, this mechanism would have been acclaimed as one of the greatest triumphs of the human mind. Its misfortune is the double one that it is not the product of human design and that the people guided by it usually do not know why they are made to do what they do. But those who clamor for "conscious direction"—and who cannot believe that anything which has evolved without design (and even without our understanding it) should solve problems which we should not be able to solve consciously—should remember this: The problem is precisely how to extend the span of our utilization of resources beyond the span of the control of any one mind; and, therefore, how to dispense with the need of conscious control and how to provide inducements which will make the individuals do the desirable things without anyone having to tell them what to do.

The problem which we meet here is by no means peculiar to economics but arises in connection with nearly all truly social phenomena, with language and most of our cultural inheritance, and constitutes really the central theoretical problem of all social science. As Alfred Whitehead has said in another connection, "It is a profoundly erroneous truism, repeated by all copy-books and by eminent people when they are making speeches, that we should cultivate the habit of thinking what we are doing. The precise opposite is the case. Civilization advances by extending the number of important operations which we can perform without thinking about them." This is of profound significance in the social field. We make constant use of formulas, symbols and rules whose meaning we do not understand and through the use of which we avail ourselves of the assistance of knowledge which individually we do not possess. We have developed these practices and institutions by building upon habits and institutions which have proved successful in their own sphere and which have in turn become the foundation of the civilization we have built up.

The price system is just one of those formations which man has learned to use (though he is still very far from having learned to make the best use of it) after he had stumbled upon it without understanding it. Through it not only a division of labor but also a coördinated utilization of resources based on an equally divided knowledge has become possible. The people who like to deride any suggestion that this may be so usually distort the argument by insinuating that it asserts that by some miracle just that sort of system has spontaneously grown up which is best suited to modern civilization. It is the other way round: man has been able to develop that division of labor on which our civilization is based because he happened to stumble upon a method which made it possible. Had he not done so he might still have developed some other, altogether different, type of civilization, something like the "state" of the termite ants, or some other altogether unimaginable type. All that we can say is that nobody has yet succeeded in designing an alternative system in which certain features of the existing one can be preserved which are dear even to those who most violently assail it—such as particularly the extent to which the individual can choose his pursuits and consequently freely use his own knowledge and skill.

VII

It is in many ways fortunate that the dispute about the indispensability of the price system for any rational calculation in a complex society is now no longer conducted entirely between camps holding different political views. The thesis that without the price system we could not preserve a society based on such extensive division of labor as ours was greeted with a howl of derision when it was first advanced by von Mises twenty-five years ago. Today the difficulties which some still find in accepting it are no longer mainly political, and this makes for an atmosphere much more conducive to reasonable discussion. When we find Leon Trotsky arguing that "economic accounting is unthinkable without market relations"; when Professor Oscar Lange promises Professor von Mises a statue in the marble halls of the future Central Planning Board; when Professor Abba P. Lerner rediscovers Adam Smith and emphasizes that the essential utility of the price system consists in inducing the individual, while seeking his own interest, to do what is in the general interest, the differences can indeed no longer be ascribed to political prejudice. The remaining dissent seems clearly to be due to purely intellectual, and more particularly methodological, differences.

A recent statement by Professor Joseph Schumpeter in his *Capitalism, Socialism and Democracy* provides a clear illustration of one of the methodological differences which I have in mind. Its author is preeminent among those economists who approach economic phenomena in the light of a certain branch of positivism. To him these phenomena accordingly appear as objectively given quantities of commodities impinging directly upon each other, almost, it would seem, without any intervention of human minds. Only against this background can I account for the following (to me startling) pronouncement. Professor Schumpeter argues that the possibility of a rational calculation in the absence of markets for the factors of production follows for the theorist "from the elementary proposition that consumers in evaluating ('demanding') consumers' goods *ipso facto* also evaluate the means of production which enter into the production of these goods."[1]

Taken literally, this statement is simply untrue. The consumers do nothing of the kind. What Professor Schumpeter's *"ipso facto"* presumably means is that the valuation of the factors of production is implied in, or follows necessarily

[1] J. Schumpeter, *Capitalism, Socialism, and Democracy* (New York, Harper, 1942), p. 175. Professor Schumpeter is, I believe, also the original author of the myth that Pareto and Barone have "solved" the problem of socialist calculation. What they, and many others, did was merely to state the conditions which a rational allocation of resources would have to satisfy, and to point out that these were essentially the same as the conditions of equilibrium of a competitive market. This is something altogether different from showing how the allocation of resources satisfying these conditions can be found in practice. Pareto himself (from whom Barone has taken practically everything he has to say), far from claiming to have solved the practical problem, in fact explicitly denies that it can be solved without the help of the market. See his *Manuel d'économie pure* (2nd ed., 1927), pp. 233–34. The relevant passage is quoted in an English translation at the beginning of my article on "Socialist Calculation: The Competitive 'Solution,'" in *Economica*, New Series, Vol. VIII, No. 26 (May, 1940), p. 125.

from, the valuation of consumers' goods. But this, too, is not correct. Implication is a logical relationship which can be meaningfully asserted only of propositions simultaneously present to one and the same mind. It is evident, however, that the values of the factors of production do not depend solely on the valuation of the consumers' goods but also on the conditions of supply of the various factors of production. Only to a mind to which all these facts were simultaneously known would the answer necessarily follow from the facts given to it. The practical problem, however, arises precisely because these facts are never so given to a single mind, and because, in consequence, it is necessary that in the solution of the problem knowledge should be used that is dispersed among many people.

The problem is thus in no way solved if we can show that all the facts, *if* they were known to a single mind (as we hypothetically assume them to be given to the observing economist), would uniquely determine the solution; instead we must show how a solution is produced by the interactions of people each of whom possesses only partial knowledge. To assume all the knowledge to be given to a single mind in the same manner in which we assume it to be given to us as the explaining economists is to assume the problem away and to disregard everything that is important and significant in the real world.

That an economist of Professor Schumpeter's standing should thus have fallen into a trap which the ambiguity of the term "datum" sets to the unwary can hardly be explained as a simple error. It suggests rather that there is something fundamentally wrong with an approach which habitually disregards an essential part of the phenomena with which we have to deal: the unavoidable imperfection of man's knowledge and the consequent need for a process by which knowledge is constantly communicated and acquired. Any approach, such as that of much of mathematical economics with its simultaneous equations, which in effect starts from the assumption that people's *knowledge* corresponds with the objective *facts* of the situation, systematically leaves out what is our main task to explain. I am far from denying that in our system equilibrium analysis has a useful function to perform. But when it comes to the point where it misleads some of our leading thinkers into believing that the situation which it describes has direct relevance to the solution of practical problems, it is time that we remember that it does not deal with the social process at all and that it is no more than a useful preliminary to the study of the main problem.

appendix 2

THE ECONOMIC ORGANISATION OF A P.O.W. CAMP

R. A. RADFORD

Introduction

After allowance has been made for abnormal circumstances, the social institutions, ideas and habits of groups in the outside world are to be found reflected in a Prisoner of War Camp. It is an unusual but a vital society. Camp organisation and politics are matters of real concern to the inmates, as affecting their present and perhaps their future existences. Nor does this indicate any loss of proportion. No one pretends that camp matters are of any but local importance or of more than transient interest, but their importance there is great. They bulk large in a world of narrow horizons and it is suggested that any distortion of values lies rather in the minimisation than in the exaggeration of their importance. Human affairs are essentially practical matters and the measure of immediate effect on the lives of those directly concerned in them is to a large extent the criterion of their importance at that time and place. A prisoner can hold strong views on such subjects as whether or not all tinned meats shall be issued to individuals cold or be centrally cooked, without losing sight of the significance of the Atlantic Charter.

One aspect of social organisation is to be found in economic activity, and this, along with other manifestations of a group existence, is to be found in any P.O.W. camp. True, a prisoner is not dependent on his exertions for the provision of the necessaries, or even the luxuries of life, but through his economic activity, the exchange of goods and services, his standard of material comfort is considerably enhanced. And this is a serious matter to the prisoner: he is not "playing at shops" even though the small scale of the transactions and the simple expression of comfort and wants in terms of cigarettes and jam, razor blades and writing paper, make the

Reprinted by permission from *Economica*, vol. 12, November 1945.

urgency of those needs difficult to appreciate, even by an ex-prisoner of some three months' standing.

Nevertheless, it cannot be too strongly emphasised that economic activities do not bulk so large in prison society as they do in the larger world. There can be little production; as has been said the prisoner is independent of his exertions for the provision of the necessities and luxuries of life; the emphasis lies in exchange and the media of exchange. A prison camp is not to be compared with the seething crowd of higglers in a street market, any more than it is to be compared with the economic inertia of a family dinner table.

Naturally then, entertainment, academic and literary interests, games and discussions of the "other world" bulk larger in everyday life than they do in the life of more normal societies. But it would be wrong to underestimate the importance of economic activity. Everyone receives a roughly equal share of essentials; it is by trade that individual preferences are given expression and comfort increased. All at some time, and most people regularly, make exchanges of one sort or another.

Although a P.O.W. camp provides a living example of a simple economy which might be used as an alternative to the Robinson Crusoe economy beloved by the text-books, and its simplicity renders the demonstration of certain economic hypotheses both amusing and instructive, it is suggested that the principal significance is sociological. True, there is interest in observing the growth of economic institutions and customs in a brand new society, small and simple enough to prevent detail from obscuring the basic pattern and disequilibrium from obscuring the working of the system. But the essential interest lies in the universality and the spontaneity of this economic life; it came into existence not by conscious imitation but as a response to the immediate needs and circumstances. Any similarity between prison organisation and outside organisation arises from similar stimuli evoking similar responses.

The following is as brief an account of the essential data as may render the narrative intelligible. The camps of which the writer had experience were Oflags and consequently the economy was not complicated by payments for work by the detaining power. They consisted normally of between 1,200 and 2,500 people, housed in a number of separate but inter-communicating bungalows, one company of 200 or so to a building. Each company formed a group within the main organisation and inside the company the room and the messing syndicate, a voluntary and spontaneous group who fed together, formed the constituent units.

Between individuals there was active trading in all consumer goods and in some services. Most trading was for food against cigarettes or other foodstuffs, but cigarettes rose from the status of a normal commodity to that of currency. RMk.s existed but had no circulation save for gambling debts, as few articles could be purchased with them from the canteen.

Our supplies consisted of rations provided by the detaining power and (principally) the contents of Red Cross food parcels—tinned milk, jam, butter, biscuits, bully, chocolate, sugar etc., and cigarettes. So far the supplies to each person were equal and regular. Private parcels of clothing, toilet requisites and cigarettes were also received, and here equality ceased owing to the different numbers despatched and the vagaries of the post. All these articles were the subject of trade and exchange.

The Development and Organisation of the Market

Very soon after capture people realised that it was both undesirable and unnecessary, in view of the limited size and the equality of supplies, to give away or to accept gifts of cigarettes or food. "Goodwill" developed into trading as a more equitable means of maximising individual satisfaction.

We reached a transit camp in Italy about a fortnight after capture and received 1/4 of a Red Cross food parcel each a week later. At once exchanges, already established, multiplied in volume. Starting with simple direct barter, such as a non-smoker giving a smoker friend his cigarette issue in exchange for a chocolate ration, more complex exchanges soon became an accepted custom. Stories circulated of a padre who started off round the camp with a tin of cheese and five cigarettes and returned to his bed with a complete parcel in addition to his

original cheese and cigarettes; the market was not yet perfect. Within a week or two, as the volume of trade grew, rough scales of exchange values came into existence. Sikhs, who had at first exchanged tinned beef for practically any other foodstuff, began to insist on jam and margarine. It was realised that a tin of jam was worth 1/2 lb. of margarine plus something else; that a cigarette issue was worth several chocolate issues, and a tin of diced carrots was worth practically nothing.

In this camp we did not visit other bungalows very much and prices varied from place to place; hence the germ of truth in the story of the itinerant priest. By the end of a month, when we reached our permanent camp, there was a lively trade in all commodities and their relative values were well known, and expressed not in terms of one another—one didn't quote bully in terms of sugar—but in terms of cigarettes. The cigarette became the standard of value. In the permanent camp people started by wandering through the bungalows calling their offers—"cheese for seven" (cigarettes)—and the hours after parcel issue were Bedlam. The inconveniences of this system soon led to its replacement by an Exchange and Mart notice board in every bungalow, where under the headings "name", "room number", "wanted" and "offered" sales and wants were advertised. When a deal went through, it was crossed off the board. The public and semipermanent records of transactions led to cigarette prices being well known and thus tending to equality throughout the camp, although there were always opportunities for an astute trader to make a profit from arbitrage. With this development everyone, including non-smokers, was willing to sell for cigarettes, using them to buy at another time and place. Cigarettes became the normal currency, though, of course, barter was never extinguished.

The unity of the market and the prevalence of a single price varied directly with the general level of organisation and comfort in the camp. A transit camp was always chaotic and uncomfortable: people were overcrowded, no one knew where anyone else was living, and few took the trouble to find out. Organisation was too slender to include an Exchange and Mart board, and private advertisements were the most that appeared. Consequently a transit camp was not one market but many. The price of a tin of salmon is known to have varied by two cigarettes in 20 between one end of a hut and the other. Despite a high level of organisation in Italy, the market was morcellated in this manner at the first transit camp we reached after our removal to Germany in the autumn of 1943. In this camp—Stalag VIIA at Moosburg in Bavaria—there were up to 50,000 prisoners of all nationalities. French,

Russians, Italians and Jugo-Slavs were free to move about within the camp: British and Americans were confined to their compounds, although a few cigarettes given to a sentry would always procure permission for one or two men to visit other compounds. The people who first visited the highly organised French trading centre, with its stalls and known prices, found coffee extract—relatively cheap among the tea-drinking English—commanding a fancy price in biscuits or cigarettes, and some enterprising people made small fortunes that way. (Incidentally we found out later that much of the coffee went "over the wire" and sold for phenomenal prices at black market cafés in Munich: some of the French prisoners were said to have made substantial sums in RMk.s. This was one of the few occasions on which our normally closed economy came into contact with other economic worlds.)

Eventually public opinion grew hostile to these monopoly profits—not everyone could make contact with the French—and trading with them was put on a regulated basis. Each group of beds was given a quota of articles to offer and the transaction was carried out by accredited representatives from the British compound, with monopoly rights. The same method was used for trading with sentries elsewhere, as in this trade secrecy and reasonable prices had a peculiar importance, but as is ever the case with regulated companies, the interloper proved too strong.

The permanent camps in Germany saw the highest level of commercial organisation. In addition to the Exchange and Mart notice boards, a shop was organised as a public utility, controlled by representatives of the Senior British Officer, on a no profit basis. People left their surplus clothing, toilet requisites and food there until they were sold at a fixed price in cigarettes. Only sales in cigarettes were accepted—there was no barter—and there was no higgling. For food at least there were standard prices: clothing is less homogeneous and the price was decided around a norm by the seller and the shop manager in agreement; shirts would average say 80, ranging from 60 to 120 according to quality and age. Of food, the shop carried small stocks for convenience; the capital was provided by a loan from the bulk store of Red Cross cigarettes and repaid by a small commission taken on the first transactions. Thus the cigarette attained its fullest currency status, and the market was almost completely unified.

It is thus to be seen that a market came into existence without labour or production. The B.R.C.S. may be considered as "Nature" of the text-book, and the articles of trade—food, clothing and cigarettes—as free gifts—land or manna. Despite this, and despite a roughly equal distribution of resources, a market came into spontaneous operation, and prices were fixed by the operation of supply and demand. It is difficult to reconcile this fact with the labour theory of value.

Actually there was an embryo labour market. Even when cigarettes were not scarce, there was usually some unlucky person willing to perform services for them. Laundrymen advertised at two cigarettes a garment. Battle-dress was scrubbed and pressed and a pair of trousers lent for the interim period for twelve. A good pastel portrait cost thirty or a tin of "Kam". Odd tailoring and other jobs similarly had their prices.

There were also entrepreneurial services. There was a coffee stall owner who sold tea, coffee or cocoa at two cigarettes a cup, buying his raw materials at market prices and hiring labour to gather fuel and to stoke; he actually enjoyed the services of a chartered accountant at one stage. After a period of great prosperity he overreached himself and failed disastrously for several hundred cigarettes. Such large-scale private enterprise was rare but several middlemen or professional traders existed. The padre in Italy, or the men at Moosburg who opened trading relations with the French, are examples: the more subdivided the market, the less perfect the advertisement of prices, and the less stable the prices, the greater was the scope for these operators. One man capitalised his knowledge of Urdu by buying meat from the Sikhs and selling butter and jam in return: as his operations became better known more and more people entered this trade, prices in the Indian Wing approximated more nearly to those elsewhere, though to the end a "contact" among the Indians was valuable, as linguistic difficulties prevented the trade from being quite free. Some were specialists in the Indian trade, the food, clothing or even the watch trade. Middlemen traded on their own account or on commission. Price rings and agreements were suspected and the traders certainly co-operated. Nor did they welcome newcomers. Unfortunately the writer knows little of the workings of these people: public opinion was hostile and the professionals were usually of a retiring disposition.

One trader in food and cigarettes, operating in a period of dearth, enjoyed a high reputation. His capital, carefully saved, was originally about 50 cigarettes, with which he bought rations on issue days and held them until the price rose just before the next issue. He also picked up a little by arbitrage; several times a day he visited every Exchange or Mart notice board and took advantage of every discrepancy between prices of goods offered and wanted. His knowledge of prices, markets and names of those who had received cigarette parcels was phenomenal. By these means he kept himself smoking steadily—his profits—while his capital remained intact.

Sugar was issued on Saturday. About Tuesday two of us used to visit Sam and make a deal; as old customers he would advance as much of the price as he could spare then, and entered the transaction in a book. On Saturday morning he left cocoa tins on our beds for the ration, and picked them up on Saturday afternoon. We were hoping for a calendar at Christmas, but Sam failed too. He was left holding a big black treacle issue when the price fell, and in this weakened state was unable to withstand an unexpected arrival of parcels and the consequent price fluctuations. He paid in full, but from his capital. The next Tuesday, when I paid my usual visit he was out of business.

Credit entered into many, perhaps into most, transactions, in one form or another. Sam paid in advance as a rule for his purchases of future deliveries of sugar, but many buyers asked for credit, whether the commodity was sold spot or future. Naturally prices varied according to the terms of sale. A treacle ration might be advertised for four cigarettes now or five next week. And in the future market "bread now" was a vastly different thing from "bread Thursday". Bread was issued on Thursday and Monday, four and three days' rations respectively, and by Wednesday and Sunday night it had risen at least one cigarette per ration, from seven to eight, by supper time. One man always saved a ration to sell then at the peak price: his offer of "bread now" stood out on the board among a number of "bread Monday's" fetching one or two less, or not selling at all—and he always smoked on Sunday night.

The Cigarette Currency

Although cigarettes as currency exhibited certain peculiarities, they performed all the functions of a metallic currency as a unit of account, as a measure of value and as a store of value, and shared most of its characteristics. They were homogeneous, reasonably durable, and of convenient size for the smallest or, in packets, for the largest transactions. Incidentally, they could be clipped or sweated by rolling them between the fingers so that tobacco fell out.

Cigarettes were also subject to the working of Gresham's Law. Certain brands were more popular than others as smokes, but for currency purposes a cigarette was a cigarette. Consequently buyers used the poorer qualities and the Shop rarely saw the more popular brands: cigarettes such as Churchman's

No. 1 were rarely used for trading. At one time cigarettes hand-rolled from pipe tobacco began to circulate. Pipe tobacco was issued in lieu of cigarettes by the Red Cross at a rate of 25 cigarettes to the ounce and this rate was standard in exchanges, but an ounce would produce 30 home-made cigarettes. Naturally, people with machine-made cigarettes broke them down and re-rolled the tobacco, and the real cigarette virtually disappeared from the market. Hand-rolled cigarettes were not homogeneous and prices could no longer be quoted in them with safety: each cigarette was examined before it was accepted and thin ones were rejected, or extra demanded as a make-weight. For a time we suffered all the inconveniences of a debased currency.

Machine-made cigarettes were always universally acceptable, both for what they would buy and for themselves. It was this intrinsic value which gave rise to their principal disadvantage as currency, a disadvantage which exists, but to a far smaller extent, in the case of metallic currency;—that is, a strong demand for non-monetary purposes. Consequently our economy was repeatedly subject to deflation and to periods of monetary stringency. While the Red Cross issue of 50 or 25 cigarettes per man per week came in regularly, and while there were fair stocks held, the cigarette currency suited its purpose admirably. But when the issue was interrupted, stocks soon ran out, prices fell, trading declined in volume and became increasingly a matter of barter. This deflationary tendency was periodically offset by the sudden injection of new currency. Private cigarette parcels arrived in a trickle throughout the year, but the big numbers came in quarterly when the Red Cross received its allocation of transport. Several hundred thousand cigarettes might arrive in the space of a fortnight. Prices soared, and then began to fall, slowly at first but with increasing rapidity as stocks ran out, until the next big delivery. Most of our economic troubles could be attributed to this fundamental instability.

Price Movements

Many factors affected prices, the strongest and most noticeable being the periodical currency inflation and deflation described in the last paragraphs. The periodicity of this price cycle depended on cigarette and, to a far lesser extent, on food deliveries. At one time in the early days, before any private parcels had arrived and when there were no individual stocks, the weekly issue of cigarettes and food parcels occurred on a Monday. The non-monetary demand for cigarettes was great, and less elastic than the demand for food:

consequently prices fluctuated weekly, falling towards Sunday night and rising sharply on Monday morning. Later, when many people held reserves, the weekly issue had no such effect, being too small a proportion of the total available. Credit allowed people with no reserves to meet their non-monetary demand over the week-end.

The general price level was affected by other factors. An influx of new prisoners, proverbially hungry, raised it. Heavy air raids in the vicinity of the camp probably increased the non-monetary demand for cigarettes and accentuated deflation. Good and bad war news certainly had its effect, and the general waves of optimism and pessimism which swept the camp were reflected in prices. Before breakfast one morning in March of this year, a rumour of the arrival of parcels and cigarettes was circulated. Within ten minutes I sold a treacle ration, for four cigarettes (hitherto offered in vain for three), and many similar deals went through. By 10 o'clock the rumour was denied, and treacle that day found no more buyers even at two cigarettes.

More interesting than changes in the general price level were changes in the price structure. Changes in the supply of a commodity, in the German ration scale or in the make-up of Red Cross parcels, would raise the price of one commodity relative to others. Tins of oatmeal, once a rare and much sought after luxury in the parcels, became a commonplace in 1943, and the price fell. In hot weather the demand for cocoa fell, and that for soap rose. A new recipe would be reflected in the price level: the discovery that raisins and sugar could be turned into an alcoholic liquor of remarkable potency reacted permanently on the dried fruit market. The invention of electric immersion heaters run off the power points made tea, a drug on the market in Italy, a certain seller in Germany.

In August, 1944, the supplies of parcels and cigarettes were both halved. Since both sides of the equation were changed in the same degree, changes in prices were not anticipated. But this was not the case: the non-monetary demand for cigarettes was less elastic than the demand for food, and food prices fell a little. More important however were the changes in the price structure. German margarine and jam, hitherto valueless owing to adequate supplies of Canadian butter and marmalade, acquired a new value. Chocolate, popular and a certain seller, and sugar, fell. Bread rose; several standing contracts of bread for cigarettes were broken, especially when the bread ration was reduced a few weeks later.

In February, 1945, the German soldier who drove the ration waggon was found to be willing to exchange loaves of bread at the rate of one loaf for a bar of chocolate. Those in the know began selling bread and buying chocolate, by then almost unsaleable in a period of serious deflation. Bread, at about 40, fell slightly; chocolate rose from 15; the supply of bread was not enough for the two commodities to reach parity, but the tendency was unmistakable.

The substitution of German margarine for Canadian butter when parcels were halved naturally affected their relative values, margarine appreciating at the expense of butter. Similarly, two brands of dried milk, hitherto differing in quality and therefore in price by five cigarettes a tin, came together in price as the wider substitution of the cheaper raised its relative value.

Enough has been cited to show that any change in conditions affected both the general price level and the price structure. It was this latter phenomenon which wrecked our planned economy.

Paper Currency—Bully Marks

Around D-Day, food and cigarettes were plentiful, business was brisk and the camp in an optimistic mood. Consequently the Entertainments Committee felt the moment opportune to launch a restaurant, where food and hot drinks were sold while a band and variety turns performed. Earlier experiments, both public and private, had pointed the way, and the scheme was a great success. Food was bought at market prices to provide the meals and the small profits were devoted to a reserve fund and used to bribe Germans to provide grease-paints and other necessities for the camp theatre. Originally meals were sold for cigarettes but this meant that the whole scheme was vulnerable to the periodic deflationary waves, and furthermore heavy smokers were unlikely to attend much. The whole success of the scheme depended on an adequate amount of food being offered for sale in the normal manner.

To increase and facilitate trade, and to stimulate supplies and customers therefore, and secondarily to avoid the worst effects of deflation when it should come, a paper currency was organised by the Restaurant and the Shop. The Shop bought food on behalf of the Restaurant with paper notes and the paper was accepted equally with the cigarettes in the Restaurant or Shop, and passed back to the Shop to purchase more food. The Shop acted as a bank of issue. The paper money was backed 100 per cent. by food; hence its name, the Bully Mark. The BMk. was backed 100 per cent. by food: there could be no over-issues, as is permissible with a normal bank of issue, since the eventual dispersal of the camp and consequent redemption of all BMk.s was anticipated in the near future.

Originally one BMk. was worth one cigarette and for a short time both circulated freely inside and outside the Restaurant. Prices were quoted in BMk.s and cigarettes with equal freedom—and for a short time the BMk. showed signs of replacing the cigarette as currency. The BMk. was tied to food, but not to cigarettes: as it was issued against food, say 45 for a tin of milk and so on, any reduction in the BMk. prices of food would have meant that there were unbacked BMk.s in circulation. But the price of both food and BMk.s could and did fluctuate with the supply of cigarettes.

While the Restaurant flourished, the scheme was a success: the Restaurant bought heavily, all foods were saleable and prices were stable.

In August parcels and cigarettes were halved and the Camp was bombed. The Restaurant closed for a short while and sales of food became difficult. Even when the Restaurant reopened, the food and cigarette shortage became increasingly acute and people were unwilling to convert such valuable goods into paper and to hold them for luxuries like snacks and tea. Less of the right kinds of food for the Restaurant were sold, and the Shop became glutted with dried fruit, chocolate, sugar, etc., which the Restaurant could not buy. The price level and the price structure changed. The BMk. fell to four-fifths of a cigarette and eventually farther still, and it became unacceptable save in the Restaurant. There was a flight from the BMk., no longer convertible into cigarettes or popular foods. The cigarette re-established itself.

But the BMk. was sound! The Restaurant closed in the New Year with a progressive food shortage and the long evenings without lights due to intensified Allied air raids, and BMk.s could only be spent in the Coffee Bar—relict of the Restaurant—or on the few unpopular foods in the Shop, the owners of which were prepared to accept them. In the end all holders of BMk.s were paid in full, in cups of coffee or in prunes. People who had bought BMk.s for cigarettes or valuable jam or biscuits in their heyday were aggrieved that they should have stood the loss involved by their restricted choice, but they suffered no actual loss of market value.

Price Fixing

Along with this scheme came a determined attempt at a planned economy, at price fixing. The Medical Officer had long been anxious to control food sales, for fear of some people selling too much, to the detriment of their health. The deflationary waves and their effects on prices were inconvenient to all and would be dangerous to the Restaurant which had to carry stocks. Furthermore, unless the BMk. was convertible into cigarettes at about par it had little chance of gaining confidence and of succeeding as a currency. As has been explained, the BMk. was tied to food but could not be tied to cigarettes, which fluctuated in value. Hence, while BMk. prices of food were fixed for all time, cigarette prices of food and BMk.s varied.

The Shop, backed by the Senior British Officer, was now in a position to enforce price control both inside and outside its walls. Hitherto a standard price had been fixed for food left for sale in the shop, and prices outside were roughly in conformity with this scale, which was recommended as a "guide" to sellers, but fluctuated a good deal around it. Sales in the Shop at recommended prices were apt to be slow though a good price might be obtained: sales outside could be made more quickly at lower prices. (If sales outside were to be at higher prices, goods were withdrawn from the Shop until the recommended price rose: but the recommended price was sluggish and could not follow the market closely by reason of its very purpose, which was stability.) The Exchange and Mart notice boards came under the control of the Shop: advertisements which exceeded a 5 per cent. departure from the recommended scale were liable to be crossed out by authority: unauthorised sales were discouraged by authority and also by public opinion, strongly in favour of a just and stable price. (Recommended prices were fixed partly from market data, partly on the advice of the M.O.)

At first the recommended scale was a success: the Restaurant, a big buyer, kept prices stable around this level: opinion and the 5 per cent. tolerance helped. But when the price level fell with the August cuts and the price structure changed, the recommended scale was too rigid. Unchanged at first, as no deflation was expected, the scale was tardily lowered, but the prices of goods on the new scale remained in the same relation to one another, owing to the BMk., while on the market the price structure had changed. And the modifying influence of the Restaurant had gone. The scale was moved up and down several times, slowly following the inflationary and deflationary waves, but it was rarely adjusted to changes in the price structure. More and more advertisements were crossed off the board, and black market sales at unauthorised prices increased: eventually public opinion turned against the recommended scale and authority gave up the struggle. In the last few weeks, with unparalleled deflation, prices fell with alarming rapidity, no scales existed, and supply and demand, alone and unmellowed, determined prices.

Public Opinion

Public opinion on the subject of trading was vocal if confused and changeable, and generalisations as to its direction are difficult and dangerous. A tiny minority held that all trading was undesirable as it engendered an unsavoury atmosphere; occasional frauds and sharp practices were cited as proof. Certain forms of trading were more generally condemned; trade with the Germans was criticised by many. Red Cross toilet articles, which were in short supply and only issued in cases of actual need, were excluded from trade by law and opinion working in unshakable harmony. At one time, when there had been several cases of malnutrition reported among the more devoted smokers, no trade in German rations was permitted, as the victims became an additional burden on the depleted food reserves of the Hospital. But while certain activities were condemned as antisocial, trade itself was practised, and its utility appreciated, by almost everyone in the camp.

More interesting was opinion on middlemen and prices. Taken as a whole, opinion was hostile to the middleman. His function, and his hard work in bringing buyer and seller together, were ignored; profits were not regarded as a reward for labour, but as the result of sharp practices. Despite the fact that his very existence was proof to the contrary, the middleman was held to be redundant in view of the existence of an official Shop and the Exchange and Mart. Appreciation only came his way when he was willing to advance the price of a sugar ration, or to buy goods spot and carry them against a future sale. In these cases the element of risk was obvious to all, and the convenience of the service was felt to merit some reward. Particularly unpopular was the middleman with an element of monopoly, the man who contacted the ration wagon driver, or the man who utilised his knowledge of Urdu. And middlemen as a group were blamed for reducing prices. Opinion notwithstanding, most people dealt with a middleman, whether consciously or unconsciously, at some time or another.

There was a strong feeling that everything had its "just price" in cigarettes. While the assessment of the just price, which incidentally varied between camps, was impossible of explanation, this price was nevertheless pretty closely known. It can best be defined as the price usually fetched by an article in good times when cigarettes were plentiful. The "just price"

changed slowly; it was unaffected by short-term variations in supply, and while opinion might be resigned to departures from the "just price", a strong feeling of resentment persisted. A more satisfactory definition of the "just price" is impossible. Everyone knew what it was, though no one could explain why it should be so.

As soon as prices began to fall with a cigarette shortage, a clamour arose, particularly against those who held reserves and who bought at reduced prices. Sellers at cut prices were criticised and their activities referred to as the black market. In every period of dearth the explosive question of "should non-smokers receive a cigarette ration?" was discussed to profitless length. Unfortunately, it was the non-smoker, or the light smoker with his reserves, along with the hated middleman, who weathered the storm most easily.

The popularity of the price-fixing scheme, and such success as it enjoyed, were undoubtedly the result of this body of opinion. On several occasions the fall of prices was delayed by the general support given to the recommended scale. The onset of deflation was marked by a period of sluggish trade; prices stayed up but no one bought. Then prices fell on the black market, and the volume of trade revived in that quarter. Even when the recommended scale was revised, the volume of trade in the Shop would remain low. Opinion was always overruled by the hard facts of the market.

Curious arguments were advanced to justify price fixing. The recommended prices were in some way related to the calorific values of the food offered: hence some were overvalued and never sold at these prices. One argument ran as follows:—not everyone has private cigarette parcels: thus, when prices were high and trade good in the summer of 1944, only the lucky rich could buy. This was unfair to the man with few cigarettes. When prices fell in the following winter, prices should be pegged high so that the rich, who had enjoyed life in the summer, should put many cigarettes into circulation. The fact that those who sold to the rich in the summer had also enjoyed life then, and the fact that in the winter there was always someone willing to sell at low prices were ignored. Such arguments were hotly debated each night after the approach of Allied aircraft extinguished all lights at 8 p.m. But prices moved with the supply of cigarettes, and refused to stay fixed in accordance with a theory of ethics.

Conclusion

The economic organisation described was both elaborate and smooth-working in the summer of 1944. Then came the

August cuts and deflation. Prices fell, rallied with deliveries of cigarette parcels in September and December, and fell again. In January, 1945, supplies of Red Cross cigarettes ran out: and prices slumped still further: in February the supplies of food parcels were exhausted and the depression became a blizzard. Food, itself scarce, was almost given away in order to meet the non-monetary demand for cigarettes. Laundries ceased to operate, or worked for £s or RMk.s: food and cigarettes sold for fancy prices in £s, hitherto unheard of. The Restaurant was a memory and the BMk. a joke. The Shop was empty and the Exchange and Mart notices were full of unaccepted offers for cigarettes. Barter increased in volume, becoming a larger proportion of a smaller volume of trade. This, the first serious and prolonged food shortage in the writer's experience, caused the price structure to change again, partly because German rations were not easily divisible. A margarine ration gradually sank in value until it exchanged directly for a treacle ration. Sugar slumped sadly. Only bread retained its value. Several thousand cigarettes, the capital of the Shop, were distributed without any noticeable effect. A few fractional parcel and cigarette issues, such as one-sixth of a parcel and twelve cigarettes each, led to momentary price recoveries and feverish trade, especially when they coincided with good news from the Western Front, but the general position remained unaltered.

By April, 1945, chaos had replaced order in the economic sphere: sales were difficult, prices lacked stability. Economics has been defined as the science of distributing limited means among unlimited and competing ends. On 12th April, with the arrival of elements of the 30th U.S. Infantry Division, the ushering in of an age of plenty demonstrated the hypothesis that with infinite means economic organisation and activity would be redundant, as every want could be satisfied without effort.

appendix 3

THE PARABLE OF
THE PARKING LOTS

HENRY G. MANNE

IN a city not far away there was a large football stadium. It was used from time to time for various events, but the principal use was for football games played Saturday afternoons by the local college team. The games were tremendously popular and people drove hundreds of miles to watch them. Parking was done in the usual way. People who arrived early were able to park free on the streets, and latecomers had to pay to park in regular and improvised lots.

There were, at distances ranging from 5 to 12 blocks from the stadium, approximately 25 commercial parking lots all of which received some business from Saturday afternoon football games. The lots closer to the stadium naturally received more football business than those further away, and some of the very close lots actually raised their price on Saturday afternoons. But they did not raise the price much, and most did not change prices at all. The reason was not hard to find.

For something else happened on football afternoons. A lot of people who during the week were students, lawyers, school teachers, plumbers, factory workers, and even stock brokers went into the parking lot business. It was not a difficult thing to do. Typically a young boy would put up a crude, home-made sign saying "Parking $3." He would direct a couple of cars into his parents' driveway, tell the driver to take the key, and collect the three dollars. If the driveway was larger or there was yard space to park in, an older brother, an uncle, or the head of the household would direct the operation, sometimes asking drivers to leave their keys so that shifts could be made if necessary.

Some part-time parking lot operators who lived very close

The Public Interest, no. 23, Spring 1971, 10–15. Copyright © 1971 by National Affairs, Inc. Reprinted by permission of *The Public Interest* and the author.

to the stadium charged as much as $5.00 to park in their driveways. But as the residences-turned-parking-lots were located further from the stadium (and incidentally closer to the commercial parking lots), the price charged at game time declined. In fact houses at some distance from the stadium charged less than the adjacent commercial lots. The whole system seemed to work fairly smoothly, and though traffic just after a big game was terrible, there were no significant delays parking cars or retrieving parked cars.

•

BUT one day the owner of a chain of parking lots called a meeting of all the commercial parking lot owners in the general vicinity of the stadium. They formed an organization known as the Association of Professional Parking Lot Employers, or APPLE. And they were very concerned about the Saturday parking business. One man who owned four parking lots pointed out that honest parking lot owners had heavy capital investments in their businesses, that they paid taxes, and that they employed individuals who supported families. There was no reason, he alleged, why these lots should not handle all the cars coming into the area for special events like football games. "It is unethical," he said, "to engage in cutthroat competition with irresponsible fender benders. After all, parking cars is a profession, not a business." This last remark drew loud applause.

Thus emboldened he continued, stating that commercial parking lot owners recognize their responsibility to serve the public's needs. Ethical car parkers, he said, understand their obligations not to dent fenders, to employ only trustworthy car parkers, to pay decent wages, and generally to care for their customers' automobiles as they would the corpus of a trust. His statement was hailed by others attending the meeting as being very statesmanlike.

Others at the meeting related various tales of horror about nonprofessional car parkers. One homeowner, it was said, actually allowed his fifteen-year-old son to move other people's cars around. Another said that he had seen an $8,000 Cadillac parked on a dirt lawn where it would have become mired in mud had it rained that day. Still another pointed out that a great deal of the problem came on the side of the stadium with the lower-priced houses, where there were more driveways per block than on the wealthier side of the stadium. He pointed out that these poor people would rarely be able to afford to pay for damage to other people's automobiles or to pay insurance premiums to cover such losses. He felt that a professional group such as APPLE had a duty to protect the public from their folly in using those parking spaces.

Finally another speaker reminded the audience that these "marginal, fly-by-night" parking lot operators generally parked a string of cars in their driveways so that a driver had to wait until all cars behind his had been removed before he could get his out. This, he pointed out, was quite unlike the situation in commercial lots where, during a normal business day, people had to be assured of ready access to their automobiles at any time. The commercial parking lots either had to hire more attendants to shift cars around, or they had to park them so that any car was always accessible, even though this meant that fewer cars could park than the total space would actually hold. "Clearly," he said, "driveway parking constitutes unfair competition."

Emotions ran high at this meeting, and every member of APPLE pledged $1 per parking space for something mysteriously called a "slush fund." It was never made clear exactly whose slush would be bought with these funds, but several months later a resolution was adopted by the city council requiring licensing for anyone in the parking lot business.

•

THE preamble to the new ordinance read like the speeches at the earlier meeting. It said that this measure was designed to protect the public against unscrupulous, unprofessional and under-capitalized parking lot operators. It required, *inter alia*, that anyone parking cars for a fee must have a minimum capital devoted to the parking lot business of $25,000, liability insurance in an amount not less than $500,000, bonding for each car parker, and a special driving test for these parkers (which incidentally would be designed and administered by APPLE). The ordinance also required, again in the public's interest, that every lot charge a single posted price for parking and that any change in the posted price be approved in advance by the city council. Incidentally, most

members were able to raise their fees by about 20 per cent before the first posting.

Then a funny thing happened to drivers on their way to the stadium for the next big game. They discovered city police in unusually large numbers informing them that it was illegal to pay a non-licensed parking lot operator for the right to park a car. These policemen also reminded parents that if their children were found in violation of this ordinance it could result in a misdemeanor charge being brought against the parents and possible juvenile court proceedings for the children. There were no driveway parking lots that day.

Back at the commercial parking lots, another funny thing occurred. Proceeding from the entrance of each of these parking lots within twelve blocks of the stadium were long lines of cars waiting to park. The line got larger as the lot was closer to the stadium. Many drivers had to wait so long or walk so far that they missed the entire first quarter of the big game.

At the end of the game it was even worse. The confusion was massive. The lot attendants could not cope with the jam up, and some cars were actually not retrieved until the next day. It was even rumored about town that some automobiles had been lost forever and that considerable liabilities might result for some operators. Industry spokesmen denied this, however.

Naturally there was a lot of grumbling, but there was no agreement on what had caused the difficulty. At first everyone said there were merely some "bugs" in the new system that would have to be ironed out. But the only "bug" ironed out was a Volkswagen which was flattened by a careless lot attendant in a Cadillac Eldorado.

The situation did not improve at subsequent games. The members of APPLE did not hire additional employees to park cars, and operators near the stadium were not careful to follow their previous practice of parking cars in such a way as to have them immediately accessible. Employees seemed to become more surly, and the number of dented-fender claims mounted rapidly.

Little by little, too, cars began appearing in residential driveways again. For instance, one enterprising youth regularly went into the car wash business on football afternoons, promising that his wash job would take at least two hours. He charged five dollars, and got it—even on rainy days—in fact, especially on rainy days. Another homeowner offered to take cars on consignment for three hours to sell them at prices fixed by the owner. He charged $4.00 for this "service," but his subterfuge was quickly squelched by the authorities. The parking situation remained "critical."

POLITICAL pressures on the city council began to mount to "do something" about the inordinate delays in parking and retrieving cars on football afternoons. The city council sent a stern note of warning to APPLE, and APPLE appointed a special study group recruited from the local university's computer science department to look into the matter. This group reported that the managerial and administrative machinery in the parking lot business was archaic. What was needed, the study group said, was less goose quills and stand-up desks and more computers and conveyor belts. It was also suggested that all members of APPLE be hooked into one computer so that cars could really be shifted to the most accessible spaces.

Spokesmen for the industry took up the cry of administrative modernization. Subtle warnings appeared in the local papers suggesting that if the industry did not get its own house in order, heavy-handed regulation could be anticipated. The city council asked for reports on failures to deliver cars and decreed that this would include any failure to put a driver in his car within five minutes of demand without a new dent.

Some of the professional operators actually installed computer equipment to handle their ticketing and parking logistics problems. And some added second stories to their parking lots. Others bought up additional space, thereby raising the value of vacant lots in the area. But many simply added a few additional car parkers and hoped that the problem would go away without a substantial investment of capital.

The commercial operators also began arguing that they needed higher parking fees because of their higher operating costs. Everyone agreed that costs for operating a parking lot were certainly higher than before the licensing ordinance. So the city council granted a request for an across-the-board ten per cent hike in fees. The local newspaper editorially hoped that this would ease the problem without still higher fees being necessary. In a way, it did. A lot of people stopped driving. They began using city buses, or they chartered private buses for the game. Some stayed home and watched the game on TV. A new study group on fees was appointed.

Just about then several other blows fell on the parking lot business. Bus transportation to the area near the stadium was improved with a federal subsidy to the municipal bus company. And several new suburban shopping centers caused a loss of automobile traffic in the older areas of town. But most dramatic of all, the local university, under severe pressure from its students and faculty, dropped intercollegiate football altogether and converted the stadium into a park for underprivileged children.

The impact of these events on the commercial parking lots was swift. Income declined drastically. The companies that had borrowed money to finance the expansion everyone wanted earlier were hardest hit. Two declared bankruptcy, and many had to be absorbed by financially stronger companies. Layoffs among car parkers were enormous, and APPLE actually petitioned the city council to guarantee the premiums on their liability insurance policies so that people would not be afraid to park commercially. This idea was suggested to APPLE by recent Congressional legislation creating an insurance program for stock brokers.

A SPOKESMAN for APPLE made the following public statement: "New organizations or arrangements may be necessary to straighten out this problem. There has been a failure in both the structure of the industry and the regulatory scheme. New and better regulation is clearly demanded. A sound parking lot business is necessary for a healthy urban economy." The statement was hailed by the industry as being very statesmanlike, though everyone speculated about what he really meant.

Others in the industry demanded that the city bus service be curtailed during the emergency. The city council granted every rate increase the lots requested. There were no requests for rate decreases, but the weaker lots began offering prizes and other subtle or covert rebates to private bus companies who would park with them. In fact, this problem became so serious and uncontrollable that one owner of a large chain proclaimed that old-fashioned price competition for this business would be desirable. This again was hailed as statesmanlike, but everyone assumed that he really meant something else. No one proposed repeal of the licensing ordinance.

One other thing happened. Under pressure from APPLE, the city council decreed that henceforth no parking would be allowed on any streets in the downtown area of town. The local merchants were extremely unhappy with this, however, and the council rescinded the ordinance at the next meeting, citing a computer error as the basis for the earlier restriction.

The ultimate resolution of the "new" parking problem is not in sight. The parking lot industry in this town not very far from here is now said to be a depressed business, even a sick one. Everyone looks to the city council for a solution, but things will probably limp along as they are for quite a while, picking up with an occasional professional football game and dropping low with bad weather.

MORAL: If you risk your lot under an apple tree, you may get hit in the head.

NEW YORK HANGS OUT
THE FOR-RENT SIGN

ELEANORE CARRUTH

Sixteen months ago Manhattan's speculative developers were in the throes of an unprecedented office-building boom, and avid customers were bidding rents through the roofs of unfinished skyscrapers. At that time FORTUNE, after some detailed analysis, concluded that the boom had got out of hand and that the supply of incoming space was running far ahead of prospective demand. (See "Manhattan's Office Building Binge," October, 1969.) This melancholy prediction has become a reality, and the full implications of the gigantic spree are now beginning to emerge.

All of 27,498,000 square feet of spanking new office space will be open for occupancy in Manhattan this year. It should be noted that this is not only a record volume, but in itself represents a 16 percent addition, in a single year, to Manhattan's total supply. The new buildings are arriving hard behind 24 million square feet built in the two previous years, and 12,135,000 square feet are scheduled for completion by the end of 1972. About a third of this year's space, some of last year's, and two-thirds or more of the next's is still in search of tenants. And in the midst of all this plenty, new leasing activity has dropped sharply.

By FORTUNE's current projections, the surplus of Manhattan office space at the end of 1971 will amount to at least 7,500,000 square feet and more probably 16,500,000 square feet—the equivalent of a dozen or so new skyscrapers—and the surplus is likely to grow a little next year. Provided there is a virtual cutoff of new building after 1972, demand may catch up with supply by 1974 or 1975 in the normal course of white-collar employment growth in New York. The latest building-by-building count of new office space—63,825,000

square feet between 1969 and 1972—comes to a few million square feet more than was calculated sixteen months ago, and delays in actual construction have pushed some completion dates from 1970 toward 1972. Meanwhile, demand has been running a few million square feet lower than previously estimated because of the recession slowdown in job growth.

But even the current calculation may well be far too optimistic. Prospects for normal demand are fading before the great new uncertainty about the business future of New York. Fourteen major corporations have departed the nation's headquarters town in the last couple of years and at least forty other companies are talking about following them. Great segments of such big space users as the banks and insurance companies are lining up to go, as well as whole divisions of corporations already headquartered elsewhere.

The Hardened Lenders

What is also unprecedented, and alarming, about the situation is the short-term way in which the buildings are financed. The 1971-72 buildings being brought in by the speculative developers cost something like $1.75 billion in all. By FORTUNE's count, at least two-thirds of the incoming space this year and next is not covered by conventional permanent mortgages. Long-term lenders have virtually deserted the Manhattan market. New York Life, for instance, called a halt on mortgages for new and proposed New York office buildings over a year ago, and Vice President William Lutz says, "If anything, I'm more hardened in that position." Most other insurance companies, pension funds, and savings banks take a similar stand, except for very special cases.

The developers, of course, build with construction loans from the banks, which generally come due within six months after completion of the building. Right now, the commercial banks are holding well over $1 billion in construction loans that are not backed by conventional mortgage commitments. Some developers think the banks will be "nice," and not call the construction loans when they are due, but others, like Donald Harvey Sr., chairman of the finance committee for Uris Buildings, are not so complacent about the deadline. "These great financial institutions like you to live up to the contract," he says.

Both the plethora of buildings and the short-term nature of their financing came about through a breakdown over the years of the traditional financial controls that had governed the production of new office space. It used to be that the developer got the bank's interim financing only if he already had in hand a commitment from the long-term lender for permanent financing to "take out" the construction loan when the building was finished. To get full permanent financing the builder first had to have tenants in hand, on firm long-term leases, for 75 to 80 percent of the space. If he could not line up that many leases to begin with, he could start with a partial construction loan on the strength of a partial mortgage, a "floor loan," for which the insurance company wanted 40 to 50 percent of the space pretty well committed. The developer finished getting tenants while he was building, and then he got the full mortgage. So, in the old days, both the interim and the permanent financing were tied from the start to the market—the tenants.

This "production control," however, was relaxed over the years as builders began to get mortgages with a minimum of leases, floor loans without tenants, and construction loans without tenants or mortgages. As Chase Manhattan's executive vice president, Raymond O'Keefe, puts it, "We feel we have built up the expertise to evaluate a developer and his building, know whether it is going to go, and find the financing to take us out."

But national banks are legally required to have a takeout against the construction loan, so there has been a proliferation of ersatz takeouts called "standby" commitments, many of which have been issued by the commercial banks themselves. The terms of the standby (high interest rates and rapid repayment) are so onerous for the builder—"ruinous," says one—that obviously he never plans to fall back on it. He agrees to its terms only in the expectation that his property will rent out so well that he can, before the necessary moment, get a conventional permanent mortgage on favorable terms.

Now the necessary moment is arriving at an unpropitious time, and the short-term deadline, the maturity of the con-

struction loan, is putting an additional pressure on the developer and on his rental rates. For in order to get the mortgage, the developer must first get tenant leases.

"You Have to Dance to the Music"

As a result of these converging forces—surplus space and a financial squeeze—rental rates have already fallen and appear to be heading a good bit lower. Uptown, on Sixth Avenue, one developer who managed to find a tenant recently for a large chunk of space in his nearly finished building admits that he had to cut 30 percent from last year's asking price. "And we weren't greedy then. We wanted to rent and are taking what we can get." A few months ago, in order to rent 399,600 square feet of space at 1 Astor Plaza coming in early this year with 1,300,000 square feet of office space, the Minskoffs (old-time Manhattan builders) not only took somewhat lower rates from W.T. Grant than they had hoped for (and named the building for the tenant), but agreed as well to take over Grant's old lease for 400,000 square feet of space, much of which they will have to modernize. And another developer says flatly, "You have to dance to the music. If my building were nearing completion, I would have to accept the facts of life and take the price being offered."

So far, most developers have not retreated dramatically, though some of course have had to lower their sights considerably from the really spectacular rents commanded in mid-1969 at the height of the bull market in space. On the average, if they were charging large users of prime space $10 per square foot last fall, developers are now cutting the price by one dollar, or even two, depending upon the location and character of the building. Smaller space users, who have always paid more, are getting a bigger break. Developers are asking more for structures that are coming in next year, reflecting the higher level of costs going into them for land, construction, and money. But practically all of the developers are making "concessions"—i.e., throwing in additional partitions, lighting fixtures, and other extras.

Some insist that they are holding the price line. Robert V. Tishman, president of Tishman Realty & Construction, which will bring in two big uptown office buildings next year, is one of them. "Our jobs," he says, "are still listing at $12 a square foot and we expect to get $12 a square foot." The Kaufmans, another of New York's old building families, insist they haven't moved rentals "a quarter of a cent." To which one real-estate man rejoins cynically, "Wouldn't you rather list space that you can't rent anyway at $12 than at $8?"

Just as the new buildings are hunting for customers, the developers are also having to compete with a mounting volume of sublease space. Companies that leased new space and took something extra for future expansion are in some cases cutting back on it now and offering the space at bargain rates. National Student Marketing, for instance, took six months to unload some 30,000 square feet at a new Park Avenue address and wound up losing $800,000 on the deal.

Companies moving to new quarters, moreover, have been and will be leaving behind older space that will be a problem for everybody. The company itself will be trying to sublet the old space if its lease has time to run. The owner of the new building, if he has offered to take over the company's old lease, will be looking for a tenant for the space. And if the lease has expired, the owner of the old building will be searching for a new customer. "These older buildings will be fighting for their lives," says New York Life's William Lutz, who foresees a fierce battle of rates developing. Pressure is mounting now as buildings still in progress approach completion, and, says one knowledgeable real-estate veteran, "The moment of truth for these developers will come sometime in the next six months or so."

Stuck with the Surplus

Most of the industry refuses to recognize that it is in any such bind. The builders regard their problems as short term and blame most of their woes on the troubles of the economy. "A couple of good quarters and companies will look again for space," says Robert Tishman. And of course there is an element of truth in the argument. The recession *has* hurt the market for office space, partly because it has slowed the growth of white-collar employment, and even more so because it has made corporations less disposed to make commitments for new costs.

The developers concede that some buildings in offbeat locations—e.g., Broadway on the West Side, Second Avenue on the East Side—may be slow to rent, but they insist things will look up soon. They like to point out that the industry successfully weathered a slump in 1962, when space was in surplus and renting lagged for a year. "If the economy turns around," says Richard Seeler, executive vice president of Cross & Brown, real-estate broker, "we will have a brisk leasing market. Every year can't be a 1969. That's just impossible."

But the fundamental problem that the industry faces, or, rather, refuses to face, is a huge oversupply and not just sub-

normal demand. And the oversupply problem is of far greater dimension than it was a decade ago, two to four times as great as then.

In its early stages, the current building spree made sense. As Fortune explained in the 1969 article, a serious shortage of office space had developed in New York between 1966 and 1968 after new construction declined sharply just when white-collar employment began to boom. At the end of 1968 Manhattan had a total of 165 million square feet of office space and needed between 12 and 17 million additional square feet simply to catch up with pent-up demand. An additional 11 million square feet was needed in 1969. Fortune's computation allowed for a 4 percent increase during the year in white-collar employment, and the new offices needed to maintain a steady, long-run uptrend in average space per employee and to replace demolished buildings.

Builders brought in 16,147,000 square feet of office space in 1969, reducing the backlog by 5 million, to a deferred demand for between 7 and 12 million square feet. In 1970, on account of construction delays, only 8,045,000 square feet of office space came on the market. But new demand fell to less than 6 million square feet, as white-collar employment increased only a little over 1 percent during the year. The backlog of demand was cut further, by 2 million feet or so.

So builders are going into 1971 with a backlog cushion of between 5 and 10 million square feet. New demand this year may be less than last year's 6 million square feet and will almost certainly be no more than 10 million square feet. Putting together this new demand and the old, unfulfilled need, the requirement is for something between 11 and 20 million square feet of space in 1971. But the builders are bringing in 27,498,000 square feet—i.e., from 7,500,000 to 16,500,000 square feet more than is needed.

Up Goes the Vacancy Rate

It is perfectly plain, then, why builders are having trouble finding takers. There is no *net* demand for such additional space; developers are wooing tenants in older buildings in order to fill the new space. But these tenants in turn are leaving behind quantities of vacant space in other buildings. According to a computerized study made by Cross & Brown, more than 6 million square feet of office space is available for sublet in Manhattan. And on top of that, there is more than 11 million square feet available in new 1970–71 buildings. The surplus, whoever turns out to hold it, could send the vacancy rate anywhere from a painful 7 all the way to 10 percent by year-end.

In 1972 another 12,135,000 square feet will come on the market. Demand will amount to about 10 million square feet if white-collar employment increases 3 percent, the average for the past decade. So it seems that builders will go into 1973 still carrying a surplus of perhaps 10 to 18 million square feet, the equivalent of about one or two years' supply. If there is very little new building after 1972, developers might catch up with themselves by 1974 or 1975. In the best of all possible worlds, builders could dig themselves out a year sooner. If employment booms again as it did in 1967 and 1968 when it increased 10 percent in two years, demand would rise by an extra 4 million square feet annually and the surplus might be absorbed before the end of 1974 or even 1973. In the worst case, the surplus might hang on well past 1975.

In view of the surplus space, the case for cutting rents seems overwhelming. FORTUNE's estimates do not allow for the damper that recent high prices might have put on demand, and a cut could remove that damper. Lower rents might also stimulate the move from old buildings into new ones. Obviously there are companies that need to consolidate operations or want newer quarters for reasons of prestige, convenience, and comfort. But the irresistible force of the market is meeting an object that builders contend is immovable: their breakeven point. Money rates, taxes, and operating costs have escalated so sharply in recent years that the breakeven rent on prime space coming in right now is at an all-time high, ranging from about $8.50 per square foot to pretty near $10, with even higher costs for 1972 buildings. "We can't sell for much less," says one developer. "Because of these fixed costs, it's not a supply and demand situation in the usual sense of the word," explains builder Sol Atlas.

A Lever That Works Both Ways

And, indeed, space is not like a manufactured commodity whose production can be halted in midstream if need be. The profit or loss on a real-estate venture represents not a month's production, but years of effort. And, because real estate is a game of leverage in which a developer operates essentially with other people's money, the capital stakes are very, very large—hard to believe, and traumatic to face if the game goes against the player.

But on the other hand, as one of Manhattan's biggest real-estate brokers puts it, "You can only get what the market

gives. Developers are out of their minds when they say rental rates are not a case of supply and demand. What they mean is that *they* can't afford to rent for less." In other words, the developer would have to put up a large amount of capital to hold the building, and he could conceivably be forced to sell it. That is the great hazard of the business. For leverage, which in good times works wonders for the developer, can also work against him.

The object in real estate is to make money on other people's money by creating a property whose market value so greatly exceeds its cost that the developer's own cash investment in the project is little or nothing by the time it is completed. The value of a building is established by capitalizing its net cash flow at a rate that reflects both the current long-term interest rate and the lender's judgment of the building's prospects. An insurance company will lend up to 75 percent of this valuation.

If, for example, it cost $55 million to erect a Manhattan building of one million square feet, the developer's breakeven point would be about $9 per square foot, assuming that he paid $3.75 for taxes and maintenance and $5.25 for debt service. If he could rent for $10.50 per square foot, he would not only have a handsome operating profit, but the extra $1.50 a foot would do wonders for the value of the building. Annual cash flow from the building (after taxes and maintenance but before debt service) would be $6,750,000. Capitalized at, say, 10 percent, the rate being used by long-term lenders to arrive at property values, the building would be worth $67,750,000—i.e., $6,750,000 divided by 10 per cent. The builder could then borrow 75 percent of that, $50 million, and his own investment in the building would be only $5 million. His return would be 30 percent, plus the tax advantage, and the resale value of the building would be $12,750,000 more than it cost. But if the developer could get only $9 per square foot, the same building would return much less income, $5,250,000, and so be worth only $52,500,000. The developer could borrow only $39,500,000, and his own investment would have to increase to $15,500,000. His return on that sum would be only 7.4 percent, a little less than the interest he could get on his money in the bond market; if he could rent only 85 percent of the space—the usual breakeven level—he would lose $1,350,000 annually in carrying the property. And the resale value of the building would be $2,500,000 less than it cost. Obviously, at an $8 rental, his situation would be piteous. A developer can thus lose a fortune on a drop in the rental rate.

Changes in interest rates also have a profound effect on

the builder's situation, for financing costs (including some amortization) have been accounting for about 60 percent of the total cost of operating a property. A drop of 1 percent in mortgage reates would reduce total operating costs by 4 1/2 percent. This would produce either extra cash flow for the builder or some leeway for cutting rents.

Even more important, a reduction in interest rates would in most cases mean that net cash flow would be capitalized at a more favorable rate, thus yielding a higher valuation on the building. That developer who was facing a $2,500,000 loss at a capitalization rate of 10 percent would be almost home free at 9 percent. At an 8 percent rate he would have a potential resale profit on his building of about $5 million.

Long-term interest rates have in fact been dropping, offering a possible lifeline to the developers. Interest rates on new high-grade corporate bonds have been dropping sharply and are down 2 percent from the high of last June. Most financial observers expect them to go lower, some by as much as another percentage point. Mortgage-money rates lag behind the corporate-bond market but have come down to about 9 percent from their peak of 10 3/4 or 11 percent. If bond rates stay where they have been recently, mortgages will go to 8 1/2, and they could possibly (not necessarily) go lower if bond rates continue to fall.

The Importance of Guessing Right

The developer always plays with variables, juggling them endlessly to arrive at the best possible conclusion. Right now he is confronting two moving variables: a favorable decline in interest rates and an unfavorable decline in the rental market. He knows that he can barely afford to rent for $9 per square foot at year-end mortgage (and capitalization) rates, but he could get by at a rental a bit under $8 if mortgage rates go all the way down to 7 1/2 percent. (That would not give him a reward for his risk or enterprise, for which he likes to get $1 per square foot more.)

So the questions the developer is asking himself these days are especially agonizing. Will mortgage rates keep going down during the year? Or will they stop declining at the end of the first quarter, as some experts expect? Should I cut rent now, figuring on lower interest rates later? Or, should I hold off cutting rents until I see where mortgage rates and the rental market come out? And so on. An error in judgment has long-term consequences, for major leases in Manhattan generally run for about fifteen years, and mortgage agreements usually cannot be renegotiated for eight to ten years.

Sol Atlas is a walking example of how even a successful builder can guess wrong. About three and a half years ago Atlas turned down a 6 percent mortgage at 1 New York Plaza because he thought he could do better by waiting. "We never anticipated that interest rates would rise the way they did." Like some other builders, he once turned down good tenants, too, in the belief that rents would go higher. The cream is off his profit.

The Coming Scramble for Mortgages

The banks, instead of calling all those construction loans, will probably be urging the builders to "clean them up," which means rent the buildings, make permanent mortgage deals, and pay off the loans. Thus the developers are living, if not with a hard-and-fast cutoff date, at least with a sense of deadline. How any given developer reacts will depend on his individual situation: his own financial resources, when the space is coming in, and how much of it is rented. Even when he can afford it, a developer will not want to carry empty floors for very long. A $55-million building would probably cost about $550,000 a month to carry empty. And besides, there is nothing a builder dreads so much as the aura of failure that surrounds a lot of vacant space. Every building acquires a personality of its own—"successful" and teeming with tenants, or "unsuccessful" and a dog to rent.

There will be a lot of competition for the supply of commercial mortgage money available, and the scramble will be fierce. The most favored will be those whose buildings are already well rented. Next at the trough will be developers who obtained floor loans from insurance companies but need a lot more tenants to qualify for full mortgages. Other developers, in order to get mortgage money, will have to fill up their long-term rent rolls at their own short-term expense by taking over new tenants' old leases (as the Minskoffs did). Some will be forced to take still another road to mortgage money, through surrender of equity. Harry Helmsley and Lawrence Wien, veteran operators, recently let Metropolitan and Equitable Life take a half interest in 1 Penn Plaza, where only 40 percent of the office space is rented.

In theory, a bank can call the construction loan, and the builder can walk away if the terms of his standby commitment are so onerous that he can't live with them. He would lose his equity, of course, but in order to get the loan he only promised to complete the structure. He is usually not personally responsible for paying off the construction loan; that is the obligation of a separate corporation set up for the particular property. But in practice the situation is considerably more complicated. The developers "live on their names," as one banker puts it; they don't like the idea of having their loans called. Neither do the banks in many instances, especially when the loan is backed by a standby commitment that has been made by the bank itself.

The banks, of course, have other options depending on individual circumstances. One thing they can always do is extend the construction loan, and postpone the problem, hoping that it will disappear. "There have been very few tests for the last ten years," says one investment banker. "But when something happens in the banking fraternity, it is cumulative. Once somebody blows the whistle and calls a construction loan, the real trouble will start."

Many of the banks remain optimistic about the long-term outlook. "We have our fingers crossed in a couple of cases, like everyone else," says Robert E. Spencer, vice president for mortgages at Chemical Bank, "but we are counting on these builders to do what they have been doing for a number of years—rent the buildings successfully."

With the financial institutions reinstating the old controls over production—first get the tenants, then you get the money —the building boom is drawing to an end. Mortgage broker Jack Sonnenblick says that builders probably cannot even get floor loans today without signed leases in hand. Only a very few developers are finding it possible to go ahead with new projects. For example, in partnership with Arlen-Gramco, the Tishmans have begun excavation at 1166 Avenue of the Americas for a 1,430,000-square-foot building on land that cost some $35 million. Other developers are having to surrender options on their land or sell it in order to avoid heavy carrying expenses. For without the Tishman's name and track record, not many will be able to swing the financing arrangements for new buildings.

The drastic curtailment of new construction will at least give the developers a breather in which to work their way out of the surplus. The optimists among them—and most of these entrepreneurs must be optimists to be in the business that built New York—hope to be at it again before very long.

"A Helluva Town"

Even the optimists, however, pale at the possibility that "normal" demand will not reappear in the future because of the flight of business from New York. "What bothers me is whether the city environment will support the office space we have and are bringing in," says Warren Lindquist, former executive vice president of the Downtown Lower Manhattan Association. Says one old-time developer: "The thing that

is really disturbing is that the percentage of people *talking* about going is higher than ever before."

There is scarcely a company of consequence whose name has not been mentioned in the past few months as a candidate for greener pastures. Leonard Yaseen, chairman of Fantus, a firm specializing in locational counseling, estimates that upwards of seventy-five corporations, large and small, are thinking of moving out. The loss could be less, of course, or it could be more—but the prospect is bleak.

A recent study of Karen Gerard, economic consultant on urban affairs for Chase, suggests that New York has already begun to slip as a headquarters town. In 1969 seven of the 131 Manhattan-based corporations that were among the FORTUNE 500 moved out and only one moved in. Last year twelve corporations among the 500 either departed or signaled their intention to do so—including five of the top fifteen; only one new arrival is clearly in sight. By contrast, over the previous decade arrivals about equaled departures.

But more than headquarters space is at stake. Whole divisions of corporations are departing too. And there are rumors that several banks and insurance companies plan to move out parts of their work. There is fear that a real Manhattan exodus will diminish the city's growth in its rich business-service lines—lawyers, accountants, consultants.

The New York celebrated in song as "a helluva town" has become just plain hell to the disenchanted. The city is dirty, disorderly, noisy, and generally out of hand, and good help is hard to find for almost any job slot. "You can't get good clerical people," says an insurance executive. "You can get bodies, but for proper help you have to go where they have gone, to the suburbs."

Killing the Goose

A great number of companies complain about the increasing difficulty of recruiting middle management for New York jobs and of persuading executives located elsewhere in the company to transfer there. "If you can't get management," says one, "you're lost." Continental Oil, for example, reports that even a 20 percent cost-of-living differential has not been enough to persuade a number of its people to move to the big city. Manhattan rents are too high, and commuting is a nightmare. "The New Haven Railroad is responsible for moving more companies out of town than any other single thing," declares one real-estate man. At a time when emphasis on quality of life is greater than ever, New York no longer seems worth the trouble to a lot of people. "The situation is really bad," says Charles Urstadt, State Housing Commissioner. "Without our backbone, which is offices, what is going to happen to the city?"

Practically all the developers blame Mayor John Lindsay for the decline of New York. "He doesn't seem as acutely aware of what's really going on as he should be," complains one developer. "We know the heads of many important companies are talking of leaving because of filth and crime in the city, and we see no effort to curtail them." Business leaders have tried to talk to the mayor, one disgruntled builder says, but "it's just very discouraging where you don't get when you talk to this man Lindsay."

The Lindsay administration has set up an Economic Development Administration, but its director, Kenneth Patton says: "I'm terribly concerned and somewhat discouraged by the attitudes, values, and posture of business leadership." Patton believes that surplus office space will help New York keep business, because corporations will have more flexibility in meeting their space requirements. He is reconciled to "pruning" efforts that send parts of companies out of New York. But the loss of headquarters offices does disturb him.

Lately the developers themselves have begun to be concerned, and one member of the real-estate fraternity thinks it's about time. "They just haven't cared," he says. "Most of them are greedy beyond anybody's conception. The builders are selling New York, but they haven't added to it. Park Avenue is a canyon, Sixth Avenue is almost there, and now Fifth. They are part of the reason people don't want to be here. We are losing the people who can make the contribution."

The developers have helped form the Association for a Better New York, consisting of over two hundred leaders of the business community, to work with government authorities in trying to turn the city around. If nothing else, real-estate developers and brokers, working through the association, will now be mobilized as an early-warning system to spot companies that are thinking of leaving New York while there is still time to try to dissuade them.

Manhattan, after all, still has a lot going for it. But it will take a concerted effort by all the forces that have become involved in Manhattan's office-building binge to make a better New York. That includes not just the developers, but the great financial institutions, the major corporations, the city government, the Port Authority, and the state. As for the chances of success, only time will tell and only one thing is sure: the stakes are bigger than the buildings.   END

A sequel to this article appeared in the February 1975 issue of *Fortune.*

MONEY SUPPLY IN THE CONDUCT
OF MONETARY POLICY

ARTHUR F. BURNS

*   *   *

Role of Money Supply

For many years economists have debated the role of the money supply in the performance of economic systems. One school of thought, often termed "monetarist," claims that changes in the money supply influence very importantly, perhaps even decisively, the pace of economic activity and the level of prices. Monetarists contend that the monetary authorities should pay principal attention to the money supply, rather than to other financial variables such as interest rates, in the conduct of monetary policy. They also contend that fiscal policy has only a small independent impact on the economy.

Another school of thought places less emphasis on the money supply and assigns more importance to the expenditure and tax policies of the Federal Government as factors influencing real economic activity and the level of prices. This school emphasizes the need for monetary policy to be concerned with interest rates and with conditions in the money and capital markets. Some economic activities, particularly residential building and State and local government construction, depend heavily on borrowed funds, and are therefore influenced greatly by changes in the cost and availability of credit. In other categories of spending—such as business investment in fixed capital and inventories, and

consumer purchases of durable goods—credit conditions play a less decisive role, but they are nonetheless important.

Monetarists recognize that monetary policy affects private spending in part through its impact on interest rates and other credit terms. But they believe that primary attention to the growth of the money supply will result in a more appropriate monetary policy than would attention to conditions in the credit markets.

Needless to say, monetary policy is—and has long been—a controversial subject. Even the monetarists do not speak with one voice on monetary policy. Some influential monetarists believe that monetary policy should aim strictly at maintaining a constant rate of growth of the money supply. However, what that constant should be, or how broadly the money supply should be defined, are matters on which monetarists still differ. And there are also monetarists who would allow some—but infrequent—changes in the rate of growth of the money supply, in accordance with changing economic conditions.

It seems self-evident that adherence to a rigid growth-rate rule, or even one that is changed infrequently, would practically prevent monetary policy from playing an active role in economic stabilization. Monetarists recognize this. They believe that most economic disturbances tend to be self-correcting, and they therefore argue that a constant or nearly constant rate of growth of the money supply would result in reasonably satisfactory economic performance.

But neither historical evidence nor the thrust of explorations in business-cycle theory over a long century gives support to the notion that our economy is inherently stable. On the contrary, experience has demonstrated repeatedly that

A letter sent on November 6, 1973, by Arthur F. Burns, chairman of the board of governors of the Federal Reserve System, to Senator William Proxmire, vice-chairman of the Joint Economic Committee of Congress, and subsequently printed in the *Federal Reserve Bulletin* November 1973. The letter was in response to a request from Senator Proxmire for comment on certain criticisms of monetary policy. It is reprinted here with the permission of Arthur F. Burns.

blind reliance on the self-correcting properties of our economic system can lead to serious trouble. Discretionary economic policy, while it has at times led to mistakes, has more often proved reasonably successful. The disappearance of business depressions, which in earlier times spelled mass unemployment for workers and mass bankruptcies for businessmen, is largely attributable to the stabilization policies of the last 30 years.

The fact is that the internal workings of a market economy tend of themselves to generate business fluctuations, and most modern economists recognize this. For example, improved prospects for profits often spur unsustainable bursts of investment spending. The flow of personal income in an age of affluence allows ample latitude for changes in discretionary expenditures and in savings rates. During a business-cycle expansion various imbalances tend to develop within the economy—between aggregate inventories and sales, or between aggregate business investment in fixed capital and consumer outlays, or between average unit costs of production and prices. Such imbalances give rise to cyclical movements in the economy. Flexible fiscal and monetary policies, therefore, are often needed to cope with undesirable economic developments, and this need is not diminished by the fact that our available tools of economic stabilization leave something to be desired.

There is general agreement among economists that, as a rule, the effects of stabilization policies occur gradually over time, and that economic forecasts are an essential tool of policymaking. However, no economist—or school of economics—has a monopoly on accurate forecasting. At times, forecasts based largely on the money supply have turned out to be satisfactory. At other times, such forecasts have been quite poor, mainly because of unanticipated changes in the intensity with which the existing money stock is used by business firms and consumers.

Changes in the rate of turnover of money have historically played a large role in economic fluctuations, and they continue to do so. For example, the narrowly defined money stock—that is, demand deposits plus currency in public circulation—grew by 5.7 per cent between the fourth quarter of 1969 and the fourth quarter of 1970. But the turnover of money declined during the year, and the dollar value of gross national product rose only 4.5 per cent. In the following year, the growth rate of the money supply increased to 6.9 per cent, but the turnover of money picked up briskly and the dollar value of GNP accelerated to 9.3 per cent. The movement out of recession in 1970 into recovery in 1971 was thus closely related to the greater intensity in the use of money. Occurrences such as this are very common because the willingness to use the existing stock of money, expressed in its rate of turnover, is a highly dynamic force in economic life.

For this as well as other reasons, the Federal Reserve uses a blend of forecasting techniques. The behavior of the money supply and other financial variables is accorded careful attention. So also are the results of the most recent surveys on plant and equipment spending, consumer attitudes, and inventory plans. Recent trends in key producing and spending sectors are analyzed. The opinions of businessmen and outside economic analysts are canvassed, in part through the nationwide contacts of Federal Reserve Banks. And an assessment is made of the probable course of fiscal policy and also of labor-market and agricultural policies, and their effects on the economy.

Evidence from all these sources is weighed. Efforts are also made to assess economic developments through the use of large-scale econometric models. An eclectic approach is thus taken by the Federal Reserve, in recognition of the fact that the state of economic knowledge does not justify reliance on any single forecasting technique. As economic research has cumulated, it has become increasingly clear that money does indeed matter. But other financial variables also matter.

In recent years, the Federal Reserve has placed somewhat more emphasis on achieving desired growth rates of the monetary aggregates, including the narrowly-defined money supply, in its conduct of monetary policy. But we have continued to give careful attention to other financial indicators, among them the level of interest rates on mortgages and other loans and the liquidity position of financial institutions and the general public. This is necessary because the economic implications of any given monetary growth rate depend on the state of liquidity, the attitudes of businessmen, investors, and consumers toward liquidity, the cost and availability of borrowed funds, and other factors. Also, as the Nation's central bank, the Federal Reserve can never lose sight of its role as a lender of last resort, so that financial crises and panics will be averted.

I recognize that one advantage of maintaining a relatively stable growth rate of the money supply is that a partial offset is thereby provided to unexpected and undesired shifts in the aggregate demand for goods and services. There is always some uncertainty as to the emerging strength of aggregate demand. If money growth is maintained at a rather stable rate, and aggregate demand turns out to be weaker than is consistent with the Nation's economic objectives, interest rates will tend to decline and the easing of credit markets should help to moderate the undesired weakness in demand. Similarly, if the demand for goods and services threatens to outrun productive capacity, a rather stable rate of monetary growth will provide a restraining influence on the supply of credit and thus tend to restrain excessive spending.

However, it would be unwise for monetary policy to aim at all times at a constant or nearly constant rate of growth of money balances. The money growth rate that can contribute most to national objectives will vary with economic conditions. For example, if the aggregate demand for goods and services is unusually weak, or if the demand for liquidity is unusually strong, a rate of increase in the money supply well above the desirable long-term trend may be needed for a time. Again, when the economy is experiencing severe cost-push inflation, a monetary growth rate that is relatively high by a historical yardstick may have to be tolerated for a time. If money growth were severely constrained in order to combat the element of inflation resulting from such a cause, it might well have seriously adverse effects on production and employment. In short, the growth rate of the money supply that is appropriate at any given time cannot be determined simply by extrapolating past trend or by some preconceived arithmetical standard.

Moreover, for purposes of conducting monetary policy, it is never safe to rely on just one concept of money—even if that concept happens to be fashionable. A variety of plausible concepts merit careful attention because a number of financial assets serve as a convenient, safe, and liquid store of purchasing power.

The Federal Reserve publishes data corresponding to three definitions of money and takes all of them into account in determining policy. The three measures are: (a) the narrowly defined money stock (M_1), which encompasses currency and demand deposits held by the nonbank public: (b) a more broadly defined money stock (M_2), which also includes time and savings deposits at commercial banks (other than large negotiable time certificates of deposits); (c) a still broader definition (M_3), which includes savings deposits at mutual savings banks and savings and loan associations. A definition embracing other liquid assets could also be justified—for example, one that would include large-denomination negotiable time CD's, U.S. savings bonds and Treasury bills, commercial paper, and other short-term money market instruments.

There are many assets closely related to cash, and the public can switch readily among these assets. However money may be defined, the task of determining the amount of money needed to maintain high employment and reasonable stability of the general price level is complicated by shifting preferences of the public for cash and other financial assets.

Variability of Money Supply Growth

In the short run, the rate of change in the observed money supply is quite erratic and cannot be trusted as an indicator of the course of monetary policy. This would be so even if there were no errors of measurement.

The record of hearings held by the Joint Economic Committee on June 27, 1973, includes a memorandum that I submitted on problems encountered in controlling the money supply. As indicated there, week-to-week, month-to-month, and even quarter-to-quarter fluctuations in the rate of change of money balances are frequently influenced by international flows of funds, changes in the level of U.S. Government deposits, and sudden changes in the public's attitude toward liquidity. Some of these variations appear to be essentially random—a product of the enormous ebb and flow of funds in our modern economy.

Because the demands of the public for money are subject to rather wide short-term variations, efforts by the Federal Reserve to maintain a constant growth rate of the money supply could lead to sharp short-run swings in interest rates and could risk damage to financial markets and the economy. Uncertainties about financing cost could reduce the fluidity of markets and could increase the costs of financing to borrowers. In addition, wide and erratic movements of interest rates and financial conditions could have undesirable effects on business and consumer spending. These adverse effects may not be of major dimensions, but it is better to avoid them.

In any event, for a variety of reasons explained in the memorandum for the Joint Economic Committee, to which I have previously referred, the Federal Reserve does not have precise control over the money supply. To give one example, a significant part of the money supply consists of deposits lodged in nonmember banks that are not subject to the reserve requirements set by the Federal Reserve. As a result, there is some slippage in monetary control. Furthermore, since deposits at nonmember banks have been reported for only 2 to 4 days in a year, in contrast to daily statistics for member banks, the data on the money supply—which we regularly present on a weekly, monthly, and quarterly basis —are estimates rather than precise measurements. When the infrequent reports from nonmember banks become avail-

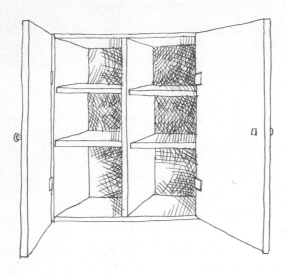

able, they often necessitate considerable revisions of the money supply figures. In the past 2 years, the revisions were upward, and this may happen again this year.

* * *

In our judgment, there is little reason for concern about the short-run variations that occur in the rate of change in the money stock. Such variations have minimal effects on the real economy. For one thing, the outstanding supply of money is very large. It is also quite stable, even when the short-run rate of change is unstable. This October the average outstanding supply of M_1, seasonally adjusted, was about $264 billion. On this base, a monthly rise or fall in the money stock of even $2½ billion would amount to only a 1 per cent change. But when such a temporary change is expressed as an annual rate, as is now commonly done, it comes out as about 12 per cent and attracts attention far beyond its real significance.

The Federal Reserve research staff has investigated carefully the economic implications of variability in the growth of M_1. The experience of the past two decades suggests that even an abnormally large or abnormally small rate of growth of the money stock over a period of up to 6 months or so has a negligible influence on the course of the economy—provided it is subsequently offset. Such short-run variations in the rate of change in the money supply may not at all reflect Federal Reserve policy, and they do not justify the attention they often receive from financial analysts.

The thrust of monetary policy and its probable effects on economic activity can only be determined by observing the course of the money supply and of other monetary aggregates over periods lasting 6 months or so. Even then, care must be taken to measure the growth of money balances in ways that temper the influence of short-term variations. For example, the growth of money balances over a quarter can be measured from the amount outstanding in the last month of the preceding quarter to the last month of the current quarter or from the average amount outstanding during the preceding quarter to the average in the current quarter. The first measure captures the latest tendencies in the money supply, but may be distorted by random changes that have no lasting significance. The second measure tends to average out temporary fluctuations and is comparable to the data provided on a wide range of nonmonetary economic variables, such as GNP and related measures.

*   *   *

Experience of 1972–73

During 1972, it was the responsibility of the Federal Reserve to encourage a rate of economic expansion adequate to reduce unemployment to acceptable levels. At the same time, despite the dampening effects of the wage-price control program, inflationary pressures were gathering. Monetary policy, therefore, had to balance the twin objectives of containing inflationary pressures and encouraging economic growth. These objectives were to some extent conflicting, and monetary policy alone could not be expected to cope with both problems. Continuation of an effective wage-price program and a firmer policy of fiscal restraint were urgently needed.

The narrowly defined money stock increased 7.4 per cent during 1972—measured from the fourth quarter of 1971 to the fourth quarter of 1972. Between the third quarter of 1972 and the third quarter of 1973, the growth rate was 6.1 per cent. By the first half of 1973, the annual growth rate had declined to 5.8 per cent, and a further slowing occurred in the third quarter.

Evaluation of the appropriateness of these growth rates would require full analysis of the economic and financial objectives, conditions, and policies during the past 2 years, if not longer. Such an analysis cannot be undertaken here. Some perspective on monetary developments during 1972–73 may be gained, however, from comparisons with the experience of other industrial countries, and by recalling briefly how domestic economic conditions evolved during this period.

Table 1 compares the growth of M_1 in the United States with that of other industrial countries in 1972 and the first half of 1973. The definitions of M_1 differ somewhat from country to country, but are as nearly comparable as statistical sources permit. It goes without saying that each country faced its own set of economic conditions and problems. Yet it is useful to note that monetary growth in the United States was

Table 1 GROWTH IN MONEY SUPPLY
Percentage change at annual rates

Country	1971 Q4 to 1972 Q4	1972 Q4 to 1973 Q2
United States	7.4	5.8
United Kingdom	14.1	10.0
Germany	14.3	4.2
France	15.4	8.7
Japan	23.1	28.2

Table 2 shows, in summary fashion, the rates of change in the money supply of the United States, in its total production, and in the consumer price level during 1972 and 1973. The table is based on the latest data. It may be noted in passing that, according to data available as late as January 1973, the rate of growth of M_1 during 1972 was 7.2 per cent, not 7.4 per cent; and that the rate of increase in real GNP was 7.7 per cent, not 7.0 per cent. In other words, on the basis of the data available during 1972, the rate of growth of M_1 was below the rate of growth of the physical volume of overall production.

Table 2 indicates that growth in M_1 during 1972 and 1973 approximately matched the growth of real output, but was far below the expansion in the dollar value of the Nation's out-

Table 2 MONEY SUPPLY, GNP, AND PRICES IN THE UNITED STATES
Percentage change at annual rates

Item	1971 Q4 to 1972 Q4	1972 Q4 to—	
		1973 Q2	1973 Q3
Money supply (M_1) ..	7.4	5.8	5.6
Gross national product			
Current dollars	10.6	12.1	11.7
Constant dollars	7.0	5.4	4.8
Prices			
Consumer price			
index (CPI)	3.4	7.1	7.8
CPI excluding food	3.0	4.0	4.1

put. Although monetary policy limited the availability of money relative to the growth of transactions demands, it still encouraged a substantial expansion in economic activity; real output rose by about 7 per cent in 1972. Even so, unemployment remained unsatisfactorily high throughout the greater part of the year. It was not until November that the unemployment rate dropped below $5\frac{1}{2}$ per cent. For the year as a whole, the unemployment rate averaged 5.6 per cent. It may be of interest to recall that unemployment averaged 5.5 per cent in 1954 and 1960, which are commonly regarded as recession years.

Since the expansion of M_1 in 1972 was low relative to the demands for money and credit, it was accompanied by rising short-term interest rates. Long-term interest rates showed little net change last year, as credit demands were satisfied mainly in the short-term markets.

In 1973, the growth of M_1 moderated while the transactions demands for cash and the turnover of money accelerated. GNP in current dollars rose at a 12 per cent annual rate as prices rose more rapidly. In credit markets, short-term interest rates rose sharply further, while long-term interest rates also moved up, though by substantially less than short-term rates.

The extraordinary upsurge of the price level this year reflects a variety of special influences. First, there has been a worldwide economic boom superimposed on the boom in the United States. Second, we have encountered critical shortages of basic materials. The expansion in industrial capacity needed to produce these materials had not been put in place earlier because of the abnormally low level of profits between 1966 and 1971 and also because of numerous impediments to new investment on ecological grounds. Third, farm product prices escalated sharply as a result of crop failures in many countries last year. Fourth, fuel prices spurted upward, reflecting the developing shortages in the energy field. And fifth, the depreciation of the dollar in foreign exchange markets has served to boost prices of imported goods and to add to the demands pressing on our productive resources.

In view of these powerful special factors and the cyclical expansion of our economy, a sharp advance in our price level would have been practically inevitable in 1973. The upsurge of the price level this year hardly represents either the basic trend of prices or the response of prices to previous monetary or fiscal policies—whatever their shortcomings may have been. In particular, as Table 2 shows, the explosion of food prices that occurred this year is in large part responsible for the accelerated rise in the overall consumer price level.

The severe rate of inflation that we have experienced in 1973 cannot responsibly be attributed to monetary management or to public policies more generally. In retrospect, it may well be that monetary policy should have been a little less expansive in 1972. But a markedly more restrictive policy would have led to a still sharper rise in interest rates and risked a premature ending of the business expansion, without limiting to any significant degree this year's upsurge of the price level.

Concluding Observations

The present inflation is the most serious economic problem facing our country, and it poses great difficulties for economic stabilization policies. We must recognize, I believe, that it will take some time for the forces of inflation, which now engulf our economy and others around the world, to burn themselves out. In today's environment, controls on wages and prices cannot be expected to yield the benefits they did in 1971 and 1972, when economic conditions were much different. Primary reliance in dealing with inflation—both in the near future and over the longer term—will have to be placed on fiscal and monetary policies.

The prospects for regaining price stability would be enhanced by improvements in our monetary and fiscal instruments. The conduct of monetary policy could be improved if steps were taken to increase the precision with which the money supply can be controlled by the Federal Reserve. Part of the present control problem stems from statistical inadequacies—chiefly the paucity of data on deposits at nonmember banks. Also, however, control over the money supply and other monetary aggregates is less precise than it can or should be because nonmember banks are not subject to the same reserve requirements as are member banks.

I hope that the Congress will support efforts to rectify these deficiencies. For its part, the Federal Reserve is even now carrying on discussions with the Federal Deposit Insurance Corporation about the need for better statistics on the Nation's money supply. The Board of Governors also expects shortly to recommend to the Congress legislation that will put demand deposits at commercial banks on a uniform basis from the standpoint of reserve requirements.

Improvements in our fiscal policies are also needed. It is important for the Congress to put an end to fragmented consideration of expenditures, to place a firm ceiling on total Federal expenditures, and to relate these expenditures to prospective revenues and the Nation's economic needs.

Fortunately, there is now widespread recognition by Members of the Congress of the need to reform budgetary procedures along these broad lines.

It also is high time for fiscal policy to become a more versatile tool of economic stabilization. Particularly appropriate would be fiscal instruments that could be adapted quickly under special legislative rules, to changing economic conditions—such as a variable tax credit for business investment in fixed capital. Once again I would urge the Congress to give serious consideration to this urgently needed reform.

We must strive also for better understanding of the effects of economic stabilization policies on economic activity and prices. Our knowledge in this area is greater now than it was 5 or 10 years ago, thanks to extensive research undertaken by economists in academic institutions, at the Federal Reserve, and elsewhere. The keen interest of the Joint Economic Committee in improving economic stabilization policies has, I believe, been an influence of great importance in stimulating this widespread research effort.

I look forward to the continued cooperation with the Committee in an effort to achieve the kind of economic performance our citizens expect and deserve.

appendix
6

A STATISTICAL HISTORY OF
THE 1974-75 RECESSION-INFLATION

	YEAR	1973		1974				1975		
	QUARTER	3rd	4th	1st	2nd	3rd	4th	1st	2nd	3rd
1 Gross national product		1,308.9	1,344.0	1,358.8	1,383.8	1,416.3	1,430.9	1,416.6	1,440.9	1,497.8
2 Disposable personal income		913.9	939.4	950.6	966.5	993.1	1,008.8	1,015.5	1,078.5	1,079.1
3 Personal consumption expenditures[1]		816.3	823.9	840.6	869.1	901.3	895.8	913.2	938.6	970.0
4 Personal saving	(in billions of current dollars) (seasonally adjusted annual rates)	73.2	89.3	84.4	71.5	65.5	86.5	75.9	113.8	82.9
5 Gross private saving[2]		210.3	229.4	224.1	207.3	196.2	227.5	222.6	266.3	
6 Gross private domestic investment		209.0	224.5	210.5	211.8	205.8	209.4	163.1	148.1	174.9
7 Government purchases of goods		276.9	286.4	296.3	304.4	312.3	323.8	331.6	338.1	343.1
8 Federal government expenditures		263.4	270.6	281.0	291.6	304.7	319.3	338.5	355.0	
9 Federal government receipts		261.8	268.3	278.1	288.6	302.8	294.7	284.1	250.5	
10 Federal government deficit		1.7	2.3	2.8	3.0	1.9	24.5	54.4	104.6	
11 Net exports (exports minus imports)		6.7	9.3	11.3	−1.5	−3.1	1.9	8.8	16.2	9.8
12 Gross national product	(in billions of 1958 dollars)	840.8	845.7	830.5	827.1	823.1	804.0	780.0	783.6	804.6
13 Personal consumption expenditures		555.4	546.3	539.7	542.7	547.2	528.2	531.5	539.7	548.9
14 Personal saving[3]		49.8	59.2	54.2	44.6	39.8	51.0	44.2	65.4	46.9
15 Gross private domestic investment		135.8	145.8	133.3	130.3	122.7	120.5	89.3	80.7	94.9
16 Government purchases of goods		143.7	145.7	146.0	145.8	145.9	146.3	147.7	149.2	149.6
17 Per capita disposable income, 1958 dollars		2,952	2,952	2,887	2,850	2,842	2,798	2,775	2,907	
18 Implicit GNP deflator		155.7	158.9	163.6	167.3	172.1	178.0	181.6	183.9	186.2

[1]In the national income and product accounts, disposable personal income is equal to personal *outlays* plus personal saving. Personal consumption expenditures plus interest paid by consumers and personal transfer payments to foreigners comprise personal outlays.
[2]Sum of personal saving, capital consumption allowances, and undistributed corporate profits minus net corporate losses attributable to revaluation of inventory. Personal saving plus gross business saving.
[3]Personal saving in current dollars divided by implicit price deflator for overall personal consumption expenditures.

	1973		1974				1975		
QUARTER	3rd	4th	1st	2nd	3rd	4th	1st	2nd	3rd
MONTH	Jy Ag Se	Oc No De	Ja Fe Mr	Ap My Je	Jy Ag Se	Oc No De	Ja Fe Mr	Ap My Je	Jy Ag Se
19 Consumer price index	132.7 / 135.1 / 135.5	136.6 / 137.6 / 138.5	139.7 / 141.5 / 143.1	144.0 / 145.5 / 146.9	148.0 / 149.9 / 151.7	153.0 / 154.3 / 155.4	156.1 / 157.2 / 157.8	158.6 / 159.3 / 160.6	162.3 / 162.8 / 163.6
20 Wholesale price index	134.3 / 142.1 / 139.7	138.7 / 139.2 / 141.8	146.6 / 149.5 / 151.4	152.7 / 155.0 / 155.7	161.7 / 167.4 / 167.2	170.2 / 171.9 / 171.5	171.8 / 171.3 / 170.4	172.1 / 173.2 / 173.7	175.7 / 176.7 / 177.7
21 Money stock: M_1, seasonally adjusted	266.4 / 266.3 / 265.5	266.6 / 269.4 / 271.5	270.9 / 273.1 / 275.2	276.6 / 277.6 / 280.0	280.4 / 280.5 / 280.7	281.6 / 283.6 / 284.4	281.6 / 282.4 / 285.0	285.8 / 288.5 / 293.0	293.5 / 294.2 / 294.6
22 Money stock: M_2, seasonally adjusted	552.1 / 555.1 / 556.8	561.9 / 567.2 / 572.2	575.5 / 580.8 / 585.5	589.4 / 591.5 / 596.7	599.6 / 601.9 / 603.4	607.6 / 611.6 / 613.5	614.8 / 619.1 / 625.1	628.9 / 635.9 / 646.1	650.5 / 653.7 / 656.3
23 Federal funds rate, average of daily rates	10.40 / 10.50 / 10.78	10.01 / 10.03 / 9.95	9.65 / 8.97 / 9.35	10.51 / 11.31 / 11.93	12.92 / 12.01 / 11.34	10.06 / 9.45 / 8.53	7.13 / 6.24 / 5.54	5.49 / 5.22 / 5.55	6.10 / 6.14 / 6.24
24 Prime rate (4–6 months), average of daily rates	9.18 / 10.21 / 10.23	8.92 / 8.94 / 9.08	8.66 / 7.82 / 8.42	9.79 / 10.62 / 10.96	11.72 / 11.65 / 11.23	9.36 / 8.81 / 8.98	7.30 / 6.33 / 6.06	6.15 / 5.82 / 5.79	6.44 / 6.70 / 6.85
25 Noninstitutional population (in thousands)	148,361 / 148,565 / 148,782	149,001 / 149,208 / 149,436	149,656 / 149,857 / 150,066	150,283 / 150,507 / 150,710	150,922 / 151,135 / 151,367	151,593 / 151,812 / 152,020	152,230 / 152,445 / 152,646	152,840 / 153,051 / 153,278	153,585 / 153,824 / 154,052
26 Civilian labor force, s.a. (in thousands)	88,902 / 88,816 / 89,223	89,568 / 89,852 / 90,048	90,465 / 90,551 / 90,381	90,324 / 90,753 / 90,857	91,283 / 91,199 / 91,705	91,844 / 91,708 / 91,803	92,091 / 91,511 / 91,829	92,262 / 92,940 / 92,340	92,916 / 93,146 / 93,191
27 Civilian employment, s.a. (in thousands)	84,679 / 84,582 / 84,983	85,452 / 85,577 / 85,646	85,800 / 85,861 / 85,779	85,787 / 86,062 / 86,088	86,403 / 86,274 / 86,402	86,304 / 85,689 / 85,202	84,562 / 84,027 / 83,849	84,086 / 84,402 / 84,444	85,078 / 85,352 / 85,418
28 Unemployment, s.a. (in thousands)	4,223 / 4,234 / 4,240	4,116 / 4,275 / 4,402	4,665 / 4,690 / 4,602	4,537 / 4,691 / 4,769	4,880 / 4,925 / 5,303	5,540 / 6,019 / 6,601	7,529 / 7,484 / 7,980	8,176 / 8,538 / 7,896	7,838 / 7,794 / 7,773
29 Employment rate (27 ÷ 25)	57.1 / 56.9 / 57.1	57.3 / 57.4 / 57.3	57.3 / 57.3 / 57.2	57.1 / 57.2 / 57.1	57.3 / 57.1 / 57.1	56.9 / 56.4 / 56.0	55.5 / 55.1 / 54.9	55.0 / 55.1 / 55.1	55.4 / 55.5 / 55.4
30 Unemployment rate (28 ÷ 26)	4.8 / 4.8 / 4.8	4.6 / 4.8 / 4.9	5.2 / 5.2 / 5.1	5.0 / 5.2 / 5.2	5.3 / 5.4 / 5.8	6.0 / 6.6 / 7.2	8.2 / 8.2 / 8.7	8.9 / 9.2 / 8.6	8.4 / 8.4 / 8.3

Sources: Bureau of Economic Analysis; Bureau of Labor Statistics; Board of Governors, Federal Reserve System.
Note: Data for recent quarters and months are subject to minor revisions as more accurate information becomes available.

INDEX

This book was designed and illustrated by Barbara Ravizza
with technical art by the House of Graphics
and design coordination by Patricia Faust
set in Palatino with Stymie Medium display by Typothetae
printed and bound by the Kingsport Press
sponsored by Bruce Caldwell and
edited by George Oudyn

6789/54321